RESEARCH HANDBOOK ON HEDGE FUNDS, PRIVATE EQUITY AND ALTERNATIVE INVESTMENTS

T0320160

RESEARCH HANDBOOKS IN FINANCIAL LAW

Series Editor: Rosa Lastra, *Queen Mary, University of London, UK*

This important new *Handbook* series presents high quality, original reference works that cover a range of subjects within the evolving field of financial law. National, regional and global financial markets are at the epicenter of economic, political and social developments. They are shaped by their own intrinsic dynamics, but are also at the receiving end of potent external forces, including monetary developments, state regulation and policies towards international and regional financial integration and free trade areas.

Under the general editorship of Rosa Lastra, these *Handbooks* are edited by leading scholars in their respective fields, and comprise specially commissioned contributions from distinguished academics, who critically, innovatively and substantially analyze a wide range of current issues in financial law.

Each of the individual handbooks is a definitive reference work, essential for both scholars of financial law as well as for practicing lawyers. The comprehensive coverage and thorough examinations of the significant topics and ideas in financial law signify the handbooks' position as authoritative and scholarly information resources.

Titles in the series include:

Research Handbook on International Insurance Law and Regulation
Edited by Julian Burling and Kevin Lazarus

Research Handbook on Hedge Funds, Private Equity and Alternative Investments
Edited by Phoebus Athanassiou

Research Handbook on Hedge Funds, Private Equity and Alternative Investments

Edited by

Phoebus Athanassiou

Senior Legal Counsel, European Central Bank, Germany

RESEARCH HANDBOOKS IN FINANCIAL LAW

Edward Elgar
Cheltenham, UK • Northampton, MA, USA

© The Editor and Contributors Severally 2012

All rights reserved. No part of this publication may be reproduced, stored in a retrieval system or transmitted in any form or by any means, electronic, mechanical or photocopying, recording, or otherwise without the prior permission of the publisher.

Published by
Edward Elgar Publishing Limited
The Lypiatts
15 Lansdown Road
Cheltenham
Glos GL50 2JA
UK

Edward Elgar Publishing, Inc.
William Pratt House
9 Dewey Court
Northampton
Massachusetts 01060
USA

A catalogue record for this book
is available from the British Library

Library of Congress Control Number: 2011932892

ISBN 978 1 84980 278 9 (cased)

Typeset by Servis Filmsetting Ltd, Stockport, Cheshire
Printed and bound by MPG Books Group, UK

Contents

Contributors

John Adams, Associate, Shearman & Sterling LLP, US.

Phoebus Athanassiou, PhD, Senior Legal Counsel, European Central Bank, Germany.

Alon Brav, Professor of Finance, Duke University, Fuqua School of Business, US.

Thomas Bullman, Senior Compliance Manager at Legal & General Investment Management Ltd, UK.

Ludwig Chincarini, Academic Council of IndexIQ.

Dilip K. Das, PhD, Professor of International Economics and International Finance, Director, The Institute of Asian Business, SolBridge International School of Business, Woosong University, Daejeon, Republic of Korea.

Alex Erskine, Chief Economist, Australian Securities and Investments Commission, Australia.

Felix Goltz, Senior Research Engineer, EDHEC Business School, Nice, France.

Nathan Greene, Partner, Shearman & Sterling LLP, US.

Andrea Hankova, Senior Hedge Fund Analyst, Kedge Capital (Suisse) S.A., Switzerland.

David Harrison, Associate, Bond Pearce LLP, UK.

Wei Jiang, Associate Professor of Finance and Economics, Columbia Business School, US.

Mark Jickling, Specialist in Financial Economics, Congressional Research Service, US.

Hyunseob Kim, PhD Candidate, Duke University, Fuqua School of Business, US.

Veronika Krepely Pool, Assistant Professor of Finance, Indiana University Kelley School of Business, US.

Marco Lamandini, Professor of Commercial Law, Faculty of Economics, University of Bologna, Italy.

Norbert Lang, Legal counsel, SEB Asset Management, Germany.

François-Serge Lhabitant, Associate Professor of Finance, EDHEC Business School, Nice, France; Chief Investment Officer, Kedge Capital Fund Management Ltd, Jersey.

Harry McVea, Reader in Law, School of Law, University of Bristol, UK; and Associate Research Fellow, Institute of Advanced Legal Studies, London.

Thomas Oatley, Associate Professor of Political Science, Department of Political Science, The University of North Carolina at Chapel Hill, US.

Ludovic Phalippou, Lecturer in Finance, University of Oxford, Saïd Business School, UK; formerly, Associate Professor of Finance, University of Amsterdam, Amsterdam Business School, The Netherlands.

David Schröder, Lecturer in Finance, Birkbeck College, UK.

Maria Strömqvist, PhD, Brummer & Partners Asset Management, Sweden; formerly, senior economist at the Financial Stability Department, Sveriges Riksbank, Sweden.

W. Kindred Winecoff, PhD Candidate, Department of Political Science, The University of North Carolina at Chapel Hill, US.

Peter Yeoh, Lecturer in Law, School of Law, Social Sciences and Communications, University of Wolverhampton, UK.

Abbreviations

ADI	Abu Dhabi Investment Authority
AIF	Alternative Investment Fund
AIFM	Alternative Investment Fund Manager
AUM	Assets Under Management
ASX	Australian Stock Exchange
ASIC	Australian Securities and Investments Commission
BaFIN	Bundesanstalt für Finanzdienstleistungsaufsicht (Germany)
BIS	Bank for International Settlements
bop	Balance of payments
CAC	Collective Action Clause
CDS	Collateralised Debt Obligation
CEO	Chief Executive Officer
CFTC	Commodity Futures Trading Commission (US)
CEPRES	Center for Private Equity Research
CIC	China Investment Corporation
CRA	Credit Rating Agency
CRMPG	Counterparty Risk Management Policy Group
EDP	Excessive Deficit Procedure
EEA	European Economic Area
EME	Emerging-market Economy
EMU	Economic and Monetary Union
ERM	Exchange Rate Mechanism
ESMA	European Securities and Markets Authority
ESRB	European Systemic Risk Board
ETF	Exchange-Traded Fund
EU	European Union
FAIFs	Funds of Alternative Investment Funds (UK)
FDIC	Federal Deposit Insurance Corporation (US)
FINRA	Financial Industry Regulatory Authority (US)
FoFs	Funds-of-funds
FoHFs	Funds-of-hedge-funds
FSA	Financial Services Authority (UK)
FSB	Financial Stability Board
FSOC	Financial Stability Oversight Council
FUM	Funds Under Management
GAPP	Generally Accepted Principles and Practices

GCC	Gulf Cooperation Council
GDP	Gross Domestic Product
GFC	Global Financial Crisis
G-7	Group of Seven
G-20	Group of Twenty
HFWG	Hedge Fund Working Group (UK)
HLI	Highly Leveraged Institution
HNWI	High Net Worth Individual
IAIS	International Association of Insurance Supervisors
IMA	Investment Management Association
IMF	International Monetary Fund
IMFC	International Monetary and Financial Committee
IOSCO	International Organisation of Securities Commissions
IPO	Initial Public Offer
IRR	Internal Rates of Returns
KIA	Kuwait Investment Authority
LBO	Leveraged Buyout
LPs	Limited Partners
LSE	London Stock Exchange
LTCM	Long-Term Capital Management
MiFID	Markets in Financial Instruments Directive
MIS	Managed Investment Scheme
NAV	Net Asset Value
NPV	Net Present Value
NURs	Non-UCITS retail schemes (UK)
NVCA	National Venture Capital Association
OCC	Office of the Comptroller of the Currency (US)
OECD	Organisation for Economic Co-operation and Development
OFT	Office for Fair Trading (UK)
OTC	Over-the-Counter
PDS	Product Disclosure Statement
PE	Private Equity
PSI	Permanent Subcommittee on Investigations (US Senate)
PWG	President's Working Group on Financial Markets (US)
QIS	Qualified Investor Schemes (UK)
RBA	Reserve Bank of Australia
SEC	Securities and Exchange Commission (US)
SMSF	Self-managed Superannuation Funds
SRO	Self-regulatory organisation
SWFS	Sovereign Wealth Funds
TFEU	Treaty on the Functioning of the European Union

UCITS	Undertakings for Collective Investment in Transferable Securities
UK	United Kingdom
US	United States
VaR	Value at Risk
VC	Venture Capital

Preface and acknowledgements

I wish to thank the publisher and Professor Rosa Maria Lastra of Queen Mary College, University of London, for entrusting me with the challenging but rewarding task of editing this book. I am also grateful to all contributors for making this book possible.

I owe a debt of gratitude to my managers at the ECB and, in particular, to Antonio Sáinz de Vicuña, Director General of the Legal Services of the ECB, and Dr Chiara Zilioli, formerly Head of the Legal Advice Division, for their support throughout the years of my service at the ECB. Last but not least, to Dr Dimitris Tsibanoulis, of Tsibanoulis & Partners Law Firm, Athens, for the opportunities that he has opened up for me, and for his trust and friendship.

I am forever indebted to Virge Juurikas for her forbearance, her unconditional love and her unfailing support in all of my endeavours, not least those associated with the editing of this book.

This book is dedicated to my family, those of its members who are no longer with us and those who are to hopefully take their place in the coming months and years.

Phoebus Athanassiou
Frankfurt am Main, Germany, 25 May 2011

Introduction

This book is published at a time of unprecedented crisis. A few words on its origins, their link to the activities of alternative investment funds and the recent surge to regulate them are deemed appropriate, by way of introduction.

The progressive deregulation of the European and US banking and financial systems, in conjunction with the galloping pace of financial globalization, have been amongst the salient characteristics of the last two decades of the history of finance. One of the most enduring legacies of the deregulation era, which was to see a flurry of promising financial innovation, has been the greater susceptibility of the European and US economies to asset and market bubbles, corporate scandals and failures and, more recently, to generalized financial sector and, in some cases, sovereign crises. As for globalization, one of its most lasting legacies has been the increasing vulnerability of national economies to financial meltdowns in the face of large, 'imported' shocks.

While globalization is, to some extent at least, something of a natural phenomenon, with technological innovation greatly facilitating the flow of capital from one corner of the world to the other, exposing market players to cross-border risks, deregulation is more a matter of choice. The policy makers' conscious decision to substitute the 'heavy hand of government' with the wisdom of the markets and the promise of financial innovation to contribute to the better pricing and spreading of risk have seen the US Congress repeal the Depression-era Glass-Steagall Act, which prevented depository (commercial) banks from competing with investment banks, European lawmakers liberalize the UCITS funds' investment policies, hedge funds thrive on both sides of the Atlantic and OTC derivatives markets grow dramatically in size and importance. The gradual dismantling of government regulation and the replacement of 'black letter' rules with reliance on market discipline were to set the scene for an extraordinary crisis that, largely due to the globalization-sponsored interdependencies amongst financial markets and their participants, nearly wiped out entire segments of the financial services industry, threatened the global financial system with a meltdown of epic proportions, cost taxpayers and the future generations dearly and, since late 2009, driven a growing number of European Union Member States to the brink of default.

The policy of fostering financial innovation through deregulation and the dismantling of normative barriers thought to impede free competition and constrain consumer choice, have both proved incapable of shielding national economies from the impact of financial crises and exposed as naïve the policy makers' reliance on market discipline as a substitute for regulation, against the dictates of common sense and the average man's knowledge of human nature and its foibles. It has also exposed the limits of economic analysis as the definitive tool for financial regulation, and cast doubts on the assumption that markets behave rationally. Three recent examples suffice to illustrate some of the deficiencies associated with reliance on market discipline and economic analysis as substitutes for external regulation; first, the massive Madoff fraud, facilitated by deficient due diligence, a lack of transparency and a combination of regulatory and supervisory inadequacies; second, the implosion of the structured finance markets, which brought to light the inability of purportedly sophisticated investors and seemingly well-regulated, by contemporary standards, market intermediaries to perform any manner of due diligence over the instruments they had created, or in which they had invested and to correctly price the risks that those carried; finally, the collapse of the housing market in the US, where what started with the best of intentions (the noble idea of promoting home ownership for the less wealthy) resulted in a market crash of unparalleled proportions due to the 'creative' but, ultimately, irresponsible financing techniques used in its context and the excessive risks that these were accompanied by.

Financial crises often lead to regulatory backlashes. The Wall Street Crash of 1929 was one example of that and the crisis that began fermenting in 2007 was to be no exception. The recent adoption of the Alternative Investment Fund Managers (AIFM) Directive, in Europe, and of the Dodd-Frank Act, in the US, are said to support the claim that financial crises provide opportunities for reforms with little (or no) link to the root causes of the crises themselves. While it is probably true that the financial crisis was not directly caused by hedge funds, nor was it the product of the market activities of private equity or sovereign wealth funds, these and other alternative investment vehicles are very much the products or manifestations of the deregulation trend that swept through financial markets in the last two decades. The new regulatory frameworks that alternative investment funds are now preparing for, on both sides of the Atlantic, are, thus, not as unwarranted as some would have one believe, however legitimate it may be to disagree on their precise scope and concrete contents. For, in the run up to the crisis, alternative investment funds have been beset by a litany of shortcomings, common to their more conventional competitors, including failures in management, oversight and control, asset segregation and valuation, as well as transparency, contributing to corporate governance distortions, the exacerbation of market risks and the accentuation of systemically significant imbalances. Similarly, the pre-crisis liberalization of alternative investment products and the policy makers' surge to widen investment choice for retail investors were symptomatic of the same financial deregulation trend that helped usher in one of the most catastrophic sequences of events to hit financial markets in recent history. In the same vein, alternative investment managers were to prove no more capable of grasping the full significance of their regulatory and societal responsibilities (those that the abdication by governments of their own role allowed room for) than their peers from the more stringently regulated banking and mutual fund sectors, while their clients, however experienced and sophisticated, were to fall no less victim to momentous errors of appreciation and to show no sounder judgement than the clients of other market intermediaries. That rules in the field of alternative investment funds have become the focus of particular attention and that wide-ranging regulatory changes have been proposed or enacted to help address the weaknesses brought to light by the financial downturn should, therefore, not come as a surprise, even if it is possible to disagree on the concrete rules proposed for their regulation.

The policy issues that alternative investment funds raised, their perceived externalities – due to their involvement in speculative trading, their use of leverage and short-selling, their participation in spurious corporate governance practices, as well as their inadequate levels of disclosure and transparency, in conjunction with the opportunities for market manipulation that these are conducive to – combined with their potential for systemic disruptions, had been identified as concerns well before the onset of the financial crisis but never seriously addressed, despite the wide attention that they had attracted. The public scrutiny of the LTCM and Amaranth failures pointed to specific areas where vigilance was essential and action was necessary. However, the regulatory fall-out of those high-profile failures turned out to be very short-lived across the Atlantic, as the SEC's modest attempt to indirectly regulate hedge funds by imposing a registration obligation on their managers was defeated in court. In the EU, the Commission was to staunchly oppose hedge fund or private equity fund regulation until 2009. It took the financial crisis for policymakers and regulators alike, on either side of the Atlantic, to change their tune and acknowledge the existence of genuine issues at stake that had to be addressed as matters of urgency. It remains to be seen how successful their hitherto or future responses will turn out to be. That the opportunity for the imposition of normative constraints on alternative investment funds was to be provided by a major financial crisis, not directly attributable to their operation, inevitably increases the probability that those constraints will turn out to have been less the products of mature reflection and rather more the fruits of haste and urgency, with the regulatory process leading up to their adoption having, to some extent, fallen victim to the vagaries of political pressure and to the whims of public opinion. But on the need for action, as such, there is little room for dispute.

In light of the above, there has hardly ever been a more appropriate time than now to explore alternative investment funds, their merits and weaknesses, their *modus operandi* and their regulation. The aim of this book is to do precisely that, devoting to alternative investment funds the attention they deserve as an important, but often misunderstood or misrepresented, component of contemporary financial markets. To achieve that aim, this book is divided in four Parts. Part A (Chapters 1–4) provides the background information necessary to understand the contemporary alternative investment fund industry's profile. Part B (Chapters 5–11) is an account of some of the main areas of regulatory policy concern arising from the activities of alternative investment funds. Part C (Chapters 12–14) traces the history of the involvement of alternative investment funds in financial crises and outlines past failures, with a view to assessing the role of alternative investment funds in the former and the lessons drawn from the latter. Finally, Part D (Chapters 15–18) provides an account of alternative investment fund regulation in selected jurisdictions, including an overview of the expected impact of the Dodd-Frank Act and the AIFM Directive on the sector, on both sides of the Atlantic.

The handbook's introductory chapter discusses hedge funds, including the legal and business structures that are typical of this asset class in the US. Chincarini also compares hedge funds to other types of investment vehicles, such as private equity funds, mutual funds, and ETFs. The author then examines briefly the claims regarding the benefits of hedge funds as well as their relationship to the financial crisis of 2008. Chapter 1 concludes with a discussion of some of the regulatory developments across the Atlantic and whether hedge fund regulation is necessary or reasonable.

Chapter 2 provides a comprehensive overview of the European hedge fund industry, its structure, players, and major strategies, as well as its historical performance. Hankova and Lhabitant argue that, while the European industry remains heavily centred in London, recent efforts to tighten the UK tax regime, combined with the regulatory changes recently introduced at the EU level (such as the adoption of the AIFM Directive and the liberalisation of the regulatory framework for harmonized collective investment schemes), are likely to reduce London's appeal as a management jurisdiction of choice. The authors also find that, compared to their US counterparts, European hedge funds under-perform; that the common belief that smaller funds outperform larger ones is unfounded;

and that the financial crisis has brought substantial changes to the *modus operandi* of European hedge funds, increasing the likelihood of further consolidation within the sector.

Chapter 3 is devoted to sovereign-wealth funds (SWFs), from the start of the previous decade until the onset of the financial crisis, a period which has seen SWFs emerge as an important investor group, providing much needed liquidity, including at times of crisis. Das argues that the concerns about SWFs and their activities voiced prior to the start of the financial crisis were exaggerated or misplaced, and that the focus of the debate surrounding them has in any event shifted since the start of the crisis. Going forward, it is important to ensure that the market turmoil, and the change of priorities that it has signalled, do not deflect attention from the need for improvements in their transparency, so as to alleviate concerns about their activities and avert the risk of a protectionist backlash. The author outlines some of the policy measures available to ensure a balance between more transparency and accountability in the operations of SWFs and the avoidance of unnecessary strictures on their activities.

Chapter 4 provides a comprehensive review of the literature on the risks and returns of private equity funds, comparing the different datasets used in academic research. Phalippou finds that average returns are lower than those of public equity and, in any event, less spectacular than often conjectured. The author also finds that buyout funds appear to bear a moderate market risk, although their exposure to liquidity and distress risk is significant. Phalippou conjectures on why industry benchmarks show different returns than those documented in Chapter 4. Finally, he discusses the issue of fund selection, emphasizing the importance of a bottom-up approach when investing in private equity, showing that top-quartile returns and evidence of performance persistence are to be approached with caution, and describing variables that can help predict returns.

Part B of the book begins with Chapter 5, which explores the rationale for allowing retail investors' wider access to alternative investment products, focusing, in particular, on the FSA's response to pressures for wider retail investor access to such products. McVea describes the new regulatory landscape, which has emerged from the liberalization policy on retail investor access to alternative investments, and assesses critically the outcome of that policy, the contours of which are only now beginning to take shape. The author's basic claim is that while the EU's desire to create a 'state of the art' onshore investment fund industry is understandable and even laudable, there are serious shortcomings with the thrust of the EU's policy of liberalization in this sphere; and that regulatory authorities in Europe, and especially the UK, have placed too much faith in market discipline and tailored regulatory rules, despite their awareness of certain risks associated with greater retail investor access to alternative investment products.

The complexity of hedge fund investments poses challenges when it comes to a detailed analysis of their returns, a condition precedent for an adequate and comprehensive hedge fund reporting. Goltz and Schröder outline in Chapter 6 the major challenges for hedge fund reporting, providing an overview of the set of tools available to report the performance and risk of hedge fund investments. The authors examine the existing regulatory framework as well as guidelines and best practices issued by governmental working groups and industry associations on hedge fund reporting. They then take a closer look at the performance and risk measures currently used for hedge fund reporting, which, from a theoretical standpoint, are not always suitable. Finally, they examine specific issues of relevance to hedge fund disclosure, such as leverage, liquidity, and operational risk.

Over the last decade, activist hedge funds have emerged as significant agents of corporate change, capable of generating operational, financial, and wider governance reforms in their target firms. Chapter 7 reviews the objectives of hedge fund activists, their tactics and their choice of target firms. It then analyzes the value-creation process initiated by activist hedge funds, distinguishing the value effect from alternative hypotheses such as stock-picking and wealth transfer. Brav, Jiang and Kim conclude that the evidence available from different studies generally supports the view that hedge fund activism creates value for shareholders by effectively influencing the governance, capital structure decisions, and operating performance of target firms, instead of destroying value or focusing on short-term profits.

The recent hedge fund fraud scandals have raised questions about how wide-spread fraud in the industry is and to what extent the sector's opaqueness creates opportunities for unscrupulous behaviours. The recent high profile fraud cases have also re-ignited the debate on hedge fund regulation. The purpose of Chapter 8 is to synthesize existing research on hedge fund fraud. Focusing on fraud detection, Pool examines both the performance and the operational red flags proposed in previous studies. The author also discusses the effectiveness of these flags for fraud prediction and detection. The author claims that both operational and performance red flags relate to fund transparency and have important implications on current calls for greater regulatory oversight.

Chapter 9 reviews the pros and cons of external versus self-regulation in the context of hedge funds. Lamandini suggests that, despite the theoretically clear distinction between these two types of regulation, the practical differences between them are less prominent than one might have assumed. Similarly, the deterrence associated with self-regulatory versus command and control rules is in practice not very dissimilar. As a result, self and external regulations are bound to coexist, considering the natural inadequacy of any national or regional institution, due to its territorially limited sovereignty, in properly responding to the regulatory challenges posed by genuinely global investment vehicles, such as hedge funds.

The final chapter of Part B examines the role that competition law could play in mitigating some of the risks associated with the activities of alternative investment funds. The financial crisis has seen many a commentator point to the destabilising effects of herding and correlated behaviour by financial market participants, linking those to price distortions and asset price bubbles. Chapter 10 inquires into those questions from the point of view of Union competition law, with particular reference to alternative investment funds. Harrison argues that applying competition law principles more rigorously in the financial services sector in general, and to alternative investment funds, in particular may reduce the need for detailed alternative investment fund regulation, while at the same time generating wider benefits for markets, their participants and investors alike.

Part C of the handbook begins with Chapter 11. This explores some of the most spectacular hedge fund failures in recent years, *inter alia* assessing the nature of the activities of hedge funds and how these were conducive to failures, their risk management practices and the role of supervisors in the run-up to their collapse and in their restructuring or recapitalization. As Jickling observes, drawing on the lessons of those failures, many of the dynamics that made the financial crisis so severe were anticipated in the reports issued in the aftermath of the collapse of *LTCM* and *Amaranth*. And yet, in 2007–2008, regulators were to prove unable to prevent those dynamics from materializing. Ironically, some of the major policy concerns raised by hedge funds and their activities were to be dealt with in response to the financial crisis, one in the creation of which hedge funds are generally considered to have played no more than a secondary role.

A discussion of the impact of hedge funds on systemic stability is a recurring feature of every financial crisis. Chapter 12 discusses the impact of hedge funds on systemic stability, first from a historical perspective and then in relation to the recent financial crisis. The analysis conducted by Strömqvist does not lend much support to the proposition that hedge funds have had a greater impact on financial crises than other investors, whether in general or specifically with regard to the recent financial crisis.

Chapter 13 addresses the thorny issue of the involvement of vulture funds in the recent sovereign default episodes within the EU. Traditionally associated with emerging economies, the threat of sovereign default has recently made its appearance in the context of several advanced economies, including those of the Member States participating in the Economic and Monetary Union, partly as a consequence of the ongoing global financial crisis. The speculative activities of some private funds have *inter alia* been blamed for the sovereign default crisis in some of those Member States, attracting calls for their tighter regulation. Yeoh discusses the underlying reasons for the acute sovereign default risks faced by certain European Union Member States, and the possible impact of the activities of vulture funds on their emergence.

Part D of the handbook begins with Chapter 14. Since the end of 2008, lawmakers around the world have been grappling with the question of how best to react to the global financial crisis, with the outcome of their reflections also having an impact on the private funds industry. The Dodd-Frank Act, adopted in July 2010, is to radically change the landscape for the registration and regulation of private investment fund advisers – whether located within, or outside the US. In addition to significantly widening the registration requirements for investment advisers, the legislation and related implementing rules proposed by US regulators impose increased compliance, recordkeeping and reporting obligations on investment advisers. Other, entirely new, rules such as derivatives regulation, systemic risk regulation, and the 'Volcker Rule', may also deeply affect the operations of private fund advisers. Greene and Adams summarize, in this chapter, the pre-July 2011 legal framework applicable to investment advisers, before analyzing the groundbreaking changes brought forth by the Dodd-Frank Act, and its consequences for the private funds industry.

Chapter 15 addresses the issue of alternative investment fund regulation in Germany. Alternative investments in open-ended investment funds and, especially, hedge funds are topics of debate in recent political discussions. Lang argues that, surprisingly, there is no coherent political and regulatory discussion in Germany on how to build up a solid hedge fund industry while, at the same time, ensuring investor protection and financial stability. What is more, questions concerning investor protection are only being asked in relation to hedge funds and funds of hedge funds, ignoring the huge certificate-emitting branch, which presents the same inherent risks as hedge funds, but which operates in a less transparent manner and at a higher cost for investors.

Chapter 16 examines the growth and regulation of hedge fund, private equity and other types of alternative investment funds in Australia. The growth of investment in these alternative asset classes has been supported substantially by the retirement income system established in Australia in the early 1990s. Investment in alternative investment products has also been buoyed by almost two decades of uninterrupted economic growth and the 'search for yield', as well as by taxation arrangements. Erskine outlines the overall size of the market, the number of investments marketed, the largest players, typical industry structures, the impact of the global financial crisis and some of the future challenges for the Australian industry.

Chapter 17 provides an overview of one of the most controversial pieces of European Union law in recent years: the AIFM Directive. Inspired by the perceived need to impose regulatory constraints on non-harmonized and, mostly, lightly-regulated funds, in response to the outbreak, in 2008, of the financial crisis, its earlier drafts were to cause controversy and deep divisions, with transatlantic ripple effects. The final rules, adopted in late 2010, were welcomed with relief by market players, for erecting less hurdles to market access than those originally proposed, and for imposing fewer obligations upon fund managers than the Commission had envisaged in its original proposal. However, the AIFM Directive remains a contentious piece of legislation, with wide-ranging implications for the way in which alternative investment funds are to conduct their business within the European Union in the coming years. Athanassiou and Bullman explore the merits and drawbacks of the Directive and reflect on its likely impact on the European and global alternative investment fund industries.

The final chapter of the handbook explores the probability that the recent financial crisis will prompt governments to establish comprehensive and effective global regulation for financial institutions. Viewing the history of post-war financial regulation through the lens of contemporary positive theories of regulation, Oatley and Winecoff conclude that the answer is 'no'. Although a case for global regulation can be made on market efficiency grounds, policymakers are less responsive to market pressures than they are to political incentives and the strong pressures that the latter create to retain national control over financial rules. The authors also argue that whilst crises trigger discussions and reforms, in each instance, adherence to global rules has been *voluntary* rather than obligatory and that the resulting agreements have failed to move towards anything that is even remotely akin to a global regulatory regime.

The law is stated as of 1 May 2011. Prospective changes are, where relevant, noted. Website citations were valid on the same date.

PART A

FOUNDATIONS

1. Hedge funds – an introduction
*Ludwig Chincarini**

INTRODUCTION

Alternative investment vehicles are vastly misunderstood and, amongst them, hedge funds are perhaps the most grossly misunderstood. While many are those who understand what the S&P 500 or a mutual fund is, few know what 'hedge funds' are, apart from believing them to be evil (Braithwaite (2009)). This is ironic, considering that the first hedge fund – started in 1949 by Alfred Winslow Jones – sought to *help* investors. Its founder was good at selecting stocks that would perform well, but rather less skilled at predicting the direction of the market. At the time, most equity portfolios were offered as mutual funds regulated by the Securities and Exchange Commission (SEC). Most of them were prohibited from shorting stocks and, therefore, had a long exposure to the overall equity market. Thus, even if their portfolio manager was exceptional at selecting stocks, a drop in the overall market would inevitably result in a simultaneous drop in the value of its portfolio. If instead the portfolio manager could simultaneously invest in 'good' stocks *and* short-sell 'bad' stocks, its portfolio would be less vulnerable to overall market risk.[1] Even the most sceptical investor could not deny the logic of the practice of selling stocks both short and long, which is where hedge funds derive their name

* CFA, PhD, Member of the Academic Council of IndexIQ. I would like to especially thank Erin Toothaker and Coady Smith as well as Jason Blauvelt, Anthony Gonzales, Andrew Oetting, Matt Walkup, Jing Wen, and Jae Sae Won for research assistance; Neer Asherie, Cliff Asness, Aaron Brown, Steward Hodges, Jacques Pezier, Eric Rosenfeld, and Paul Schulstad for helpful comments; Salvatore Bruno for data help, as well as *Global Financial Data*, David Hsieh and William Fung for their straddle data available at http://faculty.fuqua.duke.edu/̃dah7/DataLibrary/TF-FAC.xls, Kenneth French and Eugene Fama for their factor data available at http://mba.tuck.dartmouth.edu/pages/faculty/ken.french/data library.html, and *Hedge Fund Research* for both hedge fund index data and individual hedge fund data.

[1] For example, if the equity market went down due to a decline in consumer confidence or a major recession, 50% of the portfolio (the long side) would decline, while the other 50% of the portfolio would rise due to the portfolio manager's ability to sell stocks short.

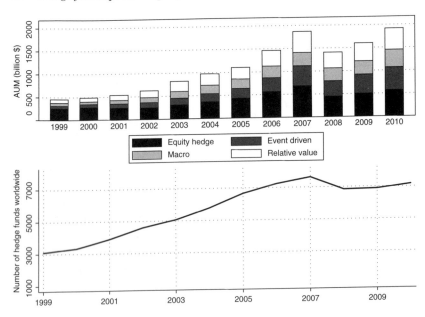

Source: Hedge Fund Research.

Figure 1.1   Hedge fund world wide assets over time

from: the portfolio manager has, in principal, 'hedged out' the portfolio's market risk by having both long and short components in it. The remaining risks are the stock-specific risks. However, in order to operate in the above way, the first hedge fund had to be set up as a legal entity that avoided the SEC's regulation. This lack of regulation marks the beginning of the public wariness and wide-spread misconceptions vis-à-vis hedge funds.

The industry has changed and grown substantially since 1949, when the first hedge fund was formed. Concerning *quantitative* changes, the number of hedge funds worldwide has grown from 530 in 1990 to 7164 at the beginning of 2011, and their publicly reported assets under management (AUM) have also increased from US$39 billion in 1990 to US$1.9 trillion at the beginning of 2011. Figure 1.1 shows the growth in hedge fund assets and number of funds since 1990. The original concept has also changed over time. Nowadays, the term 'hedge' may or may not be appropriate depending on the individual hedge fund. Moreover, the hedge fund world has become divided into the 'mammoths' and all the rest. This is clearly reflected in Figure 1.2, which shows that 78 per cent of all hedge funds' AUM is managed by funds with over US$1 billion in assets. These only

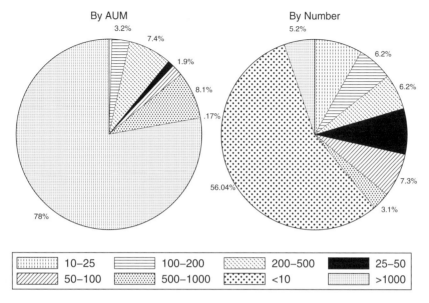

By AUM

3.2%
7.4%
1.9%
8.1%
.17%
78%

By Number

5.2%
6.2%
6.2%
7.3%
3.1%
56.04%

10–25	100–200	200–500	25–50
50–100	500–1000	<10	>1000

Source: Hedge Fund Research.

Figure 1.2 Hedge fund assets composition by number of hedge funds and hedge fund assets (in millions)

represent about 5 per cent of all hedge funds. Almost 80 per cent of hedge funds have less than US$100 million under management and 56 per cent have less than US$10 million.

This chapter will discuss hedge funds in some detail, including the legal and business structures that characterize them. It will also compare hedge funds to other investment vehicles, such as private equity funds, mutual funds, and Exchange Traded Fund (ETFs). It will then examine briefly the claims regarding their benefits as well as their relationship to the financial crisis of 2008. This chapter will then discuss some of the developments in their regulation, assessing the extent to which regulation is necessary or reasonable in the context of hedge funds.

1. UNDERSTANDING HEDGE FUNDS

1.1 The Legal Structure

An understanding of the laws governing portfolio management companies is necessary to understand why hedge funds are formed, in the

United States (US), in a specific manner. After the Great Depression and the stock market crash of 1929, the US government introduced a variety of security laws designed to protect investors and the domestic financial system, of which the most important[2] were (i) the Securities Act of 1933; (ii) the Securities Exchange Act of 1934; (iii) the Investment Company Act of 1940; and (iv) the Investment Advisors Act of 1940. Table 1.1 summarizes those laws. While all of them had some bearing on portfolio management companies, the most significant amongst them was the Investment Company Act of 1940 (also known as the mutual fund act, as most mutual funds must comply with it), which placed rules on leverage, fees, and mandatory disclosure of fund holdings. We briefly discuss, below, each of the above regulations and how a portfolio management company can be set up in order to avoid it.

The Securities Act of 1933 imposes upon portfolio management companies a duty to file quarterly and annual statements, as with any other company offering securities to the public. It can be avoided, however, through a careful reading of 'Regulation D', which allows companies to avoid registration with the SEC provided that all of the following conditions are met: (i) all but 35 of their investors must be 'accredited investors';[3] (ii) the shares or units of the fund must be privately placed; and (iii) the shares of the fund sold to US investors must be acquired for investment purposes only and not for immediate resale or distribution. This is why most hedge funds are only accessible to high net worth investors: it is not that hedge fund managers seek to exclude the poor but, in order to *inter alia* avoid the costs of regulation, the majority of their investors must be accredited ones.

The Securities Act of 1934, also known as the 'broker act', governs the trades made by brokers to ensure that these are in the best interests of the brokers' clients. Under the Act, brokers must keep detailed records of trades and avoid conflicts of interest when trading for their own account. The way around the Securities Act is to trade *for the fund as a whole* rather than on behalf of individual customers. As this is the natural business of

---

[2]   There are numerous other security laws which impact hedge funds and/or portfolio management companies, some of which can be avoided and some of which cannot. These include, amongst others, the Employee Retirement Income Security Act (ERISA) of 1974 (relating to retirement assets), and the Commodity Exchange act of 1936.

[3]   An accredited investor is an individual with a net worth of US$1 million or more, or had an annual income of US$200 000 or more in each of the last 2 years (or US$300 000 jointly with spouse) and a reasonable expectation of reaching the same income in the current year.

Table 1.1 *Major investment company regulation and hedge fund exemptions*

Regulation	Main requirements	Technique to avoid	Comments
Securities Act of 1933	Companies that issue shares to the public must disclose regular reports about the state of their company (e.g. annual financial reports like the 10-K).	Regulations S and D allow for exemption to rule. No need to register if investors are foreign investors or if investors are domestic, and all but 35 are accredited, no re-sale of securities, and privately placed shares.	Accredited investor definition is changing, but used to be a net worth of $1M or $200K in annual income.[a] Many hedge funds still issue offering memorandums with information similar to a prospectus.
Securities Exchange Act of 1934	Companies that trade on the behalf of customers must keep detailed records of trades and avoid conflicts of interest.	Trade only on behalf of the fund and not act as broker for customers.	Hedge funds keep detailed records of their trades, but since trades are done for the fund which everyone is interested in, conflict of interest does not exist, unless there are separate accounts.
Investment Advisers Act of 1940	Requires companies that give investment advice to individuals for a fee, which naturally includes a group that trades on the behalf of customers, to file an adviser registration form.	Exemption is enjoyed if: (1) the hedge fund manager or general manager manages less than $25 million in assets or (2) the fund has fewer than 15 clients in any 12-month period.	The SEC is expanding the rules for this in 2011 so that hedge funds cannot count the fund itself as just one client to avoid registration, but will have to look-through the fund and count actual clients.

Table 1.1 (continued)

Regulation	Main requirements	Technique to avoid	Comments
Investment Company Act of 1940 (a.k.a Mutual Fund Act)	Requires companies that manage portfolios on the behalf of customers to register a prospectus, restricts leverage, restricts fees, has rules of diversification, and has rules for distribution related to tax status, among others.	Exemption if the fund has less than 100 beneficial investors not counting the partners. Institutions count as one investor unless they own more than 10% of the fund.	Some hedge funds have more than 100 investors and are still exempt, this is due to the National Securities Markets Improvement Act (discussed below).
Employee Retirement Income Security Act of 1974	Focused on rules on how performance fees are calculated and paid. Restrictions on certain types of transactions. Custody of foreign assets outside the country would be limited. Expense charges would have restrictions. Fund might have to make periodic reports to the Department of Labor.	Exemption if a hedge fund has less than 25% of its assets from retirement programs.	

Commodity Exchange Act of 1974	Established CFTC as regulatory body of institutions trading commodity futures, futures, or options. Requires such institutions to file a registration form, quarterly statements to investors, annual audited statements, and performance presentation standards.	Exemptions if (1) the fund has less than $200K in capital and fewer than 15 clients, (2) the fund is restricted to family members, (3) the fund trades in OTC instruments, (4) the fund limits itself to qualified eligible persons, as well some others.	Although some hedge funds are exempt from this act, the ones that make heavy use of futures trading usually must register. The OTC limitation is particularly worrisome. A hedge fund must report all of its exchange related positions but none of its OTC positions.
National Securities Markets Improvement Act of 1996	Established additional exemptions for hedge funds by increasing exemption criteria if investors are qualified purchasers and by getting rid of look-through provisions at the 10% limitation for institutions.	Increased exemptions on previous regulations.	Allowed for hedge funds to expand, especially in terms of size.

Note: [a] An accredited investor is one that has $200000 in annual income if single and $300000 in annual income if married, or has a net worth of $1 million. A qualified purchaser is an individual or family having investments totalling $5 million, plus certain investment advisers, trusts, and companies with at least $25 million that are composed entirely of qualified purchasers.

portfolio management companies, overcoming this regulation has caused no particular difficulties for hedge funds.

The Investment Company Act of 1940 covers a large range of rules, including but not limited to the imposition of obligations and restrictions on leverage, shorting, and reporting. For many portfolio management companies, certain types of investing would be entirely excluded under the Act, making its avoidance paramount to the operation of hedge funds. Exemption from this Act can be obtained in a variety of ways. One way is by limiting the number of beneficial owners or investors of the fund to fewer than 100 and the offering is a private offering (see Section 3(c)(1) of the Act).[4]

The last major piece of legislation, the Investment Advisers Act of 1940, requires those who give investment advice to register with the SEC. Portfolio managers implicitly give investment advice by choosing the investments for the portfolio in which their clients are invested. In order to avoid registration, one of two conditions must be met: (1) the hedge fund manager or general manager must manage less than US$25 million in assets; or (2) the hedge fund must have fewer than 15 clients in any 12-month period. This might seem confusing, but hedge funds tend to form their company with two principle agents, one of which is the Investment Advisor. The Investment Adviser makes the investment decisions for the fund's single client: its investment portfolio. Therefore, as long as fewer than 15 portfolios are being managed, the management company can obtain an exemption from the registration requirement.

In 2004, the SEC amended the Investment Advisers Act to mandate advisors to 'look through' the hedge fund and, instead of counting it as a single client, count each individual investor in the fund as a discrete client. The new rule (Rule 203(b)(3)-2) which was to take effect as of 1 February 2006 and which would have resulted in many more hedge funds having to register with the SEC than the case currently is, was eventually vacated by the US Court of Appeals for the District of Columbia Circuit, which agreed with hedge fund manager Phillip Goldstein that the new Rule was 'arbitrary' and that the agency lacked the authority to impose it. One might ask why the SEC would want to broaden the scope of hedge fund regulation. There were two reasons for that: one was an increase in malpractice and fraud by hedge funds and another was the enormous growth in hedge fund assets. Interestingly, the new rules left a loophole for hedge

---

[4]   A company is also considered one beneficial owner, unless the company owns more than 10% of the portfolio management company. In that case, the company would have 'look through' to all of the investors in its company and count those as additional investors (see Section 3(c)(1)(A) of the Act). To avoid this problem, hedge funds typically keep the institutional ownership less than 10%.

funds. Because hedge funds and private equity funds have similarities, discussed later in this chapter, an exemption was made for hedge funds with lock-up periods of longer than 2 years.[5] This had the effect of excluding private equity funds (which typically keep money locked up for 3–5 years) from registration but, also, of encouraging many hedge funds to extend their lock-up periods beyond 2 years to avoid registration.

In summary, hedge funds are established as portfolio management companies that manage money by investing mainly in publicly traded securities on the behalf of their investors and seek to avoid registration with the SEC. Having said that, hedge funds were not created for devious purposes: the primary engine behind their business structure is not to avoid regulatory compliance but, rather, to ensure that regulatory constraints do not prevent them from achieving their specific investment objectives.

1.2   The Business Structure

The typical hedge fund is set up with three objectives in mind: avoid SEC registration, benefit from 'pass-through' taxation, and assume limited liability.

Despite the many ways in which hedge funds can avoid SEC regulation, many of them still voluntarily choose to register with the SEC. The final column of Table 1.2 shows that about 44 per cent of hedge funds register with the SEC, many of them to enhance their transparency and credibility, especially vis-à-vis the more risk-averse institutional investors.

'Pass-through' taxation entails that it is a hedge fund's investors who pay taxes when profits are distributed to them, rather than the hedge fund itself.[6] Hedge funds are also structured to assume limited liability, meaning that, if the hedge fund incurs losses greater than its assets or investors sue the fund, the personal assets of the fund's limited partners and/or of its investors are off-limits. Most hedge funds are formed as limited liability partnerships, the second most common business structure being limited liability companies, and the third most common being corporations (see Table 1.3).[7]

The business of a hedge fund is simple. Its managers offer to manage investor money in exchange for a fee, typically consisting of a *management*

---

[5]   This means that when an investor invests in a hedge fund with a lock-up of one year, the investor cannot withdraw his or her money for a minimum one year.

[6]   This avoids the double taxation that is problematic with US corporations. Hedge funds also set up funds in the Mirror fund or Master-Feeder set up to benefit different types of investors. Details of this can be found elsewhere.

[7]   For more details, see Bagley and Dauchy (2007).

Table 1.2 *Characteristics of hedge funds*

Group	Investability				Firm size (Bil.)	Liquidity			Transparency
	Minimum invest. (mil.)	Subscription	Open for investment	Country located		Redemption	Advance notice	Lockup	SEC registered
Equity hedge	0.84	35.34	0.91	64.64	12.18	70.55	34.59	127.49	46.74
Event-driven	1.21	39.17	0.92	84.89	8.12	114.32	55.53	189.54	53.54
Macro	1.63	25.64	0.90	62.63	11.05	33.66	18.48	30.33	26.37
Relative val	1.08	31.96	0.92	68.72	8.79	65.98	43.55	98.40	50.67
Live funds	1.15	30.37	0.94	59.19	10.28	60.79	36.64	107.50	52.31
Dead funds	0.99	36.49	0.88	74.79	11.69	73.84	33.98	114.03	35.67
All	1.07	33.32	0.91	66.94	10.94	67.11	35.36	110.60	44.05

Note: This table reports the average of the fund characteristics as of June 2009. Minimum Invest. reports the average minimum investment required, subscription reports the average frequency that investors are allowed to make subscriptions, Open for Investment reports the percentage of hedge funds that are open for new investments, Country located is the percentage of hedge funds with a US address, Firm Size is the average size of the entire firm in billions of dollars, Redemption reports the average frequency for redemption, Advance Notice reports the average number of days the hedge fund requires for notice to withdraw funds, Lockup reports the average number of days that investor funds cannot be withdrawn, SEC registered reports the percentage of hedge funds that are registered with the SEC. This selection of data includes only hedge funds that report to HFR. Equity Hedge, Event Driven, Macro, and Relative Value are hedge fund categories described in the text. Live funds represent the existing hedge funds as of June 2009 and Dead funds represents all of the hedge funds that reported at some point to HFR, but did not report as of June 2009. All represents all hedge funds, including both live and dead funds.

Table 1.3 *Characteristics of hedge funds*

Group	Leverage	Legal structure							Regional investment focus				
		L.P.	Corp.	L.L.C.	M.A.	I.C.	U.T.	Other	North America	Latin America	Asia	Europe	Other
Equity hedge	73.51	39.52	10.48	19.44	7.97	4.09	1.55	16.94	43.85	1.26	16.77	19.97	18.02
Event-driven	66.88	43.89	8.36	24.92	5.79	6.75	0.00	10.29	67.03	1.31	4.37	7.42	19.87
Macro	80.52	18.69	13.46	20.19	6.81	3.25	19.40	18.21	10.47	1.08	2.29	1.56	84.60
Relative val	79.45	29.85	15.10	21.45	9.65	3.04	1.97	18.95	51.98	1.61	6.31	8.79	31.19
Live funds	74.95	32.18	13.48	16.95	10.54	3.69	3.66	19.51	38.27	1.66	10.66	14.98	34.33
Dead funds	75.65	36.05	9.86	24.06	5.07	4.31	6.40	14.24	49.88	0.33	11.27	8.29	30.16
All	75.30	34.10	11.68	20.48	7.82	4.00	5.02	16.89	41.45	1.29	10.83	13.14	33.19

Note: This table reports the average of the fund characteristics as of June 2009. Leverage reports the percentage of funds that use leverage, legal reports the percentage of firms set up as various legal entities, including limited partnerships (L.P.), L.L.C. (limited liability companies), corporations (Corp.), and other, which represented all other forms of legal entities. Regional Investment Focus reports the percentage of funds that focus on investing in a particular region, including North America, Latin America, Asia, Europe, and Other. This selection of data includes only hedge funds that report to HFR. Equity Hedge, Event Driven, Macro, and Relative Value are hedge fund categories described in the text. Live funds represent the existing hedge funds as of June 2009 and Dead funds represents all of the hedge funds that reported at some point to HFR, but did not report as of June 2009. All represents all hedge funds, including both live and dead funds.

and an *incentive* fee. The management (or 'operating') fee is intended to cover the costs of running the hedge fund and is charged as a percentage of the assets under management. The average management fee for hedge funds is 1.49 per cent (see Table 1.4). More specifically, about 33 per cent of hedge funds charge a 1 per cent management fee, 25 per cent charge a 1.5 per cent fee, and another 25 per cent charge a 2 per cent fee. Thus, 83 per cent of hedge funds charge either 1, 1.5, or 2 per cent in management fees.[8] The incentive fee serves as compensation to the hedge fund managers for good performance and seeks to align their incentives with those of their clients.[9] The average incentive fee is 18.95 per cent. The *timing* for the collection of those fees will differ from one hedge fund to another. Some collect monthly, some quarterly, and others yearly. The most common incentive fee charged is 20 per cent, with around 80 per cent of hedge funds charging this amount. About 5 per cent of hedge funds charge no incentive fee, 3 per cent charge a 10 per cent incentive fee, 6 per cent charge a 15 per cent incentive fee, and 4 per cent charge a 25 per cent incentive fee.

In addition to those fees, hedge funds may have 'high-water marks' or 'hurdle rates'. A high-water mark represents the level at which the incentive fees begin to accrue. Typically, it is the highest net asset value or cumulative return received by a client over the duration of their investment. High-water marks seek to protect investors from hedge fund managers collecting incentive fees twice, by ensuring that the hedge fund is rewarded only for real growth in the clients' assets.[10] A hurdle rate is usually a reference return on a specific security that the hedge fund manager has to outperform before incentive fees are charged. For example, if the hurdle rate is the return on US 3-month Treasury bills, which are 6 per cent for that particular year, and the portfolio rises from US$100 million to US$130 million, the incentive fees collected are US$4.8 million (0.20 (US$30 −

---

[8]   Suppose the fee for a hedge fund manager that has US$100 million under management was 2%. This would mean that every year, the management company would take US$2 million as a fee for managing the investors' money.

[9]   Suppose a hedge fund with a 20% incentive fee starts with US$100 million in investor assets and by the end of the year the fund grows to US$130 million. This represents a 30% return, and the hedge fund would collect incentive fees of US$6 million (0.20 US$30 million).

[10]   Suppose a hedge fund begins year 1 with US$100 million, which it increases to US$130 million by the end of that year. Then in year 2, the fund falls to US$100 million again, before returning to US$130 million in year 3. The hedge fund would be collecting incentive fees for both year 1 and year 3, even though it did nothing for the investor between year 1 and year 3. The high-water mark prevents this by establishing a threshold of US$130 million at the end of year 1, under which incentive fees cannot be collected until the fund rises above US$130 million

Table 1.4 *Hedge fund database summary statistics*

Group	Total number	Avg. number	Avg. AUM	Avg. growth	Avg. M. fee	Avg. I. fee	Avg. Age	High water (%)	Hurdle rate (%)
Equity hedge	3348	1414	103.29	0.15	1.41	18.91	6.92	89.67	13.71
Event-driven	622	284	168.28	0.05	1.51	19.52	7.54	95.02	7.72
Macro	1263	542	131.93	0.11	1.79	19.27	7.33	84.88	9.58
Relative val	1119	459	157.26	0.06	1.40	18.43	6.67	84.18	17.43
Live funds	3198	1495	147.39	0.14	1.52	18.96	7.43	91.59	12.66
Dead funds	3154	1205	92.87	0.09	1.45	18.94	6.60	84.91	13.25
All	6352	2699.83	125	0.11	1.49	18.95	7.02	88.27	12.96

Note: This table reports the time-series averages of annual cross-sectional averages from January 1994–June 2009 using the Hedge Fund Research database. Avg. Number is the average number of hedge funds across monthly observations, Avg. AUM represents the average assets under management across months, Avg. Growth computes the average growth rate of new assets into the average hedge fund using the formula for monthly growth in flows as: g_t = News Flow$_t$/AUM_{t-1}, where New Flows$_t$ = $AUM_t - AUM_{t-1} \cdot (1 + r_{it})$, where r_{it} is the net returns of fund i from $t - 1$ to t, Avg. M. Fee is the average management fee across hedge funds, Avg. I. Fee is the average incentive fee across hedge funds, Avg. Age is the average number of years of existence of a fund in a particular category, High Water (%) is the percentage of hedge funds in the database with a high-water mark across funds and time, and Hurdle Rate (%) is the percentage of funds with a hurdle rate across funds and time. This selection of data includes only hedge funds that report to HFR. Equity Hedge, Event Driven, Macro, and Relative Value are hedge fund categories described in the text. Live funds represent the existing hedge funds as of June 2009 and Dead funds represents all of the hedge funds that reported at some point to HFR, but did not report as of June 2009. All represents all hedge funds, including both live and dead funds.

US$6) million). While almost 90 per cent of hedge funds have high-water marks, only around 12 per cent have hurdle rates. Table 1.4 presents statistics on fees and other items related to hedge funds.

Unlike in the case of stocks, which anyone can choose to buy at any time, hedge funds usually (i) have minimum investment thresholds, (ii) they are not continuously open for new investments (iii) even if they are, they may have subscription intervals and (iv) they are relatively illiquid. The well-known hedge fund Long-Term Capital Management (LTCM) had a minimum investment threshold of US$10 million. Hedge funds may be open or closed to new investors, depending on whether their manager feels that it has too much money relative to the opportunities of its investment strategy and, in any event, they may only be open to new investments at (regular) quarterly or annual intervals. Finally, hedge funds are typically not as liquid as stocks traded on the stock exchange, meaning that investors cannot choose the moment to sell their position in the hedge fund. Instead there are rules for withdrawing money from a hedge fund (the lock-up periods discussed above). What is more, even when an investor *can* withdraw money, there are redemption periods (for instance, withdrawals may only be allowed at quarterly intervals, with the investor receiving the funds right after the end of a quarter). In addition, investors typically have to give a number of days of advance notice before making a withdrawal.[11]

Hedge funds may be located onshore or offshore. Onshore hedge funds are subject to US tax regulations and are thus not tax-efficient for non-US residents and citizens. For this reason, many hedge funds are based in foreign jurisdictions, or have at least one fund set up in a foreign jurisdiction that caters for foreign investors and avoids US tax laws. Some of the more popular locations include Bermuda, the Cayman Islands, Curaçao, and the Bahamas. All of those jurisdictions have certain characteristics in common that make them attractive for offshore investments, including a good public image, convenience in terms of travel and language, suitability for the target foreign investors' tax situation, and organized legal structures. Figure 1.3 shows the distribution of hedge fund locations for 2010.

1.3 The Cousins of Hedge Funds

The differences between hedge funds and other alternative investment vehicles, such as private equity funds, or between them and other portfolio management companies, such as mutual funds and ETFs, are not clear to

---

[11]   The average number of days of notice is 35 from Table 1.2.

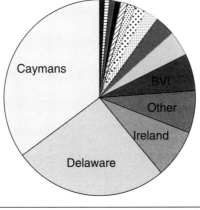

Note: BVI = British Virgin Islands.

Source: Hedge Fund Research.

Figure 1.3   Hedge funds by location of registration

all. Figure 1.4 shows the shares of the portfolio management universe by investment vehicle. Despite its enormous growth, the hedge fund industry is still a small part of the asset management universe.[12]

The main distinction between hedge funds and mutual funds is that mutual funds are portfolio companies, which are subject to the Investment Company Act of 1940 and must be registered with the SEC. Amongst other things, they have limits on their leverage and on the types of instruments they can use. However, it should be noted that, over the past 10 years, many mutual funds have been approved by the SEC to invest with more leverage and short selling. Thus, the main advantage of a hedge fund

---

[12]   However, with the leverage of its positions, the actual impact on the financial markets may be much larger than reflected in its asset size. Credit Suisse estimates that hedge funds contribute more than half of the average trading volume in equity and corporate bond markets.

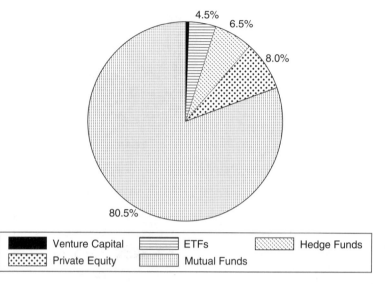

Note: Total pie: $29 trillion

Source: Hedge Fund Research, Investment Company Institute, the City UK and Blackrock.

Figure 1.4   Share of assets in professional management world in 2010

resides in its degree of flexibility in terms of its investments, while the main drawback to being in a hedge fund, as opposed to being a mutual fund is in terms of the marketing limitations applicable to hedge funds, which are not allowed to advertise or market their products to the general public.

ETFs are the latest revolution in portfolio management.[13] ETFs, of which there are currently over 2459 worldwide, are essentially passively managed portfolios that invest in a transparent way for their investors. The main difference between most ETFs and hedge funds is that ETFs are generally *not* actively managed (that is, not managed to outperform).[14] In most cases, ETFs do not use the sophisticated instruments to which hedge funds resort, nor do they take advantage of arbitrage opportunities; they

---

[13]   In fact, IndexIQ (www.indexiq.com) has launched the first series of hedge fund replicating ETFs. One for risk arbitrage (Ticker Symbol: MNA) and one to track the overall hedge fund industry returns (Ticker Symbol: QAI), and even an ETF to hedge against inflation (Ticker Symbol: CPI). The reader should be aware that the author is on the Academic Council of IndexIQ.

[14]   Some ETFs are actively managed.

usually invest according to a specified rule, like purchase companies with high dividend payout ratios. Another major difference to hedge funds is that ETFs charge much smaller fees.

Private equity (PE) funds raise money from investors, just like hedge funds, but for a different reason namely, in order to use it, in conjunction with other financing methods, to purchase private or public companies (with the intention of turning the latter into private companies). Just like hedge funds, PE funds charge fees to their investors for their services and, if the performance of their portfolio of companies is good, their investors can turn a profit. The main distinction between the two is linked to their respective (i) strategies, (ii) typical portfolio holdings, and (iii) fees and lockups. *First*, the typical holdings of a hedge fund are more liquid and tradeable compared to those of a PE fund, consisting in publicly traded stock as opposed to private companies that cannot be purchased or traded by other investors, making them very illiquid.[15] *Second*, the typical strategy of a hedge fund is to create value for its investors through an investment philosophy, which is often at times very complex and which can result in abnormally high returns for its portfolio. A PE firm, on the other hand, attempts to create value for its investors through the use of financing,[16] improving the target company's business processes or focusing on a long-term minded investment process, which may add more value to the company than focusing on short-term financial results. To reduce short-termism, a PE fund will often convert a public into a private company, so that its managers do not need to worry about pleasing investors and market analysts with every quarterly report, focusing, instead, on long-term value-enhancing projects. *Third*, because hedge funds typically can buy or sell many of their investments in a relatively short period of time, their investment performance can be assessed on a monthly or yearly basis. PE firms, on the other hand, may hold a company private for many years before eventually selling it to another private buyer or taking the company public again through an initial public offering. This makes it more difficult to measure their performance on a short-term basis. *Fourth*, although their fee structure is similar, there are some subtle differences. Just like hedge funds, PE funds charge management fees that are typically 1–2 per cent of their AUM. One of the differences – which is also sometimes a cause for criticism – is that PE funds begin accumulating management fees from the day they close the

---

[15] One should note that some hedge funds trade very illiquid assets as well, such as OTC derivatives, that are not priced very often, or real-estate funds. Some hedge funds may even purchase private companies.

[16] For more on this, the reader is referred to the discussion of the Modigliani and Miller Theorem in any corporate finance textbook.

fund, even though it might take many months before they invest all of the proceeds into one or more private companies. Thus, they are, in essence, getting paid to hold cash. Hedge funds, on the other hand, typically invest all of their assets rather quickly. Also similar to hedge funds, PE funds charge an incentive fee, more commonly called 'carried interest'.[17] Again, the typical fee is 20 per cent of the appreciation of the value of the fund.

1.4   Hedge Fund Strategies

As mentioned above, the first hedge fund was started with the simple idea of creating a portfolio that eliminated or, at least, mitigated its overall market exposure. Since then, the variety of hedge funds has grown enormously, with some of them no longer hedging at all. Others yet may have elements of hedging in their strategies even if it turns out that the hedging element was not particularly strong.

Hedge fund data collectors classify hedge funds into broad categories. The main hedge fund databases are the *Hedge Fund Research* (HFR) database, the *Dow Jones Credit Suisse* (DJCS) database, the *Lipper Trading Advisor Selection System* (TASS) database, and the *Center for International Securities and Derivative Markets* (CIDSM) database. Each of those companies has created certain hedge fund categories and lumped existing hedge funds into them.[18] We will be discussing in this chapter the categories used by HFR, the main of which are equity hedge, event-driven (ED), macro, and relative value.[19] A summary of the properties of each type of hedge fund appears in Table 1.5.

The composition of the hedge fund universe has changed over the last 30 years. In 1990, the largest group by assets was macro funds (39 per cent of the total), with equity hedge a close second (37 per cent), and ED and relative value accounting for 10 per cent and 14 per cent of the assets, respectively. By 2010, the macro category had declined enormously to 20

---

[17]   The term 'carried interest' owes its name to the way it is paid to the managers of the fund. Since the investments of PE funds are typically illiquid, the incentive fee is paid as additional capital ownership of the fund, which is only taxed at a later date as capital gains. This offers a tax advantage, which has been criticized by those outside the industry who believe that the gains should be taxed at income tax rates, not as capital gains taxes, which are lower.

[18]   The reader should note that lumping individual hedge funds into broad categories is often difficult, since every hedge fund has its own specificities.

[19]   In this chapter, we have chosen not to discuss fund-of-funds, which are investment funds that invest in a portfolio of hedge funds. For a detailed list of all categories, please visit https://www.hedgefundresearch.com/index. php?fuse=indices-new&1294509584.

Table 1.5   Different types of hedge funds

Strategy	Description	Example trade
Equity hedge	Portfolios can be of a variety of types, including market neutral portfolios that are generally constructed to be neutral to one or multiple variables, such as broader equity markets in dollar or beta terms, and leverage is frequently employed to enhance the return profile of the positions identified. Portfolios that are long equity with value or growth strategies, more quantitative directional strategies, portfolio that specialize in a particular sector like energy or healthcare, short-biased funds are generally short the market, and multi-strategy hedge funds.	A market neutral trade: After the accounting scandals in 2003 with Freddie Mac, a market-neutral fund may have been long Freddie and short Fannie in anticipation that Fannie would face similar problems.
Event driven	Portfolios can be of many varieties within this category, including activist funds which take board interest in companies and influence the direction of company events, distressed funds which typically interest themselves in the bonds and equity of bankrupt companies in hope to make higher returns off a turnaround or workout, risk arbitrage funds which buy and sell securities after a public announcement of a merger has been made hoping to profit from price convergence, private issue funds which tend to buy private companies, special situations which can include a variety of events, including spin-offs, and credit arbitrage funds that focus on finding unique opportunities in corporate debt securities, and multi-strategy funds.	A risk arbitrage trade: Company A is offering 1 share of A for every share of a company B to convince investors to tender their shares. The current price of company B is $80 (before the offer). The current price of Company As shares is $100. Strategy is to buy 1 share of Company B and short 1 share of company A and wait for the merger to close. Potential 20% return.
Macro	The strategies involve trading in global fixed income and equity, hard currency and commodity markets. Managers employ a variety of techniques, both discretionary and systematic analysis, combinations of top down and bottom up theses, quantitative and fundamental approaches and long and short term	A macro trade: Country A has an interest rate of r, while country B has an interest rate of r', where $r > r'$. Borrow in the currency of country B at r' and

Table 1.5   (continued)

Strategy	Description	Example trade
	holding periods. Within this strategy, there are hedge fund managers that focus more on commodity trading, more on currency trading, and some that follow a multi-strategy approach.	invest in country A at r. In the absence of exchange rate movements, expect to make $r - r'$.
Relative value	Relative value hedge funds invest based upon a thesis that there are different securities that are trading at a valuation discrepancy. The managers can use qualitative or quantitative techniques to invest in a variety of securities across the equity, fixed income, and derivatives spectrum. The types of strategies can vary in focus from fixed income asset backed securities, such as mortgage backed and credit card securities, fixed-income convertible arbitrage securities (which might involve trading spreads between corporate equities and convertible bonds), fixed-income corporate which involves trading bonds of various corporations, fixed-income sovereign involves trading spreads between the bonds issued by different country governments, volatility trades involved trading segments of implied volatility using options and other derivatives, and other yield related fixed income trades.	A relative value trade: The manager might feel that the Freddie Mac bonds are trading at too narrow of spread to Treasuries. Thus, the trade would go short the Freddie Mac bond, long the U.S. Treasury bond of similar maturity with an overall duration exposure of zero.

Note: Hedge fund strategy categories are from the HFR definitions.

per cent, with equity hedge at 30 per cent, and both ED and relative value accounting for a large share of assets (26 per cent and 24 per cent respectively). By numbers of hedge funds, the equity hedge category is by far the greatest with over 45 per cent of the total.

Equity hedge funds are typically involved in investments in stocks. However, there are many types of hedge funds within this universe. Some equity hedge funds are outright long stocks, just like any other portfolio that invests in stock. They are not hedged in any sense and they are simply long the stock market with stocks they believe will outperform. Some equity hedge funds are directionally short stocks (that is, they might be partially hedged, but generally are not fully hedged and are just betting that the US stock market or a group of particular stocks will decline). A growing category of equity hedge funds are known as 'equity market neutral'. Those hedge funds are closer in spirit to the original hedge fund in the sense that they attempt to be both long and short so as to have little directional exposure to the overall stock market and derive their returns primarily from the difference in the returns of the stocks that they short and stocks that they buy. Within the equity hedge funds category, there are also those hedge funds that are more quantitative and those that are more qualitative in nature. Quantitative equity hedge funds tend to use statistical and mathematical models in order to build their portfolios. Qualitative managers, on the other hand, tend to use human judgement, company fundamentals and other sources of information that are then interpreted by human portfolio managers who make their investment decisions.

ED funds are a very diverse mix of hedge funds. Their only common characteristic is that they base their investment decisions on a certain trigger event, such as a merger, spinoff, or the sale of a division of a company. Some ED hedge funds are activists, in the sense that, in their capacity as shareholders, they attempt to steer their target companies towards certain actions that will ultimately benefit their shareholders (as well as the hedge fund's investors), as opposed to taking on a passive role. Risk arbitrage funds represent, perhaps, the most well-known ED hedge fund category. As mentioned above, those hedge funds mainly engage in investments related to companies involved in a merger or an acquisition. Their typical strategy is to wait until a merger has been announced between two companies and then proceed to invest in them in order to profit from the merger. At times, risk arbitrage funds also take speculative positions in companies they feel might be bought out or where a bidding war appears likely. The overwhelming majority of transactions, however, involve trading on companies whose deals have already been publicly announced.

The distressed debt fund category is a fascinating subset of the ED category. Distressed debt funds typically invest in debt and, sometimes, in the equity of companies in bankruptcy (or on the verge of bankruptcy) with the hope of recovering a higher value for them in the future. They are often actively engaged in the management of those companies and in the court proceedings, including the renegotiation of payments to bondholders, and they may invest in private and public companies. In the case of distressed hedge funds, the 'event' is a company bankruptcy, although it is usually not as clear cut as that. Within the ED group, there is also a class of hedge funds devoted to investing in private companies, which are classified as private issue/Regulation D hedge funds. These are similar in nature to their PE fund counterparts. Other hedge funds in the ED space are those involved in events related to corporate actions, including new security issuances, asset sales, spin-offs of parts of a company, and other corporate events. Hedge funds can purchase the debt or equity of those companies with the hope of making money, based on stylized patterns before, during or after those events.

The investment process of macro funds is based on the underlying global macroeconomic picture and its impact on equity, fixed income, currency, and commodity markets around the world.[20] Within this broad category, there are hedge funds focusing on commodity investments, currency investments, and relative economic relationships between countries. A prime example of a global macro hedge fund is *Brevan Howard Asset Management*, the biggest macro hedge fund in Europe and the fourth largest globally with more than US$26 billion under management. During the financial crisis, which ruined numerous hedge funds, the conservative strategy of *Brevan Howard*, which began raising cash early in 2008 and put more funds in short term securities, worked profitably, earning the fund a 20.4 per cent return in 2009, when the average hedge fund lost about 19 per cent. One of the most famous macro hedge funds was the *Quantum Fund*. In 1992, its founder George Soros correctly bet that the UK would not raise interest rates to levels comparable to other participants in the European Exchange Rate Mechanism (ERM) and would exit the ERM. On 6 September 1992, the fund sold short more than US$10 billion worth of pound sterling, making US$1 billion within a day as the British Government could not stop the pound's depreciation outside the target zone. Julian Robertson led the *Tiger Fund*, which posted compounded annual returns of 31.7 per cent from 1980–1998, growing to US$22.8 billion under management. In the next two years, the fund lost half of that for a variety of reasons, including a US$2 billion bad bet on the Japanese yen. The fund was closed in 2000, with Robertson stating 'There is no point in subjecting our investors to risk in a market which I frankly do not understand . . .'[21]

The relative value (RV) category consists of funds with exposure to fixed-income markets. RV funds are also referred to as fixed-income arbitrage or relative-value arbitrage funds, although they also include hedge funds that simply have some exposure to fixed-income. The types of hedge funds and strategies employed in this area differ vastly from one fund to another. Their strategies may involve using quantitative techniques to measure relationships between various fixed-income securities and identifying mis-

---

[20]   The term 'macro' is derived from the managers' attempts to use macro-economic principles to identify dislocations in asset prices.

[21]   See Lowenstein (2000).

pricings or statistical anomalies leading to profitable opportunities. In the larger RV group of funds, there are those that utilize more specific strategies. Convertible arbitrage hedge funds focus on exploiting opportunities between convertible and non-convertible securities of the same issuer. For example, a company may have issued a bond which converts into common equity given certain conditions. The hedge fund might use pricing tools to value the bond in terms of the equity and find that the bond is trading too cheaply compared to the equity. They might then purchase the company's convertible bond and short sell its common stock, waiting until their prices converge and, thus, capturing a quasi-arbitrage profit. Fixed-income asset-backed funds are involved in trading the spread between a fixed-income instrument that is backed by collateral, such as loans, mortgages, or credit card receivables, and another fixed income instrument. For example, a fixed-income asset-backed hedge fund might make a trade that is long a *Freddie Mac* bond and short a US Treasury bond or it might be involved in a trade based upon the relative spread between alternative asset-backed securities. In all cases, a model or thought process indicates a 'rich' or 'cheap' spread between the instruments.

Other strategies involve the trading of corporate bonds. For example, a hedge fund may trade on the spread between corporate bonds of the same company, different companies, or on the spread between a company and a government bond. Another type of strategy is to invest in sovereign bonds, or the bonds issued by the governments of different countries depending on economic or relative valuation models. For instance, in the late 1990s, when several European countries were coming closer to a common currency, their bond yields were slowly tightening since the currency risk embedded in them would eventually disappear. Other hedge funds engage in fixed-income volatility trading: essentially, by purchasing and writing options on fixed-income instruments, those hedge funds might be betting on the volatility of bond returns being higher or lower in the future, or higher or lower on one part of the curve than on another. Those hedge funds might also invest heavily in over-the-counter (OTC) and exchange-listed derivatives, or in non-fixed-income types of instruments. Although some of those hedge funds take outright bets in the fixed-income markets in which they are involved, most of them remain true to the 'hedge' concept of hedge funds, due to their focus on spread betting.[22]

---

[22]   When an investor buys outright a corporate bond, he takes on full interest-rate exposure risk as well as other types of risk. However, when the hedge fund purchases one type of corporate bond, while shorting another, it has effectively hedged out most of the interest rate risk, as well as other types of risk.

2.   ARE HEDGE FUNDS BENEFICIAL?

One of the biggest debates in financial circles is whether anyone managing money is really adding value. This is due in part to the theoretical foundations of finance, which postulate that prices must accurately reflect all information in an efficient way. Thus, it would be impossible for a group of investors to be able to constantly find mispriced securities and earn abnormal profits from investing in them.

Before discussing how we might measure the benefits (or the lack thereof) of hedge funds, we should discuss the potential reasons why hedge funds could theoretically be superior to other forms of investing. First, hedge funds are flexible in their investments, including leveraging, shorting, and investing in all sorts of OTC derivatives that other investment vehicles cannot. Second, hedge fund managers usually have their personal assets invested in their funds, receiving incentive fees for good performance; thus, their incentives to perform well are very high and they are aligned with those of their investors. Third, hedge funds often attract talented individuals, many of whom already have a track record of achievement at major investment banks or mutual fund companies, and have decided to branch-out on their own.[23] It follows that hedge funds could provide higher net returns than other investment vehicles.[24] The next sections examine whether this is indeed the case, as well as the diversification benefits of hedge funds to an existing portfolio.

2.1   A Performance of Hedge Funds versus Other Investment Vehicles

2.1.1   The raw performance
One way to assess hedge funds is to compare their returns with those of standard investment vehicles to determine whether they offer higher after-fee returns. Such a comparison is, no doubt, simplistic, since different investment vehicles might take different levels of risk. Thus, one would ultimately need to determine the return per unit of risk, using as the standard of measurement the Sharpe or the Sortino ratio. The idea behind those measurements is that when comparing two after-fee invest-

---

[23]   It should be acknowledged, though, that this is a generalization. There are currently 7164 hedge funds, and to claim that every manager is amongst the best in the world of finance would be, without question, an incautious extrapolation.

[24]   Hedge funds may also be beneficial to the market as a whole, to the extent that they arbitrage mis-priced securities, making security prices more efficient. We will not examine that particular aspect of hedge funds.

ment returns, the said returns should be compared at the same level of risk.[25]

Table 1.6 shows the average returns of various hedge fund categories versus standard asset classes from January 1994 to December 2010. The first thing to note is that, with the exception of real estate, most of the hedge fund categories have higher average returns than the standard asset classes.[26] One of the selling points of hedge funds, which will be discussed later, is their low correlation with the S&P 500 when compared with other asset classes. From this group of asset classes, one can see that bonds and other instruments have a much lower correlation with equities than any of the hedge fund categories do. The risk-adjusted performance ratios also show that hedge fund investments have a higher return per unit of risk than any of the conventional asset classes. This has been one of the arguments for investing in hedge funds. For the Sortino ratio, the highest value for the standard asset classes is US Corporate bonds at 0.28. All of the hedge fund categories have a Sortino ratio higher than this. The Sortino ratio for the S&P 500 is 0.14, while all hedge fund categories have a value that is at least twice that. The evidence on the hedge funds' raw returns suggests that this can be an attractive investment vehicle for many types of investors. There are two further issues to discuss with respect to Table 1.6.

First, the hedge fund returns for various categories are based upon hedge fund indices that hold a group of hedge funds in a portfolio. This is typically not the way an investor would invest in hedge funds, unless he were to be doing so through a fund-of-funds. The diversification presented by this group of hedge funds is undoubtedly substantial. Thus, in addition to looking at the index of hedge fund returns, we also look at the statistics from picking a portfolio of one random hedge fund from the group. This might be more representative of the choices an investor might actually make. In order to do this we performed a bootstrap, where each month we selected a random hedge fund return to create a series of hedge fund returns, using monthly data during the period from January 1994 to June 2009. We repeated this procedure 1000 times to create a series of 1000 different simulated return series. We then compiled statistics on these 1000 series. The statistics for this simulation are listed in Table 1.6 under 'Random Fund'. The random fund had an average annualized return of

---

[25]   That is, if one vehicle has a lower return, but also a lower risk, then an investor could borrow and invest more in the lower return asset bringing its return to the level of the other vehicle. Only then can a fair comparison be made of the two. These risk-adjusted measures essentially make that comparison.

[26]   Furthermore, all of the hedge fund categories represent after-fee returns, while the indices do not have fees or transaction costs subtracted from them.

Table 1.6 Performance statistics of hedge fund strategies

Group	Mean	S.D.	Max.	Min.	ρ	Risk-adjusted return measures				
						Sharpe	Sortino	Omega	Calmar	Sterling
Equity hedge	11.31	9.36	10.88	−9.46	0.75	0.86	0.34	1.66	1.51	1.62
Event-driven	10.87	6.90	5.13	−8.90	0.72	1.10	0.40	1.86	1.91	2.00
Macro	9.16	6.74	6.82	−6.40	0.34	0.87	0.37	1.66	9.39	9.27
Relative val	8.64	4.38	3.93	−8.03	0.57	1.22	0.41	2.14	2.02	2.06
All	9.71	7.22	7.65	−8.70	0.75	0.89	0.34	1.68	1.96	2.09
Random fund	11.17	19.15	26.67	−24.73	0.25	0.40	0.18	1.38	3.12	7.33
Common indices										
S&P 500	9.00	15.71	9.78	−16.80	1.00	0.36	0.14	1.27	0.46	0.47
U.S. treasury bonds	6.42	7.73	9.57	−7.13	−0.14	0.40	0.16	1.30	2.48	3.05
U.S. treasury bills	3.32	0.57	0.52	0.00	0.09	0.04	0.01	1.02	–	–
U.S. corporate bonds	7.21	5.72	8.29	−5.91	0.24	0.68	0.28	1.55	2.42	2.48
U.S. real estate	11.73	23.40	30.93	−31.58	0.58	0.38	0.17	1.44	–	–
Global equity	7.84	15.74	11.32	−19.37	0.95	0.29	0.11	1.22	0.33	0.35
Global bonds	5.76	6.02	5.65	−5.42	0.14	0.41	0.16	1.30	1.21	1.25

Note: This table reports the time-series averages of hedge fund composites as computed by HFR from January 1994 – December 2010. Mean is the average monthly returns annualized by multiplying by 12. S.D. is the standard deviations of returns over the period annualized by multiplying by $\sqrt{12}$. Max. and Min. are the maximum (minimum) monthly return of the hedge fund index over the period. ρ represents the correlation of the returns of the hedge fund index over time with the S&P 500 returns. The Risk-Adjusted measures are the standard Sharp ratio, Sharpe $= \bar{r}_{it} - \bar{r}_{rf}/ \sigma_p$, the Sortino ratio is given by Sortino $= \bar{r}_{it} - \bar{r}_{rf}/\sqrt{LPM_2(\bar{r}_{it})}$, the Omega is given by Omega $= \bar{r}_{it} - \bar{r}_{rf}/LPM_{1i}(\bar{r}_{it}) + 1$, where $LPM_n(\bar{r}_{it}) = 1/T$ $\sum_{t=1}^{T} [\max(\bar{r}_{it} - r_{it}, 0)]^n$. The latter two are similar to the Sharpe ratio but use downside-risk measures rather than variance. The Calmar ratio is given by Calmar $= \bar{r}_{it} - \bar{r}_{rf}/ -MD_{i1}$, and the Sterling ratio is given by Sterling $= \bar{r}_{it} - \bar{r}_{rf}/\Sigma_{j=1}^{N} -MD_{ij}$, where MD_{i1} is the maximum drawdown of the fund from peak to trough during the existence of the fund in percentage terms, MD_{i2} is the next largest drawdown of the hedge fund index in percentage terms, and so on. In the case of the Sterling measure, we take $N = 4$ to represent the four largest drawdowns for the fund during the period of concern. The drawdowns are computed by creating an index series of the fund based upon net returns. S&P 500 total return data and the 10-year Treasury bond total return data were obtained from Global Financial Data. Random Fund are statistics of a randomly selected hedge fund (see text for more details).

11.17 per cent, which is comparable to the hedge fund index returns, but at a much greater cost. The standard deviation of the returns was 19.15 per cent. In some senses, one can think of the difference between 19.15 per cent and 7.22 per cent of the composite hedge fund index as the gains from a diversified portfolio of hedge funds. Drawing a random fund rather than examining a diversified index of hedge funds has a large effect on the Sharpe and the Sortino ratios, which are about half that of the composite hedge fund index. These ratios are still higher than some standard asset classes, but the disparity is much smaller. The Calmar and Sterling ratios are still quite high, reflecting the fact that the maximum drawdowns are smaller with respect to the larger mean return of this random hedge fund.

Second, even the Sharpe and the Sortino ratios are not adequate for comparing two investment vehicles when one is distributed normally and the other is distributed abnormally, with excess kurtosis and skewness, which might not be represented in the sample data. Table 1.7 shows the performance of the hedge fund indices and tests for the normality of the hedge fund returns.[27] The test of the normality of monthly returns is rejected for all of the hedge fund returns as well as the common asset class returns. Although the Sortino and the Omega ratios seek to adjust for some of the asymmetry in the return distribution, they are not perfect for comparing distributions.

Some authors have proposed new measures to deal with non-normal distributions and with some of the failures of the common measures, such as the Sharpe ratio. In particular, Hodges (1997) has proposed the use of the Generalized Sharpe Ratio (GSR), which is difficult to compute, but more accurate. Pezier (2004, 2010) has proposed the Adjusted Sharpe Ratio (ASR) which considers the third and fourth moments of the distribution and is equal to

$$ASR = SR\left[1 + \frac{m_3}{6}SR - \frac{m_4 - 3}{24}SR^2\right],$$

where SR is the standard Sharpe ratio, while m_3 and m_4 are the standarized third (i.e. skewness) and fourth moments (i.e. kurtosis) of the return distribution.[28] Since there is still no measure that is accurate in all situations, we do not compute these for the hedge fund returns in this chapter.

---

[27]   As a reminder, a Normal Distribution has a skewness of zero and a kurtosis of 3. The Jarque-Bera test is a test for the normality of the return distribution.

[28]   These measures also have problems, but in many cases, the GSR more accurately reflects the intuitive choice of investors. A simple example where the Sharpe ratio gives a very intuitive and incorrect answer is for two gambles. Gamble A gives 40%, 10%, or −20% returns with probabilities of 1/9, 7/9, and 1/9 respectively.

Table 1.7   Performance statistics of hedge fund strategies

	Mean returns					Non-normality		
	Up	Down	94–00	00–10	08	Skewness	Kurtosis	Jarque-Bera
Equity hedge	26.65	–16.21	20.88	6.10	–29.79	–0.11	3.96	8.27
Event-driven	21.67	–8.51	15.84	8.15	–23.90	–1.00	6.39	130.50
Macro	15.39	–2.01	12.02	7.60	4.91	0.34	3.34	4.85
Relative val	13.44	0.03	10.67	7.53	–19.27	–2.16	13.70	1121.39
All	21.62	–11.68	15.04	6.80	–20.48	–0.54	4.79	36.89
Random fund	33.79	–5.25	16.67	9.27	–16.28	0.65	14.47	2158.18
Common indices								
S&P 500	41.09	–48.57	22.27	1.77	–43.15	–0.62	3.73	17.60
U.S. treasury bonds	4.31	10.21	5.68	6.83	19.17	0.09	4.26	13.62
U.S. treasury bills	3.42	3.16	4.88	2.47	1.24	–2.28	12.57	946.42
U.S. corporate bonds	10.01	2.17	6.35	7.67	2.58	0.01	5.16	39.25
U.S. real estate	43.92	–35.23	–10.64	14.78	–35.23	–1.20	8.90	250.36
Global equity	38.19	–46.61	17.18	2.75	–47.45	–0.71	4.21	29.42
Global bonds	6.55	4.33	5.72	5.77	–7.40	–0.22	3.45	3.36

Note: This table reports the average returns of individual fund returns over the entire sample period from January 1994–December 2010. Mean is the average monthly returns annualized by multiplying by 12 in up or down markets respectively. Up months are those for which the S&P 500 has a positive return and down markets are those for which the S&P 500 has a negative return. Skewness is a measure of skewness of the sample distribution of the hedge fund index returns, Kurtosis is a measure of kurtosis of the sample distribution, and Jarque-Bera reports the average Jarque-Bera test statistic for the normality of the hedge fund index returns. Random Fund are the statistics of a randomly selected hedge fund (see text for more details).

As we mentioned at the beginning of this chapter, many hedge funds aim to hedge out the general market movements. In this section, we show to what extent they do this for investors. With the exception of Treasury Bill investments, that was indeed the case. Table 1.7 also shows how hedge fund strategies behave in up and down markets. If hedge funds are providing their 'hedge' one would expect to see them declining less in down markets and also perhaps rising less in up markets. That is, hedge fund returns should not be as susceptible to general market movements. Table 1.7 classifies an up market as one in which the S&P 500 has a positive monthly return and a down market as one where the S&P 500 has a negative monthly return. If we look at the equity hedge category, its natural counterpart is the S&P 500. Here we see that it is generally well hedged in both up and down markets. This is also true with respect to global equity and real-estate. It is hard to make comparisons for the other hedge fund categories and asset classes. But, on average, it does seem that the word 'hedge' applies to many hedge funds.

It is also important to look at our randomly chosen hedge fund statistics. The high performance in up markets of 33.79 per cent and the relatively good performance in down markets of −5.25 per cent is strong support for the idea that even the randomly chosen hedge fund provides much more cushion in down market scenarios than some of the major asset classes. Although the bond asset classes have higher returns in down markets, they also have very little upside in up markets. In 2008, the worst financial crisis since the Great Depression, the randomly chosen hedge fund was down 16 per cent compared to the S&P 500, global equities, and real-estate of −43 per cent, −47 per cent, and −35 per cent respectively.

2.1.2   Criticisms of hedge fund return data

Many academics have pointed out that hedge fund return data is not relia-ble.[29] The main issue is with how hedge fund return data is collected. Data collection procedures for hedge funds tend to entail biases, most of which stem from the fact that hedge funds are not required to share their return data. Some of them volunteer to do so, while others do not. The most

---

Gamble B pays 76%, 10%, and −20% with the same probabilities. Clearly, gamble B is the better choice and stochastically dominates gamble A. The Sharpe ratio would rank gamble A better than B (0.70 to 0.58). The ASR or the GSR would choose correctly gamble B. But in this case, so would the Sortino ratio with semi-variance used. There is also the more general issue of whether a better measure of risk is to compare everything as a deviation from the risk-free rate or an existing benchmark and compute an information ratio.

[29]   For example, see Brown et al. (1992, 1999), Fung and Hsieh (1997), Liang (2000), and Lhabitant (2002).

common biases are *survivorship bias, selection bias, backfill bias, double-counting bias*, and *reporting bias*.

Survivorship bias occurs when a hedge fund data-set does not include hedge funds, which have closed down or stopped reporting for another reason.[30] The general assumption is that hedge funds that close do so because of poor performance. If kept in the data-set, they would drag down the computed returns. There are many hedge funds that close or stop reporting for other reasons, including very good performance. Thus, *ex-ante* it's not clear which way the survivorship bias would skew the report, but it has been estimated that it is likely an upward bias of between 1–3 per cent of the annual performance of hedge funds. As of 1994, many of the premier hedge fund databases, like HFR and TASS, have kept a database of 'live' and 'dead' funds, the latter being those that stop reporting or go into liquidation. By using both live and dead databases in a study of hedge funds, one can eliminate most of the survivorship bias. Nevertheless, some survivorship bias lingers. First, not all hedge fund data providers contain the same hedge funds. A very detailed study of four hedge fund databases showed that the four major hedge fund databases had less than 7 per cent of common hedge funds amongst them (Fung and Hsieh (2009)). Thus, a given hedge fund database may or may not use a representative sample of hedge funds, which can be an argument against them (Liang (2000)). A better approach is to take all existing hedge fund databases and merge them together to achieve a more complete sample of hedge funds for any return-based analysis. Even if this is done, a potential remains for survivorship bias in that, once the fund stops reporting, we cannot know all of the subsequent returns. For example, during the financial crisis of 2008, many hedge funds stopped reporting in October 2008 due to poor performance, but their worst month ever was in November 2008 on the order of −70 per cent.[31] This poor performance would never be captured by the hedge fund databases. A bias in the other direction is also possible. For example, small funds may report performance as an advertising campaign to acquire assets, then stop reporting once they have gathered enough assets. In those cases, even if the fund continues to do well, its performance is missing from the data-set.

Selection bias occurs due to the voluntary nature of hedge fund reporting.

---

[30]   If the hedge fund database started with a random sample of 100 hedge funds in 2000 and, over time, hedge funds closed or stopped reporting but were still kept in the database, then survivorship bias would be less of an issue. If they threw out those hedge funds that closed or stopped reporting altogether, the computed performance of the group from 2000–2010 would report biased returns, due to a failure to account for the returns of those that closed.

[31]   See Chincarini (2011) for more details.

It is not clear which direction the bias may affect the databases. It could result in downward estimated returns if large hedge funds performed strongly but without reporting their performance during times when they do not need to raise capital. Examples of that can be seen in some of the most successful hedge funds, which have never reported their performance to database providers, including *LTCM*, Goldman Sachs's *Alpha* and *Global Equity Opportunities* funds, *AQR Capital*, *Renaissance Technologies*, and various others. Conversely, poorly performing hedge funds that never report their performance to the hedge fund database could result in an upward bias on measured hedge fund returns. Finally, selection bias can be a result of the listing criteria of the databases themselves, such as a minimum asset size.

Back-fill bias occurs when a hedge fund database adds a new hedge fund in their database in a given year and then 'backfills' their performance prior to that year, based upon return data supplied by that hedge fund. This is not an issue with most of the premier databases, since they only report hedge fund returns on a going-forward basis.

Double-counting bias can occur if a hedge fund is included in two different categories. This is not a concern for most studies and databases, provided that the database compiler and researcher exercise care.

Finally, *reporting bias* can occur when a hedge fund reports an initial performance number, based on illiquid instruments or preliminary estimates of value, which it then updates.[32] For example, the HFR database allows the past four months of hedge fund performance to be revised if more accurate estimates become available. A more severe form of reporting bias occurs when hedge funds report a smoothed month-to-month performance, rather than their true performance, that is, when performance is bad for a particular month, they might report a slightly smaller decrease in assets and, on a particularly good month, slightly lower increases, making performance look less volatile (Goetzmann et al. (2007), Getmanksky et al. (2004), and Jagannathan and Korajcsyk (1986)).

2.2   Performance of Hedge Funds after Accounting for Passive Risk Exposure: α

Notwithstanding the many potential issues with the published hedge fund returns, we continue to use the data available to perform a more refined analysis of whether hedge funds add value or not. One of the problems of using measures such as return or, even, risk-adjusted returns, is that it may

---

[32]   Mutual fund data is also subject to this bias.

not capture the portfolio manager's genuine potential to add value. While this point has been discussed in detail elsewhere, a brief discussion of this topic will follow.

Suppose a hedge fund manager bought a portfolio of S&P 500 stocks and leveraged it by two times. Let us assume that, over a 36-month period, the S&P 500 has rallied strongly, with almost no volatility. The manager would have both a high Sharpe ratio, due to a very high average return, and a correspondingly low measured volatility. By some of the measures discussed previously, we would consider this to be an excellent manager. However, one could argue that an equity hedge fund manager that simply bought a portfolio of S&P 500 stocks and leveraged it really provided no services.[33] Thus, financial economists have attempted to account for this illusory performance by running econometric regressions of the returns of a particular hedge fund against some common investment alternatives that might capture the passive exposure of those hedge fund managers. The most well-known applied regression is, probably, the Fama-French three-or-four factor regression (Fama-French (1993, 1996)).[34] However, this specification has proved to be unsatisfactory for hedge funds as they engage in non-linear strategies that would not be captured by a linear model of security returns. Moreover, while the Fama-French factors are equity-based indices, many hedge funds are not equity-based and engage in the trading of bonds, foreign exchange, commodities, and other asset classes. Thus, a more general estimation model has been proposed that regresses the hedge fund returns on many more factors (Fung and Hsieh (1997, 2001, 2004)). The model is:

$$\tilde{r}_{it} = \alpha_{iT} + \beta_{1iT}RMRF + \beta_{2iT}SMB + \beta_{3iT}HML + \beta_{4iT}MOM + \beta_{5iT}10yr$$

$$+ \beta_{6iT}CS + \beta_{7iT}BdOpt + \beta_{8iT}FXOpt + \beta_{9iT}ComOpt + \beta_{10iT}EE + \varepsilon_{it}$$

$$t = 1, 2, \ldots, T \qquad (1.1)$$

where
$\tilde{r}_{it} = r_{it} - r_{ft}$ is the net-of-fee return on a hedge fund portfolio in excess of the risk-free rate,

---

[33] The argument might be somewhat more complicated if the manager was also in charge of asset allocation and actually chose the US stock market over less attractive world equity markets. In this study, we refrain from this discussion.

[34] Prior to that, the single-factor CAPM model was the norm.

RMRF is the excess return on a value-weighted aggregate market proxy, SMB, HML, and MOM are the returns on a value-weighted, zero-investment, factor-mimicking portfolios for size, book-to-market equity, and one-year momentum in stock returns as computed by Fama and French,[35]

10yr is the Lehman US 10-year bellwether total return;
CS is the Lehman aggregate intermediate BAA corporate bond index return minus the Lehman 10-year bond return;
BdOpt is the lookback straddle for bonds;
FXOpt is the lookback straddle for foreign exchange;
ComOpt is the lookback straddle for commodities; and
EE is the total return from an emerging market equity index.

If the constant term, known as α, is positive and significant, the hedge fund manager is said to be 'adding value' above and beyond what simple static investing could do. In many cases, α captures selection ability; that is, picking superior investment assets and assessing whether or not the portfolio manager is able to accurately shift in and out of asset classes appropriately.[36] For example, in the simple situation described above, of the manager levering an S&P 500 portfolio, a regression of the hedge fund returns against the S&P 500 returns and other standard investment classes would result in a constant term of 0. Thus, in industry jargon, the manager has no α.

Table 1.8 contains the results from running these regressions on the major hedge fund returns from January 1994 to March 2010.[37] The t-statistics of the coefficients are contained in parentheses. The overall hedge fund composite index has a positive α of 0.21, and is significant. This suggests that, on average, these hedge funds add 21 bps per month or 2.52 per cent per year after fees.[38] The results for the sub-categories of equity hedge and ED funds are also positive, with even higher αs of 29 bps per month for each. The Macro and RV categories have positive αs, but

---

[35]   Source: http://mba.tuck.dartmouth.edu/pages/faculty/ken.french/datalibra ry.html.
[36]   Many authors have found that hedge fund managers produce positive alphas, including Chen (2007), Chen and Liang (2007). Chincarini (2010), and Fung et al. (2002).
[37]   The Straddle factors had only been updated to March 2010 at the time of writing this chapter.
[38]   The standard caveats apply: this is a mix of hedge funds that may not be investable for the average investor. However, it shows that a group of hedge funds put together and equal-weighted do provide an apparent risk-adjusted return.

Table 1.8   Hedge fund alphas measured from Hsieh-Fung Model

Strategy	α	β_{RMRF}	β_{SMB}	β_{HML}	β_{MOM}	β_{10yr}	β_{CS}	β_{BdOpt}	β_{FXOpt}	β_{ComOpt}	β_{EE}	R^2	N
Equity hedge	0.28 (2.57)	0.35 (10.51)	0.16 (4.53)	-0.04 (-1.60)	0.10 (4.53)	0.16 (3.18)	0.34 (5.10)	0.00 (0.88)	0.00 (0.94)	0.00 (0.07)	0.07 (2.90)	0.83	195
Event-driven	0.29 (3.16)	0.20 (7.96)	0.13 (4.56)	0.05 (2.51)	0.03 (1.34)	0.20 (3.86)	0.44 (8.67)	-0.01 (-1.48)	0.00 (-0.87)	-0.00 (-0.30)	0.06 (3.58)	0.78	195
Macro	0.18 (1.31)	0.04 (0.89)	0.06 (1.88)	-0.02 (-0.52)	0.07 (3.53)	0.27 (2.36)	0.10 (0.65)	-0.00 (-0.36)	0.02 (2.94)	0.02 (2.24)	0.13 (6.05)	0.42	195
Relative val	0.16 (1.72)	0.06 (2.73)	0.02 (1.00)	0.03 (2.11)	0.03 (2.15)	0.29 (5.37)	0.54 (6.41)	-0.01 (-1.48)	-0.00 (-1.07)	-0.00 (-1.07)	0.03 (1.95)	0.67	195
Hedge fund composite	0.21 (2.86)	0.20 (9.09)	0.11 (4.23)	-0.04 (-2.05)	0.06 (4.66)	0.14 (3.29)	0.26 (5.21)	-0.00 (-0.69)	0.01 (1.96)	0.00 (0.18)	0.11 (8.53)	0.87	195

Note: This table shows the abnormal returns of hedge fund index returns from January 1970 to December 2010. The results are from the following ordinary least squares (OLS) regressions with standard errors corrected by the Newey-West (1997) procedure with round $[4(N/100)^{2/9}]$ lags: $\bar{r}_{it} = \alpha_{iT} + \beta_{1iT}RMRF + \beta_{2iT}SMB + \beta_{3iT}HML + \beta_{4iT}MOM + \beta_{5iT}10yr + \beta_{6iT}CS + \beta_{7iT}BdOpt + \beta_{8iT}FXOpt + \beta_{9iT}ComOpt + \beta_{10iT}EE + \varepsilon_{it}$ $t = 1, 2, \ldots T$ where $= \bar{r}_{it} (= r_{it} - r_{ft})$ is the net-of-fee return on a hedge fund portfolio in excess return on a value-weighted aggregate market proxy, SMB, HML, and MOM are the returns on a value-weighted, zero-investment, factor-mimicking portfolios for size, book-to-market equity, and one-year momentum in stock returns as computed by Fama and French, 10yr is the Lehman US 10-year bellwether total return, CS is the Lehman aggregate intermediate BAA corporate bond index return minus the Lehman 10-year bond return, BdOpt is the lookback straddle for bonds, FXOpt is the lookback straddle for foreign exchange, ComOpt is the lookback straddle for commodities, and EE is the total return from an emerging market equity index, and ε_{it} is the residual. α estimates are multiplied by 100. t-statistics are in parentheses.

these are not statistically significant. Thus, it is less clear that they added value over this period.

2.3   Diversification Benefits

Now that we have discussed the raw performance methods for evaluating hedge fund performance, we turn to examining the potential diversification benefits that hedge funds may offer to a typical investor. Much research has discussed the benefits of hedge funds as diversification tools. Table 1.9 produces a correlation matrix of the monthly returns of the main hedge indices and other asset classes.[39]

The correlations, with the S&P 500, of the main equity hedge and ED categories are over 0.70. The macro strategy offers a greater diversification benefit with a correlation of 0.30. The hedge fund categories offer diversification with respect to bonds, but not much more than the S&P 500 would offer. The hedge fund categories are less correlated with real-estate than the S&P 500, but also much less so than government bonds and treasury bills. The hedge fund indices offer more diversification to global equity than the S&P 500 does. This is, of course, a very simplistic illustration of the potential hedge fund diversification benefits. A more accurate description would consider a group of asset classes, including the hedge fund asset class, and examine whether or not the efficient frontier expanded with the inclusion of hedge funds. A study that did this found that adding hedge funds to a global portfolio of equities and bonds moved the efficiency frontier sufficiently outwards (L'Habitant (2002)).[40]

3.   HEDGE FUNDS AND THE FINANCIAL CRISIS OF 2008

Contrary to popular belief, hedge funds did not cause the 2008 financial crisis. This was caused by a massive housing bubble, fuelled through cheap credit that originated in both the regulated and the unregulated parts of the banking and mortgage industries. Nevertheless, some hedge funds took advantage of the crisis and made billions shorting the housing market. Many others, especially RV funds were destroyed during the crisis

---

[39]   Some authors argue that this correlation is strongly influenced by whether the hedge fund returns are adjusted for serial correlation or not (Asness et al. (2001)). We used the unadjusted monthly returns.

[40]   This study did not include a wide variety of asset classes, such as real-estate, commodities, treasury bills or high-yield bonds.

Table 1.9   *Correlation matrix of hedge fund strategies with major indices*

	EH	ED	M	RV	ALL	SP500	BONDS	BILLS	CBONDS	RESTATE	GEQUITY	GBONDS
EH	1.00	0.86	0.57	0.71	0.97	0.75	-0.18	0.16	0.22	0.42	0.79	0.15
ED	–	1.00	0.52	0.81	0.91	0.72	-0.23	0.12	0.24	0.48	0.75	0.13
M	–	–	1.00	0.31	0.64	0.34	0.15	0.06	0.21	0.10	0.37	0.16
RV	–	–	–	1.00	0.74	0.57	-0.17	0.14	0.34	0.48	0.61	0.20
ALL	–	–	–	–	1.00	0.75	-0.19	0.11	0.23	0.42	0.79	0.13
SP500	–	–	–	–	–	1.00	-0.14	0.09	0.24	0.58	0.95	0.14
BONDS	–	–	–	–	–	–	1.00	0.06	-0.05	-0.03	0.04	0.00
BILLS	–	–	–	–	–	–	–	1.00	0.62	-0.09	0.18	0.52
CBONDS	–	–	–	–	–	–	–	–	1.00	0.29	0.27	0.63
RESTATE	–	–	–	–	–	–	–	–	–	1.00	0.59	0.26
GEQUITY	–	–	–	–	–	–	–	–	–	–	1.00	0.23
GBONDS	–	–	–	–	–	–	–	–	–	–	–	1.00

Note: Correlations are the correlations of monthly returns from January 1994 to December 2010.

due to movements in the credit markets that were more than three times the magnitude of the LTCM crisis in 1998. Total assets in the hedge fund industry dropped by an estimated US$461 billion. The Equity Hedge category was hit the worst, falling by 34 per cent in assets while the RV category came second, falling by 25 per cent.

From 2008 to 2009, a total of 2494 hedge funds closed, while only 1443 opened, meaning that during this time period there was a net decline of 1051 hedge funds. Hedge funds are born and die every year, but 2008 was the first year since 1996, with more hedge funds going out of business than launched. Table 1.7 depicts the returns of various hedge fund categories during the 2008 financial crisis. During this time, the S&P 500 had an average annualized return of −43 per cent. The US real-estate index was down 35 per cent, global equities were down 47 per cent, and global bonds were down 8 per cent, while US Treasury bonds went up by 19 per cent. In the previous section we spoke of the diversification benefits of hedge funds. One might argue that the most important time to offer diversification benefits is during extreme movements in asset prices. In this respect, hedge funds did offer some diversification.[41] Indeed, the equity hedge strategy was down less than the S&P 500, at −30 per cent, and the equity market neutral category was down by only 5.97 per cent (not shown in Table 1.7), thus providing some protection. The ED category was down −24 per cent, while the macro hedge fund class was up by 5 per cent, and the RV hedge fund class was down by −19 per cent.

Hedge funds, on the whole, did better than most standard market indices during the 2008 financial crisis, with the exception of bonds. Moreover, they did not contribute to the housing bubble, which was driven by excessive lending to home purchasers. Many of the hedge funds exposed to the risks of the housing market simply went out of business. When the bubble burst, many of the investors who invested in equities lost typically half their wealth, while those with more diversified portfolios across different asset classes or who invested in hedge funds faired better.

4.   ON REGULATING HEDGE FUNDS

Since the financial crisis of 2008, there has been a closer examination of the role that deregulation may have played in the crisis. As some of the most

---

[41]   Bonds were the best performing asset class to have owned in 2008. Chincarini (2010) shows that quantitative hedge funds actually performed even better than qualitative hedge funds during the crisis.

unregulated institutions, hedge funds have received much negative attention. This is ironic for several reasons. First, they did not cause the crisis;
on the contrary, many of them, especially RV funds, were its victims.
Second, many of the hedge funds that were linked to the crisis were located
inside regulated public companies, like *Bear Stearns* and *Goldman Sachs*.
Third, there were no reports of any hedge funds threatening to bring down
the financial system, as in the case of LTCM.

Two main reasons have been put forth for hedge fund regulation: investor protection and the industry's potential externalities. Both rationales
will be discussed below, along with the issue of whether regulation can
help address those concerns.

4.1   Are Hedge Funds Dangerous?

Most direct investors in hedge funds are either institutions or high net-
worth investors (HNWIs). One might argue that both groups should be
sophisticated enough to appreciate the risks of their investments. That
is, it would seem unlikely that additional disclosure or regulation of the
hedge fund investment strategies would be necessary for those investors.
Besides, most large, well-established hedge funds, which attract significant
sums of money from institutions or HNWIs, already provide their investors with much information, including monthly performance reports, a
summary of their exposures, and an offering memorandum. Additionally,
many of those investors are registered as investment advisors or with the
Commodity Futures Trading Commission as a result of their involvement
in commodity trading. Thus, when proposing new regulation one should
be clear about whether such regulation would genuinely benefit hedge
fund investors.

The SEC has argued that hedge funds should be regulated due to the
number of hedge fund fraud cases. The most famous example is the
Madoff scandal. Bernie Madoff extracted billions of US$ from investors
and, instead of actually managing it, he falsified returns, which encouraged the pouring of new money into the fund, while using new investments to pay off share redemptions. He continued to post false returns
until 2008, when he was no longer able to meet large investor redemptions
(Weiss (2008)). Madoff was finally arrested and imprisoned. His fraud is
estimated to have cost investors between US$10 – US$17 billion. While
the Madoff fraud made headline news when it was uncovered, there were
others prior to Madoff, including *International Hedge Fund Associates*,
one of the largest black-owned hedge funds. Kirk Wright obtained funds
mainly from wealthy NFL players, as well as doctors and entrepreneurs
(MacDonald and Bauerlein (2006)). It was later discovered that the hedge

fund had falsified its returns, with Wright having defrauded investors of a total of US$180 million, which he channelled into cars, houses and artwork. When investors finally became suspicious, he went on the run, before being caught by the FBI after three months. Facing a cumulative potential of up to 710 years in jail, he committed suicide in prison before sentencing. Whilst there are other similar stories, the amount of hedge fund fraud is relatively small. From 2001–2009, there were a total of 497 hedge fund frauds which amounts to about 1 per cent of hedge funds committing fraud per year (Dimmock and Gerken (2010)). The most common method of fraud is direct theft, rather than Ponzi schemes or other complicated methods. An example of direct theft is taking people's deposits into the fund and rather than investing them, using them for the personal benefit of the fund owner. It is also interesting to note that the number of frauds is equal amongst hedge funds that registered under the Advisors Act and those that didn't, suggesting that further regulation would not necessarily reduce fraud.

An argument against further regulation is that this would not necessarily prevent such cases from arising. All of those hedge fund cases involved fraud, which is illegal, falling within the remit of criminal law. Even if the SEC, or another regulatory body, had increased disclosure requirements, hedge fund disclosures could have been falsified, as in the case of Madoff. It is not clear what form of regulation could have prevented such fraudulent activities, short of an external agency that reconciled every dollar of investor money with every investment on a daily basis. Prime brokers already do that to some extent but, perhaps, the requirement could be more formalized by demanding that every hedge fund with more than US$100 million in AUM must safekeep all of its assets with another firm, with daily reconciliations with investor statements.[42] Besides, regulation costs money, both for the regulated firms themselves and for their investors.

Hedge funds could also adversely affect unrelated third parties involved in the financial system of which they are parts. This is called 'systemic risk'. When LTCM was at risk of collapsing, the New York Federal Reserve coordinated a consortium to inject extra capital in it and avoid its collapse. This was primarily because of fears that, due to LTCM's massive positions, its bankruptcy could lead to a massive distortion in the demand and supply of various financial instruments, creating a risk to

---

[42]   Madoff custodied his own assets and hence there was no outside reconciliation. However, about 26% of investment advisors custody their own assets without committing fraud.

the entire financial system. Regulation could be necessary to mitigate the impact of hedge funds on other parts of the financial system. What types of activities could be regulated so as to limit the impact of hedge funds on the financial system? One approach would be to regulate hedge fund activities. Examples of this type of regulation could include the imposition of restriction on the leverage that hedge funds use, the types of instruments that they invest in, the types and number of counterparties that they have, and the transparency of their positions. Another approach would be to regulate the instruments and the system that hedge funds use, by creating a clearinghouse for recording OTC transactions, such as OTC swaps. Many of the rules and ideas for regulation that have been mentioned in this section would apply to any investment institution, not just hedge funds. Thus, it seems narrow minded to focus the discussion of regulation on hedge funds, rather than on investment companies in general.

4.2 Can Regulation Help?

Even if areas in which hedge funds pose risks or dangers to either investors or the financial system can be identified, one must question whether regulation can mitigate those risks. Frequently, regulation creates additional problems and distorts incentives rather than solving the problem it was intended to address. Some recent examples of this include the new rules for banks regarding credit cards. The Dodd-Frank Act *inter alia* stipulated that the fees charged by banks per credit card swipe should decline by 84 per cent, from the typical 44 cents per average swipe to 7–11 cents per swipe. Banks have already begun responding. They are initiating fees on customer deposit accounts, considering annual credit card fees, and restricting credit card purchases to minimum sizes, all of which will negatively affect consumers by passing on fees from businesses to consumers.

As discussed above, it is not clear that hedge fund investors need protection. Let us, however, assume that the opposite is the case. That is, let's assume that some of them are incapable of understanding how their money is being invested. What type of information might help in such a case? One might argue that certain minimal disclosures should be made to hedge fund clients and that this might, in theory, be more relevant to smaller hedge funds, currently not reporting as much to their clients as they might be to the SEC or to another regulatory body. However, such additional reporting from smaller hedge funds would entail a considerable burden for regulators and it is unlikely that the staff of the competent regulatory bodies would be in a position to meticulously examine each report to detect areas of concern. There is already evidence of that in the corporate sector, where thousands of public corporations disclose their financial statements to the SEC, yet the SEC has not always been very effective at discovering fraud (e.g. Enron). Forced reporting mandates for hedge funds could be similarly ineffective and the result could be similar to the situation seen with public companies, which spend more time writing legal protection clauses into their annual reports than providing substantial and useful information to their investors and the public. If hedge funds were to be regulated also for consumer protection, regulators should take the broader approach of requiring informational documents about the fund and the fund's owners (although most of this information is usually presented in an offering memorandum). The regulation may also require information on the history of the partners and any questionable actions in their professional histories. Lastly, the compulsory disclosure of monthly performance information to an external public data provider would be beneficial, both for investors and for research on the hedge fund industry. These measures would not be too onerous to hedge funds, but would increase transparency, and may give more standardized information to potential investors. It should be noted, however, that most of those measures would not necessarily protect investors from the risk of hedge fund failure or fraud. LTCM supplied a vast amount of information to its investors, with the exception of the investment strategies it was utilizing. The background of the partners was exceptional, and yet they ended up losing almost 90 per cent of their portfolio in the financial markets. In addition, Bernie Madoff had no history of fraud and his published returns looked impressive, yet he was defrauding his investors. The publishing of returns may have allowed a shrewd analyst to notice some odd patterns in his returns, but again, most likely not.[43]

What might regulators do to prevent systemic risk? Limiting leverage might be a step in the right direction.[44] Also, regulators could force hedge funds to publicly report returns. Publicly reported returns probably would not result in a less fragile financial system, but it would make analysis of

---

[43]   In 1999, Harry Markopolos was asked by his bosses at *Rampart* to find out how they could match Madoff's double-digit returns. Markopolos was assigned to deconstruct Madoff's strategy and try to replicate it. Again and again, he could not simulate Madoff's returns, using information he had gathered about Madoff's trades. Markopolos eventually concluded that it was not legally or mathematically possible for Madoff to produce the gains he claimed to deliver. He was convinced that Madoff was either paying old clients with newer clients' money (a Ponzi scheme) or trading with inside information. He warned the SEC, but they ignored him.

[44]   It should be remembered, however, that many brokers and banks have higher leverage ratios than the typical hedge fund with much less liquid assets on hand. This is true even with the new capital requirements for banks. Also, leverage limitations are related to underlying risk. Thus, one size does not fit all.

hedge fund performance much more transparent. It might also enable shrewd analysts to understand what types of and how much risk hedge funds are implicitly taking.

4.3 What is in the Works?

With the passing of the Dodd-Frank Wall Street Reform Act, there are new regulations for hedge funds that will be effective on July 1, 2011. Section IV of the Act deals with the Private Fund Investment Advisers Registration Act of 2010. In addition to this, Section VI, entitled 'Improvements to Regulation of Banks and Savings Association Holding Companies and Deposit Institutions', prohibits banks from owning hedge funds. The Act also imposes registration obligations on many hedge funds, by amending the Investment Advisers Act of 1940. Table 1.10 provides a summary of the main regulations that may affect hedge funds due to Dodd-Frank.

The main change consists in the elimination of the 15-client rule. This will compel all large hedge funds to register. The asset exemption will increase from US$25 million to US$100 million, placing the burden of registration on the few larger hedge funds (20 per cent of the hedge fund world in numbers and about 97 per cent in terms of AUM). The SEC would also be permitted to conduct periodic inspections of hedge funds when deemed appropriate. It is not clear what burden that will place on hedge funds, but it is also not clear how this will aid investors or the financial system.

Perhaps one of the most burdensome regulations is Major Modification #8 listed in Table 1.10. This would render hedge funds classified as systemically significant non-bank financial firms subject to a series of regulations that also apply to bank holding companies, such as risk-based capital requirements, limits on short-term debt, and others. Many hedge funds already have those controls in place, but it is unclear how helpful these will be in preventing systemic risk in the future.[45] Many commercial banks that were regulated and had to follow strict capital adequacy rules still posed large risks to the financial system, mainly because risk-weights on mortgages were incorrectly specified and out-of-date.

---

[45]　The Fed and the Office of the Comptroller of the Currency engage in a continuing dialog with major commercial banks covering all aspects of their business. The degree of familiarity with the business and specificity of the controls would be difficult to reconcile with the hedge fund organization. This is because hedge funds are each very unique and thus it would be very costly and difficult to come up with a set of regulations that fit them all. This is another reason why it is hard to see the feasibility of such regulation.

Table 1.10 Major proposals from Dodd-Frank Act with respect to hedge fund regulation

Major modification	Comments	Effectiveness
1. Elimination of 15 client rule. Now, hedge funds must register regardless of number of clients. (Sec. 403)	This will force almost every hedge fund to register who got around this rule by having each fund as a client rather than looking through to the investors.	Will certainly increase registration unless hedge funds move off-shore or convert to family offices.
2. Increase in the minimum number of assets to be exempt to $100 million. (Sec. 410)	This actually will reduce the number of hedge funds that register with the SEC, since the criterion has risen from $25 million. The smaller ones will have to register with the state in which they are located.	Will reduce the SEC administrative costs, but put a slightly larger burden on states.
3. Adviser must maintain detailed records for each hedge fund. (Sec. 404)	Records include (1) Amounts of AUM; (2) Use of Leverage – including off-balance sheet; (3) Counterparty credit risk exposure; (4) Trading and Investment Positions; (5) Valuation Policies and Practices; (6) Types of assets held; (7) Side arrangements or side letters; (8) Trading Practices; (9) Other information deemed necessary by SEC or Financial Stability Oversight Council (FSOC).	Has the potential to understand risks more thoroughly, but not all leverage is the same. Thus, expert interpretation needed, but may not be available.
4. SEC can conduct periodic inspections of advisers when deemed appropriate for systemic risk and may request additional records related to the cause. (Sec. 404)	Hedge funds have never been subject to compulsory disclosure in the normal course of business. Of course, this collected information must be kept confidential. However, the information may be disclosed	Might not be very important. Remember, Lehman Brothers was not only registered with SEC, but had Fed and SEC officials within the firm monitoring the situation these actions

to Congress, any government agency or self-regulatory body, or pursuant to a court order with the condition of confidentiality.

The Act generally refers to the "fund," but its ambiguity could lead to client names.

5. The pursuit of information on systemic risk is sufficiently vague that it could imply the disclosure of private fund investor names and other highly confidential details of hedge funds. (Sec. 404)

Revealing names of investors would not be beneficial in reducing major risks. It might serve other purposes like money laundering and/or conflicts of interest. It might also lead to hedge funds moving off-shore entirely.

6. Disclosure at least annually of the votes cast with respect to U.S. public companies and a report on the aggregate amount of short sales each month.

Would not help with major issues. Might aid with conflicts of interest, which is not the main concern of the act.

7. Verification of client assets by independent public accountants. (Sec. 223)

Would not help with major issues, but would help with hedge fund fraud cases.

8. Large hedge funds qualifying as SSNFs will be subject to Federal Reserve oversight similar to that of banks and bank holding companies including cease and desist orders and some new conditions as well. A SSNF is a significant nonbank financial firm, that either (1) material financial distress at the firm could pose a threat to financial stability or the economy; or (2) the nature, scope, size, scale,

The additional regulations include (1) risk-based capital requirements; (2) continent capital requirements; (3) risk management requirements; (4) liquidity requirements; (5) credit exposure and other reporting requirements; (6) limits on short-term debt, including margin and REPOs; (7) semi-annual stress tests; (8) "Living will" plans in case of liquidation; (9) restrictions on investments in banks and other financial companies; (10) separation of banking

This would be an enormous burden for large hedge funds. With all these requirements, but no benefits from being a bank holding company, it might put them at a disadvantage. Of course, some of these items are already implemented by them. It would put some controls on large hedge funds, but it depends on the criteria. Remember, even LTCM had very reasonable checks on all these items.[53]

did not really prevent or reduce the severity of the bankruptcy.

Table 1.10 (continued)

Major modification	Comments	Effectiveness
	activities from other activities; (11) other prudential standards deemed appropriate by the Fed.	
9. Any firm with greater than $10 billion in total assets will have to perform annual stress tests and report to the Federal Reserve. (Sec. 165)		Not a large cost to hedge funds, but it is not clear that this will provide much useful information. Most hedge funds that collapsed in 2008 maintained regular stress tests, but still did not perform a sufficiently large test to predict what eventually occurred.
10. The Volcker Rule will prohibit banks from investing or sponsoring hedge funds.		May be useful in removing hidden risks within the walls of banks. For example, Bear Stearns had two major hedge funds collapse within the firm. Goldman had to bailout one of its internal hedge funds. Thus, may protect banks or investors in banks from hidden risks of hedge fund entities within firm.
11. Major Swap participants must register with CFTC and/or SEC. (Sec. 721)	Includes position limits, trade reporting obligations, capital and conduct requirements, mandatory central clearing of certains Swaps, amongst others. A major swap participant (1) maintains	Many hedge funds that deal in Swaps, deal with futures as well and are probably already registered with the CFTC. Not a large burden, and won't necessarily affect major issues.

a major position in swaps in any swap category; (2) engages in Swaps that create substantial counterparty exposure that could have adverse effects on financial system; (3) is a highly-leveraged financial entity, not subject to U.S. bank capital requirements, and maintains substantial position in Swaps.

The alternative definitions of accredited investors will slightly reduce the pool of available investors, but existing investors are not required to withdraw.

It makes sense to index the threshold of investors, but won't really go a long way to protecting investors or preventing future crises.

12. Other items include (1) altering the definition of high net-worth to remove home value; (2) periodic reviews of accredited investor definition; (3) inflation indexing of qualified client threshold; (4) a host of government studies to be initiated that may result in additional rules in the future.

Note: Based upon Title IV of the Dodd-Frank Act (2010) and the summary notes from Cadwalder, Wickersham & Taft (2010). Compliance date is July 1, 2011.

Overall, the new regulations for hedge funds do not seem excessively burdensome with the exception of Major Modification #8 in Table 1.10 on the regulation of significant non-bank financial firms. However, it is also not clear how these regulations will actually help maintain financial stability.

5. CONCLUSION

The goal of this chapter was to clarify the 'hedge fund' concept. This chapter discussed the business and legal characteristics of hedge funds, the various hedge fund strategies, the question of whether hedge fund managers really add value or not, and the regulatory environment of hedge funds in the US. The chapter also discussed how the Dodd-Frank Act may affect hedge funds in the future and offered some insights into whether these regulations will reduce the risks posed by hedge funds to investors and the financial system.

Overall, we found, as in previous studies that hedge funds do offer superior returns and hedging benefits as compared to traditional asset classes. Hedge funds tended to do better than many major indices during the financial crisis of 2008. We also found that many of the regulations proposed for hedge funds will probably do little to prevent financial crises, especially since the financial crisis was started by main street with the helping hand of the government agencies and Wall Street.

BIBLIOGRAPHY

Ackermann, C., R. McEnally and D. Ravenscraft (1999), 'The Performance of Hedge Funds: Risk, Return, and Incentives', *Journal of Finance*, **54**, 833–74.
Angel, J. and D. McCabe (2009), 'The Business Ethics of Short Selling and Naked Short Selling', *Journal of Business Ethics*, 239–49.
Asness, C., R. Krail and J. Liew (2001), 'Do Hedge Funds Hedge?', *Journal of Portfolio Management*, Fall.
Bagley, C.E. and C.E. Dauchy (2007), *The Entrepreneur's Guide to Business Law*, Southwestern College, New York.
Braithwaite, T. (2009), 'Hedge Funds Suffer from Image Problem', *The Financial Times*, October 19.
Brown, S.J., W.N. Goetzmann and R.G. Ibbotson (1999), 'Offshore Hedge Funds: Survival and Performance 1989–1995', *Journal of Business*, **72**, 91–117.
Brown, S.J., W.N. Goetzmann, R.G. Ibbotson and S.A. Ross (1992), 'Survivorship Bias in Performance Studies', *Review of Financial Studies*, **5**, 553–80.
Cadwalader, Wickersham and L.L.P. Taft (2010), 'Hedge Fund Protection Under the Dodd-Frank Wall Street Reform and Consumer Protection Act', Clients and Friends Memo, July.
Chen, Y. (2007), 'Timing Ability in the Focus Market of Hedge Funds', *Journal of Investment Management*, 66–98.

Chen Y. and B. Liang (2007), 'Do Market Timing Hedge Funds Time the Market?' *Journal of Financial and Quantitative Analysis*, December.

Chincarini, L.B. (1998), 'The Failure of LTCM', available at SSRN: http://ssrn.com/abstract=952512, October 8.

Chincarini, L.B. (2007), 'The Amaranth Debacle. Failure of Risk Measures or Failure of Risk Management', *Journal of Alternative Investments*, Winter, 91–104.

Chincarini, L.B. (2008), 'A Case Study on Risk Management: Lessons from the Collapse of Amaranth Advisors L.L.C', *Journal of Applied Finance*, Spring/Summer 2008, 152–74.

Chincarini, L.B. (2010), 'A Comparison of Quantitative and Qualitative Hedge Funds', available at SSRN: http://ssrn.com/abstract=1532992, January.

Chincarini, L.B. (2012), 'The Crises of Crowding: Quant Copycats, Ugly Models, and the New Crash Normal, Wiley, forthcoming.

Chincarini, L.B. and A. Nakao (2010), 'Measuring Hedge Fund Timing Ability Across Factors', *Journal of Investing*, forthcoming available at SSRN: http://ssrn.com/abstract=1544452, January.

Chincarini, L.B. and D. Kim (2006), *Quantitative Equity Portfolio Management: An Active Approach to Portfolio Construction and Management*. New York, McGraw-Hill.

Credit Suisse First Boston (2005), 'Hedge Funds and Investment Banks', *Equity Re-search Sector Review*, March 9.

Dimmock, Stephen G. and William C. Gerken (2010), 'Finding Bernie Madoff: Detecting Fraud by Investment Managers', unpublished Working Paper, April.

Fama, E. and K. French (1993), 'Common Risk Factors in the Returns on Bonds and Stocks', *Journal of Financial Economics*, 3–53.

Fama, E. and K. French (1996), 'Multifactor Explanations of Asset Pricing Anomalies', *Journal of Finance*, 55–84.

Fuhr, D. (2011), 'ETF Landscape: Industry Highlights', Blackrock Presentation, January.

Fung, H., X. Xu and J. Yau (2002), 'Global Hedge Funds: Risk, Return, and Market Timing', *Financial Analysts Journal*, 19–30.

Fung, W. and D. Hsieh (1997), 'Empirical Characteristics of Dynamic Trading Strategies: The Case of Hedge Funds', *Review of Financial Studies*, 275–302.

Fung W. and D. Hsieh (2001), 'The Risk in Hedge Fund Strategies: Theory and Evidence from Trend Followers', *Review of Financial Studies*, 313–341.

Fung, William and David A. Hsieh (2004), 'Hedge Fund Benchmarks: A Risk Based Approach', *Financial Analysts Journal*, September/October, 65–80.

Getmansky, M., Andy W.Lo and I. Makarov (2004), 'An Econometric Model of Serial Correlation and Illiquidity in Hedge Fund Returns', *Review of Financial Studies*, 529–610.

Hodges, S. (1997), 'A Generalization of the Sharpe Ratio and its Applications to Valuation Bounds and Risk Measures', Working Paper of the Financial Options Research Centre at the University of Warwick, pages 1–18.

Ingersoll, J., M. Speigel, W. Goetzmann and I. Welch (2007), 'Portfolio Performance Manipulation and Manipulation-proof Performance Measures', *Review of Financial Studies*, 1503–1546.

Investment Company Institute (2010), 'Worldwide Mutual Fund Assets and Flows: 3rd Quarter 2010', ICI Publication, January 27.

Jagannathan, R. and R. Korajcsyk (1986), 'Assessing the Market Timing Performance of Managed Portfolios', *Journal of Business*, 217–235.

L'Habitant, Francois-Serge (2002), *Hedge Funds: Myths and Limits.* West Sussex, England: John Wiley and Sons.

Liang, Bing (2000), 'Hedge Funds: The Living and the Dead', *Journal of Financial and Quantitative Analysis*, **35**, 309–326.

Lowenstein, Roger (2000), 'Manager's Journal: The Tiger Fund is Gone; Who's Next?', *The Wall Street Journal*, April 3.

McDonald, Ian and Valerie Bauerlein (2006), 'Southern Discomfort: Troubles at Atlanta Hedge Fund Snare Doctors, Football Players; Mr. Wright Drops From Sight As SEC and

Investors Sue; Ex-Broncos Seek Payback; "I Haven't Made Myself Scarce"', *The Wall Street Journal*, March 9.

McGrane, Victoria, Dan Fitzpatrick and Randall Smith (2010), 'Fed's New Debit-Card Fee Rules Hit Hard; Issuers Howl', *The Wall Street Journal*, December 16.

Pezier, Jacques, (2004), *The Professional Risk Manager's Handbook*, Chapter "Risk and Risk Aversion", pages 19–60, Wilmington, Delaware, PRMIA Publications.

Pezier, Jacques (2010), 'Maximum Certainty Equivalent Excess Returns and Equivalent Preference Criteria', Unpublished Working Paper, pages 1–47.

Sidel, Robin (2011), 'At Banks, New Fees Replacing Old Levies', *The Wall Street Journal*, January 5.

The City UK (2010), 'Private Equity 2010', The City UK Publication, August.

Weiss, Andrew (2008), 'Madoff Scandal Rips Apart Close World of Jewish Philanthropy', Forward, December 26.

2. Europe's hedge fund industry – an overview
Andrea Hankova and François-Serge Lhabitant*

INTRODUCTION

Due to their strong appetite for eclectic asset classes and strategies, hedge funds have played an important role in the expansion of capital markets and economic growth worldwide. They have stimulated corporate activism, facilitated the restructuring of failed companies, financed the development of emerging sectors, improved market efficiency by acting as liquidity providers in a variety of situations and, in some cases, successfully designed trading strategies to profit from turmoil and volatility. However, hedge funds have also been the target of political blame, particularly in Continental Europe. Several European governments have expressed their displeasure over the increasing role played by hedge funds in financial markets and called for additional controls and regulation, at best, and shutting them down, at worst. Surprisingly, relatively little seems to be known of the *European* hedge fund industry. The focus of most of the research efforts so far has been on the United States (US) where more data and information are available. The purpose of this chapter is to fill this gap by providing a comprehensive review of the European hedge fund industry, its structure, players, and major strategies, as well as its historical performance.

1. KEY INDUSTRY STATISTICS

Hedge fund statistics should always be considered with caution due to the absence of a central, authoritative source combined with the severe restrictions imposed on advertising and reporting of hedge fund performance. In this chapter, we therefore use commercial databases and index providers, which themselves rely on information provided voluntarily by hedge fund managers.

*   A. Hankova, PhD, CAIA, is a Senior Hedge Fund Analyst at Kedge Capital. F.S. Lhabitant is the Chief Investment Officer of Kedge Capital and a Professor of Finance at the EDHEC Business School.

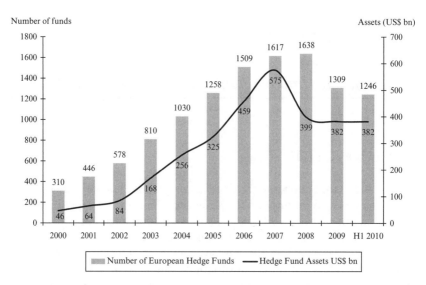

Source: Data from EuroHedge Database.

Figure 2.1   Evolution of the European hedge fund industry as of June 2010

1.1   Conventional Hedge Funds

According to *EuroHedge*, at the end of 2009 one could count 1309 European hedge funds managing approximately US$382 billion worth of assets – see Figure 2.1. By comparison, this represents 15 per cent of the hedge fund managers and 20 per cent of the hedge fund assets under management (AUM) worldwide. These numbers have varied significantly over time. From 2000 to 2007, the European hedge fund industry experienced a dramatic growth, primarily fuelled by a strong demand for active money management, an increasing quest for alternatives as a source of portfolio diversification and a structurally supportive environment for hedge fund strategies (clear trends in equity and credit markets, strong deal flow in mergers and acquisitions, a benign credit environment, availability of financing, etc.). Assets peaked at the end of 2007 (US$575 billion) before declining sharply in 2008, as a result of the financial crisis. The number of managers remained stable in 2008, but declined severely in 2009 as a result of several hedge fund closures and very few start ups. In 2010, both the number of managers and AUM seem to have stabilized, with 1246 hedge funds managing US$382 billion, according to the semi annual (H1 2010) *EuroHedge* Survey.

In terms of geography, the United Kingdom (UK) and, more spe-

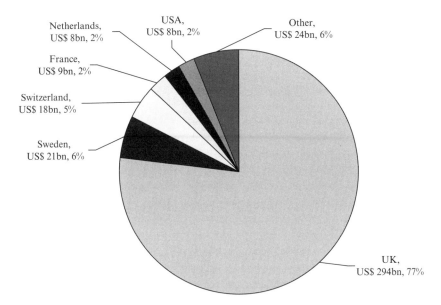

Netherlands,
US$ 8bn, 2%

USA,
US$ 8bn, 2%

Other,
US$ 24bn, 6%

France,
US$ 9bn, 2%

Switzerland,
US$ 18bn, 5%

Sweden,
US$ 21bn, 6%

UK,
US$ 294bn, 77%

Source: Data from EuroHedge Database.

Figure 2.2 *European hedge fund assets by management location as of June 2010*

cifically, London remains the primary location in Europe for hedge fund *management* with 77 per cent of the assets and 59 per cent of the funds – see Figure 2.2. The UK is also a leading centre for hedge fund service providers such as administration, prime brokerage, custody and auditing. Other important locations for hedge fund managers in Europe include Sweden (6 per cent), Switzerland (5 per cent) and France (2 per cent). Although these numbers have been stable historically, they could change in the future as some of the historical advantages offered by the UK – particularly in terms of taxes – are progressively disappearing. In addition, UK hedge funds will be affected by the European Union (EU) capital requirements directive (CRD3), which is set to seriously limit bonuses, as well as introduce a number of other requirements. So far, only two large hedge funds (*Brevan Howard* and *BlueCrest*) have relocated their teams from the UK to Switzerland, but more could follow. The economic impact could potentially be dramatic: according to the Alternative Investment Management Association, the UK hedge fund industry employs 40 000 people, including 10 000 directly employed by hedge funds, with the remainder being active as advisers and service providers to the industry.

Table 2.1   European hedge fund domicile as of January 2010

Domicile of hedge fund	Number of funds	Assets US$ million
Cayman Islands	746	244 267
Ireland	84	35 754
BVI	70	31 435
Luxembourg	54	7 264
Sweden	50	13 911
Bermuda	49	10 926
Guernsey	31	5 514
France	28	3 496
Netherlands	16	8 638
Italy	15	2 834
Jersey	13	3 807
Other	78	10 179
Undisclosed	78	5 823
Total	**1312**	**383 848**

Source: Data from EuroHedge Database.

In terms of legal structures, the majority of European-based managers use vehicles that are registered in offshore jurisdictions – see Table 2.1. The preferred offshore location remains the Cayman Islands (57 per cent of the funds), which offer significant tax advantages, a well-developed and sophisticated legal and judicial system, flexible structures to operate complex investments, and the availability of professional services such as accountants, attorneys, administrators and directors. For those willing to register a European onshore hedge fund, the preferred destinations are Ireland (9 per cent assets) and Luxembourg (4 per cent of the assets).

Similar to the US, the European hedge fund industry exhibits a substantial barbell structure, with some large-scale firms getting bigger at one end, lots of very small boutiques staying small at the other end, and very few firms in the middle. As an illustration, the four largest players (*Brevan Howard, Man AHL, BlueCrest* and *Winton*) have a market share close to 22 per cent, and the 21 largest firms manage more than 50 per cent of the overall European AUM. These firms continue to grow because they possess more professional sales and client service capabilities to reach a wider distribution channel. They attract institutional investors because they have strong operations for performance reporting, risk management, compliance, and so on. However, as a result, they have started to experience some fee erosion due to institutional client pressure and product

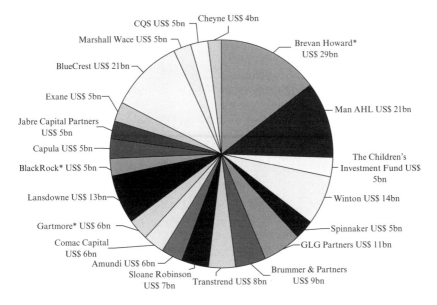

CQS US$ 5bn — Cheyne US$ 4bn

Marshall Wace US$ 5bn

BlueCrest US$ 21bn

Exane US$ 5bn

Jabre Capital Partners US$ 5bn

Capula US$ 5bn

BlackRock* US$ 5bn

Lansdowne US$ 13bn

Gartmore* US$ 6bn

Comac Capital US$ 6bn

Amundi US$ 6bn

Sloane Robinson US$ 7bn

Transtrend US$ 8bn

Brummer & Partners US$ 9bn

GLG Partners US$ 11bn

Spinnaker US$ 5bn

Winton US$ 14bn

The Children's Investment Fund US$ 5bn

Man AHL US$ 21bn

Brevan Howard* US$ 29bn

Note: *European funds only.

Source: Data from EuroHedge Database.

Figure 2.3 *Top European hedge fund firms by AUM as of June 2010*

commoditization. At the other side of the barbell, numerous small alpha boutiques are struggling to perform and raise capital. Their primary client targets are high-net worth and other highly risk-tolerant investors. Provided that their underlying performance remains strong, these smaller firms are less likely to suffer future fee erosion.

Although it is more diversified than a few years ago, in terms of strategies, the European hedge fund industry is still largely dominated by managed futures (18 per cent of the assets), European long/short equity (17 per cent), and global macro (14 per cent). All three are very liquid strategies – and European investors are known for favouring liquid hedge funds. However, it is important to stress that, thanks to the increase in hedge fund activity, some European markets (convertibles, high yields, etc.) are now enjoying more liquidity and the associated strategies have grown in importance. As a result, today there is sufficient breadth in the industry to create a diversified hedge fund portfolio consisting of European managers only, should one wish to make such an investment.

The above statistics do not include the recently appeared UCITS single manager hedge funds, which are discussed in the next section.

Table 2.2   Hedge fund assets by strategy as of June 2010

Strategy	Number of funds	AUM (US$ million)	% of universe by AUM
Managed futures	100	69 379	18.18%
European equity	272	66 252	17.36%
Macro	93	52 576	13.78%
Mixed arbitrage & Multi strategy	84	37 751	9.89%
Global equity	126	29 023	7.60%
Event driven	49	21 083	5.52%
Fixed Income	34	15 211	3.99%
Emerging market equity	108	11 955	3.13%
Market neutral	66	11 417	2.99%
Emerging market debt	30	10 605	2.78%
Credit	50	10 534	2.76%
Commodities	33	10 005	2.62%
Convertibles	23	8 757	2.29%
Asian Equity	80	8 491	2.22%
Distressed	15	6 749	1.77%
Currency	40	3 914	1.03%
Global insurance risk	8	3 105	0.81%
Volatility trading	12	2 068	0.54%
US equity	13	1 554	0.41%
Others	10	1 243	0.33%
Total	**1246**	**381 672**	**100%**

Source: Data from EuroHedge Database.

1.2   UCITS Hedge Funds (Newcits)

The framework for Undertakings for Collective Investments in Transferable Securities (UCITS) was created in 1985, to standardize rules for the authorisation, supervision, structure and activities of collective investment schemes in the European Communities, as they then were. Once registered in one EU country, a UCITS fund can be freely marketed across the EU including to retail investors. Also, offshore funds are usually treated more harshly, for tax purposes, in some European jurisdictions than UCITS funds. To gather assets, many European hedge fund managers have therefore launched UCITS-compliant scaled-down versions of their hedge funds – also called 'Newcits'.

Setting up a UCITS-compliant hedge fund involves a considerable amount of effort and resources. Nevertheless, US$34 billion of assets had

Table 2.3   UCITS assets by strategy as of January 2010

Strategy	Number of funds	AUM (US$ million)	% of universe by AUM
European equity	32	10456	46.13%
Volatility trading	2	3718	16.40%
Managed futures	4	2773	12.23%
Mixed arbitrage & multi-strategy	5	1333	5.88%
Global equity	7	932	4.11%
Asian equity	7	703	3.10%
Currency	3	463	2.04%
Emerging market equity	4	434	1.91%
Fixed income	3	416	1.84%
Credit	1	397	1.75%
Market neutral	9	304	1.34%
Emerging market debt	2	283	1.25%
Convertibles	3	278	1.22%
Event driven	1	77	0.34%
Macro	3	51	0.22%
US Equity	1	50	0.22%
Total	**87**	**22667**	**100%**

Source: Data from EuroHedge Database.

been raised through that channel as of June 2010 – an evidence for marketers that their hard work pays off. According to *Eurohedge*, Newcits have grown from 87 funds managing US$22 billion at the start of 2010 to 165 funds with US$34 billion six months later. This remains very small compared to the traditional, long-only UCITS universe, which accounts for around US$7 trillion under management. Nevertheless, some consultants estimate the size of UCITS-compliant hedge funds to reach US$350 billion in the not-too-distant future.[1]

Given the heavy restrictions on leverage, liquidity and underlying assets imposed on Newcits, it is not surprising to see that the dominant strategy is long/short equity, followed by volatility trading, global macro and managed futures – see Tables 2.3 and 2.4.

Not surprisingly the number of new European equity UCITS funds jumped from 32 to 53 within six months, which can be explained by the low additional cost of moving to a UCITS-compliant strategy as well as

[1]   Peters (2010), p. 36.

Table 2.4   UCITS assets by strategy as of June 2010

Strategy	Number of funds	AUM (US$ million)	% of universe by AUM
European equity	53	13 013	38.20%
Volatility trading	6	5 953	17.48%
Macro	10	4 176	12.26%
Managed futures	10	2 817	8.27%
Global equity	15	1 875	5.51%
Market neutral	20	1 517	4.45%
Asian equity	12	941	2.76%
Credit	3	896	2.53%
Currency	7	860	2.53%
Emerging market equity	7	716	2.10%
Mixed arbitrage & multi-strategy	10	363	1.07%
Convertibles	3	278	0.82%
Emerging market debt	2	231	0.68%
Event driven	3	227	0.67%
Fixed Income	2	113	0.33%
US Equity	1	67	0.20%
Commodities	1	19	0.06%
Total	**165**	**34 062**	**100%**

Source: Data from EuroHedge Database.

by the relatively low tracking error for some strategies (as discussed later in this chapter). However, in relative terms, the change of assets managed in the strategy has not been impressive and effectively declined as a percentage of the total universe. Global Macro, in contrast, sparked immense interest and the strategy now ranks third, accounting for a share of 12.26 per cent of all assets of the universe.

However, a key remaining issue is how Newcits will perform with respect to their offshore cousins. It might be a cynical accident that the timing of writing this chapter coincides with BlueCrest's announcement, in late October 2010, that it would wind down its BlueTrend UCITS fund, one of the largest (US$630 million) and most successful UCITS funds offered. When it launched, the fund expected tracking errors of 1 per cent to 2 per cent between the UCITS and the Cayman offshore version. However, UCITS constraints have prevented it from accurately tracking opportunities in bonds and commodities and have resulted in an unacceptable level of tracking error (3.5 per cent). The case is not unique.

According to the latest HedgeFund Intelligence research, global macro, fixed income and managed futures UCITS hedge funds show the highest level of tracking error at 4.12 per cent. Partially justifying their growth and success, Equities UCITS hedge funds have the lowest but still considerable tracking error (2.94 per cent). It remains to be seen whether UCITS clients will be willing to accept the opportunity loss.

2.   MAJOR SERVICE PROVIDERS

The magnitude of the 2008 financial crisis has emphasized the importance of the operational aspects of hedge funds and resulted in a migration to third-party administration, quality prime brokers and other specialized services.

2.1   Administrators

Citco is the leading administrator in Europe by number of funds (147 funds, 11 per cent of the total) as well as by AUM (US$54 billion, 14 per cent of the total). However, this represents only approximately half the assets Citco used to administer at the beginning of 2008 and is down by 25 per cent when measured by number of mandates. The second largest provider of administration services is *Citi* (including the former BiSys) with 115 funds (9 per cent) and US$30 billion (11 per cent) in AUM. Meanwhile, *BNY Mellon* completed its acquisition of *PNC Global Investment Services* and, as of July 2010, created the number two provider for fund accounting, administration and transfer agency services to fund managers globally. See Table 2.5.

Interestingly, while not as popular as a fund domicile, Ireland is by far the leading centre for administration, servicing 670 funds with a total value of US$247 billion. See Table 2.6.

The European administrators' landscape is rapidly changing. On the UCITS side, almost half the funds and half the assets are administered from Luxembourg, and although Ireland takes second place in terms of number of funds, it still lags behind the UK and France when measured by assets. Another evidence of the changing environment is the fact that only three administrators were able to secure more than 10 new mandates throughout 2009. This is a consequence of the slowdown of new hedge fund launches, but also the result of administrators being confronted with increased demand for more labour and operation intensive tasks, especially in the case of managed accounts as well as with requirements from investor's operational due diligence (this puts more pressure on

Table 2.5   Administrators of European hedge funds as of 1 January 2010

Administrator	No. of funds	Assets (US$ million)
Citco	147	53 582
Citi	115	29 831
PNC Global Investment Servicing	95	15 206
HSBC Securities Services	71	24 809
GlobeOp Financial Services	60	37 091
JP Morgan	49	8 899
Goldman Sachs	45	13 806
State Street/International Fund Services	36	35 436
Northern Trust	36	7 793
Daiwa Securities	34	9 222
BNY Mellon	33	7 764
SEB	26	3 234
CACEIS/Fastnet	25	4 633
UBS	24	4 454
RBC Dexia Investor Services	24	2 816
Fortis Prime Fund Solutions	22	17 063
Custom House	21	14 944
Other*	449	93 265
Total	**1312**	**383 848**

Source: Data from EuroHedge Database.

the profitability of the hedge fund administration business). Some consolidation seems inevitable, as illustrated by the recent examples of BNY Mellon/PNC and Credit Suisse/Fortis.

2.2   Prime Brokers

On the prime brokerage side, the *Lehman Brothers* collapse in September 2008 has dramatically changed the shape of the industry. When the European prime brokerage arm of *Lehman* went into administration, many hedge funds suddenly lost control of their assets, becoming creditors in the Lehman bankruptcy, essentially as a consequence of a small technical difference of regulation between the US and Europe.[2] This has

---

[2]   Re-hypothecation is a procedure by which one bank lends securities that its clients have pledged as collateral. In the US, prime brokers can only re-hypothecate securities held on margin while in Europe prime brokers can claim ownership of

*Table 2.6   Location of administrators of European hedge funds as of
1 January 2010*

Location of administrator	No. of funds	Assets (US$ million)
Ireland	670	247 492
Cayman Islands	112	49 456
Luxembourg	67	8 159
Sweden	50	13 911
Bermuda	36	6 618
Guernsey	31	5 270
France	29	3 510
Netherlands	29	8 721
UK	26	7 329
Isle of Man	25	3 214
Other	137	16 184
Undisclosed	100	13 985
Total	**1312**	**383 848**

Source: Data from EuroHedge Database.

placed the spotlight on the exact content of prime brokerage agreements, the prime brokerage model in general, the crucial role that both play in dealing with prime broker credit risk and the necessity of having multiple prime brokers. See Table 2.7.

The biggest winner of the crisis was *Credit Suisse*, which, by adding more than 100 mandates in 2008 already, surpassed UBS by number of mandates and took the largest share of the business by AUM at the end of 2009. *Deutsche Bank*, another beneficiary of the 2008 turmoil, was the other sole exception among the top five providers that was able to extend its asset base over 2009. According to the latest *EuroHedge* annual survey, *Goldman Sachs* still defended its top ranking in terms of total mandates but achieved only third place by total assets managed in the brokerage business. Together with *Morgan Stanley*, which has traditionally been the winner of the ranking, both have been hit by a drop in mandates and assets as sole mandates went for a multi-prime broker solution after the collapse of *Lehman*. However, no player in the top five was able to build

---

all cash and securities held with them. In September 2008, many European hedge funds were informed that assets they had posted as collateral with their prime broker had ended stuck somewhere within Lehman Brothers, even though they were not using Lehman as a prime broker.

Table 2.7   European hedge fund Prime brokerage as of 1 January 2010

Prime broker	Sole mandates	Split mandates	Total mandates	Assets (US$ million)
Goldman Sachs	147	158	305	52 453
Morgan Stanley	115	174	289	48 434
Credit Suisse	62	156	218	59 313
UBS	71	131	202	36 551
Deutsche Bank	55	109	164	33 451
NewEdge	82	23	105	15 506
Bank of America – Merrill Lynch	40	55	95	11 264
Citi	29	42	71	9 516
SEB	64	4	68	14 681
JP Morgan	19	36	55	22 742
Barclays Capital	11	25	36	13 439
None	123	0	123	20 191
Other (incl. undisclosed)	124	47	171	46 307
Total	**942**	**960**	**1902**	**383 848**

Source: Data from EuroHedge Database.

a significant distance to its competitors in terms of either assets or mandates. Notably, some newer providers like *JP Morgan* (which inherited the prime broker business of *Bear Stearns*) and *SEB* showed the highest rates of growth by assets. The case of the latter is particularly interesting as its strategy as a niche player has paid off – *SEB* dominates the Scandinavian market.

Prime brokers have only moderately benefited from the UCITS growth via the swap business so far, as these structures typically use custodians rather than prime brokers.

3.   THE RISK AND PERFORMANCE CHARACTERISTICS OF EUROPEAN HEDGE FUNDS

3.1   Available Databases, Indices and Performance Biases

In the US, investors have difficulties in choosing between the numerous commercial databases and indices tracking hedge fund performances. The problem is usually exacerbated as these indices and databases are highly heterogeneous and subject to various construction biases.[3] In Europe, the problem is just the opposite – there are not many good sources of European hedge fund data. To our knowledge, the only two European-focused databases commercially available are those of *EuroHedge* and *Eurekahedge*. Both firms are providers of hedge fund data and information since 1998 and 2001 respectively, both in Europe and globally. Both firms calculate proprietary indices based on their databases, using, nevertheless, different criteria.

To include a fund in its index, *EuroHedge* requires it to be at least 80 per cent managed from or based in the appropriate region and have at least a three-month track record. At the time of writing, there was no minimum size to qualify. Once a fund fits the above-mentioned criteria, it is classified into one of the existing strategy categories in agreement with the fund managers. *EuroHedge* then calculates a composite index as well as single-strategy indices as the median performance of each group. All funds, live and liquidated, are included in the historical figures.

By contrast, to include a fund in its index, *Eurekahedge* requires it to have at least 90 per cent of its mandate in the appropriate region. The location of the fund is therefore irrelevant. In addition, Eurekahedge uses the respective mathematical means (average) of the monthly returns of all hedge fund constituents in the index at that time, equally weighted and irrespective of currency denomination. All funds, live and liquidated, are included in the historical figures. It is noted that *Eurekahedge* includes new hedge funds in their indices with all their performance history. That is, if a fund enters the index at date t, the index performance prior to date t is recalculated as if the fund had been included since day one – see Lhabitant (2006).

3.2 Risk and Returns

In order to analyze the risks and returns of European hedge funds and compare them to those of their US counterparts in a fair way, we have decided to (i) use both *EuroHedge* and *Eurekahedge* indices; and (ii) pair each European index with its US equivalent calculated from the same data provider. The strategies we have considered for *Eurohedge* are as follows:

- *Composite*: all funds included in the database.
- *Global Equity*: Funds investing in equities across the world, following long/short strategies.

---

[3] See, for instance, Lhabitant (2006) for a review.

- *Event Driven*: Funds which take positions in companies involved in corporate events, such as mergers, spin-offs, take-overs and special situations.
- *Managed Futures*: Funds that take long and short positions in various asset classes through futures markets, usually with a systematic trend following approach.
- *Global Macro*: Funds that take long and short positions in various asset classes based on macro-economic analysis.
- *Convertible Arbitrage*: Funds that invest in convertible securities, normally also taking short positions in its underlying common stock, and using leverage to generate returns from movements in volatility, equity or credit.
- *Fixed Income Arbitrage*: Funds generally investing long and short and with leverage in government bonds but may also invest in corporate bonds and global fixed income securities.
- *Credit*: Funds investing in all types of credit instruments other than government debt, i.e. asset back securities, corporate or municipal bonds.
- *Multi-Strategy*: Funds which allocate capital dynamically to various strategies.

Eurekahedge uses similar definitions for its Managed Futures, Event Driven, Fixed Income Arbitrage, Global Macro and Multi-Strategy strategies. In addition, it offers the following three categories:

- *Distressed Debt*: Funds investing in or trading in debt securities from bankrupt or financially stressed issuers.
- *Long/Short Equity*: Funds having long and short positions in equities from a specific region (US or Europe).
- *Relative Value*: Funds using generally market neutral strategies that combine long and short positions in related securities.

Table 2.8 compares the performance of the various strategies using *EuroHedge* European and US indices. While all long-term performances are positive, there seems to be a substantial underperformance by European funds in each of the considered strategy. Risk/reward differences were most notable in the Event Driven strategy indices whereby the differential in volatility of −2.80 per cent was the largest between the European and US indices. Coincidentally the US Event Driven index showed three times higher maximum drawdown of −21.73 per cent compared to the European Event Driven index while the volatility of the US Event Driven index hardly made the double size of the European peer. The comparison of European

Table 2.8 Comparative performances of European vs. US hedge funds using EuroHedge indices, January 1998 to October 2010

	Annualized Return (%)	Annualized Volatility (%)	Max drawdown (%)	Return differential EU vs. US (% p.a.)	Volatility differential EU vs. US (% p.a.)	Drawdown differential EU vs. US (% p.a.)	Perf. 2010 (%)	Perf. 2009 (%)	Perf. 2008 (%)	Perf. 2007 (%)
Composite Index – Europe	7.89	3.90	−6.37	−1.76	0.28	2.79	4.28	8.94	−4.65	7.22
Composite Index – US	9.65	3.62	−9.15				6.78	15.54	−6.87	10.07
Global Equity Europe	7.07	5.49	−14.63	−4.16	−1.71	0.63	1.63	8.73	−13.43	8.23
Global Equity – US	11.23	7.20	−15.26				4.75	18.55	−13.65	15.24
Event Driven – Europe	6.48	3.33	−6.42	−2.88	−2.8	15.31	4.54	7.49	−3.55	3.76
Event Driven – US	9.36	6.13	−21.73				10.28	25.72	−20.35	7.38
Managed Futures – Europe	7.02	8.65	−9.51	−1.95	1.53	−3.82	8.75	−7.36	21.95	8.77
Managed Futures – US	8.97	7.12	−5.70				6.18	1.29	16.99	10.95
Global Macro – Europe	6.10	2.90	−2.87	−4.67	−1.05	−0.75	0.80	6.28	4.05	7.56
Global Macro – US	10.77	3.96	−2.12				5.85	8.00	3.49	12.89
Convertible Arbitrage – Europe	4.46	9.42	−34.59	−2.46	2.29	−7.67	5.37	37.40	−33.41	6.22
Convertible Arbitrage – US	6.92	7.13	−26.92				9.72	45.59	−25.12	4.71
Fixed Income Arbitrage – Europe	4.81	1.93	−3.26	−3.21	−1.45	7.57	6.04	9.77	0.08	3.20
Fixed Income Arbitrage – US	8.02	3.38	−10.84				8.11	15.66	−7.22	8.10
Credit – Europe	3.22	5.50	−27.14	−6.52	1.50	−19.62	11.49	24.07	−23.45	0.38
Credit – US	9.74	4.00	−7.52				10.24	25.60	−4.80	7.87
Multi-Strategy – Europe	4.36	3.69	−11.60	−5.28	−0.54	2.15	5.50	14.53	−9.76	9.29
Multi-Strategy – US	9.64	4.23	−13.75				6.32	19.92	−12.82	10.12

and US Credit hedge fund indices showed the largest differential in return of −6.52 per cent and drawdown of −19.62 per cent respectively. Interestingly, this underperformance does not seem related to an increase or decrease of risk, whether measured as volatility or as maximum drawdown. However, further analysis of the annual performance of European hedge funds between 2007 and 2010 shows that 2008 was an exception in various respects even though European hedge funds generally underperformed their US counterparts over the four year period. In 2008 all but two European strategies outperformed their corresponding US peer indices. Notably, that year also marked the widest dispersion in the European and US index performance differentials ranging from +16.8 per cent in Managed Futures and −18.65 per cent in Credit. Furthermore, in the following year, the performance gap widened the most, as evidenced by the difference in the composite (Europe vs. US −6.6 per cent in 2009 vs. +2.22 per cent in 2008 and −2.85 per cent in 2007) as well on the basis of average or median strategy data.

Table 2.9 compares the performance of the various strategies using *Eurekahedge* European and US indices. A similar underperformance is observed for all strategies except for Global Macro and Multi-Strategy. However, in the risk / reward context the result is not surprising as both strategies show significantly higher volatility and maximum drawdown for European hedge funds. For Global Macro, the annualized volatility of the European hedge fund index was +28.59 per cent vs. +8.54 per cent for the US index. Even more significant is the differential in maximum drawdown, which amounted to 49.54 per cent between the European and US indices of the same strategy. Findings for the Multi-Strategy indices are similar; however they are showing smaller spreads. In the case of Global Macro, the relatively small number of funds in each index (4 and 4, respectively) makes it difficult to reach any firm conclusions. With respect to the analysis of the annual performance between 2007 and 2010 there is less analogy in the findings when comparing the returns of *EuroHedge* and *Eurekahedge*. The values of return differentials between the European and US indices are largely distorted by the results of the above-mentioned strategies. By way of example, the dispersion of the return differentials ranges between −67.74 per cent (Global Macro) to −2.69 per cent (Long Short Equity) in 2008. Also contrasting *EuroHedge* with *Eurekahedge* data, its is not 2009 but 2008, which marks the year with the largest performance differential whereby average European hedge funds underperformed its US peer index by 9.78 per cent.

The bottom section of Table 2.9 compares the performance of funds by size, regardless of their strategy. The results seem to contradict the common belief that smaller hedge funds outperform larger ones, both in the US and in Europe.

Table 2.9   Comparative performances of European vs. US hedge funds using Eurekahedge indices, January 2000 to October 2010

	Annualized return (%)	Annualized volatility (%)	Max drawdown (%)	Return differential EU vs. US (% p.a.)	Volatility differential EU vs. US (% p.a.)	Drawdown differential EU vs. US (% p.a.)	Perf. 2010 (%)	Perf. 2009 (%)	Perf. 2008 (%)	Perf. 2007 (%)
Composite – Europe	9.42	7.19	−20.98	−1.73	1.15	−8.72	5.65	20.25	−18.87	7.80
Composite – US	11.15	6.04	−12.26				9.03	23.54	−9.09	12.78
Arbitrage – Europe	3.18	6.67	−27.88	−6.33	2.65	−16.16	6.30	11.93	−16.30	−6.92
Arbitrage – US	9.51	4.02	−11.72				7.91	28.83	−7.27	7.52
Managed Futures – Europe	7.71	6.43	−7.72	−7.84	−1.86	−0.89	3.78	7.75	0.55	11.32
Managed Futures – US	15.55	8.28	−6.83				8.56	8.19	27.15	19.82
Distressed – Europe	8.76	10.57	−39.63	−4.46	1.28	−9.11	9.49	33.61	−32.29	4.66
Distressed – US	13.22	9.29	−30.52				22.53	40.67	−25.61	9.30
Event Driven – Europe	7.53	6.30	−18.93	−3.98	−3.16	9.13	12.51	29.35	−14.60	4.81
Event Driven – US	11.51	9.46	−28.06				13.36	48.18	−24.37	5.47
Fixed Income Arbitrage – Europe	5.63	7.17	−21.27	−5.11	2.75	−6.87	8.83	25.98	−16.55	0.65
Fixed Income Arbitrage – US	10.74	4.42	−14.40				12.54	28.24	−13.44	8.42
Long Short Equity – Europe	9.47	7.76	−21.72	−0.30	−0.59	−2.65	4.80	20.59	−19.26	8.26
Long Short Equity – US	9.77	8.36	−19.07				7.32	24.09	−16.57	12.86
Global Macro – Europe	17.32	28.59	−56.03	4.84	20.06	−49.54	11.79	23.78	−49.36	1.07

Table 2.9 (continued)

	Annualized return (%)	Annualized volatility (%)	Max drawdown (%)	Return differential EU vs. US (% p.a.)	Volatility differential EU vs. US (% p.a.)	Drawdown differential EU vs. US (% p.a.)	Perf. 2010 (%)	Perf. 2009 (%)	Perf. 2008 (%)	Perf. 2007 (%)
Global Macro – US	12.48	8.54	−6.49				6.12	5.57	18.38	14.52
Multi-Strategy – Europe	11.81	11.82	−30.83	0.91	6.49	−19.48	7.92	19.24	−27.23	14.09
Multi-Strategy – US	10.90	5.32	−11.35				7.79	20.52	−6.39	13.38
Relative Value – Europe	6.78	7.92	−10.58	−5.04	1.27	3.21	4.23	0.23	−6.18	6.44
Relative Value – US	11.82	6.65	−13.79				10.00	28.92	−10.00	8.14
Small Funds (<$100 million) – Europe	9.63	8.40	−26.85	−0.85	2.10	−14.41	5.35	22.60	−24.10	8.26
Small Funds (<$100 million) – US	10.48	6.30	−12.43				8.98	21.54	−8.86	12.56
Medium Funds ($100 to $500 million) – Europe	11.77	6.27	−14.79	−0.67	0.04	−0.07	6.50	20.15	−13.00	8.06
Medium Funds ($100 to $500 million) – US	12.43	6.23	−14.71				8.16	30.77	−12.82	12.75
Large Funds (above $500 million) – Europe	9.78	4.60	−3.61	−4.57	−1.18	8.79	3.17	10.71	4.94	12.43
Large Funds (above $500 million) – US	14.35	5.78	−12.40	−0.85	2.10	−14.41	13.77	38.76	−7.49	12.26

4. IMPACT OF CURRENT TRENDS

4.1 Regulation of European Hedge Funds

US regulators have historically adopted a rather Coasean approach. Rather than imposing mandatory 'one-size-fits-all' requirements on hedge funds, they have set default rules but have in parallel given sophisticated investors and hedge fund managers the flexibility to opt out and set up negotiated contracts. This flexibility has provided an important safety valve against the risk of overregulation for the US onshore hedge fund industry. In contrast, many European regulators – particularly in Continental Europe – have attempted to adopt strict operating rules or restrict the sale of interests in hedge funds without conceding any real alternative. In addition, as each country in Europe had maintained its own system of financial regulation and supervision, European hedge funds had to grapple with a multiplicity of legal systems, regulators, supervisors and tax codes, several official languages, domestic investment laws and country-specific distribution rules, as well as less tangible, difficult to define, yet very real cultural barriers. Cross-border distribution was therefore complex, burdensome and costly and, as a result, almost nonexistent. Consequently, most European hedge funds tended to be created, managed, administered and distributed almost exclusively on a national scale.[4]

The 2008 financial crisis has led to calls to reform the financial regulatory system, both in the US and around the world. Even though they were amongst the victims of (rather than the culprits of) the crisis, hedge funds became the immediate target of the European Parliament and national governments willing to establish rules to clamp down on hedge funds and private equity.

After almost two years of intense debate, negotiation and lobbying, the European Parliament plenary session of 11 November 2010 has finally agreed on the text of an Alternative Investment Fund Managers (AIFM) Directive. The Directive will introduce, for the first time, a harmonized European regulatory regime governing the authorisation and supervision of AIFM. It will apply to all AIFM established in the EU, which manage alternative investment funds (AIF) irrespective of whether their fund is established inside or outside the EU, whether the AIFM manages AIF directly or by delegation, whether the AIF belong to the open or

---

[4] For a rigorous review of national hedge fund regulations in Europe, including comparisons with the situation in the US, see Athanassiou (2009).

close-ended type and whatever the legal structure of the AIF and of the AIFM. In addition, non-EU AIFM will also need to be authorized to manage EU-based AIF. In return for more regulation, the Directive provides for the introduction of a 'passport' enabling AIFM to offer their management services and market their AIF throughout the EU under a single authorization. To become authorized, AIFM have to comply with a range of obligations laid down in the Directive, relating to effective governance, organizational structure, monitoring and safeguards, capital requirements, rules of conduct, remuneration, conflict of interest, risk management and marketing, third party oversight, financial resources and liability insurance cover as well as meet enhanced reporting and disclosure requirements.

EU member states now have two years to implement the Directive into their respective national laws, following the publication of the official text. At the time of writing, the full impact of the Directive is not clear, as a number of points of detail will hinge on further regulations (including secondary legislation and implementation measures).

4.2 UCITS and Newcits

The case of UCITS hedge funds is arguably an interesting phenomenon as, in contrast to the stale flows to the traditional hedge fund strategies, the inflows into UCITS grew by more than 50 per cent in the first six months of 2010. Despite their remarkable growth, the question is whether that growth is sustainable and to what extent the UCITS framework (regulating the onshore structure) may overtake the classic offshore structure in the context of the future shape of the European hedge fund industry.

In particular, one should remember that the UCITS framework has a number of restrictions that limit the implementation of hedge fund strategies. The most important ones are the following:

- The ban on shorting cash securities: UCITS funds willing to short need to create their exposure synthetically through the use of derivatives such as swaps or contract for differences.
- The ban on investment in physical commodities or their derivatives: only exposure to commodity indices is allowed.
- Some limits on leverage: total gross exposure including derivatives is limited to 200 per cent of NAV.
- A diversification requirement: for positions exceeding 5 per cent NAV issuer limit, the aggregate shall not exceed 40 per cent of NAV.
- A 10 per cent of NAV limit on exposure to any single issuer.
- The need to offer liquidity to investors at least every two weeks.

- A limit of 10 per cent of NAV in unlisted securities, plus 10 per cent of NAV in recently unlisted securities destined to list in less than 12 months.

As a result, several hedge fund strategies are extremely difficult to implement under the UCITS format. Nevertheless, some hedge fund managers may be tempted to abuse the spirit of the UCITS rules and use the UCITS framework as a means of dodging, effectively, the AIFM directive and as an easier path to raise capital. The risk to UCITS as a brand is that these funds are likely to fail and tar all UCITS with the same brush.[5] Alternatively, they could severely underperform their offshore cousins, which could greatly disappoint investors.

5.   MAJOR FRAUD CASES/BLOWUPS AND THEIR IMPACT

The European hedge fund industry did not experience as many fraud cases or blowups as in the US and the associated losses were in no way comparable in magnitude to those of a *Madoff* or an *Amaranth*.[6] Nevertheless, there *have* been a few cases that are worth mentioning, namely *Absolute Capital Management*, *Peloton*, *Weavering Capital*, and the *K1 Group*. We will also briefly discuss the case of Bernard Madoff, as it had severe consequences for some of the European players.

5.1   Absolute Capital Management (September 2007)

Created in March 2002 by Sean Ewing and Florian Homm, Absolute Capital Management Holdings (ACMH) was a Mallorca-based long/short equity fund manager with a bias towards Germany, Switzerland and Austria. ACMH was nominated 'Best Hedge Fund Group' at the June 2006 Hedge Fund Review European Performance Awards. At its peak in 2007, it managed 12 hedge funds with total assets above US$3.1 billion.

ACMH's troubles started in July 2007, when its chief executive and

---

[5]   The usual perception of investors is that UCITS are strongly regulated products and are therefore deemed to be safer. One should, nevertheless, remember that there were several UCITS funds amongst the investors in Madoff's funds.

[6]   An interesting open question is whether this is due to different regulatory systems or if it is just a question of where Europe stands in terms of hedge fund industry lifecycle.

chairman, Sean Ewing, retired to spend more time with his family. In September 2007, its co-CIO and co-founder, Florian Homm, announced his resignation with immediate effect in an open letter to shareholders, due to a conflict with the Board on the adequate compensation to retain top-level fund managers. He also announced in this letter that he had donated 5 million shares of ACMH, worth approximately €33 million, to the funds he was running in August so that they 'ended up positive or neutral for the month'. When investors placed in their redemptions, it did not take long to discover that the funds, even though they were Europe-focused, had large allocations in US small and even micro-caps with shallow liquidity. ACMH subsequently had to suspend redemptions, shut down some funds and create a €500 million side pocket. ACMH shares, which were listed on the AIM, dropped by 70 per cent. A lawsuit was brought against Mr Homm who was accused of misrepresenting the share of illiquid investments in the portfolio. The court finally dismissed the claim in May 2010 as the claimants failed to plead the fraud with the degree of specificity required by the corresponding act, referring to an article in Hedge Fund Law Report.

5.2   Peloton (February 2008)

Peloton Partners was founded in 2005 by two *Goldman Sachs* alumni, Ron Beller and Geoff Grant. It focused primarily on credit arbitrage and mortgages. Peloton made the headlines as one of the best performing hedge funds in 2007, after delivering a stellar 87 per cent gain as a result of successful trades against US subprime mortgages. It won two awards at the annual *EuroHedge* (2007) event, including the much-vaunted 'new fund of the year' award, and became one of London's highest-profile funds.

Peloton was essentially running a strategy known as capital structure arbitrage, betting that slices of the same bond portfolio with different ratings would diverge sharply in price. It entered 2008 with a long leveraged exposure of about US$17 billion of Alt-A, subprime and other mortgage debt versus US$6 billion in shorts in lower-rated subprime paper. When the credit crisis hit, banks started cutting credit lines to hedge funds after they had taken large write downs on their own balance sheets. Peloton's positions dropped in value by 10 to 15 per cent and its creditors immediately posted additional collateral requests that it was unable to meet. Peloton therefore had to wind down its US$2 billion ABS hedge fund and to suspend redemptions in its US$1.6 billion multi-strategy fund, which had a very large position in the busted ABS fund. It ultimately had to liquidate it, with massive losses for investors.

5.3 Weavering Capital (November 2008)

Founded in 1998 by its Swedish-born CEO Magnus Peterson, Weavering Capital was originally a London-based independent firm, providing macro research to proprietary traders at banks and hedge funds. In March 2000, the firm decided to migrate to asset management and started its first hedge fund, the Weavering Capital Fund. It generated stellar performance (+140 per cent in its first 10 months), but lost 15 per cent in March 2001, 16 per cent in April and 47 per cent in June. The fund was ultimately shut down.

In April 2003, Weavering started a brand new hedge fund called the Weavering Macro Fixed Income Fund. This second fund was relatively successful: it generated returns in the 10 to 12 per cent p.a. range for five years and ultimately reached US$639 million of assets. The truth came to light in November 2008 when the fund received redemption requests exceeding US$200 million but was unable to honour them. The only position in the fund was a US$637 million interest rate swap, established against an offshore company controlled by Magnus Peterson's father. Magnus Peterson became the first hedge fund manager to be arrested in Britain, and his hedge fund was put in liquidation. At the time of writing, an investigation by the UK Serious Fraud Office was still ongoing.

And as with most fraud cases, there were numerous 'red flags'. Let us quote some of them: (a) the marketing material never disclosed the existence of the first fund; (b) both funds had unusual broking relationships, including financial interest in broking desks that generated a profit from the volume of trades, i.e. a clear conflict of interest; (c) the company employed family members of Magnus Peterson; (d) the firm had developed a reputation for its lavish hospitality, owning its own chalet for corporate entertainment in the exclusive Alpine ski resort of Verbier. Allenbridge, a reputable London-based hedge fund research house, warned against investing in Weavering in 2001; its calls were, largely, ignored.

5.4 The K1 Group (October 2009)

The K1 Group shows some interesting similarities with the Madoff fraud. The founder of the K1 Group, Helmut Kiener, was a psychologist by training who worked from 1988 to 2000 as an advertising salesman for German telephone books. In 1995, he created in parallel the K1 Group. K1 was essentially a fund of hedge funds based on the 'K1 Fund Allocation System' – a semi-automatic hedge fund allocation system developed by

Kiener in 1996. The official performance was impressive, with returns of 844 per cent from 1996 through July 2009 – and these were after a 3 per cent management fee and a 30 per cent performance fee.

In fact, Kiener was making false statements about the profits in the K1 funds. Several hedge funds that Kiener was investing with were apparently run by Oceanus Asset Management, a company that was just a front for none other than Helmut Kiener himself. Most of the money allocated there seems to have gone right back into Kiener's pocket to buy aircraft and property and maintain his luxurious lifestyle. In total, Kiener defrauded about 4924 investors and two banks (*Barclays Capital* and *BNP*) of €345 million. Ironically, the BaFin, Germany's financial regulator, had tried, since 2001 to stop K1 from soliciting German investors or working as a fund manager in Germany. Kiener had nevertheless managed to carry on his activities in the EU after moving the funds to the British Virgin Islands.

Dieter Frerichs, managing director of the K1 group funds K1 Global and K1 Invest, committed suicide. Both vehicles were shut down in 2009. In November 2010, Mr. Kiener, the self-proclaimed hedge fund manager, was charged with 35 counts of aggravated fraud and 68 counts of forgery after a year-long probe, according to the *Financial Times*.

6.   CONCLUSIONS

While the European hedge fund industry is no longer at its infancy, with 1246 hedge funds managing US$382 billion in September 2010, it is far from maturity, especially when compared to the US. The industry is heavily centred in London, which has become the primary location in Europe not only for hedge fund management companies but also for hedge fund service providers such as administrators, prime brokers, custodians and auditors. However, the recent efforts to tighten the historically advantageous UK tax regime combined with several regulatory changes introduced by the EU, such as the new Capital Requirements Directive (CRD3) and the Alternative Investment Fund Managers Directive (AIFM), are expected to negatively impact the attractiveness of London in the medium to long term. Switzerland as a non-EU country may profit from these developments but so far only two very large hedge funds decided to leave the UK and relocate in Switzerland.

At the same time, the European efforts to standardize the rules for the authorisation, supervision, structure and activities of collective investment schemes in the EU countries has kicked off a trend of Newcits launches, essentially UCITS-compliant scaled-down versions of the offshore hedge funds. Despite requiring considerable amount of effort and resources to set up, Newcits became very successful and popular products, particularly for retail investors. Since January 2010 the UCITS industry has doubled in number of funds and manages US$34 billion in assets as of June 2010. However, whether its growth will be sustainable going forward will depend on the tracking error between the UCITS and the Cayman offshore versions as a result of restrictions on leverage, liquidity and underlying assets imposed by regulators.

Our risk and returns analysis between European and US hedge funds has shown that while all long-term performances are positive, there seems to be a substantial underperformance by European funds in each of the considered hedge fund strategies using the *EuroHedge* database. When using the *Eurekahedge* database, we observe some exceptions for two strategies, namely Global Macro and Multi Strategy. By using the data of the latter provider, we have also shown that the common belief that smaller funds outperform larger ones was more a myth than reality.

With regard to the hedge fund service providers, the major trends in this area started as a result of the 2008 financial crisis when migration to third-party administration, demand for lower dependency on a single prime broker (diversification) and other specialized services have been observed. Furthermore, with the slowdown of new hedge fund launches but also the result of administrators being confronted with increased demand for more labour and operation intensive tasks, some consolidation seems inevitable.

Apart from the financial crisis of 2008 it was also the case of frauds and blowups that have shaped the development of hedge funds. Fortunately, Europe did not experience as many fraud cases or blowups as the US, both in terms of numbers as well as magnitude of the losses.

Lastly the greatest challenge we see for the European industry is the trend towards more regulated and supposedly more harmonized hedge fund landscape. In contrast to the US, Europe follows a 'one-size-fits-all' approach that will translate into a centralized regulatory regime governing the authorisation and supervision of alternative investment managers as proposed by the AIFM Directive. At the time of writing, the full impact of the Directive is not clear.

However, we still believe in growth of the European hedge fund industry in the near future, due to an increasing appetite from smaller and institutional investors, such as pension funds and life insurers, who want to increase quite substantially their currently modest allocations in hedge funds. In our opinion, this could accelerate the establishment of an institutional quality European hedge fund industry.

BIBLIOGRAPHY

Amenc N., Sender S. (2010), *Are hedge fund UCITS the cure-all?*, Nice, France: EDHEC.

Athanassiou, Phoebus (2009), *Hedge Fund Regulation in the European Union: Current Trends and Future Prospects*, Amsterdam, The Netherlands: Wolters Kluwer Law & Business.

Athanassiou, Phoebus (2010), 'New-look prime broking market takes shape in Europe', *EuroHedge*, **12**(4), 7–9.

Athanassiou, Phoebus (2010), 'Fund administrators adapting to a rapidly changing world', *EuroHedge*, **12**(5), 20–21.

Athanassiou, Phoebus (2010), 'New hedge fund launches start to pick up pace in first half of 2010', *EuroHedge*, **12**(7), 10–11.

Athanassiou, Phoebus (2010), 'Recovery in European hedge fund asset growth stalls in the first half', *EuroHedge*, **12**(8), 10–11.

Harris, J. (2010), 'Fund of funds struggle', *Hedge Funds Review*, July/UCITS Supplement, 20–22.

Ineichen, A.M. (2004), 'European hedge funds', *Journal of Portfolio Management*, **30**(4), 254–67.

Lhabitant, François-Serge (2006), *Hedge Fund Indices for Retail Investors: UCITS Eligible or not Eligible?*, Swiss Finance Institute Research Paper Series No.6–14, available at SSRN: http://ssrn.com/abstract=935214.

Peters, N. (2010), 'Q&A with Paul Holmes of BoA Merril Lynch: UCITS funds could soon be a $350 billion market', *The Hedge Fund Journal*, **55**, 34–5.

3. Sovereign-wealth funds – a paradigm shift in capital flows in the global economy
*Dilip K. Das**

INTRODUCTION

Financial globalization has gained momentum in recent years. Over the last two decades the rate of increase in global cross-border investment was twice that of the rate of growth of multilateral trade in goods and services, which in turn exceeded the rate of global GDP growth (Lane and Milesi-Ferretti, 2006). State-owned and managed sovereign-wealth funds (SWFs) have played an increasingly important role in underpinning, sustaining and expanding financial globalization and in supporting financial diversification. At the same time, they have not escaped criticism over their activities, nor have they been spared losses on their investments since the onset of the global financial crisis.

SWFs have grown considerably in significance in the course of the last few years. The global financial crisis has made of them a more visible group of investors, while their participation in global financial markets appeared likely to grow in importance for as long as inflows from trade surpluses and commodity exports continued (IFS, 2010). At the same time, given their limited disclosure and lack of transparency, SWFs have prompted economic nationalists to threaten with a protectionist backlash. Pre-crisis, threats of financial protectionism had been mounting in proportion to the increase in their global investments. As a result, despite being significant liquidity-enhancing and financial resource allocation agents, SWFs had also become the focus of a controversy, with both public and private sector policy conclaves expressing concerns over their activities, reflecting on how to reconcile the policy measures necessary to keep them in check with the promotion of an open, global financial system.

*   PhD, Professor of International Economics and International Finance; Director, The Institute of Asian Business, SolBridge International School of Business, Woosong University, Daejeon, Republic of Korea. The author is grateful to the handbook's editor for helpful comments and suggestions. The usual disclaimer applies.

The purpose of this chapter is to provide readers with the basic conceptual strands of the debate surrounding SWFs, their genesis and their coming into prime. The structure of this chapter is as follows. Section 1 focuses on the definition of and tracks the origin, growth and *raison d'être* of SWFs. Section 2 addresses the specificities of SWFs as a somewhat atypical international financial markets phenomenon. The various types of SWFs, their different objectives and management styles are covered in Section 3. Section 4 explores the market size and growth prospects of SWFs, while Section 5 examines the ramifications of their activities, providing some insights into whether the fears aroused by their operations are founded. Section 6 attempts to provide answers to some of the more controversial policy questions raised by the activities of SWFs, while Section 7 sums up the conclusions of this chapter.

1.   DEFINITION AND CONCEPTUAL UNDERPINNINGS

1.1   Definition

Despite the lack of a universally accepted definition of 'sovereign wealth funds', these can be defined, in functional terms, as pools of capital owned and run by the governments of sovereign nations, with a view to managing national savings, budget surpluses or excess foreign exchange reserves, investing them globally into corporate stocks, bonds and other financial instruments.[1] Thus viewed, SWFs can be defined as sovereign government investment vehicles that invest in and hold foreign assets for long-term purposes. The rationale, objectives and investment behavior of SWFs are very similar to those of other funds, including trusts (mutual funds), hedge funds or private-equity funds. However, as the assets of SWFs belong to sovereign nations, the funds that manage them are commonly known as 'sovereign wealth funds' (a term that was not in vogue until 2005). Although little is known of the precise nature and degree of government intervention in the operations of individual SWFs, a majority of them are thought to be semi-autonomous, self-directed entities, dedicated to professional portfolio management.

---

[1]   While the foreign currency assets in which SWFs invest are held separately from the official reserves of the respective monetary authorities, whether or not they are part of the reserve assets of the respective country is ambiguous.

Enhancing risk-adjusted returns on their investment is their overarching objective.

Several of the export-oriented Asian emerging-market economies (EMEs)[2] and, in particular, China, have been steadily building-up trade surpluses in recent years. At the same time, the progressive rise in oil and gas prices has contributed to a significant increase in the revenues of the members of the Gulf Cooperation Council (GCC)[3] and of the Russian Federation, turning them into globally significant net investors. Of the EMEs' sub-group of economies, China has been the largest global investor, with almost twice the amount of foreign investment as the next largest EME, the Russian Federation, and three times as much as the Republic of Korea, the third largest investing EME (MGI, 2008). Economies that are Asia's financial hubs, namely, the Hong Kong SAR, Singapore and Taiwan (but, interestingly, not Japan) have been expanding their global investments in the course of the last decade (MGI, 2008).

The source of the accumulated pool of assets managed by an SWF can be foreign currency deposits earned through recurrent balance of payments (bop) surpluses or revenue earned from the exports of non-renewable natural resources, such as oil and gas, or income from the export of commodities (or a combination thereof). At the end of 2009, SWFs funded by commodity exports totalled US$2.5 trillion, while non-commodity SWFs, funded by a transfer of assets from official foreign exchange reserves, totalled US$1.3 trillion (IFS, 2010). Non-commodity funds accounted for an increasing share of global SWF assets (IFS, 2010). The rise in gross official international reserves, in the run-up to the financial crisis, led to an unprecedented concentration of official sector liquid foreign exchange resources, with the fiscal surpluses of certain governments representing another major source of excess liquidity in the public sector. Finally, it is worth noting that some SWFs are domestic pension funds, funded in domestic currencies, which diversify their portfolio by making global investments. Pension and non-pension fund-type SWFs nevertheless share many characteristics in common, making them practically indistinguishable from one another.

---

[2] Emerging-market economy is a term coined by Antoine W. van Agtmael of the International Finance Corporation in 1981. It is a sub-set of developing economies. For an explanation of what emerging-market economies (EMEs) are and how are they defined, see Das (2004), Chapters 1 and 2.

[3] The GCC was established in 1981. Its members are Bahrain, Kuwait, Oman, Qatar, Saudi Arabia and the United Arab Emirates (UAE).

1.2   Genesis of SWFs

SWFs were an outgrowth of the expanding foreign exchange reserves of the official sector. An economy's foreign exchange reserves, typically held in US\$, € or ¥, are the official sector external surpluses, which have traditionally been managed by the respective central banks or monetary authorities, with the explicit short-term objective of preserving the stability of the domestic currency and of protecting banks during crisis periods, as well as for liquidity management purposes. Several EMEs suffered from currency and banking crises during the 1990s and/or in the early 2000s. Since foreign exchange reserves are intended for use during such exchange rate or financial emergencies, they were conventionally invested in assets that could be liquidated quickly and easily. In managing reserves, the preference of the central banks had been for liquidity to cover bop needs. The rate of return on their investments was not an important consideration. Therefore, low-return investments in United States (US) Treasury bonds or other equivalent instruments were regarded as acceptable.

Unlike those bop-specific investments by central banks or monetary authorities, the foreign assets of SWFs are mostly placed in less liquid instruments, representing, for the most part, longer-term investments. When, in the early 2000s, the foreign exchange reserves of a number of EMEs began growing, beyond what was regarded as necessary to serve the shorter-term bop objectives highlighted above, the mind-set of investing governments began to change. The new line of thinking was that, as this money represented *surplus public wealth*, possibilities for higher-returns on it had to be explored. The managing governments concluded that, at least part of the growing foreign exchange reserves should be placed in high-yielding, higher-risk (but less liquid) longer-term investments. With these considerations in mind, a number of sovereign governments launched SWFs, so as to maximize the risk-adjusted long-term returns on their accumulated surplus financial resources. Consequently, large amounts of state-controlled liquidity began flowing into private assets globally. The continuous growth in sovereign assets over the last decade, at least until the onset of the financial crisis, resulted in the official sector becoming an active and prominent investor group.

1.3   Antecedents to and Objectives of Contemporary SWFs

Despite the fact that professional and academic interest in them had, until recently, remained subdued, SWFs are not a new institutional investor class. Indeed, SWFs have operated in the international capital markets since the early 1950s. Although the term SWF is of recent vintage, the first fund-making international investments on behalf of a sovereign government began operations in 1953, when the Kuwait Investment Authority (KIA) was launched, to invest some of Kuwait's substantial oil revenues. The second such venture was the Kiribati Revenue Equalization Reserve Fund, which was created by the British administration of the Gilbert Islands in 1956.[4] Temasek Holdings of Singapore and the Alaska Permanent Fund, both of which began operating in 1974, as well as the Mubadala Development Company of Abu Dhabi and the Alberta Heritage Fund of Canada, which began operations in 1976, are amongst the oldest state investment funds.

Depending on their objectives, SWFs can take the form of *non-renewable resource funds, stabilization funds* or government-owned *pension funds* and *investment companies*. The age-old adage that 'necessity is the mother of invention' applies aptly to the birth of SWFs. Where countries have excess liquidity, whatever its source, it is neither desirable nor always possible to channel it to consumption by increasing the level of imports. Exploring possibilities for its inter-temporal utilization may, indeed, be the most prudent way to utilize it. This applies, a fortiori, if the sources of excess liquidity are exports of natural, non-renewable resources, such as mineral wealth, precious stones, other commodities or strategic raw materials (such as oil) which are bound to, sooner or later, stop being available for exploitation. In these conditions, SWFs can act as provident saving instruments for the benefit of future generations. Prudently investing present financial assets to generate future sources of revenue is, therefore, one of the main objectives of those financial entities. Moreover, even where the prospect of an eventual discontinuation in the supply of mineral wealth or other exhaustible commodities is distant, economies can face price and supply volatility, leading to unsteady revenue streams. SWFs can help eliminate that volatility by stabilizing revenue streams. A less frequently encountered motive for the creation of SWFs has been preparing domestic financial markets for the creation of an active international financial center. The governments of the Republic of Korea and Singapore had that consideration in mind when they created the Korean Investment Corporation and the Singapore Government Investment Company (GIC), respectively. Presently, the SWF industry comprises over 40 such institutions in operation, run largely by Asian and Middle Eastern governments. To the extent that SWFs are an instrument for the accumulation and investment of savings that cannot (or should not) be invested domestically

---

[4] A levy on the export of phosphates from Kiribati resulted in rich revenues, creating an investment pool of over half a billion US $.

or spent on imports in the short-term, they can become lucrative sources of global investible resources. In a globalizing world economy, the owner governments may want to channel such surplus capital to mature industrial economies (MIEs), where profitable investment opportunities in real or financial terms are available in abundance. Some of the MIEs, such as the US, need capital to meet their current account deficits. These capital resources may, alternatively, also be channeled to *other* EMEs where investment opportunities may present themselves, or be kept at home to meet the savings gap.

1.4 Maturing of SWFs

In spite of the large volume of their operations, SWFs had for a long time remained low-key and obscure financial market players. Only recently did SWFs become the focus of argumentative debate, even sour controversy, in the popular and financial media when they attempted to make large and conspicuous acquisitions in the industrialized economies. As of the last quarter of 2007, *The Financial Times* and *The Wall Street Journal* began covering SWFs extensively, with a new class of SWF experts emerging. Esteemed institutions like the *Deutsche Bank*, *Morgan Stanley* and *Standard Chartered* began publishing well-researched pieces on SWFs. The growing role of SWFs also began attracting a great deal of attention from central bankers and finance ministers in the industrialized economies. In the Group-of-Seven (G-7) meeting held in October 2007 the leaders of industrialized economies expressed concern about the investments made by SWFs drawing attention, in particular, to the lack of transparency in their operations.[5] The US Senate Banking Committee held lengthy and repeated hearings on SWFs in October and November 2007.[6] In mid-November 2007, the International Monetary Fund (IMF) convened its first annual roundtable on sovereign assets. The US Treasury discussed SWF operations for the first time in its *Semi-Annual Report on International Economic and Exchange Rate Policies*, published in June 2007.

The global financial crisis, which began with the US sub-prime mort-

---

[5] The reference is to the G-7 meeting hosted by the then US Treasury Secretary Henry Paulson and Federal Reserve Chairman Ben S. Bernanke in Washington DC, on 22 October 2007.

[6] Several noted scholars including Kenneth Rogoff, Patrick Mulloy and Edwin Truman participated in these hearings. Christopher Cox, the Chairman of Securities and Exchange Commission, expressed his concern regarding the operations of the SWFs in a speech at the Harvard University on October 24, 2007.

gage crisis of 2007 and resulted in catastrophic losses for the banking industry, with an additional US$34 billion in troubled loans that disrupted the US$57 trillion US financial system (Dodd, 2007), represented a window of opportunity for SWFs, which played a salvaging role in the midst of the crisis. The credit crunch brought SWFs into the centre of market and academic attention. Cash-rich and enterprising SWFs became active even *before* the monetary authorities of the industrialized countries joined forces to ease the liquidity squeeze.[7] Amidst the crisis, some of the largest financial institutions, including the *Citigroup*, *Union Bank of Switzerland* (UBS), *Morgan Stanley* and *Merrill Lynch*, found themselves in need of fresh liquidity injections, with SWFs coming to their rescue. The Abu Dhabi Investment Authority (ADIA) provided an emergency capital injection of US$7.5 billion to the *Citigroup*, Singapore's GIC provided SFr 11 billion to UBS and Temasek Holdings of Singapore helped Merrill Lynch enhance its capital position by US$6.2 billion. By January 2008, SWFs from Kuwait, Korea and Singapore had invested US$21 billion in *Citigroup* and *Merrill Lynch*, helping them restore some of the serious losses they had taken as a result of the credit crisis (*The Economist*, 2008).[8] High-profile participation in these leading investment activities helped SWFs emerge as investors of global significance, with a role to play in contributing to the stability of the global financial system.[9]

Since the start of the global financial crisis, many SWFs took losses on the investments they had made prior to its onset, which forced them to retreat to their domestic markets in late 2008. According to early 2009 estimates, SWFs shrunk in size by approximately 30 per cent, putting their aggregate assets under management (AuM) at below US$3 billion (Setser and Ziemba, 2009). The financial crisis adversely affected their

---

[7]   This synchronized central bank policy action was taken on 12 December 2008. The Federal Reserve Board, the European Central Bank, the Bank of Canada and the Swiss National Bank were its initiators, while the central banks of Japan and Sweden stood by to step in and act as necessary.

[8]   At the same time it is worth remembering that the collapse of Lehman Brothers in September 2008 was sealed by the refusal of the state-run Korea Development Bank, on 9 September 2009, to fund a bail-out for the troubled US mortgage lender.

[9]   This wave of sizeable investments by SWFs was partly driven by the boom in petroleum prices. Towards the end of September 2007, average petroleum spot price (APSP) of benchmark West Texas Intermediate (WTI) shot up to US$83.90 per barrel and in early November it topped US$99. This was 65% increase in petroleum prices in one year. The global consumption of oil has been growing at an average annual rate of 1.9%; 2007 was the sixth consecutive year of oil price increases.

main two sources of funding namely, oil and export revenues. The price of oil decreased sharply to below US$70 per barrel, from the record levels it had reached in mid-2008, while the export revenues of the Asian EMEs declined, as a result of a financial crisis-motivated drop in demand from the MIEs. It is only in early 2010 that SWFs once again began acquiring international assets, but only very slowly.

2.   AN IRONY OF THE GLOBAL FINANCIAL SYSTEM?

Both SWFs and their operations are unprecedented, even atypical, in several respects. *First*, SWFs presently manage substantial assets, which are much larger compared, for instance, to those of hedge funds (IFC, 2010). *Second*, a clear majority of SWFs are owned by the governments of EMEs. *Third*, SWFs have changed the character and composition of investments made by sovereign states, which conventionally placed their excess foreign exchange reserves in low-risk, high-grade assets, such as US Treasury Bonds. By investing through SWFs, states have moved towards riskier assets, including equities and corporate bonds, and diversified their portfolios, with a view to securing higher risk-adjusted returns. *Fourth*, the foreign sovereign government-ownership of SWFs has become a source of concern for the host economies, exposing SWFs to the accusation that their investments are motivated by strategic and political rather than purely economic or profit-maximization considerations. *Fifth*, as more SWFs buy into prestigious firms and business corporations in the MIEs, an uncomfortable scenario of share croppers is conjured up, where foreign-owned firms employ the highly-skilled workforce of the MIEs with the sole objective of returning high, 'take-away' profits.

Theoretical and empirical research has focused on the benefits that can be derived from international capital inflows as well as on the risks that those entail (see, for instance, Edwards, 2001, Klein and Olivei, 1999 and Rodrik, 1998). In an appropriate policy environment, external capital inflows can contribute to the smoothing of consumption or to capital accumulation and to growth and economic diversification. They can also be instrumental in institutional readjustments that are the necessary underpinning for improvements in terms of economic performance (Kose et al., 2006). According to standard, neoclassical economic theory, it is normal for the MIEs to invest in developing or emerging market economies. One would, therefore, expect capital flows to move from the rich, high capital/labour ratio economies to the poorer, lower capital/labor ratio economies. SWFs reverse that relationship: it appears ironic that the EMEs, which should have been attracting global capital, are instead investing in the MIEs, with the latter tapping, effectively, the EMEs' surplus savings, in what is known as the 'Lucas paradox' (Lucas, 1990). Prima facie this is capitalism at work: productive capital flows from where it is available to where it is needed. However, this evidently is '. . . a paradigmatic change from a world in which private investors from wealthy industrialized countries used to invest around the globe to one in which emerging-market governments become major share-holders in Western companies' (DBR, 2007).

At the end of 2009, Asia and the Middle East each accounted for 40 per cent of SWF assets. European SWFs held a large share of the remaining 20 per cent. SWFs from China (US$928 billion) and the UAE (US$677 billion) were the largest global investors, followed by Norway (US$445 billion) and Saudi Arabia (US$436 billion) (IFS, 2010). In terms of individual economies, China was the largest exporter of net capital, surpassing Germany, Japan, the Russian Federation and Saudi Arabia. On the other side of the equation, the US has become, since 2001, the largest net consumer of external capital, absorbing around 70 per cent of the global savings to meet its domestic current account deficits. No parallels are available in the modern economic history of a situation where the largest global economy turns into a huge capital importer for such a sustained a period of time.

The precise amount of the aggregate AuM of SWFs is not known because a majority of them keep their operations confidential. It is only very imprecisely that the SWFs' AuM can be estimated, based on publicly available market statistics. Several informed estimates have been attempted in recent years. Pre-crisis, Morgan Stanley put the value of the global corporate AuM of SWFs at US$2.5 trillion (Jen, 2007a). Another source put that figure at anything between US$2 trillion and US$3 trillion (Johnson, 2007). The US Department of Treasury estimated the range of the SWFs' aggregate assets between US$1.5 trillion and US$2.5 trillion (The US Department of Treasury, 2007). The estimated range of the IMF stood at between US$1.9 trillion and US$2.9 trillion (IMF, 2007a). For its part, Deutsche Bank Research put the number a tad higher, at US$3 trillion (DBR, 2007). These are very substantial amounts of capital for which SWFs from the EMEs could find investment opportunities in their own economies or, at least, in their respective regions. Despite the fact that, due to the global financial crisis, the SWF's AuM fell by 3 per cent in 2009, when, according to some estimates, it was thought to stand at around US$3.8 trillion, recent projections made by International Financial Services, London, expected SWF assets to increase to US$5.5 trillion in 2012 (IFS, 2010). According to another estimate, assuming a moderate return on investment of 5 per cent p.a., and that around half of the official sector external surpluses would be transferred to SWFs, their AuM could exceed US$5 trillion by 2014 (Beck and Fidora, 2009). It follows that, while their growth will be slower than expected, there is no indication that SWFs will stop representing an important investor group. *How* they will invest their large pools of capital in the future will be a matter of crucial concern in business, financial and political circles.

3.   CATEGORIZATION AND MANAGEMENT

As we have suggested earlier in this chapter, SWFs can be categorized according to their *sources of wealth* and their *policy objectives*.

Starting with the former, the source of wealth of a number of SWFs has been exports (or taxes on exports) of non-renewable resources or commodities (in the recent past, commodity prices, including oil, have risen sharply). Many of the SWFs originally established for the purpose of fiscal stabilization have changed their principal *raison d'etre* and been transformed into savings funds. The latter have a different portfolio composition, investing in a broader range of longer-term assets than those of stabilization funds. Oil-producing economies have established funds for both of the above objectives. There are 31 oil-producing economies, of which 21 have established one sort of SWF or other; 16 of these were created after 1995. Two of the oil-producing economies (Chad and Ecuador) folded their funds in 2005–2006. In all, ten of these funds have stabilization as their essential objective, while the others are committed to the twin-objectives of saving and stabilization (IMF, 2007b). Although the newer oil revenue-based funds have stabilization as their central policy focus, they began to emphasize their long-term saving objective after oil prices began stabilizing. Their asset management techniques changed accordingly. Oil-producing economies, such as Azerbaijan, that have recently increased their oil production, have also established funds to improve the management of additional oil revenue. As the revenues of commodity exports frequently accrue directly to governments, foreign currency earnings are not converted into domestic currency. In such cases, foreign currency does not enter the domestic economy and, therefore, does not need to be sterilized through the issuance of domestic debt by central banks. Second, non-commodity producing countries have earned foreign exchange through persistent current account surpluses and set up SWFs. Many of the Asian EMEs, particularly China, built up resources for their SWFs in this manner. These EMEs have established themselves as successful exporters of manufactured and other high-value-added products in the global economy. Economies such as Korea and Taiwan are major exporters of information technology products. In many cases, their current account surpluses went hand in hand with capital account surpluses. This group of Asian EMEs is marching to a different beat from the MIEs, giving a clear impression of decoupling from them, as they are long on capital when the MIEs are short of capital. The resulting expansion of foreign exchange reserves in this country group led to the decision to transfer excess foreign exchange reserves into 'stand-alone funds' (US Department of Treasury, 2007). Third, fiscal surpluses or public savings generated through privatization can also provide a source of financial wealth channelled into SWFs. SWFs created on the basis of that type of financial resources are comparable to SWFs created on the back of non-renewable resources. Finally, there are examples of SWFs established on the back of large pension reserve funds, which are, however, entirely based on domestic financial resources.

The second possible distinction in the context of SWFs is on the basis of their *policy objectives*. First in this categorization are 'stabilization funds', which are set up by countries exporting commodities and non-renewable natural resources. The basic objective of these funds is to insulate, or at least to stabilize, the government budget and the national economy from price volatility. Their *modus operandi* is to simply build up assets when the revenue inflows are strong, in anticipation for leaner periods. These funds smooth the net flow of revenue into the budget, while depositing a predetermined part of it into the stabilization fund. Second, as alluded to earlier in this chapter, economies exporting non-renewable resources can launch savings funds with the objective of storing wealth for the future generations when those natural resources will have been exhausted. Financial saving for this purpose has been termed 'intergenerational equity' (IMF, 2007b). These savings funds convert non-renewable resources into a portfolio of diversified financial assets. A third objective for creating an SWF is for the purpose of economic development. To that end, SWFs will accumulate financial wealth to meet the priority socio-economic objectives of the domestic economy. Infrastructure development, which is a capital-intensive process, takes high priority in this set of objectives. Pension reserve funds are the last type of SWF. Their principal objective is to achieve high risk-adjusted returns by astutely investing in the global marketplace. These two types of SWFs (i.e. those created with the objective of economic development in mind and pension reserve funds) can be regarded as a 'subset of SWFs' that is explicitly or implicitly linked to long-term fiscal commitments (IMF, 2007a). Without prejudice to the above, SWFs often have multiple objectives, with many of them moving on an ever-changing spectrum of objectives, adjusting to newly emerging situations as global economic circumstances and financial conditions change.

An SWF's objective has a strong bearing (and, ultimately, determines) its asset allocation strategy. For the most part, the investment horizon of SWFs is long-term, which is a blessing for the recipients of their funds (receiving large amounts of long-term capital from discreet investing institutions that do not demand major management alterations can indeed be a providential development). Each SWF has its own asset allocation and risk management strategy. The challenge for SWFs is to strike a balance between generating high returns on investments, and achieving an appropriate level of liquidity, fund management efficiency and the socio-economic objectives they have been assigned by their sovereign owners.

As pointed out earlier in this section, one can assume that, in terms of asset allocation, stabilization funds usually adopt a relatively shorter-term approach than the savings-oriented SWFs, which obviously prefer investing in long to very long-term assets. Although there are statutes governing them, these give them a high degree of autonomy in choosing from a large range of global assets. An additional element of freedom that SWFs enjoy is that, unlike private pension and investment funds, they do not have to work under investment rules binding them to asset classes or norms regarding currency exposure. Thus, in deciding among competing investment options, SWFs are more similar to hedge funds than they are to other regulated segments of the fund industry.

4.   MARKET SIZE AND GROWTH DYNAMICS

SWFs have proliferated after 2000 and so has the volume of their global investments, at least up until the onset of the financial crisis.

The banking and financial sector has been one of their favored areas of investment. By January 2008, they had invested close to US\$69 billion on recapitalizing some of the largest financial institutions in the MIEs. As alluded to earlier in this chapter, the majority of SWFs publicize few of their operational details, as a result of which the markets only have scant knowledge of their activities. Going by what is available, Deutsche Bank Research (DBR, 2007) has compiled some basic statistical data on SWFs. According to that compilation, the ADIA fund of Abu Dhabi was the largest SWF, with an estimated US\$875 billion of AuM, while Singapore's GIC was the second largest, with US\$330 billion worth of AuM. Norway's GPFG came next with US\$322 billion of AuM. The fourth in this reckoning was Saudi Arabia's SWF with US\$300 billion of AuM. KIA, the first SWF to be launched, came fifth with US\$250 billion in AuM and

China's more recently established China Investment Corporation (CIC) was the sixth largest with US$200 billion in AuM. Hong Kong Monetary Authority Investment Portfolio managed assets worth US$140 billion and was the seventh largest, followed by the Stabilization Fund of the Russian Federation with US$127 billion in AuM. The ninth position was held by Temasek Holdings of Singapore with US$108 billion in AuM while the tenth by the Central Hujin Investment Corporation of China, with US$100 billion in AuM.

Present day estimates of the AuM of SWFs have been provided in Section 2. Although their global operations are larger than those of hedge funds (with an estimated AuM of US$1.8 trillion in March 2010, according to *Hedge Fund Intelligence* estimates), SWFs account for less than one-eighth of the global investment fund industry, which, at the time of writing, had an estimated US$21 trillion worth of AuM. Another revealing comparison can be made with the assets held by the global banking sector (US$63.5 trillion). In 2007, SWFs managed only 5 per cent of the total assets held by the global banking sector (DBR, 2007).[10] Thus, at present, SWFs are much smaller in size when compared to other large institutional investors, although their importance and weight in the global financial market are expected to grow. Due to the financial crisis, the projections made in 2007 that SWFs would continue accumulating global assets at the rate of US$800 billion to US$900 billion annually (IMF 2007a) have not been confirmed; the same is true of the estimates according to which, given that rate of expansion, the aggregate AuM of SWFs could reach US$12 trillion by 2012 (DBR, 2007).

The expansion of the aggregate AuM of SWFs will be a function of the competitiveness and of the official reserves situation in the EMEs of Asia, particularly China, the Hong Kong SAR, Korea, Singapore and Taiwan, whose weight in the total stock of global official foreign currency reserves has markedly increased in the recent past. As we have suggested in Section 2 of this chapter, the two main assumptions underlying all future projections of the SWF sector's growth are that a large segment of incremental bop surpluses will be channeled to SWFs and that the return on their investments will be higher than that on the sovereign bond holdings of central banks. While the projections made by Morgan Stanley in 2007 that SWFs would grow rapidly in the medium term have not been confirmed, amidst the global financial crisis, the sector's AuM of US$3.8 trillion at the end of 2009 was quite substantial, even if not yet rivaling, as it had been expected, the size of the official foreign exchange reserves (Jen, 2007a).

---

[10]   See DBR (2007), Table 4.

5.   RAMIFICATIONS OF THE OPERATIONS OF SWFS

As with any group of unleveraged, cash-rich and passive investors, with a preference for large-volume long-term investments, one would expect SWFs to have been treated as a wholesome development for capital markets. The accumulation and channeling of capital to productive pursuits are, after all, constructive and welfare-enhancing activities that the global economy can only benefit from: as purveyors of capital, SWFs have, in principle, a positive role to play in enhancing market liquidity, stemming price volatility and promoting the better allocation of financial resources.[11] However, instead of being greeted, especially by business corporations and financial institutions seeking long-term capital, SWFs were treated with mistrust, in political and business circles alike, at least until the start of the financial crisis. There are several reasons behind the generalized mistrust vis-à-vis SWFs, some of which are highlighted below.

In search of higher returns, many SWFs have in recent years taken significant stakes in important business corporations and banks, provoking, in the process, the ire of political leaders and rankling public opinion in the host economies.[12] Some of the observers of that trend began questioning whether this could lead to the cash-rich governments of EMEs investing in sensitive sectors in the MIEs, whether politically (such as the mass media) or economically (such as energy), or in large exporting corporations. The key trigger for concern was the taking by SWFs of stakes in high-profile US and European corporations.[13] For instance, in 2004, China's Lenovo Group took over IBM's personal computer business for US$1.7 billion,

---

[11]   According to estimates made by Jen (2007b), capital flows from SWFs should have a far-reaching impact, by raising the 'safe' bond yields by 30 to 40 basis points over the next ten years. They would also drive down the average return on equities by 50 to 70 basis points and reduce the equity premium by 80 to 110 basis points.

[12]   Some of the more striking recent examples include: the investment, in 2007, by China Investment Corporation (CIC) of US$3 billion in initial public offering (IPO) of Blackstone, a large private equity group, buying 9.9% stake in it. Qatar Investment Authority (QIA) that owns 25% of J. Sainsbury, a large British supermarket chain, unsuccessfully tried to gain total control. Vneshtorgbank, a Russian state-owned bank took 6% stake in the EADS, the maker of Airbus. Dubai International Capital (DIC), one of the smallest SWFs, bought a stake in EADS as well as making a large acquisition of HSBC stocks. SWFs from China and Singapore succeeded in acquiring a 5.2% stake in Barclays Bank. Gazprom, the Russian gas monopoly, tried to buy the gas pipelines and storage facilities in the EU, which was trenchantly opposed.

[13]   For some examples, see Section 3 of this chapter.

creating a large splash in the world of business. What the macroeconomic and strategic implications of the growth in the SWFs' investments in global corporate assets could be, in the medium- and long-term, are questions that have occupied the minds of the professional and policy-making communities. For Truman (2007) the very fact that the EMEs have accumulated 'a vast amount of international assets' raised 'profound questions about the structure and stability of international financial systems in the first decade of the 21st century'.[14]

Another reason underlying the pre-crisis concerns expressed vis-à-vis SWFs was related to the *motivation* underlying their investments. In a capitalist system, the common objective of shareholders is to see their wealth increase. However, when the shareholders are sovereign governments, it is far from obvious that the engine behind their activities will be the maximization in the value of their shares or, instead, the pursuit of a myriad of other non-economic objectives. Indeed, some SWF observers and critics have not entirely ruled out the possibility that SWFs could follow nationalistic, political and non-profit-maximizing objectives, which are apt to create uneasiness – to put it euphemistically – about their expanding operations. There is, arguably, considerable scope for corporate governance and corporate strategies being unconventionally influenced by SWFs, not least because SWFs are being increasingly viewed as turning from creditors into owners.

A closely related and understandable source of anxiety surrounding SWFs is linked to their *state-ownership*. It is commonly observed that governments in the developing economies, are more actively involved in international investment decisions than those in the MIEs. Although these controls have been loosening in the recent years, as domestic financial sector liberalization in the Asian and Middle-Eastern economies continues, they still exist. This element of state-ownership can intensify the apprehension, in the MIEs, of foreign government intervention in decisions of relevance to resource allocation (*The Economist,* 2008). Besides, large private sector corporate assets in the hands of foreign governments 'are at sharp variance with today's general conception of a market-based global economy and financial system' in which commercial decisions are made by individual entrepreneurs based on profit maximizing motives (Truman, 2007).

Another reason behind the reservations expressed vis-à-vis the activities

---

[14]   With respect, the argument seems a tad unconvincing, considering the high degree of financial globalization in the 21st century economy, where activities such as those pursued by SWFs should be taken in stride, rather than being questioned.

of SWFs is to do with their *opacity*. As the majority of SWFs make little information available about their operations and investment strategy, there is the widespread perception in 'countries with liquid and efficient capital markets that SWFs are intransparent if not incalculable participants in global financial markets' (DBR, 2007). In terms of secretiveness, SWFs rank even below the most secretive hedge funds, revealing little regarding their basic philosophy, investment strategy, portfolio composition, operations and return on investments. This opacity has created misgivings regarding their operations and mistrust in their motives. Angst regarding their ability to destabilize markets has been candidly expressed by electronic and print media, politicians and opinion leaders.

Notwithstanding their state-ownership and the government control element inherent in their activities – which can, in and of themselves, explain why the public debate surrounding them has taken on such negative overtones, raising the spectre of protectionism – SWFs do not differ fundamentally, in terms of their investment operations, management and *modus operandi*, from other public or private sector investment funds. Like them, SWFs look for the highest risk-adjusted returns. Similarly, their investment activities and mode of operation do not seem strikingly different from those of large pension funds, whether in the private or in the public sector. That SWFs have a good deal of autonomy in their operations has been noted earlier in this chapter, but the same is also true of other 'unconventional' investors, including hedge funds and private equity funds. Moreover, so far, SWFs have not shown any signs of indulging into 'mischievous behavior' as investors. Indeed, while recommending a policy of caution vis-à-vis SWFs, some commentators have expressed the view that, so far, SWFs have acted as 'model investors' and that those advocating their tougher oversight would first need to furnish proof of the risks inherent in their 'political dimension' before additional rules are devised to constrain their activities (Epstein and Rose, 2009). Moreover, empirical evidence suggests that, like private equity funds, SWFs largely play a passive role as shareholders, avoiding to intervene in the management of their target companies (despite the fact that the stakes that they take are, sometimes, quite substantial) and that it is only very infrequently that SWFs become actively involved in corporate governance. With the prospect of SWFs taking ownership stakes in important commercial enterprises against the will of their management and shareholders being remote, the spectre of unwelcome and objectionable intrusion by cash-rich SWFs into the business activities of flagship corporate entities, especially in the MIEs, is over-blown and, so far, unsupported by empirical evidence.

If the concerns caused by the state-ownership of SWFs were exaggerated or misplaced pre-crisis,[15] many of them would appear to have lost some, at least, of their relevance since the start of the global financial crisis. The financial crisis has seen a shift in the debate from the potentially adverse effects of their activities to their market stabilizing role. The shifting focus of the debate surrounding SWFs reflects the rapid switch of priorities of policy-makers from insulating their economies from SWFs to attracting much needed funds amidst tight liquidity conditions. As it has aptly been observed, '[T]he concerns about excessive investment of sovereign wealth funds in advanced economies that seemed widespread prior to the crisis, while not having disappeared, are now being voiced less frequently'(Beck and Fidora, 2009). Given that some of the concerns underlying that debate were unwarranted, the above is a positive development. It should, however, not deflect attention from the need for improvements in those areas where SWFs are lacking, with an emphasis on their transparency and accountability.

6. SQUARING THE POLICY CIRCLE: THE ROLE OF TRANSPARENCY

The scale and scope of the operations of SWFs has grown considerably in recent years, even if SWFs cannot, at present, move markets. Empirical experience so far suggests that their large and diversified portfolio investments entail few risks of destabilizing international financial markets. Those who regard investments by SWFs as a source of instability would thus need to reassess the validity of some of their concerns. As stated in the previous section, there is little evidence of unwarranted, undesirable or offensive conduct by SWFs. If anything, investment flows by SWFs should be welcomed by the host country governments. The long-term investment horizon of their investments and their lack of interest in speculative activities should make them a strong stabilizing force in the international financial market. Arbitrary restrictions and a rise of financial protectionism would, effectively, work as a barrier against financial globalization; besides, erecting barriers to foreign investment while, at the same time, demanding open access to the economies of EMEs would be patently hypocritical.

That said, the participation of SWFs in the international financial system can be decisively improved and the concerns to which their operations have given rise can be considerably alleviated by policy initiatives

---

[15] In this regard, see our discussion in Section 6.4.

at the SWF level, at the host economy level and at the level of international institutions, placing the emphasis on their transparency and accountability.

6.1   Host Economy-level Solutions

Arguably the thorniest policy issue regards investments by SWFs that may enable them to take on management stakes. A knee-jerk reaction of analysts and policy-makers in the host economies could be to limit the stakes that SWFs can have in specified economic sectors or industries, keeping it below a prescribed threshold, with both the target industries and the respective stake limits being determined by the regulatory authorities of the host country. However, that measure is not easy to implement, as it is difficult to identify the specific investors or funds that should be subjected to such restrictions. Besides, some host country corporations and pension funds may well be averse to such limitations on investments by SWFs.

One policy solution to this prickly issue could be to allow SWFs to only invest in non-voting shares in specified sectors of the domestic economy. Care should be taken in determining the industrial sectors to which such restrictions would apply. Trying to keep a supermarket chain from falling into the hands of a SWF would not seem rational, as a grocery business is not of so strategic an interest for the host economy that decisions made by a SWF could adversely affect the economic well-being of the local retail purchasing community.

6.2   Self-correcting Policy Measures for SWFs

One strategy that SWFs may want to consider in order to alleviate the concerns surrounding their operations is to voluntarily increase their levels of transparency and accountability. Improvements in terms of their transparency and accountability would no doubt result in reducing the risk of reflexive financial protectionism or, at least, in containing its expansion. Legitimate concerns regarding the motivation underlying their investments could be alleviated if SWFs were to become more transparent, as transparency is indispensable for the smooth operation of international capital markets. As a commentator has argued, transparency is necessary to advance *horizontal accountability* among the participants and stakeholders as well as *vertical accountability* along the policy-making process (Truman, 2007). The example of GPFG of Norway is frequently cited in financial circles for having exemplary levels of disclosure and for being a paragon of transparency. The Permanent Reserve Fund of Alaska (US), the Alberta Heritage Savings Trust Fund (Canada), Singapore's Temasek

Holdings and Malaysia's Khazanah Nasional BHD are also regarded as highly transparent by financial markets and government authorities (*The Economist*, 2008).

If SWFs were not to voluntarily adopt higher standards of transparency they could, indeed, be internationally coaxed to publish audited information about their balance sheets, annual and quarterly reports as well as to provide information on their investment rationale, basic philosophy and objectives, portfolio composition, investment strategy and return on investment. This could be achieved through best-practices recommendation groups, with the participation of both industry representatives and national authorities. SWFs that are averse to comply with calls for high standards of voluntary disclosure and transparency could be restricted to purchasing up to a specified level of non-voting shares in their target companies. In fact, given the scale and scope of the operations of SWFs, it would seem in order to consider making, in the future, most stringent norms of disclosures mandatory.

6.3 Establishing a Code of Conduct

International financial institutions, such as the IMF have initiated a third line of policy action in the matter of SWFs. It has been argued that the international investment operations of sovereign governments warrant 'collective effort to establish an internationally agreed standard to guide the management of their cross-border investments' (Truman, 2007). Therefore, recognizing the positive liquidity enhancing and financial resource allocation roles of SWFs, policy-makers at an international level have begun deliberations on how to forestall financial protectionism so that an open global financial system can be promoted and buttressed. What code of conduct SWFs may need to follow for those purposes has become a legitimate issue of debate in the international financial community.

The International Monetary and Financial Committee (IMFC) of the IMF, a committee of the Board of Governors of the IMF comprising representatives of 185 IMF member countries, charged the IMF with analyzing the relevant policy issues, both from the perspective of investors and from that of the recipients of SWF flows. The IMFC stressed the imperative need for a candid dialogue on identifying best practices so that the spectre of financial protectionism can be avoided. In the November 2007 roundtable of the IMF, attended by senior level delegates from central banks, ministries of finance and sovereign asset managers from 28 countries, it was decided that the IMF would take into consideration the viewpoints of the two sides and identify sound practices to be followed in the management of SWFs. Dominique Strauss-Kahn, the Managing Director of the IMF, emphasized the imperious need for SWFs to function 'in ways that are consistent with global financial stability' (IMF, 2007c). An agreed upon set of best practices could go a long way in maintaining an open global financial system and discourage the host countries from imposing unilateral restrictions on SWF operations.

The IMFC established a 26-member International Working Group on Sovereign Wealth Funds, which met on 30 April 2008 in Washington DC. The Working Group met thrice at Washington DC, Singapore and Santiago to draft a set of generally accepted principles and practices (GAPP), reflecting the investment objectives and practices of SWFs. At the end of the third meeting in October 2008 the members of the group agreed to the 'Santiago Principles'. In carrying out its work, the Working Group used the findings of an IMF-commissioned voluntary survey of SWFs on their current structure and practices, and drew on related international principles and practices of broad acceptance. The GAPP laid down a set of 24 principles to which the members agreed, covering a wide area of SWF operations and seeking to establish a framework of generally accepted principles and practices that properly reflect appropriate governance and accountability arrangements as well as the conduct of investment practices by SWFs on a prudent and sound basis.

A recent account of the implementation of the Santiago Principles points to the conclusion that their implementation has not been even across jurisdictions, and that a:

> small group of SWFs, predominantly from democratic countries, shows a high degree of commitment to the principles. A second group shows partial implementation, and a third group, mainly from the Gulf Arab region, has yet to reach satisfactory implementation levels. The Santiago Principles and the commitment of their sponsors—some of the biggest SWFs—are an important test for the viability of new forms of global governance. However, as it has aptly been observed, 'although the Principles comprise some elements of transparency, disclosure requirements are only limited', which is why 'a further enhancement of the Principles and the surrounding governance Framework will be mandatory in order to alleviate protectionist pressures in recipient countries once the financial crisis is overcome' (Beck and Fidora, 2009). Moreover, their sluggish implementation risks devaluing the Principles, thereby increasing SWFs' political risk exposure (Behrendt, 2010).

6.4 Regulations for Guarding Against Foreign Stakes

SWFs are already subject to a variety of regulations, especially in the MIEs, the purpose of which is to keep those foreign investors out whose investments are not deemed to be welcome.

The US is, perhaps, the best equipped to prohibit or to suspending any unwelcome foreign investment. Commentators have identified two main types of regulatory and/or legal powers that can be exercised to block investments by SWFs, namely, (i) notification or reporting requirements for future transactions involving foreign investors and (ii) specific, often sector-based, restrictions limiting a foreign investor's ownership or control of certain assets (Walker and Chorazak, 2008). For instance, the Exon-Florio Amendment, which is part of the Defense Production Act, has been in place since 1950.[16] In addition, the US Committee on Foreign Investment (CFI) has been active in identifying and blocking any foreign takeovers that it regards as injurious to the US commercial or strategic interests (the CFI was able to stop UNOOC in its tracks).[17] Japan, the second largest economy according to 2009 IMF estimates, also has stringent limits on inward foreign investment in place as well as the power to suspend investments by foreign controlled enterprises in specific industrial sectors. Canada also has legislation restricting foreign ownership to minority shares in a long list of industries. Without discouraging investments by SWFs, it has recently demanded more transparency in their operations and declared that scrutiny of takeovers by them will be higher. By contrast, Australia and New Zealand have been far more welcoming to SWFs. As a result, Asian SWFs and those from oil-exporting economies have large investments in both of these economies.

The situation is not dissimilar in the European Union (EU), whose regulatory environment comprises both hard law and soft law instruments applicable to SWFs, starting from the *acquis* and its exceptions and exemptions to free movement of capital, as in the case of 'public security' and 'legitimate national interests' (Mezzacapo, 2009) through to national country restrictions, such as Germany's Foreign Trade and Payments Act, as amended in 2006, to restrict investment transactions involving foreign persons[18] or the United Kingdom (UK), where the corresponding

---

[16] The Exon-Florio Amendment is a law that was enacted by the US Congress in 1988 to review foreign investment within the US. The amendment was passed into law under the Omnibus Trade and Competitiveness Act of 1988 and amended Section 721 of the Defense Production Act of 1950. All foreign investments that might have an impact on national security may be reviewed and if deemed to pose a threat to national security, the US President may block them.

[17] CFI is an inter-agency committee authorized to review transactions that could result in control of a US business by a foreign person ('covered transactions'), in order to determine the effect of such transactions on the national security of the United States.

[18] The focus of German rules appears to be on the protection of its defense-related industries, in connection with which Germany wants to be extra

protective regime makes use of 'golden shares'[19] and is more potent and versatile compared to its German law counterpart. The UK also has a 29.5 per cent cap on foreign shareholdings in what it regards as strategic industries. The on-going deliberations in the European Commission seem to favor the idea of 'golden shares', as these can prevent outright takeovers of strategic holdings as well as of politically and economically sensitive commercial assets. Among the members of the EU there is, so far, disagreement on whether there should be a collective policy on restricting SWFs, or whether individual member economies should devise their own policies. While France and Germany strongly favored, pre-crisis, an EU-wide stand, to curb uncontrolled access to stakes in their business firms, enthusiasm in the UK was not so high. The same is true of Ireland, which has traditionally followed an open investment regime and may be wary of an EU-led restrictive regime on SWF investments. Although unequivocal in their demand for transparency, the French and German governments have shown a preference for a code of conduct instead of rigid regulations.

Are new, SWF-specific regulations necessary, whether at the national or at the supranational level? At least one commentator has responded negatively (Mezzacapo, 2009), invoking the adequacy of the combination of the regulatory framework and the soft law measures already in place, while others have taken a less unequivocal stance vis-à-vis the idea of regulation, despite being against SWF-specific regulation (Epstein and Rose, 2009).

7.   SUMMARY AND CONCLUSIONS

SWFs have gradually become established as major institutional investors and important participants in the global financial system. With a total AuM of around US$3.8 trillion at the end of 2009 and with the prospect of an increase in the international reserves of EMEs, their growth dynamics appear strong. Despite their liquidity enhancing and financial resource allocation instrumentality, and the decisive role they can play in underpinning, sustaining, and expanding financial globalization, SWFs have attracted controversy, mainly on account of their state-ownership and their lack of transparency, and the considerable anxiety that these

---

cautious in allowing SWFs from China and the Russian Federation to take stakes in them.

[19]   Golden shares are nominal shares that can outvote all other shares under certain specified circumstances.

have created in connection with their operations. It has been argued in this chapter that concerns about their activities are exaggerated and that protectionist restrictions from host economies on their activities could deprive international financial markets of a significant cash-rich market player at a critical time for the recovery of large corporate entities in the MIEs. It has also been argued that the fears generated by the participation of SWFs in the international financial system could be considerably alleviated through policy initiatives at various different levels.

BIBLIOGRAPHY

Athanassiou, Phoebus (2009), *Hedge Fund Regulation in the European Union – Current Trends and Future Prospects*, Alphen aan den Rijn: Kluwer Law International.

Beck, Roland and Michael Fidora (2009), 'Sovereign Wealth Funds – Before and Since the Crisis', *European Business Organisation Law Review* **10**(3), 353–67.

Behrendt, Sven (2010), 'Sovereign Wealth Funds and the Santiago Principles: Where Do They Stand?', Carnegie Middle East Center, Carnegie Papers No.22, May.

Das, Dilip K. (2004), *Financial Globalization and the Emerging Market Economies*, London and New York: Routledge.

Deutsche Bank Research (2007), 'Sovereign Wealth Funds: State Investment on the Rise', Frankfurt, Germany, September 10.

Dodd, Randall (2007), 'Subprime: Tentacles of a Crisis', *Finance and Development,* **44**(4), 15–19.

Edwards, Sebastian (2001), 'Capital Mobility and Economic Performance: Are Emerging Economic Different?', Cambridge, MA, National Bureau of Economic Research, NBER Working Paper No. 8076.

Epstein, Richard A. and Amanda Rose (2009), 'The Regulation of Sovereign Wealth Funds: The Virtues of Going Slow', *The University of Chicago Law Review*, **76**(1), 111–134.

International Financial Services (2010), 'Sovereign Wealth Funds 2010', Report, London.

The International Monetary Fund (2007a), 'Global Financial Stability Report', Washington DC, September.

The International Monetary Fund (2007b), 'The Role of Fiscal Institutions in Managing the Oil Revenue Boom', Washington DC, March 5.

The International Monetary Fund (2007c), 'IMF Convenes First Annual Roundtable of Sovereign Asset and Reserve Managers', Washington DC. Press Release No. 07/267, November 16.

Jen, Stephen L. (2007a), 'How Big Could Sovereign Wealth Funds Be?' *Global Economic Forum,* New York, Morgan Stanley Research, May 4.

Jen, Stephen L. (2007b), 'Sovereign Wealth Funds', New York, Morgan Stanley Research, October.

Johnson, Simon (2007), 'The Rise of Sovereign Wealth Funds', *Finance and Development,* **44**(3), 56–7.

Klein, Michael W. and Giovanni Olivei (1999), 'Capital Account Liberalization, Financial Depth and Economic Growth', Cambridge, MA, National Bureau of Economic Research, NBER Working Paper No. 7384.

Kose, Ayhan M., Eswar Prasad, Kenneth N. Rogoff and Shang-Jin Wei (2006), 'Financial Globalization: A Reappraisal', Washington DC, The International Monetary Fund, Working Paper No. 06/189, August.

Lane, Philip R. and Gian Maria Milesi-Ferretti (2006), 'The External Wealth of Nations Mark II', London, Center for Economic Policy Research, CERP Discussion Paper No. 5644.

Lucas, Robert E. (1990), 'Why Doesn't Capital Flow from Rich to Poor Countries?' *American Economic Review*, **80**(2), 92–6.

McKinsey Global Institute (2008), 'Mapping Global Capital Markets: Fourth Annual Report', San Francisco.

Mezzacapo, Simone (2009), 'The so-called "Sovereign Wealth Funds": regulatory issues, financial stability and prudential supervision', European Economy, Economic Papers, 378, April.

Rodrik, Dani (1998), 'Who Needs Capital Account Convertibility?' In *Princeton Essays in International Finance* No. 207, Princeton, NJ, Princeton University Press.

Setser, Brad W. and Rachel Ziemba (2009), 'GCC Sovereign Funds: Reversal of Fortune', Washington DC, Council on Foreign Relations Working Paper, January.

Summers, Lawrence (2007), 'Funds that Shake Capitalist Logic', *The Financial Times,* July 29.

Truman, Edwin M. (2007), 'Sovereign Wealth Funds: The Need for Greater Transparency', Washington DC, Peterson Institute for International Economics, Policy Brief No. 07-06, August.

The Economist (2008), 'The Invasion of the Sovereign-Wealth Funds', January 19.

The US Department of Treasury (2007), 'Semi-Annual Report on International and Exchange Rate Policies', Washington DC, June.

Walker, John L. and Mark J. Chorazak (2008), 'Sovereign Wealth Funds: The Evolving Legal and Regulatory Landscape', Washington Legal Foundation Critical Legal Issues Working Paper Series No. 159 August.

4. Private equity funds' performance, risk and selection

*Ludovic Phalippou**

INTRODUCTION

The purpose of this chapter is to assess the risks and returns of private equity funds, based on the different datasets used in the literature and to point out some issues in fund selection.

This chapter is divided into *two* main sections, namely private equity fund risk and return; and private equity fund selection. The first section provides an overview of the academic evidence on the risk and return of investing in private equity funds (buyout and venture capital). We find that the average private equity fund return is comparable or inferior to that of public equity, a finding that is in contrast to what industry associations report. We show that differences in methodology may explain, in part, this paradox. We also find that venture capital funds have market betas of 2.7, whilst buyout funds have lower market betas (1.3). Estimates of cost of capital are around 15 per cent (in excess of risk-free rate) for both buyout and venture capital funds. The second section is dedicated to fund selection. Years of large capital inflows from investors have poorer returns. New evidence on performance persistence is presented, showing that investors may have difficulties exploiting return persistence as this is too short-lived. Finally we report that the most important explanatory variable for the cross-section of buyout returns is the number of investments a private equity firm is holding at the same time.

In terms of vocabulary convention, the term '(portfolio) company' shall refer, throughout, to an entity receiving financing from a private equity fund, while the term 'private equity firm' shall refer to an organization running private equity funds (e.g. KKR).[1]

---

* Lecturer, University of Oxford, Said Business School.

[1] In this chapter, private equity comprises buyout investments (typically mature companies purchased with a substantial amount of debt) and venture capital investments (typically companies in early stage of their life, often with negative earnings and no possibility to borrow money).

1. PRIVATE EQUITY FUNDS PERFORMANCE AND RISK EXPOSURES

1.1 Past Academic Evidence on Performance with Thomson Data

The *Thomson* cash flow dataset was used until 2009 to generate the industry's performance report. *Thomson* would generate aggregate performance figures over various horizons, while industry associations, such as the National Venture Capital Association (NVCA), would issue press releases discussing these benchmarks. Financial newspapers would then widely propagate these numbers.

Thomson obtains data mostly from fund investors. In principle, these cash flows should represent the amount and timing of all the cash transfers to/from investors, including fees. Kaplan and Schoar (2005) and Phalippou and Gottschalg (2009) had access to the *Thomson* database. Kaplan and Schoar (2005) reported that buyout funds had returns below those of the S&P 500, while venture capital funds had returns slightly above those of the S&P 500. Phalippou and Gottschalg (2009) argued otherwise: they found that the net asset value (NAV) reported by mature and inactive funds were suspiciously high. They also noted that a number of mature funds (i.e. those that had reached their 10th year anniversary) had no cash flow activities for 2 years or more (most of them for 6 years or more) and reported the exact same NAV every quarter over the last 2 years or more (most of them over the last 6 years or more). In addition, those funds were those which were performing worse. In light of the above pattern, they argued that it was more reasonable to write-off those NAVs.[2] Phalippou and Gottschalg (2009) also showed that different aggregation choices and sampling choices lead to findings of lower returns.

In addition, Phalippou and Gottschalg (2009) assessed a lower bound to the sample selection bias. Investors providing data to *Thomson* may have fund selection capabilities, as a result of which the performance resulting from this dataset may be exaggerated. Using a wider sample of funds, Phalippou and Gottschalg (2009) found that the funds in the *Thomson* dataset were indeed slightly above average.[3] With all these considerations

---

[2] Note that Driessen et al. (2011) constructed a model that converts NAVs into market values using a statistical model. The model predicts that the market value of these NAVs is less than 10% of reported NAVs.

[3] They use a separate and widely available 'investment dataset' known as VentureXpert. Data include information about 29 739 companies (location, industry description, age), their investment characteristics (time of investment, stage, equity invested, exit date and mode), and funds that invested in them (fund size,

in mind, they found that returns for both buyout and venture capital funds were below those of the S&P 500 index.

1.2 Past Academic Evidence on Risk Exposure with Thomson Data

Knowledge of past performance would not be helpful without knowledge of the risks associated to it. But risk is even more difficult to quantify than returns. Yet, recent research *has* developed some tools and methodologies. In this section, we examine one of these tools and methodologies, developed by Driessen, Lin and Phalippou (2009) and applied to *Thomson* data.

The idea is that with the right asset pricing model and, therefore, with the right alphas and betas, the expected net present value of private equity cash flows (investments and dividends) should be zero. So we assume an asset pricing model and search for the alphas and betas that are most consistent with expected net present value of cash flows be zero. Later in this chapter, we cover other tools applied to other datasets but all these methods rely on this basic idea.

Driessen, Lin and Phalippou (2011) have used a 'Method of Moment'. A method of moment is somewhat natural in this context since one needs to look for the alphas and betas that make the expected value of a variable equal to zero. This, however, is a method that needs to be adapted to the particularities of the data: the highly idiosyncratic risk of private equity investments calls for forming portfolios. In addition, the identification of alphas and betas comes from observing funds alive at different moments in time, meaning that portfolios should not mix funds alive at different moments in time. Driessen et al. (2011), therefore, create portfolios of funds based on fund vintage years (i.e. starting years).

For venture capital funds, Driessen et al. (2011) find a market beta of 2.7 and a negative alpha. In addition, they simulate a typical fee structure, quantifying the effect of the non-linear fee structure on beta. They find that, after fees, beta is smaller. This is due to the fact that fees are convex in performance, thus smoothing the pay-offs. A smaller beta, in turn, makes alpha higher. It follows that, while fees are about 6 per cent per year, the difference between pre-fees alpha and post-fees alpha is only 4 per cent

---

investment focus, vintage year, headquarter). The unique feature of their dataset is that they have a link between the 'investment' dataset and the 'cash-flow' dataset. In the 'investment' dataset, they can observe the characteristics of funds that are not included in the 'cash-flow' dataset. They find that funds that are *not* part of Thomson cash flow dataset are indeed inferior in the sense that they have fewer investments exited successfully (i.e. via an IPO or an M&A).

Table 4.1   Buyout funds – Thomson summary cash flow data

Panel A: Buyout funds raised from 1980 to 1997						
Year	N	Cash in	Cash out	Stock out	NAV	Total
2003	453	1089	9917	350	70068	n.m.
2007	453	84	3830	103	41598	n.m.
Total		148694	202927	13944	41598	258469
Multiples			1.36	0.09	0.28	1.74
Panel B: Buyout funds raised from 1980 to 1993						
Year	N	Cash in	Cash out	Stock out	NAV	Total
2003	246	22	886	63	13452	n.m.
2007	246	0	176	47	10465	n.m.
Total		60447	103650	9458	10465	123573
Multiples			1.71	0.16	0.17	2.04

Note: This table shows statistics from Thomson for the cash flows of buyout funds for the years 2003 and 2007. Performance is as of December 2007. The total amount invested (Cash in), distributed in cash or in stock (cash out, stock out) and NAV at the end of the year are all in millions of US$. The total is taken over all the years (1980–2007). Multiple is the total value distributed divided by amount invested. All figures are net of fees. Ever green and mezzanine are excluded.

per annum. For buyout funds, Driessen et al. (2011) find a market beta of 1.3.

1.3   Recent Evidence on Performance with Thomson Data

The two academic studies mentioned in Section 1.1 have a sample that stops in 2001 and 2003, respectively. Given the strong growth in the private equity asset class and the fact that one needs to wait at least 10 years before a final performance number becomes available, there is an obvious need for an updated report.

Table 4.1 shows performance statistics for buyout funds from *Thomson* as of December 2007.[4] Panel A shows results for all funds raised between 1980 and 1997 (US and Europe). The first line shows the cash flows they generated in 2003 and the Net Asset Value (NAV) at the end of year 2003. The second line shows the cash flows they generated in 2007 and their

---

[4]   The analysis in this section was repeated with venture capital funds instead of buyout funds and results were similar.

NAV at the end of 2007. Next, we show the sum of the cash flows across time. The 453 funds in the sample invested a total of US$149 billion, distributed a total of US$217 billion (US$203 billion in cash and US$14 billion in stocks) and valued all on-going investments at US$42 billion at the end of 2007.

Here, we only have one performance measure available, namely a cash multiple (i.e. the total amount distributed divided by the total amount invested); this is displayed in the last line. The realized multiple is 1.45, which is likely to be less than public markets.[5] However, it is reported that there is still a substantial amount of on-going investments, the total value of which is measured by the funds' NAV as of December 2007. The final NAV is about 30 per cent of the amount invested, which appears quite high given that these funds are 10 years or older. If we were to add these NAVs to the total distributed, the (total) multiple would be 1.74. But, even then, an investment that returns only 10 per cent per annum for 6 years would have such a cash multiple.

These results are consistent with previous research despite the fact that the sample has doubled with the passage of time, with performance appearing to be close or below that of public equity. In addition, a substantial part of the performance of these mature funds is supposed to yet be realized since the latest reported NAV is relatively high.

Panel B shows funds covered by Phalippou and Gottschalg (2009), i.e. funds raised between 1980 and 1993. A polemical aspect of the Phalippou and Gottschalg (2009) study was the choice of writing-off the NAVs of mature and inactive funds. This choice was justified by the fact that, for most of these funds, the same NAV was repeated for many quarters/ years without any cash flow activity. Hence, the authors considered that what this entails is that the relevant fund is effectively liquidated and has no valuable investments. It is therefore interesting to see how much cash was actually paid out of these on-going investments after the end of their sample time period. Panel B shows the US$13 billion NAV reported as of the end of 2003, which was written-off by Phalippou and Gottschalg (2009). Four years later, this NAV amount has hardly changed and hardly any cash had been paid in the meantime. This would confirm the idea defended by Phalippou and Gottschalg (2009) that these investments are so-called 'living-deads'. They keep on repeating the same NAV but no cash flow is coming out.

Another possibility is that *Thomson* data are flawed. The worse kind

---

[5] For example, an investment returning only 4% per annum for 10 years would have a cash multiple higher than 1.45.

Table 4.2   US venture capital index returns

For the period ending	Qtr.	1 year	3 years	5 years	10 years	15 years	20 years
September 30, 2009	2.3	−12.4	1.3	4.9	8.4	36.6	23.1
June 30, 2009	0.2	−17.1	1.3	5.7	14.3	36.3	22.7
September 30, 2008	−2.9	−0.9	10.2	10.7	40.2	33.3	22.2
Other indices at September 30, 2009							
DJIA	15.8	−7.4	−3.3	1.8	1.6	8.7	9.2
NASDAQ Composite	15.7	1.5	−2.0	2.3	−2.5	7.0	7.8
S&P 500	15.6	−6.9	−5.4	1.0	−0.2	7.6	8.0

Note: US venture capital index returns for the periods ending 9/30/2009, 3/30/2009 and 9/30/2008.

Source: Cambridge Associates LLC.

would be that *Thomson* may not have cash-flow reports for some funds. For example, assume that for fund $i = 1,..,N$ *Thomson* stops receiving cash flow information at date T_i and thereafter they report for every quarter t that $NAV(t)$ equals $NAV(T_i)$. If that is the case, then performance derived from this database is most likely underestimated. This is because investments tend to happen in the early years of a fund (and are therefore more likely to be recorded) while dividends tend to happen in the later years of a fund (and are therefore more likely to be distributed after date T_i, being thus omitted). As *Thomson* provides no description of how they maintain their dataset, it is very difficult to determine whether or not performance is, indeed, underestimated.

1.4   Other Datasets and Evidence

As mentioned above, the main dataset used in previous research might not be accurate. It is thus important to use other datasets to compare results. This is what we do in this sub-section.

1.4.1   CEPRES

The Center for Private Equity Research (CEPRES) offers a dataset giving the cash flows generated by a General Partner (i.e. the private equity fund manager) on each one of its investments. Cash-flows are gross of all fees charged to the fund investors. The *Thomson* dataset mentioned above (or that of *Cambridge Associates* mentioned below and in Table 4.2) give the cash flows generated by a given fund for limited partners (i.e. investors in a private equity fund), net of all fees. The CEPRES dataset, therefore, differs from the aforementioned two datasets in terms of data aggregation level (fund versus investment) and fees (gross versus net).

CEPRES is a private consulting firm established in 2001 as a co-operation between the University of Frankfurt and *Deutsche Bank Group*. Data is obtained from private equity firms who make use of the 'Private Equity Analyzer' service. Participating firms sign a contract, undertaking to provide the correct cash flows (before fees) generated for each investment they have made in the past. In return, the firm receives statistics such as risk-adjusted performance measures. CEPRES does not benchmark private equity firms to peer groups. This improves data accuracy and representativeness as it eliminates incentives to manipulate cash flows or cherry-pick past investments. A subset of this database, covering mainly venture capital investments, is used by Cumming, Schmidt and Walz (2009), Cumming and Walz (2009) and Krohmer, Lauterbach, and Calanog (2009).

The buyout side of this dataset was used by Franzoni, Nowak and Phalippou (2009). Data contain all liquidated buyout investments and their cash flows as of December 2007. Franzoni et al. (2009) computed modified Internal Rates of Returns (IRRs) and the alphas/betas of buyout investments. They found modified IRRs in the range of 20 per cent gross of fees across time periods and continents. According to Phalippou (2009) this means that the modified IRR is about 12 per cent *net of fees*. These numbers are consistent with those mentioned above, in sub-section 1.1.

In addition, Franzoni et al. (2009) also find that market beta for buyout investments is 1.3. This low beta may be surprising at first sight because the higher leverage used in buyout investments should increase the (equity) beta. There are several (non-mutually exclusive) possibilities. First, higher leverage may reduce the beta on asset (e.g. the disciplinary role of debt may reduce risk and private equity ownership may increase profitability). Second, private equity firms may target companies with lower beta on asset or may be better at handling debt. Third, private equity firms also engage in a number of non-levered investments.

Finally, Franzoni et al. (2009) find that buyout investments are exposed to liquidity and distress risks (the Fama-French HML and SMB factors). Adding up all these risk components, they estimate that the cost of capital for buyout investments is 18 per cent (in excess of risk-free rate).

1.4.2   Fundraising prospectuses

The prospectuses that private equity firms provide investors with when raising funds contain cash multiples and IRRs of all their previous investments. We have collected performance information on 12000 investments from the prospectuses of buyout firms. These data, however, do not give underlying cash flows and are gross of fees. These data are analysed in Lopez-de-Silanes, Phalippou and Gottschalg (2010). One way to think of these data is that they are similar to those of CEPRES but without the detailed cash flows. This point is important because without the detailed cash flows saying anything about average performance is next to impossible. This is because the average IRR of investments is usually very different from the IRR of all investments pooled together. This is also true at the fund level, but the difference is larger at the investment level.

The value weighted multiple is a more relevant figure, although without a precise duration measure it is of limited statistical value. As a result, these data cannot be used to provide an informed insight to average performance. Yet, these data are useful to explain cross-sectional differences between investments and hence they will be used in Section 2 below. The usefulness of IRR and cash multiples in the cross-section stems from the fact that these measures of performance are highly correlated at the investment level to more accurate measures. This was shown with CEPRES data by Franzoni et al. (2009). Plain IRR and modified IRR (a more accurate measure) have a correlation of 97 per cent. The Public Market Equivalent (PME) and the cash multiple have a similar correlation.[6] The only caveat is that IRR and multiple need to be winsorized (e.g. at the 95th percentile), otherwise outliers make any regression analysis meaningless.

1.4.3   Investor records

Some researchers have had access to the detailed track record of certain investors, observing the cash flows amount and the date for each portfolio company. An example is the proprietary dataset of Ljungqvist and Richardson (2003), which contains 207 private equity funds.

On the one hand, these are ideal data as they leave no room for cherry-picking from GPs, all fees paid would be expected to be reported and all fund track records would be expected to be uninterrupted. Finally, the timing and amount of cash flows would be expected to be precise. The downside, however, is that investors who are willing to share their data may be above average. It would be surprising if investors who lost signifi-

---

[6]   As mentioned above, the problem with a cash multiple is that it does not take into account the time value of money. A multiple of 1.3 is high for an investment held for one year but low for an investment held for 10 years. A Public Market Equivalent (PME) is like a cash multiple but does take into account the time value of money. PME is the present value of all dividend paid (and final residual value, if anything) divided by the present value of the investments made.

cant amounts in an asset class would be happy to provide information on how poorly they have performed. In addition, even if all investors were equally happy to share their track record, there would still be the survival issue to reckon with. If an investor still invests in private equity, then it is likely to be the case that its performance was satisfactory. Having said that, there appears to exist no alternative to this type of data: one needs to have the exact track record of, hopefully, a large number of investors in order to be in a position to know if at least one group thereof had a satisfactory return in private equity.

1.4.4 Preqin

A source of data that is becoming increasingly important is that of Preqin (previously known as 'Private Equity Intelligence'). Preqin offers two types of data. The *first* is a list of a number of private equity funds and their most recent performance, measured by IRR or cash multiple (i.e. total distributed, divided by total invested). The data mainly come from pension funds in the US, since the said funds are under a legal obligation to provide a full list of all the funds they are investing in and the most up-to-date performance figure for each one of them. The *second* type of data is a cash flow dataset, very much like the one of *Thomson*. The coverage is not as comprehensive as that of *Thomson* for earlier years but, with the passage of time, coverage is improving. At the moment, about one in three mature funds in the first dataset is present in the cash flow dataset; the ratio is higher for buyout funds and lower for venture capital funds.[7]

We provide some descriptive statistics derived with the first dataset, which is the most comprehensive one. We select all funds raised before 2000 and separate venture capital from buyout funds. The performance is as of December 2009. Where size is missing, we replace it by the median size (US$300 million in buyout and US$100 million in venture capital). For the missing multiple and IRR, we use the following formula to infer one from the other: Multiple = $(1+IRR)$ ^ (duration) and we assume a duration of 6 years for all funds; this is the effective duration of PE funds estimated by Phalippou and Gottschalg (2009).

We count 492 buyout funds (a fairly substantial sample). The (size-weighted) mean and median IRR for buyout funds is 12 per cent. The (size-weighted) mean and median multiple is 1.7 for buyout funds. These

---

[7] A quick check of the data indicates that the funds present in the cash flow dataset seem to have better performance than the average fund in the comprehensive dataset.

numbers are consistent with an effective duration of 5 years (an investment returning 12 per cent a year for 5 years would have a multiple of about 1.7). Most importantly, these numbers are similar to what has been documented in earlier studies (see Section 1.1). So, for mature buyout funds, it seems that we have some consistent answers. One problem, however, with judging performance for buyout is that the growth has been very strong and that performance has been extreme in recent years. Funds raised between 2001 and 2004 seem to have experienced high returns in their early years. Funds raised in 2004–2007 have invested about as much as all the buyout funds before them and what their performance is, is not really known. The financial crisis seems to have significantly hit buyout fund performance but whether that is indeed the case and to what extent will only be known in 5 to 10 years.

For venture capital funds there are even more mature funds. We count as many as 892 of them. Their median IRR is 7.5 per cent and their value-weighted IRR is 10 per cent (despite some IRRs above 500 per cent). Similarly, median multiple is 1.5 and value-weighted multiple is 1.8. Again, these statistics are consistent with those previously reported (see Section 1.1). The advantage of these data is that anyone can subscribe to and verify their accuracy. Simple analysis like the one conducted above shows that returns are indeed low.

1.4.5   Round data

In the context of real estate, art (e.g. paintings) and venture capital, the data may consist of market values observed at different points in time, with only negligible cash flows in-between. Each time a building or a painting changes hands, we observe a market value. Each time a venture-capital-financed company reaches a so-called 'round milestone', we observe a valuation. We call such data 'round data'.

For venture capital, the most comprehensive 'round data' source is Sand Hill Econometrics, who combined data from existing databases (VentureOne and Venture Economics), adding information from proprietary data sources. These data give the value of a company at each valuation round until the exit (trade sale, IPO or bankruptcy). By analyzing these data, one can draw conclusions about the risk and return profile of the target company. However, the risk and return faced by the private equity fund investor is bound to be different. For example, in case of an IPO-exited project, the return observed will be based on the IPO offering price and not on the price at which the investors have sold. An extreme example where this distinction has mattered a lot is the eBay IPO. Benchmark Partners' return in eBay was 20 times the investment at the time of the IPO. However, investors received the eBay stocks 6 months after the IPO, when their price had increased by more than 3000 per cent, making their stake worth 700 times the investment. Hence the return from each financing rounds to the IPO can be very different than the return of the private equity fund investors. Moreover, it is unclear whether the equity stake of a venture capitalist changes across rounds and how that would impact on estimated returns.[8] What this means is that results on risk and return drawn from data on round valuation will be different from those drawn from data on cash-flows to/from investors. This is an important caveat to bear in mind in order to understand the literature.

Cochrane (2005) is the first to have computed the alpha and beta of venture capital using these data. He finds a beta around 2 and an implausibly high alpha. At the time, however, the dataset was quite noisy and his assumption of log-normality has since been challenged (Korteweg and Sorensen, 2010). Korteweg and Sorensen (2010) use a cleaner version of the same dataset and avoid strong distributional assumptions. Formally, they combine a Tobit model with a dynamic filtering and smoothing problem. They present a Markov Chain Monte Carlo estimator using Gibbs sampling, which produces the posterior distribution by iteratively simulating from three distributions: a Bayesian regression, a draw of truncated random variables and a path from a Kalman filter. They find a beta around three, which is similar to what is found by Driessen et al. (2009) but the alpha they report appears implausibly high just like that of Cochrane, i.e. over 30 per cent per annum.

What is important to bear in mind is that return figures for these investments are not available for about half of the observations, with returns for the said investments being extrapolated by a statistical model. It would be interesting to see what the alpha would be if all these investments were assumed to have a −100 per cent rate of returns, which would not be unreasonable, as investments that do not benefit from an extra financing round are often worthless (in venture capital). It is also not very well understood why alphas are so high with the econometric approaches of

---

8   Another difference between round returns and those experienced by investor comes from fees. Fees vary across funds, over time, and are non-linear in performance. They thus affect estimates of both risk and abnormal return. In addition, the stake of fund managers in a company changes over the project's life. If the stake of a fund manager is higher when the expected return is higher then the investor's performance will be superior to that of the project. The project and investor risk/return may be close to one another but there has not been any evidence on this yet and it is not obvious they will be.

Cochrane (2005) and Korteweg and Sorensen (2009). It seems that some of it comes from a volatility correction and the estimate of volatility is always very high with these data.

1.4.6 Listed vehicles

Publicly traded private equity firms are essentially closed-end funds.[9] As such, they are publicly traded just like any stock. They got in the spotlight recently as a number of indices based on these stocks were launched in the course of the last decade (e.g. S&P Listed Private Equity Index, PowerShares Listed Private Equity Fund, LPX50).

Most of the private equity money is invested via private partnerships, not via listed vehicles. The research reviewed above focuses solely on private equity partnerships. As Jegadeesh, Kräussl and Pollet (2009) aptly point out, however, some of these listed vehicles are funds-of-funds (FoFs), which themselves invest in private partnerships. As a result, we can observe regular market prices for a pool of partnerships. At first sight this is an extremely attractive feature. In addition, sample selection bias may be low although FoFs are supposed to select the best private equity partnerships.

These FoFs inform their investors annually of the total investment, distribution, net asset value and fees faced by the fund-of-fund. The general perception of NAVs in private equity is that these are not reliable. Hence, the information they provide cannot enable the computation of a reliable return. When conducting a due diligence, large investors would gather a good deal of information about the accounting of portfolio companies to evaluate the NAVs and therefore form an opinion on the market values and actual returns. Investors in listed FoFs do not have access to such detailed information. But even if these investors did have access to all the information possible, could they process it efficiently? Large investors in private equity tend to invest directly in private partnerships, not via listed vehicles. Investors in listed vehicles are typically small and with little knowledge of the intricacies of such a complex asset class (e.g. Cumming, Fleming and Johan, 2010). So the question is: can investors come up with a reasonable market price? Do variations in such a market price have anything to say about the risk/return profile of the asset class?

There are two main applications for which we need the risk/return of a publicly traded stock. The first is to obtain expected returns and expected covariance so as to build an optimal asset allocation. The second applica-

---

[9] In the UK, these vehicles are commonplace in private equity, mainly due to some special tax alleviation provisions.

tion is to compute the cost of capital to be used by the chief financial officer to assess whether projects have a positive Net Present Value (NPV) or not. For the first application, even if the risk/return profile we compute from market prices is not that of the underlying business, that is not relevant. What investors want to know is the type of risk/return payoff they will face when investing in a given stock. So, back to the private equity case, if an investor wants to invest in these FoFs, what she cares about is the risk/return that these vehicles exhibit. It does not matter to her if the said risk/return coincides with the true underlying risk/return.

Different considerations apply to the second application. The cost of capital should be based on the true risk of the business. If the market does not provide the right answer, that is an issue. For example, let us assume that, for whatever reason, the market dislikes value stocks. As a result, value stocks have a high return. Should the value corporations use this high return in their NPV calculations? Perhaps not, or else they would invest in too few projects. Back to the private equity case, if one wants to know the risk profile of a private partnership, it is crucial that the market provides the right answer. To make the case more concrete, assume that the market under-reacts to news for private equity listed vehicles, possibly because it does not observe most of them. In that case, the stock may follow the market return more closely than it would otherwise do. Without such an under-reaction, the beta may be very different. Similarly, recent literature (e.g. Barberis and Shleifer, 2003) has pointed out that stocks tend to co-move more with those that are included in the same index than with those that are classified in the same industry. A chemical company that belongs to the S&P 500 may co-move more with Microsoft (as they both belong to the S&P 500) than with a chemical company that is not in the S&P 500. Hence, private equity listed vehicles may co-move more closely with the stock-market than with the underlying business. While some of the above are only assumptions, we believe that bearing them in mind is apposite.

Nonetheless, it is interesting to know what private equity listed vehicles offer in terms of risk and return profile.[10] Jegadeesh, Kraussl and Pollet (2009) find an alpha close to zero. In addition, Jegadeesh, Kraussl and Pollet (2009) observe that 12 months after an IPO the discount (market price to NAV) stabilizes at about 10 per cent. Given the fees of these funds, they compute that this discount implies that investors expect that the

---

[10] Studies of listed private equity vehicles include Jegadeesh, Kraussl and Pollet (2009), Bergmann, Christophers, Huss and Zimmermann (2009), and Kaserer, Lahr, Liebhart and Mettler (2010).

underlying partnerships return a small positive alpha. This is because most of the discount corresponds to future expected fees. This is an interesting and reassuring finding. Investors expect the asset class to provide a small alpha. Simply put, studies that look at actual cash flows find that reality is different from expectations. Such studies of private equity discount may also bring insights into how sentiments regarding private equity vary over time and also about the biases in NAVs. For instance, Jegadeesh, Kraussl and Pollet (2009) find that listed vehicles returns forecast future changes in the NAV that private equity funds report.[11]

1.5   Industry Benchmarks and Investor Perceptions

After reviewing the academic literature on risk and return of private equity, the picture that emerges contrasts with that of the general public that the average venture capital or private equity fund perform well. It may then be interesting to turn to the investor side and see why private equity investors think otherwise. An investor who is perceived as the most knowledgeable on this asset class, David Swensen, Yale's CIO, has stated that:

> While the value added by operationally oriented buyout partnerships may, in certain instances, overcome the burden imposed by the typical buyout fund's generous fee structure, in aggregate, buyout investments fail to match public alternatives (. . .) In the absence of truly superior fund selection skills (or extraordinary luck), investors should stay far, far away from private equity investments.(. . .) Some part of the failure of buyout managers to produce risk-adjusted returns stems from the inappropriate fee structure.(. . .) Because the incentive compensation fails to consider the investor's cost of capital, buyout partnerships capture 20 per cent of the returns generated by favorable wind at the long-term equity investor's back.(. . .) The large majority of buyout funds fail to add sufficient value to overcome a grossly unreasonable fee structure. (D. Swensen, 2005, 133–5).

It follows that, both academics and top investors seem to agree that the average venture capital or private equity fund has poor performance. Why does the general public think otherwise?

Private equity industry associations (e.g. NVCA, EVCA) announce aggregate performance every quarter (see Table 4.2). Invariably, these

---

[11]   Note, however, that this does not mean that investors in listed PE can out-guess the NAVs. It can be that NAVs are marked-to-market with some delays and that listed PE simply follows the movement of the stock-market. In this case the discount will forecast future changes in NAV, yet investors in listed PE have not outguessed anyone.

returns are above those of public equity markets over long horizons (e.g. over the previous 10, 15, 20 years). These reports are the only source of performance information for this asset class. As a result, they are widely disseminated by the press to the investment community. As seen above, two academic studies have used the same underlying data as those used by the industry associations, but different methodologies (Kaplan and Schoar, 2005, and Phalippou and Gottschalg, 2009). Both have reached results that are more sobering than those of industry associations: both buyout and venture capital funds have a performance that is at best similar to that of the S&P 500. These studies used data ending in 2001 and 2003 respectively. More recent performance may be higher, but in those years (2001–2003), the industry associations were also posting strong outperformance of private equity compared to public equity. Hence, differences in methodology probably provide a plausible explanation for the discrepancy in results.

The current industry approach measures performance from one point to the other (called end-to-end returns or point-to-point returns). This method consists in taking the sum of all NAVs (for example) as of December 2005 and treat it as if it were the amount invested at that date. All the net cash flows are then recorded for all the funds from 2006 to 2010, with all NAVs as of December 2010 being summed and treated as a dividend payment at that date. The IRR of the resulting stream of cash flows is what is called the 'past 5 years private equity return'. It is possible that these aggregated NAVs may be below the aggregate market value. This is because most of the NAV comes from young funds, which set their NAV to the amount invested. Since returns are positive on average, these NAVs are below market values. So, the aggregate NAV at one point in time may be below market values.

If the aggregate NAV is too low, as suggested above, this has two opposite effects. The effect on initial NAV exaggerates performance (because it lowers the assumed initial investment) and the effect on final NAV underestimates performance (because it decreases the final value). Which effect prevails will depend on the horizon and the performance level. Longer horizons and higher performance will lower the present value of the final NAV, making the initial NAV relatively more important and, thus, bias returns more upward. Phalippou (2010a) shows that this bias can be of sizeable magnitude and can thus, at least partly, explain the difference between the perception of the general public and the results of academic studies.

Another issue with existing benchmarks is that they are very different across data providers.[12] This sometimes gives the impression that return

---

[12]   Cornelius (2010) provides an extensive coverage of this issue.

figures depend mostly on the dataset one uses. But, as we discussed above, the different data available to researchers usually show low performance. As argued by Phalippou (2010b) the methodology used for these benchmarks results in very unstable results. Thus, differences in benchmarks may result from the methodology used rather than from any discrepancy in the underlying data. In any case, we can conclude that the common belief that returns have been spectacular has little foundation. If one does not trust the data, then no conclusive outcome is available. To argue that average performance has been high, however, one has to explain why the available data over-represent bad funds and/or misses many dividend payments.

2. FUND SELECTION

2.1   The Importance of a Bottom-up Approach in Private Equity

Before selecting funds, what an institutional investor typically does first is to decide on the allocation to each broad asset classes, of which private equity is only one (see, for example, van Bisbergen, Brandt and Koijen, 2008).[13] For that, it uses some versions of the classical mean-variance framework. The necessary inputs are an expected return for each asset class and correlations between all the asset classes. When it comes to private equity, an estimate of expected return (and, a fortiori, of correlations) is difficult to come up with. Thus, in practice, investors take what is believed to be the long-term return of private equity (shown in Table 4.2) and use it for expected return. Correlations are even more of a mystery, with investors often using some relatively low ones.[14] What usually comes out of these algorithms is that all other asset classes (bond, equity etc.) should be shorted in order for a large long position to be taken in private equity. Often, instead of questioning the assumptions (on expected returns and

---

[13]   'The investment management divisions of banks, mutual funds, and pension funds are predominantly structured around asset classes such as equities, fixed income, and alternative investments. (. . .) This induces the centralized decision maker of the firm, the Chief Investment Officer (CIO), for example, to pick asset managers who are specialized in a single asset class and to delegate portfolio decisions to these specialists. As a consequence, asset allocation decisions are made in at least two stages. In the first stage, the CIO allocates capital to the different asset classes, each managed by a different asset manager. In the second stage, each manager decides how to allocate the funds made available to him, that is, to the assets within his class' (van Bisbergen et al. (2008, 1849–50)).

[14]   E.g., the Harvard Management case study from Harvard Business School shows such low correlations.

correlations), investors impose some constraints on short sales, as a result of which private equity is brought to a supposedly more reasonable range of 20 per cent to 30 per cent of the asset allocation. The objective is then clear: if one has 10 billion under management, 2 to 3 billion should find its way into private equity. This approach is sometimes called 'top-down'.

The above approach can lead to problems that are more acute in private equity than they are in other asset classes.[15] The reason is that private equity performance is very cyclical, with low performance and small inflows following periods of particularly high performance and large inflows. In a nutshell, at some point in time, some private equity investments return very large amounts. Next, investors rush large amounts of capital to private equity. This may be because investors put in their mean-variance tool higher return expectations and, so, get as an answer that allocation should be increased. At that point, one typically witnesses much higher valuations because private equity firms compete more forcefully for a limited pool of deals (Gompers and Lerner, 2000). Since these higher valuations are the result of price pressure rather than better prospects, the ensuing returns are low. As a consequence, investors following the top-down approach end up in the worse possible situation: they increase allocation to private equity most when expected returns are at the lowest. This unfortunate outcome could be corrected by having a better estimate of expected returns. Instead of using the supposedly long-run performance of Table 4.2, one could have a forecast model for expected return based on past performance, aggregate allocation to private equity etc. (for an example, albeit simple, of such a model see Kaplan and Stromberg, 2009).

The fact that not all investors are equal poses yet another problem. If investor 'Lambda' from Toulouse-France decides to invest US$100 million in US public equity, she can expect a similar return as D. Swensen from New-Haven, Connecticut, USA. But if investor 'Lambda' invests US$100 million in private equity, she will probably not secure the same return as D. Swensen. The main reasons are that they will face different fees, they will not have access to the same funds and they may not receive the same amount and quality of co-investment opportunities.[16]

As a result, a bottom-up approach is more promising in private equity

---

[15]   See van Bisbergen et al., 2008, for a study of general problems with the top-down approach.

[16]   Large pension funds are often invited to co-invest with a fund in which they are invested. For Endowments, it is rare. Private equity firms may want to privilege their largest investors and thus cherry pick the best investments. They then invite them to increase their stake in those investments. In addition, they do not charge any fees on those co-investments.

than a top-down approach. Each year, one needs to evaluate the opportunities, try to identify which ones are positive NPVs for him/her and invest in as many positive NPV propositions as possible, probably with an upper bound of around 10 per cent to 20 per cent of the total portfolio. As positive NPVs are difficult to identify, that may not always be easy to achieve. Yet, this is the best route. A fund should probably be discarded whenever a business proposal seems unlikely to bring value (e.g. crowded strategy, no expertise in the strategy etc.), when true past performance (as opposed to the potentially window-dressed figure featuring on the prospectus) is poor and there is no reason to believe the future will be any different, when the contract does not align interests and has a high level of performance insensitive fees etc.

In some years, only a handful of funds will pass this test and the allocation to private equity will be relatively low; in other years, more funds will pass the test and the allocation will be relatively high. What is most important with that approach is that investors do not tie their hands upfront. It is the existing opportunities that dictate allocation, not the other way around.

2.2   Top Quartile

A common argument from private equity investing advisors is that the average private equity fund should be avoided as only top quartile funds deliver good returns (e.g. Fraser-Sampson, 2007). Note that this argument is consistent with the academic results reviewed above, but not with press-coverage, nor with the beliefs of most investors.

Next, advisors typically argue that investing in top quartile funds is not difficult if one is familiar with the asset class (e.g. Fraser-Sampson, 2007). While the above may be true, one still has to explain why 75 per cent of the money in private equity (invested in the bottom three quartiles) would be so-called 'dumb-money'.[17] In addition, there is an important caveat to bear in mind: a disproportionately high number of top quartile funds are from a few vintage years. This is because of the high cyclicality of private equity performance noted above, which is why investing in top quartile funds is as much about finding the top funds in any given batch as it is about market timing. Below, we will discuss why the later may be more difficult than the former.

---

[17]   The expression Dumb money was coined by Frazzini and Lamont (2008) and refers to investors who systematically allocate their money to the wrong stocks. This expression is also used on Wall Street by technical analysts and in the press.

Table 4.3 Fund selection

Panel A: Venture Capital funds

	N_obs	Value at risk (5th percentile)	Median
Top quartile funds	207	21%	39%
Every vintage year, select only funds:			
In top quartile	209	6%	31%
In top half	421	−1%	19%
Not in bottom quartile	621	−7%	12%
Not in top quartile	619	−22%	1%
Select all the funds, but select only:			
In top 5 vintage years	163	−11%	19%
Not in top 5 vintage years	665	−21%	4%
Mix of the two:			
Avoid bottom quartile in top 5 years	123	7%	26%
Top quartile, avoid bottom 5 years	104	21%	54%
Top half, avoid bottom 5 years	211	14%	32%

Panel B: Buyout

	N_obs	Value at risk (5th percentile)	Median
Top quartile funds	120	23%	31%
Every vintage year, select only funds:			
In top quartile	123	15%	28%
In top half	244	9%	22%
Not in bottom quartile	362	2%	17%
Not in top quartile	357	−15%	9%
Select all the funds, but select only:			
In top 5 vintage years	62	−9%	22%
Not in top 5 vintage years	418	−11%	11%
Mix of the two:			
Avoid bottom quartile in top 5 years	47	12%	29%
Top quartile, avoid bottom 5 years	62	22%	33%
Top half, avoid bottom 5 years	123	17%	26%

Table 4.3 shows the effect of selecting a sub-set of funds. It uses Preqin data on fund performance as of December 2009. It considers funds raised from 1985 to 2000, either venture capital (Panel A) or buyout (Panel B). For each selection criterion, it reports the number of funds selected, the IRR of the 5th percentile (value-at-risk) and the IRR of the 50th percentile (median). Top vintage years are those with the highest median IRR. If one selects the top quartile of all venture capital funds, the median IRR is 39 per cent. If one selects the top quartile of venture capital funds every single year among those offered that year, the median performance is lower at 31 per cent. However, the value-at-risk is very different. Overall top quartile funds have a value-at-risk of 21 per cent while the every-vintage top quartile funds have a value-at-risk of 6 per cent.

Similar results, although less dramatic, apply to buyout funds, suggesting that timing the market is important to avoid poor performers. Results also show that if one never invested in a top quartile fund, the median IRR is a meagre 1 per cent in venture capital and 9 per cent in buyout. Another interesting result is that if an investor missed only the top five best vintage years, representing less than one fund in five, the returns are very low. In venture capital the median IRR is 4 per cent and value-at-risk is −21 per cent. Similarly, for buyout funds, the median IRR is 11 per cent and the value-at-risk is −11 per cent.

Avoiding the worse years also matters. If an investor simply picks the top half of the funds each year but avoids the five worst years in venture capital (1986, 1996, 1998, 1999, 2000), the returns are high (especially the value-at-risk). The same holds true in buyout, with the worse five years being from 1995 to 1999. These results show that if one can always select the top quartile funds in any vintage year, median performance will be high but value-at-risk will be lower than that computed on the full sample. Also, most high-return funds and low-return funds come from the same vintage years. Finally, the importance of cycles seems higher for venture capital. But when we will have the final performance of the post-2000 buyout funds, we may find a cyclicality that is equally strong in buyout as it is in venture capital.

What the results above show is that statistics on top quartile funds derived from aggregate (cross-vintage) data may differ from what investors experience if they do not time the market well. But market timing is trickier than fund picking. If one does not invest in, say, KKR 2005 because it is a bad year to invest, KKR may not allow one to invest in KKR 2010, as private equity firms will occasionally write investors off once they skip one fund generation (they will insist on having a stable and reliable pool of capital). Another difficulty is that allocations to private equity will vary a lot over time, something that some institutions may not like.

Table 4.4 Performance persistence

Firm rank	Vintage	IRR	(next 2) Ranks 1990–1999	Vintage	IRR
1	1989	198.5	10, 363	95, 99	192, −8
2	1981	67.4	35, 121	92, 95	87, 11
3	1982	64.3	5	91	346
4	1983	51.6	76	91	48
5	1980	50.6	21, 88	92, 94	39, 125
6	1989	46.1	n.f.		
7	1988	43.4	334, 337	90, 93	−4, −10
8	1988	43.1	213, 96	91, 94	10, 34
9	1988	42.1	81, 16	93, 97	40, 135
10	1989	39.6	26, 13	92, 96	110, 167
11	1988	35.8	113, 14	94, 97	30, 160
12	1983	35.4	n.f.		
13	1989	35.1	n.f.		
14	1989	33.6	34, 24	93, 97	87, 120
15	1989	33.5	87	91	40
16	1988	31.8	311	92	−1
17	1988	30.1	207	92	11

Note: Top decile venture capital funds. Ranking is based on IRR. Funds are raised between 1980 and 1989. If a firm has several funds in the top decile, the earliest fund is kept. The rank achieved by the next two funds raised in the 1990s is shown along with the vintage of these funds and the IRR.

2.3 Predictors of Private Equity Funds Performance

We have mentioned market timing above as a tool to outperform in private equity. We now turn to fund picking (i.e., choosing among competing funds). We begin by what is the most recurring argument: there is performance persistence in private equity, so find the top firms and invest with them. Academics have been investigating issues of relevance to the performance persistence of mutual funds for some 20 years. There is a quasi-consensus: there is no persistence. In a striking example, Malkiel (1995) lists the 20 best funds in the 1970s and their ranking in the 1980s. Only two funds stayed in the top 20, with the remaining funds having had fairly low rankings.[18]

In Table 4.4, above, we repeat a similar analysis with Preqin data. We take the venture capital funds raised between 1980 and 1989 that are in the

---

[18] For example, the fund that was first in the 1970s was 151 in the 1980s (out of 260).

top 10 per cent. They belong to 17 different firms. Three firms have several funds in the top 10 per cent and we keep only the fund from the earliest vintage year. The IRRs are all above 30 per cent. Next, we record the ranking of the next two funds raised in the 1990s, along with their vintages and returns.

Results do not seem very different than with mutual funds. The average ranking for the next two funds is 114. Only one firm stayed in the top decile with all its funds. If one looks at the top venture capital firm from the 1980s, it raised a top fund in 1989, then the next fund was raised in 1995 and that fund too had a very high return, but then the third fund, from 1999, had a very poor performance. The problem is that investors in 1995 may not have known that the 1989 fund would do so well. The 1989 fund liquidated around 1999. But knowing in 1999 that this firm has high returns was not very useful because the 1999 fund did very poorly. In a sense, 1999 was too late to know that this firm was good (one should have known in 1995, when the second fund was raised).

What academics have originally called persistence is to do with the fact that two successive funds have positively correlated returns. For example, if KKR III (i.e. the third fund raised by KKR) had high returns then KKR IV (i.e. the next fund raised by KKR) also had high returns. Similarly, if ABC IV had low returns, then ABC V also had low returns. Kaplan and Schoar (2005) also find that for venture capital funds (but not for buyout funds) the result holds true if one were to skip one fund. To continue with the above example, this means that if ABC IV had low returns then ABC VI also had low returns and if ABC IV had high returns then ABC VI also had high returns.

Phalippou (2010a) investigated in detail this issue of time between two funds and found that the more time one requires between two funds of the same firm, the lower performance persistence is. Once one requires more than 5 years inbetween two funds, the persistence results disappear. Hence, while one may skip one fund in the analysis, what this means in practice is that, on average, 3 to 4 years are required between the focal fund and the previous fund. If one goes beyond this threshold, there is no longer any performance persistence. What this entails is that while some firms repeat successes, it may be difficult for investors to design an effective selection strategy based on that result. In practice, by the time they can see that a firm has generated good past performance, it may be too late, as the next fund may not perform well.

Yet, there may be ways to exploit early performance indicators to select funds. Hochberg et al. (2009), for example, find that if one takes the maximum IRR over all the funds previously raised by a firm at time t, this would help predict the performance of the fund raised at time t.

So, when firm ABC raises fund IV, the investor will look at the current performance of funds ABC I, ABC II and ABC III, and take the highest IRRs among these three funds. If that number is high ABC IV will have high returns (and vice versa). In that case, there would be a predictability that is exploitable by investors. What this shows is that analyzing the track record probably helps selecting the right funds. However, this should not be done in a naïve way.

Looking at fund size or, more specifically, at the number of portfolio companies, may also be helpful. Lopez-de-Silanes, Phalippou and Gottschalg (2010) show that the main driver of performance in buyouts is the number of investments held in parallel by a firm. The more investments a firm manages, the poorer the performance. This coincides with a widely held belief in the investor community that diseconomies of scale are important in private equity. Thus, prospective investors may pay special attention to firm scale and changes in firm scale. Related to this finding, Cumming and Dai (2010) find that, in venture capital, fund size *increases* whilst geographic proximity *decreases* valuations. All else being equal, what this would mean is that in venture capital better returns are obtained when the venture capitalist is physically close to its portfolio companies and runs smaller funds. Gompers, Kovner and Lerner (2009) have also found that specialized venture capital firms perform better.

3. CONCLUSION

We have reviewed the literature on risk and return of private equity (venture capital and buyout) and compared the different datasets used in academic research. Returns do not seem as spectacular as often conjectured. Irrespective of the datasets, the average return seems to be lower than public equity returns. Buyouts seem to bear a moderate market risk (beta is around unity), but they have a significant exposure to liquidity and distress risk. The cost of a capital buyout is 18 per cent (in excess of risk-free rate). The beta of venture capital seems much higher (around 3), implying a cost of capital of about 20 per cent (in excess of risk-free rate and any potential liquidity risk premium). The finding of low average returns is consistent across datasets and coincides with the finding of leading private equity investors. It is, however, in contrast to what industry associations advertise and what the broad public then believes. We conjecture that the methodology used by industry associations may be behind this apparent contradiction. Finally, we have addressed the issue of fund selection, emphasizing the importance of a bottom-up approach when investing in private equity, showing that top-quartile returns and evidence of performance persistence should be approached with some caveats in mind and describing variables that have predicted returns.

BIBLIOGRAPHY

Barberis, Nicholas and Andrei Shleifer (2003), 'Style Investing', *Journal of Financial Economics*, **68**, 161–99.

Bergmann, B., H. Christophers, M. Huss and H. Zimmermann (2009), 'Listed private equity', NBER Working Paper No. 9454.

Cochrane, J. (2005), 'The risk and return of venture capital', *Journal of Financial Economics*, **75**, 3–52.

Cornelius, P. (2010), 'Comparing benchmarks for private equity funds', available from the author.

Cumming, D. and N. Dai (2010), 'Local bias in venture capital investments', *Journal of Empirical Finance*, **17**(3), 362–80.

Cumming, D., Grant Flemming and Sofia Johan (2010), 'Institutional investment in listed private equity', *European Financial Management*.

Cumming, D., D. Schmidt and U. Walz (2009), 'Legality and venture capital governance around the world', *Journal of Business Venturing*, **25**(1), 54–72.

Cumming, D. and U. Walz (2009), 'Private equity returns and disclosure around the world', *Journal of International Business Studies*, **41**(4), 727–54.

Driessen, J., T.C. Lin and L. Phalippou (2009), 'A new method to estimate risk and return of non-traded assets from cash flows: the case of private equity funds', NBER Working Paper No. W14144.

Franzoni F., E. Nowak and L. Phalippou (2009), 'Private equity performance and liquidity risk', Geneva, Switzerland: Swiss Finance Institute Research Paper No. 09–43.

Fraser-Sampson, G. (2007), *Private equity as an asset class*, Chichester, West Sussex: Wiley Finance.

Frazzini, A. and O.A. Lamont (2008), 'Dumb Money: Mutual fund flows and the cross-section of stock return', *Journal of Financial Economics*, **88**(2), 299–322.

Gompers, P. and J. Lerner (2000), 'Money chasing deals? The impact of fund inflows on private equity valuation', *Journal of Financial Economics*, **55**(2), 281–325.

Gompers, P.A., A. Kovner, and J. Lerner (2009), 'Specialization and success: evidence from venture capital', *Journal of Economics and Management Strategy*, **18**(3), 817–44.

Hochberg, Y., A. Ljungqvist and A. Vissing-Jorgensen (2009), 'Informational hold-up and performance persistence in venture capital', Working Paper, Northwestern University.

Jegadeesh, N., R. Kräussl and J. Pollet (2009), 'Risk and expected returns of private equity investments: evidence based on market prices', NBER Working Paper 15335.

Kaplan, S. and A. Schoar (2005), 'Private equity performance: returns, persistence, and capital flows', *Journal of Finance*, **60**, 1791–823.

Kaplan, S. N. and P. Stromberg (2009), 'Leveraged buyouts and private equity', *Journal of Economic Perspectives*, **23**(1), 121–46.

Kaserer, C., H. Lahr, V. Liebhart, and A. Mettler (2010), 'The time varying risk of listed private equity', *Journal of Financial Transformation*, **28**, 87–93.

Korteweg, A. and M. Sorensen (2009), 'Risk and return characteristics of venture capital-backed entrepreneurial companies', Technical Report, AFA 2009 San Francisco Meetings Paper.

Krohmer, P., R. Lauterbach, and V. Calanog (2009), 'The bright and dark side of staging: Investment performance and the varying motivations of private equity', *Journal of Banking and Finance*, **33**, 1597–1609.

Ljungqvist, A. and M. Richardson (2003), 'The cash flow, return, and risk characteristics of private equity', NBER Working Paper 9454.

Lopez-de-Silanes, F., L. Phalippou and O. Gottschalg (2010), 'Giants at the gate: on the cross-section of private equity investment returns', MPRA Paper 28487, University Library of Munich, Germany.

Malkiel, B.G. (1995), 'Returns from investing in equity mutual funds 1971–1991', *Journal of Finance*, **50**(2), 549–72.

Phalippou, L. (2009), 'Beware when venturing into private equity', *Journal of Economic Perspectives*, **34**(3), 568–77.

Phalippou, L. (2010a), 'Venture capital funds: flow-performance relationship and performance persistence', *Journal of Banking and Finance*, **34**(3), 568–77.

Phalippou, L. (2010b), 'Does conservative accounting bias private equity benchmarks upwards or downwards?', available from the author.

Phalippou, L. and O. Gottschalg (2009), 'The performance of private equity funds', *Review of Financial Studies*, **22**(4), 1747–76.

Swensen, David F. (2005), *Unconventional Success: A Fundamental Approach to Personal Investment*, New York, Free Press.

van Binsbergen, Jules, Michael W. Brandt and Ralph S.J. Koijen (2008), 'Optimal decentralized investment management', *Journal of Finance*, **63**(4), 1849–95

PART B

REGULATORY ISSUES

5. Alternative investments and retail investors – a bold but risky experiment
*Harry McVea**

1. INTRODUCTION

The label 'alternative investments' is notoriously ill-defined, perhaps best characterized in terms of an attitude to risk rather than as a distinct asset class.[1] Traditionally, access to alternative investments – and to investment strategies typically associated with such investments – has largely been restricted to sophisticated (or at least wealthy) investors. Such investors are taken to know (or to be able to afford advice about) the risks they are running and, therefore, to be capable of deciding where and how much of their wealth they should invest. Furthermore, they are taken to be able to bear the loss in the event that losses do, in fact, occur.

Yet while alternative investments have traditionally been the preserve of sophisticated investors and market players, the last decade or so has witnessed a growing desire by domestic and EU regulators to facilitate retail investor access to a wider range of investments and sophisticated investment strategies through the use of authorized onshore investment vehicles. Claimed rationales for this policy are to promote greater consumer choice and to offer retail investors the opportunity to diversify risk. This chapter seeks to engage with, and contribute to, the ongoing policy debate which surrounds the liberalization of the alternative investments sector – in particular with regard to retail access to hedge funds and/or hedge-fund-like strategies – as it applies to unsophisticated investors. Furthermore, it seeks to describe and critique the regulatory landscape in the UK (and indirectly the EU) which has resulted from recent domestic and EU policy initiatives.

The chapter is structured as follows: first, it explores the rationales for allowing retail investors wider access to alternative investment products

---

* Reader in Law, School of Law, University of Bristol, UK; and Associate Research Fellow, Institute of Advanced Legal Studies, London.
[1] See, e.g., Moloney, N. (2006), 'The EC and the Hedge Fund Challenge: A Test Case for EC Securities Policy After the Financial Services Action Plan' *Journal of Corporate Law Studies*, **6**(1), 1, 3 (in the context of 'hedge funds').

and vehicles, focusing, in particular, on the FSA's response to various pressures for wider access by retail investors to alternative investment products; secondly, it describes the new regulatory landscape which has emerged from the recent liberalization of retail investor access to more sophisticated products and investment strategies; and thirdly, it assesses and critiques the outcome of that policy, the contours of which are only now beginning to take shape.

My basic claim is that while the EU's desire to create a 'state of the art' onshore investment funds industry is understandable and in part even laudable, there are nevertheless serious shortcomings with the thrust of the EU's policy of liberalization in this sphere – a policy which has received a relatively warm welcome by domestic regulators, notably the FSA. However, while the regulatory authorities both in the UK and in Europe are aware of certain risks associated with greater retail access to wider-range alternative investment products, insufficient weight has been given to these risks and too much faith has been placed in market discipline and tailored regulatory rules to address the problems identified. In short, the EU's policy, as embraced by the FSA, represents a bold but ultimately risky, perhaps even reckless, experiment.

2. WIDER RETAIL ACCESS TO ALTERNATIVE INVESTMENT FUNDS AS A POLICY STRATEGY

The development of the European investment funds industry is an important plank of the European Commission's strategy for creating a single market for financial services in the European Economic Area (EEA).[2] According to the Investment Management Association (IMA), '[t]he fundamental economic function of the investment management industry is to act as an efficient conduit for capital from those who wish to invest to those who need investment.'[3] From the perspective of retail investors – with which this chapter is primarily concerned – investment

---

[2]   See, for example, European Commission, *Green Paper on Enhancing the European Framework for Investment Funds* (July, 2005) COM(2005) 314 final; and *White Paper on Enhancing The Single Market Framework for Investment Funds* (November 2006) COM(2006) 686 final.

[3]   September 2009 IMA Submission published in House of Lords, *European Union Committee 3rd Report of Session 2009–10 Directive on Alternative Investment Fund Managers, Volume II: Evidence* (February, 2010) HL Paper 48–II, 251, www. publications.parliament.uk/pa/ld200910/ldselect/ldeucom/48/48ii.pdf, accessed 1 March 2011 (hereinafter 'IMA Submission').

funds provide access to professionally managed and diversified investments on affordable terms.[4] Moreover, as Europe's population continues to age, ever greater numbers of its citizens will need to take increasing responsibility for their long-term financial needs.[5] Central to the Commission's policy in this area has been the EU Undertakings for Collective Investment in Transferrable Securities ('UCITS') Directive 86/611/EEC ('UCITS Directive') and the 'harmonized' framework it establishes.[6] The UCITS Directive, which has proved both durable and successful, has been recast over the years – principally, by Directive 2001/107/EC (the 'Management Company Directive') and Directive 2001/108/EC (the 'Product Directive'), and referred to collectively as UCITS III.[7] A further series of reforms are soon to culminate in the implementation of UCITS IV by July 2011.[8] In essence, UCITS IV seeks to make UCITS products more efficient and to boost further the success of the UCITS brand.[9]

According to recent figures, by the end of 2009, assets under the management of UCITS funds alone stood in excess of €5 trillion, a sum which represented '75 per cent of all investment fund assets in Europe.'[10] These assets accounted for '55 per cent of the European Union's GDP at the end of 2009' and approximately '10 per cent of European households' financial assets.'[11] In line with the Commission's view as expressed in its 2006 White Paper,[12] the investment fund market has become increasingly organized on a pan-European basis, with the UCITS product passport widely used.[13] What is more, recent years have witnessed strong sales of cross-border funds outside Europe, with third-country sales – primarily in Asia – accounting for up to 40 per cent of new sales of UCITS funds.[14] More recently, and somewhat controversially, the Commission has sought to bring non-harmonized (non-UCITS funds) 'alternative funds' (or more correctly, the managers of such funds) within the regulatory fold by

---

[4]   *White Paper, supra,* fn 2.
[5]   *Ibid.*
[6]   See *infra* n 47 and accompanying text.
[7]   As to the liberalization effected by UCITS III, see *infra* n 69 and accompanying text.
[8]   Directive 2009/65 OJ 2009 L302/32.
[9]   For more details on the changes introduced by UCITS IV, see *infra* n 73.
[10]   See, HM Treasury and FSA, *Transposition of UCITS IV: Consultation Document* (December 2010) para 1.2.
[11]   *Ibid.*
[12]   *Supra,* fn. 2, 1.
[13]   HM Treasury and FSA, *Transposition of UCITS IV, supra,* fn. 10.
[14]   *Ibid.,* para 1.3.

way of its Alternative Investment Fund Management Directive ('AIFM Directive').[15]

The UK funds industry has a long and distinguished history, representing the second largest fund management market after the US and, by a distance, the largest centre in Europe.[16] UK funds account for over a third of the total EU industry, with a very wide range of domestic and overseas clients.[17] According to the IMA, the UK funds industry managed some £3 trillion worth of assets at the end of 2008,[18] and of the category of the alternative funds industry that is labelled 'hedge funds', as of December 2009, 76 per cent of European single manager hedge fund (with assets totalling US$382 billion) were managed out of the UK, the vast majority from London.[19] According to TheCityUK, fund management generally accounted for 0.67 per cent of UK GDP in 2009, and provided employment for over 50 000 people.[20] Meanwhile, net exports of UK fund management totalled £2.9bn in 2009.[21]

Yet despite the fact that the UK has been a significant beneficiary of the globalization of the fund management industry generally, and a major industry player within the context of the EU, the last decade has witnessed a contraction in its market share as a *domicile* for funds. According to the IMA, the total assets of funds domiciled in Luxembourg and Dublin in 1999 was just under twice the amount of those domiciled in the UK, but by 2009 they were four times as much.[22] The implementation of the AIFM, which has been widely derided as too wide in its scope,[23] overly protectionist,[24] and as limiting investor choice,[25] is likely to have a signifi-

---

[15]   A final agreed text was adopted by the European Parliament 11 November, 2010. The Directive is due to be implemented across the EU by the beginning of 2013.

[16]   TheCityUK, *Fund Management 2010* (October 2010), www.thecityuk.com/media/188154/fund%20management 202010.pdf, accessed 1 February 2011.

[17]   IMA Submission, *supra,* fn. 3.

[18]   *Ibid.*

[19]   International Financial Services London (IFSL), *ISFL Research: Hedge Funds* 2010 (April 2010), www.thecityuk.com/media/2358/Hedge_Funds_2010.pdf, accessed 1 February 2011.

[20]   TheCityUK, *supra,* fn. 16, 1.

[21]   *Ibid.,* 11.

[22]   *Ibid.,* 7.

[23]   Saunders, R. (2010), 'AIFM: Appalling Investment Fund Managers Directive?' *Asia News* (5 November 2010), www.ipe.com/asia/aifm-appalling-investment-fund-managers-directive_37807.php, accessed 1 March 2011.

[24]   See, Borges, A. (2010), 'Market Reality splits European and US policies towards hedge funds' (EuroHedge, June 2010), www.hfsb.org/sites/10188/files/eh_0610_borges.pdf, accessed 11 January 2011.

[25]   *Ibid.*

cant influence on the fund management sector in the UK, and is almost certain to result in a future where the UK's position as a major player is no longer assured.[26]

Broadly, and at the risk of over-simplification, the EU's investment fund sector can be split in two: on the one hand, a harmonized sector directed at retail or unsophisticated investors and based on the pan-EU UCITS framework;[27] and, on the other hand, a non-harmonized sector which, *in the main*, is directed at more sophisticated players, and currently governed by national regimes.[28] One major strand in the EU's current policy with regard to the investment funds sector generally, is to harmonize non-UCITS schemes, and the controversial AIFM Directive is the basis upon which this ambitious extension of its harmonization programme is to be achieved.[29] These developments are being played out against a background of significant market change, notably a gradual blurring of the lines between traditional retail products and products which utilize hedge-fund-like investment techniques (such as leverage, derivatives trading, and short selling).

The FSA's response to the growing international and European trend favouring wider retail access to alternative investment funds and strategies, is reflected in a number of its policy documents.[30] In summary, the FSA's policy response in this area can be characterized as being in part *principled* and in part *pragmatic*, reflecting a number of overlapping considerations and constraints, namely:

---

[26]   In particular, concerns have been expressed that leading fund managers will decamp to less heavily regulated centres. See Borges, *ibid.*

[27]   See, *supra*, fn. 47, and accompanying text.

[28]   This separation is by no means clear cut. Some non-harmonized products are clearly geared towards the retail market – e.g. the FSA's non-UCITS retail schemes (NURS). Although these are non-harmonized, as their name indicates, they are retail-oriented funds. See also, investment trust companies (i.e. companies which invest in other companies) which despite being non-harmonized are widely viewed as suitable for the retail market.

[29]   See, *supra*, fn. 23.

[30]   Some of the most important are: *Wider-range Retail Investment Products Consumer Protection in a Rapidly Changing World* (Discussion Paper, 05/3, June 2005) (hereinafter DP 05/3); *Wider-range Retail Investment Products Consumer Protection in a Rapidly Changing World – Feedback on DP 05/3* (Feedback Statement, 06/3, March 2006) (hereinafter FS 06/3); FSA, *Funds of Alternative Investment Funds (FAIFs)* (Consultation Paper 07/6, March 2007) (hereinafter CP 07/6); *Funds of Alternative Investment Funds (FAIFs): Feedback on CP 07/6 and further consultation* (Consultation Paper, 08/4, February 2008) (hereinafter CP 08/4); and *Funds of Alternative Investment Funds (FAIFs) (Including feedback on CP08/4)* (Policy Statement 10/3, February 2010c) (hereinafter PS 10/3).

(a)   the FSA's desire to ensure that retail investors were afforded greater exposure to more appropriate wider range (i.e. alternative investment) products (the 'investor choice' argument);

(b)   the fact that since retail investors were already exposed to alternative investments in a variety of ways and subject to varying regulatory controls and protections, there was a need for greater consistency in terms of the regulatory protections available (the 'regulatory fragmentation' argument); and

(c)   the realisation that, in the light of international and EU developments (e.g. UCITS III and the E-Commerce Directive)[31], the FSA had limited scope for unilateral action (the 'external influences' argument).

These arguments are assessed, below.

2.1   The 'Investor Choice' Argument

According to the FSA, allowing consumers access to a wider range of innovative investment strategies through authorized onshore vehicles would facilitate greater consumer choice. Restrictions on investor choice would, in the FSA's view, have the undesirable effect of denying some retail consumers access to what might otherwise be suitable investment products, notwithstanding the fact that such products were slightly further along the continuum in terms of risk, volatility, illiquidity and complexity than products typically associated with the retail market.[32] The FSA was also concerned that undue restrictions on investment choice might impair retail investors' ability to develop their knowledge of financial markets,[33] or to take appropriate responsibility for their investment decisions as required under the Financial Services and Markets Act 2000 (FSMA, 2000).[34] Finally, the FSA was of the view that removing restrictions on investor choice could help investors to better manage risk exposure through access to more advanced diversification strategies.[35]

   In essence, this latter diversification claim is rooted in portfolio theory, which 'rests on the insight that risk averse investors will always hold a diversified "portfolio" of capital assets'[36] According to Mnookin and Gilson, the overall risk associated with an asset's return is comprised of two components:

---

[31]   2000/31/EC of 8 June 2000. See, *infra* n 52 and accompanying text.
[32]   DP 05/3, para 4.17.
[33]   Section 5(c). FSMA 2000.
[34]   Section 5(d). FSMA 2000.
[35]   CP 07/6 Annex 1, para 3; and CP 08/4, para 4.19.
[36]   Gilson, R. and Mnookin, R. (1985), 'Sharing Among the Human Capitalists:

systematic (or market) risk; and unsystematic risk.[37] Systematic risk refers to the fact that most securities have 'at least some correlation to external market movements such as interest rates, consumer spending, and exchange rates, and thus, to some extent, move up and down in tandem.'[38] In other words, investors are exposed to, and cannot diversify away, the risk of those events that impact on the value of *all* asset classes. By contrast, unsystematic risk is the risk associated with holding any particular asset or asset class. In respect of unsystematic risk, modern finance theory posits that investors can reduce such risk by investing their capital in a range of assets and asset classes (e.g., shares, bonds, commodities, real estate, and so on).[39] According to Shadab 'Hedge funds' pursuit of absolute returns is just another way of stating that they pursue returns uncorrelated with general market factors, or returns with low systematic risk'[40] In sum, a large and sophisticated body of academic and practitioner research finds that access to wider range investments (including hedge-fund-like strategies) can enable investors to generate absolute returns even in falling markets.[41] An outright prohibition on retail access to such strategies would have the effect of denying these investors the opportunity to benefit from alternative investment strategies and further entrench these investments as the domain of the sophisticated/wealthy.

2.2 The 'Regulatory Fragmentation' Argument

A second driver of the FSA's policy making strategy on wider-range retail investment products revolved around the fact that retail consumers were already subject to differing regulatory requirements, largely as a consequence of historical accident and as a result of the particular nature of the investment vehicle selected.[42] The effect of this fragmentation was that 'retail consumers [were] confronted with wider range products in a variety of circumstances, and subject to differing conditions.'[43] In the FSA's view,

---

An Economic Inquiry into the Corporate Law Firm and How Partners Split Profits' *Stan Law Rev*, **37**, 313, 322 (footnote omitted).

[37]   *Ibid.*

[38]   Shadab, H. (2007–2008), 'Fending for Themselves: Creating a U.S. Hedge Fund Market for Retail Investors' *N.Y.U. J. Legis. & Pub. Pol'y* 11, 251, 267.

[39]   *Ibid.*, 268.

[40]   *Ibid.*, footnotes omitted.

[41]   Funds included in a portfolio of funds of funds may, in practice, carry some hidden risks. See, Kovas (2004), 'Should Hedge Fund Products be Marketed to Retail Investors? A Balancing Act for Regulators', Institute for Law and Finance, Johann Wolfgang Goethe-Universitat Frankfurt, Working Paper Series No. 10.

[42]   DP 05/3, para 1.4.

[43]   *Ibid.*

this situation was potentially confusing for investors, and required a reassessment with regard to whether there was a need for greater clarity and consistency in terms of the regulatory controls and protections on offer. According to the FSA, important in achieving consistency was the principle of treating like cases alike:[44] In short, the complexity and heightened fragmentation through which investors were already able to gain access to wider-range 'alternative' products meant that there was a risk that consumers could be confused by the different products on offer and the different distribution channels though which such products were made available. In the FSA's opinion, this confusion was liable to result in mis-buying or mis-selling.[45]

2.3　The 'External Influences' Argument

A third and final factor which shaped significantly the FSA's policy concerned external influences, in particular international developments and EU legal constraints. With regard to the former, the FSA thought it notable that developed countries such as Australia, Switzerland and Canada permitted retail investors readier access to a wider range of investment products than was the case in the UK.[46] However, a more important influence – indeed constraining factor – was the impact of EU legal developments, which significantly reduced the FSA's scope for unilateral action.

Unless amendments are needed to primary legislation, the FSA implements EU law via changes to its Handbook. One major change which required FSA action was with regard to UCITS schemes. Although originally designed for unsophisticated, highly risk averse investors, UCITS III introduced important and far-reaching changes to the UCITS regime,[47] liberalising the range of financial products in which a UCITS scheme could invest. Accordingly, the FSA has been obliged to give effect to such liberalizations through changes to its Handbook. What is more, the implementation of UCITS IV and the AIFM Directive will require more significant modifications to the FSA's Handbook.

The presence of EU law as an external factor – and the liberalizations which it has introduced – has therefore circumscribed the FSA's freedom of action.[48] Indeed, the FSA also recognized that its scope for manoeuvre

---

[44]　*Ibid.*, para 4.19.
[45]　*Ibid.*, p 9.
[46]　*Ibid.*, para 4.17.
[47]　See, *supra,* fn. 7, and accompanying text.
[48]　See, DP 05/3, para 1.7.

was further limited by the E-Commerce Directive which provides a framework to enable cross-border marketing of e-commerce/online services – including the cross-border marketing of online investment products – by electronic means. The FSA's approach to the Directive has been based on the self-evident reality that websites advertising products in one Member State may be accessed by consumers in other Member States. Since different Members States have different rules as to the provision of alternative investments to consumers, the E-Commerce Directive – by permitting the cross-border marketing of certain alternative investment products – severely limited the FSA's ability to prohibit the advertising of certain types of investments to UK consumers, save in exceptional circumstances.[49] The effect of the Directive is that 'a fund of hedge funds authorized in Germany can be offered to and purchased by retail investors in the UK, even though such a fund established in the UK or outside the EEA could not be.'[50] Thus, to the extent that EU law permitted the UK to adopt a stricter regime than other EU Members states, the FSA recognized that UK investors would nevertheless be able to have unrestricted product access outside the UK (a situation which would also have had the effect of placing UK product providers at a competitive disadvantage to providers based in certain other Member States).

Limiting further the FSA's discretion to apply its own protective host State provisions is Article 19(6) of the Markets in Financial Instruments Directive (MiFID), which requires segregation of products into 'complex' and 'non-complex'. Under MiFID, only non-complex products can be sold on an execution-only basis (i.e. without advice or any form of test to determine the appropriateness of the investment for the consumer). By contrast, the sale of so-called 'complex products' is in all cases subject to a consumer-specific suitability test. Determining what is and what is not a complex product is therefore critical. According to MiFID, shares admitted to trading on a regulated market, money market instruments, bonds and other forms of securitized debt, and all UCITS, are non-complex instruments.[51] Accordingly, UCITS can be sold cross-border on an execution-only basis, without advice or a

---

[49]   The FSA can seek to make use of certain derogations in the Directive which require, for example, the provision of essential information to UK consumers.

[50]   DP 05/3, para 2.21.

[51]   On 8 December 2010, the European Commission launched a consultation on the review of MiFID. According to the Commission, one possible change is the removal of the *automatic* classification of UCITS schemes as non-complex.

test of appropriateness. In view of the fact that UCITS III has expanded the range of eligible assets for UCITS schemes, the net result has been a significant liberalization of what products can legally be sold to UK retail investors without the need for advice or the satisfaction of a suitability test.

Following lengthy consultation, the FSA embraced the EU's liberalization policy but sought to buttress it by way of a three-pronged regulatory strategy:[52] first, by reinforcing its existing consumer information and awareness work in a way which 'stress[ed] the need for consumers to invest proportionately in investment products';[53] second, by emphasising product provider responsibility as part of its broader initiative on Treating Customers Fairly (TCF); and thirdly, by expanding its range of Non-UCITS Retail Schemes (NURSs) (which were already widely marketable to retail consumers) to include funds of unregulated schemes, subject to appropriate regulatory safeguards.

The end result of the FSA's policy response to the issue of greater retail access to wider-range investments, is a complex and fragmented regulatory landscape, the contours of which we now set out to explore and subsequently critique.

3.   THE REGULATORY LANDSCAPE

Currently, retail investors in the UK have access to alternative ('wider-range') investment products and funds (some of which are more easily accessible than others) in a number of different ways set out and discussed below. In certain key respects, wider access has been the result of significant changes initiated at the EU level and subsequently given effect to in the UK by amendments to the FSA's Handbook. Imminent reforms to harmonized retail investment funds via UCITS IV, and the implementation of the AIFM Directive, are sure to result in further changes, as market players position themselves to take advantage of new market options and/or avoid new regulatory burdens.

In the UK, retail access to alternative investments may follow as a result of access to any combination of the following:[54]

---

[52]   FS 06/3, para 1.4.
[53]   *Ibid.*
[54]   Note also, that UK retail investors can access wider-range, alternative, investments available in some other EEA countries by virtue of the E-Commerce Directive – investment products in relation to which the FSA has limited control.

**3.1   Onshore or Offshore 'Unregulated Collective Investment Schemes'
Managed by Onshore UK Managers**

For the purposes of UK law, most hedge funds constitute unregulated
collective investment schemes.[55] This is because of the potentially unlimited range of products and asset classes in which they are free to invest,
the investment strategies typically deployed and the governance arrangements around which funds are structured. However, despite the fact that
unregulated schemes do not need to comply with the sort of detailed
regulatory provisions applying to regulated schemes (in particular, with
regard to their investment powers and governance arrangements) any
persons operating and establishing such schemes by way of business in the
UK are subject to the FSMA 2000. Most significantly, such persons must
be either *authorized* or *exempt* persons.[56] They must also comply with the
FSA's Principles for Business, its requirements on 'Senior Management
Arrangements, Systems and Controls' (e.g. to 'take reasonable care to
establish and maintain such systems and controls as are appropriate to
its business' (SYSC 3.1.1R)), and the market abuse regime. In addition,
any individuals performing 'controlled functions' in accordance with s 59
will require approval by the FSA. Furthermore, as unregulated schemes
they cannot be marketed to the public. Instead, the promotion of such
schemes must comply with the relevant parts of the FSA's Handbook (e.g.
Conduct of Business Sourcebook (COBS)), which governs the means by
which authorized persons may market unregulated schemes, as well as the

---

[55]   See FSMA, 2000 s 235 (which defines a 'collective investment scheme'
(CIS)). Only three types of funds – schemes – may be marketed to the general
public in compliance with the FSA's CIS Sourcebook (COLL): UCITS schemes;
non-UCITS retail schemes (NURS) and 'recognized' schemes from outside the
UK. The term 'unregulated collective investment schemes' refers to all CISs that
fall outside the category of regulated schemes (whether those regulated schemes
are domestic or overseas).

[56]   Authorization is typically acquired by way of securing what is known as a
'Part 4 permission' granted under the FSMA 2000, Part 4. Applicants must satisfy
the 'Threshold Conditions' set out in Schedule 6 of the Act. Once an applicant has
been granted a permission to engage in a particular type (or types) of 'regulated
activity' the applicant is deemed an 'authorized person' for the purposes of the Act.
However, the practice of hedge fund management does not currently constitute a
separate regulated activity under the Regulated Activities Order (RAO) for which
a *specific* permission is required. As a result, hedge fund managers/advisors who
are located in the UK – and who provide investment advice and make day-to-day
investment decisions for offshore 'master funds' – will be authorized to do so as a
consequence of their permission to manage or advise on investments generally (see
arts 37 and 53 of the RAO, respectively).

provisions of the Financial Services and Markets Act 2000 (Promotion of Collective Investment Schemes) (Exemptions) Order 2001 (SI 2001/1060) (as amended), which exempts certain communications in respect of the promotion of unregulated schemes.

In essence, the relevant rules in relation to the promotion of unregulated schemes as contained in the FSA's Handbook,[57] stipulate that authorized persons may only promote such schemes to 'eligible counterparties'[58] and 'professional clients' (both groups being deemed sufficiently sophisticated to take care of their own interests) and, in very limited circumstances, to less sophisticated investors.[59] Accordingly, in certain – admittedly very limited circumstances – some so-called 'sophisticated retail investors' may have access to such funds in so far as they fall within the above definitions. Given that to date many hedge funds commonly stipulate very high minimum investment amounts – typically US$ 100000 or more – retail customers have not featured highly as potential investors in individual hedge funds. However, the indications are that minimum levels of investment are beginning to fall, offering some, albeit limited, scope for sophisticated retail investors to take advantage of such schemes.[60]

3.2   Onshore Listed Hedge Funds and Funds of Hedge Funds

In certain circumstances, an actual hedge fund or, more likely, a 'fund of funds' hedge fund, may find it advantageous to seek an onshore listing as

---

[57]   See COBS 4.12 (and its accompanying Annex). Similar rules also apply to the promotion of authorized 'qualified investor schemes' (QISs)). QIS are a type of FSA authorized investment fund (AIF). See *infra* n 81, and accompanying text.

[58]   See FSA, Handbook, Glossary.

[59]   See the FSA's Conduct of Business Sourcebook (COBS) 4.12.4 (i.e. a so-called category 8 person). If the customer approaches the intermediary and asks about investing in a hedge fund, then it is possible for the firm to give advice through a one-off communication under Article 15 of The Financial Services and Markets Act 2000 (Promotions of Collective Investment Schemes) (Exemptions) Order 2001 (SI 2001/1060) (as amended). According to FSMA 2000 s 241, authorized persons who communicate (in breach of FSMA 2000, s 238) or approve (in breach of FSMA 2000, s 240) an invitation or inducement to participate in an unregulated investment scheme are liable for damages under s 150 at the suit of a private investor who has suffered loss. See also, *Seymour v Ockwell* [2005] EWHC 1137; [2005] PNLR 39 (concerning the promotion of an unregulated scheme in breach of similar provisions in the Financial Services Act 1986).

[60]   Retail investors – even very unsophisticated investors – may of course be exposed indirectly to unregulated collective investment schemes by virtue of the fact that pensions funds and other institutional investors in which they have invested have themselves invested in such funds.

a *corporate vehicle* on the main market of the London Stock Exchange.[61] Although such funds will have access to a deeper pool of investment capital – primarily because of a wider investor base – they are, however, subject to stricter regulatory requirements than would be the case if the fund remained offshore.[62]

As their name implies, funds of funds hedge funds invest only in other hedge funds, with diversification benefits for their investors.[63] Domestic hedge funds and 'funds of funds' investment companies can, in principle, secure a 'listing' for their securities on the Official List provided they comply with certain requirements set out in the Listing Rules. Under the new listing regime,[64] the only route open to a closed-ended or open-ended investment company seeking a listing of its equity securities on the Official List is by way of a Premium Listing.[65] A Premium Listing denotes a company which satisfies the UK's highest standards of regulation and corporate governance (as opposed to a 'Standard Listing' which denotes that the company has met minimum EU standards). That said, a closed-ended

---

[61]   See: ss 833 and 834 of the Companies Act 2006. Such companies do not need to seek authorisation from the FSA. However, the manager of an investment trust company must seek authorisation from the FSA, since such a manger is carrying on a regulated activity under the FSMA 2000. It should also be noted that investment companies that are quoted on the Alternative Investment Market (AIM) do not currently qualify for investment trust company status. However, it is proposed that this will be amended so that the shares of an investment trust can be listed on any regulated market: On July 27, HMRC, HM Treasury and the Department for Business, Innovation & Skills published a consultation document which sets out proposals for a new investment trust regime.

[62]   See, *infra* n 64, and accompanying text.

[63]   The downside is, of course, that additional management fees are incurred. Furthermore, investment trust companies are usually closed-ended vehicles. Thus if the investor wishes to redeem his investment he must do so by selling his shares in the secondary market. The share price of a closed ended vehicle is a function of the supply and demand for its shares. Thus there is a risk that the price at which an investor sells his shares is at a discount to the net asset value of the company.

[64]   The relevant regime has undergone significant reform recently. The current rules are the culmination of a three-year review of the structure of the UK Listing Regime which had its origins in the FSA's 2007 Listing Review of Investment Entities – a review which, in fact, formed the catalyst for a much broader review of the whole Listing Regime.

[65]   Closed-ended funds are not CIS within s 235 FSMA 2000: art 21 FSMA 2000 (Collective Investment Schemes) Order made under s 235(5), FSMA 2000. Accordingly they are not subject to the usual promotion restrictions which apply to unregulated CIS. Open-ended investment companies (OEICs) are defined in s 236 FSMA 2000 and are subject to the Open-ended Investment Companies Regulations 2001.

investment fund or open-ended investment company is permitted to have a Standard Listing for any *additional class* of equity shares it issues, but only if it already has (and intends to maintain) a premium listing of an existing class of its equity shares.

Closed-ended investment funds must comply with Chapter 15 of the Listing Rules which, as well as stipulating rules specific to closed-ended investment companies, also includes other Listing Rules with which such companies must comply (e.g. related party transactions).[66] Open-ended investment companies must comply with LR 16 and any other relevant Listing Rules stipulated therein.

Where the company is an investment trust company (and the above rules have been complied with), its shares may be marketed to the public in much the same way, and subject to the same protections under the FSMA 2000, Part 6, as is the case with respect to the shares of any other commercially listed company.[67]

In sum, although it is difficult for hedge funds to meet the criteria for listing in the UK (and, accordingly, the listing of such funds is uncommon), 'fund of funds' hedge funds can (and do) list in the UK, because they invest in portfolios of hedge funds on a conventional long-term basis. In this way, retail investors are capable of gaining exposure to alternative investment products and strategies, albeit of a somewhat limited nature.

3.3   Domestic UCITS III Funds (Newcits)

As we have already seen, the governance structures and nature of the investment activity typical of most hedge funds mean that it is not easy for them to satisfy the requirements set out in the regime for listed investment entities. For similar reasons, hedge funds are also unable to fit within the UCITS regime (governed by the UCITS Directives and given effect to in the UK by way of the FSA's Handbook). The fact that many alternative investment funds are not covered by UCITS means that they cannot

---

[66]   As noted earlier, actual hedge funds are likely to encounter difficulties in complying with these rules since they must, *inter alia*, have an adequate spread of risks, and engage in material disclosures with regard to investment policies and expenses. Brevan Howard's BH Global Macro hedge fund was the first such fund to list in the UK. (2007), 'Freshfields and Simmons List the First Closed-end Fund on LSE', *The Lawyer*, 13 February.

[67]   Consequently, a person who has, for example, acquired securities in a fund, or a fund of hedge funds, as result of defective listing particulars, may (provided they can show loss in respect of the securities) bring an action for compensation under the FSMA 2000 s 90.

benefit from the Directive's passport arrangements, and so cannot be marketed throughout the EU. However, as a result of certain liberalizations contained in UCITS III (which makes provision for sophisticated, albeit relatively heavily regulated, UCITS III funds), this situation has begun to change rapidly, enabling the pan-European marketing of so-called UCITS hedge funds (or Newcits, as they are sometimes known).[68]

Accordingly, UCITS III now makes provision for retail investors to have wider access to alternative investments, albeit within the context of a relatively heavily regulated environment. As noted above,[69] greater retail exposure to alternative investments was principally achieved by liberalising the range of assets in which a UCITS scheme could invest. Significantly, this freedom was clarified in 2007 by the Eligible Assets Directive (2007/16/EC) ('EAD') which provided detailed definitions for certain terms contained in UCITS III pertaining to 'eligible assets' for investment by UCITS funds.[70] Consequently, although UCITS funds are still prohibited from investing directly in hedge funds, they can nevertheless gain exposure to hedge funds indices through financial derivatives instruments.[71] Moreover, such derivatives can be used to leverage the fund by up to 100 per cent of the fund's assets, subject to an overarching requirement to prudently spread the fund's investment risk.[72] Although a UCITS investment manager must still comply with a variety of investment restrictions – e.g. that no more than 10 per cent of net asset value ('NAV') of the UCITS fund is invested in any single security – under UCITS IV,

---

[68] Elias, C. (2010), 'Hedge Fund Regulation: UCITS Provide Sweet Alternative' *Westlaw Business Currents* (23 September, 2010). Almost half of institutional investors invested in hedge funds already invest in, or are considering an allocation to, UCITS style hedge funds: (2010), 'Hedge Funds warming to UCITS III', 10 March, 2010, *Hedge Funds Review*, www.hedgefundsreview.com/hedge-funds-review/news/1596110/investors-warming-ucits-hedge-funds, accessed 10 January 2011.

[69] *Supra,* fn. 7 and accompanying text.

[70] Mason, I. and Cornish, M. (2009), 'United Kingdom' in Mason, I. and Cornish, M. (eds), *International Guide to Hedge Fund Regulation*, Bloomsbury Professional, para 19.11.

[71] For an argument critical of the inclusion of hedge fund indices in the list of eligible assets under UCITS III, see, Lhabitant, F. (2007), 'Hedge Fund Indices for Retail Investors: UCITS Eligible or Not Eligible?' *Derivatives Use, Trading and Regulation* 12, 275.

[72] Mason and Cornish, *supra*, fn. 70. Before these changes, UCITS schemes were only allowed to invest in derivatives "for the purposes of 'efficient portfolio management' (EPM), that is to say, for the purposes of reducing risk or costs, or in order to generate additional capital or income for the scheme in accordance with an acceptably low level of risk." FSA DP 05/3, para 2.12.

new structural arrangements will be available for the first time which will enhance opportunities for funds to adopt new structural innovations. In particular, UCITS IV will facilitate the use of so-called 'master-feeder structures', permitting a UCITS 'feeder' fund to invest as much as 85 per cent of its NAV in another UCITS 'master' fund.[73] Furthermore, simplified notification procedures and improved supervisory co-operation are thought likely to boost the success of the UCITS brand.[74]

The overall effect of these reforms to the UCITS framework as it was originally designed, is to provide retail investors with considerably wider access to wider-range 'alternative' products than have hitherto been passportable throughout the EU. Moreover, when coupled with changes brought about by the MiFID Directive classifying UCITS as non-complex products, and thus as being capable of being sold on an execution-only basis, there has been a significant extension of the range of investment products which can legally be sold to UK retail investors without the need for advice or the satisfaction of a suitability test.[75]

3.4   Non-UCITS Retail Schemes (NURS)

Non-UCITS retail schemes are authorized funds which – as the name indicates – do not comply with the UCITS framework (and therefore are not currently harmonized and therefore not currently passportable). Such schemes have wider investment and borrowing powers than those laid down under the UCITS Directives (but not as wide as NURS that operate as funds of alternative investment funds – see 3.5 below – or as wide as Qualified Investor Schemes – see 3.6 below). In view of the fact that NURS are retail schemes, they may be marketed to the general public, but subject to strict promotion rules. Managers wishing to offer NURS need to become authorized persons and to abide by the FSA's rules as set out in COLL 5.6: 'Investment powers and borrowing limits for non-UCITS retail schemes'. For example, NURS may (a) invest up to 10 per cent of the value of scheme property in transferable securities or money-market instruments issued by any single body; (b) invest up to 20 per cent in aggregate of the value of the scheme property in transferable securities, which are not approved securities and unregulated schemes; (c) invest in a wider range of schemes, which do not comply with the requirements of the UCITS Directive; (d)

---

[73]   *Ibid.* The remaining 15 per cent can be invested in ancillary liquid assets and derivatives for hedging purposes. *Ibid.*, para 19.11.

[74]   HM Treasury and FSA, *Transposition of UCITS IV: Consultation Document* (December 2010) para 1.2.

[75]   However, see, *supra,* fn. 51.

include gold in the scheme property (up to a limit of 10 per cent of the value of the scheme property); (e) include immovables in the scheme property; and (f) borrow on a non-temporary basis without any specific time limit as to repayment of the borrowing. Authorized managers must nevertheless ensure the NURS provides a 'prudent spread of risk'.[76]The overall effect of the NURS regime is the granting of significant investment freedoms (and greater retail exposure to wider-range 'alternative' investments), subject to what are seen by the FSA as suitable regulatory controls.

3.5   Non-UCITS Retail Schemes (NURS) Operating as Funds of Alternative Investment Funds (FAIFs)

In March 2010, following extensive FSA consultation, a new type of NURS vehicle was introduced into the UK retail market: funds of alternative investment funds (FAIFs). The introduction of this investment vehicle mirrors developments in some other EU Members states, such as France, Germany, Spain, and Ireland. The introduction of FAIFs into the UK market therefore provides retail investors with a domestic based open-ended alternative to close-ended UK-listed, non-FSA-authorized, investment trust companies which operate as funds of hedge funds. In essence, an FSA authorized FAIF takes the form of a NURS (and thus shares many of the characteristics and investment restrictions which apply to NURS),[77] save that in certain respects they have wider investment powers. These powers are set out in the FSA's Handbook, COLL 5.7: 'Investment powers and limits for non-UCITS retail schemes operating as funds of alternative investment funds'. Most significantly, whereas NURS may not invest more than 20 per cent of scheme assets in unregulated collective schemes, this rule is relaxed with regard to FAIFs.

In order to ensure adequate unitholder protection, FAIF managers are required to carry out initial and ongoing due diligence in selecting underlying funds to determine, inter alia, whether: (a) the fund provides sufficient information upon which to base responsible decision-making; (b) the assets in the underlying scheme are held by a third party independently of its manager; (c) the valuation of schemes within the FAIF and the maintenance of a fund's accounting records are segregated from the scheme's investment management process;[78] and (d) each of the funds in which the

---

[76]   COLL 5.6.3R.

[77]   For example, (a) the funds in which a FAIF invests cannot themselves invest more than 15% of their value in other funds; (b) a FAIF's borrowing powers are restricted to 10%; and (c) a FAIF cannot invest in commodities.

[78]   There is, however, no obligation to have an independent valuer.

FAIF invests is independently audited in accordance with international accounting standards. The effective operation of these mechanisms is critical to the aim of promoting investor protection, since FAIFs are more likely to have greater exposure to more complex, less liquid, and thus more difficult to value, assets than ordinary NURS.

FAIFs are also able to take advantage of certain structural freedoms that are not available to ordinary NURS, such as the use of master-feeder structures. In effect, such structures enable a UK-managed fund to invest all of its capital in an existing FAIF (provided that the scheme operates in a way that is consistent with the FSA's rules). Typically, the 'master' fund and its service operations are based offshore (often for tax purposes) and UK investors invest in the master fund by way of the onshore based and managed 'feeder' fund. This is an option denied to NURS since they are prohibited from investing more than 35 per cent of the scheme's assets in any single collective investment scheme.

Since FAIFs are non-UCITS they are unable to benefit from the single passport regime and, accordingly, may not be marketed throughout the EEA – though they may be marketed to the public in the UK by an authorized person in compliance with the FSA's Handbook.[79] It should also be noted that the impact of the AIFM Directive, which introduces new regulations affecting the operators of all collective investment schemes investing in alternative investments, will impact on the FSA's general NURS regime and the regime as it applies to FAIFs.[80] As a result, the FSA expects that the FAIF rules will require further refinement in the future.

3.6   Qualified Investor Schemes (QIS)

In 2004, the UK introduced Qualified Investor Schemes (QIS).[81] QIS are a type of FSA authorized investment fund (AIF) which have wider investment and borrowing powers than other AIFs, such as NURS, and which are 'open' only to 'eligible investors'.[82] In substance, this means that they

---

[79]   In view of the fact that UCITS III funds afford managers more flexible investment powers and benefit from passporting arrangements, they provide a serious rival to the new FAIF regime (which does not benefit from the passport arrangements).

[80]   PS 10/3, para 1.16.

[81]   See COLL 8 Annex 1R. Accordingly certain sophisticated retail investors may have access to such 'alternative' schemes, albeit only in very limited circumstances.

[82]   See COLL 8 Annex 1R.

can only be promoted to corporations, other institutional investors (such as pension funds and charities) or sophisticated individual investors who regularly invest significant sums and can be expected to understand the risks involved in investing in a wider range of investments.[83] However, to the extent that certain retail investors can demonstrate that they have sufficient expertise, experience, and knowledge to make their own investment decisions and understanding of the risks involved, such investors will also have access to QIS schemes.

4.   ASSESSING THE NEW REGULATORY LANDSCAPE

According to orthodox regulatory theory, where investors are sophisticated, the justification for regulatory intervention – particularly in the form of product regulation – is weak. The idea that such investors are able to protect their own interests is predicated on the assumption that since both parties – investors and fund operators/advisers – are of roughly equal bargaining power and have access to roughly equal amounts of relevant information, the agreements reached will be mutually beneficial and not one-sided. The claimed absence of significant information asymmetries means that there is said to be no market failure which requires regulatory action in the form of state-mandated investor protection measures.

As a result, any investment vehicle directed in the main at sophisticated players ought, within this characterisation, to be subject to no or, at most, 'light touch' regulation. As the Hedge Fund Standards Board (HFSB) – a London-based self-regulatory body for the pan-European hedge fund sector – has argued:[84]

> [m]ost hedge funds rely on sophisticated investors . . . with an increasing share of institutional monies. These are knowledgeable and sophisticated—or they have the resources to hire knowledgeable and sophisticated advisors—and therefore do not need the protection of regulators in the way retail investors do.

Underpinning this view is the idea that the combination of enlightened self-interest and the desire to avoid any loss of reputational capital result-

---

[83]   According to s 238(5) FSMA 2000 the FSA has the power to make rules permitting the promotion of certain unregulated CISs 'otherwise than to the general public'. In this respect, see: COBS 4.12.

[84]   *Submission from the Hedge Fund Standards Board (HFSB) to the European Commission public consultation on hedge funds,* www.hfsb.org/sites/10109/files/hfsb_submission_to_european_commission.pdf, (at 19), accessed 10 January 2011.

ing from the interplay of market forces, provides the optimal level of protection for such investors *given the costs of regulation*.

By contrast, where investors are less experienced and less able to exert bargaining power, significant market failures are thought likely to occur, particularly in relation to informational problems. Informational problems represent the most commonly cited market failure justification for much financial services regulation since, within the classical paradigm of exchange, it is on the basis of adequate amounts of accurate information that investors seek to make rational choices about where and how much to invest. However, in so far as the interplay of markets forces cannot supply a socially optimal level of information for investment decision-making, there is a risk that resulting transactions will infringe the notion of a mutually beneficial exchange, and lead to unfairness and a resultant misallocation of resources. Furthermore, even where good quality information is available, there may be factors – such as bounded rationality constraints, biases, framing issues, and the use of heuristics – which prevent individual investors from appreciating this information and making informed investment decisions based upon it.

Where regulation satisfies some form of cost-benefit criteria to ensure that it does not make the problem worse (that is to say, it does not lead to the imposition of regulation which has disproportionate costs or adverse unintended consequences), then regulation is said to be justified in correcting the identified market failures. In view of the likely market and informational failures associated with exposure to alternative investments, such as hedge funds, significant investor protection measures would seem to be necessary in order to protect retail consumers who invest in such products. In other words, greater retail exposure to wider-range 'alternative' investments would seem to require some concomitant commitment by the regulatory authorities to a proportionate regulatory response, which seeks to ensure that retail investors have protections commensurate with the risks they face.

In the UK, this market failure analysis may go some way towards explaining the FSA's approach to translating the EU's policy of liberalization in relation to certain alternative investments into regulatory action. In essence, increased retail exposure to wider-range, 'alternative', investments is most likely to be associated with UCITS III (newcits) investment vehicles, NURS vehicles, and the new NURS-FAIF regime – all retail vehicles with investment powers that are wider than those traditionally associated with retail investments. Central to this exposure is the FSA's attempts to address perceived market failures via regulatory requirements, principally, by embedding a process of due diligence and proactive risk management by authorized fund managers as the cornerstone of its liberalization policy.

Emphasis is thus placed on a combination of *ex ante* and *ex post* monitoring by authorized fund mangers in relation to the underlying funds' investment policy, risk management techniques, operational infrastructure, commercial terms, and governance arrangements.[85] Accordingly, fund mangers need to ensure that they have adequate amounts of information upon which to make rational judgements so as to maximize the chances of generating superior returns, while at the same time minimizing exposure to unnecessary risks. Insofar as retail investors are unable to perform due diligence on the underlying funds and their investments (which will almost always be the case in view of the complexity associated with the underlying investments), expert fund managers – subject to FSA rules and FSA discipline – will in effect act as surrogates for such investors and perform due diligence and an ongoing monitoring role on their behalf.

4.1 Transparency Concerns

A distinguishing feature of increased exposure to alternative investments (and, in particular, hedge funds) is, however, a general lack of transparency regarding their holdings, investment strategies, and governance structures.[86] This lack of transparency makes it difficult for even supposedly sophisticated investment managers, acting on behalf of their retail customers, to ensure that the necessary standards of care are initially and on an ongoing basis adhered to. Despite the fact that information flows about hedge funds and the investment strategies employed by them have shown some signs of improvement, the widely acknowledged opacity of the hedge fund industry, and the complexity of the instruments traded, militate against self-protection of the type envisaged by the FSA's rules – even by supposedly more sophisticated investors or investment managers. Consequently, significant informational asymmetries are likely to arise, resulting in sub-optimal investment decision-making. As the FSA has previously acknowledged:[87]

---

[85] At the EU level for packaged retail investment products generally, see, the European Commission's Communication on Packaged Retail Investment Products (PRIPS) (2009) (COM (2009) 204) which represents an attempt to revamp the EU's harmonized disclosure and advice rules with regard to investment products.

[86] Transparency concerns have long been perceived as a source of potential problems associated with hedge funds: Kovas, *supra,* fn. 41, 7. For an excellent discussion of general concerns about retail exposure to alternative investments, see, Moloney, N. (2010), *How to Protect Investors: Lessons from the EC and the UK*, Cambridge, Cambridge University Press, 168–79.

[87] DP 05/04, at 33.

it may be difficult for some investors to truly understand the increasingly complex strategies various hedge funds are pursuing, or track style drift. Hedge fund prospectuses are deliberately drafted in a very broad manner so that they do not restrict the manager's flexibility to seize new investment opportunities.

This is likely to be the case not only for supposedly sophisticated private investors, but also for skilled FSA-authorized fund managers.[88] Furthermore, according to the SEC: '[i]n practice, even very large and sophisticated investors often have little leverage in setting [the] terms of their investment and accessing information about hedge funds'.[89] Again, to the extent that this holds true, many hedge fund investors and investment managers investing in other hedge funds are offered 'membership' of the fund on what effectively amounts to a 'take it or leave it' basis, rather than as the result of any meaningful form of 'bargain'.[90] Accordingly, the protections that are offered to retail investors through the putative due diligence of authorized, supposedly expert fund managers are, in practice, more limited than they might at first sight seem.

These concerns are explored, below, in greater detail, focusing in particular on: the funds' freedoms to adopt new organisational structures; difficulties associated with the valuation of hedge fund assets; and preferential treatment associated with the use by hedge funds of 'side letters'.

4.2 Organisational Structures

Recent reforms – some of which have taken effect and some which have yet to be implemented – make it feasible for fund managers to deploy new and potentially more efficient, organisational arrangements, such as master-feeder structures. In effect, these freedoms remove 'the necessity to replicate onshore an existing offshore fund purely to gain access to the UK retail market.'[91] However, the use of such master-feeder structures amounts in effect to a double structural layer which is liable to exacerbate

---

[88] See Kovas, *supra*, fn. 41, 13. Since a major source of risk resides in the quality and integrity of the hedge fund manager himself, and since the manger is in the best position to provide information in relation to the assessment of attendant risks, there is inevitable an acute information asymmetry.

[89] Securities and Exchange Commission (SEC), *Implications of the Growth of Hedge Funds* (September 2003) at 47 (and sources cited therein).

[90] However, see *infra* n 98 and accompanying text in relation to so-called 'cornerstone' investors who may be able to bargain for preferential terms at the expense of other investors. Such investors are, however, the exception rather than the rule.

[91] CP 08/4, Annex 1, p 1.

opacity concerns in relation to the underlying funds.[92] Moreover, the introduction of master-feeder structures lends itself to greater opacity with regard to management fees.[93] In view of the fact that consumers may not fully appreciate the effect that such charges have on fund performance, a lack of clarity about the way in which management fees are calculated has the potential to lead to considerable consumer detriment. Finally, the use of such structures militates against proportionate and effective regulatory protections, since the FSA would 'only be authorising the onshore FAIF investment "shell" without having any direct regulatory control over the underlying investments [i.e. the offshore master fund]'.[94]

4.3 Valuation and Liquidity Problems

This general lack of transparency for both retail investors and their FSA-authorized fund managers is likely to be particularly acute in relation to the valuation of the underlying hedge fund assets, the credibility of which is a fundamental aspect of widening retail access to alternative investment products. Again, despite the fact that significant strides forward have been made in helping to address concerns about valuations, acute difficulties subsist in ensuring accurate valuations.[95] Robust and reliable valuations are central to the operation of the hedge fund industry and in securing investor protection, since the NAV of each fund's portfolio of financial instruments represents the means by which subscriptions and redemptions are calculated. To the extent that the fund's assets are liquid, and traded on a recognized investment exchange (such as the London Stock Exchange) or some other liquid market for which prices are readily available, valuations will be relatively uncontroversial. However, where complex and/or illiquid financial instruments represent a not insignificant proportion of the fund's assets, serious problems are likely to arise. These problems stem from the fact that such instruments are infrequently traded and, thus, are inherently more difficult to value.

Furthermore, difficulties associated with highly complex, illiquid assets are compounded by the conflict of interest between the hedge fund manager and the fund's other investors. Because illiquid instruments do not trade regularly, managers are more likely to be involved in helping to

---

[92] *Ibid.*, p 2.
[93] *Ibid.*
[94] *Ibid.*, para 4.5.
[95] McVea, H. (2008), 'Hedge Fund Asset Valuations: The Work of the International Organisation of Securities Commissions (IOSCO)' *International and Comparative Law Quarterly* 57, 1.

facilitate valuations by, for example, providing relevant information and price quotes.[96] Accordingly, there is a risk that management's decisions in this respect will be polluted by the fact that the valuation of certain instruments within the fund's portfolio will influence the level of performance fees that managers receive. The use of leverage – with its capacity to amplify potential losses – heightens further a manager's incentive to inflate valuations. Overvalued assets are, in turn, likely to adversely impact on investors and to hamper price formation more generally.

An additional problem is that the underlying investments in the fund may give risk to liquidity problems in as much as they are difficult to liquidate, especially when the holders of such assets seek to exit the market in and around the same time.[97] Such exits are more likely during a crisis period, potentially resulting in forced asset sales and, in turn, compounding difficulties with market liquidity and efficient pricing. The existence of master-feeder structures as described above may exacerbate these difficulties, since keeping track of valuations and associated liquidity concerns in a *variety of underlying funds*, each specialising in a different portfolio of complex assets, is likely to be a more difficult task than monitoring the valuation and liquidity of complex assets in a *single* fund.

4.4   Preferential Treatment (Side Letters)

The existence of so-called 'side letters' represents a recurrent problem associated with alternative investment products generally and hedge funds in particular. In essence, these are supplementary agreements between the hedge fund and favoured investors. Such investors are often 'cornerstone' investors whose financial support is critical to the operation of the fund and who are therefore better able to negotiate for a 'bespoke' service.[98] As a result, a major strength associated with alternative products – that management and investors interests are strongly aligned – is likely to be absent. Preferential treatment for these investors typically includes fee waivers or fee rebates as well as special liquidity terms or redemption rates. The effect

---

[96]   To the extent that assets are 'marked to model' (i.e. where mathematical models are used to calculate value), further problems arise. These problems have been evident in relation to the models used to price structured finance instruments. Here, even supposedly sophisticated investors routinely purchased complex instruments which proved to be hugely overvalued.

[97]   'Lock up' periods may also operate such that investors are unable to redeem their units at will.

[98]   Spangler, T. (2010), *A Practitioner's Guide to Alternative Investment Funds*, 2nd edn., City & Financial Publishing 88.

of the existence of side letters has previously been recognized by the FSA.[99] Although the FSA is alert to the investor protection issues surrounding the use of side letters by alternative investment funds, UK authorized fund managers will need to monitor the existence of such arrangements in the hedge funds in which they invest, so as to ensure that any potential adverse effects associated with them are minimized or rendered nugatory.

4.5 The Financial Crisis: The Watchword is 'Caution'

The recent liberalization associated with wider-range, alternative, investment products plays out against a backdrop of unprecedented market and regulatory failures which were at the root of one of the most cataclysmic financial disasters in recent history. Three examples are perhaps sufficient to illustrate some of the deficiencies associated with regimes based on market discipline and supplemented by tailored 'external' regulation – in essence the basis upon which wider retail access to wider ranger investment in both the EU and the UK is predicated. First, the Madoff scandal – probably the largest investment fund fraud in history, involving losses estimated to be in the region of US\$50 billion. Here, weaknesses in market discipline, due diligence, and a lack of transparency, as well as regulatory incompetence facilitated 'a stunning fraud of epic proportions.'[100] Secondly, the implosion of the structured finance markets also illustrates glaring failures by supposedly sophisticated investors and often heavily regulated market-players in performing adequate due diligence over the instruments to which they were exposed. Moreover, despite the use of supposedly sophisticated risk assessment techniques, many mainstream financial institutions failed to price risk accurately. Indeed, as the FSA has itself recognized more generally, '[o]ne of the striking features of the recent financial crisis is how frequently governance bodies appear not to have challenged the major assumptions upon which their organization's investment strategy was based.'[101] Finally, in relation to the safe-keeping of clients' assets and clients' money – a crucial pillar of the FSA's investor protection framework under its CASS regime – FSA research has revealed

---

[99] FSA, *Hedge Funds: A Discussion of Risk and Regulatory Engagement* (Discussion Paper 05/04) 48.

[100] A. M. Calamari as quoted in Spangler, *supra*, fn. 98, 89.

[101] FSA (2010c), 'How developments in regulation may affect investment companies' (Speech by Tony Hanlon, Manager of the Asset Management Sector Team, FSA, 20 April 2010), www.fsa.gov.uk/pages/Library/Communication/Speeches/2010/0420_th.shtml, accessed 29 February 2011.

a regime seemingly honoured more in the breach than in the observance.[102] Failures include: poor management oversight and control; segregation errors during transitional periods resulting from operational and structural changes; and incomplete or inaccurate records. Although these failures have been the spur for renewed regulatory activity by the FSA to help clarify and strengthen its CASS regime, these efforts nevertheless represent yet another example of regulatory authorities attempting to 'close the stable door after the horse has bolted'.

Wider retail access to alternative, investments requires meaningful transparency, effective market discipline, assiduous due diligence and on-going monitoring, robust valuations, and the safe-keeping of clients' assets and money. The above examples offer little confidence that regulatory oversight over what are complex assets will prove in any way sufficient. On the contrary, these examples, suggest that the FSA's faith in the alchemy associated with a combination of market discipline supplemented by carefully crafted regulatory rules is misplaced. Yet, in the face of evidence that would seemingly counsel caution, the FSA persists with attempts to widen investment choice for retail investors. In this respect, choice is almost elevated to a fetish. In principle, denying choice is viewed as problematic since it limits autonomy; and evident dangers are downplayed in part on the basis that investors will not be forced to exercise choice.

The recent crisis has revealed our limited understanding of financial markets. It has also revealed failures at all levels (*market* and *regulatory* failures) and amongst investors generally (both sophisticated and unsophisticated) and market players with significant reputational capital. These *failures* should give us pause for thought. What is more, the fact that there has already been significant liberalization within the UCITS framework is not a sound argument for compounding potential problems associated with that framework through further liberalizations. Somewhat naively, this policy of deregulation which seeks to dismantle barriers impeding competition and constraining consumer choice is in large part reliant on a paradigm of regulation (and forms of regulation) which has hitherto proved incapable of meeting some of the key challenges it has been designed to address. In many key areas – e.g. valuations – the 'external regulation' amounts to little more than exhortations that valuations should be fair and robust and that there should be increased emphasis on the integrity of individuals and entities that have routinely

---

[102]   According to FSA findings 'compliance with CASS across the industry is poor': FSA (2010a), *Client Money & Asset Report* (January 2010) para 1.6.

shown themselves unwilling to grasp the full significance of their regulatory responsibilities.

5. CONCLUSION

The European investment funds sector is entering a period of unprecedented change. The implementation of the highly controversial AIFM Directive will establish for the first time a pan-EU harmonized regime for alternative investment products and strategies. Although this regime is directed at sophisticated investors, a significant feature of the funds industry both globally and in Europe, is a gradual erosion of the lines of demarcation separating investments and strategies traditionally associated with the retail market and those typically associated with the alternative investment sector, in particular with respect to hedge funds products and strategies. Most significantly, liberalizations associated with the UCITS brand (stemming from UCITS III reforms), as well as reforms at the Member State level – for example the FSA's own revamping of its NURS regime through the introduction of its new FAIFs – have enabled the market to evolve in such a way as to afford retail investors wider access to alternative investment products and strategies than ever before, and to those that have hitherto been associated with only sophisticated investors and/or non-harmonized funds.

As we have sought to argue above, while the impetus to encourage Europeans to take responsibility for their own financial future is understandable, and although the desire to facilitate the development of the 'state of the art' EU funds industry is laudable, there are nevertheless serious shortcomings with key aspects of the EU's policy of liberalization in this sphere – aspects which have received a relatively warm, if cautious, welcome by domestic regulators, notably the FSA. With regard to the FSA, much of the Agency's work is this area can, of course, be explained by a desire to rationalize an otherwise fragmented set of regulatory arrangements, and to respond to the practicalities and realities associated with implementing EU law. However, to the extent that the FSA's reforms in this area are based on a principled belief in the benefits of greater retail exposure to alternative investment products and strategies, this policy seems seriously deficient and short-sighted – shortcomings which go right to the heart of the EU's policy of liberalization in this sphere more generally.

Although many of the risks associated with greater retail exposure to wider-range alternative investments are widely known, insufficient weight appears to have been given to them. In other words, these acknowledged risks are not viewed as providing sufficient reasons for denying investor choice though regulatory prohibition. Rather, they are characterized as incidental difficulties that need only to be finessed in order to facilitate investor choice. What is more, the risks associated with such developments are downplayed inasmuch as the freedom of choice they confer on investors, need not in fact be exercised. Yet, faith in the ability of market discipline, enlightened self-interest and appropriately tailored regulatory rules, seems curiously misplaced, especially so in the light of previous failures associated with providing retail investors with exposure to wider range investment (e.g. the 'split caps' debacle) and with recent events associated with the financial crisis more generally (e.g. the Madoff scandal). Indeed, without better investor education and clear risk warnings, liberalization of the type being pioneered at both the EU and the national levels risks creating the impression that, as part of the new regulated universe for unsophisticated investors, the products on offer are safer than they actually are. Moreover, in the light of the moral hazard problems exposed by the recent bank bailouts, this new policy is untimely and ill-judged, since it is likely to exacerbate moral hazard by potentially extending the protection offered by compensation schemes to a wider range of funds than ever before, and by implying that the authorities will 'ride to the rescue' if fund failures expose retail customers to significant losses.[103] The inability or unwillingness of Europe's policy makers to put a much needed break on the liberalization of the alternative investment sector transforms what might otherwise be characterized as a bold development into a risky, even reckless, experiment.

BIBLIOGRAPHY

Borges, A. (2010), 'Market Reality Splits European and US Policies Towards Hedge Funds' (EuroHedge, June), www.hfsb.org/sites/10188/files/eh_0610_borges.pdf, accessed 11 January 2011.
Elias, C. (2010), 'Hedge Fund Regulation: UCITS Provide Sweet Alternative' *Westlaw Business Currents* (23 September).
European Commission (2005), *Green Paper on Enhancing the European Framework for Investment Funds* (July) COM(2005) 314 final; and *White Paper on Enhancing The Single Market Framework for Investment Funds* (November 2006) COM(2006)686 final.
Financial Services Authority (FSA) (2005), *Wider-range Retail Investment Products Consumer Protection in a Rapidly Changing World* (Discussion Paper, 05/3, June).

---

[103]   HM Treasury proposes extending scope of Financial Services Compensation Scheme to cover Ucits IV rules, http://citywire.co.uk/wealth-manager/treasury-proposes-extending-fscs-scope-under-ucits-iv-rules/a459779, accessed on 1 April, 2011.

FSA (2006), *Wider-range Retail Investment Products Consumer Protection in a Rapidly Changing World – Feedback on DP 05/3* (Feedback Statement, 06/3, March).

FSA (2007), *Funds of Alternative Investment Funds (FAIFs)* (Consultation Paper 07/6, March).

FSA (2008), *Funds of Alternative Investment Funds (FAIFs): Feedback on CP 07/6* and further consultation (Consultation Paper, 08/4, February).

FSA (2010a), *Client Money & Asset Report* (January).

FSA (2010b), *Funds of Alternative Investment Funds (FAIFs) (Including Feedback on CP08/4)* (Policy Statement 10/3, February).

FSA (2010c), 'How Developments in Regulation may Affect Investment Companies' (Speech by Tony Hanlon, Manager of the Asset Management Sector Team, FSA, 20 April), www.fsa.gov.uk/pages/Library/Communication/Speeches/2010/0420_th.shtml,

Gilson, R. and R. Mnookin (1985), 'Sharing Among the Human Capitalists: An Economic Inquiry into the Corporate Law Firm and How Partners Split Profits', *Stan. Law Rev.* **37**, 313.

Hedge Fund Standards Board, *Submission from the Hedge Fund Standards Board (HFSB) to the European Commission public consultation on hedge funds,* <www.hfsb.org/sites/10109/files/hfsb_submission_to_european_commission.pdf>.

HM Treasury and FSA (2010), *Transposition of UCITS IV: Consultation Document* (December).

IMA Submission published in House of Lords, *European Union Committee 3rd Report of Session 2009–10 Directive on Alternative Investment Fund Managers, Volume II: Evidence* (February, 2010) HL Paper 48–II, 251, www.publications.parliament.uk/pa/ld200910/ldselect/ldeucom/48/48ii.pdf, accessed 1 March 2011.

International Financial Services London (IFSL), *ISFL Research: Hedge Funds* 2010 (April 2010), www.thecityuk.com/media/2358/Hedge_Funds_2010.pdf, accessed 1 February 2011.

Lhabitant, F. (2007), 'Hedge Fund Indices for Retail Investors: UCITS Eligible or Not Eligible?' *Derivatives Use, Trading and Regulation*, **12**, 275.

Kovas (2004), 'Should Hedge Fund Products be Marketed to Retail Investors? A Balancing Act for Regulators', Institute for Law and Finance, Johann Wolfgang Goethe-Universitat Frankfurt, Working Paper Series No. 10.

Mason, I. and Cornish, M. (2009), 'United Kingdom' in Mason, I. and Cornish, M. (eds), *International Guide to Hedge Fund Regulation*, Haywards Heath, Bloomsbury Professional.

McVea, H. (2008), 'Hedge Fund Asset Valuations: The Work of the International Organisation of Securities Commissions (IOSCO)' *International and Comparative Law Quarterly* **57**, 1.

Moloney, N. (2006), 'The EC and the Hedge Fund Challenge: A Test Case for EC Securities Policy After the Financial Services Action Plan' *Journal of Corporate Law Studies* **6**(1), 1.

Moloney, N. (2010), *How to Protect Investors: Lessons from the EC and the UK*, Cambridge, Cambridge University Press.

Saunders, R. (2010), 'AIFM: Appalling Investment Fund Managers Directive?' *Asia News* (5 November 2010), www.ipe.com/asia/aifm-appalling-investment-fund-managers-directive_37807.php, accessed 1 March 2011.

Shadab, H. (2007–2008), 'Fending for Themselves: Creating a U.S. Hedge Fund Market for Retail Investors' *N.Y.U. J. Legis. & Pub. Pol'y* **11**, 251.

Spangler, T. (2010), *A Practitioner's Guide to Alternative Investment Funds*, 2nd edn., London: Sweet & Maxwell.

TheCityUK, *Fund Management 2010* (October 2010), www.thecityuk.com/media/188154/fund%20management 202010.pdf, accessed 1 February 2011.

6. Hedge fund reporting
*Felix Goltz and David Schröder**

INTRODUCTION

Hedge funds employ dynamic investment strategies and enjoy a high degree of freedom with regard to the instruments that they can hold in their portfolio. In addition, they can use short selling of securities and leverage. Consequently, alternative strategies are infinitely more complex than those of traditional funds. The complexity of hedge fund investments poses a challenge when it comes to an adequate and comprehensive hedge fund reporting. Although some of the key elements of hedge fund returns can easily be captured by appropriate indicators, other aspects are much more of a qualitative nature, and are thus more difficult to formalize.

This chapter serves as theoretical background to the question of appropriate hedge fund reporting practices. We outline the major challenges for hedge fund reporting and give an overview of the set of tools that is available to report the performance and risk of hedge fund investments. This chapter is divided in four sections. Section 1 demonstrates the importance and the challenges of hedge fund reporting, the regulation framework, as well as guidelines issued by governmental working groups and industry associations. Section 2 looks at the performance and risk measures used in hedge fund reporting. Although some of the standard measures are widely employed in practice, they are not always suitable from a theoretical standpoint. Section 3 examines specific issues that are of importance for hedge fund disclosure, such as leverage, liquidity, and operational risk. A final section concludes this chapter.

*   EDHEC-Risk Institute and University of London, Birkbeck College, respectively.

1. HEDGE FUND REPORTING: IMPORTANCE, CHALLENGES AND REGULATION

1.1 Motivation and Challenges of Hedge Fund Reporting

In an illustrative example, Foster and Young (2008b) show why detailed hedge fund reporting is indispensable – and difficult to achieve at the same time. They consider the case of a hedge fund manager who sells options that pay their holders a specific amount of money in case that a rare event occurs.[1] Then he invests the money obtained from selling the options and the collected hedge fund capital in treasury bonds – and does nothing. If he is lucky, the rare event does not occur over the option's lifetime, and consequently his fund will yield a rather high return, obtained from selling the options and the interest gained on the proceeds. In contrast, if the rare event occurs, investors incur a heavy loss. This hypothetical example makes clear why good hedge fund reporting is difficult to achieve: the mere disclosure of past returns may not be sufficient to reflect the underlying risk of a portfolio. What is more, even a very detailed risk reporting might not be helpful for investors: managers can in principle just add noise trading to their main investment strategy to disguise the underlying bets.

The example raises the question what the possible means are to establish more confidence for hedge fund investors. In the remainder of this section, we describe some of the possibilities to reduce informational asymmetries between investors and hedge fund managers, and their limitations.

1.1.1 Detailed reporting

The most important instrument to reduce the informational asymmetries between hedge fund management and investors is a detailed, consistent, and accurate hedge fund reporting. Return-based reporting allows investors to get a comprehensive picture of the past risks and returns. A comprehensive description of the most important performance and risk indicators is provided in Section 2 below. However, even a very detailed reporting cannot completely solve the problems related to hedge fund opaqueness. First of all, return-based hedge fund reporting is only backward looking. All information contained in a hedge fund report contains therefore only valuable information about the fund's expected future development under the premise that the investment strategy remains largely unchanged in the future and that the fund's overall investment

---

[1]   Such a rare event can be, e.g., a decline of the S&P500 by more than 20 per cent within one year.

environment is similar to the past. The rapidly changing strategies of hedge fund managers and occurrences of spectacular hedge fund closures following sudden changes in the markets prove that this is not always the case (even if the manager has positive intentions). Another problem is the abundance of the proposed performance and risk measures. Academics constantly propose new indicators, thereby improving and complicating things at the same time. Eling and Schumacher (2007) argue that many of the proposed performance measures lead to highly correlated rankings of hedge funds. On the other hand, Do et al. (2005) point out that traditional measures, such as the Sharpe ratio, can be very misleading when evaluating hedge funds. Next, many of the hedge fund performance measures can be gamed by managers. Examples of such techniques are provided by Goetzmann et al. (2007), while empirical evidence is provided by Bollen and Pool (2009). Reported returns of hedge funds are often much smoother than their true returns would be. Thus, smooth returns may be a sign of a manager that is gaming performance measures. This issue will be discussed in more detail in Section 3.2. Although Goetzmann et al. (2007) propose performance measures which are manipulation-proof, they are rarely used so far. A potential solution to the problems related to the disclosure of past returns is the holdings-based reporting approach. It aims to disclose the current holdings of hedge funds – which might however face opposition by managers. We come back to this reporting style in Section 3.3.

1.1.2   Auditing and external platforms

Another possibility to enhance trust between hedge funds and their investors is to include independent third parties in the reporting process. The involvement of such outside parties to validate the reported figures can take place at different stages. One possibility is to run the hedge fund via a managed account which then carries out the trading activity as directed by the hedge fund manager. The managed account platform can thus provide investors with the required information. Another option is to rely on external platforms, i.e. not to manage the hedge fund itself, but just to calculate the risk and performance measures of the fund which then can be forwarded to investors. Finally, a hedge fund can decide to let its reports be audited by a third party. Besides these external devices, hedge funds can also opt to implement internal controls such as delegating the determination of a fund's net asset value to an independent administrator. We come back to the issue of involving third parties in Section 3.6.

Third party audit or internal controls are, however, no guarantee of the correctness of a report – but only a signal in that direction. There are conflicts of interest between hedge funds and the audit company, which can lead to a suboptimal audit quality. Another drawback of hedge fund auditing is the high expertise required by audit companies. Since the investment strategies implemented by hedge fund managers evolve very quickly, auditing has sometimes difficulties in keeping up. Nevertheless, audit seems to have some positive effects on reporting quality. Liang (2003) shows that audited funds have more coherent data in hedge fund databases, which can be interpreted as a signal for higher reporting reliability.

1.1.3 Hedge fund fee structure

The rather complex fee structure of hedge funds with performance fees and high-water marks might lead to the conclusion that hedge fund managers' payment schemes are designed to align the interest of managers and investors. Unfortunately, this is not the case. Although fees help to mitigate the different interests of both sides to some extent, Foster and Young (2008a) show that it is generally impossible to design an incentives scheme that allows distinguishing between skilled managers and unskilled managers (including the fraudulent manager of the introductory example). Hence, unskilled managers may successfully mimic the behavior of a good manager over a certain time period, and thus earn high fees, without delivering any investment skill. In the light of their impossibility theorem, the fee structure of hedge funds does not seem to be a feasible way to increase investor confidence.

Overall, despite many caveats, hedge fund reporting remains a sensible way to reduce informational asymmetries between investors and managers, and thus create investor confidence. Any hedge fund reporting system will have its drawbacks, but detailed information on the hedge fund performance which is audited by an independent third party seems to be a reasonable basis for investors. Finally, regulators or industry associations can play a role in creating generally accepted reporting standards. We turn to this issue in the following sections.

1.2 Existing Regulation of Hedge Fund Disclosure

Although hedge fund disclosure is largely unregulated, hedge funds face a few governmental regulations in many countries. Hedge funds that are registered in the United States (US) have to comply with the US GAAP accounting standards. Many of the standards are concerned with valuation principles and thus do not affect hedge fund disclosure itself (e.g. FASB 157). However the FASB statement 107 (Disclosures about Fair Values of Financial Instruments) imposes some regulations for hedge funds. In the United Kingdom (UK), the Financial Services Authority has decided to use a principle-based regulation instead of setting up exact rules that specify all that is permitted or prohibited. Also, many regulatory issues regard other aspects than information disclosure. In the US, more recent attempts to regulate hedge fund disclosure have failed.[2] In the European Union, the proposed new directive on alternative investment fund managers (AIFM) is also aimed at hedge funds, and will therefore certainly have an impact on hedge fund disclosure.[3] A detailed overview on hedge fund regulation in other European countries has been provided by the European Fund and Asset Management Association (2005) and, more recently, by Athanassiou (2009).

1.3   Reporting Guidelines

Besides existing governmental regulation, there are attempts to impose 'best practices' or 'sound guidelines' on the hedge fund industry. Some of these proposals are issued by governmental organizations and financial authorities, often with the aim of reducing systematic risks in financial markets by encouraging better hedge fund governance and detailed hedge fund reporting standards. On the other side, national hedge fund manager associations and initiatives propose best practice guidelines in order to prevent increasing governmental regulation of the hedge fund industry, and to hinder the business of the industry's black sheep. Table 6.1 gives an overview on the most important guidelines on hedge funds.

The above list includes only the most important guidelines. Many other countries have their own guidelines, such as the AIMA Australia, or the FSA Dubai. In addition, there are other standards for risk management practices that are not specifically designed for hedge funds, such as those of the Risk Standards Working Group, the CFA, or the Investor Risk Committee. Many of the best practices are of very general nature, and remain very undemanding. They do not specify exact rules for hedge fund managers, but give a rather broad overview of what the hedge fund

---

[2]   In 2004, the SEC designed a new rule that would have required hedge fund managers to register as investment advisors, including disclosure on many critical issues about hedge fund governance. However, in 2006, the US Court of Appeals vacated the rule.

[3]   The AIFM Directive was adopted in November 2010 and is to be implemented by January 2013 at the earliest. However, only a small Section of the AIFM Directive is devoted to hedge fund reporting. Most of these disclosure requirements are already contained in many of the voluntary guidelines published over the past years (see Section 1.3). Only hedge funds with high levels of leverage will be subject to major additional reporting and disclosure requirements under the AIFM Directive.

Table 6.1 Best practices and guidelines for hedge funds

Date	Region	Name	Organization	Content
2008	US	Best Practices for the Hedge Fund Industry – Asset Managers' Committee	PWG (President's Working Group on Financial Markets)	Overarching Guidelines for asset managers
2008	US	Best Practices for the Hedge Fund Industry – Investors' Committee	PWG (President's Working Group on Financial Markets)	Overarching Guidelines for hedge fund investors
2007	US	Sound Practices for Hedge Fund Managers	MFA (Managed Funds Association)	Overarching Guidelines for asset managers
2007	Europe	Guide to Sound Practices for Hedge Fund Managers	AIMA (Alternative Investment Management Association)	Overarching Guidelines for asset managers
2007	International	Principles for the Valuation of Hedge Fund Portfolios	IOSCO (International Organization of Securities Commissions)	Hedge Fund Valuation
2007	UK	Guide to Sound Practices for Hedge Fund Valuation	AIMA (Alternative Investment Management Association)	Hedge Fund Valuation
2008	UK	28 Best Practice Standards	HFSB/HFWG (Hedge Fund Standards Board/Hedge Fund Working Group)	Overarching Guidelines for asset managers

management should do in order to improve the governance of a fund. Especially the sections on hedge fund disclosure are somewhat vague, and mainly touch upon issues of relevance to the hedge funds' general set up, as displayed in Table 6.2.

Minimum compliance with such recommendations is unlikely to give substantial help to investors, as Naik (2007) points out. What is more, the multitude of guidelines imposes a challenge to hedge fund managers, since some of the points addressed in the best practices might be in conflict to each other, reflecting differences in market practices between the US and Europe. Fortunately, all these guidelines are very similar in nature, so that

Table 6.2   Common standards for hedge fund disclosure

Requirement	Description or example
Private placement memorandum	Existence of a private placement memorandum
Counterparties	Disclosure of counterparties and third parties on request
Strategy of the fund	Hedge fund style, permissible investment, use of leverage, regional exposure
Key management	Names and vita of the hedge fund management
Conflicts of interest of managers	Managers running several hedge funds
Conflicts between investors	Disclosure on side letters and parallel managed accounts
Legal framework	Hedge fund structure, including fee structure and redemption rights
Timely disclosure	Disclosure of past hedge fund performance at regular intervals
Valuation framework	Detailed description of the valuation framework used

compliance with one of the guidelines often implies the compliance with other guidelines as well.[4]

Another difference between the various best practice standards is the enforcement of such principles in practice. The newly issued best practices of the Presidents Working Group (PWG) are of a completely voluntarily basis. The Hedge Fund Working Group (HFWG) Best Standards in contrast want to establish a 'comply or explain' practice. However, it is not clear whether and how this practice could be actually enforced.

The future is likely to see more guidelines on valuation and disclosure for hedge fund managers. For example, the Global Investment Performance Standards (GIPS) Executive Committee has announced its intention to extend its guidance on how to calculate and report investment results to clients to address the specific issues of hedge funds.[5] Hopefully, existing and new proposals will converge over time to an internationally accepted standard.

Clear rules for hedge fund disclosure, either by governmental regulation

---

[4]   In October 2008, major hedge fund organizations set up an internet site where different guidelines can easily be compared. This overview is available at: www.hedgefundmatrix.com.

[5]   However, the new GIPS 2010 standard, effective from January 1st, 2011 does not yet include any extension to hedge fund investments.

or by industry standards, can have many advantages. Investors are better informed, and more importantly, are equally well informed – thereby eliminating the advantages of privileged investors over others. Fund managers will appreciate a set of clear and simple rules which they can expect would satisfy authorities and investors across the globe. Finally, regulators similarly benefit from a unified disclosure framework, allowing them to compare and better assess the overall risks involved in hedge funds investments.

2. PERFORMANCE AND PERFORMANCE RISK MEASURES OF HEDGE FUNDS

The typical investor is risk-averse, i.e. he has a preference for high returns, but dislikes the risk related to his investment. All risk and performance risk measures thus aim to satisfy the investor's needs to be informed about the returns, but also the related risks he faces. Some measures focus on the return component; others try to capture the riskiness of the hedge fund investment. Finally, risk-adjusted performance measures and factor analysis combine both dimensions by relating return and risk to each other.

The literature on stocks and mutual funds has proposed an abundance of measures that can be employed to measure risk and return of these investments. The crucial question is whether these risk indicators can be similarly used for hedge fund portfolios. First works that analyzed hedge fund risk and performance, including the papers by Elton et al. (1987), Brown et al. (1999), and Ackermann et al. (1999), drew on these standard measures to obtain answers to the question whether hedge funds perform better than the market or not. However, as subsequent works by Agarwal and Naik (2000c), Fung and Hsieh (2001), Lo (2001), and Brooks and Kat (2002) have shown, hedge funds exhibit some particularities which make them very different to standard equity investments. First, hedge funds returns are not normally distributed. Second, they are non-linear with respect to the standard market factors, such as equity and bond markets. Indeed, hedge funds often modify their investment style so that their exposure to risk factors is highly dynamic over time. These differences cause the standard risk and return indicators – although still widely used – not to be appropriate for hedge funds.

In this section, we briefly describe the most important performance and risk indicators used in hedge fund reporting. Lhabitant (2004), Amenc et al. (2005) and Géhin (2006) provide more comprehensive surveys on most of the measures currently employed by hedge funds. Le Sourd (2007) gives an overview on measures aimed at traditional investment universes, but equally used by hedge funds.

2.1   Analysis of Hedge Fund Returns

A first assessment of hedge fund returns involves the analysis of past returns using descriptive statistics and statistical tests.

2.1.1   Returns, return persistence, and volatility

Past hedge fund returns no doubt provide important information on hedge funds. Standard presentations include monthly and annual returns – net of fees – in absolute terms, and relative to a benchmark.[6] Since investors care essentially not about past returns, but future returns, persistence measures are important as well. Gain frequency, calculated as the percentage of positive monthly returns are a first indicator of performance persistence. Closely related, but more complicated to calculate, is the Hurst (1951) coefficient. Finally, the volatility of monthly returns gives a first assessment of the riskiness of a hedge fund. Simpler, but equally informative measures about a hedge fund's volatility are minimal and maximal past monthly returns, or – more generally – their upper and lower declines (or quartiles).

2.1.2   Downside risk

Next, there are some key figures which help assess the downside risk of returns – an issue which is of particular interest to hedge fund investors. The maximal past drawdown is a simple but informative indicator for downside risk. Next, skewness and kurtosis of fund returns are jointly important in assessing the downside risk: a return distribution that is negatively skewed combined with a positive (excess) kurtosis is a strong indicator of high downside risk. Semi-deviation and other lower partial moments of hedge fund returns are similarly useful. Finally, hedge fund returns during extremely negative equity markets are a good measure on a fund's ability to hedge downside stock market movements.

2.1.3   Non-normality and auto-correlation of hedge fund returns

Information can also be gained by applying statistical tests on the returns of hedge funds. Statistical tests, such as the Jarque-Bera test (Jarque and Bera, 1980), allow one to assess the normality of hedge fund returns. If normality is rejected, the fund is likely to exhibit a larger downside risk

---

[6]   The calculation of past returns is not as simple as it appears, since it is premised on a determination of each hedge funds' value, an issue which is tackled again in Section 3.6. Moreover, there are several ways to calculate returns. For more details see e.g. Chapter 2 of Lhabitant (2004).

than standard equity investments. Tests of autocorrelation, such as the Ljung-Box test (Ljung and Box, 1978), are generally used to detect the degree of illiquid assets in the hedge fund portfolio. If the test of no auto-correlation is rejected, the portfolio is likely to contain a large fraction of illiquid and thus hard-to-value assets. Consequently, return figures have to be treated with caution. Since both issues are of special interest for hedge fund reporting, we come back to theses issues in Sections 3.1 and 3.2.

2.2 Extreme Risk Measures

Because of their non-normal return structure and, thus, relatively higher downside risk, simple volatility measures underestimate a fund's riskiness. It is therefore crucial to specifically assess the risk of extremely negative returns in the case of hedge funds.

2.2.1 VaR and related measures
Value-at-risk (VaR) is perhaps the most important extreme risk measure. The VaR of a portfolio is the maximum amount of capital that can be expected to be lost within a specific time period (usually one month), given a specified confidence level (usually 95 per cent or 99 per cent). There are several ways to calculate VaR. The simplest approach is to assume a normal distribution of returns, which has to be estimated in order to cal-culate the expected maximal loss. Since hedge fund returns are usually not normally distributed, an alternative is to use non-parametrical estimation based on the historical distribution of hedge fund returns. This way, the non-normality is captured automatically. Another approach uses Monte-Carlo simulation techniques to estimate the expected maximal loss. Such simulations can either simply assume normally distributed returns or more complex distributions that account for the asymmetry and fat tails of hedge fund returns.

Besides the standard VaR, there are more sophisticated VaR measures that try to better capture the specific needs of hedge fund reporting. The so-called Cornish-Fisher VaR, see e.g. Favre and Galeano (2002) – also called modified VaR (MVaR) – is an extension of the standard VaR incorporating the effect of skewness and fat tails of hedge fund returns. Incremental VaR (Jorion, 2001) aims to measure the change in VaR when introducing a particular asset class to the portfolio. Closely related, Component VaR (see again Jorion (2001)) indicates the contribution of a specific asset to the VaR of the overall portfolio. The conditional VaR (also called Expected Shortfall) is another extension of the VaR approach. Compared to the VaR, it does not specify the maximal expected loss within a specific confidence level, but the average amount of loss conditional on the fact that such a significant loss actually occurs. Conditional VaR thus is very important if the distribution of returns has very fat tails, since the loss might be much larger than specified by VaR.[7] Applications of the conditional VaR to hedge funds are by Agarwal and Naik (2004) and De Souza and Gokcan (2004). Finally, Shortfall Probability can be considered as the inverse of VaR: instead of estimating the maximal loss given a confidence interval, the shortfall probability indicates the probability that a given loss will actually occur.

Another approach to calculate a VaR estimate relies on style analysis, the so-called Style VaR Lhabitant (2001, 2004). This methodology first examines the relation of different investment styles on the portfolio,[8] and then analyzes the impact of the worst variation of each style on the portfolio. Laporte (2003) proposed an extension of the Style VaR to include liquidity risk faced by hedge fund investors through look-up constraints.[9] By adding an additional factor to the Style VaR, this model easily allows one to analyze the impact of such clauses on a fund's VaR. Finally, it is important to mention the Extreme Value Theory (EVT) (Embrecht et al., 2008; Lhabitant, 2004). Actually, it is not a variant of VaR, but an important tool to calculate it. EVT just focusses on the modelling of the tails of a distribution, leaving the rest unspecified. However, since rare negative events are of high importance for hedge funds, this approach allows for a rather good evaluation of the risks related to such events. The distribution of the tail can then be used to estimate the VaR.

2.2.2   Stress tests

Besides the different VaR approaches, hedge funds often use stress tests to assess extreme risks. As opposed to VaR, stress testing requires no assumption on a fund's return probability distribution, and is therefore essentially a non-statistical risk measure. It rather relies on Monte-Carlo techniques to evaluate the impact of extreme but probable situations on hedge fund performance. The crucial difference to VaR and EVT is the stress test's ability to simulate shocks that have never occurred in the past, or which are more likely to occur than the historical evidence suggests. Stress tests can also be used to analyse the impact of structural shocks or

---

[7]   Strictly speaking, conditional VaR and expected shortfall are two different concepts. Conditional VaR calculates the expected shortfall given a pre-specified confidence level, whereas the expected shortfall can also be calculated using another loss limit.

[8]   See Section 2.4 for more details on style analysis.

[9]   This is an important difference to the general notion of liquidity risk, which usually denotes the liquidity risk within the hedge fund.

breaks of the financial system on hedge fund returns. The basic idea of stress test is simple: evaluating the impact of sudden changes in key determinants of hedge fund returns on their performance. Such stress tests can either simulate the consequences of changes in one particular key variable (also called 'sensitivity testing') on hedge fund performance, or the impact of an extreme variation of many critical factors jointly (called 'multidimensional scenario analysis'). Stress tests can be set up both rather simply, by assuming a one-shot deviation from the variables under consideration, or involve more complicated models that reflect the impact of so-called spiral effects ('second round effects') on a hedge fund's performance.[10]

2.3 Risk-adjusted Performances Measures

The last sections presented measures to analyze both hedge fund returns and their related risks. However, The most interesting part of hedge fund reporting are indicators that combine both types of analysis, because above-average returns are not a surprise when running high-risk strategies. The real challenge consists in delivering a good performance while keeping the risk exposure limited. Risk-adjusted performance measures are designed to detect investments that exhibit a good risk-return trade-off.

2.3.1 Sharpe ratio and related measures

The Sharpe (1966) ratio is the most famous measure that relates the return of an investment to its risks. It is defined as the quotient of the portfolio's expected excess return over the risk-free rate $E[r_p] - r_f$ and its standard deviation σ_p:

$$S_p = \frac{E[r_p] - rf}{\sigma_p} \tag{6.1}$$

The higher the Sharpe ratio, the better is the risk-return relation of the investment. Intuitively, it can be interpreted as a fund's excess return per unit risk. In fact, apart from slight modifications, all risk-adjusted performance measures follow this principle by relating returns to units of risk. Almost three decades after the Sharpe ratio, Sharpe (1994) proposed a generalization of his original ratio, the so-called Information Ratio (IR). It is defined as the quotient of the portfolio's excess return over another portfolio (usually a benchmark) and the standard deviation of the return difference between both portfolios. Thus, it captures the fact that managers often try to outperform a benchmark, while maintaining

---

[10] See Jorion (2001) for a detailed review of stress testing.

a low tracking error. The M^2 measure, owing its name to the authors' names Modigliani and Modigliani (1997), also focuses on how to evaluate a performance compared to a benchmark. They suggested adjusting the portfolio to have the same risk as the benchmark before comparing them. The M^2 is, hence, equivalent to the return the fund would have achieved if it had the same risk as the benchmark, which is often the market index. In essence, it is equal to the Sharpe ratio times the standard deviation of the benchmark.

Closely related to the Sharpe ratio is the Treynor (1965) ratio, which divides the expected excess return of a portfolio by its beta, where the beta is calculated on the basis of the CAPM (Sharpe, 1964; Lintner, 1965). The advantage of the Treynor ratio is that it only focusses on the systematic component of risk, and not total risk. Along with the evolution of multi-factor models, such as the Fama and French (1992, 1993) three-factor model, a generalization of the Treynor ratio has been proposed, including the portfolio's sensitivities to more than one factor (Hübner, 2005).

Although the Sharpe ratio is easy to calculate and widely used, it is not very appropriate for measuring hedge fund performance, since it is based on the assumption of normally distributed fund returns – an assumption which is rarely met. The Sortino ratio (Sortino and Price, 1994) offers a slightly different measure by replacing the standard deviation with the downside deviation. Consequently, the Sortino ratio is more appropriate for hedge funds. Another variant of the Sharpe ratio is the Modified Sharpe ratio, also called return over VaR, which has been proposed by Gregoriou and Gueyie (2003). The Modified Sharpe replaces the standard deviation in the denominator of the Sharpe ratio by the earlier presented Modified VaR (or Cornish-Fisher VaR). This replacement is motivated by the fact that the MVaR takes skewness and kurtosis of the return distribution into account.

2.3.2   Other risk-adjusted performance measures

Besides the Sharpe ratio and modifications thereof, some other risk-adjusted performance measures are explicitly tailored for the non-normal distribution of hedge fund returns. The Stutzer (2000) index tries to capture a behaviorial element of investors, which are thought to minimize the probability that the excess return of their investment will be negative over a long time horizon. Since a high likelihood of severe losses increases the probability of negative excess returns, the Stutzer index punishes hedge funds with a strongly negative skewness and a high kurtosis. The Omega ratio has been put forward by Keating and Shadwick (2002). Its advantage is that it also includes its third and fourth moment while requiring no assumption on a fund's return distribution. More precisely,

Omega is a relative gain-to-loss function of using exogenously (and arbitrary) return threshold. The Omega is then defined as the quotient of the (expected) excess return over a threshold and the expected loss below the same threshold. Hence, the higher the Omega, the better. With the aim of creating a measure that combines the positive aspects of Omega ratio (reflecting higher moments) and Sharpe ratio (easy interpretation), Kazemi et al. (2004) proposed a Sharpe-Omega ratio. While identical in terms of ranking to the Omega ratio, it uses the expected excess return in the numerator of the ratio – similar to the Sharpe ratio.

Compared to the previous ratios, the Alternative Investment Risk Adjusted Performance measure by Sharma (2004) is an indicator that incorporates an individual risk-aversion parameter when comparing hedge fund performance. Based on a constant relative risk aversion utility function, it also allows capturing the effect of the third and fourth moments of hedge fund returns on investor's expected utility.

Two simple ratios of average returns relative to downside risk are the Calmar and Sterling ratio. These ratios divide the average annual excess return by a maximum drawdown indicator (Kestner, 1996; Young, 1991)

2.4 Beta or Correlation Analysis: Factor Models

All previous indicators focus on measuring the risk-adjusted performance of hedge fund returns. However, they leave aside the source of hedge fund returns and risks. Beta or correlation analysis aims to detect a fund's underlying return driving factors by explaining hedge fund returns through the fund's exposure to various risk factors. Factor analysis is especially important for investors that consider hedge fund investment only as a part of their overall portfolio, such as institutional investors. Pension funds or insurance companies have to care about their overall portfolio risk, and not only a hedge fund's specific risks. Similarly, fund of hedge fund investors face the same situation when deciding about the asset allocation across funds.

2.4.1 Linear factor models

Most factor models used to analyze hedge fund returns are linear models:

$$r_t = \alpha + \sum_{k=1}^{K} \beta_k F_{k,t} + \varepsilon_t \qquad (6.2)$$

where r_t is the monthly return of the hedge fund, α its abnormal performance, β_k the sensitivity of the hedge fund to the risk factor k, $F_{k,t}$ the return of risk factor k and ε_t the disturbance term. The primary advantage of linear models is their simplicity: their calculation is straightforward and easy to understand. In addition, since commonly used, the use of linear models simplifies the comparisons between hedge funds. Most famous factor models try to explain portfolio returns by stock return factors. The most prominent model is the CAPM (Sharpe, 1964; Lintner, 1965), which uses the return of the market portfolio as the single factor to explain portfolio returns. Three and four factor extensions are by Fama and French (1992, 1993) and Carhart (1997). They include the return spreads between value and growth stocks, small and big stocks, and past winners and past losers, respectively. Another variant of the linear factor model is returns-based style analysis by Sharpe (1988, 1992). This approach explains portfolio returns by benchmark returns of different asset classes, investment styles or categories.

Although very popular for traditional investment universes, these linear factor models using standard asset classes as factors tend to have poor explaining power for hedge fund returns. The primary reason for this low quality is the non-linear and non-normal structure of hedge fund returns (Fung and Hsieh, 2000; Agarwal and Naik, 2000c; Fung and Hsieh, 2001), which cannot be captured by simple equity factor models. Hence, several extensions or adaptations of previous models have been proposed for hedge fund factor analysis.

A first approach, proposed by Fung and Hsieh (1997) is to include the returns of other asset classes to the set of factors, such as commodities (Agarwal and Naik, 2000b; Fung and Hsieh, 2004), exchange rates (Agarwal and Naik, 2000a), or hedge fund indices (Lhabitant, 2001). Also called hedge fund style analysis, these additional factors then capture the non-linear and dynamic trading strategies as employed by hedge funds in the linear factor model. A second possibility has been proposed by Agarwal and Naik (2000c), who use equity option portfolios as factors in their model to account for non-linearities.

2.4.2 Non-linear and dynamic factor models

Instead of employing factors in the linear model that exhibit non-linear features, an alternative is to directly model the non-linearity or dynamics in the estimation. Again, there are many ways to model these non-linearities: higher moment adjusted models of the CAPM (Favre and Ranaldo, 2003; Xu et al., 2004), conditional regression models (Kat and Miffre, 2002; Kazemi and Schneeweiss, 2006), or regime switching models (Billio et al., 2007). Finally, truly dynamic models use either Kalman filter techniques to incorporate the dynamic betas of hedge funds (Posthuma and van der Sluis, 2005; Swinkels and Van Der Sluis, 2006), or explicitly model the time-varying structure of a hedge fund's risk exposure (Berk et al., 1999; Zhang, 2004).

2.4.3   Alpha analysis

Alpha analysis is the flip side of beta analysis. In fact, it is just the intercept of the factor model presented in (2): the residual or abnormal return that cannot be explained by the fund's risk exposure. Accordingly, alpha can be calculated by any of the factor models outlined above – and the value of alpha depends on the chosen model. Alpha reflects returns without taking on risk exposures.[11]

3.   SPECIFIC ISSUES WITH HEDGE FUND PERFORMANCE

3.1   Non-normality of Hedge Fund Returns

Hedge funds returns are generally not normally distributed, see e.g. Lhabitant (2004).[12] This has considerable consequences on a number of hedge fund risk measures. Simple measures, such as the Sharpe ratio, are then of limited use when assessing a hedge fund. The same applies to all value-at-risk measures assuming normally distributed returns.

Non-normality of hedge fund returns can easily be detected with statistical tests of normality. The most popular tests are the Jarque-Bera test (Jarque and Bera, 1980) and the Lilliefors (1967) test.

As presented in Section 2, many adjustments of standard risk measures have been proposed that account for the non-normality of hedge fund returns. For example, the Sortino ratio is a good improvement over the Sharpe ratio, and the Cornish-Fisher VaR a suitable extension of standard value at risk measures. Hence, it is important to be aware that hedge fund return might not be normally distributed. Tools that take this into account are often straightforward to implement.

3.2   Smoothed Hedge Fund Returns

Another particularity of hedge fund returns is so-called return smoothing which can be explained by investments in illiquid assets and deliberate misreporting.

Since hedge funds often invest in illiquid assets, their net asset value is

---

[11] Since the main purpose of Alpha analysis is to calculate risk-adjusted returns, it is often classified as risk-adjusted performance measure, see Section 2.3.

[12] It is important to mention that the returns of stocks and mutual funds are not normally distributed either, but the normality assumption is less violated compared to hedge fund returns.

not always straightforward to determine. Sometimes, there are no market prices for securities available, and the manager linearly extrapolates the price between two observable prices. Or there might be various quotes for thinly traded securities so that the manager is inclined to use smoothed broker-dealer quotes. The returns so-obtained will be usually much flatter than those of similarly risky, but liquid investments. On the other side, returns may be deliberately smoothed by hedge fund managers to let their fund appear less volatile than it actually is.

Smoothed returns data has considerable consequences for the evaluation of hedge funds. Most of all, the funds' volatility does not reflect its true riskiness, but is biased downwards (Asness et al., 2001). As a direct consequence, risk-adjusted performances measures are no longer accurate.

There is quite some empirical evidence that return data of hedge funds is too smooth. Getmansky et al. (2004) show that illiquidity is the major reason for smoothing of hedge fund returns. Bollen and Pool (2006) develop a model, which allows detecting deliberate cheating in hedge fund returns. They find that, for some funds, the most likely reason for return smoothing is that the managers misreport return figures to reduce the volatility of the fund's returns, thereby achieving higher Sharpe ratios.

Return smoothing, either on purpose or not, can be detected by serial correlation in hedge fund returns. A simple test is the already mentioned autocorrelation test of Ljung and Box (1978). It is also possible to construct risk measures that overcome this problem. Getmansky et al. (2004), for example, propose adjustments to the standard Sharpe ratio that corrects for the bias caused by illiquid assets contained in hedge fund portfolios.

3.3   Holdings-Based Reporting

All risk measures discussed in Section 2 are based on past return data: risk-adjusted performance measures relate past returns to past risk exposure, and factor analysis explains the sources of past returns by common risk factors.

Holdings-based reporting takes a completely different approach. It consists in disclosing the exact portfolio composition of a fund, which then allows investors to analyze each of the securities that make up the portfolio. The individual risks are then aggregated over the entire fund to obtain the overall risk exposure.

Holdings-based reporting thus offers many advantages. First, by definition, it allows a much more detailed analysis of all the risks involved. Second, it avoids the estimation errors inherent to return-based reporting. From an investor's perspective, holdings-based reporting enables them to choose their own technique to aggregate the risk of different asset or security classes and thus reflect individual risk preferences. Finally, holdings-based reporting reduces the problems related to the lack of hedge fund transparency since the investor is informed about the portfolio composition.

The last point, in particular, is also one of the major drawbacks of holdings-based reporting. Full portfolio disclosure may be counterproductive to good hedge fund performance, since other market participants can make use of this information to trade against a hedge fund's strategy. This is why holdings-based reporting for hedge funds cannot be too detailed; instead of individual securities, only the holdings of the different security classes are made public. In addition, hedge funds publish their portfolio composition only with a time-lag, such that the risk profile obtained only reflects the positions the fund had some considerable time before. Next, holdings-based reporting requires the processing of a good deal of data, and know-how and time to analyze it. Risk analysis using portfolio holdings does not only require current and past portfolio holdings, but also the risk characteristics of each of the holdings involved. If not done accurately, one can easily obtain the wrong conclusions.

3.4   Liquidity Risk Indicators

Investments in illiquid assets do not only cause return smoothing of hedge funds, but they are also a source of risk in their own right. Liquidity problems can quickly increase the risk of a fund's failure. Since illiquid positions are very common in hedge funds, liquidity risk is much more of a problem for hedge funds than it is for mutual funds.

Liquidity and liquidity risk is unfortunately not clearly defined. In this section, we describe the two main versions of liquidity risk and liquidity risk measures: asset liquidity risk and funding liquidity risk. Asset liquidity risk denotes a fund's risk of not being able to sell positions in its portfolio. Funding liquidity risk refers to the risk of a fund not being able to meet financial obligations when they are due. Although both kinds of risk are closely related to one another, that distinction is important. Whereas asset liquidity is much more of an asset management task, funding liquidity is more concerned about cash management.[13]

Asset liquidity risk measures aim to indicate the liquidity of the assets contained in the portfolio. The earlier mentioned Ljung-Box test (Ljung

---

[13]   Note that both kinds of liquidity risk refer to risks within the hedge funds. In addition to these risks, investors face usually an additional liquidity risk due to look-up periods of their hedge fund stakes, as already mentioned in Section 2.2.

and Box, 1978) of autocorrelation of hedge fund returns is a practical test for evaluating to what extent the fund contains illiquid assets. Since illiquid assets tend to exhibit relatively constant prices, the returns of a portfolio containing illiquid assets are more likely to be auto-correlated (Getmansky et al., 2004). The percentage of hard-to-value (non-marketable or illiquid) assets is another convenient asset liquidity risk indicator. Average liquidation periods for a specified part of the portfolio are also a good measure to capture the liquidity risk of a portfolio, although estimating such liquidation periods is not straightforward. Hedge funds can also provide estimated impact costs, i.e. the differences between market and realized prices, when unwinding large investments. Finally, similarly to extreme performance risks, stress tests can help to analyze the impact of critical market situations on a portfolio's liquidity.

Funding liability risk indicators try to capture the provision of cash to meet obligations when due. A simple class of funding liquidity risk measures are liquidity ratios, such as cash-to-equity or VaR-to-cash ratios. Asset liability match analysis tries to examine the timing of the various portfolio transactions. By relating future payments and redemptions to each other, this analysis helps to detect possible mismatches and, thus, liquidity constraints well in advance. Similarly to asset liquidity, hedge funds can simulate funding liquidity stress tests to evaluate the impact of adverse market conditions on the cash situation of the fund.

3.5   Leverage Risk Indicators

In contrast to mutual funds, hedge funds can make use of financial leverage by borrowing large amounts of capital. Although leverage is not per se a source of risk, being a convenient tool to adjust a portfolio towards the desired risk-return profile, it usually amplifies all other risks. Especially important is the impact of leverage on liquidity risk. Unfortunately, there is no universal leverage risk indicator that fits all situations since, which indicator is useful depends very much on the hedge fund strategy. [14]

Leverage risk indicators can be classified in two main groups: accounting and risk-based leverage measures. Accounting-based leverage indicators are usually simple ratios of information contained in a hedge fund's financial statement. These measures, such as gross assets-to-equity, debt-to-equity, or their inverses allow a first assessment of a fund's leverage. The problem of these ratios is that they do not capture off-balance-sheet leverage. For example, futures can imply a high leverage without appear-

---

[14]   For an overview of leverage indicators, see Rahl (2003).

ing in the financial statements. Neglecting this leverage exposure can be misleading. That is why Breuer (2000) suggested incorporating off-balance-sheet leverage exposure into the ratios (as contained in futures) by calculating their balance sheet equivalent.

Another possibility of capturing off-balance-sheet leverage is through risk-based indicators. Risk-based leverage indicators aim to capture the leverage of a fund by relating its risk exposure to some balance sheet component, which is usually again net asset value of equity. Some of the prominent ratios are VaR-to-equity, volatility-to-equity, or stress loss-to-equity. Here, off-balance sheet leverage risk is automatically included via the risk component in the numerator. McGuire et al. (2005) propose another risk-based leverage measure using hedge fund style analysis. They observe that the coefficients of the different factors in style analysis should add up to one if no leverage is used. This observation led the authors to the conclusion that the sum of the coefficients is a very useful leverage indicator, since any deviation from one is a clear sign of using leverage, both on and off-balance sheet. For example, a sum of beta coefficients of two indicates a portfolio risk exposure twice as large as the investors' capital, and hence a leverage of 100 per cent.

3.6   Operational Risk Disclosure

Although often neglected as an independent source of risk, operational risk is perhaps the most important risk to hedge fund investors. As Giraud (2005) shows, half of all hedge fund failures are caused by operational risk problems, such as misrepresentation of a fund's net asset value, fraud, or trading activities outside of the fund's mandate. The significance of this cause of hedge fund failure draws attention to why disclosure of operational risk is essential for a thorough hedge fund reporting. It is clear that no investor can expect to be fully insured against fraud by the hedge fund management, but detailed operational risk disclosure can reduce its impact significantly. In what follows, we shortly describe the basic ingredients of operational risk disclosure. Since risk related to a fund's valuation framework is the most important part of operational risk disclosure, it is presented in a separate paragraph below.

First of all, each hedge fund should issue a private placement memorandum that gives an overview on the hedge fund strategy, including its investment style, employed asset classes and regional exposure, and the planned use of leverage. This includes also a detailed description of the organization of the fund: the legal framework, information on proxy voting, redemption rights or the fee structure of the fund should be stated clearly. Next, the hedge fund should provide as much information as possible on the hedge fund management itself, e.g. the vita of the managers and the possible conflicts of interests of the management team. Apart from the problems already mentioned, relating to fee incentives versus hedge fund performance (see e.g. Section 3.2), such internal conflicts can also arise for instance when managers run different hedge funds so that they could be inclined to manage the fund's allocation to optimize their joint fee income. Conflicts of interest can also occur between different hedge fund investors, such as those induced by side-letters and accounts managed in parallel for specific investors. Hence, any fund should disclose the existence of such arrangements. The involvement of third parties represents another source of operational risk. The hedge fund team should consequently disclose its main counterparties and give a short analysis of the risks involved by outsourcing activities to partners. Finally, hedge funds should arrange for special event reporting, i.e. an irregular disclosure of important information on the occasion of significant market or strategy changes.

By far the most important part of operational risk disclosure relates to the valuation framework. Since hedge funds invest in many different and complex financial products, some of which are not regularly traded, calculation of its net asset value is not simple. Often there are many ways to calculate the current value of a specific asset, and different methodologies may yield very different results. This is why a clear statement of a fund's valuation principles is indispensable. We now briefly present the main valuation principles used by hedge funds.

For liquid assets, market prices are available. However, prices can be either ask, bid, or mid-prices, and they can be calculated as an average over a certain time period. Obtaining a value for illiquid asset is much more difficult. One possibility is to employ pricing models, such as stochastic pricing models or discounted cash flow models. If related financial instruments are traded in the market, no-arbitrage pricing models are useful. Counterpart quotes or estimates represent another means of estimating an asset's value. Sometimes, the valuation of difficult and complex assets is assigned to independent appraisals of third parties.

Besides the existence of a clear and transparent valuation framework, it is important to have clear control mechanisms that ensure that the valuation principles are followed. A first control mechanism is to assign the determination of the fund's net asset value to a third party valuation service provider or administrator. If the valuation is carried out in-house, it is possible to ensure compliance with the valuation framework by a strict separation of duties between a fund's manager and its administrator, who is in charge of the fund's valuation. Finally, hedge fund managers might opt to carry out the valuation themselves, while at the same time mandating an on-going validation of their valuation policy to an external auditor.

4. CONCLUSION

This chapter presents an overview of the issues at stake when hedge fund managers provide information on performance and risk to investors. It shows that, as a result of the importance of the quality of reporting, industry associations and policy working groups have set up guidelines and 'best practices' for reporting with the aim of enhancing hedge fund transparency and thus investor confidence. Our description of those guidelines shows that these rarely provide concrete guidance. Often, they are very vague, predominantly covering topics where there is not much contention between managers and investors, such as consistent, clear and timely reporting of past returns. The guidelines fall short of encouraging hedge funds to provide information on important aspects of hedge fund risks.

Hedge funds differ from other investments. It is thus important to reflect on the appropriateness of performance and risk measures. We list different available indicators and emphasize that standard measures of performance are often not suitable to report risk-adjusted hedge fund returns. While we have taken a closer look at widely used performance and risk measures, we have also examined specific issues that are of special importance for hedge fund disclosure, such as leverage, liquidity, and operational risk. Such a theoretical background to sound hedge fund reporting is a necessary prerequisite for improving the quality of hedge fund reporting in practice. The issues raised in this chapter lie at the heart of creating a more transparent industry environment. Better hedge fund transparency is likely to have many advantages. First, it can lead to increased investor participation – and less money withdrawal during financial crises. Second, better informed investors can contribute to a better discipline of hedge fund providers. Finally, a better market place for hedge funds can have a positive effect on market efficiency and deeper financial markets.

BIBLIOGRAPHY

Ackermann, C., R. McNally and D. Ravenscraft (1999), 'The performance of hedge funds: Risk, return, and incentives', *Journal of Finance*, **54**(3), 833–74.

Agarwal, V. and N. Y. Naik (2000a), 'Generalised style analysis of hedge funds', *Journal of Asset Management*, **1**(1), 93–109.

Agarwal, V. and N. Y. Naik (2000b), 'On taking the alternative route: Risks, rewards, style and performance persistence of hedge funds', *Journal of Alternative Investments*, **2**(4), 6–23.

Agarwal, V. and N. Y. Naik (2000c), 'Performance evaluation of hedge funds with option-based and buy-and-hold strategies', London Business School, Working Paper.

Agarwal, V. and N. Y. Naik (2004), 'Risks and portfolio decisions involving hedge funds', *Review of Financial Studies*, **17**(1), 63–98.

Amenc, N., P. Malaise and M. Vaissié (2005), 'EDHEC funds of hedge funds reporting survey'. Nice, EDHEC publication.

Asness, C. S., R. J. Krail and J. M. Liew (2001), 'Do hedge funds hedge?', *Journal of Portfolio Management,* **28**(1), 6–19.

Athanassiou, Phoebus (2009), *Hedge Fund Regulation in the European Union – Current Trends and Future Prospects*, New York, US: Kluwer Law International.

Berk, J. B., R. C. Green and V. Naik (1999), 'Optimal investment, growth options, and security returns', *Journal of Finance*, **54**(5), 1553–1607.

Billio, M., M. Getmansky and L. Pelizzon (2007), 'Dynamic risk exposure in hedge funds', University of Venice, Working Paper.

Bollen, N. P. B. and V. K. Pool (2006), 'A screen for fraudulent return smoothing in the hedge fund industry'. Owen Graduate School of Management, Working Paper.

Bollen, N. P. B. and V. K. Pool (2009), 'Do hedge fund managers misreport returns? evidence from the pooled distribution', *Journal of Finance,* **64**(5), 2257–88.

Breuer, Peter (2000), Measuring off-balance-sheet leverage. IMF, Working Paper WP/00/202.

Brooks, C. and H. Kat (2002), 'The statistical properties of hedge fund returns', *Journal of Alternative Investments*, **5**(2), 26–44.

Brown, S. J., W. N. Goetzmann and R. G. Ibbotson (1999), 'Offshore hedge funds: Survival and performance, 1989–95', *Journal of Business,* **72**(1), 91–117.

Carhart, Marc M. (1997), 'On persistence in mutual fund performance', *Journal of Finance*, **52**(1), 57–82.

De Souza, C. and S. Gokcan (2004), 'Allocation methodologies and customizing hedge fund multi-manager multi-strategy products', *Journal of Alternative Investments*, **6**(4), 7–21.

Do, V., R. Faff and J. Wickramanayake (2005), 'An empirical analysis of hedge fund performance: The case of Australian hedge fund industy', *Journal of Multinational Financial Management,* **15**, 377–93.

Eling, M. and F. Schumacher (2007), 'Does the choice of performance measure influence the evaluation of hedge funds?', *Journal of Banking and Finance,* **31**(9), 2632–47.

Elton, E. J., M. J. Gruber and J. C. Rentzler (1987), 'Professionally managed, publicly traded commodity funds', *Journal of Business*, **60**(2), 175–99.

Embrecht, P., C. Klüppelberg and T. Mikosch (2008), *Modelling External Events for Insurance and Finance*, Heidelberg, Germany: Springer.

European Fund and Asset Management Association (2005), 'Hedge funds regulation in Europe', EFAMA Survey.

Fama, E. F. and K. R. French (1992), 'The cross-section of expected stock returns', *Journal of Finance*, **47**(2), 427–65.

Fama, E. F. and K. R. French (1993), 'Common risk factors in the returns on stocks and bonds', *Journal of Financial Economics*, **33**, 3–56.

Favre, L. and A. Ranaldo (2003), *How to price hedge funds: from two to four-moment CAPM*. Nice, EDHEC publication.

Favre, L. and J.A. Galeano (2002), 'Mean modified value-at-risk optimization with hedge funds', *Journal of Alternative Investment*, **5**(2), 21–25.

Foster, D. P. and H. P. Young (2008a), 'The hedge fund game: incentives, excess returns, and piggy-backing'. Wharton Financial Institutions Center, Working Paper.

Foster, D. P. and H. P. Young (2008b), 'Hedge fund wizards', *The Economists' Voice*.

Fung, W. and D. A. Hsieh (1997), 'Empirical characteristics of dynamic trading strategies: The case of hedge funds', *Review of Financial Studies*, **10**(2), 275–302.

Fung, W. and D. A. Hsieh (2000), 'Performance characteristics of hedge funds and commodity funds: Natural versus spurious biases', *Journal of Financial and Quantitative Analysis*, **35**(3), 291–307.

Fung, W. and D. A. Hsieh (2001), 'The risk in hedge fund strategies: Theory and evidence from trend followers', *Review of Financial Studies*, **14**, 313–41.

Fung, W. and D. A. Hsieh (2004), 'Hedge fund benchmarks: A risk based approach', *Financial Analysts Journal*, **60**(5), 65–80.

Géhin, Walter (2006), The challenge of hedge fund performance measurement: a toolbox rather than a pandora's box. Nice, EDHEC publication.

Getmansky, M., A. W. Lo and I. Makarov (2004), 'An econometric model of serial correlation and illiquidity in hedge fund returns', *Journal of Financial Economics*, **74**(3), 529–609.

Giraud, Jean-René (2005), Mitigating hedge funds' operational risks. Nice, EDHEC publication.

Goetzmann, W., J. Ingersoll, M. Spiegel and I. Welch (2007), 'Portfolio performance manipulation and manipulation-proof performance measures', *Review of Financial Studies*, **20**, 1503–1546.

Gregoriou, G. N. and J. P. Gueyie (2003), 'Risk-adjusted performance of funds of hedge funds using a modified Sharpe ratio', *Journal of Wealth Management*, **6** (3), 77–83.

Hübner, Georges (2005), 'The generalized Treynor ratio', *Review of Finance*, **9** (3), 415–35.

Hurst, Harold Edwin (1951), 'Long term storage capacity of reservoirs', *Transactions of the American Society of Civil Engineers*, **116**, 770–99.

Jarque, C. M. and A. K. Bera (1980), 'Efficient tests for normality, homoscedasticity and serial independence of regression residuals', *Economics Letters*, **6** (3), 255–9.

Jorion, Philippe (2001), *Value at Risk – the New Benchmark for Managing Financial Risk*, New York, US: McGraw-Hill.

Kat, H. M. and J. Miffre (2002), 'Performance evaluation and conditioning information: the case of hedge funds'. Cass Business School, Working Paper.

Kazemi, H., T. Schneeweis and B. Gupta (2004), 'Omega as a performance measure', *Journal of Performance Measurement*, **8**(3), 16–25.

Kazemi, H. and T. Schneeweiss (2006), 'Conditional performance of hedge funds'. CISDM, Research Paper.

Keating, C. and W. Shadwick (2002), 'A universal performance measure', *Journal of Performance Measurement*, **6**(3), 59–84.

Kestner, Lars N. (1996), 'Getting a handle on true performance', *Futures*, **25**(1), 44–6.

Laporte, N. (2003), 'Modelling liquidity risk in a VaR model'. MSCI, Working Paper.

Le Sourd, Véronique (2007), 'Performance measurement for traditional investment'. Nice, EDHEC publication.

Lhabitant, François Serge (2001), 'Assessing market risk for hedge funds and hedge fund portfolios', *Journal of Risk Finance*, **2**(4), 1–17.

Lhabitant, François Serge (2004), *Hedge Funds – Quantitative Insights*, Chichester, UK: John Wiley & Sons.

Liang, Bing (2003), 'The accuracy of hedge fund returns', *Journal of Portfolio Management*, **29**(3).

Lilliefors, H. (1967), 'On the Kolmogorov-Smirnov test for normality with mean and variance unknown', *Journal of the American Statistical Association*, **62**, 399–402.

Lintner, John (1965), 'The valuation of risk asset and the selection of risky investments in stock portfolios and capital budgets', *Review of Economics and Statistics*, **47**, 13–37.

Ljung, G. M. and G. E. P. Box (1978), 'On a measure of lack of fit in time series models', *Biometrica*, **65**(2), 297–303.

Lo, A. (2001), 'Risk management for hedge funds: Introduction and overview', *Financial Analysts Journal*, **57**(6), 16–33.

McGuire, P., E. Remolona and K. Tsatsaronis (2005), 'Time-varying exposures and leverage in hedge funds', *Bank for International Settlement Quarterly Review* (March), 59–72.

Modigliani, F. and L. Modigliani (1997), 'Risk-adjusted performance', *Journal of Portfolio Management*, **23**, 45–54.

Naik, Narayan (2007), 'Hedge funds, transparency and conflict of interest', Technical report, European Parliament.

Posthuma, N. and P. J. van der Sluis (2005), 'The Hedge Fund Paradigm', in Michael K. Ong (eds), *Risk Management: A Modern Perspective*, Burlington, MA: Academic Press.

Rahl, Leslie (2003), *Hedge Fund Risk Transparency*, London, UK: Risk Books.

Sharma, Milind (2004), 'A.I.R.A.P. – alternative risk-adjusted performance measures for alternative investments', *Journal of Investment Management*, **2**(4), 34–65.

Sharpe, William F. (1964), 'Capital asset prices: A theory of market equilibrium under conditions of risk', *Journal of Finance,* **19**, 425–42.

Sharpe, William F. (1966), 'Mutual fund performance', *Journal of Business,* **39**(1), 119–138.

Sharpe, William F. (1988), 'Determining a fund's effective asset mix', *Investment Management Review,* (December), 59–69.

Sharpe, William F. (1992), 'Asset allocation: management style and performance measurement', *Journal of Portfolio Management,* **19**, 7–19.

Sharpe, William F. (1994), 'The Sharpe ratio', *Journal of Portfolio Management,* **21**, 49–58.

Sortino, F. A. and L. N. Price (1994), 'Performance measurement in a downside risk framework', *Journal of Investing,* **3**(3), 59–65.

Stutzer, Michael (2000), 'A portfolio performance index', *Financial Analysts Journal,* **56**(3), 52–61.

Swinkels, L. and P. J. Van der Sluis (2006), 'Return-based style analysis with timevarying exposures', *European Journal of Finance,* **12**(6–7), 529–52.

Treynor, Jack. L. (1965), 'How to rate management of investment funds', *Harvard Business Review,* **43**(1), 63–75.

Xu, X. E., J. Yau and H. Fung (2004), 'Do hedge fund managers display skill?', *Journal of Alternative Investments,* **6**(4), 22–31.

Young, Terry W. (1991), 'Calmar ratio: A smoother tool', *Futures,* **20**(1), 40.

Zhang, Hong (2004), 'Dynamic beta, time-varying risk premium, and momentum'. Yale ICF Working Paper No. 04-26.

7. Hedge fund activism
Alon Brav*, Wei Jiang† and Hyunseob Kim‡

INTRODUCTION

During the past decade, hedge fund activism has emerged as a new type of corporate governance mechanism, capable of bringing about operational, financial, and governance reforms in target firms. Shareholder activism (Gillan and Stark (2007), Karpoff (2001)) and, more broadly, the monitoring of corporate managers by large investors (Shleifer and Vishny (1986), Grossman and Hart (1980)) are not new phenomena in global capital markets. In the United States (US), institutional investors, including pension funds and mutual funds, have actively engaged in the management of target public companies as far back as the 1980s with the intention of creating long-term shareholder wealth. Early institutional shareholder activism was constrained by regulatory and structural barriers, including the 'free-rider problem' and inherent conflicts of interest between target firms and institutional investors (Black (1990)). As a result, no conclusive results exist in the academic literature on the effect of activist investing by institutional shareholders.

On several levels, hedge fund activism distinguishes itself from the activism of other institutional shareholders who seek to induce changes in public corporations. First, stronger financial incentives exist in the case of hedge funds than in the case of other institutional activists. On average, hedge funds earn significant performance fees, normally around 20 per cent of excess returns in addition to fixed management fees. Moreover, hedge fund managers invest a substantial proportion of their personal wealth in the funds that they manage, alongside their limited partners. This *sui generis* compensation structure, which is different from that of other institutional investors such as mutual fund and pension fund managers, provides a stronger motivation for hedge fund managers to generate a high investment return.

Second, hedge funds are lightly regulated, not widely available to the

*   Duke University and NBER.
†   Columbia University.
‡   Duke University. Kim gratefully acknowledges financial support from the Kwanjeong Educational Foundation.

general public and cater mainly to institutional clients and a limited number of wealthy individuals. Therefore, hedge funds are not subject to the strict fiduciary mandates embodied in the Employee Retirement Income Security Act of 1974 (ERISA), which in turn allows them greater flexibility to intervene in target firms. For example, as US law does not require hedge funds to maintain diversified portfolios, as in the case of some other institutional investors, hedge funds can more easily establish large and concentrated stakes in target firms. In addition, hedge funds can also trade on margin, and use derivative instruments to hedge or leverage their stake in the target firms. These crucial advantages empower activist shareholders and provide them with greater sway when negotiating with the senior management of their target companies.

Third, hedge funds face fewer conflicts of interest than other institutional investors, such as mutual funds and pension funds, who often maintain business relationships with the invested companies or may pursue non-financial agendas and goals that do not necessarily translate into creating shareholder value. Hedge fund managers rarely face conflicts of this sort.

Fourth, hedge funds usually maintain 'lock-up' provisions that restrict investors from withdrawing their principal capital. As hedge fund activists often invest in target firms, on average, for more than a year in pursuit of their strategies, this feature of locked-up capital allocated towards longer-term investments provides hedge fund managers pursuing an activist investing mandate with extended flexibility to focus on investment objectives that require intermediate and long-term investment horizons to materialize.

In this chapter we provide an overview of the academic literature on hedge fund activism. In our review of the academic literature, we find that hedge fund activists target 'value' firms with low valuations relative to their respective fundamentals including return on assets, return on equity and market-to-book ratios. In addition, activist hedge funds tend to target firms that are characterized by sound operating cash flows, low growth rates of sales, leverage, and dividend payout ratios. Therefore, these target firms may be broadly characterized as 'cash-cows' that face low potential for growth and may suffer from the agency problem of free cash flow (Jensen (1986)). Prior academic studies of shareholder activism by institutional shareholders identify that target companies were characterized instead by poor operating performance (Gillan and Stark (2007)).

Target firms are generally smaller relative to comparable firms. Hedge funds target small firms, in part due to the greater ease and flexibility with which a given amount of capital can lead to the accumulation of a significant ownership stake in the target. Moreover, the target companies chosen by hedge fund activists exhibit relatively high trading liquidity, institutional ownership, and analyst coverage. In essence, these characteristics enable activist investors to accumulate significant stakes in target firms quickly, without adverse price impact, and to gain greater support for their agendas from sophisticated investors. Finally, we find that target firms tend to have incorporated weaker shareholder rights relative to comparable firms, which is consistent with the argument that hedge fund activists target poorly-governed firms where the potential for wealth creation is greater.

By and large, the consensus in the literature is that hedge fund activism is successful in achieving the goals of creating value for the shareholders of target firms. The short-term average abnormal returns around the announcement of the intervention of hedge funds are significantly positive across various studies, on the order of 5 per cent to 10 per cent. However, the perceived increase in firm value through hedge fund activism shows considerable cross-sectional differences. The categories that achieve the highest abnormal short-term returns are the sale of the target firm and changes in business strategy. In contrast, hedge fund activism that targets purely capital structure or corporate governance related reforms earns lower returns. In sum, investors believe that activism that facilitates the efficient re-allocation of capital in target firms has the highest impact on shareholder value.

Furthermore and equally importantly, post-event long-run returns, up to multiple years, suggest no reversion in target firm stock price, which indicates that the initial market perception of value creation is justified. No less importantly, target firms tend to exhibit improvements in operating performance as measured by return on assets or equity after the activism event. The evidence also demonstrates increases in Chief Executive Officer (CEO) turnover, in leverage and in payouts by target firms as well as a decrease in CEO compensation. These results are consistent with the view that hedge fund activism creates value in the areas of operational, financial, and governance performance in the target firms.

The remainder of this chapter is organized as follows: Section 1 describes the data on hedge fund activism. Section 2 examines the goals and tactics employed by hedge fund activists. Section 3 details the characteristics of firms that activist hedge funds target. Section 4 addresses the fundamental question of whether hedge fund activism creates value for shareholders through the analysis of short-run and long-run stock returns and changes in operating performance of target firms. Lastly, Section 5 examines returns to investors in activist hedge funds. The final section summarizes our conclusions.

1.   DATA ON HEDGE FUND ACTIVISM

As no centralized database exists for analyzing hedge fund activism events, the most reliable source for such events in the US is Schedule 13D filings. Section 13(d) of the 1934 Securities Exchange Act requires investors who are beneficial owners of 5 per cent or more of any class of publicly traded securities of a company with the intent to influence corporate control to disclose the size of their stake and the nature of their purpose within 10 days of crossing the 5 per cent ownership threshold. Schedule 13D filings provide information about the identity of the filer, the filing date, ownership and its changes, the cost of purchase, and most importantly, the purpose of the investment as noted in Item 4 ('Purpose of Transaction').

Brav, Jiang, Partnoy and Thomas (2008a) apply a top-down approach to construct a comprehensive sample of activism events that includes events from both Schedule 13D filings and major financial media outlets tracked by Factiva (for events that involve ownership below the 5 per cent threshold). The list of hedge funds filing Schedule 13D filings is filtered through a complete list of all Schedule 13D filers over the 2001 to 2006 period. Next, all Schedule 13D filings and amendments are gathered for this sample of hedge funds through the SEC's EDGAR system. They also search for activism events where hedge funds acquire stakes below 5 per cent, identifying 27 additional events. Filings associated with risk arbitrage, distress financing, and non-regular corporations such as closed-end funds, are excluded so that the resulting sample consists of 236 activist hedge funds and 1059 fund-target firm pairs between 2001 and 2006. Finally, Brav et al. (2008a) rely on a combination of information from SEC filings and news search from Factiva to code key elements of activism events, including but not limited to announcement date, ownership stake, stated objectives, managerial responses and outcomes. Brav, Jiang and Kim (2009) follow the same procedure and extend the sample in Brav et al. (2008a) by one more year to 2007, expanding the sample to a total of 1172 events.

Klein and Zur (2009) construct their sample by identifying all Schedule 13D filings between 2003 and 2005. The sample is then filtered so that only transactions that present an explicit activist agenda are analyzed. Events that only present a general agenda of maximizing shareholder value are excluded from their study. This procedure generates 101 activist hedge funds and 151 confrontational target events (and 154 events for 134 other types of activist investors, including individuals). Clifford (2008) identifies hedge fund activists through the Dow Jones Newswires 'CFA Weekly Summary of Key 13D Filings to the SEC' and supplements his sample with additional activist hedge funds by searching Factiva for relevant news articles. Active and passive block holdings are aggregated for these funds from 1998 to 2005 and extracted from SEC filings. This procedure yields 788 activist blockholder events for 197 distinct hedge funds. Boyson and Mooradian (2007) obtain their sample of hedge funds from CSFB/ Tremont. They identify 111 hedge funds and collect all Schedule 13D filings by these funds for the period 1994 to 2004. This process yields 418 unique hedge fund-target firm pairs for 397 target firms. Lastly, Greenwood and Schor (2009) collect activism events by hedge funds from Schedule 13D filings and definitive proxy statements filed by non-management entities. This process yields 784 unique events initiated by 139 hedge funds across the 1993 to 2006 time period.

Finally, researchers have sought to study and describe hedge fund activism in global capital markets including the UK, Germany, and Japan. Becht, Franks, Mayer, and Rossi (2009) collect their sample of activism events in the UK using proprietary data from one hedge fund: the Hermes UK Focus Fund. Mietzner and Schweizer (2008) construct their sample from the disclosure of acquisition of at least 5 per cent ownership in shares of public firms registered with the German Federal Financial Supervisory Authority. Stokman (2008) performs extensive news/media searches to collect his sample of hedge activism throughout Europe. Similarly, Uchida and Xu (2008) collect a sample of Japanese activism events by searching for activism related to two activist funds: the Murakami Fund and the Japanese arm of American Warren Lichtenstein's *Steel Partners* hedge fund. Hamao, Kutsuna and Matos (2010) collect a larger sample of institutional activism in Japan by gathering mandatory filing on block-shareholdings that exceed the 5 per cent threshold.

2. CHARACTERISTICS OF HEDGE FUND ACTIVISM EVENTS

2.1 Objectives and Tactics of Activist Hedge Funds

Brav, Jiang and Kim (2009) and Brav et al. (2008a) both conduct detailed analyses of the stated objectives by activist funds when they announce their intent to intervene in target firms and calculate their respective success rates. Both studies classify the intentions of activist hedge funds into five general categories: (i) General Undervaluation/Maximization of shareholder value, (ii) Capital Structure, (iii) Business Strategy, (iv) Sale of Target Company, and (v) Corporate Governance. Excluding the intent of activist hedge funds to 'maximize shareholder value', the remaining four objectives are not mutually exclusive as one activist hedge fund

Table 7.1   Annual summary statistics

Year	No. of events	Composition by stated objectives					% Hostile	% Success	% Partial success
		General	Capital structure	Business strategy	Sales	Gover-nance			
2001	92	59.8%	16.3%	12.0%	16.3%	21.7%	12.0%	38.9%	13.9%
2002	120	49.2%	15.8%	19.2%	18.3%	27.5%	28.3%	31.1%	24.6%
2003	122	54.9%	9.0%	21.3%	17.2%	18.9%	19.7%	25.9%	14.8%
2004	144	46.5%	16.7%	22.2%	18.1%	25.7%	34.0%	39.0%	22.1%
2005	234	47.0%	17.9%	26.9%	18.4%	17.9%	30.8%	39.3%	23.8%
2006	252	46.4%	22.2%	25.4%	19.8%	29.0%	27.0%	24.1%	31.0%
2007	208	41.3%	17.8%	24.5%	27.9%	26.9%	23.1%	31.1%	15.6%
Total	1172	47.9%	17.4%	23.0%	20.1%	24.2%	27.5%	31.3%	21.1%

may target multiple issues in pursuit of creating shareholder wealth in a target firm. An event is classified as successful if the hedge fund achieves its main stated goal, while a partial success is achieved if the hedge fund and the target company reach a negotiated settlement that partially meets the fund's initially stated objective. Table 7.1, below, provides annual summary statistics for the distribution of events across these five classifications and their eventual success rates:

The first category, labeled 'General', includes events in which the hedge fund believes that the target firm is undervalued and that there is potential for the fund to collaborate with the target firm's management to maximize shareholder value. All events in this objective involve communication with management and simultaneously exclude more aggressive tactics such as proxy fights that are publicly observed and followed by major media outlets. Half of the sample of hedge fund activism events is limited to this categorization.

The second category of activism events represents 17.4 per cent of the full sample and includes activism targeting a firm's payout policy and capital structure. This category includes events in which the hedge fund proposes changes focused on reallocating excess cash, an increase in firm leverage or higher payouts to shareholders. This sub-sample of events also involves the issuance of securities by target firms, such as adjusting seasoned equity offerings or restructuring the target firm's debt load.

The third set of activism events includes hedge fund activism that targets issues broadly defined as business strategy and, more particularly, operational efficiency, business restructuring, mergers and acquisitions activities and growth strategies. This category represents 23 per cent of all events in the sample.

The fourth category of activism events involves activism urging the sale of the target by two different strategies. Either a hedge fund attempts to force a sale of the target company to a third party or, as demonstrated in a small minority of cases, a hedge fund will look to acquire the company itself. Partial success for this group is achieved when a firm agrees to transform itself, even though it maintains its status as an independent entity.

The fifth and final sub-sample of events includes activism that targets corporate governance issues that the activist hedge fund believes detract from the target firm's objective to maximize shareholder wealth. Common agendas pursued by hedge funds include rescinding takeover defenses, ousting the CEO or chairman, challenging board independence and fair representation, demanding more information disclosure or questioning potential fraud and challenging the level or the pay-for-performance sensitivity of executive compensation.

The two rightmost columns in Table 7.1 provide the year-by-year success rate of activism across each of these activist objectives. Aggregated across both hostile and non-hostile events, hedge funds achieve either complete or near complete success in 31.3 per cent of all events, which we define as achieving their main stated goals. In 21.1 per cent of the cases, we observe a partial success, with hedge funds gaining major concessions from their targets; in 22.1 per cent of the cases the fund fails to achieve its stated objectives or withdraws its investment in the target firm. Given that target firms often demonstrate a strong tendency to resist, these rates of success or partial success are impressive. Both Klein and Zur (2009) and Boyson and Mooradian (2007) report that the overall success rate of hedge fund activism in their samples is approximately two-thirds. The remaining 25.5 per cent of the activism events were either ongoing, toward the end of the sample collection, or no information on outcome was available through any news service or SEC filing. Furthermore, Brav, Jiang and Kim (2009) find that activism events where a goal was clearly stated (categories (2)–(5)) and were met with managerial resistance are generally associated with lower complete success rates and higher partial success rates. This result implies that a middle-ground resolution achieved through negotiation is a more probable outcome for events with a public confrontation. Unsurprisingly, the total success rate for the hostile sample is significantly larger, at 60.6 per cent, relative to the non-hostile sample, at 43.9 per cent. This evidence is best interpreted as an equilibrium outcome whereby hostile tactics are adopted when the perceived resistance from the target firm's management is higher or following failed initial approaches that were less confrontational.

Brav et al. (2008a) also categorize the tactics employed by hedge funds from least to most aggressive. Events in which the activist hedge fund attempts to communicate with the board or management on a regular basis with the purpose of enhancing shareholder value are relegated to the first category. Almost none of the filings in this group reveal any specific agenda by the activist hedge fund by way of either SEC filings or news media articles. These cases occur at a frequency of approximately 50 per cent in the sample. The second group of tactics is categorized as events where a hedge fund seeks board representation without pursuing a proxy contest or confrontation with existing senior management or the board of directors. The third category of tactics includes cases where the hedge fund makes formal shareholder proposals or publicly criticizes the management and demands changes. Events in which the hedge fund threatens to wage a proxy fight in order to earn board representation or to sue management for breach of duty fall into the fourth category. The fifth category is assigned to events in which the hedge fund launches a proxy contest in order to replace board representation. The remaining two groups of tactics include events in which the hedge fund sues the company or intends to take control thereof (e.g., with a take-over bid).

As these categories are not mutually exclusive, an activism event can be composed of tactics and strategies in more than one of these categories. Hostile activism events belong to tactic categories four through seven, although some occur in the third category in which we see stated hostile intentions such as the intent by a hedge fund to oust the CEO of a target firm. Following this criterion, Brav, Jiang, and Kim (2009) determine that hostile events comprise 27.1 per cent of the sample. The evolution of activism events in which an explicit agenda is pursued is traced by following both media articles and subsequent SEC filings for the 611 events in the sample analyzed by Brav, Jiang and Kim (2009). Through an activist hedge fund's intervention, target firms accommodate at a rate of 35.3 per cent, negotiate at a rate of 22.3 per cent and resist at a rate of 42.4 per cent.

2.2   Activist Hedge Funds' Investment in Target Firms

Below we examine the ownership percentage and the monetary value of stakes that activist hedge funds seek when pursuing activist tactics in target firms. Brav, Jiang and Kim (2009) aggregate data on investments made by hedge fund activists measured both in US$ value (at cost) and as a function of the percentage of shares outstanding in the target company. The median initial percentage stake when a hedge fund files its 13D filing with the SEC for its target is 6.3 per cent and reaches a maximum percentage stake of 9.5 per cent. Meanwhile, the median initial US $ stake at cost is 15.0 reaching a maximum of 24.8 million when adjusted to constant 2007 US $. It is important to note that hostile activist cases exhibit larger ownership stakes in target firms and greater capital commitments by hedge funds, especially at the higher percentiles of the sample.

One important pattern that emerged from the data is that hedge fund activism does not generally involve controlling blocks. At the 95th percentile of the sample, Brav, Jiang and Kim (2009) find that hedge funds hold 29.2 per cent in the target firms—a considerably lower investment than the majority requirement. Boyson and Mooradian (2007) also document that the mean initial (maximum) percentage ownership by hedge funds in target firms is 8.8 (12.4) per cent, while Greenwood and Schor (2009) report a 9.8 per cent average initial ownership in their sample. We therefore infer that activist hedge funds generally do not seek to take control of target firms. Instead, hedge funds effectively pursue strategies and tactics with the purpose of creating value from the perspective of minority shareholders. Activists face the challenge of working to garner support from other shareholders, especially when shareholder voting is necessary to facilitate changes in the target firm. These patterns distinguish activist hedge funds from the corporate raiders of the 1980s who sought complete control of the target organization with the purpose of deriving all profits and benefits from their actions. Brav, Jiang and Kim (2009) also report the various forms of exit strategies, where selling in the open market accounts for two-thirds of all complete events.

One major source of controversy in the public debate surrounding hedge fund activism is the intended investment horizon of the activists. Critics have accused activist funds of aiming for short-term trading gains at the expense of longer-term shareholder value. Brav, Jiang and Kim (2009) measure the 'exit date' when the activist hedge fund significantly reduces its investment in the target company by way of multiple sources. 'Exit Date' is defined as when ownership decreases below the required 5 per cent disclosure threshold in amendments to 13D filings. The date when the outcome of the target firm's sale or the fund's withdrawal from the intervention is announced is applied as a second source to determine 'Exit Date'. As the sample period is across the time frame of 2001 to 2007, many recent events remain unresolved at the close of data collection, with exit information only being available for 42.9 per cent of activist events.

In the sub-sample of completed events where information to determine exit date is available, Brav, Jiang and Kim (2009) find the median duration of investment from first filed Schedule 13D to divestment to be 266 days. The average duration of investment is 376 days, which implies that the distribution of the duration is right-skewed. The respective 25th and 75th percentile figures for the full sample are 126 days and 487 days. Furthermore, the investment horizon for activism events initiated with hostility is of shorter duration than non-hostile investments in target firms. One shortcoming of these data is that the numbers generally underestimate the unconditional duration of hedge funds' investments in their target firms for two principal reasons: investments censored at the end of the sample period are excluded, while the end of an investment is measured when ownership decreases below 5 per cent. When applying annual portfolio turnover rates of activist hedge funds as measured by quarterly holdings disclosed in their 13F filings, Brav et al. (2008a) find the average holding period in a position to be nearly two years. The evidence regarding the duration of investment is supported by Boyson and Mooradian (2007), who show that for hostile and non-hostile events, the average duration of activist hedge funds' investment in their sample is 496 and 773 days, respectively.

3.   CHARACTERISTICS OF TARGET FIRMS

What type of companies do activist hedge funds target? Brav, Jiang and Kim (2009) find that target firms are generally smaller than comparable, non-target firms. This result is consistent with evidence supplied by Klein and Zur (2009), Greenwoord and Schor (2009), Clifford (2008), Boyson and Mooradian (2007) and Mietzner and Schweizer (2008). Hedge funds are less likely to engage larger firms due to the associated cost of capital that is needed to build a meaningful stake in the target firm. Moreover, given that the median activist hedge fund manages less than US$1 billion in assets, acquiring a sizeable stake in a large firm might introduce an inordinate amount of idiosyncratic risk in their portfolio.[1]

Activist hedge funds often resemble 'value investors' as the probability of activism is higher in the case of firms with low market-to-book valuations. The analysis suggests that activist investors seek to identify undervalued companies where the potential for improvement is high. Our analysis is supported by the fact that, in two-thirds of events in the sample, the activist hedge fund has explicitly stated its belief that the target firm is undervalued. In pursuit of abnormal returns, activists seek to profit from improvement in the target firms' operations and strategies, so that hedge funds tend to target firms whose stock prices have yet to reflect potential for improvement. Target firms tend to demonstrate a significantly higher ability to achieve profits in terms of return on assets relative to their peers

---

[1]   This was demonstrated anecdotally when Bill Ackman chose to create a fund in 2007 to hold shares in Target and bring about changes in what was a significantly larger corporation.

and tend to be low growth. Our analysis also shows that the target firms' dividend payouts are significantly lower relative to peers, when measured by their dividend yield. Coupled with the results on the return on assets for target firms, this is evidence that target firms generate handsome cash flows but are reluctant to pay out to investors – one symptom of the agency problem of free cash flow according to Jensen (1986). Apart from providing insights into the current state of hedge fund activism, this evidence also suggests a crucial evolution in activist investing, as earlier institutional activism focused on poorly performing companies (Gillian and Starks (2007)).

The aforementioned characteristics are consistent across different studies. In particular, Boyson and Mooradian (2007) report that target firms have a lower Tobin's q, sales growth rate, payout ratio and dividend yield relative to the industry/size/book-to-market-matched firms. They also find that target firms have a higher operating profitability in terms of return on assets and cash flow relative to matched firms. Clifford (2008) also finds that firms in the active blocks earn higher returns on assets and on equity and have lower market-to-book and leverage ratios than those in the passive blocks. Overall, these characteristics suggest that hedge fund activists target firms characterized by stable but undervalued businesses, generating sound cash flows, rather than firms facing operational problems or having uncertain business prospects. On the investment side, target firms spend less than their peers on research and development, scaled by lagged assets. This finding is corroborated by Boyson and Mooradian (2007).

Brav, Jiang and Kim (2009) find that target firms are also characterized by significant higher institutional ownership and analyst coverage relative to peers. However, the effect of analyst coverage is not robust. Both institutional ownership and analyst coverage proxy for shareholder sophistication, which is crucial for activist hedge funds as they must rely on the understanding and support of fellow shareholders when attempting to implement changes due to the minority stake they hold in the target.

Brav, Jiang and Kim (2009) also find that target firms exhibit higher trading liquidity than comparable firms. The main benefit of high liquidity for hedge fund activists is that they may accumulate a stake in the target company within a short period of time while avoiding the associated costs of adverse market impact. Norli, Ostergaard, and Schindele (2010) provide evidence that stock market liquidity facilitates intervention by activist investors. Lastly, both Brav, Jiang and Kim (2009) and Brav et al. (2008a) measure governance characteristics by the Gompers, Ishii, and Metrick (2003) governance index that tracks 24 takeover defenses that firms can adopt, as well as the laws of the state in which the targets are incorporated.

Both studies find that target firms tend towards greater takeover defenses which impose limitations on shareholder rights in target firms.

The characteristics of target firms in activism events in international capital markets are broadly consistent with those in the US. Uchida and Xu (2008) and Hamao, Kutsuna and Matos (2010) show that hedge fund activism in Japan tends towards targets perceived as undervalued when proxied by low market-to-book ratios and targets that use less leverage than matched firms. For activism events in the UK, Becht, Franks, Mayer, and Rossi (2009) report evidence that is consistent with the hypothesis that the target firms in an activist hedge fund's portfolio are small, 'value' firms.

In summary, the characteristics of target firms suggest that the potential problems that hedge funds identify tend to be general issues, including changes in governance and payout policies, as opposed to issues that are unique to individual firms, such as a decline in sales. At the same time, targeted firms do not appear to suffer from serious operational difficulties as indicated by their sound cash flows and profitability. The potential problems that these firms face are likely related to the agency problem of free cash flow, such as relatively low dividend payouts and diversifying investments that may not be in the best interest of shareholders or, more broadly, in that of the operation of the target firm relative to its industry peers and/or main competitors. These targeting patterns seem sensible given that hedge funds are normally not experts in the specific business of their target firms. Focusing on issues that are generalizable to other potential target firms helps lower the marginal cost of launching activism on a new company (Black (1990)) and, simultaneously, increases the likelihood that the details of the intervention are understood by the market (Kahn and Winton (1998)). In short, activist hedge funds perform the service of re-aligning interests with incentives when perceived and, often, real conflicts of interests arise between management and shareholders.

4.   DO HEDGE FUND ACTIVISTS CREATE VALUE FOR SHAREHOLDERS?

The fundamental question for hedge fund activism is whether it achieves the stated goal of creating sustainable value for shareholders, and if so, across what investment horizon. We address this question by examining short-run stock returns around the announcement of activism events as well as subsequent long-run returns. This analysis addresses how the stock market perceives, *ex-ante*, the effect of hedge fund activism on shareholder value and whether the long-run measures are consistent with the market's initial perception.

4.1 Event-day Returns Around the Announcement of Activism

Brav, Jiang and Kim (2009) adopt short-run and long-run event windows around the announcement of activism events, defined as the Schedule 13D filing date if available, or the first announcement of targeting in media articles if the hedge fund ownership stake is lower than 5 per cent. A run up in stock price of about 2.6 per cent is observed between ten days and one day prior to filing with the SEC. An increase of 1.0 and 1.2 per cent occurs on the filing day and the following day, respectively. Afterwards the abnormal return keeps trending up for a total of 6.0 per cent in 20 days. Klein and Zur (2009) report the average market-adjusted abnormal return is 7.2 per cent for the [-30, +30] window surrounding the announcement date. Both Clifford (2008) and Boyson and Mooradian (2007) document significant and positive average abnormal announcement-day returns ranging from 3.4 to 8.1 per cent for various event windows. Greenwood and Schor (2009) find that the average abnormal return for the [-10, +5] window is 3.6 per cent for their sample and is highest for events related to asset sales and block mergers for the target firm.

The evidence, outside the US, for the market's belief that activist hedge funds create value in target firms is consistent with the documented evidence in US capital markets. Becht, Franks, and Grant (2009) calculate the average cumulative abnormal return around the [-25, +25] announcement-day window to be about 6.0 per cent for their sample of activism events in Europe. Stokman (2008) also reports a similar magnitude of abnormal returns for European cases: the average cumulative abnormal return during the [-25, +25] window is 12.2 per cent. For activism events in Germany, Mietzner and Schweizer (2008) report the average abnormal return of 6.24 per cent for the [-20, +20] window around the announcement of activists' acquisition of stakes. For Japan, Uchida and Xu (2008) document an average excess return of 5.6 per cent for the [-2, +2] window around the announcement of activism events although Hamao, Kutsuna and Matos (2010) find a lower 1.8 per cent abnormal return for the [-5, +5] event window. Market reaction is higher at 3.8 per cent in activist events classified as hostile. Thus, the evidence suggests that investors believe that hedge fund activism adds value to target firms.

Brav, Jiang and Kim (2009) also find that the average abnormal return during the [-20, +20] event window is higher for earlier sample years rather than for later ones. The average abnormal event-day return is nearly 14 per cent on average in 2001 and decreases to less than 4 per cent in 2006 and 2007. This decline in return may be driven by competition: as this activist 'arbitrage' strategy proved fruitful more players entered the field, which in turn reduced the equilibrium returns to activism. The study also finds that activism aimed at the sale of the target generates the highest abnormal return at 8.54 per cent. Becht, Franks, and Grant (2009) document a similar difference in average abnormal returns between acquired firms at 8.1 per cent and non-acquired targets at 5.2 per cent for their sample of activism events in Europe. Brav, Jiang and Kim (2009) report that activism related to business strategy generates a significant abnormal return of 5.95 per cent. Meanwhile, activists who target capital structure and governance generate lower positive abnormal announcement returns that are statistically insignificant. Similarly, Becht, Franks, and Grant (2009) show that the announcement of board turnover outcomes produces abnormal returns close to zero. These results contrast, however, with the evidence in Boyson and Mooradian (2007), who report that activist investing related to corporate governance is associated with the most favorable stock market reaction. Thus, the evidence on the market's perception of governance-related activism is mixed.

4.2   Long-term Returns in Target Firms Resulting from Hedge Fund Activism

The high event-day abnormal return documented in the previous section is consistent with alternative hypotheses that refute value-creation by activist hedge funds. These include a temporary upward price pressure created by the lead hedge fund or followers, and market over-reaction. If the price change is interpreted purely as a temporary impact we should expect to observe evidence of negative abnormal returns shortly after the event. Brav, Jiang and Kim (2009) conduct additional tests and extend the sample through one year post-activism and do not find evidence consistent with mean-reversion, thus refuting the 'temporary price impact' hypothesis. These results are comparable to those in Clifford (2008). Overall, the evidence in the literature suggests that abnormal returns around event time are positive for targets of hedge fund activism and that positive abnormal returns do not revert up to a year after the initiation of activism. This evidence clearly refutes the market over-reaction hypothesis and supports the hypothesis that hedge fund activism creates value for shareholders.

4.3   Performance of Target Firms Before and After Activism

If hedge fund activism creates shareholder value by intervening in target firms, one would also anticipate improvements in terms of operating performance, capital structure and corporate governance following the intervention by activist hedge funds. This section reviews the evidence on the changes in target firms post-activism along various measures of corporate policy and performance.

Brav, Jiang and Kim (2009) and Brav et al. (2008a) proxy for the target firm's operating profitability by measuring its return on assets, prior, at, and after the activism event. Both studies find that targeted companies generally achieve higher operating profitability relative to their corresponding industry/year/size matched peers. However, the performance of targeted firms deteriorates during the event year and roughly recovers to the pre-event level two years following the event.

The change in payout policy occurs sooner with hedge fund intervention. Total payout (including both dividends and share repurchases by the target firm) increases during the year of intervention and peaks in the following year. Compared to the pre-event year level the average total payout by target firms increases 0.1 to 0.2 percentage points in post-event years. However, these changes are not statistically significant. Dividend initiation to shareholders increases the year following the event, with a 1.2 percentage point significant difference in the probability of initiation between the year prior to and year after the intervention. The net leverage ratio[2] increases by 1.0 to 1.3 percentage points compared to the level in the year before the event (these changes are also not statistically significant at conventional levels).

Several other studies provide similar evidence on the effect of hedge fund activism on target firm performance and policy. Boyson and Mooradian (2007) demonstrate that target firms exhibit increases in return on assets, cash flow, Tobin's q, and payout and a decrease in cash holdings one year after intervention by activist hedge funds. Clifford (2008) provides additional evidence that firms targeted by activist hedge funds experience a decrease in cash levels and increases in operating profitability, leverage, and dividend yield. Similarly, Klein and Zur (2009) document that one year after activist intervention, target firms decrease cash balances and increase leverage and dividend payout. Furthermore, evidence in Kim (2009) suggests that, following the intervention of activist hedge funds, the managers of target firms are less involved with self-interested over-investment using the firms' cash flow compared to the pre-event period. Hamao, Kutsuna and Matos (2010) find that targets in Japan experience an increase in payouts although there is no evidence that other financial and governance policies have changed significantly. Lastly, Becht, Franks, Mayer, and Rossi (2009) find that target firms in the UK experience decreases in

---

[2] Net leverage is defined as total debt minus cash holdings scaled by book assets, within two years post intervention.

total assets and numbers of employees and an increase in return on assets during activism events. This result suggests that activist funds facilitate active restructuring and slack-cutting in the target firms. Collectively, the evidence in these studies broadly supports the hypothesis that hedge fund activism enhances firm performance by reducing agency costs associated with free cash flow and by subjecting managers to increased discipline.

Concerning the financial strength of target firms, changes in Altman's (1968) Z-score, a widely used proxy for bankruptcy risk in the literature, suggest that although overall credit worthiness improves in years following activist intervention, the changes are not statistically significant. An alternative measure of financial strength, the distance to default, measures the number of standard deviation decreases in the firm value before it fails the debt obligations based on Merton's (1974) bond pricing model. Target firms experience improvements in the safety of debt claims from the event-year to two years following the event. Moreover, differences between the post-event years and the year prior to activism are highly significant. Overall, these results suggest that credit worthiness of debt claims issued by target firms improves after the intervention of activist hedge funds.

A relevant question is what the impact of hedge fund activism is on executives. Brav, Jiang and Kim (2009) classify an event as 'CEO turnover' if the name of the target firm's CEO differs from the prior year in the ExecuComp database. Their analysis shows that one year after the activism event, the CEO turnover rate among surviving target firms increases significantly when benchmarked to one year prior to intervention, with an increase of 5.5 percentage points. These measurements underestimate CEO turnover as CEO departures resulting from the liquidation or sale of the firm are excluded. The study also finds that CEO compensation at target firms is higher relative to peers leading up to the event year and decreases in the years following activism investing (the differences are statistically insignificant), becoming indistinguishable from peer levels one year after hedge fund targeting. A related pattern is the increase in pay-for-performance sensitivity, which is measured as the percentage of CEO's total compensation that results from equity-based incentives such as shares and options: targeted firms experience a significant increase in pay-for-performance two years after the event year compared to the year before the event. Overall, hedge funds succeed at reducing executive compensation to industry standards, enhancing pay-for-performance, and ousting CEOs. These actions appear to be far more widespread than implied by the activist hedge funds' publicly stated objectives as in only 5.6 per cent of all activism events hedge funds openly request CEOs of target firms to step down and only in 4.7 per cent of all events hedge funds demand a reduction in compensation. It follows that hedge funds carry out governance-related agendas more frequently than stated in the public domain.

To summarize, hedge fund activism has proved successful in improving operating performance, increasing dividends and share repurchases and reducing agency costs at target firms. Activist investing is also associated with heightened discipline of senior management as measured by actions taken vis-à-vis the CEO of the target firm including but not limited to removal and reduction in pay. These crucial results imply that one small group of block holders – activist hedge funds – are effective at influencing corporate policies and enhancing corporate governance.

4.4 Value Creation, Stock Picking, or Wealth Transfer?

The primary competing hypothesis to explain the positive market reaction to hedge fund activism is that hedge fund activists simply identify and alert the market to the presence of undervalued companies without, however, adding to the firms' fundamental value. According to this hypothesis, the positive market reaction results from new information regarding the identification of an undervalued, publicly listed corporation and not from the announcement that a hedge fund has committed to intervene to enhance value to shareholders. Given the strong evidence stated earlier in this review that hedge funds target 'value' firms, it is plausible that obtaining the value return is indeed a part of the hedge funds' strategy.

Brav et al. (2008a) present several types of evidence that refute this alternative hypothesis as a viable explanation. For instance, they examine the sub-sample where activist hedge funds revealed a significant ownership in the 13F filing prior to the filing of a Schedule 13D and the associated abnormal returns at the time of the 13D filing. This sub-sample of events sheds light on the controversy surrounding whether activists engage in stock-picking or create value through intervention, since the new information in the subsequent 13D filing signals intervention rather than simply stock-picking. Based on the results of the cross-sectional regression in which the dependent variable is the announcement-day abnormal return, Brav et al. (2008a) report that the coefficient on the dummy variable for the existence of the 13F filing prior to the 13D filing is, indeed, significantly negative. However, they find that this sub-sample of events displays a significant announcement window return that is comparable to that in the full sample despite the little additional information regarding ownership stakes disclosed in the 13D filing. These results suggest that it is the expectation regarding the hedge fund's intervention instead of the information on stock-pricking that drives the positive announcement returns.

Brav et al. (2008a) further argue that activist hedge funds are not merely stock-pickers because hedge funds would be incentivized to sell either shortly after the announcement or simultaneously as the market re-adjusts its valuation of the target firm. Prior evidence, however, is that activist hedge funds continue to hold their stakes in their target firms for relatively long periods of time. Moreover, their analysis finds that in 94 per cent of events, hedge funds exit only following a resolution of their stated goals. Thus, the price reaction likely reflects not only the market's expectation of the hedge funds' identifying an undervalued firm, but also their intent and commitment to implement the proposed changes. It is quite difficult for a hedge fund to consistently exit at a high price without following-through on its proposed course of action.

The second alternative hypothesis attributes the positive excess returns to shareholders to a wealth transfer from other stakeholders. Brav et al. (2008a) examine the 'wealth transfer' hypothesis by focusing on two other important groups of stakeholders of a target firm: creditors and senior management, as represented by the CEO. Regarding creditors, the study shows that if target company shareholders gain at the expense of its creditors by the process of increasing leverage and lowering the firm's debt rating, then the gains earned by shareholders should be higher in companies with higher levels of leverage. This is likely to be the case for firms with long-term debt, as the terms for short-term debt can be adjusted quickly to reflect the new leverage conditions. However, the relation between abnormal announcement-window returns and the long-term debt ratio (scaled by the market value of capital) is economically small, holding constant other covariates. A cleaner test is obtained from the sub-sample of 174 targets that do not hold long-term debt, thus implying no creditors to expropriate. This sub-sample exhibits somewhat higher announcement window returns than the remaining sample that has long-term debt. The overall evidence, therefore, suggests that it is unlikely that the expropriation of bondholders is a meaningful source of shareholder gains in the wake of the announced activism.

Aslan and Maraachlian (2009) also focus on the dynamics of wealth transfers between creditors and shareholders through the process of activist investing by hedge funds. Based on a data set of activist filings at the SEC from 1996 to 2008, they find that target *bondholders* earn a mean excess return of 2 per cent around the nine-day announcement window. Furthermore, their study finds that activism events with well-defined objectives in areas of reform (such as corporate governance) are associated with higher excess bondholder returns than events that simply target the general and ambiguous identification of asset undervaluation. Their findings provide additional support for the perspective that increased shareholder value is driven by the active intervention of hedge funds instead of by wealth transfers from bondholders. Not surprisingly, they document that certain sub-samples of hedge fund activism, such as aiming to sell all or part of the target firms' assets, produces negative excess bond returns on average; moreover, the loss is driven by the sample of bonds with weak covenant protections.

Huang (2010) identifies leveraged buyouts (LBO) as a potential channel through which activist hedge funds create value for shareholders. He samples 237 buyout proposals in the US from 1990 to 2007 and documents that pre-announcement equity holdings by hedge funds (but not other institutional investors, such as pensions and mutual funds) are positively associated with the initial LBO premium offered by the acquirer. Furthermore, he finds that this positive relation holds only for activist hedge funds (i.e., filers of the Schedule 13D form) and that activist hedge funds increase their stakes in targets following the announcement of buyout offers. The latter result suggests that hedge fund activists protect the shareholder wealth of target firms by increasing their stakes in the firm in order to enhance their bargaining power against the acquirer. Overall, his findings suggest that activist hedge funds create value for target shareholders in LBO transactions through their bargaining power over potential buyers.

Similarly, Cheng, Huang and Li (2010) show how hedge fund activists are able to bring about changes in target firms' financial reporting decisions, leading to an increase in accounting conservatism. The basic premise is that conservatism improves hedge funds' ability to monitor the target's managers, as it reduces information asymmetry and therefore leads to higher firm value. They gather a sample of 1901 activist events over the period 1994 to 2005 and find that after the intervention target firms indeed exhibit greater timeliness in recognizing losses than gains. Conservatism is highest when hedge funds have built large financial stakes and undertaken hostile tactics. They conclude that hedge funds' intervention brings about improvements in target firms' financial reporting policies and, as a result, improved monitoring of the target firms' management.

Jiang, Li, and Wang (2010) deliver the same message but from a different perspective, by analyzing a sample of US bankruptcy filing firms during the 1996 to 2007 time period. Their study finds that abnormal stock returns during the bankruptcy filing process are higher among the sub-sample where a hedge fund is among the largest unsecured creditors. The fact that when hedge funds act as creditors does not come at the expense of shareholders indicates that they enhance the overall value of firms in Chapter 11 proceedings by providing fresh capital, reducing the frequency of inefficient liquidations and smoothing out the frictions among different classes of claims.

To summarize, the evidence in the literature indicates that hedge fund activism *creates* value for shareholders, mainly through the active intervention of activist funds in the management of their target firms or, occasionally, through their negotiation of deals with potential acquirers rather than through the simple extraction of value from creditors or through the exercise of superior stock-picking skills by activist hedge funds.

5.   RETURNS TO HEDGE FUND ACTIVISM

In this section we examine whether hedge fund activists create value for *their own* investors. Given that activist funds carry the burdens associated with the costs of intervention and only receive a small proportion of the direct gain resulting from their efforts, a priori, it is unclear whether such activities are profitable for their investors. If one perceives activist investing as a form of arbitrage,[3] this question is illuminating for at least two reasons. First, activist hedge fund profitability is a necessary condition for their survival and long-term success. Like other types of arbitrage, profitability decreases as interest in the new strategy arises and subsequent competition by other hedge funds engaged in activism increases in pursuit of earning excess returns with minimal risk, as evidenced by trends over the past few years. The continuous process of discovery of a stable equilibrium strategy in pursuit of profitability ensures that hedge fund activism will remain a staple of corporate governance in the foreseeable future.

Second, if markets are efficient, abnormal returns to an investment strategy should persist only when activists have access to private information. In conventional settings, superior information on the value of the target firm is assumed to be outside the control of the investors and unknown at large to the market. Within the context of activist investing, the value of the firm could be potentially affected by the activist's action. As a result, the fund's superior information on its own intention to intervene becomes valuable. This non-conventional form of private information calls for potential extensions of existing regulation regarding informed trading. For example, when a lead hedge fund 'tips' a small set

---

[3]   Bradley, Brav, Goldstein, and Jiang (2010) analyze shareholder activism (mostly by hedge funds) in closed-end funds. Closed-end funds serve as an ideal laboratory for analyzing value improvement from activism because their discount (the deviation of actual from potential value) can be accurately measured. They find that activism during 1988 to 2003 reduces the close-end fund discounts to a half of their original level on average.

of investors, such as members of an alleged 'wolf-pack', on its intention to engage a target firm with activist intentions prior to filing the Schedule 13D, the informed parties can gain at the expense of uninformed sellers. However, such actions do not violate the existing rules, as such private information is not considered proprietary about the firm. In a similar vein, the hedge fund could trade derivative instruments based on the private information regarding its own agenda (Hu and Black (2006), Brav and Mathews (2011)), which has evolved into a contentious issue in the recent debate regarding disclosure.

5.1 Returns to Activist Funds

Brav et al. (2008b) offer a detailed analysis of the returns to activist hedge funds based on two data sources: a combination of databases of self-reporting hedge funds and the institutional quarterly holdings maintained by the Thomson 13F database. They succeed at matching 103 unique funds with at least 12 months of return data across a time period stretching from January 1995 (or an earlier available date) through June 2007 (or the latest report date).

To analyze the performance of activist hedge funds, their study measures one- and four-factor alphas for each activist hedge fund using either 36-month or as many months as possible, conditioned on the fact that funds report at least 12 months of data, and rolling window factor loadings. This process allows for time-varying loadings on the factors by the hedge funds. To benchmark activist performance against other self-reported hedge funds that do not engage in activist investing, they measure fund alphas relative to two hedge fund samples: the first includes all hedge funds followed by *HedgeFund.net*; and the second includes all equity-oriented hedge funds in *HedgeFund.net*. Based on this sample of returns to activist and non-activist hedge funds, Brav et al. (2008b) find that the performance of activist hedge funds exceeds that of the full sample of self-reported hedge funds and the sub-sample of equity-oriented hedge funds for both one-factor and four-factor alpha measures. Specifically, they report that the respective average (median) of one- and four-factor monthly alphas for the sample activist hedge funds is 0.71 per cent (0.68 per cent) and 0.64 per cent (0.63 per cent), as compared to 0.41 per cent (0.33 per cent) and 0.39 per cent (0.29 per cent) for the full sample of hedge funds. Brav et al. (2008b) find that activist hedge fund returns tend to commove with the returns of both small and value-oriented hedge funds. In addition, the relatively low sensitivity to the market factor indicates that activists probably establish positions beyond buy-and-hold stakes in the common stock. However, the commonly used non-equity factors are not significant in the return regressions for activist funds. The size and value tilt is also consistent with the characteristics of target firms described in Section 3.

The returns discussed above do not accrue entirely to hedge funds, as launching activism is costly. Gantchev (2009) is the only study that seeks to calibrate the net return after incorporating such costs, in particular at the crucial and costly stage of a proxy contest. Analyzing a dataset of 1492 hedge fund campaigns between 2000 and 2007, he finds that the average activist campaign costs US$10.5 million, or one-third of the average gross return for the deal.

6.   CONCLUSION

This review serves as a comprehensive survey of research on hedge fund activism, a new phenomenon that has emerged during the past decade and has been widespread across various sectors of industry and multiple countries. Overall, the research we survey supports the belief that, by way influencing the governance, capital structure decisions and operating performance of target firms, hedge fund activism creates value for shareholders.

BIBLIOGRAPHY

Altman, E.I. (1968), 'Financial ratios, discriminant analysis and the prediction of corporate bankruptcy', *Journal of Finance,* **23**(4), 589–609.

Aslan, H. and H. Maraachlian (2009), 'Wealth effects of hedge fund activism on bondholders', Working Paper, University of Houston.

Becht, M., J. Franks, C. Mayer, and S. Rossi (2009), 'Returns to shareholder activism: Evidence from a clinical study of the Hermes UK Focus Fund', *Review of Financial Studies,* **22**(8), 3093–3129.

Becht, M., J. Franks, and J. Grant (2009), 'Hedge fund activism in Europe', Working Paper, London Business School.

Black, B. (1990), 'Shareholder passivity reexamined', *Michigan Law Review,* **89**(3), 520–608.

Boyson, N. and R. M. Mooradian (2007), 'Hedge funds as shareholder activists from 1994–2005', Working Paper, Northeastern University.

Bradley, M., A. Brav, I. Goldstein, and W. Jiang (2010), 'Activist arbitrage: A study of open-ending attempts of closed-end funds', *Journal of Financial Economics,* **95**(1), 1–19.

Brav, A., W. Jiang, F. Partnoy, and R. Thomas (2008a), 'Hedge fund activism, corporate governance, and firm performance', *Journal of Finance,* **63**(4), 1729–75.

Brav, A., W. Jiang, F. Partnoy, and R. Thomas (2008b), 'The returns to hedge fund activism', *Financial Analysts Journal,* **64**(6), 45–61.

Brav, A. and R. Mathews (2011), 'Empty voting and the efficiency of corporate governance', *Journal of Financial Economics,* **99**(2), 289–307.

Brav, A., W. Jiang, and H. Kim (2009), 'Hedge fund activism: A Review', *Foundations and Trends in Finance,* **4**(3), 185–246.

Cheng, C.S.A., H.H. Huang and Y. Li (2010), 'Hedge fund intervention and accounting conservatism', Working Paper, Louisiana State University.

Clifford, C. (2008), Value creation or destruction? 'Hedge funds as shareholder activists', *Journal of Corporate Finance,* **14**(4), 323–36.

Gantchev, N. (2009), 'The cost of activist monitoring: Evidence from a sequential decision model', Working Paper, Wharton School.

Gillan, S. L. and L. T. Starks (2007), 'The evolution of shareholder activism in the United States', *Journal of Applied Corporate Finance,* **19**(1), 55–73.

Gompers, P., J. Ishii, and A. Metrick (2003), 'Corporate governance and equity prices', *Quarterly Journal of Economics,* **118**(1), 107–155.

Greenwood, R. and M. Schor (2009), 'Hedge fund investor activism and takeovers', *Journal of Financial Economics,* **92**(3) 362–75.

Grossman, S. J. and O. D. Hart (1980), 'Takeover bids, the free-rider problem, and the theory of the corporation', *The Bell Journal of Economics,* **11**(1), 42–64.

Hamao, Y., K. Kutsuna, and P. Matos (2010), 'Investor activism in Japan: The first 10 years', Working Paper, University of Southern California.

Hu, H. and B. Black (2006), 'The new vote buying: empty voting and hidden (morphable) ownership', *Southern California Law Review,* **79**(4), 811–908.

Huang, J. (2010), 'Hedge funds and shareholder wealth gains in leveraged buyouts', Working Paper, National University of Singapore.

Jensen, M. (1986), 'Agency cost of free cash flow, corporate finance and takeovers', *American Economic Review,* **76**(2), 323–9.

Jiang, W., K. Li, and W. Wang (2012), 'Hedge funds and Chapter 11', *Journal of Finance,* **67**(2), 513–560.

Kahn, C. and A. Winton (1998), 'Ownership structure, speculation, and shareholder intervention', *Journal of Finance,* **53**(1), 99–129.

Karpoff, J. M. (2001), 'The impact of shareholder activism on target companies: A survey of empirical findings', Working Paper, University of Washington.

Kim, H. (2009), 'Agency, investment, and corporate governance', Working Paper, Duke University.Klein, A. and E. Zur (2009), 'Entrepreneurial shareholder activism: Hedge funds and other private investors', *Journal of Finance,* **64**(1), 187–229.

Merton, R. C. (1974), 'On the pricing of corporate debt: The risk structure of interest rates', *Journal of Finance,* **29**(2), 449–70.

Mietzner, M. and D. Schweizer (2008), 'Hedge fund versus private equity funds as shareholder activists – differences in value creation', Working Paper, European Business School.

Norli, Ø., C. Ostergaard, and I. Schindele (2010), 'Liquidity and shareholder activism', Working Paper, Norwegian School of Management.

Stokman, W. A. N. (2008), 'Influences of hedge fund activism on the medium term target firm value', Working Paper, Erasmus University Rotterdam.

Shleifer, A. and R. Vishny (1986), 'Large shareholders and corporate governance', *Journal of Political Economy,* **94**(3), 461–88.

Uchida, K. and P. Xu (2008), 'US barbarians at the Japan gate: Cross border hedge fund activism', Working Paper, The Bank of Japan

8. Hedge funds and the detection of managerial fraud
Veronika Krepely Pool*

INTRODUCTION

Hedge funds are among the most active financial markets participants. While no official statistics exist, it is commonly cited that they account for at least half of the daily trading volume on the major exchanges.[1] Yet hedge funds are perhaps also the least transparent financial institutions. Taking advantage of the safe harbor provisions of the securities statues, hedge funds have historically escaped registration with the Securities and Exchange Commission (SEC) as well as disclosure requirements and are currently only subject to the anti-fraud provisions of the law.[2] Their lack of transparency raises questions about how common fraud is in the industry and whether the sector's opaqueness increases the propensity for unscrupulous managerial behavior. Recent hedge fund scandals have further exacerbated these suspicions. Moreover, while the number of scandals (and that of regulatory enforcement cases against hedge funds) is relatively small, the instances of fraud that do come to light tend to be very brazen. Could this suggest that, while perhaps common, hedge fund fraud is often undetected, especially if it does not lead to the fund's demise? What do we know about managerial wrongdoing in the hedge fund industry?

The purpose of this chapter is to address those questions by surveying academic research on hedge fund fraud. This is a relatively new but fast-growing research area. While managerial wrongdoing can take many different forms, the literature and this survey focus on what Bollen and Pool (2010) refer to as 'reporting violations'. These involve untruthful

---

* Indiana University, Bloomington, IN 47405.

[1] 'As Lenders, Hedge Funds Draw Insider Scrutiny', *New York Times*, October 16, 2006 by Jenny Anderson.

[2] The anti-fraud provision of the Investment Advisers Act of 1940 (Rule 206(4)–8) defines fraud as 'any untrue statement of a material fact or [omission] to state a material fact necessary to make the statements made [. . .] to any investor or prospective investor in the pooled investment vehicle; or otherwise [engaging] in any act, practice, or course of business that is fraudulent, deceptive, or manipulative [. . .].'

statements or disclosures about various aspects of the fund with the aim to mislead current or prospective investors, including misrepresenting performance or risk. The misrepresentations often hide lost or stolen funds as a result of high-stakes trading, misappropriation of investors' assets, or even running a Ponzi scheme. Alternatively, managers may engage in what Bollen and Pool (2010) categorize as 'trading violations'. Insider trading or illegal short selling are examples of those regulatory offenses. Recent media attention highlighting the complexities of insider networks indicates that insider trading by hedge funds may indeed be wide-spread, raising important concerns. However, because the detection of such activities requires transaction-level data that are generally not available to researchers, academic research on hedge fund trading violations is scarce.

What makes the investigation of hedge fund fraud very different from that of corruption[3] in other areas of finance is that due to the lack of transparency, researchers are often confined by the limited amount of available information on hedge funds. Securities law does not yet require hedge funds to report to any regulatory agency. Nor is there a comprehensive directory of hedge funds or an industry association that would systematically collect information about individual funds or the industry as a whole. Instead, some funds voluntarily report to commercial databases. These voluntary reports, largely unverified and unaudited as well as characterized by self-selection bias, comprise the main source of hedge fund research. In some cases, researchers supplement these voluntary reports with novel, but, often, less comprehensive sources. For instance, in 2006, following the adoption by the SEC of short-lived Rule 203(b)(3)-2, requiring hedge funds to register as investment advisers, a large number of hedge funds filed with the SEC Forms ADV (filed by investment advisers who register with the SEC). Since the registration requirement was overturned by the US Court of Appeals the following year, the only comprehensive collection of hedge fund Form ADV filings appeared in 2006 and has since been withdrawn. An additional source of information is the sample of SEC Form 13F filings. These filings report long positions in publicly-traded securities by investment advisers with assets under management (AUM) of US$100 million or more. Hedge funds that hold 13F securities and have assets of at least US$100 million are to be found in this data sample. Finally, in a few cases, researchers have access to proprietary hedge fund information collected by due diligence firms.

---

[3]   Corruption and fraud are used interchangeably in this survey though the two concepts are different in the context of law. See, for instance, Snyman, CR. 2002. *Criminal Law*. 4th edition. Durban: Butterworths.

Existing studies have followed two main approaches in order to detect potentially fraudulent behavior among hedge fund managers. The first approach is to look for suspicious patterns in reported returns using voluntarily reported performance results from data vendors. These suspicious patterns are referred to as *performance (red) flags*. If a manager manipulates returns so that reported performance is different from the fund's true performance, the manipulation is likely to leave a trail behind. Uncovering that trail is, however, complicated by the fact that true realized returns are not observable, nor do we have precise knowledge about the underlying data-generating process (that is, researchers have no way of knowing what truthfully reported returns should look like). To circumvent these difficulties, researchers often start with a careful examination of managerial incentives. They then derive econometric models of managerial behavior based on these incentives, as well as the return patterns resulting from that behavior. Examples of performance flags include return smoothness, a discontinuity at zero in the reported return distribution, or low return correlation with a large set of asset classes.

The second approach is to rely on *operational flags*. Operational flags are based on the characteristics of the fund's organizational structure. For instance, the use of affiliated brokers or custodians, or the absence of independent fund audits may create more opportunities for fraud, and, as a result, constitute a red flag. Similarly, managers with a disciplinary record may be more likely to violate the law in the future. Studies in this area obtain data on the funds' organizational structure and characteristics from SEC Form ADV. These forms contain conflict of interest disclosures and information on the manager's disciplinary history. As mentioned above, for hedge funds, the only comprehensive sample of Form ADV data is from 2006. However, those requirements are expected to be reintroduced in 2011 under the Dodd-Frank Wall Street Reform and Consumer Protection Act, thereby reinstating the role of operational flags in fraud detection.

Performance and operational flags complement each other and are both useful tools for investors or investigators. While the fund characteristics they describe do not necessarily imply the presence of fraud in and of themselves, existing studies discussed below find that they are indeed frequently associated with more egregious forms of misbehavior and do help predict fraud. Accordingly, the SEC has been adopting new strategies to combat fraud in the post-Madoff era, which incorporate the risk-based screening of financial firms for potential audits. In describing these risk-based filters, the SEC lists operational flags, such as offering custodian services for clients or using unknown auditors, as well as performance flags, such as smooth or outlier returns as indicators of a heightened risk of fraud.

The aforementioned two sets of flags also provide non-overlapping indicators and accommodate relatively low levels of transparency. Transparency is an important subject of debate within the hedge fund industry. Proponents of transparency argue that more transparency would allow investors to assess fund risk accurately, including the risk of fraud. It could also increase the probability that fraud is detected, and may serve as a deterrent for wrongdoing. Opponents argue that hedge funds' proprietary trading strategies require secrecy. Moreover, extending the regulatory umbrella to hedge funds may result in the latter resembling the mutual fund industry, which, due to the strict regulatory restrictions to which it is subject, is largely unable to participate in more illiquid and more complex markets (Stulz (2007)). As a result, extensive regulation of hedge funds may impede market efficiency. Developing performance and operational flags to detect hedge fund fraud can help address those concerns. In particular, both flag types are easy to implement and their existence should serve as a deterrent for fraud. Moreover, they can be screened for without compromising proprietary trading secrets. Performance flags can be tested in any set of reported returns, including the privately distributed periodic reports investors receive from their funds. Operational flags only require information on the fund's organizational structure and managerial history, yet again allowing funds to keep their trading strategies and portfolio holdings confidential.

The rest of the chapter revisits the issues of regulation and transparency, and the indicators of managerial fraud. This chapter is organized as follows. Section 1 provides a brief summary of the regulatory environment in the hedge fund industry. Section 2 discusses known hedge fund fraud cases. Sections 3 and 4, introduce performance and operational flags, respectively. Section 5 briefly describes additional approaches to fraud detection. Finally, Section 6 provides a conclusion.

1. REGULATORY BACKGROUND

1.1 Brief Regulatory History

To understand the approaches researchers adopt in their study of hedge fund fraud, it is important to first review the US hedge fund industry's regulatory environment, which determines the amount and type of publicly available information.

Interests in hedge funds are securities interests, which are governed by the Securities Exchange Act of 1933, the Investment Company Act of 1940, and the Investment Advisers Act of 1940. While these statutes impose very strict rules on other investment companies (such as mutual funds) in terms of reporting, record-keeping, the use of leverage or complex strategies, and fund fees, hedge funds typically escape most of these requirements due to the safe harbor provisions of those laws. For instance, the Investment Company Act offers exemptions in Sections 3(c)(1) and 3(c)(7). In particular, Section 3(c)(1) exempts from its scope of application investment companies with 100 or fewer investors. Section 3(c)(7) provides an exemption to investment companies that meet two requirements. First, fund investors must be limited to qualified purchasers, that is, high net worth individuals or institutions with a set of minimum liquid wealth requirements and second, the fund can have no more than 499 investors. In addition to these criteria, in order to meet the registration exemption, hedge funds cannot publicly offer their securities. The relevant exemption in the Investment Advisers Act of 1940 is Section 203(b)(3), which also places restrictions on the number of clients and on the ability of the managers to advertise publicly and to act as advisers to registered funds.

Due to the above provisions, from the industry's birth in 1949 – when Alfred W. Jones formed the first hedge fund – until today, hedge funds have been mostly unregulated investment pools. The registration exemptions also mean that no information is systematically collected on the hedge fund industry and the managers. The only exception to this was a temporary change in the regulatory environment, in 2006. Specifically, in December 2, 2004 the SEC amended the Advisers Act with the introduction of Rule 203(b)(3)-2, which eliminated the private adviser exemption of funds with AUM of at least US$25 million and lock up periods of less than two years. Under Rule 203(b)(3)-2, all such funds were required to register with the Commission by February 1, 2006. Several developments prompted this change. For instance, the industry grew considerably throughout the 1990s: while its size was estimated to be around US$50 billion in 1990, the SEC estimated that US$870 billion of assets were under hedge fund management by 2004 (according to BarclayHedge, fund assets were around US$1.91 trillion by 2007 and US$1.6 trillion in the second quarter of 2010)[4]. This tremendous growth was accompanied by the retailization of hedge funds, with retail investors gaining increasing exposure through pension funds and endowments/foundations. In addition, the late trading/market timing scandals in 2003–2004 illustrated how wrong doing by hedge funds had the potential to also harm non-hedge fund investors.

The new Rule was to, however, prove short-lived. Within one year

---

[4]   http://www.barclayhedge.com. These statistics exclude fund of funds assets.

of its adoption, the US Court of Appeals had overturned the vacation requirement in *Phillip Goldstein et al. vs the Securities and Exchange Commission*. Although that requirement was quickly withdrawn, the majority of hedge funds did register with the SEC within 2006. Therefore, for a one-year snapshot, public information on hedge funds became richer with Form ADV filings. These filings pertain to information on the operational and organizational structure of the funds, as well as to important background information about the manager. While these are no longer available for most hedge funds (except for a subset of hedge funds that continue being registered even after 2006), the Private Fund Investment Advisers Registration Act of 2010 (enacted on July 21, 2010 as Title IV of the Dodd-Frank Wall Street Reform and Consumer Protection Act) yet again eliminates the private adviser exemption (Section 203(b) (3)), requiring hedge funds previously organized under Sections 3(c)(1) or 3(c)(7) of the Investment Company Act of 1940 to register with the SEC. The Act will become effective on July 21, 2011. In addition to the regular form ADV filings, the Act also provides for new data collection and record keeping requirements, amounting to a new regulatory regime going forward.

Finally, it is worth noting that although hedge funds have avoided most of the restrictions governing the behavior of other investment companies, they remain under the anti-fraud provisions of the securities statues. In 2007, the SEC expanded the anti-fraud provision, which applies to both registered and unregistered investment advisers, allowing the SEC to impose fines, bar individuals from investment management activities, or even pursue criminal proceedings against them. The expanded rule prohibits false or misleading statements to existing or prospective investors expressed verbally or in writing.

1.2 Regulatory Debate and Transparency

A recurring theme in the financial services field, which is of relevance also to hedge funds, is whether the lack of transparency increases the likelihood of fraud. In particular, the SEC and many commentators have argued that the lack of regulatory scrutiny may attract unscrupulous characters to the hedge fund industry, bent on defrauding investors, and that 'registration may help the hedge fund industry to the extent it discourages persons intent on committing fraud from entering the industry and damaging the reputation of the legitimate managers' (Registration Under the Advisers Act of Certain Hedge Fund Advisers; Final Rule, p. 72058, http://www. sec.gov/rules/final/ia-2333.pdf). While no comprehensive proof exists for this claim, there is some evidence to that effect in the academic literature.

For example, Liang (2003) finds that audited funds display better data quality and that transparency, such as exchange listing, also results in more consistent reporting of hedge fund performance. Bollen and Pool (2009) show that funds that operate in more liquid markets, in which the verification of their performance is easier, have a lower tendency of avoiding negative returns (i.e., mark up returns).

2.   KNOWN FRAUD CASES

In recent years, several highly publicized fraud cases have come to light, including the collapse of the *Bayou Hedge Fund Group* in 2005 and the Madoff scandal in 2008. In both of these cases, theft and misappropriation were concealed for a surprisingly long period of time. In other cases, high operational risks were allowed to spiral out of control, due to a lack of internal risk management systems. One recent example is the failure of *Amaranth Advisors*, which involved market manipulation and misrepresentations by a single energy trader. Although the collapse of *Amaranth* had a much smaller impact on the financial industry than that of *Long-Term Capital Management* in 1998, large fund failures remain a concern due to the risk they represent for the entire financial system, due to the complex and highly leveraged positions that these funds often take.

The industry has experienced a series of other scandals that received less visibility, but which were equally damaging to the reputation of hedge funds. While no official statistics exist on the frequency of fraud events, Bollen and Pool (2010) assemble a comprehensive database of regulatory and legal actions against hedge funds, using a number of sources. *First*, they comb the litigation section of the SEC's website, which publishes the SEC litigation releases and administrative actions against hedge funds. *Second*, the authors collect information from the websites of the Department of Justice and the Commodity Futures Trading Commission on regulatory violations by hedge funds, news releases by the Financial Industry Regulatory Authority, and from the Stanford Law School's Securities Class Action Lawsuit Clearinghouse website on investor lawsuits against hedge funds. Information from these sources is augmented by a collection of fund problem cases from a leading due diligence firm. Finally, Bollen and Pool scan the financial press for additional funds and identify several new cases, including several funds involved in the Madoff scandal. After merging the hedge fund cases, their final list contains over 1000 unique fund names. Of this list, close to 400 fund names are identified in the CISDM/TASS merged data files, representing roughly 2 per cent of all funds. These funds are associated with a wide range of fund problems, from relatively minor regulatory violations to much more serious offenses. Bollen and Pool (2010) categorize each case into two types of violations: *reporting violations* and *trading violations*. Reporting violations include problem funds that are charged with misappropriation, overvaluation, misrepresentation, or running a Ponzi scheme, while trading violations include those cases in which the fund engages, for instance, in illegal short selling or insider trading.

In many instances of the uncovered fraud cases, especially in the reporting violations sample, the fraud is brazen and often leads to the fund's collapse, with large losses for investors. For instance, the emergency enforcement action filed by the Commission in 2002 concerning *Beacon Hill Asset Management* or in 2005 concerning *KL Group* reveal that only a small fraction of investor capital remained by the time the SEC intervened to freeze fund operations. In a large number of the cases, litigation documents reveal that fund managers attempted to misrepresent fund values by overstating performance in order to hide large trading losses or the misappropriation of fund assets.

Perhaps instances of fraud that do not lead to the fund's demise are much less likely to be caught and may never come to light. Other cases may not meet the materiality condition of fraud but, nevertheless, constitute dishonest or harmful behavior. For instance, funds may simply misrepresent or inflate the value of their positions periodically, but mark positions back to market when the opportunity arises. Throughout this chapter, it is argued that uncovering any misrepresentation by fund managers is useful, even if some of these misrepresentations are not material to prompt SEC action. For instance, Bollen and Pool (2008) find that in many SEC cases against hedge funds, intentionally overstated returns often accompany misappropriation or other fraudulent behavior. Hence, screening for a potentially benign pattern in fund returns may identify funds with increased operational risks and an increased probability of fraud; therefore, such benign patterns may serve as a leading indicator of more serious offenses.

Misrepresentations affect investors in two different ways. *First*, they may distort the true risk return tradeoff of the fund by, for instance, under-representing risk. As a result, investors may allow investments in hedge funds to be over-represented in their portfolio, leading to a suboptimal resource allocation in the economy. *Second*, misrepresentations may result in wealth transfers among investors who are leaving the fund and those that are incumbent or entering. For instance, the SEC litigation release for the hedge fund *Marque Partners* provides details on how incumbent investors were able to leave the fund at inflated prices.

3.   PERFORMANCE FLAGS

This section, reviews existing research on performance flags. As mentioned above, the focus of performance flag studies is to identify suspicious patterns in the self-reported performance of hedge funds. Subsections A and B provide the background for performance related fraud research by describing the nature of the available performance data and the managerial incentives, respectively. Subsection C summarizes the extant research in the area.

3.1   Hedge Fund Data

Hedge fund managers in the US are prohibited from publicly advertising their funds. Therefore, to gain publicity, hedge funds often report to data vendors, who then sell their information to potential clients. These fee-based hedge fund data sources are self-reported and unverifiable, both of which characteristics represent handicaps for research on the performance and risk profile of those funds. Interestingly, for forensic fraud analysis, some of these shortcomings are an advantage. For academic research, the three most popular data sources are *Lipper/TASS*, *CISDM*, and *HFR*. Other data sources include *Hedgefund.net*, *BarclayHedge*, *Eureka*, *MSCI*, *Morningstar Altvest*, *Cogenthedge*, and *MARHedge*. Recent papers often combine several data sources, most typically, *Lipper/TASS* and *CISDM*. In the broader hedge fund literature, more comprehensive data pools are assembled in two studies. Agarwal, Daniel, and Naik (2010) and Agarwal, Fos, and Jiang (2010) examine the overlap between five commercially available data sources (TASS, CISDM, HFR, MSCI, and Eureka) to create the most comprehensive collection of self-reported fund returns. Those efforts are important for the insights that they provide into commercially available hedge fund data. Agarwal et al. (2010) find that 71 per cent of the funds in the pooled sample only report to a single database and that the overlap between the individual databases is very low. In a combined sample of the five databases, CISDM features the largest percentage of unique funds (25.8 per cent), followed by TASS (16.7 per cent), but clearly, adding new data sources expands information to previously unstudied funds.

In addition to the differences in coverage, the databases may also differ in the information they contain on particular funds that enter multiple databases. In an early study of hedge fund databases, Liang (2000) compares the information funds report to the HFR and TASS databases. He finds that reported returns, net asset values and several fund characteristics, such as fees or investment objectives, often differ across the two samples. While generally not considered in previous research, those data discrepancies may also represent warning signs of potentially fraudulent conduct in the spirit of Straumann's (2008) data quality flags discussed below.

Finally, since reporting is purely voluntary in the current regulatory environment, self-selection bias is also an important concern. Are available performance histories a good representation of the performance history of the hedge fund universe? And in particular, are fraudulent firms more or less likely to report? While the literature shows that successful firms are less likely to report (Ackermann, McEnally, and Ravenscraft (1999)), and that poor performers are more likely to drop out of the databases (Agarwal, Fos, and Jiang (2010)), there is no direct evidence as to whether fraudulent funds are over or underrepresented in commercially available databases. However, the sample construction in Bollen and Pool (2010) does provide some suggestive evidence. Bollen and Pool report that close to two-thirds of the fund names recorded from litigation or news releases cannot be mapped in the combined *TASS/CISDM* sample. However, the severity of the offenses does not seem to play an important role in the reporting decision. The only exception is the category of Ponzi schemes.

3.2   Managerial Incentives

Since performance reports to data vendors are generally not verified by a third party, they provide a good laboratory for studying suspicious reporting patterns. Unfortunately researchers cannot observe the fund's true performance; therefore, it is not possible to directly identify where reported returns deviate from the actual ones to pinpoint wrongdoing. Instead, researchers look for suspicious patterns derived from the agents' incentives. Of particular interest are outcomes around which payoffs are highly asymmetric. This approach is not unique to hedge funds: several important examples are featured in other research areas, such as proxy voting, sports economics, or accounting. For instance, Listokin (2008) finds that management is much more likely to win by a small margin than lose by a small margin on management-sponsored resolutions. Duggan and Levitt (2002) show that Japanese sumo wrestlers finish the 15 bout tournament with seven wins less frequently than expected but win eight games more frequently than expected. Coincidentally, winning eight matches insures the players' advancement in the official rankings, making eight wins a pivotal outcome. Therefore, wrestlers with seven completed wins have an incentive to win their next match by any means possible, while players with no chance to make it to eight with the remaining games can afford to lose. This asymmetry around eight gives rise to the potential for collusion and fraud. Chandar and Bricker (2002), who subdivide the returns of closed-end funds into returns on restricted securities and unrestricted securities, are perhaps closest to the hedge fund setting. Restricted securities are valued with managerial discretion, while unrestricted securities are liquid and therefore, allow for no discretion in valuation. The authors argue that managers will have an incentive to provide an overly optimistic valuation for restricted securities, when the return on the unrestricted assets is slightly below the benchmark.

Similarly, in the hedge fund industry, a careful examination of the incentive structure points to the conclusion that certain outcomes, such as reporting returns above zero or reporting exceptional returns in December, may be especially desirable. Managerial incentives are driven by two main determinants of the manager's payoffs: the fund's fee structure and its capital flows that ultimately determine the assets under the manager's control. *First*, the fund's fee structure generally contains an incentive fee, which allows managers to capture a portion of the profits. Therefore, zero[5] or the high-water mark may be return hurdles around which manipulation is expected. *Second*, capital flows affect AUM, hence the asset base used for determining the US$ value of the compensation that accrues to the manager. If flows are affected by the fund's performance, managers will have an incentive to manipulate performance in a way that maximizes subsequent flows. Consistent with the well-established result in the mutual fund literature, Agarwal and Nai (2004) find that hedge fund investors reward funds that perform well with large inflows. This means that reporting higher returns is always tempting. Moreover, the results in Agarwal et al. (2010) and Bollen and Pool (2009) also point to the conclusion that managers have an incentive to avoid reporting losses. These papers show that investors are more likely to invest in hedge funds with a higher percentage of positive returns. That is, when two funds have the same average (or cumulative) past performance, but one fund has more positive return months than the other, it receives more investor capital flow. This again motivates zero as a quantitative anchor for reported returns. In addition to achieving good performance, managers also have strong incentives to avoid losses, as those raise the risk of capital withdrawals, leading to a decline in the fund's asset base. Moreover, large outflows often result in costly liquidations, presenting a feedback mechanism that further erodes performance. This

---

[5]   Hedge funds are absolute return funds (Waring and Siegel (2006)), which also suggests that zero may be an important mark.

may be especially true of hedge funds, which are often associated with less liquid holdings or arbitrage strategies that may take time to converge. Therefore, mitigating outflows is another incentive that requires careful consideration. Fund managers may employ lock ups and redemption notice requirements to do so. However, less innocuous techniques may also help achieve the same goal.

3.3 Major Work on Performance Flags

In Subsection 3.2 above, it has been argued that hedge fund managers have an incentive to avoid reporting losses. They also have an incentive to smooth returns more aggressively when non-discretionary returns are low, or at fiscal year ends, when their compensation is determined. Managers who manipulate returns are likely to leave statistical footprints behind. Researchers will then track those footprints or, in other words, performance flags in the self-reported hedge fund returns. Some of the footprints described in this section are the result of managerial behavior that is not material enough to be prosecuted by regulators. However, as mentioned above, these may be important in the sense of signaling larger problems ahead. Other footprints will be associated with much more egregious forms of misbehavior.

Research has identified two ways for managers to avoid reporting losses and alter returns. *First*, Goetzmann et al. (2007) suggest that fund fees are a potential tool as these are accrued monthly but, generally, paid annually. A manager could use, over the year, the accrued fees that are kept in an escrow account to temporarily enhance AUM, with the hope that the fee account can be repaid before year end. While accrued fund fees may give a lot of flexibility to managers to artificially inflate returns, it is difficult to derive the statistical footprints of such actions. This is because the true value of the escrow account is generally intractable for researchers as different investors enter the fund at different times and, as a result, have different high-water marks. Therefore, the majority of existing research concentrates on a second, perhaps even more controversial approach to avoiding losses. In particular, managers may simply misreport or manage realized returns by, for instance, artificially marking up the value of the portfolio in periods when true returns are poor and possibly marking them down in periods of good performance. Such 'return-smoothing' may be more possible when the fund's assets are very illiquid, although the lack of holdings' disclosure may allow similar opportunities in some of the more liquid funds. For instance, Abdulali (2006) argues that in markets where trade prices are not readily available, managers may receive a number of different broker quotes for the same security. Since there is no regulatory guidance on how to select the quote used in valuing assets, managers can distort returns by choosing the most favorable quotes. Moreover, Skeel and Partnoy (2007) argue that, for some assets that require complex valuation models, model inputs may also be manipulated to arrive at auspicious values. Even more blatantly, some managers may simply fabricate returns, as was the case with Madoff. Gregoriou and Lhabitant (2008) report that Madoff's fabricated returns were nearly always positive: *Fairfiled Sentry*, a Madoff feeder-fund only had 10 negative months (5 of which equaled −0.1 per cent) in its 215-month return history.

Several studies focus on the smoothness of hedge fund returns and its implications for return manipulation. Asness, Krail, and Liew (2001) argue that if, in the underlying asset market, the fund's portfolio holdings are traded very infrequently and, as a result, prices are not always available, portfolio marks may simply represent extrapolation from past trade prices. They also argue that the absence of recent traded prices can leave hedge funds with the 'flexibility' to manage reported returns. Stale prices, whether produced by an honest best effort to mark hard-to-price securities to market or by intentional price management, will downward-bias the fund's volatility and distort its correlation with other asset classes. Moreover, the low volatility will also inflate the risk-adjusted performance of the funds. Borrowing from studies that model non-synchronous stock prices (see Scholes and Williams (1977) and Dimson (1979)), Asness et al. regress reported hedge fund index returns on contemporaneous and lagged S&P 500 returns to test for staleness and find that lagged market returns have an important role in explaining hedge fund index returns. Additionally, Asness et al. also attempt to test whether the return smoothness is the result of intentional managerial manipulation or illiquidity. The authors separate S&P 500 returns into up and down markets and estimate lagged betas for both. The results show that lagged betas are larger in down markets than in up markets, which the authors interpret as evidence of intentional managerial smoothing. In particular, the summed lag beta coefficients for the aggregate hedge fund index is 0.17 in up markets and equals 0.79 in down markets, with the difference between the two sums being statistically significant. However, the interpretation of these results can be challenged on the basis of Jagannathan and Korajczyk (1986), who show that option-like returns can also exhibit such asymmetries when they are regressed on linear factors.

Smoothness remains a key concept in hedge fund research. The idea of return smoothness is formalized in Getmansky et al. (2004). In that paper, true hedge fund returns follow a factor model of the following form:

$$R_t = \mu + \beta\Lambda_t + \varepsilon_t, \quad E[\Lambda_t] = E[\varepsilon_t] = 0, \quad \Lambda_t, \varepsilon_t \sim \text{independent},$$
$$\text{Var}[R_t] = \sigma^2 \tag{8.1}$$

where R_t is the true return of a hedge fund in period t. True returns are not observable however. Instead, fund investors observe reported returns modeled as follows:

$$R_t^o = \theta_0 R_t + \theta_1 R_{t-1} + \ldots + \theta_k R_{t-k} \quad \text{where}$$
$$\theta_j \in [0,1] \quad \text{for} \quad j = 0, \ldots, k \tag{8.2}$$
$$1 = \theta_0 + \theta_1 + \ldots + \theta_k$$

That is, the authors assume that returns are not fully revealed contemporaneously. Just as in the Asness et al. framework, Equation 2 can capture several sources of smoothing, including innocuous smoothing due to the illiquidity of hedge fund assets and possible intentional return smoothing by the manager. Getmansky et al. make no attempt to differentiate between the possible alternative explanations. Using Equations 1 and 2, they derive several statistical properties of the reported returns. They show that the transformation described in Equation 2 does not alter the mean return: the mean reported return equals the mean true returns. This is true because, in this framework, the smoothing coefficients θ sum to one. However, smoothing lowers volatility, which means that reported returns will appear less volatile when true returns are smoothed. When interpreted as a risk measure, this means that hedge funds whose reported returns are accurately characterized by Equation 2 appear less risky than they truly are. Moreover, return smoothing also introduces autocorrelation in reported returns, even though successive observations of true returns are not correlated. These properties of smoothness are summarized in Equation 3.

$$E[R_t^o] = \mu$$

$$\text{Var}[R_t^o] = \sigma^2 \sum_{j=0}^{k} \theta_j^2$$

$$\text{Cov}[R_t^o, R_{t-m}^o] = \begin{cases} \sigma^2 \sum_{j=0}^{k-m} \theta_j \theta_{j+m} & \text{if } 0 \le m \le k \\ 0 & \text{if } > k \end{cases} \tag{8.3}$$

Getmansky et al. (2004) find that smoothness is an important feature of hedge fund returns, especially for funds that feature more illiquid holdings, such as the Fixed-Income Directional fund category that displays an estimate of θ_0 that equals 0.76, that is, only about 76 per cent of the actual return gets reported contemporaneously. The authors compare their hedge fund results to the smoothness coefficients they estimate for mutual funds and equity and bond indices. For these later groups smoothness is not a characteristic of returns.

Bollen and Pool (2008) extend the framework of Getmansky et al. (2004) to differentiate between intentional return manipulation and other innocent causes of smoothness. In their paper, they model managerial incentives using an asymmetric reporting algorithm. In the spirit of Chandar and Bricker (2002), Bollen and Pool decompose returns into a discretionary and a non-discretionary component, using factor regressions. Specifically, in the context of Equation 1 above, the non-discretionary component of hedge fund returns is given by the fitted value of the model, while the discretionary component is the error term. They then argue that, when the fund's non-discretionary returns are positive, managers will have no incentive to misvalue the discretionary portion of their portfolios. On the other hand, if non-discretionary returns are negative, some managers may use inflated valuations on the discretionary assets to show favorable performance for the month. The asymmetric reporting scheme is summarized in Equation 4, below, and is motivated by competition among hedge funds and the compensation structure of the hedge fund industry. Of particular interest is the managers' incentive to avoid outflows and generate additional inflows, as discussed in Subsection 3.2, above. The algorithm is also consistent with several known hedge fund fraud cases and is well illustrated by the scandal involving the *National Australia Bank* in 2004 discussed in Bollen and Pool.

Bollen and Pool (2008) modify the Getmansky et al. (2004) smoothing model to capture the asymmetry in the manager's incentives to smooth when true returns are good versus when true returns are poor:

$$R_t^o = (\theta_0(1 - I_t) + \psi_0 I_t) R_t + (\theta_1(1 - I_{t-1}) + \psi_1 I_{t-1}) R_{t-1} + \ldots$$

$$+ (\theta_k(1 - I_{t-k}) + \psi_k I_{t-k}) R_{t-k}$$

$$I_{t-j} = 1 \quad \text{if} \quad R_{t-j} \geq c \quad \text{for} \quad j = 0, \ldots, k$$

$$I_{t-j} = 0 \quad \text{if} \quad R_{t-j} < c \quad \text{for} \quad j = 0, \ldots, k \tag{8.4}$$

where R_t and R_t^o are true and reported returns, respectively, I_{t-1} is an indicator variable that takes the value of one if $R_{t-1} \geq c$ and zero otherwise, and c may represent zero or the non-discretionary component of fund returns. The asymmetric smoothing model implies an asymmetric serial correlation in hedge fund returns; therefore, it provides an empirical framework to test for asymmetrically smoothed returns. This is described as follows:

$$R_t^o a + (b_1^- (1 - I_{t-1}) + b_1^+ I_{t-1}) R_{t-1}^o + \eta_t, \qquad (8.5)$$

that is, if the manager smoothes asymmetrically between good and bad times, the coefficient that measures the association between contemporaneous and lagged reported returns will be higher when lagged returns are poor. In the empirical implementation of the test, the authors redefine the indicator variable so that it turns on, when the fund's non-discretionary return is negative, and off, when it is positive. They approximate non-discretionary returns by the fitted value of the reported returns from factor regressions. The authors estimate equation 5 for each individual fund in their sample and flag funds for which the estimated betas are asymmetric. In cross-sectional analyses, they find that the probability of being flagged is related to the risk of capital flight: funds with more volatile flows are more likely to display asymmetric conditional serial correlation in their returns.

The asymmetric smoothing model of Bollen and Pool (2008) describes an econometric model that uses a specific set of assumptions about managers' reporting behavior. Therefore, it represents only one possible algorithm for screening for potentially suspicious patterns in reported returns. A careful examination of managerial incentives may imply other algorithms that could be similarly used by sophisticated fund investors and regulators.

While the smoothing models in equations 2 and 3 aim to provide an exact mechanism that connects *reported* to *actual* returns (which, in turn implies specific time-series features for reported returns), another approach is to simply look at the behavior of reported returns around specific hurdles that affect the manager's payoff. In particular, one possibility is to examine the return distribution around zero or the high-water mark. Abdulali (2006) and Bollen and Pool (2009) use this insight to propose two approaches to pinpoint performance manipulation by hedge funds. Abdulali (2006) creates a measure called 'bias ratio' for detecting managerial mark-ups in individual funds. The idea of this measure is to count the number of monthly reported returns that fall within one standard deviation to the left as well as to the right of zero. The author argues that funds with very high bias ratios or, in other words, funds with an unusually high number of positive returns, should be flagged as suspicious.

Bollen and Pool (2009) study misreporting in the hedge fund industry using the pooled cross-sectional, time-series returns of hedge funds. The idea is to pinpoint wrongdoing (not at the individual fund level, but for the industry as a whole) by identifying discontinuities in the pooled distribution around important hurdle points, such as zero. The authors develop a powerful econometric technique to determine points of discontinuity. In particular, they first identify a distribution that follows the empirical distribution of hedge fund returns as closely as possible with the constraint that the mimicking distribution is continuous. To achieve a very close fit, the authors fit non-parametric kernel densities serving as the mimicking distribution. The smooth kernel distribution is used as a reference. This is because when the fit is very close, the true distribution of hedge fund returns is not, in statistical terms, significantly different from the mimicking distribution at any point, where the true distribution is also continuous. The two distributions will diverge, however, when reported returns display a discontinuity.

The test statistic, which describes the statistical significance of a deviation from continuity, is derived analytically, as well as using a simulation approach. For the latter, the study generates a large number of draws from the mimicking distribution, each time summarizing the generated information in histograms and recording the number of observations that fall into each of the histogram bins. For each bin, the expected number of observations is then determined by the average number of observations that fall in the bin across all draws, and the standard deviation by the standard deviation of the number of observations in a given bin across all draws. The authors then compute the actual number of observations in each of the bins, using the actual empirical distribution of reported returns. The test statistic, which is available for each of the historgram's bins, is based on comparing the actual number of observations to the number of observations one could expect under continuity.

Using this approach, Bollen and Pool show that the return distribution of the hedge fund industry is quite smooth everywhere except at zero. The large discontinuity at zero reveals the paucity of small negative returns. This finding is consistent with the claim that hedge fund managers artificially manage returns in order to avoid reporting negative results. The authors also address and discard potential alternative explanations and show that return inflation reverses over time, that is, managers correct mark-ups subsequently. This later point is crucial because, if mark-ups are uncorrected, the fund would eventually blow up. For the hedge fund sample as a whole, the authors estimate that approximately 10 per cent of the returns are distorted.

The incentives for return inflation may also vary over time. Agarwal, Daniel, and Naik (2010) argue that managerial mark-ups will be more likely in December due to the compensation structure of hedge funds. In particular, hedge funds pay incentive fees at the end of the year, hence what matters is the fund's value around the payday. Therefore, managers may be tempted to report stronger performance measures in December, in order to earn higher fees. The authors provide evidence on a December spike and connect this spike to the strength of managerial incentives. After controlling for risk, funds with higher incentives display a significant premium (between 34 to 70 basis points) in December above the average return they earn from January to November. Greater incentives are associated with higher pay-for-performance sensitivities, short lock-ups and restriction periods, and high management fees. The authors also show that the December spike is more pronounced for funds that operate in a more favorable environment for opportunistic reporting, such as high volatility or illiquid funds.

Finally, in addition to return mark-ups and smoothing (that are likely to be reversed for most funds before deviations from true values are large enough to risk irreversible consequences), for Ponzi schemes or otherwise misappropriating managers, the footprints of fraud in reported returns can be very simple. For instance, in his whistleblower letter to the SEC, Harry Markopolos detailed several warning signs about the characteristics of the reported returns in the Bernie Madoff feeder-funds. Among these is the simple observation that a Madoff feeder-fund reported an unrealistically low number of negative monthly returns for a long (215-month) time period encompassing a great variety of market conditions. Similarly, he also noted the lack of correlation between Madoff's returns and the S&P 500 index, which was especially troublesome as Madoff's stated strategy implied a positive correlation. Indeed, anecdotal evidence suggests that correlation between a fund's return and the return on existing asset classes is a popular screen for fraud in the industry. While investing in hedge funds is valuable in large part because of the low correlation between these funds and other asset classes, the non-correlation of fund returns with *any* asset class raises a red flag.[6]

Straumann (2008) proposes data quality measures that can be used to identify artificial patterns in fund returns. For instance, managers who fabricate returns may report strings of identical values, too many observations that are exactly equal to zero, frequently repeating observations, or numbers whose last digit is not uniformly distributed. Straumann scores hedge funds based on five such data quality indicators, but does not take a

---

[6]   It is important to note, however, that two papers in the hedge fund literature interpret the lack of correlation as managerial skill (see Sun et al. (2009) and Titman and Tiu (2008))

strong stand on whether these indicators reveal made-up returns or simple recording errors by the manager or the data vendor.

Studies use subsets of these indicators to evaluate hedge fund returns. For instance, Brown et al. (2010) use the Bollen and Pool (2009) filter and also add the Hasanhodzic and Lo's (2007) hedge fund return replication technique, and Treynor and Mazuy's (1966) timing measure to distinguish between manipulated and non-manipulated returns. Cassar and Gerakos (2011) use a database of due diligence reports from *Hedge Fund Due Diligence Group* to differentiate innocuous smoothing from more unscrupulous behavior, and find that return patterns are consistent with intentional smoothing for funds that use less verifiable pricing methods or provide the manager with more discretion. Interestingly, Cassar and Gerakos find that having a more reputable accountant does not reduce the likelihood of misreporting.

Given the abundance of proposed indicators for problem funds in the literature, it is important to ask how well these screens work in predicting hedge fund fraud. This task is undertaken by Bollen and Pool (2010). The authors build a sample of problem funds from SEC litigation releases, news announcements, other regulatory action releases by the CFTC, DOJ, or FINRA, and from information provided by a leading due diligence firm. They then compare the return characteristics of the problem funds to the return characteristics of all other funds in the hedge fund database, using the data filters discussed above. These screens include a low correlation flag with other asset classes, the conditional and unconditional return smoothing coefficients, the data quality measures proposed by Straumann (2008), as well as a measure that flags funds with a discontinuity at zero. The discontinuity measure in this paper is applied at the fund level; therefore, the originally proposed method using kernel densities is not feasible. Instead, the study adopts the approach of Burgstahler and Dichev (1997) from the accounting literature to evaluate whether the actual number of reported returns in a given bin is different from what would be expected under continuity.

The Bollen and Pool fraud sample features two types of offenders: trading violators and reporting violators. While the flags are well motivated in the reporting violation sample, they are not likely to be useful predictors for trading violations. This is indeed what the authors find. Reporting violators trigger the flags statistically significantly more often than non-problem funds in the hedge fund database, while trading violators are not associated with the flags in the sample. Among the performance flags, the authors find kink/discontinuity at zero, low correlation with other asset classes, and the general lack of negative reported returns to be especially useful in predicting hedge fund fraud.

4. OPERATIONAL FLAGS

The papers reviewed in this section use SEC disclosure forms to flag firms with heightened levels of operational risk. While operational risk is hard to quantify, these papers argue that operational flags exist when the organizational structure or the internal processes of the fund easily lend themselves to fraudulent activity. This is based on the commonly cited definition of operational risk, described in Basel II, which defines it as 'risk of loss resulting from inadequate or failed internal processes, people and systems, or from external events'. For instance, conflict of interest arrangements, such as affiliated brokers or auditors, the lack of personnel oversight systems or featuring infrequent audits may indeed signal an environment that facilitates unscrupulous behavior. This has been emphasized in media reports on the most recent scandals: Bernie Madoff, for instance, provided trade clearing and custodian services to his clients. The manager's past criminal or disciplinary history may also be considered an operational flag.

4.1 Disclosure Data

Information on the fund's internal processes and the manager's disciplinary or criminal history is disclosed on SEC Form ADV. Form ADV is filed by registered investment advisers on an annual basis to register with the SEC and the relevant securities authorities at the state level. Part 1 of Form ADV is divided into 12 items, which cover information on the portfolio managers, their advisory affiliates, and the characteristics of the fund, its investors, and employees. The first 6 items include details on the form of organization and legal structure, and the fund's general operations. Items 7 to 10 disclose potential conflict-of-interest arrangements, such as affiliations, control, participation in clients' transactions, and the arrangements concerning the custody of clients' assets. Item 11 (Disclosure Information) is the disciplinary disclosure section of the form. It asks whether the investment advisers or their advisory affiliates have any history of criminal, regulatory, or civil judicial actions filed against them. These include felony convictions, misdemeanor charges, or charges of violations of the SEC or CFTC statues or regulations. If any of the questions of Item 11 are answered in the affirmative, the fund must also submit a disclosure reporting page (DRP) to detail the nature of the offenses.

Effective in 2011, the SEC also requires that investment advisors provide a narrative brochure written in plain English for their investors, which constitutes part 2 of Form ADV. This brochure contains a summary of the salient disclosures in part 1, information about the fund's fee structure, and the educational background of the fund manager and members of the advisory panel. Thus, part 2 of Form ADV aims to highlight the fund's operational risk to fund investors in a more accessible manner.

It is important to note that conflict of interest arrangements are not illegal as long as they are properly disclosed. Nor are they uncommon. For instance, Dimmock and Gerken (2011) report that in their comprehensive sample of Form ADV filings (which includes non-hedge fund filers as well) 26 per cent of investment advisers also serve as custodians of the assets they manage. Similarly, 32.2 per cent of the cases in the Dimmock and Gerken sample, firms have an interest in client transactions. Surprisingly, investment advisers also report past disciplinary problems. In particular, while minor regulatory violations are more common (13.4 per cent), civil or criminal offenses are reported by 4.4 per cent of the firms in the sample.

Do conflict of interest arrangements or past offenses by fund managers help predict fraud? This question is addressed in the next subsection.

4.2   Major Work on Operational Flags

Brown et al. (2008) provide the first important assessment of the role of operational flags in fraud detection. The authors recognize the unique opportunity created by the brief regulatory change in 2004, and use the 2006 snapshot of hedge fund ADVs in their study. The authors search Form ADVs for managers who report prior legal or regulatory problems. Funds whose managers are in this sample are designated as problem funds. The authors identify 368 problem funds in their sample of 2299 funds. Their study then analyzes how the fund's organizational structure and its systems in place are related to whether the fund is classified as a problem fund. The results indicate that problem funds are more likely to feature conflict-of-interest arrangements, indicating that disclosing previous disciplinary history may be useful for investors in assessing operational risk.

The analyses provided in the paper also allow the researchers to evaluate whether mandatory disclosures of the type featured on Form ADV are useful for investors. In particular, such filings are said to be very costly for hedge funds; therefore, it is important to investigate the type of benefits they provide. Brown et al. argue that while knowing about disciplinary history appears valuable, this information may be available to the market through other channels, such as through due diligence firms or personal contacts. The information redundancy hypothesis implies that disclosure requirements serve no benefit. The paper's results are mixed with respect to the role of disclosure. On the one hand, the authors find that problem funds display lower leverage levels and more concentrated ownership, perhaps signaling that some lenders and investors may be aware of the heightened risk of fraud, even in the absence of disclosures. On the other hand, the flow-performance analyses are less supportive of the information redundancy hypothesis. Specifically, Brown et al. find that investors do not reward problem and non-problem funds differently when observing superior returns. This implies that many investors may not be able to differentiate between problem and non-problem funds without disclosures.

Brown et al. (2009a) argue that since the future of ADV filings is uncertain, information on the manager's criminal or other disciplinary background may not be available in the future. Therefore, they develop a new instrument for operational risk, the w-score, by connecting Form ADV information to readily available fund characteristics from self-reported accounts collected by data vendors, such as fund returns, fees, or size. The study then finds that the failure rate of funds is increasing in the fund's w-score. Whilst fund failures are not necessarily caused by fraud, they are frequently associated with poor performance. For example, Brown et al. (2001) show that attrition probabilities are decreasing in returns and increasing in volatility. Gregoriou (2002) finds that performance deteriorates in the last six months of the life of the fund, while Liang and Park (2010) show that downside risk is an especially well-performing predictor of fund failures.

Dimmock and Gerken (2011) also use form ADVs to study whether operational flags can help predict fraud. They broadly focus on investment advisers (not only hedge funds) and create a historical panel of ADVs. The panel dataset allows them to investigate whether past flags of operational risk, such as conflicts-of-interest arrangements or disciplinary history, are associated with subsequent SEC violations. They show that the fund's or the manager's past operational problems are, indeed, a good predictor of future offenses.

Finally, Brown et al. (2009b) use a sample of due diligence reports to create a more direct measure of operational risk. The due diligence reports are based on a large collection of data sources, which include documents that fund managers provide to the due diligence firm, questionnaires, and on-site interviews with the manager or other key employees of the fund. The due diligence firm also makes an attempt to verify all available information by performing background checks as well as cross-checking through third party records from auditors, brokers, administrators, or custodians to verify fund performance and reported AUM. As a result, the final reports contain detailed information about the fund's internal controls, pricing methods, and any misrepresentation or inconsistency by the manager concerning the performance of the fund or past disciplinary problems. The authors show that 41 per cent of the managers in their sample are associated with past legal or regulatory problems, which represents more than twice the rate reported in Form ADV filings, suggesting that managers may even misreport to the SEC. This, in turn, questions the effectiveness of mandatory disclosure requirements. The authors also show that their direct measure of operational risk constructed from due diligence information is a good predictor of poor future performance out of sample, which suggests that due diligence firms and other third-party evaluators may play an important role in curtailing fraud in the hedge fund industry.

5.   OTHER WORK ON FRAUD DETECTION

In addition to the performance and operational screens discussed in the previous sections, a promising new approach to detect unscrupulous behavior is to examine the characteristics and pricing of hedge fund portfolio positions disclosed in Form 13F filings. Cici, Kempf, and Puetz (2010) follow this approach in a working paper circulated at the time of writing, providing direct evidence on intentional valuation manipulation by hedge fund managers. The authors examine the valuation fund managers submit for their 13F securities, mostly concentrating on the most liquid stocks in the sample. For these securities, pricing should be very straightforward: fund managers must use the closing market prices of the holdings disclosure date in their filings. The paper reports significant discrepancies between the fair price and the price hedge funds use to mark the value of their positions. In particular, managers tend to mark-up asset values following periods of poor performance but push their valuations down after experiencing good returns. Moreover, strategic portfolio smoothing is more prevalent when the likelihood of being caught is lower, for instance, when the fund is not regularly audited. Cici et al. show the intentional mismarkings are motivated by managerial incentives and display patterns that are consistent with the papers discussed in Section 3 above.

6.   CONCLUSION

Hedge funds are important financial markets participants. Their large positions, active trading, and presence in many different asset categories are widely believed to enhance market efficiency and contribute to the well functioning of the markets. However, the sheer size and complexity of their positions also pose considerable risks to the financial system; therefore, it is crucial to understand the risk of operational failure in the hedge fund industry, as well as the risk of fund fraud. Assessing those risks is nevertheless difficult, due to the general lack of publicly available information on hedge funds.

How to assess the risk in the current regulatory environment or how to change the regulatory environment to increase transparency yet preserve the proprietary nature of these funds have been important questions for both regulators and researchers in recent years. This chapter has commented on these issues by surveying the academic literature on hedge fund fraud. Current academic knowledge on detecting fraud in the industry and measuring the risk of wrongdoing concentrates on two approaches. First, researchers use self-reported performance and other fund information to develop performance flags to screen for suspicious reporting behavior. The advantage of this approach is that it utilizes readily available information and is easy to apply to any set of reported returns, including the privately distributed periodic reports investors receive from their funds. Second, researchers develop operational flags from mandatory disclosures or due diligence documents on the structure of the fund, its systems in place, and on background information concerning the fund manager. Operational flags only require information on the fund's organizational structure and managerial history, yet again allowing funds to keep their trading strategies and portfolio holdings a secret. Overall, the fund fraud literature finds that both operational and performance flags have predictive power for hedge fund fraud. Moreover, the literature shows that the two approaches utilize non-redundant information and as such, they complement each other. Therefore, they provide a diverse set of tools for regulators and, perhaps more importantly, for individual investors to screen funds for suspicious patterns or behavior. The findings also suggest that these tools may be viewed as an alternative to costly transparency in the hedge fund industry; hence future research in the area is needed to further extend the variety and predictive power of the available flags.

BIBLIOGRAPHY

Abdulali, Adil, 2006, 'The bias ratio: Measuring the shape of fraud', *Protégé Partners Quarterly Letter*.

Ackermann, Carl, Richard McEnally, and David Ravenscraft (1999), 'The performance of hedge funds: Risk, return, and incentives', *Journal of Finance* **54**, 833–874.

Agarwal, V. and N. Naik (2004), 'Risks and portfolio decisions involving hedge funds', *Review of Financial Studies*, **17**, 63–98.

Agarwal, V., N. Daniel, and N. Naik (2010), 'Do hedge funds manage their reported returns?' *Review of Financial Studies*, forthcoming.

Agarwal, V., F. Fos, and W. Jiang (2010), 'Inferring reporting-related biases in hedge fund databases from hedge fund equity holdings', Working Paper, Georgia State University.

Asness, C., R. Krail, and J. Liew (2001), 'Do Hedge Funds Hedge?' *Journal of Portfolio Management* **28**, 6–19.

Bollen, N., and V.K. Pool (2008), 'Conditional return smoothing in the hedge fund industry', *Journal of Financial and Quantitative Analysis*, 267–98.

Bollen, N., and V.K. Pool (2009), 'Do hedge fund managers misreport returns? Evidence from the pooled distribution', *Journal of Finance*, 2257–88.

Bollen, N., and V.K. Pool (2010), 'Predicting hedge fund fraud with performance flags', Working Paper.

Brown, S., W. Goetzmann, and J. Park (2001), 'Careers and Survival: Competition and Risk in the Hedge Fund and CTA Industry', *Journal of Finance* **56**, 1869–86.

Brown, S., W. Goetzmann, B. Liang, and C. Schwarz (2008), 'Mandatory disclosure and operational risk: Evidence from hedge fund registration', *Journal of Finance* **63**, 2785–2815.

Brown, S., W. Goetzmann, B. Liang, and C. Schwarz (2009a), 'Estimating operational risk for hedge funds: The w-score', *Financial Analysts Journal* **65**, 43–53.

Brown, S., W. Goetzmann, B. Liang, and C. Schwarz (2009b), 'Trust and delegation', New York University Working Paper.

Brown, S., M. Kang, F. In, and G. Lee (2010), 'Resisting the Manipulation of Performance Metrics: An Empirical Analysis of the Manipulation-Proof Performance Measure', New York University Working Paper.

Burgstahler, David and Ilia Dichev (1997), 'Earnings management to avoid earnings decreases and losses, *Journal of Accounting and Economics*, **24**, 99–126.

Cassar, G., and J. Gerakos (2011), 'Hedge funds: Pricing controls and the smoothing of self-reported returns', *Review of Financial Studies*, forthcoming.

Chandar, N. and R. Bricker (2002), 'Incentives, discretion, and asset valuation in closed-end mutual funds', *Journal of Accounting Research*, **40**, 1037–1070.

Cici, G., A. Kempf, and A. Puetz (2010), 'Caught in the act: How hedge funds manipulate their equity positions', Working Paper.

Dimmock, S., and W. Gerken (2010), 'Finding Bernie Madoff, Detecting fraud by investment managers', Michigan State University Working Paper.

Dimson, E. (1979), 'Risk measurement when shares are subject to infrequent trading', *Journal of Financial Economics*, **7**, 197–226.

Duggan, M., and S. Levitt (2002), 'Winning isn't everything: Corruption in sumo wrestling', *American Economic Review*, **92**, 1594–1605.

Getmansky, M., A. W. Lo, and I. Makarov (2004), 'An econometric model of serial correlation and illiquidity in hedge fund returns', *Journal of Financial Economics*, **74**, 529–609.

Goetzmann, W., J. Ingersoll, M. Spiegel, and S. Ross (2003), 'High-water marks and hedge fund management contracts', *Journal of Finance*, **58**, 1685–1717.

Goetzmann, W., J. Ingersoll, M. Spiegel, and I. Welch (2007), 'Portfolio performance manipulation and manipulation-proof performance measures', *Review of Financial Studies* **20**, 1503–1546.

Gregoriou, G. (2002), 'Hedge fund survival lifetimes', *Journal of Asset Management*, **3**, 237–52.

Gregoriou, G., and F. Lhabitant (2009), 'Madoff: A riot of red flags', *Journal of Wealth Management*, **12**, 89–98.

Hasanhodzic, J., and A. W. Lo (2007), 'Can hedge fund returns be replicated? The linear case', *Journal of Investment Management*, **5**(2), 5–45.

Jagannathan, R., and R. A. Korajczyk (1986), 'Assessing the Market Timing Performance of Managed Portfolios', *Journal of Business*, **59**, 217–235.

Liang, B. (2000), 'Hedge funds: The living and the dead', *Journal of Financial and Quantitative Analysis*, **35**, 309–326.

Liang, B. (2003), 'The accuracy of hedge fund returns', *The Journal of Portfolio Management*, 111–122.

Liang, B. and H. Park (2010), 'Predicting hedge fund failures: A comparison of risk measures', *Journal of Financial and Quantitative Analysis*, **45**, 199–222.

Listokin, Y. (2008), 'Management always wins the close ones', *American Law and Economics Review*, **10**, 159–184.

Scholes, M., Williams, J. (1977), 'Estimating betas from non synchronous data', *Journal of Financial Economics*, **5**, 309–328.

Skeel, D. and F. Partnoy (2007), 'The promise and perils of credit derivatives', *University of Cincinnati Law Review*, **75**, forthcoming.

Straumann, D. (2008), 'Measuring the quality of hedge fund data', *RiskMetrics Journal*, Winter, 65–93.

Stulz, R.M. (2007), 'Hedge funds: Past, present, and future', *Journal of Economic Perspectives*, **21**, 175–94.

Sun, Z., A. Wang, and L. Zheng (2009), 'The road less traveled: Strategy distinctiveness and hedge fund performance', Univeristy of California, Irvine Working Paper.

Titman, S., and C. Tiu (2008), 'Do the best hedge funds hedge?', University of Texas at Austin Working Paper.

Treynor, J., and K. Mazuy (1966), 'Can Mutual Funds Outguess the Market?', *Harvard Business Review*, **44**, 131–6.

Waring, M. and L. Siegel (2006), 'The myth of the absolute-return investor', *Financial Analysts Journal*, **62**, 14–21.

9. Self-regulation – what future in the context of hedge funds?
*Marco Lamandini**

1. INTRODUCTION

In a study on *whether* and *how* to regulate hedge funds, published shortly before the outbreak of the financial crisis, in August 2008, Professor Paredes[1] summarized four basic regulatory choices: (i) do nothing; (ii) regulate hedge funds *directly*; (iii) regulate hedge funds *indirectly*, focusing on their *managers*, and (iv) regulate hedge fund *investors*. Comparative legislative history offers a wealth of examples of each of those approaches having been followed. However, the first option was to prevail, for a very long time, both in the United States (US) and in the European Union (EU), in the field of hedge funds, before the financial crisis tilted the balance in favor of external (direct) regulation. This chapter compares external to self-regulation, with a view to assessing what the practical differences between them are and to evaluating the role of self-regulation, in the post-financial crisis era, as a hedge fund regulatory tool.

2. AN OVERVIEW OF THE US REGULATORY APPROACH TO HEDGE FUNDS UNTIL THE OUTBREAK OF THE FINANCIAL CRISIS

Dr. Alfred Winslow Jones is generally credited with forming the first hedge fund in 1949, in the US.[2] The industry was to grow substantially over the

---

*   Full Professor of Company and Securities Law, University of Bologna.

[1]   Paredes, Troy (2007), 'Hedge Funds and the SEC: Observations on the How and Why of Securities Regulation', Washington University, Faculty Working Paper Series, paper no. 07-05-01, 3; Id., (2006), 'On the Decision to Regulate Hedge Funds: The SEC's Regulatory Philosophy, Style and Mission', Washington University, Faculty Working Paper Series, paper no. 06-03-02, (both advocating a best practice-oriented mode of regulation).

[2]   Verret, Jay W. (2007), 'Dr. Jones and the Raiders of Lost Capital: Hedge Fund Regulation, Part II, A Self-Regulation Proposal', *Delaware Journal of Corporate Law*, **32** (3) 799–802.

following decades proving, however, successful at avoiding, until very recently, direct regulation. Deference to private ordering, coupled with some form of indirect regulation, had been the name of the game, despite the fact that (i) the US were (and remain) home to the majority of assets under hedge fund management worldwide, (ii) the industry has experienced tremendous growth, especially over the last decade, (iii) the US were shaken, in 1999, by the near collapse of Long-Term Capital Management (LTCM), and (iv) hedge funds were found, only a few years after the LTCM collapse, to have played an active part in the 'market-timing' scandals, brought to light by New York Attorney General Eliot Spitzer.

Some contended that this regulatory self-restraint occurred because direct regulation was in fact undesirable in this particular field. It was argued that (intrusive) direct regulation could lead hedge funds to react by moving away from the more heavily regulated to the off-shore jurisdictions, where controls are substantially weaker. Alan Greenspan made that point already in 1998 arguing, at a testimony before the US Congress, following the LTCM collapse, that, 'it is questionable whether hedge funds can be effectively directly regulated in the US alone (. . .) Given the amazing communication capabilities available virtually around the globe, trades can be initiated from almost any location. *Indeed hedge funds are only a short step from cyberspace* (emphasis added). Any direct US regulation restricting their flexibility will doubtless induce the more aggressive funds to emigrate from under (US) jurisdiction'. He concluded that, 'the best we can do is what we do today: regulate them indirectly'.[3] In turn, still in May 2006, his successor at the New York FED, Ben Bernanke, stated that, 'in the case of hedge funds, the reasonable presumption is that market discipline can work. Investors, creditors, and counterparties have significant incentives to rein in hedge funds' risk taking. Moreover, direct regulation would impose costs in the form of moral hazard, the likely loss of private market discipline and possible limits on funds' ability to provide market liquidity'.[4]

---

[3] 'Hedge Fund Operations: Hearing Before the H. Comm. On Banking and Financial Services', 105th Con. 160–61 (statement of Alan Greenspan, Chairman, Federal Reserve System Board of Governors).

[4] 'Hedge Funds and Systemic Risk', Speech at the 2006 Federal Bank of Altanta's 2006 Financial Markets Conference, Sea Island, Georgia, quoted by Jonna, Paul M. (2008) 'In Search of Market Discipline: The Case for Indirect Hedge Fund Regulation', *San Diego Law Review* (45) 989 , at 1012. A market-oriented view also prevailed in the economic literature of the time, especially in the US. Some of the studies published shortly before the unfolding of the crisis, include Cumming, Douglas and Li Que (2007), 'A Law and Finance Analysis of Hedge Funds', available electronically at http://www.degroote.mcmaster.ca/

Others argued that regulatory self-restraint was mainly the result of regulatory capture. Some others, approaching, from a public choice perspective, the bills introduced in the US Congress in 1999 and SEC's preparatory work in 2003, which eventually led to the adoption, in December 2004, of the SEC's so-called 'Hedge Fund Rule', calling for the registration of hedge fund managers as Investment Advisers under the Investors Advisers Act of 1940, even supported the view that US regulators *purposefully* 'designed initiatives that were not meant to succeed, that is they self captured their own work (. . .) in the face of a trade off between the need to show their commitment to tackle publicly demonized issues and the awareness of their limitations vis-à-vis increasingly sophisticated and powerful private actors'.[5]

Be as it may, the Hedge Fund Rule, adopted in December 2004 was vacated by the Court of Appeal for the District of Columbia on 23 June 2006, in *Goldstein*,[6] and, between then and the outbreak of the financial crisis, the US component of the global hedge fund industry had mainly relied on self-regulation. Nonetheless, as noted also by the SEC,[7] following *Goldstein*, the US regime[8] has also comprised an anti-fraud provision, which prohibits advisers to pooled investment vehicles from making false or misleading statements to, or otherwise defrauding, investors or prospective investors in those pooled vehicles, thereby conferring the clear

---

faculty/rsconference/documents/ALawandFinanceAnalysis.pdf, considering an international dataset of 2937 hedge funds from 24 countries around the world; Oesterle, Dale A. (2006), 'Regulating Hedge Funds', *Entrepreneurial Business Law Journal*, **1**(1), available electronically at http://moritzlaw.osu.edu/eblj/issues/volume1/number1/oesterle.pdf ('extensive direct regulation of hedge funds is unnecessary and may harm the country's trading markets'); Kambhu, John and Til Schuermann and Kevin J. Stiroh (2007), 'Hedge Funds, Financial Intermediation and Systemic Risk', available at SSRN: http://ssrn.com/abstract=995907, passim. Note, however, that Schmidt, Michael J. (2007), 'Investor Protection in Europe and the United States: Impacting the Future of Hedge Funds', *Wisconsin International Law Journal*, **25**(1), 185 has found that, in this field, 'the United Kingdom is clearly ahead of the United States. UK regulations appear to have much closer scrutiny over fund managers' activities': despite this more intrusive regulation and supervision, however, 'hedge fund management is thriving in Europe and not flocking to the United States', because 'Europeans are comfortable working within their regulatory schemes'.

   5   Robotti, Paola (2009), 'Private Governance of Financial Markets: the US Regulatory Regime on Hedge Funds', IBEI Working Papers, 2009/20 at 4.
   6   *Goldstein v. SEC* 451 F3d 873 (DC Cir 2006).
   7   SEC 17 CFR Parts 230 and 275, Release no. 33-8766; IA 2576; File no. S7-25-06.
   8   For a detailed illustration, Spangler, Timothy (2008) *The Law of Private Investment Funds*, New York, Oxford University Press, 123 ff.

authority to the SEC to bring enforcement actions against investment advisors who defraud investors in hedge funds or any other pooled investment vehicles and providing a legal basis for the control of their market integrity. Moreover, the requirements for determining whether an individual is eligible to invest in certain pooled investments were substantially revised, introducing the 'accredited natural person' category, which was designed to ensure, through the increase of the parameters of investor wealth (untouched since 1982, despite inflation),[9] that investors in those types of funds are sophisticated or wealthy enough to evaluate and bear the risks of their investments. Leaving aside these (slight) innovations, which ironically, in the words of the SEC at the time, were believed to have the potential to enhance substantially the protection for investors and potential investors in hedge funds and other similar funds, the US confirmed its strong reliance on market discipline until the beginning of the financial crisis. Still in February 2007, the President's Working Group on Financial Markets (PWG), which had already come up with a first set of recommendations in 1999, in the wake of the collapse of LTCM, issued a set of illustrative 'soft law' principles and guidelines 'regarding private pools of capital'.[10] Those principles were intended to cover both investor protection and systemic risk worries (or so, at least, it was claimed at the time). According to Principle no. 2, '. . . market discipline most effectively addresses systemic risk posed by private pools of capital. Supervisors should however use their existing authorities with respect to creditors, counterparts, investors and fiduciaries to foster market discipline on private pools of capital. Investor protection concerns can be addressed most effectively through a combination of market discipline and regulatory policies that limit direct investment in such pools to more sophisticated investors'. Based upon these general principles, a complete set of 'best practices for the hedge fund industry', i.e., detailed 'soft law' standards open to voluntary (but strongly recommended) adoption by alternative investment funds were published on 15 January 2009, in the form of a Report of the Asset Managers Committee to the PWG. On the same day, the Investors' Committee of the PWG issued their 'Principles and Best Practices for Hedge Fund Investors'.[11]

---

[9]   See Rules 215 and 501 of the Securities Act 1933, as amended. The Dodd Frank Wall Street Reform and Consumer Protection Act now empowers the SEC to adjust the standard.

[10]   Agreement among PWG and US Agency Principals on Principles and Guidelines regarding Private Pools of Capitals.

[11]   Note that the US industry, through the Managed Fund Association, already provided, starting from February 2000, a comprehensive set of best practices

3. AN OVERVIEW OF THE EU'S REGULATORY APPROACH TO HEDGE FUNDS UNTIL THE OUTBREAK OF THE FINANCIAL CRISIS

Europe has had no unified regulatory framework for alternative investment vehicles and showed differentiated regulatory approaches at national level. As a result, hedge fund and other private capital pool managers did not benefit from a European passport and were not able to market their products across the EU under the umbrella of an identical set of rules.

A number of European civil law jurisdictions (including France, Germany and Italy) had enacted direct hedge fund (national) regulation; however, many of the EU Member States refrained from directly regulating those funds, preferring, instead, to turn their attention to their managers. The United Kingdom, for instance – by far the leading European jurisdiction for hedge fund management services – regulated hedge fund managers but not the funds themselves.[12]

Starting from 2006, the European regulatory debate was to focus on the possible need to harmonize such divergent national regimes in order to foster pan-European market integration and overcome existing national regulatory fragmentation. In its 'Green Paper on the Enhancement of the EU Framework for Investment Funds'[13] the Commission called for a 'coherent and enlightened European approach to this sector', envisaging 'a common regulatory approach', possibly also on the concept of 'private placement', to facilitate the cross-border offer of hedge funds and private equity funds to qualified investors.[14] The Council, in turn, requested, in May 2007, a report from the Commission on the possible measures to be taken on a Single Market framework for the retail-oriented, non-harmonized fund industry, herein included some funds of hedge funds.

(now the MFA's 2005 Sound Practices for Hedge Fund Managers), including provisions and a template for anti-money laundering policies and procedures. See also the recommendations and guiding principles issued by the Counterparty Risk Management Policy Group ('Corrigan Group'), with its July 2005 Report, 'Toward Greater Financial Stability: A Private Sector Perspective', available electronically at http://www.isda.org/educat/pdf/CRMPGII_7-22-05_FINAL_v6_wcover.pdf.

[12] For an overview, see Spangler, Timothy (2008), *The Law of Private Investment Funds,* 110.

[13] COM (2005) 314 final.

[14] See also Commission of the European Communities, 'White Paper on Enhancing the Single Market Framework for Investment Funds', 15 November 2006, COM(2006) 686 final, 11–13 taking a more timid approach in respect to hedge funds and confirming action on the private placement issue.

With the Van den Burg Report,[15] the European Parliament drew attention to the 'gaps in disclosure requirements with respect to corporate
governance and investment policy, on the adaptation of rules for the
level of leverage and risk management and diversification; the quality of
supervision in off-shore locations and to step up cooperation'. As suggested earlier in this chapter, some of those concerns were already tackled
(at least in part) in various different ways at the level of the EU Member
State jurisdictions,[16] mostly through indirect regulation and supervision
(especially from the banking side) or through reliance on self-regulation.
In London where, as already noted, most of the European managers are
located,[17] self-regulation was represented by a wide array of measures set
by self-regulatory bodies within the general principles of supervision of the
Financial Services Authority (FSA) namely, the 'Principles' for authorized
firms and individuals; the rules on 'Senior Management Arrangements,
Systems and Controls'; the 'Code of Market Conduct'; and the 'Conduct
of Business Sourcebook'.[18] In fact, the FSA accepted that hedge funds
and other alternative investment funds be only lightly regulated off-shore,
regulating, nevertheless, the managers and their activities in the United
Kingdom (UK). The philosophy of the FSA was described in a position
paper issued on March 2006:[19] being fully aware of the risks of regulatory
competition in the field, the FSA found at the time (before the outbreak

---

[15]   PE384.621v01-00, 12 March 2007.

[16]   For an overview see OICV-IOSCO (2006), Technical Committee of the
International Organization of Securities Commissions, 'The regulatory environment for hedge funds: a survey and comparison – Final Report', where examples,
at 6, of restrictions on leverage, the use of derivative instruments, and quantitative restrictions in investments for registered or authorised collective investment
schemes engaging in hedge-fund-like strategies. See also PriceWaterhouseCoopers
(2004), 'The Regulation and Distribution of Hedge Funds in Europe, Changes
and Challenges'; Assogestioni and EFAMA (2005), 'Hedge Funds Regulation in
Europe: A Comparative Survey', available electronically at http://www.efama.org/
index.php?option=com-docman8task=doc-details&grid=176&Itemid=35.

[17]   It is reported that, by the end of 2006, the US hedge fund industry had a 63
per cent share of assets under management based on manager location, London
had 21 per cent, the rest of Europe had 5 per cent and Asia had 8 per cent:
Horsfield-Bradbury, John (2008), 'Hedge Fund Self Regulation in the US and the
UK', Working Paper, at 56.

[18]   Note that these principles – and namely Principle 11 – offered sufficient legal
basis to the FSA also, in a macro prudential systemic perspective, for requiring
from hedge funds' managers regular flows of information, conducting thematic
visits and set up 'relationship management' (compare AIMA (2009), 'Response
of 30 January 2009, European Commission's Consultation on Hedge Funds', 10).

[19]   FSA (2006), 'Hedge Funds: A Discussion of Risk and Regulatory
Engagement', Feedback Statement 06/2.

of the financial crisis) that it would be counter-productive to increase the burden of regulation if that were to result in managers moving off-shore, to more lightly regulated jurisdictions. It nevertheless established a dedicated supervision team to monitor, on an ongoing basis, certain risks it had identified, such as market abuse, money laundering, operational risks, and conflicts of interest, *inter alia* with regard to asset valuation, where the FSA explicitly supported the principles for the valuation of hedge fund portfolios laid down by the International Organization of Securities Commissions (IOSCO)[20] and to review, on a regular basis, also those prime brokers that did not have exposures to hedge funds. The FSA's supervisory approach was also cautious in differentiating hedge fund managers from traditional asset managers and private equity/venture capital funds.

4.   THE FINANCIAL CRISIS AND ITS AFTERMATH: AN OVERVIEW OF GOVERNMENT INTERVENTION ON ALTERATIVE INVESTMENT FUNDS IN EUROPE, THE US AND INTERNATIONALLY

The financial crisis, which was to hit severely the hedge fund industry, prompted a reconsideration of the regulatory philosophy adopted so far with regard to the alternative investment funds' sector. Only in the US, where it is reported that over 1500 hedge funds were liquidated,[21] some blamed the hedge fund industry as one of the major 'enablers of exuberance'.[22] Not surprisingly, the impetus for regulatory reform and for the inclusion of the alternative investment funds' industry into the regulatory and supervisory framework gained momentum on both sides of the Atlantic.

---

[20]   See OICV-IOSCO (2007), Technical Committee of the International Organization of Securities Commissions, 'Principles for the Valuation of Hedge Fund Portfolios – Consultation Report'; and OICV-IOSCO (2007), Technical Committee of the International Organization of Securities Commissions, 'Principles for the Valuation of Hedge Fund Portfolios – Final Report'.

[21]   Aguilar, Louis A. (2009), 'Hedge Fund Regulation on the Horizon – Don't Shoot the Messenger' Speech of the SEC Commissioner at the Hedgeworld Fund Services Conference, New York.

[22]   Taub, Jennifer S. (2009), 'Enablers of Exuberance: Legal Acts and Omissions that Facilitated the Global Financial Crisis', Working Paper, available electronically at http://ssrn.com/abstract=1472190. The prevailing view denies, though, a major role to the hedge fund industry in instigating the financial crisis.

4.1 Summary of the US Regulatory Approach Since the Outbreak of the Financial Crisis

Several bills requiring the direct regulation of hedge funds were introduced in the US Congress, starting from 2009. Both the Dodd-Frank Wall Street Reform and Consumer Protection Act (now Public Law 11-203 of 21 July 2010) and the Restoring American Financial Stability Act (introduced in Congress in April 2010) require hedge fund managers ('advisers') that manage assets in excess of US$ 150 million either in the form of private funds established in the US or stemming from US private fund investors to register with the SEC, thereby eliminating the long-standing private adviser exemption. The Dodd–Frank Act also permits the SEC to add to the existing record-keeping and reporting obligations of registered investment advisers the requirements to (i) maintain such records and file the same with the SEC 'as necessary and appropriate' for the public interest and for the protection of investors or for the assessment of systemic risk by the Financial Stability Oversight Council (FSOC), (ii) provide and make available to the FSOC systemic-risk related information concerning the amount of assets under management and the use of leverage, including off-balance-sheet leverage, counterparty credit risk exposure, trading and investment positions, the fund's valuation policies and practices, the types of assets held, any side letters, trading practices and such other information as the SEC may deem necessary or appropriate.[23] Moreover, the Dodd–Frank Act permits the SEC to conduct, at its discretion, periodic and ad hoc examinations of the records of private funds maintained by advisors.

4.2 Summary of the European Regulatory Approach Since the Outbreak of the Financial Crisis

Europe's alternative investment funds-specific regulatory reaction to the financial crisis has taken the form of the adoption, in November 2010, of the Alternative Investment Fund Managers (AIFM) Directive, which provides for registration requirements (coupled, nevertheless, with the benefits of a 'European passport') as well as for information-sharing, transparency and disclosure duties vis-à-vis investors and regulators. It also sets out provisions – yet unparalleled in the US – on risk and liquidity management, on the requirement for AIFM to make use of independent valuation providers and depositaries and on the possibility for regulators to impose

---

[23] This may include different reporting requirements for different classes of fund advisers, based on the type and size of private funds being advised.

specific limits on hedge fund leverage. Besides, the AIFM Directive also provides for the imposition of minimum ongoing capital requirements, 'to ensure the continuity and regularity of the management services provided by the AIFM', which 'should cover the potential exposure of AIFM to professional liability' (recital 11 and article 14). In addition, in order to ensure that AIFM operate 'subject to robust governance controls' and are organized 'so as to minimize conflict of interest' (recital 12 and article 10), so as to offer a 'reliable and objective asset valuation' (article 16) apt to protect investor interests, the AIFM Directive requires that 'the valuation of assets be undertaken by an entity which is independent of the AIFM'. Regarding the issue of leverage, the AIFM Directive subjects AIFM employing high levels of leverage as part of their investment strategies to special disclosure requirements on their use and sources of leverage and, in certain cases, to specific limits thereon (Articles 22–25), on the assumption that these highly leveraged AIFM 'may, under certain conditions, contribute to the build up of systemic risk or disorderly markets'. To the extent that the use of high levels of leverage could be detrimental to the stability and efficient functioning of financial markets, the Commission and, in exceptional circumstances, the competent authorities of the home Member State are therefore allowed, under article 25 to 'impose limits', either in the form of a threshold that should not be breached at any point in time or in that of a limit on the average leverage employed during a given period.

Interestingly, some of the regulatory emphasis of the AIFM Directive is placed on 'Level 2' implementing measures, to be adopted by the Commission, implementing the Directive's framework principles in the areas of conduct of business rules (e.g. conflict of interest, risk and liquidity management), capital requirements, organizational requirements, delegation of functions and transparency requirements. As stated in recital 27, 'Those measures are designed to specify the criteria to be used by competent authorities to assess whether AIFM comply with their obligations' as regards all regulated aspects of their activity. It seems therefore safe to argue that, in the European regulatory context, the AIFM Directive marks a very substantial swing of the regulatory pendulum from self-regulation or country-specific, non-harmonized regulation to external regulation, with a strong emphasis on Level 2 implementing measures. Moreover, if one were to take into account the parallel evolution of the European supervisory framework – namely, the creation of three new European Supervisory Authorities (ESAs), responsible for the coordination of micro-prudential supervision, and of the European Systemic Risk Board, responsible for macro-prudential supervision – one would also expect, eventually, an additional layer of external regulation to be imposed, consisting of a common rule book composed by Level 3 technical standards proposed by the ESAs and endorsed by the Commission.

4.3 Summary of the International Regulatory Approach Since the Outbreak of the Financial Crisis

Regional regulatory reforms in the US and the EU have coincided with a wide-ranging reconsideration, internationally, of the regulatory approach towards hedge funds. In its final report on hedge fund oversight, published in June 2009,[24] IOSCO concluded, on the one hand, that hedge funds, hedge funds managers/advisers and prime brokers should be subject to mandatory registration and appropriate, ongoing regulatory requirements[25] but, on the other hand, that regulators should encourage and take account of the development, implementation and convergence of industry good practices, where appropriate, while they should also have the authority to co-operate and share information. In fact, as correctly noted by the ECB in an opinion,[26] 'an internationally coordinated response is necessary given the highly international nature of the industry and the consequent risks of regulatory arbitrage and evasion': a conclusion which makes the intricacies of the government and self-regulatory nexus even worthier of careful consideration in this domain.

5. SELF-REGULATION VERSUS GOVERNMENT REGULATION: MARKET AND REGULATORY CONVERGENCE RECONSIDERED

Regulation is possible in several different ways. The conventional form is based on 'command and control' legal rules imposed and enforced by national governments. Where financial regulation is coupled with de-legification (i.e. the use of primary legislation only to set general framework

---

[24] OICV–IOSCO (2009), Technical Committee of the International Organization of Securities Commissions, 'Hedge Funds Oversight – Final Report'.
[25] These would relate to: (a) organizational and operational standards; (b) conflicts of interest and other conduct of business rules; (c) investor disclosure; (d) prudential regulation.
[26] See ECB, 'Opinion of 16 October 2009 on a proposal for a Directive of the European Parliament and of the Council on Alternative Investment Fund Managers', CON/2009/81, which urges the Commission to continue the dialogue with its international partners, in particular the US, to ensure a globally coherent regulatory and supervisory framework.

principles to be supplemented and implemented by secondary regulation), detailed, 'secondary' legal rules tend to be set, instead, by supervisory authorities. An alternative mode of regulation is self-regulation, consisting of self-imposed or self-enforced rules.[27] Self-regulation reflects market discipline: a private ordering, developed under marked pressure but, also, often prompted by the threat of government intervention and, often, directed at preempting it.[28]

5.1   Benefits of Self-regulation

The legal and economic literature traditionally lists a series of benefits of self-regulation in the alternative investments field. A recent study[29] summarizes the outcome of the debate as follows:

> An overview of the literature suggests that self-regulation is deemed to have a number of advantages over 'conventional' regulation. Since the burden of devising rules and policing compliance therewith is directly borne by those regulated, it is less costly [. . .]; because it draws on the relevant market participants' experience, expertise and superior knowledge of the regulatory issues at stake, it can be better informed, more focused and easier to adapt to new technological or economic developments; since its 'rules' are devised by those to whom they are to apply, they are likely to be more effective [. . .] ; because its emphasis is on ethical standards of conduct and on the spirit, rather than the letter of its rules, it is less formalistic and can, over time, lead to an overall improvement in behavioral values, engendering more commitment, pride and efficiency within a self regulated industry; moreover, contrary to so called 'command and control' regulatory regimes, self regulation is deemed to be more responsive and favorable to innovation; last but not least, unlike external

---

[27]   For a recent discussion of this mode of alternative regulation or, more often, of co-regulation, compare Cafaggi, Fabrizio (2006), 'Rethinking Private Regulation in the European Regulatory Space', in *Reframing Self-Regulation in European Private Law*, Kluwer Law Publ., *passim* where there are references to previous literature.

[28]   Self-regulation is theoretically classified as: (i) mandated private regulation, where an industry is required or designated by the government to formulate and enforce norms within a framework set by the government; (ii) sanctioned private regulation, in which a private body formulates the norms which are then subjected to governmental approval; (iii) coerced private regulation, where the industry formulates the norms in response to threats by the government that if it does not it will impose statutory regulation; (iv) voluntary private regulation, where there is no active state involvement (Cafaggi, Fabrizio, *supra*, fn. 27, 22, where there are additional references).

[29]   Athanassiou, Phoebus (2009) *Hedge Fund Regulation in the European Union – Current Trends and Future Prospects,* Wolters Kluwer, International Banking and Finance Law Series, 9, at 220 (where other references).

regulation, regulation by the hedge funds themselves would not be limited in any single jurisdiction, but could have benefits in every jurisdiction in which the funds operate

Indeed, it is widely accepted that self-regulation can respond more swiftly and with greater flexibility to industry changes, whereas conventional external regulation, at least in the form of primary rules, takes longer to enact and may become 'petrified' for too long thereafter. This is a feature of general relevance, when discussing the pros and cons of self-regulation, which nevertheless proves particularly significant with regard to hedge funds or other alternative investment funds, which, as it is widely accepted, 'are designed to fit regulatory cracks'[30] and are traditionally structured so as to escape heavy regulation.[31] In principle, therefore, self-regulation should be better placed than conventional regulation to offer a comprehensive set of detailed and efficient standards of conduct for alternative investment funds, that are in line with financial innovation and apt to help shape the industry's conduct in detail, capturing the subtleties of the market activities of alternative investment funds in an attempt to foster the 'optimal' degree of regulation and to induce best market practices.

At least theoretically, self-regulatory standards also differ from 'command and control' legal rules, in that the former identify best practices (i.e. 'optimal' and recommended outcomes) whereas the latter set (only) minimum (and mandated) requirements. Despite its qualitatively different content, due to the proximity of self-regulators to market participants, self-regulation is less costly for society at large and less prone to regulatory excesses. Indeed, there are fewer social costs in delineating and drafting self-regulatory rules and a lesser risk of regulatory overkill and false positives (i.e. the loss of conducts which, had it not been for the restrictions imposed by regulation, would have occurred and which would have caused no societal harm). Finally and, perhaps, even more importantly, self-regulation is more apt to be cross-border (or even global) compared to external (government) regulation.[32]

---

[30]   Horsfield-Bradbury, *supra*, fn. 17, 51.

[31]   It is reported that in 2006 55 per cent of hedge funds were incorporated off shore taking advantage of minimum regulation and favourable tax treatment: King, Michael R. and Philipp Maier (2009), 'Hedge Funds and Financial Stability: Regulating Prime Brokers Will Mitigate Systemic Risk', *Journal of Financial Stability*, 5 , 283 at 292.

[32]   Horsfield-Bradbury, *supra*, fn. 17, 55.

5.2   The Costs of Self-regulation

At the same time, the literature attributes significant social costs to self-regulation. It is widely accepted that private 'regulators', albeit taking decisions affecting the public interest, lack public accountability and that, 'unless properly blended within the regulatory fabric and grounded in private law, self-regulation can amount to no more than 'window dressing', a 'charade' to deflect criticism of corporate activities and pre-empt more direct and effective government intervention, while in fact serving vested private interests in conflict with the public good and institutionalizing a form of bargaining between industry and government'.[33] It must be remembered that government regulation is an answer to market failures. Experience shows that, in the financial services sector, despite the claimed sophistication of investors and counterparties, market responses have on several occasions proved ineffective in coping with agency problems and with conflicts of interest. This is hardly surprising, since, especially in the context of the alternative investment funds industry, informational asymmetries and insufficient governance or monitoring rights vested in investors and other counterparties can, *ex ante*, be conducive to aberrant behavior on the part of investment managers and to unsound or unsafe choices from the side of investors, prime brokers and other counterparties and can, *ex post*, delay (or make next to difficult or even impossible) the detecting and sanctioning of the same. What that suggests is that market discipline alone is not sufficient. In turn, the social costs of market failures have, in the recent past, proved to be very high. In light of the above, it would be rather naïve to expect that self-regulatory bodies, set up by the industry itself, would spontaneously side with the *public* rather than with the *private* interest of their principals when adopting self-imposed rules, unless there is at *least* the close monitoring of a governmental authority to ensure the quality of the outcome of the self-regulatory exercise. In addition, due to its voluntary nature, self-regulation cannot draw on the backing of a robust enforcement mechanism other than the 'name and shame' one, which has, in practice, provided a very weak 'stigma' so far associated with the voluntary deviation by a market player from the best practices recommended by the industry. Moreover, and perhaps even more importantly, hedge funds can become a source of systemic financial instability because of their impact on the market prices of securities (especially through forced sales, when they venture to liquidate positions because the market has turned against them), which is why self-regulation alone

---

[33]   Athanassiou, *supra*, fn. 29, 221 (with additional references).

would, in their case, appear to be insufficient.[34] In this respect, market discipline alone was not (and could never be) adequate to provide the market or supervisory bodies with all the information necessary to help measure such systemic risk and to help with the development of a suitable strategy to cope with it. A recent study has therefore concluded that:

> (. . .) One is tempted to a priori dismiss self regulation as a suitable instrument for the industry's governance (. . .). This is because the information asymmetries on which hedge funds thrive entail the existence of less than perfect competition [. . .], with serious implications for the successful deployment of self-regulation. In addition, the fund managers' incentives to reduce these asymmetries [. . .] are limited [. . .] Furthermore, hedge fund managers are seldom members of an association that applies common rules and practices [. . .]. It follows that hedge fund managers lack the features and representation potential of a guild or other professional body or association [. . .] and that the size, complexity and opacity of the markets where they operate do not match with the specifications determined in the literature for the successful deployment of self-regulation. Ultimately, what diminishes the likelihood that self-regulation could ever prove effective in a hedge fund context, is the fact that financial motives for breaking any self imposed rules are, in this field, very substantial meaning that, unless backed by an active regulator and a persuasive set of sanctions for non compliance, self-regulation would almost inevitably fail to meet the expectations placed upon it[35]

5.3 How Real Are the Differences Between External and Self-regulation?

At closer look, many of the theoretical differences between regulatory and self-regulatory rules tend to evaporate. Regarding the *substantive content* of these two types of rules, hedge-fund-related best practices codified by self-regulatory bodies have so far been (and have often been criticized for being) too broad and vague, thus resembling more general command and control principles than detailed standards of conduct. In the same vein, hedge-fund-specific command and control financial law rules – especially those set at Level 2 or 3 – often depart from a principle-based approach, representing a transformation into an external rule of the content of pre-existing self-regulatory standards, subject to certain amendments. Regarding the regulatory *process*, the ('coerced') self-regulatory exercise on hedge funds has proved to be substantially influenced by a 'benign

---

[34] Engert, Andreas (2010), 'Transnational Hedge Fund Regulation', *European Business Organization Law Review*, **11**(3), 329–78. On the systemic risk associated with hedge funds, compare, *inter alia*, European Commission, 'Consultation Paper on Hedge Funds', Working Document of the Commission Services, DG Internal Market, 5.

[35] Athanassiou, *supra*, fn. 29, 225.

big gun' threat, that is the threat that the government would step in and impose its own rules should the industry fail to adopt a self-imposed regulatory agenda.[36]

Thus, both regulatory settings, albeit formally having private or, instead, public officials in their respective 'driver's seat', and following different rule-making processes, may, therefore be conducive to similar outcomes. This remains the case despite the fact that, when private actors lead the (self) regulatory exercise, one is conceptually confronted with an interest-based regulatory framework, where the (presumably superior) technical expertise of the members of the private governing body called to enact the standards 'is generally instrumental to interest representation';[37] by contrast, when public officials lead the regulatory exercise, one is faced, in practice, with a technocratic approach, where most of the substance and, in respect of secondary legislation, also the form, of the resulting legal rules depend on the legal and economic assessments made by civil servants charged with government or oversight functions in the sector. This bureaucracy, however, is not truly insulated from the market (due to overlaps between political and economic oligarchies, the 'sliding doors' into and out of the private industry, group pressure and other comparable herd effects). What is also worth recalling is that, especially in recent times, this bureaucracy no longer represents, subject, perhaps, to some valuable exceptions, a segregated social group with a distinctive background, education or a deeply inculcated sense of public duty. It follows from the above that, despite the theoretically clear distinction between private ordering, on the one hand, and external regulation set by a public institution, on the other, the distance between the rules enacted by private and public regulators may, in practice, be smaller than what one would expect the case to be in theory.

Similarly, differences in enforcement may be less distinctive than one might have assumed. If courts and supervisors take, as they should, in this author's view, self-regulatory standards into account for determining liability and enforce such standards on an on-going basis – construing the standard as the expected conduct, unless a deviation from the standard is justified by the principle of proportionality or by reference to other objective reasons – self-regulation would, in practice, become next to mandatory, being enforced similarly to external regulation. In turn, supervisors are facing, in practice, severe limitations in the *ex ante* enforcement of external rules, meaning that even conventional rules are often bound to be

---

[36]   Engert, *supra*, fn. 34, 355.
[37]   Cafaggi, *supra*, fn. 27, 13.

enforced *ex post*. In other words, under certain conditions, the deterrence effect associated with self-regulatory and command and control rules might, in practice, be not too dissimilar.

5.4 The Coexistence Between Self-regulation and External Regulation

It follows from the above that, despite their differences, self-regulation and external regulation are bound to coexist: no command and control rule, at least in this field, is independent from the self-regulatory efforts of the industry itself, since both regulators and supervisors are substantially influenced in their rule making (even when they are not 'captured') by the values, beliefs and practices developed by the industry. In turn, experience suggests that no credible form of self-regulation can exist if its standards are not made into an integral part of the overall regulatory framework and duly taken into account by supervisors and courts alike when enforcing the applicable command and control rules, with an emphasis on the general principles setting out the overarching duties of soundness, transparency and integrity weighing on market actors. *Thus, as obvious as it may seem, co-regulation appears to provide the right regulatory answer.*[38] As noted in the literature, 'it would seem that both forms of regulation work best when they co-exist; that is, two tier regulation is more likely to be superior to a system wholly reliant on either self or statutory regulation'.[39]

An illustrative example of this effective coexistence can be found in the FSA's approach to hedge fund transparency *vis-à-vis* their investors as regards the issue of preferential treatment granted to specific investors through so-called 'side letters'. The FSA had stated that it understood 'acceptable market practice' to be for managers to ensure that all investors are informed when a side letter is granted. This statement is clearly illustrative of the way in which a principle-based brand of supervision, grounded on market practices, works in practice: whilst accepting to show deference to the free bargaining of sophisticated investors and refusing to impose a flat ban with respect to 'side letters' and the correlated preferential treatment negotiated among hedge fund managers and specific investors, the FSA encouraged the industry to develop a market practice conducive to full disclosure, warning, at the same time, that failure to disclose the existence of side letters would be a breach of Principle 1 of the Principles for Businesses (whereby 'a firm must conduct its business with integrity') and,

---

[38] On co-regulation see Cafaggi, *supra*, fn. 27, 27 ff.
[39] Doyle, Chris (1997), 'Self regulation and Statutory Regulation', *Business Strategy Review*, **8**(3), 42 (quoted by P. Athanassiou, *supra*, fn. 29, 226).

depending on the circumstances, even a criminal offence under section 397 of the 2000 FSMA. In this way 'government's benign big gun looms in the background, loaded and ready'.[40] Not surprisingly, the Hedge Fund Standards recommended by the Hedge Fund Working Group (the 'Large Group') were promptly made compliant (adopting Standard 2, under which 'a hedge fund manager should disclose the existence of side letters which contain material terms and the nature of such terms').

6.   SELF AND EXTERNAL REGULATION FROM AN INTERNATIONAL SUPERVISORY PERSPECTIVE: WHAT FUTURE FOR SELF-REGULATION?

The theoretical divide between self and external regulation becomes even more blurred if one approaches it from an international (or transnational) regulatory perspective. Where governments regulate through global 'soft law' provisions and recommended general principles, market-driven and institution-driven norms necessarily come even closer to one another. In this context, obviously, the potential of self-regulation to have a more 'globalized' scope compared to traditional regulation plays a crucial role in supporting the evolution of an efficient and comprehensive regulatory transnational framework. Indeed any national or regional institution fails, due to its territorially limited sovereignty, to respond with efficacy to the regulatory challenges posed by global investment vehicles that are, in the words of Greenspan, 'only a short step from cyberspace'. As it has been aptly noted,

> [I]f hedge fund activities were distributed evenly over jurisdictions, one might conjecture that the patchwork of national regulations restricts systemic risk on average by the right amount. Yet the mismatch between the national reach of government regulation and the transnational nature of systemic risk is more serious and complicated. The hedge fund industry responds to differences in national regulation by engaging in 'regulatory arbitrage'. Consequently jurisdictions find themselves competing with each other to attract hedge fund business. Instead of balancing the cost of intervention against the benefit of controlling systemic risk, successful regulators are biased towards pleasing regulated firms. To prevent such state capture, government regulation itself has to transcend national jurisdiction.[41]

While it is true that some of the above can be achieved through a regional 'hard law' harmonization effort – provided that a supranational insti-

---

[40]   Engert, *supra*, fn. 34, 356.
[41]   Engert, *supra*, fn. 34, 356.

tutional framework is in place, as it is the case of the EU – to do so effectively, a high prize would have to be paid: making the bastion also a prison.[42] It follows that, whilst having some potential, if successful, to foster a 'bottom up' alignment of the global rules and of the industry practices with those mandated within the supranational constituency (provided that the latter is sizeable enough to influence or, even, shape market behaviors),[43] a supranational (albeit regional) response to regulatory competition is certainly a second best. For a global industry accustomed to 'fit regulatory cracks' a *global* 'top down' regulatory response would remain the first best solution.[44] Moreover, concerns have been raised that, by adopting its own regulatory approach in this field, the EU would, instead of spreading its own standards, risk entering into conflict with the US,[45] a risk that could certainly be averted by international convergence.

As clearly epitomized by the 2009 IOSCO principles on hedge fund oversight, though, 'top down' convergence in an international setting that has, so far, been characterized by weak global institutions and is still lacking a proper global rule maker, can only lead to a credible outcome if intimately associated with self-regulation. Not surprisingly, in its discussion of Principle Five, IOSCO acknowledges that 'the development of a common set of industry standards remains of high value to all market participants including securities regulators, active market participants and investors. The IOSCO Technical Committee will work with industry

---

[42]   House of Lords, 'Directive on Alternative Investment Fund Managers', Volume I, Report, London, HL Paper 48-I 2010, at para 142 ('funds cannot get in and money cannot get out').

[43]   Compare also the ECB's response to the Commission Consultation on Hedge Funds (ECB, 'Eurosystem Contribution', European Commission's consultation on hedge funds, 25 February 2009, 3): 'The Eurosystem is strongly in favour of an internationally coordinated response, given the highly international nature of the hedge fund industry. (. . .) A European initiative can act as a first step towards a global consensus, but at the same time should take the competitiveness of the EU-based hedge funds and hedge fund management firms into account. A "regulated in the EU" label could prove to be an advantage for some hedge fund-like private pools of capital. Moreover, a common EU regulatory regime would benefit market integration at the European level. Given the international character of the hedge fund value chain, a purely European response, if deemed necessary, might be most effective if directed towards asset managers and investors residing in the EU'.

[44]   ECB, *supra*, fn. 26, 1.

[45]   Referring to the UK position, which was voted down in the Council see Engert, Andreas, *supra*, fn. 35, 54; compare also 56 where it is noted that 'it is hard to imagine regulatory harmonization without US leadership, although there are important counter examples'.

bodies to develop a consolidated set of industry standards which should reflect and supplement the above recommendations and should be globally consistent. Regulators should encourage hedge funds/hedge funds managers to adhere to the consolidated set of industry standards and may take into account those standards in giving effect to the above principles. Regulators should also agree to a way in which they could be informed about the take up/compliance (and consequences of non-compliance) by individual hedge funds/hedge funds managers of/with the standards'.

The above statement helps clarify a few relevant policy points.

First, it illustrates that global regulatory convergence, at least in this particular field, can only help curb regulatory competition in laxity, if the process is driven by the international organizations of supervisory authorities and if the latter are genuinely successful (or, in any event, more successful than national governments) in refraining from regulatory and supervisory competition while, at the same time, resisting any 'capture'. It is generally accepted that, although the adoption of overarching, general soft law principles remains reserved to the national government level, the degree of real international convergence in financial regulation and supervision depends crucially on the agreements reached before their intergovernmental adoption and implemented thereafter by the technocrats of the supervisory authorities involved. This indicates that the nature and size of the financial regulator matters and the mode of regulation is a function thereof: if rules are set in fact by a global cooperative nexus of regulators significantly exposed to market pressures, soft law provisions based on institutional transnational agreements mimicking market standards can represent the only workable form of international regulatory response. In a rule making perspective, what that means is that international convergence can only reasonably be expected, if at all, on the basis of a set of broad general principles. Moreover, absent a centralized and unified global supervisory authority that is genuinely independent from national interests, decisions are bound to be taken through permanent multilateral bargaining, a process which internalizes, but does not neutralize, the conflicts associated with divergent national interests (the same conflicts that, in a competitive instead of cooperative transnational regulatory and supervisory setting, are externalized in the form of regulatory competition in laxity). This suggests that – unless common rules and supervisory standards are adopted by majority rule and under the pressure associated with a major financial crisis – the regulatory output cannot be expected to be anything other than the sum of 'viable' political compromises, very much dependent also on the (global and national) industry interests.

Second, what the IOSCO observation, above, suggests is that supervisory authorities, albeit better positioned (because better informed) and (in principle, at least) more 'independent' than politicians, do need an open and on-going dialogue with the industry as part of any rule making and enforcement process. This is, in particular, true as regards detailed rules of conduct. Self-regulation can play, here, a very useful function of 'norms discovery', so as to properly complement the external regulatory framework. Most of the detailed, technical supervisory standards in this field should, in fact, incorporate by reference, one way or another, market-drawn best practices. This can occur according to different patterns of supervisory intervention. Where supervision is principle-based and supervisors are called upon to enforce a limited number of general principles set by external regulations, supervisors will necessarily (or, in any event, should) interpret such general principles – and attribute to them a more detailed content – in the light of any existing market best practices. In this setting, it is certainly up to the regulated firm to adopt the conduct that it may reasonably deem fit to abide by the mandated general principles retaining, however, full responsibility for its conduct should its decision be eventually found inconsistent with the applicable general principles. Conformity with market best practices should, in principle, amount to a safe harbor, at least for as long as such practices are not openly contested by the supervisors. By contrast, conducts below the threshold recommended by self-regulatory standards would, in principle, fall in a grey area, and could only be accepted if individually justified, according to the principle of proportionality – a principle that is recognized by regulators and reflected in the best practices themselves – or for other objective reasons, provided that the deviation from the standard does not cause any societal harm. In such a setting, private self-regulation would thus end up being publicly enforced, thereby becoming legally (quasi) mandatory; private rules, despite their self regulatory origin, would be transformed into legal norms, because non-compliance with the standard would also be a breach of a regulatory general principle (and would be sanctioned as a violation thereof). In addition, as recently recommended by the ECB, to further enforce industry compliance with best practices, the obligation for hedge fund managers to submit themselves to peer reviews could be introduced and it could be considered whether regulated institutional investors should be allowed to invest only in hedge funds managed by asset managers that comply with best practices.[46] On the other hand, where supervision is grounded on detailed (often secondary) legal rules and technical standards set by the relevant institutions, supervisors should either regulate the field

---

[46] ECB, *supra*, fn. 43, 5.

thoroughly, incorporating in their rules the standards originally set by self-regulatory bodies (replacing the 'should' of the recommendations with the 'shall' of their own mandatory requirements) – at least where the self-regulatory exercise has proved to have been of good quality and capable of drawing a fair balance of all interests concerned – or substantially include the industry positions in their more intrusive legal and economic regulatory assessment (as due in Europe under the better regulation principle).[47] Also in such a setting, private ordering is, in a way, made into an integral part of the regulatory framework, thereby becoming legally mandatory. From this perspective, self-regulation also has a future in the context of the AIFM Directive: it seems indeed quite likely that most of the Level 2 measures to be adopted by the Commission under the Directive (as well as most of the Level 3 technical standards to be endorsed by the Commission upon a proposal of the ESAs) will be drawn from the existing (or revised) industry standards.

Finally it remains questionable if and to what extent there is room for the coexistence of *detailed* external regulation (in Europe, through Level 2 and 3 implementing measures for the AIFM Directive) and self-regulatory standards. In principle, such coexistence could make sense in so far as self-imposed best practices were indeed 'optimal' standards as opposed to being the minimum requirements set by external detailed rules. If the substantive content of self-imposed and external rules could effectively differ, there would remain, in fact, a difference in the degree of 'virtuosity' (be it superior fairness or efficiency, as the case may be) of the behavior expected under the legal rules and the standards respectively, which would make possible such coexistence and would make self-regulation an 'add on' in respect to external regulation (i.e. capable of bringing about additional gains in social welfare, which would not be made, however, compulsory by external regulation). This would also entail that, by abiding by the legal rules, hedge fund conducts would already meet the legal standards, with

---

[47]   Compare e.g. AIMA 'Response to European Commission's Consultation on Hedge Funds', 30 January 2009, 14: 'we strongly believe that unified best practise standards are more likely to be effective than regulation imposed by others. We would hope that such standards would lead to a more harmonised and internationally consistent approach, reducing the risk of regulatory arbitrage. We would envisage that national regulators would make reference to such standards in their rules, although the extent to which any particular regulatory authority would wish or be able to incorporate it into its own rules would be a matter for that regulator'. Whilst such approach is certainly illustrative of how self-regulation and supervision can coexist, excessive reliance on national choice as recommended in the last sentence could, in this author's view, bring about, once again, national fragmentation and regulatory and supervisory competition in laxity.

the application of the additional, self-imposed 'add on' requirements being only optional. Compliance with external rules would become relevant for legal assessment, while compliance with self-regulatory market standards would become relevant for market assessment,[48] unless regulatory incentives are put in place to foster compliance with higher market standards. It should be noted, though, that, the optional nature of self-regulation remains such only until the hedge fund and/or its manager commits publicly to the standards. Indeed, up to that point in time, each member of the industry would, in fact, be free to opt-out of the 'add on' standard without incurring any legal sanction (except, if so provided, disclosure under the 'comply or explain' paradigm). In the hedge fund industry, self-regulatory bodies monitor the standards but do not enforce them. By contrast, once a member of the industry commits publicly to the higher self-regulatory standards, these become binding upon it, 'in the sense that non-compliance with them becomes a form of misrepresentation, leading to sanctions by regulators or the courts'.[49] Systemic consistency would, therefore, recommend that international supervisory organizations extend, also in this field, the provisions already embedded in the Basle banking principles,[50] making internal compliance compulsory not only with external rules but, also, with any code of conduct and self-regulatory standard to which the firm has committed itself.

7. CONCLUDING REMARKS

In conclusion, despite the theoretically clear distinction between the expected outcome of private ordering and external regulation, the differences between the two may, as a practical matter, be less acute, with the private or public nature of the body setting the rule being likely to matter less than expected. Also enforcement might be less

---

[48] As recently noted, e.g., by the Hedge Fund Standards Board (HFSB), 'in a sophisticated market place, it is left to investors to drive conformity with the HFSB standards. HFSB believes that this is a very powerful mechanism, since the interests of investors are closely aligned with those of the managers. Investors can vote with their money (i.e. withdrawing monies from managers who do not meet the standards or under-perform) and ultimately drive the Darwinian process that sees the weak managers eliminated and continuous improvement of Standards' (HFSB (2009), 'Public Response to the IOSCO Consultation Report on Hedge Fund Oversight', 8).

[49] *Ibid*, 9.

[50] Basel Committee on Banking Supervision (2005), High Level Paper on Compliance Risk and the Compliance Function in Banks, *passim*.

distinctive than theoretically expected. If courts and supervisors take self-regulatory standards into account to determine liability and enforce such standards on an ongoing basis – construing the standard as the expected conduct, unless a deviation from the standard is justified by the principle of proportionality or by other, objective reasons – self-regulation becomes, in practice, mandatory and is to be enforced similarly to external regulation. In other words, the deterrence associated with self-regulatory and command and control rules might be in practice not very dissimilar.

All this suggests that, despite some of the post-crisis rhetoric surrounding the issue of regulatory reform, self-regulation and external regulation are bound to coexist also in the frame of the recently approved AIFM Directive. And rightly so, if we consider that, in the field of hedge funds, transnational rule making is fraught by the natural inadequacy of any national or regional institution, due to its territorially limited sovereignty, to properly respond to the regulatory challenge posed by global investment vehicles, such as hedge funds.

BIBLIOGRAPHY

ABI (2009), 'ABI Response to the European Commission Consultation Paper on Hedge Fund', *Position Paper.*

Aguilar, Louis A. (2009), 'Hedge Fund Regulation on the Horizon – Don't Shoot the Messenger', Speech by SEC Commissioner at the Hedgeworld Fund Services Conference, New York.

AIMA (2009), 'Response to EU Commission Consultation on Hedge Funds', London: AIMA.

Athanassiou, Phoebus (2009), *Hedge Fund Regulation in the European Union*, Amsterdam, the Netherlands: Kluwer Law International.

Cafaggi, Fabrizio (2006), 'Rethinking Private Regulation in the European Regulatory Space', in *Reframing Self-Regulation in European Private Law*, F.Cafaggi (ed.), the Netherlands: Kluwer Law International.

Cumming, Douglas and Li Que (2007), 'A Law and Finance Analysis of Hedge Funds', available electronically at http://www.degroote.mcmaster.ca/faculty/rsconference/documents/ALawandFinanceAnalysis.pdf.

Doyle, Chris (1997), 'Self regulation and Statutory Regulation', *Business Strategy Review*, 8(3).

Edwards, Franklin R. (2006), 'Hedge Fund and Investor Protection Regulation', *Federal Reserve Bank of Atlanta Economic Review*, 91(4).

Engert, Andreas (2010), 'Transnational Hedge Fund Regulation', *European Business Organization Law Review*, 11(3), 329–78.

European Central Bank (2009), 'Opinion of the 16 October 2009 on a Proposal for a Directive of the European Parliament and of the Council on Alternative Investment Fund Managers and amending Directives 2004/39/EC and 2009/. . ./EC'. CON/2009/81.

European Central Bank (2009), 'Eurosystem Contribution', European Commission's Consultation on Hedge Funds, 25 February.

Hedge Fund Standards Board (2009), 'Public Response to the IOSCO Consultation Report on Hedge Fund Oversight'.

Horsfield-Bradbury, John (2008), 'Hedge Fund Self Regulation in the US and the UK', available at http://www.law.harvard.edu/programs/corp-gov/papers/Brudney2008-Horsfield-Bradbury.pdf.

Jonna, Paul M. (2008), 'In Search of Market Discipline: The Case for Indirect Hedge Fund Regulation', *San Diego Law Review*, **45**(4).

Kambhu, John and Til Schuermann and Kevin J. Stiroh (2007), 'Hedge Funds, Financial Intermediation and Systemic Risk', available at SSRN: http://ssrn.com/abstract=995907.

King, Michael R. and Philipp Maier (2009), 'Hedge Funds and Financial Stability: Regulating Prime Brokers will Mitigate Systemic Risks', *Journal of Financial Stability*, **5**.

Oesterle, Dale A. (2006), 'Regulating Hedge Funds', *Entrepreneurial Business Law Journal*, **1**(1), available electronically at http://moritzlaw.osu.edu/eblj/issues/volume1/number1/oesterle.pdf.

OICV-IOSCO (2006), Technical Committee of the International Organization of Securities Commissions, 'The regulatory environment for hedge funds: a survey and comparison – Final Report'.

OICV-IOSCO (2007), Technical Committee of the International Organization of Securities Commissions, 'Principles for the valuation of hedge fund portfolios – Consultation Report'.

OICV-IOSCO (2007), Technical Committee of the International Organization of Securities Commissions, 'Principles for the valuation of hedge fund portfolios – Final Report'.

OICV-IOSCO (2008), Report of the Technical Committee of the International Organization of Securities Commissions, 'Report on Funds of Hedge Funds – Final Report'.

OICV-IOSCO (2009), Technical Committee of the International Organization of Securities Commissions, 'Hedge Funds Oversight – Final Report'.

Paredes, Troy, (2006), 'On the Decision to Regulate Hedge Funds: The SEC's Regulatory Philosophy, Style and Mission', Washington University, Faculty Working Paper Series, paper no. 06-03-02, March.

Paredes, Troy, (2007), 'Hedge Funds and the SEC: Observations on the How and Why of Securities Regulation', Washington University, Faculty Working Paper Series, paper no. 07-05-01, May.

PriceWaterhouseCoopers (2004), 'The regulation and distribution of hedge funds in Europe, Changes and challenges', London.

PricewaterhouseCoopers (2009), *Response to EU Commission Consultation on Hedge Fund*, London.

Robotti, Paola (2009), *Private Governance of Financial Markets: the US Regulatory Regime on Hedge Funds*, Barcelona: IBEI.

Schmidt, Michael J. (2007), 'Investor Protection in Europe and the United States: Impacting the Future of Hedge Funds', *Wisconsin International Law Journal*, **25**(1).

Scott Hall, S. (2009), *International Finance: Law and Regulation*, London: Sweet and Maxwell.

Spangler, Timothy (2008), *The Law of Private Investment Funds*, New York: Oxford University Press.

Taub, Jennifer S. (2009), 'Enablers of Exuberance: Legal Acts and Omissions that Facilitated the Global Financial Crisis', electronic copy available at: http://ssrn.com/abstract=1472190.

Verret, Jay. W. (2007), 'Dr. Jones and the Raiders of Lost Capital: Hedge Fund Regulation, Part II, a Self-Regulation Proposal', *Delaware Journal of Corporate Law*, **32**(3).

10. Hedge fund regulation through competition law principles – some reflections
*David Harrison**

The condition is easily diagnosed. Over the last half century, the rise of the investment industry has created overwhelming incentives for investors to follow one another into risks they often do not understand. As a result, world markets are hopelessly synchronised. This obstructs rational pricing and, in a capitalist world that relies on markets to set prices, endangers our prosperity. Finding a cure, however, is more difficult. (John Authers, 2010, p.182)

INTRODUCTION

One could imagine a world where, by accident or design, for policy reasons or because policy-makers cannot agree, there is no dedicated hedge fund regulatory framework. In such a world there would remain the underlying rules of the market economy, including those contained in competition law, to serve as instruments to control hedge funds and their market activities.

In the European Union (EU), competition law applies to 'undertakings', i.e. to all entities engaged in the pursuit of an economic activity, regardless of their nomenclature, their precise legal status or the manner of their financing. Unlike, say, financial regulation or national taxation rules, EU competition law is not concerned with the details of the legal structure, or the precise physical location of an undertaking. Instead, the effect on EU trade is the test of whether or not competition rules apply to agreements between, or to the conduct of, undertakings (including those that are located outside the EU). The extent to which this test is met can

* David Harrison is a lawyer specialising in EU/competition law at Bond Pearce LLP, UK. He is the author of *The Organisation of Europe: Developing a Continental Market Order* (Routledge, London and New York, 1995) and the discussion paper 'The Division of Labour and the Division of Europe' (an account of the origins of the Treaty of Rome), published by the European Interdependence Research Unit, St Antony's College, Oxford, in 1999. He has previously worked on economic, financial and monetary issues.

be relatively easily ascertained: an influence, direct or indirect, actual or potential, on the pattern of trade between any two of the 27 EU Member States will suffice. Agreements relating to the buying and selling of internationally traded securities, such as those that hedge funds routinely enter into, are likely to fulfil that test.

This chapter will, first, explain some underlying principles of relevance to the general competition law rules applicable in Europe; second, consider how these may apply to financial services in general; third, look in more detail at the issue of the exchange of information between competing undertakings; and, fourth, formulate some thoughts which may be of particular relevance to the hedge fund industry. It concludes that if financial sector firms were treated the same way as firms in the real economy and if competition law principles were to be applied to them consistently it is possible that some market malfunctions might be avoided.

1.   THE IMPACT OF THE FINANCIAL CRISIS

The global financial and economic crisis has prompted introspection and soul-searching in the world of market economics. In the words of the G20 London summit declaration of April 2009, 'We face the greatest challenge to the world economy in modern times; a crisis which has deepened since we last met, and which affects the lives of women, men and children in every country.' The title of the latest book by US judge and antitrust author Richard Posner is *A Failure of Capitalism*. Commenting on the current, post-crisis, condition of the 'efficient market hypothesis', Jeremy Siegel, Professor of Finance at the Wharton School of the University of Pennsylvania remarked, perhaps ironically, on the occasion of a conference held in Cambridge in April 2010: 'there are good economic reasons why prices are where they are, despite the fact that subsequent history may show that these prices are terribly wrong'.[1]

Judged by one simple yardstick, namely the amount of state aid to the private sector, it is as if economic progress in the EU has been suspended. The long-term trend of reducing national subsidies to private firms, down from an average of 1 per cent of EU gross domestic product (GDP) in 1992 to 0.5 per cent by 2007, has come to an end. Because of the banking crisis, recorded levels of state aid have risen more than sevenfold, to an EU

---

[1]   'Efficient Market Theory and the Recent Financial Crisis': paper delivered at the Inaugural Conference of the Institute for New Economic Thinking, on the theme '*The Economic Crisis and the Crisis in Economics*'.

average of 3.6 per cent of GDP in 2009 (*see European Commission State Aid Scoreboard (Autumn 2010 Update)*).[2] In the UK, state aid has risen to 7.9 per cent of GDP, in France to 2.2 per cent and in Germany, to 4.8 per cent. In Belgium, the corresponding figure is 10.1 per cent of GDP. Most of this aid is towards the financial sector and, in some cases, states now exert substantial control over access to credit. In general, levels of state aid are now higher in Western Europe than in post-Communist Central and Eastern Europe. Banking has, paradoxically, done more to extend state control over the economy than anything else since the collapse of Communism.

Under Article 127 of the Treaty on the Functioning of the European Union (TFEU), the European System of Central Banks 'shall act in accordance with the principles of an open market economy with free competition, favouring an efficient allocation of resources.' Competition law, through the control of state aid to private firms, already provides the standards against which to judge whether or not state-financed bail-outs distort the European single market. What more might it have to say specifically in relation to financial services?

2.   COMPETITION LAW AND MARKET POWER

EU competition law has origins both in US antitrust policy and, also, in the ideas of German thinkers on how to curb excessive market (or economic) power. It was US antitrust expert Robert Bowie who wrote the key competition law articles in the 1951 European Coal and Steel Community Treaty, at the request of Jean Monnet.[3] And one of the two co-authors of the 1956 Spaak Committee Report, setting out how the future European common market should be created, was Hans von der Groeben, who went on to become the first Competition Commissioner of the European Commission. Von der Groeben had ties to the German ordoliberal group of economists and lawyers, with roots in the 1930s Freiburg school, who sought to find legal and economic answers to the collapse of the Weimar Republic and the rise of the National Socialists, by proposing frameworks to prevent concentrations and misuse of economic power (see Gerber 1994).

---

[2]   Crisis measures, including guarantees, notified to and approved by the European Commission have, according to the Spring 2010 Update, in fact reached 32.6% of EU GDP, although not all are expected to be implemented.

[3]   Monnet (1978), 352.

Competition law now extends the rules of the market economy to most of the European continent, including large parts of Central and Eastern Europe previously under Communist rule. This may be judged as a success if one recalls that quite a few of these countries belonged to the rival, non-market, Council for Mutual Economic Assistance ('Comecon') during the 1959–1991 period. Through the decentralized network system embodied in Regulation 1/2003, EU competition rules have, in the words of the European Commission, 'to a large extent become the 'law of the land' for the whole of the EU'.[4] This network system, involving national and EU authorities applying the same rules across the enlarged EU, is an 'innovative model of governance for the implementation of [EU] law by the Commission and the member state authorities'. Comparable networks of EU and national authorities are being created in those economic sectors, like energy, where liberalisation in the single market is still incomplete.

At the heart of competition law is the economic concept of market power. Competition law provides a framework for curbing and containing market power, so that dangerous concentrations thereof can, to the extent possible, be avoided. For the purposes of describing market power it is possible to use for shorthand the 2004 Guideline of the Office of Fair Trading (OFT), the national competition authority in the United Kingdom (UK), on the 'Assessment of Market Power' (*OFT 415*). Section 3.1 provides as follows:

> Market power can be thought of as the ability profitably to sustain prices above competitive levels or restrict output or quality below competitive levels. An undertaking with market power might also have the ability and incentive to harm the process of competition in other ways; for example, by weakening existing competition, raising entry barriers or slowing innovation. However, although market power is not solely concerned with the ability of a supplier to raise prices, this guideline often refers to market power for convenience as the ability profitably to sustain prices above competitive levels.

The same concept exists at the EU level, where market power has been described as 'the ability to cause negative market effects as to prices, output, innovation or the variety or quality of goods and services'.[5] It is from this orthodox analysis of the concept of market power that the range of competition law instruments, which attempt to address the problem of market power, whether exercised by one firm in a market or by several,

---

[4] Communication from the Commission on the functioning of Regulation 1/2003, April 2009, para. 47.

[5] Commission Notice: Guidelines on the applicability of Article 81 of the EC Treaty to horizontal co-operation agreements, para. 27 (OJ 2001/C 3/02).

through agreements, concerted practices or other forms of co-ordinated behaviour, flow (legal prohibitions on anti-competitive behaviour; fines of up to 10 per cent of global turnover and other sanctions; the control of mergers between firms; market investigations).

The damage to the world economy by the banking crisis far exceeds the damage caused by any one firm, or group of firms, that exercise market power in the real economy. The consequences for public finances in, for example, the UK have been compared to the economic costs of a war (Martin Wolf 2009). And it has led to Western Europe providing more subsidies for the private sector than post-Communist Central and Eastern Europe have provided to theirs. Commenting on the crisis, the European Competition Commissioner Joaquin Almunia said in a speech in March 2010:

> The financial crisis demonstrates very clearly how a lack of effective regulation created incentives for financial institutions not to compete on the basis of the best long-term business models. Rather they were incentivised to pursue excessive risk-taking in order to achieve short-term gains.

Writing retrospectively on her experience of dealing with the crisis in an article in the European Commission's first Competition Policy Newsletter of 2010, former Competition Commissioner Neelie Kroes observed, 'I have never suggested that the finance sector should be only about simple deposits and small loans. But banks do need to offer products and services they actually understand, instead of racking up massive leverage on the back of opaque alphabet soup products.' Could concentrations of market power be part of the problem? That takes us on to the next stage of the analysis.

3.   MARKET POWER IN THE CONTEXT OF FINANCIAL MARKETS

Adair Turner, Chairman of the UK Financial Services Authority, has pointed out that a striking feature of the last 30 to 40 years of economic history has been the dramatic increase in the size of the financial sector relative to the real economy, in the UK and in other developed countries.[6] According to figures he cites, the total balance sheet of the UK banking

---

[6]   Speech to the Cass Business School, 17 March 2010, 'What do banks do, what should they do and what public policies are needed to ensure best results for the real economy?'

system, defined to include all legal banking entities operating in London, had by 2007 reached around 500 per cent of GDP, compared with only 34 per cent in 1964. Moreover, this had become dominated by a complex mesh of intra-financial system claims and obligations, rather than by banks' relations with UK households and companies. Over the same period and, in particular, in the past 20 years, complex securitisation has also allowed an enormous off-balance-sheet growth in credit markets. There has also been a 'remarkable explosion' in the scale of financial trading activity relative to the real economy globally.[7] From a financial regulatory point of view, he has suggested that new 'macro-prudential tools' may therefore be needed to address the self-reinforcing exuberant upswings and subsequent downswings which result from a credit system combining securitisation and on-balance sheet lending. In his analysis, 'a system of securitised credit can further increase the risks of self-reinforcing credit and asset priced cycles and therefore further increase the case for new macro-prudential tools'.

Lord Turner has emphasized the need to understand the deep-rooted drivers of financial instability:

> If [. . .] we believe that liquid financial markets are subject for inherent reasons to herd and momentum effects, that credit and asset price cycles are centrally important phenomena, and that the widespread trading of credit securities can increase the extent to which credit and asset prices are linked in self-reinforcing cycles, then we have challenges which cannot be overcome by any silver bullet structural solution.[8]

The key point here lies in the idea that financial markets may for 'inherent reasons' tend to instability rather than equilibrium. Apart from the crisis of 2008, history provides many previous examples of financial bubbles, including the Dutch Tulip Bubble of 1636, the South Sea Bubble of 1720, the stock price bubble of the 1920s, property-related bubbles in the Nordic region and Asia in the 1980s and 1990s, and the US technology stocks boom in the 1990s.[9]

That beyond a certain point the size of the financial sector may itself

---

[7] Foreign exchange trading has risen from 11 times global trade value in 1980 to 73 times today; the value of oil futures traded has increased from 20% of global physical production and consumption in 1980 to 10 times today; and interest rate derivatives trading has grown from nil in 1980 to US$390 trillion in mid-2009.

[8] *Supra*, fn. 6.

[9] The repetitive nature of financial catastrophe is illustrated by the title of the 2009 book on the history of the subject, by Reinhart and Rogoff: *This Time Is Different: Eight Centuries of Financial Folly*.

create difficulties has also been suggested by, for example, ECB Executive Board Member Gertrude Tumpel-Gugerell, speaking in June 2010: 'The size of the financial sector is another aspect which deserves close scrutiny. When the financial system grows too large it may eventually lead to a mis-allocation of resources.'[10] As the President of the Federal Reserve Bank of Boston has pointed out, the combined size of the three largest US banks is now 40 per cent of US GDP, while in each of Germany, France, Ireland and the UK the combined size of the three largest banks is greater than national GDP.[11]

From a macroeconomic perspective, the US economist Hyman Minsky has explored the underlying 'inherent reasons' for instability. In his work *Stabilizing an Unstable Economy* Minsky argues that instability must necessarily follow from the reliance of the US economy on banking, as during a period of stability banks, which are commercial businesses, will seek to create profits from financial innovation and, in this way, create conditions for the next boom. Minsky refers to such instability as arising from 'internal processes' in the economy:

> It is necessary for the financial system to be responsive to changing business demands for financing, but if financial innovation and aggressive seeking of borrowers outpaces the demands for funds for investment financing, excess funds will be available to finance demand for existing bonds, common stock, and capital assets. This leads to a rise in the price of capital assets relative to the supply price of investment output. This, as has been explained, increases investment activity and thus profit – leading to a further rise in the price of capital assets and long-lived financial instruments. The behaviour of financial markets, then, can trigger a boom from seemingly stable expansions.[12]

From a hedge fund practitioner's point of view the comments of George Soros are particularly noteworthy. Soros' approach builds on Karl Popper's philosophy of scientific knowledge to arrive at the view that, far from being infallible, financial markets embody very imperfect, and highly fallible, knowledge. Most of the time the imperfect knowledge or expectations of financial market participants will tend to cancel themselves out, or correct themselves. But, in certain 'far from equilibrium' circumstances, expectations about a price trend can become widely shared and self-reinforcing, leading eventually to a boom-bust sequence. When this

---

[10]   Speech in Warsaw, 11 June 2010, 'Financial Integration and Stability: Efficiency Gains vs Pitfalls'.

[11]   Speech by Eric Rosengren in London, 10 November 2009, 'Can We Ensure That Global Banks Do Not Create Global Problems?'

[12]   Minsky (1986), 278.

happens financial prices do not follow fundamental real economy prices. Instead, the relationship is reversed and fundamental real economy prices follow financial prices. It is this latter phenomenon which Soros describes as the heart of his theory of 'reflexivity'.

Since at least the 1980s, Soros has rejected the hypothesis that financial markets tend towards equilibrium. His view has been that, on the contrary, some financial markets tend towards disequilibrium. By a reflexive process, expectations of market participants can have a real impact on future financial market prices, which in turn can have a real impact on the underlying assets, or collateral, to which those prices relate. In 1987, long before the latest crisis, Soros wrote that,

> I contend that such paradoxical behaviour is typical of all financial markets that serve as a discounting mechanism for future developments, notably stock markets, foreign exchange markets, banking and all forms of credit. Microeconomic theory may continue to ignore it, because there are large areas of economic activity where it occurs only occasionally or not at all; but we cannot expect to understand macroeconomic developments without taking the phenomenon into account. A world of fluctuating exchange rates and large-scale capital movements is characterised by vicious and benign circles in which the 'normal' pattern of causation, as defined by classical economics, seems to be reversed: market developments dictate the evolution of the conditions of supply and demand, not the other way round.[13]

Soros is not suggesting that most markets tend towards disequilibrium. For most markets, most of the time, the normal microeconomic rules of supply and demand appear to apply. It is those markets – the 'real economy' markets – with which competition law is traditionally concerned, by seeking to prevent the exercise of market power or to thwart the ability of firms to sustain prices above competitive levels.

However, different processes appear to be at work in financial markets, in particular those which, through improvements in technology and deregulation, now operate globally (including those where alternative investment funds are active). Because these markets involve expectations by market participants of future price levels, self-fulfilling tendencies can at times be created which affect those price levels and ultimately, by extension, the real economy assets to which they relate. For Soros, this phenomenon can mainly be observed in the creation of domestic credit by banks, but in some of his other books (see, for instance, Soros 2009) he also documents the boom-bust or bubble creation process underlying the US conglomerate boom in the 1960s; US Real Estate Investment Trusts;

---

[13]   Soros (1987), 31.

stock market prices generally; the international banking crisis of the 1980s; some commodity markets; and, of course, the recent US housing bubble.

4.   IMPLICATIONS

The sheer size of the financial sector; the reasonable suspicion (to put it no higher) that, for one reason or another, aspects of it are inherently unstable; and the scope for price movements in that sector to affect asset prices in the real world economy all suggest further analysis is needed. If prices set by financial markets can indeed affect real economy prices, either upwards (in a bubble) or downwards (in a crash), that, from a competition law point of view, appears something close to an exercise of market power. If so, is there anything that competition law might have to say or do about it?

Exuberance in financial bubbles is not necessarily irrational. From the point of view of individual financial firms it may make perfect sense to engage in financial transactions based on the presumption of a boom. Until the moment when the bubble bursts the rational firm will normally participate and maximize profits. As Posner has pointed out, at the height of a boom:

> no single bank, in the highly competitive financial-intermediation industry, could justify to its shareholders reducing its risk-taking (for example by reducing its leverage), and therefore their return on equity, merely because the risks that it and its competitors were taking might precipitate a financial crisis that could in turn usher in a depression [. . .] There would be only one effect of the bank's altruism – of its willingness to sacrifice profits enabled by taking a slight risk of bankruptcy that most financial executives would think tolerable, as the risk would be unlikely to materialise for a number of years during which they would be making huge amounts of money: the bank would lose out in competition with its daring competitors.[14]

This is the 'excessive risk-taking in order to achieve short-term gains' to which Competition Commissioner Almunia referred in March 2010.[15]

On the face of it, financial markets appear to be highly competitive between participants. But, on closer inspection, one may wonder whether that is really the case. In practice, given that markets are global, and given the huge scale of the financial sector compared to the real economy, there

---

[14]   Posner (2009), 322.

[15]   Speech to the Centre on Regulation in Europe: 'Competition v Regulation: where do the roles of sector specific and competition regulators begin and end?'

may be rather fewer firms involved than one would expect. According to press reports there are just 30 banks and insurance firms on a global systemic risks list.[16] Some markets, such as those for credit derivatives, appear particularly concentrated (but, also, particularly opaque).

What exactly is the nature of competition in a financial bubble? Within a bubble participants are not competing, as in the real economy, over the price of goods or services, so that the price reaches equilibrium by a process of supply and demand. On the contrary, in a bubble participants are collectively expecting a given price to move in a particular direction, and they are competing essentially for profits resulting from their share of that expected price movement, probably with the use of innovative trading techniques or leverage. This interdependent behaviour between ostensible competitors has features oddly similar to an oligopoly in the real economy. As an introductory practitioner text for foreign exchange dealers explains:

> For each commercial transaction he handles, the marketmaker may do ten additional trades with other marketmakers. What is going on? The answer is that foreign currency traders have become information dealers. The bulk of their trading is related to the ebb and flow of economic and political events. [. . .] Since most FX supply and demand comes from the interbank market itself, the trader knows that any news event may bring about a reaction on the part of other traders. And, perceiving an impending shift in the market, he must immediately adjust his own position according to how he thinks other traders will react. Traders are like the judges in the Keynesian beauty contest who, rather than voting for the girl they thought was most beautiful, instead voted for the girl they thought the other judges would think was the most beautiful. Market equilibrium will depend in part on what traders think other traders think about equilibrium.[17]

As US economist Kenneth Rogoff has observed in the context of bubbles, the same set of fundamentals can produce different price equilibria: 'It all depends on how market participants co-ordinate their expectations'.[18] In the analysis of Eric Rosengren, President of the Federal Reserve Bank of Boston, it is incorrect expectations by market participants of asset values which is the key characteristic of a bubble.[19] Or, to take the Soros analysis, it is at the point where the individual (and fallible) knowledge

---

[16] 'Thirty groups on systemic risk list', *Financial Times,* 30 November 2009.
[17] Grabbe (1986), 153.
[18] Rogoff, *Financial Times,* 8 April 2010: 'Spotting the tell-tale signs of bubbles approaching'.
[19] See the speech by Rosengren '*Asset Bubbles and Systemic Risk*' (Philadelphia, 3 March 2010), available at http://www.bostonfed.org/news/speeches/rosengren/2010/030310/index.htm.

and expectations of individual market participants coalesce, for whatever reason, that a trend forms, which can then become self-reinforcing. It is therefore the *collective* nature of the trend or expectation of price which is the salient feature, not a process of competition between individual participants in a market. This produces the '*herd and momentum effects*' to which Adair Turner alluded in his speech of 17 March 2010.[20]

The instruments of competition law have proved their worth in the real economy and, on the whole, they have managed to make the market economy work reasonably well. Is there anything in the armoury which might be applicable to 'herd and momentum effects' in the financial markets – including those that alternative investment funds have often been accused of contributing to?

First, it is clear that financial institutions are 'undertakings' for the purposes of competition law, and subject to the same prohibitions on anti-competitive agreements and behaviour as other firms.[21] In the *Austrian Banks* case,[22] long-standing arrangements between the 'Lombard' network of banks jointly to agree changes in interest rates in Austria were found by the European Commission to infringe the prohibition on anti-competitive agreements contained in Article 81(1) of the EC Treaty (now Article 101(1) TFEU). The European Commission rejected any argument that the 'special economic context' of the banking industry meant it should be treated differently from other sectors of the economy.

Second, this same prohibition applies not only to actual agreements between financial institutions but, also, to concerted practices. In the *Austrian Banks* case, the European Commission explained at paragraph 415:

> Conduct can therefore by caught by Article 81(1) as a concerted practice if, although they have not agreed or decided beforehand how each of them should behave on the market, the parties deliberately follow or adapt themselves to a common strategy which promotes or facilitates the co-ordination of their conduct on the market.

---

[20]   *Supra*, fn. 6.

[21]   In this regard, see Athanassiou, 'Competition Law and the European Financial Services Sector: An Overview of Recent Developments' (2008)1(3) *International In-house Counsel Journal*, 419–29, 421–3. For a discussion of the evolving relationship between competition law and financial regulation see also 'Law and regulation for global financial markets: competition law, financial stability and the rules of the game' by Martin McElwee, Freshfields Bruckhaus Deringer LLP, *Law and Financial Markets Review*, September 2010, 473–484.

[22]   Case COMP/36.571, Commission Decision of 11 June 2002, OJ 2004 L 56/1.

Third, below the level of concerted practice competition law also recognizes the concept of tacit co-ordination, or parallel behaviour. This is a phenomenon which may arise in markets which are oligopolistic – or, in other words, where market rivals are interdependent, and price competition is minimal, or non-existent. Whether tacit co-ordination shades into a concerted practice is a question of evidence. In the *Dyestuffs case*, the European Court of Justice observed that,

> Although parallel behaviour may not itself be identified with a concerted practice, it may however amount to strong evidence of such a practice if it leads to conditions of competition which do not respond to the normal conditions of the market, having regard to the nature of the products, the size and number of the undertakings, and the volume of the said market [23]

Fourth, because of the risks, the simple exchange of information between market participants in oligopolistic markets can per se constitute an infringement of Article 101 TFEU. In *Thyssen Stahl AG v Commission,*[24] the Court of First Instance (now the General Court) held that, where the structure of a market is oligopolistic, it is all the more important to ensure the decision-making independence of undertakings and residual competition, and that for that reason the exchange of recent data on market shares could infringe Article 101 TFEU. (We will look at the exchange of information in more detail in the next section.)

Fifth, in a concentrated or oligopolistic market it is also possible for one or more undertakings to abuse their dominant position, contrary to the prohibition contained in Article 102 TFEU. Normally, abuse of a dominant position will take the form of unilateral behaviour by one firm, in a position to exercise market power. However, the exact wording of Article 102 TFEU refers to abuse of a dominant position 'by one or more undertakings' and the case law of the European Court of Justice confirms that collective dominance by several firms does exist as a legal concept.[25]

The mere existence of a position of joint dominance in a particular market is not prohibited: it is the abuse of that position which is forbidden. The case-law of the European Court of Justice has, however, emphasized that a dominant undertaking has a *'special responsibility'* not to allow its conduct to impair genuine undistorted competition on the common market.

Sixth, as well as applying to the conduct of individual firms, competition

---

[23] Case 48/69 *ICI Ltd v Commission* [1972] ECR 619, paras 66 and 67.
[24] Case T-141/94 [1999] ECR II-347.
[25] Case 395/96 P *Compagnie Maritime Belge Transports SA v Commission* [2000] ECR I-1365.

law provides competition authorities with wide-ranging powers of investigation and review over entire market structures. Using such powers the Commission has in recent years investigated the malfunctioning European electricity and gas markets, as well as the market for retail financial services, where it found *'widespread competition barriers which unnecessarily raise the cost of retail banking services for European firms and consumers'*.[26] Corrective action in a number of areas has been promised.

5.   EXCHANGE OF INFORMATION BETWEEN COMPETING UNDERTAKINGS

In January 2011 the European Commission for the first time provided detailed guidance on the exchange of information between competing undertakings, in its revised Guidelines on the Applicability of Article 101 TFEU to horizontal co-operation agreements, defined as agreements between actual or potential competing firms.[27]

The Guidelines state that,

> [I]n situations where the exchange of market information is liable to enable undertakings to be aware of market strategies of their competitors it may lead to restrictive effects on competition. The competitive outcome of information exchange depends on the characteristics of the market in which it takes place (such as concentration, transparency, stability, complexity etc) as well as on the type of information exchanged, which may modify the relevant market environment towards one liable to coordination.

The main competition concerns are that,

> [T]hrough information exchange companies may reach a common understanding on the terms of coordination, which can lead to a collusive outcome on the market. Information exchange can create mutually consistent expectations regarding the uncertainties present in the market. On this basis companies can then reach a common understanding on the terms of coordination of their competitive behaviour, even without an explicit agreement on coordination. Exchange of information about intentions on future conduct is the most likely to enable companies to reach such a common understanding. However, information on current conduct that reveals intentions on future behaviour can also be very useful in this context.

---

[26]   Commission Press Release IP/07/114 of 31 January 2007.
[27]   Communication from the Commission: Guidelines on the applicability of Article 101 of the Treaty on the Functioning of the European Union to horizontal co-operation agreements (OJ C 11, 14.1.2011), at Chapter 2.

The Guidelines explain that the exchange of information between competitors about future conduct regarding prices and quantities, or indeed any strategically useful forward-looking or commercially sensitive data, is likely to be particularly problematic. Sharing strategic data can give rise to restrictive effects on competition if it reduces the parties' decision-making independence by decreasing their incentives to compete.

What about the exchange of information which is already public? The Commission's view is that exchanges of 'genuinely public information' are unlikely to constitute an infringement of Article 101 TFEU. However, and crucially:

> Genuinely public information is information that is equally easy (ie costless) to access for everyone. Even if the data is in what is often referred to as 'the public domain', it is not genuinely public if the costs involved in collecting the data discourage to a sufficient degree other companies and buyers from doing so. For information to be genuinely public, obtaining it should not be more costly for buyers and companies unaffiliated to the exchange system than for the companies exchanging the information.

The Guidelines are aimed at undertakings which are active in the real economy. Given the position taken in the *Austrian Banks* case, above, it seems improbable that similar principles would not apply to firms active in the financial sector. It is true that firms in the financial sector will be more concerned about the future prices of securities than about present, real economy prices, and this dimension of time is missing from the Commission's Guidelines. Taking into account future prices adds complexity to the analysis, but it may make the argument for competition greater, not lesser. There is an interesting passage in Minsky where he equates market power with the introduction of financing decisions taken over time as twin factors, which can lead to incoherence in the economy:

> Where monopoly power exists and when financing and investment are undertaken, present prices are not parameters for decisions. In these cases prices either vary with the unit's own decisions or the future enters in a significant way in determining behaviour. Under these conditions markets can fail to be effective control and coordinating mechanisms. We are left, then, with a split attitude towards the market. On one hand, the market is a very effective control and coordinating device if units are forced to take prices as parameters and to behave as if current prices will exist forever. On the other hand, the market can fail to achieve coherent results in situations in which units know either that their actions will have an appreciable effect upon prices or that current prices will not necessarily rule forever. [28]

---

[28] Minsky (1986), 120.

From a competition law point of view, uncertainty about the future at the level of the individual firm is essential in the real economy for the price mechanism to function. In the financial sector, irrespective of whether financial prices are right or, in fact, prove to be 'terribly wrong', the creation, through the exchange of information, of mutually consistent expectations regarding competitive behaviour is likely to be viewed with the same concern as in the real economy.

6.   SOME POINTERS FOR THE HEDGE FUND INDUSTRY

What, therefore, might one draw out of this discussion of relevance to the hedge fund industry? In his book describing their origins and development Sebastian Mallaby remarks that: 'Starting in the 1990s, hedge funds became large enough to move markets of all kinds.' [29]

The buying and selling of internationally traded securities by hedge funds and other alternative investment funds is likely to have an effect on cross-border trade and, for that reason, fall under the jurisdiction of EU competition law. The European Commission has already indicated as much in the *Austrian Banks* case, where it is stated that:

> Parts of the practices at issue either concern services of a cross-border nature, and for that reason alone are therefore capable of affecting trade between Member States, or are by their very nature closely related to cross-border goods flows. Agreements relating to cross-border payments transactions, documentary business and the buying and selling of securities also fall within this category.[30]

How might one approach a competition law analysis of the hedge fund industry? Hedge funds themselves are characterized by a conspicuously low level of concentration. Andrew Haldane of the Bank of England has pointed out that,

> Unlike banking, the hedge fund sector does not comprise a small number of large players, but rather a large number of relatively small players. The largest hedge funds typically have assets under management of less than US$40 billion, the largest banks assets in excess of US$3 trillion. Unlike banking, concentration in the hedge fund sector is low and has been falling [. . .] And unlike banking, entry and exit rates from the hedge fund industry are both high.[31]

---

[29]   Mallaby (2010), 146.
[30]   *Supra*, fn. 22, para 455.
[31]   Andrew Haldane 'Banking on the state' (Bank of England, speeches, 06.11.09)

On the other hand, hedge funds do have close links with a small number of large players in the banking sector, since some of the largest investment banks act as prime brokers, providing important services to hedge funds and trading securities with them. According to hedge fund manager Barton Biggs, hedge funds have accounted for about one-third of the total trading volume of prime brokers and, 'most important, hedge funds are a captive source of demand for the lucrative securities and margin lending activities from which a prime broker locks in a fat spread.'[32]

Unlike hedge funds, prime brokers as a class do appear concentrated. In 2003 the three market leaders Morgan Stanley, Goldman Sachs and Bear Stearns were estimated collectively to have had 79 per cent of the prime broker market; and in 2006, 62 per cent of this market.[33] The banking crisis of 2008, including the collapse and exit of Lehman Brothers and Bear Stearns from the market, has led to a situation where, at the time of writing, single hedge funds tend to use multiple prime brokers.

From a competition law point of view, relations between hedge funds and other financial market participants might be analysed as being either of a vertical or horizontal nature. A hedge fund is likely to have vertical relations with its investors, on whose behalf the fund is run. Relations with some counterparties for the buying and selling of securities will also essentially be of a vertical nature, where there is no possible competition with the hedge fund itself. Hedge funds are, however, likelier than not to be in a state of direct competition with one another (for example, to attract investor funds), and therefore relations between one hedge fund and another will be of a horizontal nature. An additional element of complexity resides in the fact that 'competitors' can be both actual and potential. Potential competitors are firms who could enter a market quickly in response to appropriate price signals.

It follows that hedge funds might have as potential competitors other financial institutions, such as investment banks, which are not hedge funds but which are (or could become) active in the same market. Banks who own hedge funds would be actual competitors. For banks who act as prime brokers, certain services to hedge funds might be termed vertical in nature (including, say, financing and settlement services), while other services, such as acting as counterparty to derivative contracts, might qualify as horizontal.

---

[32] Biggs (2006), 48.
[33] 2003 figures from Tremont, cited by J. Daníelsson, A. Taylor & J-P. Zigrand, 'Highwaymen or Heroes: Should Hedge Funds be Regulated? A Survey', *Journal of Financial Stability* 1 (2005): 522. 2006 figures from Lipper HedgeWorld prime brokerage league table.

As for any other financial undertakings, agreements or concerted practices between hedge funds and competitors would be likely to infringe EU competition law if they have any effect on the price of securities. In addition, agreements or concerted practices that fix trading conditions; limit or control production, markets, technical development or investment; share markets or sources of supply; or discriminate between other trading parties would also fall under competition law scrutiny.[34] While it may seem improbable that overt agreements or concerted practices will exist between hedge funds, there is some anecdotal evidence of co-ordinated behaviour. For example, it is suggested in a recent book that,

> Hedge funds cherish privacy and go to great lengths to stay out of the public eye, but the notion that hedge funds are secretive is something of a myth. Many hedge fund managers like to share their ideas, and they like to copy other managers' ideas because a group hug can drive the share price up in a sort of self-fulfilling prophecy, which CEOs love. Who else owns it? That's a question most hedge fund managers ask first and foremost. This clubby, influential New York City/Connecticut area hedge fund sphere was sometimes referred to as the hedge fund mafia.[35]

The opposite form of price behaviour – bear raids calculated to drive stock prices down – would, if engaged in collectively by several hedge funds, be equally likely to contravene EU competition law rules. Collective betting on the anticipated price movement of a given security is also likely to constitute an infringement.[36] The foregoing comments might also be applied, *mutatis mutandis*, to agreements or concerted practices between hedge funds and potential competitors, such as investment banks, who may be active in the same market.

There is then the more difficult question of the potential co-ordination of behaviour resulting from the very structure of the market. In the new

---

[34]   This is a list of the kinds of practices prohibited in the real economy. There is considerable case-law under each scenario as to the detailed implications.

[35]   McCullough (2010), 72.

[36]   While collective betting as such does not seem to have been addressed by the competition authorities, the Commission in 1984 condemned, as restricting competition, practices by competing zinc producers to buy up zinc before it reached the London Metal Exchange, and also to buy themselves, or through third companies, so as to support the quoted zinc price: 'Its object and effect was to influence the LME zinc price so that it did not diverge too far from the producer price [. . .] The producers thereby brought the LME price, which was determined by supply and demand, into line with the fixed producer price, thus reducing the competitive pressure exerted by the LME price.' (Commission Decision IV/30.350 of 6 August 1984, at OJ L 220 17.08.1984, at para. 72).

2011 Guidelines on horizontal co-operation, referred to above, an intriguing example is given by the Commission, entitled 'Swaps and information exchange'.[37] The swap referred to is not a credit default swap (CDS), such as those that hedge funds routinely enter into, but rather a swap agreement between two leading hypothetical competing producers of a similar commodity chemical. The analysis of the Commission is that the swap agreement itself between competitors does not give rise to competition concerns, but any exchange of internal information in relation to costs, a key parameter of competition with regard to the commodity chemical, is problematic.

The situation is clearly different where, instead of a bilateral agreement, numerous swap agreements are entered into between counterparties relating to securities. Originally, however, CDSs were bilateral agreements, under which two financial institutions agreed to swap each other's risk of default on the loans each had made, or the bonds each held, for a mutually agreed fee. At a later stage, CDSs became mass-produced, by the pooling of default risks through the use of securitized debt instruments. By 1999 the volume of credit derivatives deals was put at US$229 billion, a six-fold increase in two years.[38] According to statistics issued by the Bank for International Settlements in May 2010, the gross market value of CDSs may have peaked in 2008, at US$5.116 trillion. In common with other over-the-counter (OTC) financial derivatives markets, such as for foreign exchange and interest rate swaps, nearly all transactions were between financial institutions (dealers, banks and other securities firms). The Bank for International Settlements (BIS) records a very small proportion (about 2 per cent) as being with non-financial customers.[39]

It appears likely, therefore, that within such an interdependent market a high volume of information relevant to the parameters of competition will circulate between participants. Moreover, such information is unlikely to be 'genuinely public information', in the sense defined by the Commission, as it would either be very difficult, or very costly, for non-market participants to have access to it. It is also worth adding that, as Adair Turner has pointed out, price signals coming from the CDS market in the period immediately prior to the banking crisis appeared to have provided no

---

[37]   This is example 7 in the chapter on 'Production Agreements'.

[38]   See Chapters three and four of Tett, 2009, for a description of the creation of the credit default swap market.

[39]   BIS: 'OTC derivates market activity in the second half of 2009' (May 2010), Graph 1 and Table 4. Report available electronically on www.bis.org in the section 'Statistics'.

forewarning of the crisis. Prices generated within this market appear, therefore, to have become disconnected from reality.

Where the structure of a market itself appears faulty, rather than the behaviour of specific firms, EU competition law investigations of a particular sector of the economy, or into a particular type of agreement across various sectors, are possible. Such investigations may lead to published reports analysing the facts and the problems, and also, if necessary, lead to enforcement or other action.

Within the hedge fund industry, there do appear to be examples of group-think and consensus behaviour rather than individual decision-making independence. This, at least, is a recurrent theme of '*Diary of a Hedge Fund Manager*', (McCullough, 2010) which documents episodes in the market from 2000 to 2009. Anecdotes of consensus behaviour abound, both as the market rose and as it fell. Some evidence of co-ordination of currency attacks can also be found in Mallaby's book '*More Money than God*'.[40] The section on systemic risk in a recent industry report suggests a 'non-trivial' impact on the market of selling by hedge funds during 2007 to 2009.[41] The UK Turner Review of 2009 refers to the likely adverse effect on prices of simultaneous behaviour by hedge funds during the crisis.[42] Similarly, the recent decline in hedge fund returns has coincided with some evidence of herding, with hedge fund returns, both within and across different investment strategies, showing signs of correlation.[43]

One consequence of the banking crisis, and of the resulting tighter regulation of banks, may be the further growth of the more loosely regulated hedge fund industry. In May 2010 the global hedge fund industry was already reported, despite the crisis, to have more than US$2700 billion

---

[40]   See Mallaby 2010, 156–62 in relation to the 1992 European currency crises, and 203–206 in relation to the 1997 Thai currency crisis.

[41]   Charles River Associates, '*Impact of the Proposed AIFM Directive across Europe*', October 2009. Report prepared for the Financial Services Authority, London. Available electronically on fsa.gov.uk in the section 'FSA Library'.

[42]   'The simultaneous behaviour by many hedge funds to deleverage and meet investor redemptions may well have played an important role over the last six months in depressing securities prices in a self-fulfilling cycle.' (Financial Services Authority: *The Turner Review: A Regulatory Response to the Global Banking Crisis*, March 2009, 72)

[43]   The increasingly similar positioning of individual hedge funds within broad hedge fund investment strategies – allegedly proven by the rising correlation between the returns of different funds and different strategies – has been highlighted by the ECB as a 'major risk for financial stability which warrants close monitoring' (ECB, *Financial Stability Review* (Frankfurt am Main, 1 June 2006), 142). Evidence on hedge fund herding is mixed (in this regard, see J. Daníelsson, A. Taylor & J–P. Zigrand, *supra*, fn. 33, 522).

of assets under management, not far short of its high point in April 2008, when it reached US$2900 billion.[44] While individually perhaps relatively small, taken collectively the impact of hedge funds on the market could, therefore, be considerable.

7. CONCLUSIONS

If aspects of the financial services sector are unstable or tend towards disequilibrium one inevitable approach is tighter regulation of individual firms in that sector. This is, of course, already happening. But, as the experience in the EU with the AIFM Directive has shown, it can in practice be very difficult to devise and to agree upon specific rules. Regulators themselves may well have differing starting points, philosophies and objectives.[45] One impact of tighter regulation may turn out to be regulatory arbitrage – international firms moving business to take advantage of any available regulatory gaps and loopholes. Experience also suggests that innovators in financial services go on to create new forms of business which can avoid regulation completely, thus making it redundant.

A parallel (or alternative) approach may be to pay rather more attention to the underlying competition rules which govern the rest of the market economy, designed to counteract market malfunctions and concentrations of market power. They are intended to make the market as a whole work, rather than regulate individual firms within it. But the better a market works, the less need there may be for detailed regulation.

In his recent book, John Authers of the *Financial Times* provides details of numerous examples in recent years of disturbing correlations between previously uncorrelated global financial markets, with markets moving increasingly in unison and risk management for investors becoming difficult, if not impossible.[46] Writing in the *Financial Times* on 22 May 2010 Authers went on to say, 'Asset bubbles on the scale we have seen do not happen unless something is systematically wrong with the way in which our money is invested. It is hard to see how regulation can fix the problem. [. . .] The fundamental problem is herding.'

And yet, co-ordinated behaviour between competing undertakings is, as we have seen, contrary to basic competition law principles. It may well

---

[44] *Financial Times*, 27 May 2010.

[45] See the discussion in Athanassiou: 'The Conceptual Underpinnings of Onshore Hedge Fund Regulation: a Global and European Perspective': *Journal of Corporate Law Studies*, October 2008, 251.

[46] Authers, 2010.

be open for argument how far herding, correlated behaviour or group-think in the financial sector results from conscious co-ordination between competitors and how far it is unconscious, driven by the structure of the market, the madness of crowds or the nature of the financial incentives involved. But, for whatever reason, the absence of decision-making independence appears linked to malfunctioning markets, price distortions, and, at times, to asset price bubbles.

For individual hedge funds this may well appear paradoxical: there is, apparently, fierce competition and yet, at the same time, apparent herding and correlated behaviour. The underlying reasons are doubtless complex, and beyond the scope of this chapter.[47] But what in practical terms might be done?

A compliance audit by hedge funds of their own behaviour in the light of competition principles might be a worthwhile first step. Large firms in the real economy do this already, as a matter of course. As will be clear from the discussion so far, competition law places severe limitations on the kinds of information which competing firms can exchange with one another. There seems little reason for financial institutions to operate under different rules. How far is any information exchanged between competitors 'genuinely public information'? Calls have been made for greater transparency of hedge fund operations – might this include providing data to regulators to substantiate or refute any apparently co-ordinated position taking? Guidelines covering permissible and non-permissible practices from a competition law point of view might also be drawn up, possibly with the assistance of hedge fund representative groups, and possibly with the assistance of the competition authorities.

A competitive rather than co-ordinated industry appears desirable from the point of view of the investors it serves, and also less likely to lead to malfunctioning markets. Possibly the strongest argument for regulating the hedge fund sector is that hedge funds may pose a systemic risk to the financial system. In the words of the de Larosière Report, 'global systemic risk arises from a common exposure of many financial institutions to the same risk factors'.[48] One might speculate that financial institutions whose operations conform to competition law principles will be correspondingly less likely to pose risks to the financial system, and to the real economy. Decision-making independence should, logically, reduce the strength of

---

[47]   But see, for example, Turner and others (2010) '*The Future of Finance*' (2010) and Chapter 3 by Paul Woolley, 'Why are financial markets so inefficient and exploitative – and a suggested remedy'.

[48]   Report of The High Level Group on Financial Supervision in the EU, Chaired by Jacques de Larosière, 25 February 2009, para. 147.

the trend towards a common exposure to the same risk factors. Promoting it could, therefore, be a means of addressing systemic risk. One might speculate, moreover, that markets will be more likely to tend to equilibrium where participants in them do not have or exploit market power.

Much might perhaps be done in this area by market participants themselves, on a voluntary basis. Enforcement of competition law by the authorities may, all the same, remain useful in extreme '*far from equilibrium*' situations (to borrow the phrase from George Soros), where, for whatever reason, collective (and almost certainly mistaken) expectations among market participants turn out to have real consequences for asset prices in the real economy.

In extreme cases, where 'self-reinforcing cycles' (or bubbles) occur, a number of competition law instruments might be brought to bear. Whether they would per se succeed in stopping the creation of bubbles is, of course, difficult to predict. Although it is a matter of live debate between economists, it is possible that bubbles, like the weather, can never be stopped. However, on the whole, bubbles do not feature in markets in the real economy where competition law principles are applied, the decision-making independence of undertakings is preserved and concentrations of market power are avoided.

Within a 'self-reinforcing cycle' (or bubble) the mere exchange of information between interdependent market participants may, for example, repay detailed competition law scrutiny, to see if it might involve or lead to a concerted practice. Or, if price trends of assets in the real economy appear out of line with those resulting from competitive levels in adjacent or similar real economy markets, that may create a presumption that for some reason a financial bubble is forming, which merits investigation to establish if there is an exercise of market power.

The very fact of investigating the origins of, and relationships within, a suspect bubble may even have the effect of leading to it deflating, without the need for more comprehensive regulatory intervention or controls. Alternatively, the competition authorities, having scrutinized the economic and legal relationships involved, may be justified in recommending other remedies, or taking other measures to promote decision-making independence.

BIBLIOGRAPHY

Athanassiou, P. (2008), 'The Conceptual Underpinnings of Onshore Hedge Fund Regulation: a Global and European Perspective' *Journal of Corporate Law Studies*, October, 251.

Athanassiou, P. (2008), 'Competition Law and the European Financial Services Sector: An Overview of Recent Developments', *International In-house Counsel Journal*, **1** (3), 419–29.

Authers, J. (2010), *The Fearful Rise of Markets: A Short View of Global Bubbles and Synchronised Meltdowns*, London: Financial Times Prentice Hall.

Biggs, B. (2006), *Hedgehogging*, Malden, MA, US: John Wiley and Sons.

Danielsson, J., A. Taylor & J.-P. Zigrand (2005), 'Highwaymen or Heroes: Should Hedge Funds be Regulated? A Survey' *Journal of Financial Stability* 1 (2005): 522.

Financial Services Authority (2009), *The Turner Review: A Regulatory Response to the Global Banking Crisis*, London, UK: FSA.

Gerber, D.J. (1994), 'Constitutionalising the Economy: German Neo-liberalism, Competition Law and the "New" Europe', 42, *American Journal of Comparative Law*, 25.

Grabbe, J. (1986), *International Financial Markets*, Cambridge, MA, US: Elsevier.

Mallaby, S. (2010), *More Money than God: Hedge Funds and the Making of a New Elite*, London: Bloomsbury.

McCullough, K. (2010), *Diary of a Hedge Fund Manager*, Malden, MA, US: John Wiley and Sons.

Minsky, H. (1986), *Stabilizing an Unstable Economy*, New Haven, CT, US: Yale University Press.

Monnet, J. (1978), *Memoirs*, New York, US: Doubleday.

Posner, R. (2009), *A Failure of Capitalism*, Cambridge, MA, US: Harvard University Press.

Reinhart, C. and K. Rogoff (2009), *This Time is Different: Eight Centuries of Financial Folly*, Princeton, NJ, US: Princeton University Press.

Soros, G. (1987), *The Alchemy of Finance*, Malden, MA, US: John Wiley and Sons.

Soros, G. (2009), *The Crash of 2008 and What it Means*, US: BBS Public Affairs.

Tett, G. (2009), *Fools Gold*, London: Little, Brown.

Turner, A. and others (2010), *The Future of Finance: The LSE Report*, London: London School of Economics and Political Science.

Wolf, Martin (2009), 'Why Britain has to Curb Finance', *Financial Times*, 22 May 2009.

PART C

ALTERNATIVE INVESTMENT FUNDS – FAILURES AND FINANCIAL CRISES

11. Lessons of Long-Term Capital Management and Amaranth Advisors
*Mark Jickling**

INTRODUCTION

For two decades, hedge funds have been under intense (if intermittent) scrutiny as the most visible agents of financial speculation. Two episodes best illustrate the relevant policy concerns: the near collapse of Long-Term Capital Management (LTCM) in 1998, which was revealing of how a single hedge fund could build up counterparty exposures large enough to threaten markets with system-wide disruptions; and the failure of Amaranth Advisors in 2006, which raised fears of large-scale manipulation in commodity prices. Neither instance led to a strong regulatory response, in part because there were no visible aftershocks – LTCM was quickly recapitalized, while Amaranth's liquidation had little effect on natural gas prices. But both episodes prefigured greater financial disruptions to come. The regulators' worst-case scenario if LTCM had been allowed to fail – a spiral of forced deleveraging and plunging asset values – closely resembles the actual course of events in 2008, while the price volatility that some attributed to Amaranth's strategies was similar to but far milder relative to what was observed in energy and other market segments in 2008–2009. The Dodd-Frank Act passed by the United States (US) Congress in 2010 addressed the 'too-interconnected-to-fail' issue (by requiring large hedge funds to register and disclose trading information) and fears of excessive speculation (by increasing regulation and transparency in over-the-counter derivatives markets). Ironically, both major policy concerns about hedge funds were dealt with legislatively in response to a crisis in which hedge funds themselves played an insignificant role.

*   Mark Jickling covers financial market issues for the Congressional Research Service (CRS), which provides non-partisan analysis for the US Congress. The views expressed in this article are his own and do not reflect the position of CRS.

293

1.   THE NEAR-COLLAPSE OF LTCM AND ITS AFTERMATH: A MISSED OPPORTUNITY FOR LESSONS TO BE LEARNED

In September 1998, the Federal Reserve Bank of New York decided that the US safety net was wide enough to catch a falling hedge fund. The story is well known: LTCM, a hedge fund run by Nobel Laureates and bond trading legends, had US$3 billion in capital, which it leveraged up to US$100 billion in fixed-income assets and a US$1 trillion notional derivatives position. Such was the prestige of its founders that LTCM received extremely favorable terms from its creditors, counterparties, and brokers, who were eager to discover (and copy) its strategies.

Going into 1998, LTCM's view was that spreads between US Treasuries and other high-grade debt were unusually wide, because of the flight to safety that had accompanied the Asian crises in 1997, and that a reversion to the mean was to be expected. On 17 August 1998, however, the Russian government declared a debt moratorium, and investor confidence around the world was, once again, shaken. Spreads over US Treasury bonds increased sharply, and LTCM's short positions in US debt showed enormous losses, triggering margin and collateral calls that the fund struggled to meet. By early September, LTCM's liquidity problems became widely known, and rescue meetings began at the New York Fed. On 22 September 1998, 14 banks and securities firms, including the hedge fund's largest creditors and counterparties, agreed to contribute new capital to prevent default and took ownership of LTCM's portfolio.

The Federal Reserve Bank of New York justified its intervention by setting out a systemic risk scenario, in language that has become very familiar since 2007:

> Had Long-Term Capital been suddenly put into default, its counterparties would have immediately 'closed-out' their positions. If counterparties would have been able to close-out their positions at existing market prices, losses, if any, would have been minimal. However, if many firms had rushed to close-out hundreds of billions of US$ in transactions simultaneously, they would have been unable to liquidate collateral or establish offsetting positions at the previously-existing prices . . . Under these circumstances, there was a likelihood that a number of credit and interest rate markets would experience extreme price moves and possibly cease to function for a period of one or more days and maybe longer. This would have caused a vicious cycle: a loss of investor confidence, leading to a rush out of private credits, leading to a further widening of credit spreads, leading to further liquidations of positions, and so on.[1]

---

[1]   Testimony of William J. McDonough, President Federal Reserve Bank of

The LTCM episode caused consternation among regulators and central bankers, as well as in the US Congress. Hedge funds had been on the policy radar since the European currency dislocations of the early 1990s, but, in the consensus view, there was no public interest in preventing hedge fund failures since all investors were presumed to be sophisticated and able to bear the losses of unsuccessful speculation. With LTCM, hedge funds joined large insured depositories and others in the special class of institutions whose failure could trigger systemic disruptions and losses to markets and institutions that had no direct connection or dealings with the failing firm.

Numerous studies sought to explain the LTCM episode and recommended steps to prevent its recurrence.[2] With hindsight, we can appreciate the quality of analysis but must note that the studies did not lead to policy measures that might have been useful when something like the collapse of LTCM was replicated on a much larger scale in 2007 and 2008. The rest of this section will examine selected studies and argue that it was a case of missing the forest for the trees – the LTCM debate came to focus on how a single highly-leveraged entity could create a shock of a magnitude to threaten the normally robust forces of systemic stability. Within the studies and reports, however, there were ample findings suggesting that those stabilizing forces were weaker than generally assumed. These were lessons not learned.

1.1 The Basel Committee Report

The Basel Committee on Banking Supervision issued a report in January 1999.[3] Instead of 'hedge fund,' the term used in that report was 'highly leveraged institution'(HLI), defined as an unregulated entity, usually chartered offshore, disclosing limited information, and employing significant leverage. The analysis of the systemic risk posed by an LTCM insolvency was essentially the same as the Fed's – there were direct exposures (the losses that would be suffered by creditors and counterparties), secondary exposures (resulting from liquidating collateral and rebalancing portfolios under adverse market conditions), and stressed-market exposures (rapid, disorderly deleveraging, leading to higher volatility, lack of liquidity, and a general increase in risk aversion and uncertainty).

New York, in US House of Representatives, Committee on Banking and Financial Services (1998).

[2] For surveys of these recommendations, see Financial Stability Forum (2000), Annex C, and Becker et al. (2000).

[3] Basel Committee on Banking Supervision (1999), 29.

The report concludes that the direct exposure losses would likely have been manageable, but that the second and third types of losses could not be gauged due to the opacity of LTCM's overall position and the markets where it traded.

The Basel Committee's recommendations focused on how banks and securities firms should improve the measurement and management of their risk exposures to HLIs. This was, in essence, a 'best practices' or self-regulatory approach, based on the tacit assumption that regulated financial institutions wished to avoid excessive risk, and that their incentives were basically aligned with those of regulators concerned with systemic stability: 'The Committee recognizes that banks have the principal responsibility for managing their exposure to these and other counterparties in a safe and prudent manner.'[4]

Other recommendations that involved a more direct regulatory approach included consideration of increases in risk-based capital requirements for exposure to HLIs (and over-the-counter derivatives positions) and direct regulation of HLIs. However, the report called for implementation of these measures only if the indirect approach proved ineffective.[5]

1.2   The President's Working Group Report

The President's Working Group on Financial Markets (PWG) submitted its report on LTCM to Congress on 28 April 1999.[6] It echoed the conclusions of the Basel Committee report in many respects – positing a primary reliance on market discipline and setting out a similar set of best practices, including improvements to the credit approval process, better monitoring of credit quality, stress testing, appropriate measurement of leverage and risk, and more awareness of the interplay between market, credit, and legal risk.[7] However, the PWG went well beyond the Basel Committee in its analysis of the systemic risk implications of LTCM.

The PWG defined the systemic risk problem in broad terms: 'The central public policy issue raised by the LTCM episode is how to constrain excessive leverage more effectively.'[8] In contrast to the Basel Committee,

---

[4]   *Ibid*, 1.

[5]   *Ibid*, 5.

[6]   President's Working Group on Financial Markets (1999). The PWG consists of the Secretary of the Treasury and the Chairmen of the Federal Reserve, the Securities and Exchange Commission, and the Commodity Futures Trading Commission. It has no regulatory authority.

[7]   *Ibid*, 36.

[8]   *Ibid*, 29.

the PWG did not limit the definition of HLI to hedge funds: 'Other financial institutions, including some banks and securities firms, are larger, and generally more highly leveraged, than hedge funds.'[9] With post-2008 hindsight, this analysis should have prompted consideration of leverage limits and more abundant capital cushions for large commercial and investment banks. At the time, of course, few US policymakers were prepared to consider that Wall Street bulge bracket firms could have the same appetite for risk as the all-in gamblers at LTCM, and it was politically unthinkable to treat them as though they might.[10] Still, several observations in the PWG report lead in this direction.

The PWG describes the key financial firms as gatekeepers – hedge funds 'cannot achieve significant leverage without the credit and clearing services of the large banks and securities firms that are at the center of the securities and derivatives markets.'[11] Interestingly, this view of major firms as enforcers of market discipline is also echoed in the Basel Committee report, which envisioned a natural shrinking of HLI leverage and riskiness as risk management at banks improves.[12] The PWG observes that market discipline broke down more or less completely in the LTCM case: 'the main limitation on the LTCM Fund's overall scale and leverage was that provided by its managers and principals.'[13] And the PWG does not view LTCM as an aberration; the report notes in several places that the history of financial markets shows that firms become less concerned about risk during good times, and that the painful lessons of the inevitable corrections are soon forgotten.

In short, the PWG report concluded that market discipline was necessarily the principal defense against the possibility that HLI losses could spill over into the system as a whole, generate contagion, and cause widespread disruption of markets. Moreover, market discipline depended on firms that were themselves HLIs, and whose actions in the LTCM case suggested serious shortcomings in their incentives and capabilities to manage risk. This analysis, however, did not lead to recommendations for regulatory limits on leverage at all highly-leveraged firms, and such recommendations would almost certainly have been rejected by Congress.

---

[9]   *Ibid*, 29.
[10]   In 1999, with Robert Rubin (and later Lawrence Summers) at Treasury, Alan Greenspan at the Fed, and Senator Phil Gramm as Chairman of the Banking Committee, deregulation was predominant in Washington.
[11]   *Ibid*, 30.
[12]   Basel Committee on Banking Supervision (1999), 5.
[13]   President's Working Group on Financial Markets (1999), 15.

1.3   The Counterparty Risk Management Policy Group Report

Issued in June 1999, the report of Counterparty Risk Management Policy Group (CRMPG) was perceived as a challenge to the PWG's analysis.[14] While best practice recommendations (dealing with transparency, risk assessment, measurement, and management, market practices and conventions, and regulatory reporting) made up the bulk of the report, a brief discussion of the concept of leverage received most attention at the time of publication.[15] The PWG report had noted the difficulties in measuring leverage, but the CRMPG went much further.

The CRMPG report argued that the term leverage was not subject to a single definition – that the term encompassed balance sheet concepts, market-dependent future cash flows, and market risk. A high level of balance sheet leverage (i.e. the ratio of assets to capital) may not indicate a high degree of market risk. Conversely, market risk in a portfolio with no leverage may be quite high. Market risk may be measured by value-at-risk techniques or stress testing, but differently-leveraged portfolios with identical market risk may face different liquidity risks. The measurement of leverage must be accompanied by a multidimensional 'interpretation' of leverage. The CRMPG concluded that leverage might be a concept 'with broad intuitive appeal, [but] it is not an independent risk factor whose measure can provide useful insights to risk managers and supervisors alike.'[16]

The CRMPG study slowed any momentum toward statutory or regulatory constraint of leverage that the PWG might have generated. The term HLI soon vanished from US usage (although it persisted in a series of reports from Basel). In October 1999, a group of 31 academics issued a critique of the PWG report, arguing that the report's 'emphasis on "excessive" leverage as a systemic concern is unsupported.'[17]

The connection between hedge fund failure, leverage, and systemic risk did not remain a high-priority regulatory issue in the US. A bill similar to the PWG's recommendation that hedge funds register with the Securities and Exchange Commission (SEC) was introduced in 1999, but did not advance beyond the committee level.[18] In 2003, the SEC staff called

---

[14]   Counterparty Risk Management Policy Group, [1999]. The CRMPG's members were 12 of the firms that participated in the LTCM recapitalization. The group was convened in January 1999 at the suggestion of regulators; some viewed the report as a form of penance for actions in the LTCM case.

[15]   *Ibid*, 16–18.

[16]   *Ibid*, 17.

[17]   Financial Economists Roundtable (1999).

[18]   H.R.2924 (106th Congress), the Hedge Fund Disclosure Act.

for registration of hedge funds as investment advisers[19] and in 2004 the Commission adopted a rule implementing that recommendation. That rule was challenged in court and vacated in 2006.[20] The SEC's argument for increased hedge fund regulation was based almost entirely on investor protection, rather than systemic risk, concerns.

A joint report by the Basel Committee and the International Organization of Securities Commissions (IOSCO) in 2001 noted that virtually all of the response to the LTCM episode took the form of self-regulatory best practices, and this was not seen as cause for alarm.[21] In early 2007, the PWG also embraced self-regulation with a statement that 'creditors and counterparties of private pools of capital are generally large, sophisticated financial firms that have the incentives and the expertise to provide effective market discipline.'[22]

Within a few months of the PWG's 2007 release, the crisis gathered momentum and notions of systemic risk changed. The PWG's 'light-touch' approach in that document – for example, that 'supervisors should clearly communicate their expectations regarding prudent management of counterparty risk exposures . . .'– was suddenly out of date.

Many observers have pointed out that the systemic scenario put forward by the Federal Reserve Bank of New York in its justification of the LTCM intervention was more or less exactly what was observed, on a global scale, during the financial crisis of 2008. John Reed, Chairman of Citigroup in 1998, expressed this most clearly in a Senate Banking Committee hearing, in response to a question from Senator Jeff Merkley:

> Well, we had a situation there that was a one-institution version of what later happened to all of us, and where basically the taxpayer had to step in because there wasn't enough capital in the private sector to cover the risks that were manifesting themselves in this crisis we've gone through . . . Long-Term Capital was . . . the anatomy of the problem that we're today wrestling with. It was alone. It sat there. It was tremendously interconnected, as you say. It had counterparty lines. It had all sorts of assets, which conceivably would have been liquidated at very distressed prices and so forth, which would have impacted the market. And yet as a system, we sort of ganged together, papered it over, and went on having learned nothing.[23]

---

[19] US Securities and Exchange Commission (2003).
[20] *Goldstein v. Securities and Exchange Commission*, 451 F.3d 873 (D.C. Cir. 2006).
[21] Basel Committee on Banking Supervision (2001).
[22] President's Working Group on Financial Markets (2007).
[23] Testimony of John Reed in US Senate Committee on Banking, Housing, and Urban Affairs, (2010) (Congressional Quarterly transcript edited by author).

Many of the market dynamics that made the crisis so intractable and severe were fully anticipated in the reports on LTCM. That there could be a 'vicious circle' of deleveraging – i.e. of market losses triggering forced liquidation of assets, driving prices still lower and leading to further liquidations – was a basic premise of all LTCM studies, but in 2007–2008 regulators were unable to prevent such a cycle from taking hold.

The CRMPG report clearly warned of the liquidity shocks that swept away major US investment banks in 2008: 'The viability of a financial intermediary or large trading counterparty could be compromised by poor management of liquidity risk.'[24] The report described the interaction of credit, market, and liquidity risk as 'the single greatest risk' to the functioning of financial intermediation.[25] The CRMPG called for 'comprehensive contingency funding plans' against liquidity risk, but in the crisis such plans were shown to be nonexistent or inadequate (unless the firms had counted all along on access to public credit). Finally, the reports noted that the behavior of the large firms that play a central role in financial markets did not in all cases promote stability. All observed that LTCM was able to get unlimited credit on unusually favorable terms, despite the fact that counterparties lacked complete information about the fund's aggregate position, which meant that the size and distribution of losses that would follow an LTCM default were unknown even to its major trading partners. In addition, counterparties took proprietary positions similar to LTCM's, in effect increasing their exposure to any market circumstances that would put the fund in distress.

The reports do not comment on another destabilizing aspect of counterparty behavior: as the crisis approached and LTCM attempted to reduce the size of its losing positions, its brokers engaged in front-running, exacerbating the price movements that were destroying the hedge fund.[26] The theme of firms seeking profits on the short side when their very survival (and, with it, that of systemic stability) is riding on the long side reappears in 2008; witness the behavior of issuers and raters of mortgage-backed bonds in 2007 as problems in US housing markets were becoming clear, the Paulson/Goldman Sachs episode, and other instances where firms effectively traded against their own long-term interests. Failure to anticipate phenomena like these contributed to the overestimation of the robustness of market discipline.

---

[24]   Counterparty Risk Management Policy Group (1999), 20.

[25]   *Ibid*, 22.

[26]   This phenomenon was noted in the popular press – see Lewis (1999), 24 – and confirmed years later by empirical research on trading in Treasury futures on the Chicago Board of Trade: see Fang (2009).

LTCM's downfall remains fascinating on one level because it contains the elements of classic stories and myths of intellectual hubris. On another level, hindsight shows us that an equally fundamental error was made by regulators who studied and interpreted the LTCM story. The lesson that was extracted was that highly-leveraged funds could become so interconnected with the major financial players that fund failure could trigger systemic instability. The more valuable lesson would have been that the system itself was vulnerable to exogenous shocks wherever they might originate. This was put concisely by Andrew Lo, who wrote that the problem in 2008 was not that a shadow banking system had emerged, where intermediaries performed banking functions without prudential regulation or the explicit protection of the safety net, but rather that there was a 'shadow hedge-fund system, i.e. the banks, insurance companies, and mortgage companies that took on hedge-fund-like risks without the proper safeguards and preparations.'[27]

2. FROM LTCM TO AMARANTH

The next most spectacular hedge fund failure after LTCM was that of Amaranth Advisors, which traded heavily in natural gas derivatives markets and collapsed in September 2006 after losing about US$5 billion in less than three weeks. The Amaranth case raised the questions that are posed whenever commodity prices become unusually volatile or reach levels that do not appear to most people to be justified by the underlying economic fundamentals. Can a single speculator amass market power and manipulate prices? If not a single speculator, can speculation, in general, create artificial prices, either by means of knowing collusion among traders or through irrational herding? Do derivatives markets, where the notional amounts of the underlying commodity may exceed physical trading volumes, perform price discovery or price distortion?

Like LTCM, Amaranth's trading strategy was based on a simple idea about the direction of prices. Having earned large profits when natural gas prices rose in 2005 after Hurricane Katrina, the fund expected that hurricane activity in 2006 would again drive prices up. To profit from this intuition, Amaranth entered into massive spread positions in natural gas futures and swaps, in various combinations, with the fund shorting contracts expiring in certain months and taking long positions in certain other, more distant months. If spreads widened, which would happen if the market expected higher prices going into 2007, Amaranth would

---

[27] Lo (2009), 43.

profit. Because the fund was trading on spreads, rather than taking a simple long position, its gross positions in the market grew very large.

An investigation into Amaranth's trading was conducted by the Senate Permanent Subcommittee on Investigations (PSI) and published in 2007.[28] The report includes detailed accounts of Amaranth's positions and trades, using data obtained by subpoena. The conclusions were that Amaranth dominated natural gas trading during 2006, that because of its trading, spreads between 2006 and 2007 contracts were artificially wide (meaning that hedgers seeking price protection for 2007 paid too much), and that since prices were affected by Amaranth's large-scale trades rather than the interaction of many buyers and sellers, Amaranth's positions constituted excessive speculation.[29]

The extent to which Amaranth dominated natural gas trading becomes clear in the PSI report. It was not unusual for Amaranth to have held over 50 per cent of total open interest in Nymex futures, and at certain periods it accounted for over 70 per cent of trading volume in some contracts.[30] The report's analysis suggests that Amaranth's trading caused natural gas spreads to widen, but that when the market turned against Amaranth, the hedge fund was unable to influence the course of price changes. An interesting observation is that Amaranth became 'too big for the market it had created'[31] and that it was therefore unable to reduce its positions during May, when that would have been profitable at then-current prices. Its efforts to unwind in May caused prices to drop so quickly that the fund ultimately increased the size of its positions in June: it saw little choice but to make a one-sided 'widowmaker' bet.[32]

In August 2006, when the prospects for a bad hurricane season dimmed, the market turned decisively against Amaranth. By this time, regulators had become concerned about the effects of a disorderly liquidation of Amaranth's portfolio. On 29 August 2006, as Amaranth tried desperately to get out of its position, another hedge fund, *Centaurus*, began trading against it. Amaranth had promised that it would complete its sales before the last hour of trading, to avoid a disorderly close, and it did. *Centaurus*, however, bought heavily up to the close and bid up the price of the expiring contract (which caused spreads against future months to narrow, to

---

[28] US Senate Committee on Homeland Security and Governmental Affairs (2007).

[29] Under the US Commodity Exchange Act, the CFTC is charged with preventing 'excessive speculation,' but that term is not defined in the statute.

[30] *Ibid*, 51.

[31] *Ibid*, 74.

[32] *Ibid*, 80.

Amaranth's detriment). Amaranth later requested that *Nymex* investigate trading near the close, charging that prices had become artificial during the period when it was restrained from trading.[33]

The PSI observed that the enforcement by *Nymex* of position limits, designed to prevent price manipulation, was lax. Even when *Nymex* did insist that Amaranth reduce (or at least not expand) its positions, the hedge fund simply shifted its trading to the over-the-counter ICE exchange, which offered swaps that were economically equivalent to *Nymex* futures, but was not regulated. A major conclusion of the PSI study was that the unregulated status of the OTC derivatives market made it impossible for the Commodity Futures Trading Commission (CFTC) to exercise effective market oversight.[34]

The collapse of Amaranth raised two central issues. Is price volatility attributable to the actions of speculators, or to fundamental supply and demand factors? Second, was the unregulated status of the OTC derivatives markets a dangerous regulatory gap that needed to be closed?

The first question is one of the oldest questions in economics. The bulk of empirical evidence suggests that speculators – who must buy when prices are low and sell when they are high in order to stay in business – do not increase price volatility. At the same time, there is a long record of price bubbles and panics, suggesting that non-fundamental factors can explain certain price movements. As one of the most visible agents of speculation in the modern economy, hedge funds have been frequently at the center of this debate.

At the time of LTCM, many Asian regulators argued that hedge funds, singly or collectively, had caused or exacerbated the Asian financial crisis through currency speculation.[35] This view was not persuasive to many economists, who pointed to several plausible reasons why the Asian currencies' pegging to the US$ had resulted in these currencies being fundamentally overvalued. As a result, no consensus emerged as to the role of hedge funds in the Asian crises.[36] In the case of Amaranth, the argument that hedge funds might wield excessive market power was vitiated by the fact that the putative manipulator had collapsed. Amaranth did not lead to any major regulatory or legislative actions in the US.

The same issue reappeared in 2008, with increased urgency, when the price of oil climbed from about US$60 per barrel to US$140. Blame

---

[33] *Ibid*, 110.
[34] *Ibid*, 119–120.
[35] See, e.g., Yam (1999), 164.
[36] See, e.g., Fung and Hsieh (2000).

focused on speculators, and the mechanics of the derivatives markets came under intense scrutiny. This time, however, the alleged manipulators were not hedge funds but pension funds and other large institutional investors, who were said to have allocated a portion of their portfolios to commodity indexes, often through swap contracts linked to a published index of commodity prices. The swap dealers would then offset their price risk by taking long positions on the futures exchanges. Although the allocation by each pension fund was modest, the aggregate of institutional investment in commodities was said to be disproportionate to the amount of money usually expected in commodities trading, creating substantial and permanent upward pressure on prices.[37]

This analysis was disputed by the CFTC and others, who argued that the markets were properly reflecting the expectations of traders about future prices, and was seriously weakened by the fact that energy prices collapsed beginning in August 2008. A CFTC staff study found that commodity index trading by institutions had actually declined during the first half of 2008.[38] Nonetheless, with gasoline prices hitting record levels, the Congress considered numerous derivatives reform measures, and enacted a bill giving the CFTC jurisdiction over OTC contracts that performed a significant price discovery function.[39] This legislation, however, fell short of the comprehensive regulation of the OTC market, which the PSI report on Amaranth had advocated.

3.   REGULATORY BACKLASH: THE DODD-FRANK ACT

At the end of 2008, when the financial crisis had progressed to a point that few would have thought possible only two years earlier, the questions raised by the Amaranth and LTCM cases had not been answered. Hedge funds had their defenders – they provided liquidity, made price discovery more efficient, were a laboratory for financial innovation, and so on. Their detractors were unable to offer unequivocal proof of widespread manipulation or make the case that the funds posed a clear systemic threat, although suspicions remained. The issue of the precise nature of the risks posed by leverage was also unresolved.

---

[37]   Testimony of Michael W. Masters in Senate Committee on Homeland Security and Governmental Affairs, 'Financial Speculation in Commodity Markets', Heating, May 20, 2008.

[38]   US Commodity Futures Trading Commission (2008).

[39]   Public Law 110–246, the Food, Conservation, and Energy Act of 2008.

In early 2009, when the Obama Administration and Congress began work on financial reform legislation, those questions were no longer important to policy choices. The reform agenda was so broad that the fate of hedge funds was determined before the earliest legislative drafts appeared. The system had collapsed at tremendous cost to tax-payers, prompting regulators to demand more powers and more information, particularly regarding the 'shadow' sectors, which included hedge funds and OTC derivatives markets. The perceived urgency of the matter left little room for debate.

Over the 18 months that Congress required to enact the Dodd-Frank Wall Street Reform and Consumer Protection Act, there was, in fact, very little controversy over the proposition that large hedge funds should be made to register with the SEC and provide whatever information on whatever schedule the regulators deemed necessary for the monitoring of systemic risk. That any bill enacted would include these provisions was a foregone conclusion. It is telling that, even the hedge fund industry itself did not actively lobby against new regulation.

OTC derivatives reform, by contrast, was vigorously debated in its basic features: which contracts would have to be cleared, how reporting would take place, which entities would become 'regulated entities' and what swap exchanges would need to look like. However, a number of provisions left over from the 2008 energy speculation bills were included in Dodd-Frank and enacted with little opposition. The CFTC was given the authority to regulate margins on futures and a mandate to set position limits across exchange and OTC markets. Its anti-manipulation authority (and that of the SEC) was enhanced in various ways. This is unlikely to put an end to arguments about the role of speculators in volatile markets, as the 2010 sovereign debt crisis in Europe suggests.

In summary, many of the recommendations for regulatory and legislative action that came out of studies of LTCM and Amaranth are now law in the US, as a result of a crisis in which hedge funds are generally accepted to have played no significant role.

4. CONCLUDING REMARKS

Financial regulation in the US is notoriously piecemeal. The historical pattern has been that major financial crises are followed by the creation of a new regulatory agency and the extension of regulation to new markets and market participants. Financial innovation then develops along paths that skirt agency jurisdiction. Hedge funds are a classic example.

When the statutory provisions that allowed hedge funds to escape SEC regulation were enacted, there was no Congressional intent to accommodate entities accounting for significant shares of trading in equity, fixed-income, and derivatives markets. The core activities of hedge funds – pooling investments and managing customer money – are clearly amongst those that Congress intended to regulate with the Investment Company Act and Investment Advisers Act of 1940. Hedge funds availed themselves of what were, essentially, *de minimis* exemptions for funds with fewer than 100 investors and advisers with fewer than 15 clients. These exemptions, combined with other provisions of law and regulation that permit private, unregulated securities activity involving sophisticated investors only, allowed the hedge fund sector to boom.

Although hedge fund deregulation was fortuitous, it had many strong defenders. Hedge funds provided liquidity, were laboratories for innovation, and took on risks that others wished to avoid. Those risks could cause losses only to investors presumably able to understand and bear them. In short, not only was there no public interest in regulating hedge funds, but to do so might prove positively harmful. From that perspective, the failures of LTCM and Amaranth could be perceived to represent two isolated cases of gambler's ruin, which in no way challenged the prevailing assumptions about financial system stability or efficiency.

This chapter has argued that the near collapse of LTCM raised the problem of 'too-interconnected-to-fail,' previewing the catastrophic Bear Stearns and Lehman Brothers episodes; and that the meltdown of Amaranth raised suspicions about the potential of speculators to trigger unwarranted price volatility, both issues that have occupied regulators more or less constantly since 2008. With the Dodd-Frank legislation, which proceeded from a great loss of confidence in financial market self-regulation, hedge funds have come under a comprehensive disclosure regime (with the possibility of prudential oversight as well, for funds deemed to be systemically-significant), despite the consensus that they played little or no causal role in the global financial crisis. While there is something of a paradox in that, what the recent adoption of hedge fund-specific legislation in the US serves to show is that even necessary regulatory reforms are often impossible without a major disaster to prompt decision-makers into action. It remains to be seen how successful some of the measures adopted in response to the 2008 financial crisis will prove to be at preventing the recurrence of market failures similar to those that led to the ongoing crisis and which the LTCM and Amaranth incidents foreshadowed.

BIBLIOGRAPHY

Basel Committee on Banking Supervision (1999), 'Banks' Interactions with Highly Leveraged Institutions,' (Basel, Bank for International Settlements).

Basel Committee on Banking Supervision and International Organization of Securities Commissions (2001), 'Review of Issues Relating to Highly Leveraged Institutions (HLIs)', Mar. 2001, 12 (available at http://www.bis.org/press/p010322.htm).

Becker, Brandon and Colleen Doherty-Minicozzi (2000), 'Hedge Funds in Global Financial Markets', February, 100 (available at www.wilmer.com).

Bookstaber, Richard (2000), 'Understanding and Monitoring the Liquidity Crisis Cycle', *Financial Analysts Journal*, Sep/Oct, **56** (5), 17–22.

Chan, Nicholas, Mila Getmansky, Shane M. Haas and Andrew W. Lo (2006), 'Do Hedge Funds Increase Systemic Risk?', *Federal Reserve Bank of Atlanta Economic Review*, Fourth Quarter, **91**, 49–80.

Chincarini, Ludwig B. (2008), 'A Case Study on Risk Management: Lessons from the Collapse of Amaranth Advisors,' *Journal of Applied Finance*, Spring **18**(1), 152–74.

Counterparty Risk Management Policy Group (1999), 'Improving Counterparty Risk Management Practices,' New York: Counterparty Risk Management Policy Group p. 57.

Dunbar, Nicholas (2000), *Inventing Money: The Story of Long-Term Capital Management and the Legends Behind It*, Chichester, UK: John Wiley & Sons.

Elul, Ronel (2008), 'Liquidity Crises,' *Federal Reserve Bank of Philadelphia Business Review*, Second Quarter, 13–22.

Fang, Cai (2009), 'Trader Exploitation of Order Flow Information during the LTCM Crisis,' *Journal of Financial Research*, Fall 2009 **32** (3), 261–84.

Financial Economists Roundtable (1999), 'The Financial Economists Roundtable Statement on Long-Term Capital Management and the Report of the President's Working Group on Financial Markets,' Oct. 6, 1999 (Philadelphia, Pennsylvania, Wharton Financial Institutions Centre).

Financial Stability Board (2007), 'Update of the FSF Report on Highly Leveraged Institutions,' May 19, Basel: Bank for International Settlements, p. 34.

Financial Stability Forum (2000), 'Report of the Working Group on Highly Leveraged Institutions,' Apr. 5, Basel: Bank for International Settlements, p. 162.

Financial Stability Fourm (2001), 'Progress in Implementing the Recommendations of the Working Group on Highly Leveraged Institutions (HLIs)', May 2001, Basel: Bank for International Settlements, p. 19.

Fung, William, and David A. Hsieh (2000), 'Measuring the market impact of hedge funds,' *Journal of Empirical Finance*, **7**, 1–36.

Kambhu, John, Til Schuermann, and Kevin J. Stiroh (2007), 'Hedge Funds, Financial Intermediation, and Systemic Risk,' *Federal Reserve Bank of New York Staff Reports*, No. 291, July 31.

Lewis, Michael (1999), 'How the Eggheads Cracked,' *New York Times Magazine*, Jan. 24, p. 24.

Lo, Andrew W. (2009), 'Regulatory reform in the wake of the financial crisis of 2007–2008,' *Journal of Financial Economic Policy*, **1**(1), 4–43.

Lowenstein, Roger (2000), *When Genius Failed: The Rise and Fall of Long-Term Capital Management*, New York: Random House.

Paredes, Troy (2006), 'On the Decision to Regulate Hedge Funds: The SEC's Regulatory Philosophy, Style, and Mission', *University of Illinois Law Review*, **5**, 975–1035.

President's Working Group on Financial Markets (1999), 'Hedge Funds, Leverage, and the Lessons of Long-Term Capital Management,' Apr. 28, 109.

President's Working Group on Financial Markets (1999), 'Over-the-Counter Derivatives Markets and the Commodity Exchange Act: Report of the President's Working Group on Financial Markets', Nov. p. 35.

President's Working Group on Financial Markets (2007), 'Agreement among PWG and US Agency Principals on Principles and Guidelines Regarding Private Pools of Capital,' Feb. 22, p. 6.

US Commodity Futures Trading Commission (2008), 'Staff Report on Commodity Swap Dealers & Index Traders with Commission Recommendations', Sept. p. 70.

US House of Representatives, Committee on Banking and Financial Services (1998), *Hedge Fund Operations*, Hearing, 105th Congress, 2nd session, Oct. 1.

US House of Representatives Committee on Financial Services (2007), *Hedge Funds and Systemic Risk in the Financial Markets*, Hearing, 110th Congress, 1st session, Mar. 13 (Serial No. 110–13), p. 141.

US House of Representatives Committee on Oversight and Government Reform (2008), *Hedge Funds and the Financial Market*, Hearing, 110th Congress, 2nd session, Nov. 13 (Serial No. 110–210).

US Securities and Exchange Commission (2003), 'Implications of the Growth of Hedge Funds,' Staff Report to the [SEC], Sept.

US Senate Committee on Banking, Housing, and Urban Affairs (2010), *Implications of the 'Volcker Rules' for Financial Stability*, Hearing, 111th Congress, 2nd session, Feb. 4.

US Senate Committee on Homeland Security and Governmental Affairs (2007), Permanent Subcommittee on Investigations, 'Excessive Speculation in the Natural Gas Market,' Staff Report, June 25.

Yam, Joseph C.K. (1999), 'Capital Flows, Hedge Funds and Market Failure: A Hong Kong Perspective,' *Reserve Bank of Australia Bulletin*, Nov. p. 16.

12. Hedge funds and their impact on systemic stability
Maria Strömqvist*

INTRODUCTION

'Hedge fund' is a collective term for different types of investment fund. Generally speaking, a hedge fund is a fund with absolute return targets for financially sophisticated investors. Although many hedge funds protect their investments against losses (so-called hedging) this does not apply to all hedge funds, which, in fact, use many different investment strategies. Hedge funds do, however, have a number of common characteristics that distinguish them from other types of fund. In general, hedge funds employ more flexible investment strategies, in search for 'absolute returns'. Currently, a more liberal regulatory framework than for mutual funds enables hedge funds to pursue more dynamic investment strategies, with both long and short positions and the use of derivatives. Hedge funds can also choose to have a higher level of leverage compared to other types of fund.

Mutual funds have a relative return target, where the result of the fund is compared against a designated index. Hedge funds, on the other hand, have an absolute return target, irrespective of the development of the market as a whole, their goal being to achieve a return that has a low correlation with traditional risk factors such as stock- and bond indices. The part of the return that is independent from the risk premiums in the financial markets is known as alpha and it can be calculated as a residual.[1] Even if the goal of hedge funds is to be market neutral, research has shown that most hedge funds have *some* exposure to market risk. However, hedge

---

* Brummer and Partners. This chapter was written when I was a senior economist at the Financial Stability Department, Sveriges Riksbank. The views expressed here are those of the author and should not be regarded as Brummer and Partners' or the Riksbank's views on these issues. This chapter builds and expands on M. Strömqvist, 'Hedge funds and financial crises', published in Sveriges Riksbank Economics Review, No. 1, 2009.
[1]   Naik et al. (2007) found that the average alpha during 1994 to 2004 was 3% per year but that it differed between strategies (from zero to more than 5%). Negative alphas are uncommon.

fund returns are still less correlated with market risk than those of mutual funds.[2]

The fee structure of hedge funds also differs from that of traditional funds. In a mutual fund, the management fee represents a small percentage of their managed capital. In the case of hedge funds, it normally consists of a fixed fee of 2 per cent of the managed capital and, in addition, a variable fee of 20 per cent (or more) of any earnings over and above the return target. Some hedge funds also apply a so-called 'high-water mark', which sets a limit for when the variable fee may be levied. A high-water mark means that the variable fee is only charged if the value of the fund exceeds its highest previous value, irrespective of the earnings achieved in the period concerned.

Hedge funds are usually organised as limited partnerships, with the investors being the limited partners and the fund managers being the general partners. The managers normally invest part of their own capital in the fund so that their interests will be aligned with the interests of the investors.

With a high minimum limit for investments, hedge funds are primarily intended for institutional investors or financially-strong private individuals. A typical feature of hedge funds is also that investors can only withdraw their money from the fund on a monthly or quarterly basis, in contrast to mutual funds that provide liquidity on a daily basis. This facilitates investments in less liquid assets.

1.   THE DRAMATIC GROWTH OF HEDGE FUND MARKETS

According to Caldwell (1995) the first hedge fund was set up in 1949 by Albert Wislow Jones. It was a long/short equity fund,[3] which invested in stocks, with the risk in the portfolio being offset through 'hedging' (i.e. through short positions). The collective name 'hedge fund' is derived from that particular investment strategy, although the hedge fund market was to develop, over time, many different strategies. However, it was not until 1986 that the public's awareness of the existence and the activities of hedge funds increased. Julian Robertson's Tiger hedge fund attracted some media attention for having an average annual return of over 40 per

---

[2]   See, for example, Fung and Hsieh (2001, 2004).
[3]   Long/short equity is a strategy where the managers buy shares they believe will increase in value and short sell shares they believe will decrease in value.

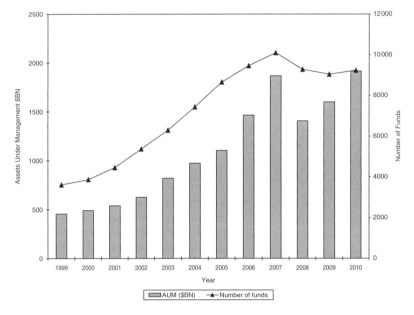

Source: International Financial Services London (IFSL) estimates and Hedge Fund Research (HFR).

Figure 12.1   Development of the hedge fund market

cent. It was at this time that the hedge fund market really started growing (Fung and Hsieh (1999)).

In the beginning, hedge funds focused on high net-worth individuals. Over time, institutional investors assumed a more prominent role. According to Fung et al. (2008), institutional investors, such as pension funds, have contributed to the sector's growth with the largest capital flows in recent years. These investors aim to diversify their portfolios with investments in funds that have a lower exposure to traditional risk factors. Recently, some hedge funds have also started to target retail investors offering lower minimum investments and higher liquidity for investors.[4]

The hedge fund market has grown exponentially over the last ten years. In 1999, hedge funds managed approximately US$380 billion and there were around 4000 funds. By the end of 2010, 9200 hedge funds including fund-of-funds managed about US$1900 billion (see Figure 12.1). This

---

[4]   According to PricewaterhouseCoopers (2008) investments by European retail investors in hedge funds are still small.

represents a fivefold increase in the capital managed by hedge funds over a period of ten years, as compared to the twofold increase only for mutual funds over the same period. In addition to the fact that hedge funds have grown in number and in size, the range of strategies they have adopted has also changed during that period. Almost a third of the total capital invested in hedge funds in 1996 was channelled to global macro funds[5] (Strömqvist (2008)). The most common strategies today are share-based (e.g. long/short equity) and arbitrage strategies that exploit cases of mispricing on the market. Global macro funds now account for only a small percentage of the market.

2.   HOW CAN HEDGE FUNDS AFFECT FINANCIAL MARKETS?

The more liberal investment rules governing the activities of hedge funds can have both positive and negative effects on financial markets.

The more liberal investment rules in question first and foremost mean that hedge funds can perform two functions on the financial markets. The *first* is to play the role of arbitrager. A common hedge fund strategy consists in the fund-manager exploiting mispricing phenomena. This may, for example, affect derivatives that are mispriced in relation to the underlying asset or shares that are mispriced in relation to the fundamental value of their issuer. Whether an asset is mispriced or not is usually assessed using statistical and economic models. When investors buy undervalued assets and sell overvalued assets, prices are pushed back towards their more fundamental values. This helps to improve pricing, making the market more effective. The *second* role is to help improve liquidity in the financial system. Higher liquidity is generally believed to lead to more effective pricing. For example, Brophy, Paige, and Sialm (2009) present evidence that hedge funds provide liquidity in niche assets when other classes of investors are reluctant to invest due to the high degree of information asymmetry.

But the flexibility of hedge fund strategies also entails risks. The most tangible risk is associated to the use of a high degree of leverage. Although leverage might help funds generate larger profits, it can also increase the risk of their collapse if their managers make the wrong investment calls. The higher degree of leverage entails risks for the hedge fund counterparties (for example the lenders), suggesting that a fund's failure may have

---

[5]   Global macro funds are based on an analysis of changes in macroeconomic variables and invest in all types of assets and markets.

contagion effects throughout the financial system. The hedge funds' use of derivatives also entails certain risks. Derivatives make it possible to adopt large positions on the market for only a small capital contribution, giving the manager additional leverage. Derivatives can, however, be used for two purposes: one is risk protection while the other is speculation. Hedge funds use derivatives for both of these purposes. The use of borrowing and of derivatives can contribute to greater fluctuations in share prices as it leads to the taking of larger positions. The more liberal investment rules for hedge funds can also be used to reinforce market movements for speculative purposes, so-called 'positive feedback trading'. Finally, if hedge funds constitute the majority of trades in a small and illiquid market it could be a problem if they were to quickly withdraw from that market.

In discussing the impact of hedge funds, it is important to distinguish between *systemic risk* and *financial risk*. Systemic risk is the one affecting an entire financial market or system, rather than just specific participants. Financial risk, on the other hand, is the possibility of loss in investment and it only affects the specific investors involved in a given transaction. Hedge funds, like all other investment vehicles, take on financial risk. But the question of wider interest is whether or not their investments also involve systemic risk.

3. HAVE HEDGE FUNDS HAD AN IMPACT ON PREVIOUS FINANCIAL CRISES?

The financial crises of the 1990s and 2000s provided an opportunity for a discussion about the role of hedge funds. Even though the course of events in these crises differed widely, the criticism levelled against hedge funds has tended to be the same. More specifically, the criticism directed at hedge funds in connection with financial crises is that hedge funds or groups of hedge funds with a high degree of leverage could exercise a strong impact on prices by making speculative attacks on, for example, certain companies' sectors or currencies. This impact on prices can be strengthened when herd behaviour is generated among investors. Hedge funds are also accused of manipulating asset prices and of contributing to the build-up of financial bubbles. A financial bubble is a situation in which the price that players pay for financial assets, for example shares or real estate, significantly exceeds the value that the asset has in terms of the income that it can realistically be expected to generate.

Four different financial crises and the impact of hedge funds thereon will be discussed in this section, in relation to the criticism presented above. The first crisis concerned European currencies and occurred at the start of the 1990s. The second was the Asian crisis that began in the autumn of 1997. The year 1998 saw the collapse of the Long-Term Capital Management (LTCM) hedge fund, which was partly a result of the near sovereign default of Russia earlier that year. The fourth crisis is the IT bubble and its resolution in and around 2000. The most recent crisis will be analysed in the following section.

3.1   George Soros and the European Currencies

A clear example of a situation when an individual hedge fund had an impact on prices relates to the well-known case of currency speculation by George Soros and his Quantum Fund in the early 1990s. The Quantum Fund was a global macro fund and Soros speculated in this case against fixed European exchange rates. The reason that the exchange rates were challenged is that they did not correspond to the macroeconomic conditions in the countries concerned. In the autumn of 1992, the Quantum Fund sold large volumes of the British pound and the Swedish krona, among other currencies, against the US$ forward rate (short positions). The attempts of the respective central banks to defend their fixed exchange rates became too costly and they were forced to abandon them. As a result, there was a rapid decline in the value of the currencies and the Quantum Fund was able to make large profits. According to Fung and Hsieh (2000), the Quantum Fund made a profit of one billion US$ on its short positions in the British pound alone. Soros came under heavy criticism for his actions but responded that since the currencies were obviously improperly valued a price adjustment would in any case have been necessary sooner or later.

Figure 12.2 shows the relative development of the two European currencies and hedge funds in the period between August and December 1992. The two graphs at the bottom of the figure show the cumulative development of the British pound and the Swedish krona relative to the US$. The upper two graphs show the cumulative earnings for an index of hedge funds with a global macro strategy and for Soros' Quantum Fund.

The Bank of England was forced to abandon its defence of the pound on 16 September. On that month, the Quantum Fund had a return of 25 per cent. The fund's return continued to be positive over the following months. The Swedish Riksbank took the decision to allow the krona to float on 19 November and, as a result, the krona lost 20 per cent of its value against the US$.

In that particular case, it is undoubtedly so that the speculative attacks of an individual hedge fund on specific currencies significantly affected their prices. On the other hand, the Quantum Fund cannot be accused

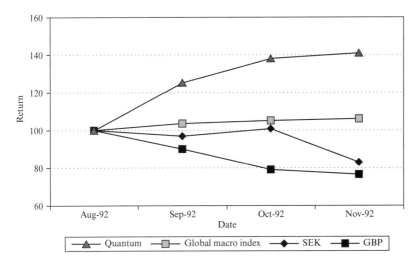

Sources: Fung and Hsieh (2000) and Strömqvist (2008).

Figure 12.2   The crisis in 1992 and global macro funds

of having manipulated prices or of contributing to the development of
the financial bubble: the latter bubble was the result of an erroneous economic policy and a price adjustment was, therefore, unavoidable. One
criticism that *could* be made, however, is that this price adjustment may
have occurred more rapidly and more dramatically due to the speculative
activities of Soros's Quantum Fund than, the case would otherwise have
been, in all likelihood. It is possible that a more orderly price adjustment
would have had a lower economic cost but, on the other hand, it may have
delayed the necessary structural adjustments enforced by the crisis. The
fact that the macro fund index in Figure 12.2 is fairly stable during the
period indicates that the currency speculations were relatively limited to
the Quantum Fund and, possibly, a few other funds. In other words, there
is little evidence of herd behaviour among the hedge funds on the occasion
of this crisis.

3.2   The Asian Crisis

Concerns with hedge fund speculation against fixed exchange rates
became current again in connection with the Asian crisis. By the mid-
1990s, a number of South-East Asian countries, such as Thailand, had
run large current account deficits. Their fixed exchange rates against the
US$ contributed to domestic borrowing in foreign currencies, which, in

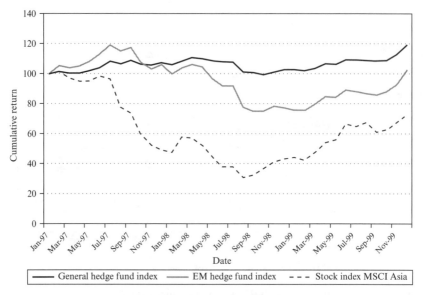

Sources: MSCI Barra and Strömqvist (2008).

Figure 12.3   Cumulative return during the Asian crisis 1997–1999

turn led to higher currency risk exposure. The development of a financial bubble was also driven by an inflow of international capital. When this inflow reversed, becoming an outflow, the fixed exchange rates became untenable. In July 1997, Thailand devalued its currency, a move that was soon to be followed by Malaysia and South Korea. The bursting of the financial bubble led to major adjustments in asset prices, for instance in share prices. The crisis raised the question whether hedge funds held extensive short positions in the Asian currencies and had, thus, pressured the respective countries to devalue so that they would then be able to make large profits from the weakening of the currencies and the falling share prices. The issue was taken so seriously that it was investigated by the IMF (Eichengreen et al. (1998)), which interviewed a number of market operators.

Figure 12.3 shows the cumulative return on the Asian stock market, an index for hedge funds with a focus on emerging markets, and a general hedge fund index. If hedge funds had collectively speculated against the economies of the Asian countries one would expect to have seen a high positive return for hedge funds during that period. However, that is not the case. The general hedge fund index shows a weak positive return during the relevant period. A more interesting point is that hedge funds with a focus on emerging markets lost 20 per cent of their value up to the middle of 1998. Thus, the Asian crisis had a negative impact on these hedge funds (although they still had a higher return compared to the share index). I have shown (Strömqvist 2008) that hedge funds investing in emerging markets mainly use long positions in shares. Their return is thus positively correlated to the stock market. A paper by Bris, Goetzmann and Zhu (2007) points out that the possibility to take short positions in emerging markets is, if not completely prohibited, at least very limited. This reduces the opportunities for hedge funds to exploit a negative market trend to generate increased profits.

As in the case of the 1992 crisis, this particular financial bubble was the result of fundamental and structural imbalances in the financial system. Hedge funds therefore played no prominent role in its development. The factor that distinguishes the Asian crisis from the crisis of 1992 is that, in the Asian crisis, it was no longer possible to identify individual investors or groups of investors who contributed more to its development than others. What happened instead was that international investors in general panicked and rapidly withdrew some of the capital they had invested in the region (Lindgren et al. (1999)). Eichengreen et al. (1998) found no evidence that hedge funds, in particular, had any involvement in undermining the economies of the Asian countries through speculation, herd behaviour or positive feedback trading. Nor could Fung and Hsieh (2000), by means of regression analysis, find any negative correlation between hedge fund returns and shifts in the value of the Asian currencies.

3.3 The IT Bubble

In 1999, the value of IT-related shares increased dramatically, resulting in record market values in relation to the companies' reported values or profits. These values proved to be untenable and in March 2000 the trend reversed, with the prices of IT-related shares falling sharply. If hedge funds had played the role of arbitragers, they should have counteracted the exaggerated price increases by taking short positions in IT shares. However, in a study of hedge fund holdings in American IT shares, Brunnermeier and Nagel (2004) found that the opposite was, in fact, the case. According to the results of this study, hedge funds held extensive long positions in IT shares during the bubble and then reduced these holdings before the crash occurred. This conclusion is confirmed by Figure 12.4, which shows the cumulative return for hedge funds in relation to the US stock market. The index for hedge funds increased at approximately the same rate as the share index in 1999 and the early part of 2000. Subsequently, the two graphs separate; the share index falls dramatically while the hedge fund

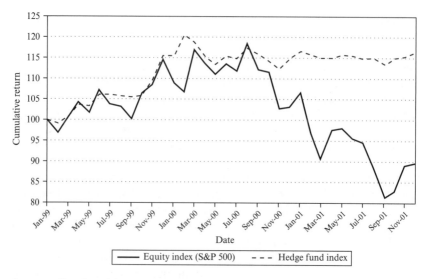

Sources: Ecowin and Strömqvist (2008).

Figure 12.4   Cumulative return during the IT bubble

index remains relatively unchanged throughout the remainder of 2000. Brunnermeier's and Nagel's (2004) explanation was that hedge funds were aware that there was a bubble and their optimal strategy was to ride the wave rather than trying to correct prices.

What criticism can, then, be levelled at hedge funds in the context of that particular crisis? It is possible that by buying IT-related shares, hedge funds helped drive up prices and, thus, increase the financial bubble. One may also ask whether they instigated the dramatic fall in prices by selling their IT shares. The stock market is, however, a relatively liquid market and large volumes must be traded in order for the general trend to be affected. The hedge funds' impact on the bubble should therefore correspond to their influence on the financial market at the time. If we assume that hedge funds realized that there was a bubble, the fact that they chose to ride the wave indicates that they believed they did not have sufficient influence on the financial markets to be able to burst the bubble themselves. Brunnermeier and Nagel (2004) found that although the hedge funds reduced their holdings in IT shares before the crash, they did not sell their entire holdings. It is reasonable to assume that they did not, at the same time, adopt short positions in these shares in order to drive prices downwards. Hence, there is no evidence that hedge funds in particular escalated the fall in share prices of IT stocks in this period.

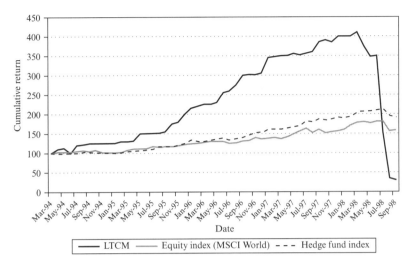

Sources: Lowenstein (2000), MSCI Barra and Dow Jones Credit Suisse.

Figure 12.5   Cumulative return for Long-Term Capital Management

3.4   The Collapse of LTCM

The three crises presented above represent episodes in which hedge funds, through various means, succeeded in getting a better return on their investments than the market as a whole. This section discusses the issue of hedge fund leverage and its effects on financial stability when a leveraged strategy fails. This is to be done by taking LTCM as an example. See Figure 12.5.

LTCM, a highly profitable Delaware-based limited partnership,[6] considered unique amongst hedge funds *inter alia* on account of the reputation of its principals, collapsed in August 1998, with a loss of an estimated US$4.4 billion, when its principals wrongly predicted that high-risk, developing countries' debt bonds would increase in value. According to Edwards (1999), with equity of approximately US$5 billion at the time of its collapse, the fund had borrowed up to US$125 billion, which entailed an extremely high degree of leverage of 25 times LTCM's equity. The fund's strategy was to exploit mispricing, particularly on the bond market. Specifically, the fund had invested large sums in the assumption that the interest rates of bonds issued at different times but with the same final date would converge.

---

[6]   Prior to its demise, LTCM had a stellar track record, producing net returns of 40% in 1995 and 20% in 1996 and 1997.

Following the financial collapse in Russia, the market situation suddenly changed and the interest rates diverged instead of converging. On account of the major losses that the fund made, given its high leverage and its positions in derivatives, the Federal Reserve was of the opinion that its collapse could have a negative impact on the entire financial system. Together with a number of investment banks, the Federal Reserve arranged a rescue for LTCM in which the positions of the fund were taken over.

The LTCM episode demonstrates partly that there are risks associated with funds with a high degree of leverage, and partly that hedge funds can be regarded as being systemically important. It is namely not only the fund's investors and counterparties that might be affected if the fund goes bankrupt but, also, other market players with varying degrees of exposure to the failed hedge fund, varying from the limited to the very tenuous. When the assets of a leveraged investor, such as a hedge fund, have to be sold-off, the value of assets of the same type may also fall, which in turn may force other leveraged investors to sell-off assets if the value of their collateral falls below the borrowed sum. This creates a vicious circle that affects financial stability. Good risk management is therefore important, not only for the hedge funds themselves but also for their counterparties that make such high leverage possible.

According to Edwards (1999), it is, however, unusual for hedge funds to have a degree of leverage of more than ten times their equity. In their study, Eichengreen and Park (2002) found that, in 1998, 74 per cent of the hedge funds had a degree of leverage less than two times their equity. The corresponding figure one year later was 89 per cent. The US President's Working Group on Financial Markets (1999) also discussed the risks associated with a high degree of leverage. The Group found that other institutional investors had the same degree of leverage as hedge funds in 1998 (although many of them had more assets under management compared to hedge funds).

4.   HOW DOES THE RECENT FINANCIAL CRISIS DIFFER FROM PREVIOUS CRISES?

The debate surrounding hedge funds and their impact on financial crises has continued in connection with the most recent turmoil. For example, in early 2007 two Bear Stearns' hedge funds collapsed, and the event placed focus on hedge funds and their systemic risks. These funds had concentrated and highly leveraged portfolios with credit instruments related to the US subprime housing bonds market. Another example is that of Iceland accusing hedge funds of speculating against the Icelandic currency and, consequently, the Icelandic economy (Thompson Financial News,

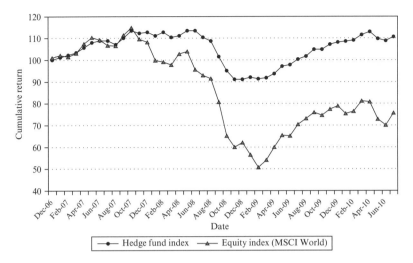

Sources: MSCI Barra and Dow Jones Credit Suisse.

Figure 12.6   *Cumulative return during the recent crisis*

2008). In September 2008, shortselling was prohibited on many markets as it was believed that the practice had been used to accelerate falls in share prices, especially in financial companies. Questions on the speculative investments of hedge funds were also raised again during Greece's sovereign debt crisis in 2010 (*The Washington Post*, 2010).[7]

The pertinent question is this: what has the role of hedge funds been during the recent crisis and how could their activities have been responsible for its outburst? A general answer is that the crisis has affected them more than they have affected the crisis. The main piece of evidence corroborating that theory is that hedge funds have experienced more problems in handling this than previous crises, and that they appear to have suffered more than they have benefited from it.

4.1   Broad Decline in Hedge Fund Returns

Figure 12.6 shows the cumulative returns on the hedge fund and stock markets during the recent crisis. The hedge fund market had a stable and, thus, superior development compared to the stock market between

---

[7]   During that period Germany temporarily banned so-called naked short selling on some financial instruments.

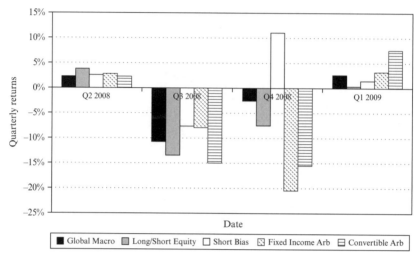

Source: Dow Jones Credit Suisse.

Figure 12.7   Quarterly returns for selected strategies

October 2007 and June 2008. Thereafter, both the hedge fund index and the share index declined, although the fall was greater for the share index. The hedge fund index was also negatively affected during the spring of 2010 when the Greek crisis occurred although, again, to a lesser extent than the equity markets.

Unlike in the case of the Asian crisis, when it was mainly funds with a focus on emerging markets that were affected, the negative development in the hedge fund industry's returns during this crisis cannot be related to a particular strategy. According to the Barclay's database on hedge funds, as much as 89 per cent of the hedge funds in that database had a negative return in September 2008. Figure 12.7 shows the quarterly strategy returns from the second quarter of 2008 to the first quarter of 2009, for five different strategies. In the second quarter of 2008, all of these strategies had a positive return. However, all strategies had a negative return in the third quarter of 2008. In the fourth quarter of 2008 only the short bias strategy[8] had a positive return. The strategies that performed worst during the fourth quarter were the convertible arbitrage and fixed income arbitrage strategies.[9] The

---

[8]   This strategy is defined in the next section.
[9]   These strategies exploit the mispricing of convertible debt instruments and interest rate instruments respectively.

poor return of the long/short equity strategy indicates that funds employing this strategy have had a predominance of long positions in the falling stock market. In 2009 the returns turned positive again, except for the short bias strategy. A number of factors that distinguish the recent crisis from previous crises, and which have contributed to the poorer hedge fund returns are discussed in the sections below.

4.2   Regulatory Changes

A unique feature of the recent crisis relates to a decision taken in the autumn of 2008, which suddenly changed the rules governing the hedge fund market. The decision to ban shortselling (primarily the shortselling of shares in financial companies) affected different strategies to different degrees. That decision had a major negative impact on certain strategies, mainly those in which shortselling is a natural element or in which there is a high degree of exposure to the financial sector. The ban affected hedge funds more than mutual funds because hedge funds use shortselling to a greater extent. A ban on shortselling in a falling market makes it more difficult to use strategies that reinforce negative market movements. This was also the aim of the ban. However, the ban on shortselling also made it more difficult to protect long positions through short positions and to use certain arbitrage strategies.

Short bias is a strategy that provides increasing returns in the case of falling asset prices, and the effect of the ban on shortselling can clearly be seen in Figure 12.7. The short bias strategy worked well during the second quarter of 2008 but not in the third quarter, when the ban on shortselling was introduced. The strategy then provided a high positive return in the fourth quarter of 2008. The strategy is not particularly opportunistic, however, as it means that the fund always has a predominance of short positions in its portfolio, irrespective of market conditions. An example of a market neutral arbitrage strategy that includes shortselling is convertible arbitrage, which is a market neutral strategy, i.e. the return should not be dependent on market movements. In this strategy, a long position is usually taken in the convertible debt instrument and a short position in the share concerned. The profits arise from the mispricing of the convertible debt instrument in relation to the share, for example it may be undervalued due to poor liquidity. Hence, the strategy does not use shortselling to bet on falling share prices and thus cannot be accused of taking positions to reinforce negative market movements. Although the shortselling ban was aimed at negative feedback trading and not arbitrage strategies, the latter were also affected negatively.

During 2009, regulators turned their attention specifically to hedge funds. During the G-20 meeting in April 2009, world leaders explicitly stressed the necessity to regulate systemically important hedge funds (Bloomberg, 2009). In Europe, a regulatory process to restrain the activities of private equity and hedge funds was initiated.[10] According to the European Commission (2009), the activities of hedge fund managers posed a series of risks for the stability of financial markets. Although hedge funds were not considered the cause of the recent crisis, the European Commission concluded that the existing regulatory environment was not enough to monitor the risks posed by hedge funds to the financial system.

4.3   Broad Decline in Asset Values

Previous crises have been limited to particular markets or asset types. In the recent crisis, many different asset types have been affected simultaneously and, what is more, globally. Normally, hedge funds receive premiums for assuming credit risk, duration risk and liquidity risk.[11] These risk premiums normally constitute a large part of a hedge fund's profits. In the latest crisis, however, a higher degree of risk taking has not led to higher profits, on the contrary. The fact that the downturn has affected many different asset types and markets at the same time has also wiped out all of the profits previously gained from these premiums. The increased risk premiums have simply not compensated for the losses made.

In the 2001–2003 period, many hedge funds generated large profits by diversifying their portfolios to include property or commodities. As investors have become more unwilling to take risks during the crisis, they have reduced borrowing in their portfolios by selling assets. This has driven the prices of almost all asset types downwards, including commodities and property, which has weakened the positive effects of diversification.

Hedge funds were better able to predict the downturn that occurred in connection with the IT bubble than the downturn during 2008 because the valuations of the companies during the IT bubble were at historically high levels. It was, therefore, easier for them to predict that a price adjustment would take place. This was not the case in the 2008 crisis and many funds were therefore taken by surprise by the dramatic fall in share prices.

---

[10]   The legislative process regarding the Alternative Investment Fund Manager Directive was finalized during 2010.

[11]   Credit risk is the risk of loss due to a debtor's non-payment of a loan or other line of credit. Duration risk is the risk associated with changes in general interest rate levels or yield curves. Liquidity risk is the risk that a given security or asset cannot be traded quickly enough in the market to prevent a loss (or make the required profit).

There has been extreme volatility in both share and commodity prices in the recent crisis. This has made it more difficult to forecast future movements in asset values. For example, many hedge funds that had invested in a negative stock market and high commodity prices experienced problems in July 2008 when the trend suddenly reversed, with a considerable increase in share prices and a considerable fall in commodity prices (ECB (2008)).

A final difference between the recent crisis and previous crises is that the recent turmoil originated in a bank crisis. The problems of banks have had a direct impact on hedge funds in the form of more restrictive lending, higher borrowing costs and assets tied-up in connection with bankruptcies (e.g. Lehman Brothers).[12] Hedge funds have been forced to sell-off assets in a falling market and this has had a negative effect on their returns.

The evidence presented in this section has shown that hedge funds appear to have suffered more from the recent crisis than they have benefited from it. Although that does not eliminate the possibility that hedge funds were responsible for causing the crisis, there is no evidence that that was the case.

5. DO HEDGE FUNDS CONSTITUTE A GREATER THREAT TO FINANCIAL STABILITY THAN OTHER INVESTORS?

This section discusses the systemic instability potential of hedge funds compared to other types of investor, especially in the light of the recent financial crisis. The possibility for an investor to influence the financial markets is greater the greater the proportion of total capital this investor manages. The question is how large a proportion of total risk capital is today invested in hedge funds, given that these have grown dramatically in numbers and size over the last ten years. The degree of leverage used by hedge funds is also an important factor, since it enables larger investments than the amount of equity would justify. Another interesting question is whether hedge funds are the only type of investment fund on today's financial markets that constitutes a threat to financial stability.

Figure 12.8 shows the capital managed by institutional investor groups between December 2007–2009. Despite the dramatic growth of

---

[12] See Aragon and Strahan (2009) for an analysis of the impact from Lehman Brothers' bankruptcy on hedge funds.

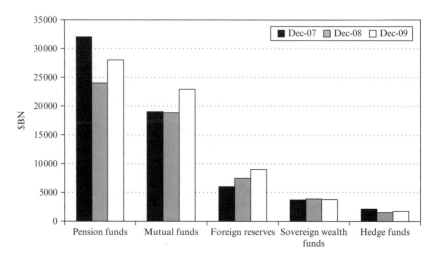

Sources: IFSL estimates, Investment Company Institute, author's own calculations.

Figure 12.8   *Capital managed by institutional investor groups (2007–2009)*

the hedge fund sector, hedge funds still account for only a small part of the total assets under management. Both pension companies and fund companies manage well over ten times as much capital as hedge funds. This counters the argument that hedge funds could, as a group, influence entire markets. In the case of major market movements it is, therefore, probable that several types of institutional investor follow the same trends.

How great is the influence of individual hedge funds? Figure 12.8 shows the total quantity of managed capital but says nothing about how the capital is distributed between the funds. That question is instead answered by Figure 12.9. According to the *Alpha Magazine journal*, one of the largest hedge funds in the world is JP Morgan Asset Management, which manages capital of around US$ 40 billion. This is only a few percentage points of the capital managed by the world's largest fund companies and pension companies.

However, the leverage of hedge funds must also be included in the analysis. Figure 12.10 shows the average gross market exposure of hedge funds as a percentage of assets under management from 2000–2009. The average leverage of hedge funds has during this period never been above two times the assets under management. The ratio decreased sharply during the turbulent 2008. Although there may be funds with significantly higher

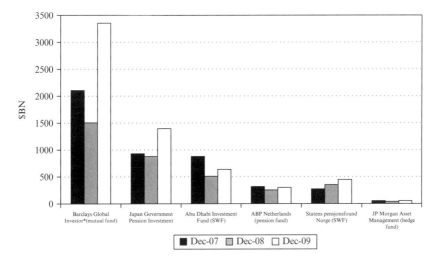

Note: *Barclays Global Investor was purchased by Black Rock in 2009.

Sources: IFSL estimates, Bloomberg, company websites and annual reports.

Figure 12.9   The largest players in terms of managed capital (2007–2009)

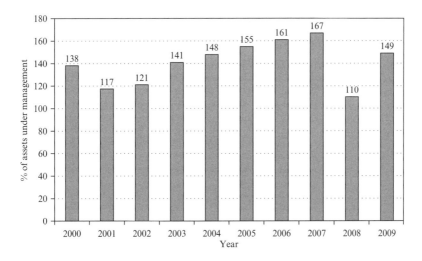

Source: IFSL estimates.

Figure 12.10   Average gross market exposure of hedge funds as % of assets under management (2000–2009)

leverage, taken together with the size of the assets under management, it is reasonable to assume that the influence of individual hedge funds on entire markets is limited.[13]

A comparison between Sovereign Wealth Funds (SWFs) and hedge funds is apposite, by way of conclusion. Both of these types of investment fund are fairly unregulated and do not need to publish information about their holdings and transactions. They can both contribute liquidity to financial markets and increase the efficiency of these markets. Even though SWFs tend to have long-term goals there are examples of speculative transactions on the part of such funds.[14] However, unlike in the case of the hedge fund market, the market for SWFs is highly concentrated in that it consists of a handful of very large funds. Individual SWFs should, therefore, be better able to influence the market than hedge funds.

6. NO SUPPORT FOR THE CLAIM THAT HEDGE FUNDS AFFECT FINANCIAL CRISES MORE THAN OTHER INVESTORS

The behaviour of hedge funds, like that of other investors, has differed widely in the previous crises and does not point to any specific pattern in terms of their impact on financial crises.

The criticism of hedge funds often stems from the fact that, in crises, they have invested money in the price adjustment of incorrectly valued assets. Under normal conditions, this has a positive impact on the effectiveness of the market. In financial crises, however, it is regarded as a factor that can make the market more unstable. It is, on the other hand, unreasonable to expect that investors that normally employ arbitrage strategies should refrain from doing so during financial crises and that mispricing should be allowed to prevail. From the policy point of view it is, thus, difficult to assess when these strategies are desirable and when they are not.

Another common criticism is that hedge funds manipulate asset prices and contribute to the development of financial bubbles. However, the

---

[13]   The exception could be small, illiquid markets in which hedge funds provide the majority of liquidity. However, the systemic impact of these markets can be discussed.

[14]   On one occasion, the Norwegian SWF short-sold bonds issued by Icelandic banks, a move that was severely criticised by the Prime Minister of Iceland (*The Economist*, 17 January 2008).

only crisis discussed in this chapter where hedge funds can be suspected of contributing to the development of the bubble is the IT crisis. In two of the other crises, the funds exploited untenable situations caused by erroneous economic policies. Generally speaking, the use of arbitrage strategies actually counteracts the development of financial bubbles but, given their profit-maximising targets, hedge funds do not assume any responsibility for preventing the creation of bubbles. One may, on the other hand, discuss whether the speculative attacks of hedge funds against bubbles can accelerate the deflation of the bubbles or aggravate its consequences once this has materialized.

The arguments for the claim that hedge funds do not have a greater impact on financial markets than other investors have already been presented by Eichengreen et al. (1998) and they are still valid today. Hedge funds alone are not large enough to be able to influence prices on liquid markets as their capital is small in relation to that of other investors, such as banks and insurance companies. It is therefore more probable that large market movements are due to several types of institutional investor following the same trends. The fact that hedge funds rode the wave during the IT bubble can be seen as a sign that they did not regard themselves as being large enough to influence the direction of the liquid stock market.

Moreover, there is no clear evidence that hedge funds generate herd behaviour. It can rather be argued that hedge funds are less prone to generate herd behaviour than other investors because they want to keep their strategies secret (Eichengreen et al. (1998)). The IT bubble exemplifies the fact that hedge funds may be those that follow other investors, rather than the other way around. Neither Fung and Hsieh (2000) or Eichengreen et al. (1998) were able to find proof that hedge funds reinforce market movements or that they are more interested in manipulating a market than other investors.

The strongest argument for the claim that hedge funds have not driven the recent financial crisis is that they have been negatively affected on a broad front. In contrast to previous crises, the downturn has affected most asset types and markets, reducing the effect of diversification. In addition, the shortselling of shares was prohibited on many markets in September 2008, with the aim of preventing an acceleration of the fall in share prices. The cost of this ban was, however, that strategies that normally employ short-selling, irrespective of the market conditions, were affected. That was unfortunate because, in the long run, restricting the possibility to conduct arbitrage reduces the effectiveness of financial markets. Implementing a general limit on hedge fund leverage is unlikely to have the intended impact on systemic risk, since a highly leveraged fund investing in short-term government bonds may be less risky than an unleveraged fund investing in equities. It is, then, more reasonable to implement stricter regulations on the risk management of hedge funds' counterparties, given their information regarding hedge funds, than to restrict the activities of hedge funds.

The fact that hedge funds have been hit by the latest crisis does not, however, rule out that they have played a role in the development of the crisis together with banks and other institutional investors. Bear Stearns' funds were two of the funds that provided liquidity for the new, complex credit instruments and which then shook the market when they collapsed. However, it is important to remember that the recent financial crisis originated in the banking sector. Hence, from a financial stability point of view, the most important thing to do is to ensure that systematically important banks can correctly review and control their risks as counterparties to hedge funds.

7.   CONCLUSIONS

A discussion of the impact of hedge funds on systemic stability is a recurring feature of every financial crisis. A common criticism has been that hedge funds manipulate asset prices and contribute to the development of financial bubbles. Rather than manipulating markets, the analysis in this chapter indicates that hedge funds exploit untenable situations caused by erroneous economic policies. It is possible, however, that the speculative attacks of hedge funds against bubbles can accelerate the deflation of the bubbles or aggravate its consequences once this has materialized.

Regarding the recent financial turbulence, there is no evidence that hedge funds caused the crisis. The fact that hedge funds have been hit by the latest crisis does not rule out that they have played a role in the development of the crisis together with banks and other institutional investors. However, the analysis conducted here does not support the claim that hedge funds, in general, have a greater impact on financial crises than other investors.

BIBLIOGRAPHY

Alpha Magazine (2008), 'Alpha Magazine's Hedge Fund 100 Rankings 2008', available at www.alphamagazinerankings.com
Aragon, G. O., and Strahan, P. E. (2009), 'Hedge Funds as Liquidity Providers: Evidence from the Lehman Bankruptcy', NBER Working Paper No. w15336.
Bloomberg (2009), 'Hedge Funds Say G-20 Crackdown Makes Industry a 'Scapegoat'', 2 April.

Bris, A., Goetzmann, W. N. and Zhu, N. (2007), 'Efficiency and the Bear: Short Sales and Markets Around the World', *Journal of Financial Economics*, **83**(1), 33–58.

Brophy, D. J., Paige P. O., and Sialm, C. (2009), Hedge Funds as Investors of Last Resort?, *Review of Financial Studies*, **22**(2), 541–74.

Brunnermeier, M. K. and Nagel, S. (2004), 'Hedge Funds and the Technology Bubble', *Journal of Finance*, **59**(5), 2013–2040.

Caldwell, T. (1995), 'Introduction: The Model for Superior Performance', in Lederman, J. and R. A, Klein (eds.), *Hedge Funds*, New York: Irwin Professional Publishing.

ECB (2007), 'Financial Stability Report', December 2007, Frankfurt, European Central Bank.

ECB (2008), 'Financial Stability Report', December 2008, Frankfurt, European Central Bank.

Edwards, F. R. (1999), 'Hedge Funds and the Collapse of Long-Term Capital Management', *Journal of Economic Perspectives*, **13**(12), 189–210.

Eichengreen, B., Mathieson, D., Chadha, B., Jansen, A., Kodres, L. and Sharma, S. (1998), 'Hedge Funds and Financial Market Dynamics', *IMF Occasional Paper no.166*, Washington, DC, International Monetary Fund.

Eichengreen, B. and Park, B. (2002), 'Hedge Fund Leverage Before and After the Crisis', *Journal of Economic Integration*, **17**(1), 1–20.

European Commission (2009), 'Proposal for a Directive of the European Parliament and of the Council on Alternative Investment Fund Managers and Amending Directives 2004/39/ EC and 2009/. . ./EC'.

Fung, W. and Hsieh, D. A. (1999), 'A Primer on Hedge Funds', *Journal of Empirical Finance*, **6**, 309–331.

Fung, W. and Hsieh, D. A. (2000), 'Measuring the Market Impact of Hedge Funds', *Journal of Empirical Finance,* **7**(1), 1–36.

Fung, W. and Hsieh, D. A. (2001), 'The Risk in Hedge Fund Strategies: Theory and Evidence from Trend Followers', *Review of Financial Studies*, **14**, 313–341.

Fung, W. and Hsieh, D. A. (2004), 'Hedge Fund Benchmarks: A Risk-based Approach', *Financial Analysts Journal*, **60**(5), 65–80.

Fung, W., Hsieh, D. A., Naik, N. Y. and Ramadorai, T. (2008), 'Hedge Funds: Performance, Risk and Capital Formation', *Journal of Finance*, **63**, 1777–1803.

Lindgren, C-J, Balino, T. J. T., Enoch, C., Gulde, A-M, Quintyn, M. and Teo, L. (1999), 'Financial sector crisis and restructuring: Lessons from Asia', *IMF Occasional Paper no.188*, Washington, DC: International Monetary Fund.

Lowenstein, R. (2000), 'When Genius Failed: The Rise and Fall of Long-Term Capital Management', New York: Random House.

Naik, N.Y., Ramadorai, T. and Strömqvist, M. (2007), 'Capacity Constraints and Hedge Fund Strategy Returns', *European Financial Management*, **13**(2), 239–56.

PricewaterhouseCoopers (2008), 'The 'Retailisation' of Non-harmonised Investment Funds in the European Union', EDT/2007/ IM/G4/95, October.

Strömqvist, M. (2008), 'Hedge Funds and International Capital Flows', doctoral thesis, Department of Finance, Stockholm School of Economics.

The Economist (2008), 'Asset-backed Insecurity', 17 January.

Thomson Financial News (2008), 'Iceland Threatens "Bear Trap" Intervention against Hedge Funds', 2 April.

The Washington Post (2010), 'Hedge Funds Probe Exposes Heart of Greek Crisis', 6 March.

US President's Working Group on Financial Markets (1999), 'Hedge funds, leverage, and the lessons of Long-Term Capital Management', Report of the President's Working Group on Financial Markets, Washington, DC.

13. Sovereign default risks in the Economic and Monetary Union and the role of vulture funds

*Peter Yeoh**

INTRODUCTION

The concept of 'sovereign debt default risk' refers to the probability that a sovereign government may be unable or unwilling to repay its public debt on schedule. The earlier international bank syndicated loans,[1] popular amongst sovereign states for the financing of their liabilities have, since the late 1980s, given their place to sovereign ('Brady') bonds,[2] created to overcome some of the more troublesome features that consortium lending packages posed for sovereign creditors. The popularity of sovereign bonds as a means of financing public debt has to a large extent been facilitated by the sovereign debt credit ratings issued by the three global credit rating agencies (CRAs), representing the summary evaluation of the ability and willingness of sovereign governments to settle their public debt on time and functioning as indicators of the probability of their default.

Investors have generally associated the risk of sovereign default with emerging economies. Sovereign debt defaults have, after all, largely occurred in Latin American, Asian or other transition economies. The threat of an advanced economy's default did not become apparent until the emergence of the Icelandic, Dubai and Greek crises. Insights into the reasons why those economies have faced sovereign debt default risks are important for academics, investors, policy makers and the general public alike. This chapter examines some of the reasons for this unusual phenomenon, inquiring into the role that vulture funds may have played in bringing about (or exacerbating) the risk of sovereign default in some of

---

* Phd, LLM, LLB, MBA, BECONS, CIM, PGCERT, Law Lecturer and Researcher, University of Wolverhampton.

[1] Fuller, G. (2009).

[2] Salomon Smith Barney (2000). Brady bonds are US$-denominated bonds issued in various emerging economies. At the time of writing, they accounted for an estimated 37 per cent of the total volume of sovereign fixed-income securities traded in the secondary markets.

the world's advanced economies and trying to identify ways of addressing sovereign default risks in the European Union (EU) and in the European Economic and Monetary Union (EMU), whether through the closer regulation of certain types of private funds or through other policy alternatives.

1. SOVEREIGN DEBT DEFAULT RISK EVALUATION

Sovereigns may default on their debts either due to severe liquidity pressures, caused by serious weaknesses in their macroeconomic fundamentals, or out of choice. While a sovereign's *ability* to settle its debts on time is directly linked to its economy's performance and its fiscal health, its *willingness* to pay may be linked to other, non-economic considerations, making the assessment of the risk of sovereign default a more complicated exercise compared to that of corporate default. Indeed, sovereign default risk evaluation extends beyond pure solvency analysis, to also include non-economic factors such as, for instance, the stability of a sovereign's political institutions and its social cohesion. In practice, eight variables are employed to help evaluate an economy's ability and willingness to settle its debt: the per capita income in the relevant sovereign, its gross domestic product (GDP) growth rate, its inflation, fiscal balance, external balance, external debt, economic development and its default history, if any.

Sovereigns may opt to default on their debt if their assessment of the costs of sovereign default is that these are more tolerable compared to the austerity measures necessary to enable them to service their ongoing debt obligations, which are likely to carry grave political risks for the government of the day. A consideration that may tip the balance in favor of a sovereign's voluntary default is that, unlike in the case of corporations, it is difficult for creditors to enforce payments on a sovereign's debt obligations by seizing, for instance, those of its assets situated outside its jurisdiction (even if sovereign immunity[3] on loans and bond contracts were to be waived). Besides avoiding opposition against unpopular austerity programmes, a default strategy could also allow the diverted repayment resources to be applied to enhance domestic consumption, gaining, in the process, popular support for the government of the day. The potential costs of default may, on the other hand, provide a (relatively stronger) source of pressure to induce sovereigns to take the measures necessary

---

[3] As provided in the 1976 Foreign Immunity Act (US) and the 1978 State Immunity Act (UK).

to honour their debt obligations, instead of opting to default. The four common costs arising from external sovereign debt default are *reputational, international trade exclusion*-related, *domestic economy* and *political* costs.[4] Although material, reputational costs (as reflected in credit ratings and interest rate spreads) are of a medium or short-term relevance only. Regarding international-trade exclusion-related costs, whilst there is no conclusive evidence of discrimination against traders based in defaulting debtor nations, empirical evidence suggests that default events have a negative impact on the creditworthiness of trading partners resident in defaulting countries, rendering trade credit more costly and less easily accessible.[5] Default events are also known to affect adversely domestic economic growth (resulting, for instance, in drops in output, enhanced vulnerability to currency risks or, in extreme cases, loss of access to international finance and domestic banking crises). Finally, sovereign default events have in most instances led to a deterioration in the political fortunes of national administrations (which helps explain why political leaders often postpone default decisions to make sure that there is a broad consensus that these are unavoidable and why the strategic default option, which is highly costly in terms of political reputation, is rarely exercised).[6] Research has shown that while economic costs are generally short-term in nature,[7] political costs are, by comparison, particularly dire for the incumbent administration, being broadly similar to those following currency crises.[8]

2. FUNDAMENTAL FACTORS UNDERLYING SOVEREIGN DEBT RISKS; SOVEREIGN DEBT CRISIS INDICATORS

The capacity and willingness of sovereigns to settle their external debt obligations determine the degree of risk faced by creditors and investors in extending credits to them. Insights from the extant literature suggest that, unless forced by very adverse and compelling circumstances, sovereign

---

[4] Borensztein, E. & Panizza, U. (2009).

[5] *Ibid.*

[6] Trebesch, C. (2009). Trebesch argues that a state's non-compliance with the generally accepted standards of 'fair debt restructurings' appears to exert significant costs on the domestic economy, leading to a deterioration in its access to foreign capital.

[7] See Ozler, S. (1993); Reinhart, C. & Rogoff, K. & Savastano, M. (2003).

[8] Borensztein & Panizza, *supra*, fn. 4.

debtors do not, in practice, voluntarily default, so as to avoid the stigma of a pariah economy.[9] Relevant macroeconomic indicators are usually helpful in providing forewarnings of a sovereign default event. These include variables such as debt services ratio, import ratio, investment ratio, variance of export revenue and domestic money supply growth. Various other macroeconomic performance indicators may also function as effective proxies in gauging the sustainability of external debt levels. As none of those approaches is without its limitations, it is safer and more effective to use them in a complementary manner. The sustainability of a debtor nation's external debt levels may be gauged by the pertinent risk premium placed on its bonds, reflecting the market's view of its debt sustainability by the additional interest it has to pay relative to the interest rate on US Treasury bonds or German Bunds. As a general proposition, the higher the risk premium the greater will be the implied probability of default and the lesser the likelihood that a sovereign's debt will be sustainable.

Ultimately, the incidence of the risk that a sovereign may be unable or unwilling to settle its external debt is the product of its economic performance, as reflected by the above variables of which the most relevant, as indicators of its economic and fiscal health, are the budgetary deficit-to-GDP ratio and the total-debt-to-GDP ratio. Balance of payments crises resulting in shortages of foreign exchange reserves can also force debtor nations to default or to reschedule their maturing foreign currency liabilities, as demonstrated in the 1997 Asian Financial Crisis.[10] Interestingly, there are no precedents of sovereigns failing to meet their debt repayment obligations on account of speculation, although there are examples of large-scale attacks on the financial interests of sovereigns, as in the 1992 case of 'Black Wednesday', when speculators effectively brought down the British currency, leading to the exit of the United Kingdom (UK) from the European Exchange Rate Mechanism.

Past experience demonstrates that debtor nations' defaults on their external debts are associated with relatively high public debts in relation to their revenues and GDP, significantly high external debt to total debt ratios and under-developed or poorly organized capital and financial markets. The cases of Dubai and Iceland show clearly how high external borrowing levels in boom times can lead to serious challenges when

---

[9]   See Sheng, A. (2009).
[10]   See Frenkel, M., Karmann, A. & Scholtens, B. (2004); Hilscher, J. & Nosbusch, I. (2008). The latter empirical study suggests that economies with more volatile fundamentals are likely to encounter a severe weakening thereof, which may compel them to go into defaults. The risk is reflected in a higher yield spread on their bonds.

global economic conditions deteriorate. External economic and political conditions may also exert varying degrees of influence on a sovereign's decision to default, depending on how dependent their economies are to external trade, global economic confidence, health and natural disasters (such as, for instance, the SAR and H2N1 worldwide epidemics or the Asian Tsunami).[11] Other external conditions of relevance to the ability of sovereigns to settle their external debt obligations include restricted or very costly access to international bond and loan financing brought about by weak domestic conditions arising from social and political instabilities or, simply, dismal debt servicing histories. The 1997 Asian Financial Crisis and the 2008 Global Financial Crisis brought to the fore the effects of fiscal contagion and the huge problems that these can cause to debtor nations already saddled with severe debt problems.

3.   THE EMU SOVEREIGN DEFAULT CRISIS AND THE PARTICULAR CASE OF GREECE

While some economies were, at the time of writing, in the process of preparing their economic stimulus package exit strategies, some others were beginning to suffer under the effects of their oversize budget deficits and their unsustainable public debts. The three most prominent examples were those of Iceland, Dubai and Greece. Of those three, Iceland's economy was a victim to the domestic effects of the global financial crisis, delivered through an overly-leveraged banking system;[12] Dubai fell victim to its excessive recourse to foreign loans to fund the global investments of its main sovereign wealth fund corporation and the untenable bubbling of its property sector;[13] while the case of Greece, a Member State participating in the EMU, was the most noteworthy, less because of the country's fundamentals and more so on account of its EMU participation. As such, the case of Greece deserves special attention.

To qualify for EMU participation, Greece had to satisfy stringent economic convergence criteria. Given its successful accession to the Third Stage of EMU, the general perception of Greece (as well as of all other EMU-participating Member States) was that its economy was sound and well-managed, implying little risk for lenders. This perception was to be proven wrong in late 2009 and early 2010, when it transpired that

---

[11]   See Porzecanski, A. (2004).
[12]   See Boyes, R. (2009); and Jonsson, A. (2009).
[13]   See Gross, D. (2009); and Mortished, C. (2009).

Greece had masked its high external debt to gain entry to the EMU. Modern financial engineering was, *inter alia*, used to make that possible. This included a 2001 deal with a Wall Street investment bank, consisting in the use of an off-balance-sheet type device to 'hide' some of Greece's debts ahead of its accession to the EMU.[14] Specifically, currency swaps, a type of over-the-counter (OTC) derivative contract under the terms of which parties agree to exchange long-term streams of interest payments in different currencies, were made use of. The usual reason for resorting to currency swaps is in order to address the threat of currency fluctuations. Arguably, these swaps operate as loans, with the two parties to a contract agreeing to an exchange of cash up front, with one of the two parties undertaking to make higher payouts in the future. Hence, when accounted for otherwise than as loans in the national government accounts, currency swaps can (and did, in the case of Greece) facilitate the reporting of reduced debt levels.[15]

Whilst Greece was, at the time of writing, at the centre of the European sovereign default crisis, it is not alone in the EU with severe budgetary and current account deficits. Other EMU Member States, including Portugal, Italy, Ireland and Spain (jointly coined, alongside Greece, as 'PIIGS'), have also been struggling to deal with acute budget deficit threats. At the time of writing, there were fears of a contagion effect,[16] with certain other economies, including Spain (with a budget deficit of 11.2 per cent of GDP), Portugal (with a budget deficit of 9.4 per cent of GDP) and Ireland (with a budget deficit of 14.3 per cent of GDP) also facing budgetary pressures, reflected in a ballooning of their bond yields and credit default swaps (CDS) spreads. These phenomena were not entirely surprising, given the EU Commission's massive difficulties in enforcing the Maastricht Stability and Growth Pact criteria and the Excessive Deficit Procedure (EDP). This was exemplified by its 2003–2004 dispute with the European Council, culminating in the July 2004 decision of the European Court of Justice, as it then was, in case C-27/04, to annul the Council

---

[14] See Story, L., Thomas, L., Jr, Schwartz, N.D. (2010); Blodget, H. (2010); Salmon, F. (2010a). It is argued here that the 'fee' associated with the Greek derivatives was, in reality, not a fee but, rather, payments to cover all of the credit and market risks that Goldman Sachs was assuming in lending money to Greece.

[15] WSJ (2010); and Fleming, S. (2010). Greece was unable to join the EMU in 1999, due to its vast deficits, but succeeded in 2001. The Greek deficit at the time stood at some 13 per cent of GDP and public debt at 113 per cent of GDP in comparison with the criteria of 3 per cent and 60 per cent, respectively. It seems that other Mediterranean economies, have resorted to similar currency trade arrangements with investment banks as Greece.

[16] Randow, J. & Thesing, G. (2010).

Conclusions of 25 November 2003 through which the Council suspended, effectively, the taking up of an EDP against France and Germany.[17] One feature that the troubled EMU Member States shared in common was the narrow spreads between the interest premium on their debt refinancing borrowing and the one paid by Germany on its debt. Even though compliance by these economies with the Maastricht criteria was suspect, their borrowing costs kept reducing, so much so that, by 2002, they were almost equal to those of Germany. Years of unmitigated credit binging were to follow, suggesting that one of the reasons why these economies failed to get their fiscal priorities in order was because issuing debt became a lot cheaper *after* their adoption of the single currency than it had been *before* it. Increased borrowing was to come at the back of accumulated budget deficits and national debts, which compared adversely, even with those of Latin American economies, some of which had previously defaulted on their sovereign debts. With investors becoming more sensitive to national macroeconomic indicators on account of the financial crisis and with news that Greece's deficit figures were considerably higher to those officially acknowledged, spreads on Greek and other EMU Member States began to widen. Concerted European efforts to calm market fears took long to materialize and, when they did, it is only very gradually that they began to generate the desired effects, *inter alia* because of doubts as to Greece's ability to implement the austerity plans it has committed to[18] without its fiscal deficit reduction efforts dragging it into a deep recession. It is worth nothing that, while austerity measures similar to those taken in Greece did work in the UK in the 1980s, they had been accompanied by sharp falls in short-term interest rates and, more importantly, by currency depreciation, none of which are possible in the case of EMU-participating Member States. The combination of sluggish growth, a budget deficit of over 10 per cent of GDP, a public-debt-to-GDP ratio of more than 100 per cent and high bond yields appeared difficult to sustain in the long run, dampening any hopes of Greece's speedy recovery from the crisis.[19]

The Greek sovereign default crisis is symptomatic of graver concerns, both about the way in which financial markets operate and about the future of the EMU. The incredible speed at which bouts of irrational euphoria alternate with spells of unwarranted introspection (amplifying movements in asset prices that are often unrelated to market fundamentals) not only points to the conclusion that financial markets are irrational

---

[17]   Chaar, S. & Odier, L. (2010).

[18]   Papic, M. & Zeihan, P. (2010).

[19]   *The Economist* (2010(b)).

and not alert to genuine risks[20] but, also, suggests that some speculative forces may be at work. Rating agencies are also deemed to have played a destabilizing role as they failed to predict the 2008 banking sector credit crisis, only to systematically overreact thereafter to fears of a sovereign debt crisis, aggravating what was an already difficult situation.[21] The rating agencies' failings in the run up to the sovereign default stage of the global financial crisis is likely to have led them to target Greece, which, on account of its severe budgetary problems, was to become the poster image of sovereign debt crisis for the peripheral EMU economies. Finally, the impact on the crisis of the hesitations and ambiguities of some of the EMU Member State governments and the EU institutions should not be disregarded.[22] Their failure to provide clear signals of their commitment to assist Greece, on account of their deep disagreements as to what the appropriate remedy to its budgetary difficulties should be, have no doubt added to the structural problems besetting the EMU, that call for urgent structural adjustment responses rather than for any kind of *ad hoc* short-term response addressing merely the immediate liquidity problems faced by some Member States, as urgent and important as those may be, instead of dealing with their root causes. The deeper causes for the high budget and fiscal deficits of some of the Member States, as well as the adverse consequences of continuing sluggish growth in the Euro zone, require careful analysis to enable the formulation of the right mix of financial and fiscal policy measures within a single currency economic zone such as the EMU. Ultimately, the sustainability of the euro needs to be ensured, by giving it the institutional support to make it work. Seen from this perspective, the ongoing crisis is as much about a loss of confidence in the sustainability of

---

[20]   Grauwe, P. D. (2010); Bernoth, K. & Wolff, G. B. (2008). The latter study suggests that creative accounting increases spreads, especially where financial markets are unsure about the actual extent of creative accounting. Also see Becker, S. (2009). The CDS market-implied probabilities particularly appear high suggesting other factors (counterparty risks, speculation, cross-hedging) other than default risks also influence pricing in these markets. The sharp sovereign CDS widening is also further attributed to the implicit transformation of bank risk into sovereign risk as a consequence of state guarantees on bank liabilities.

[21]   Grauwe, *supra*, fn. 20; Carneiro, P. E. (2009) (who argues that rating agencies appear to lose their focus at times of crisis, committing more errors immediately prior to and after the onset of a financial crisis); and Tozer-Pennington, V. (2010). The rapid downgrade of Greece prompted Michael Barnier, the European Internal Market Commissioner, to call for an investigation into CRA practices. Prior to this, the EU Parliament had, in April 2009, called for CRAs that wanted their ratings to be used within the EU to apply for registration and to be approved by the Committee of European Securities Regulators.

[22]   Grauwe, *supra*, fn. 20.

the single currency as it is about concerns over the solvency of individual Member States.

Whether or not certain private funds contributed, through their activities, to exacerbating the sovereign default crisis within the EMU is an issue that will be addressed in the following section.

4.   THE ROLE OF VULTURE FUNDS

The European sovereign default crisis has been partly blamed on the workings of certain private funds, which have allegedly indulged in speculative securities-trading to unsettle sovereign debt markets, raising borrowing costs unjustifiably and weakening, in the process, the single currency. The accusations leveled against so-called 'vulture hedge funds' and other distressed-debt investors for aggravating, through their activities, the predicament of debtor nations are worthy of closer scrutiny.

Vulture funds (mostly private equity or hedge funds) are those that invest in debt issued by sovereign nations or distressed businesses beset by weak economic fundamentals. Vulture funds seek to profit by purchasing distressed debt at substantial discounts to its face value and they are often said to be rejecting, on a systematic basis, international debt restructuring programmes through legal action (so called 'holdout litigation') for the full settlement of sovereign debt.[23] The notion of profiting from the misfortunes of troubled economies is, not surprisingly, generally condemned, explaining the bad publicity that these types of funds have attracted in recent years.[24] Other than short-selling bonds in the cash

---

[23]   Africa Action Campaign Resources (2008); Goldman, S. E. (2000); Nolan, J. (2001). Vulture funds are said to be free-riders by not agreeing to restructure their debt while other creditors and the debtor share respectively the burden of debt restructuring, including debt forgiveness, 'haircuts', or longer maturities (for the former) and fiscal tightening and economic austerity (for the latter). The success of vulture funds in getting preferential treatment over other creditors would reduce the amount of payments to the latter and inject a sense of unfairness among those creditors that accept the restructuring terms.

[24]   BBC World Service (2010). The Debt Relief (Developing Countries) Act bans vulture funds from acquiring emerging economies' debt at a discount, only to sue for full recovery in UK courts from aid assistance funds provided by rich nations or other multilateral aid agencies. Also see Berensmann, K. & Schroder, F. (2006). The Ecuador case shows how coercing dissenting creditors into the restructuring process by imposing negative amendments on the old bonds can effectively undermine the potential of free-riding by vulture hedge funds even in the absence of collective action clauses (CACs).

market, speculative funds are thought to have acquired CDS contracts in order to profit from falling sovereign bond prices resulting from increasing sovereign default risks. CDS spreads widened, as a result, and, as this trend accelerated, speculators sold their CDS contracts for a profit. More generally, concerns were expressed already before the outbreak of the sovereign default stage of the global financial crisis that vulture funds invested in sovereign debt with the intention of litigating for full recovery. In Ecuador's 2000 debt exchange, bondholders were provided with securities worth 70 cents on the dollar; however, vulture funds, which bought Peru's Brady bonds at 25 cents on the dollar, achieved hefty gains *without* resorting to legal action. On the other hand, in the more widely publicized case of *Elliot Associates L.P. v the Republic of Peru and the National Bank of Peru*, a New York-based vulture fund, which paid US$11.4 million for US$20.7 million par-value bonds, and which did not participate in the Brady bond exchange offered by Peru, started litigation in the US for the recovery of its debt in full, invoking the *pari passu* clause contained in the new loan agreements. Faced with the prospect of defaulting on its new loan agreements, Peru settled the claim with a US$58.45 million pay-out, resulting in a profit of more than 400 per cent for Elliot. The interpretation and application of the *pari passu* clause favoured in this case (i.e. that no payments could be effected to any creditors unless all creditors are paid out on a pro rata basis) has, not surprisingly, attracted a good deal of controversy.[25]

Controversy surrounds the role played by vulture funds in generating or aggravating the sovereign default crisis faced by some of the EMU-participating Member States. Greece, supported by certain other Member States, has claimed that investor manipulation of CDS has not only led the country to the brink of financial ruin but, also, damaged the credibility of the single currency. European leaders have called upon the US to join a crackdown on speculative funds, which, while reacting sympathetically, have in turn advised troubled sovereigns to focus on getting their economy back on track and lower their debts rather than blame these on their activities.[26] There is little evidence available to back the contention that hedge fund activities, whether in the sovereign CDS markets or elsewhere, have either brought about or exacerbated the Greek debt crisis, causing Greece to pay significantly more on its debt than other economies with similar economic fundamentals. The market for Greek sovereign CDS is quite small, with third country hedge funds or

---

[25]   Scott, H. & Jackson, H. (2002).
[26]   McKenna, B. (2010).

other speculative funds only holding a small slice thereof. Vulture funds are, therefore, unlikely to have been apt to cause the instability that has plagued the EMU since late December 2009. Moreover, it remains the case that vulture fund investors provide financial markets with urgently needed liquidity, which other bondholders are unwilling to provide, especially when it comes to riskier bonds from emerging economies, enabling economies to gain access to international capital markets at more affordable prices so as to help fund their development needs. At the same time, for all their negative publicity, 'holdout litigations' can serve to limit collusive behavior among majority creditors, acting against the interests of minority creditors, while at the same time discouraging opportunistic sovereign defaults or protracted delays against the completion of restructuring processes. Furthermore, it is arguable that where vulture funds acquire significant level of claims, the administrative burden associated with restructuring sovereign debt is reduced, as a result of a reduction in communication and negotiation costs.[27] In addition, it is arguable that the sharp increase in spreads, in the first and second quarters of 2010, was more a consequence of the transformation of banking sector risk into sovereign risk rather than the result of speculative activities (in the form of the massive sale of CDS contracts held by vulture funds). This transformation of risk is reflected in the large-scale fiscal outlays and in the sizeable guarantees on bank liabilities financed with tax payers' money in Europe, the US and elsewhere in the world. Hence, it could plausibly be argued that, if sovereign spreads within the EMU have risen so sharply, it is mainly because markets have commenced to be concerned about the fiscal fallout of the global financial crisis rather than because of speculation. It is no surprise that the increase in sovereign bond and CDS spreads has been sharper in Member States with high public debt-to-GDP ratios, large current account deficits and declining international cost competitiveness.

Finally, it is worth recalling how the Brady Plan itself altered the dynamics of the debt restructuring process. The Plan was formulated

---

[27]   Fisch, J. E. & Gentile, C. M. (2004); Miller, M. & Thomas, D. (2006) (who argue that the argument that holdout litigation is part of the solution, rather than of the problem of sovereign debt restructuring, is applicable only in the period of transition to CACs); Salmon, F. (2007); and Bratton, W.W. (2004). The broad interpretation in the *Elliot* case of the clause was criticised on the grounds that the past actions of market participants never intended the clause to require rateable payments to creditors. Those in favour of the narrow interpretation contend that the objective of this provision is to prevent any informal arrangements for a debtor nation's assets or revenues to service particular debts.

by former US Secretary of the Treasury Nicholas Brady to address debt crises in the emerging economies during the 1980s. It offered banks credit enhancements for their agreements to reduce claims on sovereign debtors agreeing to carry out substantial austerity reforms. Such credit enhancements were achieved through the conversion of existing commercial bank loans into bonds and then collateralizing the obligations on these bonds with US Treasury zeroes acquired through the proceeds of IMF and World Bank loans. The emergence of Brady bonds in the 1980s provided unprecedented investment opportunities for vulture funds, in the form of the trading of sovereign bonds in the secondary market. By facilitating the securitization of sovereign debts and broadening the base of investors, the Plan gave rise to more investment opportunities, *inter alia* for vulture hedge funds. It follows that, to the extent that speculation is to blame for the woes of some of the EMU Member States, the roots of the problem may not lie as much in the activities of speculative funds as in the decisions that made those activities possible in the first place.

Against the background of so unprecedented a financial crisis as the one that was unfolding at the time of writing, it is, perhaps, not surprising that concerns should have been expressed that the single currency may come under strain from vulture funds willing to launch concerted attacks against the EMU[28] or that an entire market should have developed bets on whether certain EMU Member States will, eventually, default on their debts.[29] However, it is telling that ECB President Trichet has denied that an Anglo-Saxon conspiracy was to blame for the fall in the value of the euro, attributing, instead, the current market uncertainties to the difficulties of international investors in understanding Europe and its decision-making mechanisms.[30] Earlier allegations by several European political leaders of speculative practices by hedge funds and other market participants should not detract from the urgent need for ailing economies to come to terms with the hard but necessary truth that, if speculators were able to profit from the woes of some of the EMU-participating Member States, this was more because of the deep structural weaknesses in those Member States' economies than it was because of their speculative trading tactics. Those economies urgently need to undertake serious structural

---

[28]   Bresser-Pereira, L. C. (2010).
[29]   Hartcher, P. (2010). Feldman is reported here as one of the principal names behind London's *Markit Group*, which in September 2009, launched the iTraxx-SovX Western Europe Index. By February 2010, investors bought US$85 billion worth of insurance against the risk of Greek bankruptcy. Also see Salmon, F. (2010b).
[30]   Goldstein, S. (2010).

adjustments, to ensure that third parties, with no insurable interest in their economic fortunes, cannot profit from their misfortunes.

At the same time, it is only natural that vulture funds should have come under even closer scrutiny by financial regulators, because of the Greek crisis. Moreover, Member State authorities were said to be looking into the market activities and practices of global investment banks, which paddle sophisticated derivative financial instruments to the public sector. Indeed, there is nothing to stop them from extending their scrutiny to the investment practices of hedge funds, private equity funds and investment banks, especially those said to be engaging in speculative currency trading or vulture-fund-type litigation tactics,[31] not least because it cannot be excluded that some of them may have exploited the crisis to conduct strategic acquisitions of distressed sovereign debt at very low prices. Considering the all-round condemnations that some of their perceived practices have earned them, it might be strategically wiser for hedge funds and private equity funds, in particular, to combine their profit maximization objectives with national and business sustainability societal goals if they are to escape even closer scrutiny and even more regulation as a backlash of the financial crisis. Besides, the 750 billion euro rescue package through which the Member States have declared war on markets betting against any of their peers, and the swift and decisive response from the combined resources of all 16 EMU-participating Members States should put financial speculators on enquiry if they are not to see their strategies backfire or their activities subjected to regulatory constraints.

The impact of the global and EU financial crisis on the alternative investment fund industry's pan-European regulation is briefly examined in the following section.

5. THE FINANCIAL CRISIS AND THE REGULATION OF ALTERNATIVE INVESTMENT FUNDS

The global and EU financial crises have encouraged an acceleration in the pace of the European onshore alternative investment fund industry's regulation.[32] Unlike in 2005, when Germany's initiatives to regulate onshore

---

[31]   Besides, not very long ago, albeit in a somewhat different context, a senior German cabinet member had likened hedge funds, in particular, to 'locusts' or 'parasites' which feed on the sufferings of others.

[32]   For an account of the state of play, in mid-2009, with regard to the European regulation of hedge funds, see Athanassiou, P. (2009).

hedge funds and other unregulated or lightly regulated alternative investment funds were to lead to no concrete results, both on account of the overall market circumstances and on account of the opposition of certain Member States (including the UK), this time around the Commission and the Council took on a more pro-regulatory stance vis-à-vis alternative investment fund managers (AIFM). The driving forces in the reshaping of EU AIFM regulation were, once again, a group of Member States led by Germany and France, with the backing of the European Parliament. Their initiatives were, in part, motivated by domestic political economy interests and, in part, by the perceived debunking of the Anglo-Saxon model of financial services that had informed large parts of the EU financial market rules prior to the onset of the financial crisis. With London's hitherto influential position having been weakened in the aftermath of the financial crisis (which, *inter alia*, saw the collapse of *Northern Rock*), but also because of various other financial and political difficulties at home, an alternative regulatory paradigm was to emerge from the crisis that shifted the balance of regulatory power towards the EU Member States of Continental Europe.[33] While the urge to regulate AIFM was not linked to any specific concerns with the impact of their activities on sovereign debtors (as the publication of the Commission's AIFM proposal preceded, by several months, the sovereign default stage of the global financial crisis), the transparency requirements built into the draft AIFM Directive were unlikely not to have had an impact on those of the private funds' speculative activities that could also target sovereign debtors. The sovereign default stage of the financial crisis has in all likelihood added urgency to the need to complete the work conducted on the draft AIFM Directive, which was finally adopted in November 2010, after several months of intensive negotiations and lobbying.

Even prior to the adoption of the AIFM Directive, several Member States had adopted measures to restrict the potential for financial market speculation. Germany's financial regulator, the BaFin, prohibited naked sales[34] of debt securities of euro zone countries admitted to trading on domestic regulated markets as well as CDS in which the reference liability is at least also a liability of a euro zone country and is not employed to

---

[33] See Quaglia, L. (2009).

[34] In ordinary short-selling, investors sell (or 'short') borrowed shares or securities in a bet that their price will retreat, and when it does, they buy them back at lower prices, profiting from the difference. In contrast, in naked short-selling, investors never hold the stocks but promise to deliver in the hope that the prices will drop to enable them to realize the difference between the agreed price and the (by now) lower market price.

hedge default risks (a 'naked CDS'). These prohibitions, effective from 19 May 2010, were to be subject to review on an ongoing basis. BaFin justified its actions as a response to the extraordinary volatility of debt securities of various EMU Member States, as well as to the considerable widening in the spreads of CDSs on the credit default risks of several Member States. BaFin was of the opinion that massive short selling of the debt securities involved and the conclusion of uncovered CDS on credit default risks of EMU Member States were resulting in excessive price movements posing severe threats to financial markets and seriously undermining financial stability in the EMU.[35] BaFin has since extended the ban on naked short-selling to certain quoted financial services stocks with a primary listing in Germany, with the banned transactions covering all methods of betting against companies, bonds or currencies without an underlying economic interest in the security.[36] Austria also extended, on 25 May 2010, its temporary prohibition on naked short-selling in the cash market of the shares of its leading financial institutions (subject to an exemption in the case of the positions taken by market makers or specialists).[37] The Spanish Securities Market Commission also agreed to adapt its rules on short positions to those proposed by the CESR in March 2010, inclusive of the technical details as published on 26 May 2010.[38]

It remains to be seen whether measures such as the above will curb excessive financial markets speculation. To complement their effects, some lessons could usefully be drawn from the US. There, states are prohibited from borrowing for operating expenses, such as salaries, services and transfer payments, and debts are issued primarily to finance infrastructures and related capital expenditures. Such rules over time help to make bonds issued for capital expenditure attractive to investors. The adoption of similar rules by the EMU-participating Member States could help make interest rates on sovereign bonds more manageable. The ECB could help to shape and expedite this process by restricting collateral to bonds issued by EMU Member States with satisfactory constitutional limits on their borrowing. Hence, a powerful (if discretionary) restriction could be set on fiscal deficits through a combination of the Member States self-interest in wanting to pay lower interest rates on their debts and an ECB rule on restricting collateral to bonds issued by sovereign issuers with satisfactory limits on their deficits. This would not necessitate any changes to the

---

[35]   BaFin (2010), 19 May.
[36]   Ewing, J. (2010), 25 May.
[37]   Eu Business (2010), 25 May.
[38]   Uria Menendez Newsletter (2010).

Treaty and would leave the Member States free to decide on the structure and levels of their taxes and expenditures for as long as these do not breach their constitutional limits.[39]

6.   CONCLUDING REMARKS

Speculative funds are likely to continue being the focus of attention within the EU, for as long as the sovereign default crisis persists. Attributing the blame for Greece's structural spending problems to foreign speculators operating in the CDS markets could even divert attention from the urgent need for some Member States to take the remedial measures necessary to ensure that similar crises do not occur in the future.

The banking sector's liquidity crisis has resulted in stimulus measures of an unprecedented scale, financed through tax payers' money. This, in turn, has converted the private sector's debt concerns into sovereign governments' concerns. Sovereigns already faced with high fiscal deficits and external debt challenges have come under pressure from the global financial markets. Unlike previous challenges involving emerging economies, the sovereign debt crisis has hit advanced economies through the globalization of financial markets and the contagion effects that this facilitates. For as long as sovereigns are not subject to any kind of formal bankruptcy regime and governments are unwilling to waive their sovereignty, sovereign debt crises and their resolution will continue requiring informal, cooperative global regimes. Reforms are, no doubt, necessary and the ongoing, global financial crisis presents not only an unprecedented challenge but, also, an opportunity for those reforms to be introduced, not least because those affected by it include some of the world's more advanced economies.

The Greek crisis has unveiled key weaknesses in the EMU and in European economic governance. The relative laxity over the policing of fiscal rules has enabled the PIIGS economies, in particular, to engage in excessive public spending, financed through their preferential access to international capital as a result of their EMU participation. Some governments have, in the process, aggravated the state of their public finances, adding to their external debts and budgetary deficits. The current EMU crisis is not just about specific countries: it rather is about deeper, EMU-wide economic, fiscal, structural and institutional problems and, ultimately, about the sensitive issue of a common European identity and,

---

[39]   Feldstein, M. (2010), 18 May.

ultimately, about what that entails at times of crisis, when there are difficult economic choices to be made. The unfolding of events in the first half
of 2010, with an emphasis on the vital initial stages of the sovereign default
stage of the financial crisis, and the disunity shown after its outbreak
suggest that there is an urgent need for greater efforts in terms of political
and economic cohesion if the EMU and the EU are to remain viable and
that serious efforts are necessary to address the inherent structural problems of the EMU. These are, in many respects, the result of an imbalance
between the full centralization of monetary policy and the maintenance,
at the level of the Member States, of virtually all instruments of economic
policy, including budgetary policies, wage policies, employment policies
etc. They are also attributable, in part, to the fact that, because the EMU
is not embedded in a political union, national imbalances can cause creeping divergences between Member States that no mechanism is available
to alleviate. What this lack of political and economic integration entails
is that when a crisis erupts, this is hard to resolve. As political unifica-
tion is unlikely to be feasible in the immediate future, smaller focused
steps towards that objective could instead be undertaken. The current
discussion for a European Monetary Fund (EMF)[40] could be such a step.
Another suggestion might be to issue common Euro government bonds,
with each of the Member States participating pro rata of their capital
share in the ECB.[41] To avoid moral hazard concerns, the interest rate that
each Member State would pay could be determined by the interest rates
that each of these Member States pay when they issue bonds in their own
markets. Attention should ultimately be paid to the conditions required
for the proper functioning of a currency union, which has no common
budget to compensate for asymmetric shocks. The top priority must be to
design and strengthen mechanisms targeted at preventing pro-cyclical policies and large fiscal shocks. Second, structural reforms to boost long-run
growth prospects must be accelerated to facilitate their smooth adjustment
to shocks. Last but not least, high priority needs to be accorded to labour-
market liberalization under a reinvigorated Lisbon Agenda.[42] All of those
steps, however small, could provide signals that the EMU Member States
are committing themselves to a future intensification of the process of
political union and of their desire to preserve and strengthen the EMU.[43]

Europe's political leaders may want to rely less on rhetoric and more

---

[40]   Gros, D. & Mayer, T. (2010).
[41]   Grauwe, P. D. & Moesen, W. (2009), 3 April; and Securities Industry and
Financial markets Association (SIFMA) (2008), September.
[42]   Balcerowicz, L. (2010).
[43]   EurActiv (2010a), 15 March.

on attention to fiscal and structural adjustments to achieve more viable and sustainable solutions to the economic and fiscal problems that their economies are facing. Long-term answers to those difficulties lie more in the making of serious adjustments to structural public debt, fiscal deficits, and labour immobility problems than they do in curtailing the speculative activities of vulture funds, which do not appear to have contributed to the onset of the global financial crisis, however much some funds may have profited from it. Ultimately, vulture funds may be the wrong targets, to the extent that they have simply acted as the 'messengers' of the underlying structural economic problems besetting the EMU rather than as their root causes.[44] Parallels could be drawn to the shorting activities of hedge funds in the run up to the emergence of the serious corporate problems that plagued financial markets in previous years and which went unheeded until too late.[45] 'Shooting the messenger', instead of taking steps to address the deep-rooted difficulties that some of the EMU's participating Member States are confronted with may well be the wrong thing to do.

BIBLIOGRAPHY

Africa Action Campaign Resources (2008), 'Understanding Vulture Funds: Key Terms to Know', available at http://www.africaaction.org
Athanassiou, P. (2009), *Hedge Fund Regulation in the European Union: Current Trends and Future Prospects'*, Alphen: Kluwer International Law.
Athanassiou, P. (2010), 'The Draft AIFM Directive and the Future of European Alternative Investment Fund Regulation', CESifo Dice Report 1/2010.
Balcerowicz, L. (2010), 'A More Perfect Monetary Union', Project Syndicate, available at http://www.project-syndicate.org
BBC World Service (2010), 'Vulture Funds: UK MPs Propose Law to End Debt Relief Profiteering', 26 February, available at http://www.bbc.co.uk
BaFin (2010), 'BaFin Prohibits Naked Short-Selling Transactions and Naked CDS in Government Bonds of Euro Zone', 19 May, available at http://www.bafin.de
Becker, S. (2009), 'EMU Sovereign Spread Widening: Reasonable Market Reaction or Exaggeration?', *EU Monitor* 68, 29 June.
Berensmann, K., Schroder, F. (2006), 'A Proposal for a New International Debt Framework for the Prevention and Resolution of Debt Crisis in Middle-Income Countries', Discussion Paper 2/2006, German Development Institute, available at http://www.die-gdi/die-homepage.nsf
Bernoth, K. and G. B. Wolff (2008), 'Fool the Markets? Creative Accounting, Fiscal Transparency, and Sovereign Risk Premia', *Scottish Journal of Political Economy*, **55**(4), 465–87.
Biggadike, O. and B. Levisohn (2010), 'Euro Falls on Concern Nations Still Struggle After Loan Package', *Bloomberg Businessweek*, 11 May, available at http://www.businessweek.com

---

[44]   Oakley, D., Tett, G. & Hughes, J. (2010), 1 March.
[45]   Sauer, R. (2010); Lewis, M. (2010); Zero Hedge (2010), 12 February.

Blodget, H. (2010), 'Greece Paid Goldman $300 Million to Help Hide Its Ballooning Debts', *Business Insider*, 14 February, available at http://www.businessinsider.com

Borensztein, E. and U. Panizza (2009), 'The Costs of Sovereign Default', IMF Staff Papers, **56**(4), 683–741.

Boyes, R. (2009), *Meltdown Iceland: Lessons on the World Financial Crisis from a Small Bankrupt Island*, (New York Bloomsbury Publishing).

Bratton, W. W. (2004), 'Parri Passu and a Distressed Sovereign's Rational Choices', Emory Law Journal, **53**(823).

Bresser-Periera, L. C. (2010) 'Speculation against the Euro', IDEAS, 18 February, available at http://www.networkideas.org

Chaar, S. and L. Odier (2010), 'How Bad is Greece's Debt Problem?', *This Is Money*, 15 February, available at http://www.thisismoney.co.uk

Carneiro, P. E. (2009), 'Ten Years' Analysis of Sovereign Risk: Noise-Rater, Risk, Panels, and Errors', *The Journal of Risk Finance*, **10**(2), 107–130.

Charles River Associates (2009), 'Impact of the Proposed AIFM Directive across Europe', CRA Project NO. D14806, London, CRA, October 2009.

Chamberlain, M. (2010), 'Regulating Alternative Investment Funds: Casting the Net Too Wide', *JUBFL* **72** (1), 1–9.

EurActiv (2007), 'McCreevy Defends Decision Not To Regulate Hedge Funds', 22 February, available at http://www.euraactiv.com

EurActiv (2010a), 'EU Rejects US Claims of Hedge Funds Regulation Rift', 15 March, available at http://www.euraactiv.com

EurActiv (2010b), 'Financial markets and Eurozone System Partly to Blame for Greek Crisis', 15 March, available at http://www.euraactiv.com

EUbusiness (2010), 'Austria Extends Ban on Naked Short-Selling', 25 May, available at http://www.eubusiness.com

European Commission (2009), 'Proposal for a Directive on Alternative Investment Fund Managers, (AIFM), Brussels, COM(2009) 207 final.

Ewing, J. (2010), 'Germany Draft Wider Ban on Speculative Trades', *The New York Times*, 25 May, available at http://www.nytimes.com

Feldstein, M. (2010), 'For a Solution to the Euro Crisis, Look at the States', *The Washington Post*, 18 May, A19.

Financing for Development (2004), 'Strategic Issues in Managing Sovereign Debt for Sustained Development: An Issues Paper for Multi-Stakeholder Dialogue on Debt', Financing for Development, United Nations Department of Economics and Social Affairs Paper.

Fisch, J. E. and C. M. Gentile (2004), 'Vultures or Vanguards?; The Role of Litigation in Sovereign Debt Restructuring', Emory Law Journal, 53 (1043)

Fleming, S. (2010), 'How Goldman Helped Greece Hide Its Debt', *Daily Mail*, available at http://www.thismoney.co.uk

Frankel, M., A. Karmann & B. Scholtens (2004), *Sovereign Risk and Financial Crisis* (Berlin, Springer).

Fuller, G. (2009), *Corporate Borrowing: Law and Practice*, (Bristol: Jordans).

Goldman, S. E. (2000), 'Mavericks in the Market: The Emerging Problems of Hold-Outs in Sovereign Debt Restucturing' *UCLA Journal of International Law & Foreign Affairs*, 5 (159).

Goldstein, S. (2010), 'Trichet Denies Anglo-Saxon Attack on Euro', 31 May, available at http://www.menafn.com

Grauwe, P. D. and W. Moesen (2009), 'Gains for All: A Proposal for a Common Eurobond', CEPS Commentary, 3 April, available at http://www.ceps.eu

Grauwe, P. D. (2010), 'Crisis in the Eurozone and How to Deal With It', CEPS Policy Briefs No. 204/February 2010, available at http://www.ceps.eu

Gross, D. (2009), 'Dubai World is A Symptom of the Problem', *Financial Post*, available at http://www.financialpost.com

Gross, D. and T. Mayer (2010), 'How to deal with Sovereign Default in Europe: Towards a Euro(pean) Monetary Fund', CEPS Policy Brief No.202/February 2010.

Harris, J. (2010), 'AIFM Texts Adopted by EU Parliament and Council', *Hedge Fund Review*, 18 May, available at http://www.hedgefundreview.com

Hartcher, P. (2010), 'Crunch Time for Well-Fed Cockcroach of the World Financial System', *WAtoday*, 20 April, available at http://www.watoday.co.au

Herman, B. (2004), 'Dealing with Sovereign Debt Difficulties', Initiative for Policy Dialogue (IPD) Working Paper Series, Columbia University.

Hilscher, J. and I. Nosbusch (2008), 'Determinants of Sovereign Risk: Macroeconomic Fundamentals and the Pricing of Sovereign Debt', Brandeis University Working Paper.

Jonsson, A. (2009) *Why Iceland: How One of the World's Smallest Countries Became the Meltdown's Biggest Casualty,* (New York: McGrawhill).

Kiel Institute (2010), 'Dennis Snower Criticises European Monetray Fund Proposal', Kiel Institute for World Economy, 15 March, available at http://www.ifw-kiel.de

Lehne Report (2008), available at http://www.theglobalmail.com

Lewis, M. (2010) *The Big Short: Inside the Doomsday Machine*, (New York: W. W. Norton and Company).

Lhabitant, F-S (2010), 'Commentary-The AIFM Directive, another European Storm?', Risk Center, 15 March, available at http://www.riskcenter.com

McKenna, B. (2010), 'White House Resists Greek Pressure for Crackdown on Speculators', *Globe and Mail*, 14 April, available at http://www.theglobalmail.com

Miller, M. and Thomas, D. (2006), 'Sovereign Debt Restructuring: the Judge, The Vultures and Creditor Rights', Warwick Economic Research Papers No. 757, August.

Mortished, C. (2009), 'Problems for Dubai Are Only Just Beginning Over Future of Islamic Bond', *Times Online*, 26 November, available at http://www.business.timeson-line.co.uk

Nolan, J. (2001), 'Emerging Market Debt & Vulture Hedge Funds: Free-Ridership, Legal and Market Remedies', Financial Policy Forum, Derivatives Study Center, Special Policy Report 3, 29 September.

Oakley, D., Tett, G. and J. Hughes (2010), 'Sovereign CDS Become Europe's New Bogeyman', *Financial Times*, 1 March, available at http://www.ft.com

Olivares-Caminal, R. (2008), 'Sovereign Bonds: A Critical Analysis of Argentina's Debt Exchange Offer', *Journal of Banking Regulation*, **10**(1), 28–45.

Open Europe (2010), 'AIFM Directive Would Jeopardise Billions in Tax Revenues and Development Funding', 17 May, available at http://www.openeurope.org.uk

Ozler, S. (1993) 'Have Commercial Banks Ignored History', *American Economic Review*, **83**, 608–620.

Papic, M. and P. Zeihan (2010), 'Germany's Choice', Stratfor, 8 February, available at http://www.stratfor.com

Porzecanski, A. (2004), 'Dealing with Sovereign Debt: Trends and Implications, in Chris, J. and P. Fraser (eds), *Sovereign Debt at the Crossroads* (Oxford, OUP).

Quaglia, L. (2009), 'The *Old* and *New* Political Economy of Hedge Funds Regulation in the EU', Paper Presented at the UACES Conference in Angers, September.

Randow, J. and G. Thesing (2010), 'ECB's Weber Sees Threat of Grave Contagion Effects', *Bloomberg*, available at http://www.bloomberg.com

Rasmussen Report (2008), available at http://www.europarl.europa.eu

Reinhart, C., K. Rogoff and M. Savastano (2003), 'Debt Intolerance', NBER Working Papers No. 9908.

Salmon, F. (2007), 'In Defense of Vulture Funds', 14 February, available at http://www.felixsalmon.com/000667.html

Salmon, F. (2010a), 'The Greek Derivatives Aren't Goldman's Fault', 16 February, available at http://blogs.reuters.com/felix-salmon/2010/02/16/the-greek-derivatives-arent-goldmans-fault

Salmon, F. (2010b), 'Eurozone Crisis: The Bigger Picture', 3 March, available at http://blogs.reuters.com/delix-salmon/2010/03/03/eurozone-crises-the-bigger-picture

Sauer, R. (2010) *Selling America Short: The SEC and Market Contrarians in the Age of Absurdity,* (New Jersey: John Wiley & Sons, Inc).

Scott, H. and H. Jackson (2002), 'Sovereign Debt Restructuring: Should We Be Worried About Elliott?', International Finance Seminar, Harvard Law School, May.

Securities Industry and Financial Markets Association (2008), 'A Common European Government Bond' SIFMA Discussion Paper, September.

Sheng, A. (2009), *From Asian to Global Financial Crisis: An Asian Regulator's View of Unfettered Finance in the 1990s and 2000s,* (New York: Cambridge University Press).

Smith Barney, S. (2000) 'A Primer on Brady Bonds' 9 March, available at http://www.people. hbs.edu/besty/. . ./SSBper cent 20Brady20per cent 20Primer.pdf

Story, L. L. Thomas Jr. and N. D. Schwartz (2010), 'Wall St. Helped to mask Debt Fueling Europe's Crisis', *The New York Times*, 14 February, available at http://www.nytimes.com

The Economist (2010a), 'Europe: The Sad End of the Party; The Greek Crisis', 8 May, p. 51.

The Economist (2010b), 'Greek Chorus of Boos', 8 May, p. 75.

The Luxembourg Bankers' Association (2010), 'Council to Negotiate with Parliament on Draft EU Rules for Hedge Fund Managers', 19 May, available at http://www.abbl.lu

Tozer-Pennington, V. (2010), 'Rating Agencies Under Scrutiny Once More', Operational Risk & Regulation, 06 May, available at http://www.risk.net

Trebesch, C. (2009), 'The Cost of Aggressive Sovereign Debt Policies: How Much is the Private Sector Affected', IMF Working Paper, February.

Uria Menendez Newsletter (2010), 'Capital Markets', June 2010, available at http://www. uria.com

Waterfield, B. (2010), 'EU Bailout Is Built On a Lie', 9 May, available at http://blogs.euroo-bserver.com/waterfield/2010/05/09/eu-bailout-is-buils-on-a-lie

WSJ (2010), 'Goldman and Greece: What the Heck are Currency Swaps?', 17 February, available at http://blogs.wsj.com/marketbeat/2010/02/17/goldman-and-greece-what-the-heck-are-currency-swaps

Zero Hedge (2010), 'Just How Ugly is the Sovereign Debt Truth? How Self Delusions Prevent Recognition of Reality', 12 February, available at http://www.goldseek.com

PART D

COMPARATIVE PERSPECTIVES AND FUTURE PROSPECTS

14. US regulation of investment advisers and private investment funds – a concise overview

Nathan Greene[†] and John Adams[*]

INTRODUCTION

On 31 July 2010, President Obama enacted the single largest financial regulatory reform in the US since those of the Depression-era, in the 1930s and early 1940s. Considering the breadth of its scope, few, if any, financial market participants will not be affected in some way by the Dodd-Frank Wall Street Reform and Consumer Protection Act of 2010 (the 'Dodd-Frank Act' or the 'Act'). While there is little in the way of additional regulation placed directly on private funds themselves, the Act increases the scope of the US Investment Advisers Act of 1940, as amended (the 'Advisers Act'), by eliminating or tightening certain of its exemptions. These changes, which were clearly targeted at investment advisers to private funds, impose a universal registration of all larger hedge fund and private equity fund managers, at least those based in the United States (US).

The Dodd-Frank Act also regulates the private investment fund industry in other ways. Notably:

- Derivatives, and especially over-the-counter (OTC) swap contracts, will be significantly more regulated and major users of swaps, including many private funds, will likewise be more regulated.
- The 'Volcker Rule' will limit the role that banks can play in sponsoring, managing or investing in hedge funds and private equity funds.
- There will be new systemic risk-related reporting by hedge funds and private equity funds.
- There is the potential, if still rather unlikely, that private funds or private fund managers could be regulated as systemically significant financial institutions.

[†]   Partner, Shearman & Sterling LLP, US.
[*]   Associate, Shearman & Sterling LLP, US.

As the Dodd-Frank Act cannot be seen in isolation, this chapter will first summarize the existing legal framework applicable in the US to the regulation of investment advisers and then turns to analyse in some detail key aspects of the Dodd-Frank Act and its implementing regulations adopted or proposed by various US regulators.

1.   AN INTRODUCTION TO THE ADVISERS ACT

1.1   Who Registers?

Any investment adviser doing business in the US or dealing with US persons as clients is required (unless an exemption applies) to register with the US Securities and Exchange Commission ('SEC') under the Advisers Act. An 'investment adviser' is, in pertinent part:

> . . . any person who, for compensation, engages in the business of advising others, either directly or through publications or writings, as to the value of securities or as to the advisability of investing in, purchasing, or selling securities, or who, for compensation and as part of a regular business, issues or promulgates analyses or reports concerning securities.[1]

As discussed below, the primary exemption that investment advisers to private funds historically relied upon to avoid registration with the SEC is the so-called '14-or-fewer clients' or 'private adviser' exemption. This provision was especially attractive in that a fund typically counted as a single client, so that a fund manager could operate a business servicing 14 investment funds, each with, potentially, hundreds of investors, while still avoiding SEC registration – so long as the manager also limited its profile to non-public marketing. That exemption was repealed by the Dodd-Frank Act.

1.2   The Registration Application: Form ADV

To register with the SEC, an investment adviser must file a Form ADV registration application together with a nominal fee. The SEC is required to approve or reject the application within 45 days.[2]

---

[1]   Section 202(a)(11) of the Investment Advisers Act of 1940 (15 U.S.C. § 80b-2(a)(11)). Unlike in many other jurisdictions (including in the European Union), the Advisers Act definition of 'investment advisers' makes no distinction between advisers with no discretionary management authority and discretionary investment managers: all are 'investment advisers.'

[2]   This time-frame can be favourably compared with registration applications in

Form ADV comprises two parts: what amounts to mainly a 'check-the-box' Part 1 and a narrative Part 2 that has the character of a disclosure brochure about the firm's business. The whole of Part 1 and most of Part 2 is filed electronically and becomes publicly available at www.adviserinfo. sec.gov. The remainder of Part 2, which takes the form of a supplement detailing certain information about the firm's principals, is not required to be filed or made public, but does need to be provided to each of the adviser's clients at or before the time that services are first provided.

1.3   Once Registered

Upon becoming registered as an investment adviser with the SEC, a firm becomes subject to the Act's various requirements, including those relating to: (i) advisory contracts and advisory fees, with limits on performance fees charged to non-eligible clients and fund investors, (ii) fiduciary duties and standards of care to clients, (iii) disclosures to clients and regulators, (iv) custody and possession of client assets, (v) recordkeeping, (vi) advertising, use of placement agents and other sales practices, (vii) trading and investment practices, (viii) supervision, compliance, and code of ethics practices, policies and procedures, including a requirement to have a qualified chief compliance officer; and (ix) the SEC's examinations, discipline and disqualification authority.

1.4   Regulatory Examinations and Ongoing Compliance and Record-Keeping

The duties to which an SEC-registered investment adviser are subject that many consider the most burdensome are that the adviser is:

- Obligated to open the business to regulatory examinations by the SEC on demand, and
- Expected to maintain a robust compliance and record-keeping program tailored to the adviser's business.

An SEC examination can be conducted without notice (though typically provides for about ten days' prior notice) and can last from a week or two to several months. Examinations typically are conducted in person at the investment adviser's offices and typically focus on trading and sales

---

the EU. As an example, the FSA in the UK has six months to determine an application (extendable to 12 months if the FSA deems an application 'incomplete').

practices, although the SEC can extend the review to cover analysis of any books and records it chooses. As one might expect, resource constraints coupled with a 'follow the money' philosophy historically resulted in larger fund managers receiving more frequent visits than smaller managers. Non-US firms also tend to be examined much less frequently, and may be examined on what the SEC calls a 'desktop' basis (i.e., by phone and email).

A meaningful part of the examination process focuses on a firm's compliance infrastructure. When analysing a fund manager's compliance policies, the SEC will expect to see detailed written procedures and an appropriately senior and experienced individual formally designated as the chief compliance officer. The SEC also expects to see evidence that the program is in daily operation, so may ask for records of compliance tests performed, completed checklists, task calendars, etc., as well as evidence that the program is not static and responds to changes at the firm or in the broader industry. Failure to have sufficiently robust procedures is an offence in itself, regardless of whether or not other failings exist. Registered investment advisers also are subject to detailed rules relating to the types of books and records that must be maintained, the medium in which they should be maintained, and the duration for which they should be kept. The effectiveness of a firm's record-keeping inevitably will be tested by an SEC examination of the firm, as the process tends to require compilation and delivery to SEC staffers of large volumes of records in short order.

1.5   Capital Requirements

A significant philosophical divergence from regulatory regimes in the EU is that SEC-registered investment advisers are not required to meet capital requirements. However, the SEC can (although apparently it only rarely does) take into consideration an adviser's financial soundness when considering whether or not to approve an application for registration. The SEC also has access to the firm's financial books and records during an examination, so has the opportunity to ask questions at that point.

1.6   Custody

Custody over client assets is present under US law whenever a registered adviser or the adviser's 'related person'[3] holds, directly or indirectly, client

---

[3]   A 'related person' will include anyone who controls, is controlled by, or is under common control with, the adviser (Advisers Act Rule 206(4)-2(d)(7)).

funds or securities or has authority to obtain possession of them. Because of the level of control that an investment adviser tends to have over the funds it manages, an adviser often will be deemed to have custody over a fund's assets even when those assets are placed with a bank or brokerage unaffiliated with the advisory firm. Whenever an investment adviser has custody of client assets, those assets must be maintained with a 'qualified custodian' such as a bank, registered broker-dealer, or non-US financial institution that commonly segregates client assets from its own assets. The investment adviser itself – or a related person – is allowed to hold assets directly, assuming either is a 'qualified custodian' for this purpose. However, post-Madoff, a registered adviser that itself or through a related person has either direct or deemed custody must provide for a third-party annual securities count, an annual internal control report (but only for true 'self-custody' and not for deemed custody), and precise guidelines to be followed with regard to providing account statements to clients. Private funds whose accounts are audited each year are exempted from these account statement guidelines, as well as from the annual securities count, but still must use a qualified custodian.

2. DODD-FRANK AND REPEAL OF '14-OR-FEWER CLIENTS' EXEMPTION (JULY 2011 FORWARD)

With the repeal of the long-standing '14-or-fewer clients' exemption from the registration requirements of the Advisers Act, effective 21 July 2011, many presently unregistered investment advisers, both within and outside the US, will register with the SEC. Those advisers will find themselves subject to the rules and regulations of the Advisers Act, including those discussed above.

While the general theme of the Dodd-Frank Act is increased financial regulation, Congress recognized that the provisions of the Advisers Act should be applied with some flexibility across different types of investment advisers.[4] For example, those investment advisers providing advice solely to family offices are excluded from all provisions of the Advisers Act.[5]

---

[4] A similar differentiation between different types of fund managers is contemplated in the EU by the Alternative Investment Fund Managers Directive (Directive 2011/61/EU, published in the *Official Journal of the European Union* on 1 July 2011).

[5] The SEC's final rulemaking regarding the family office exclusion was published on 22 June 2011, *available at* http://www.sec.gov/rules/final/2011/ia-3220.pdf.

Additionally, the Dodd-Frank Act provides for limited exemptions for (i) certain non-US investment advisers; and (ii) what the SEC calls 'exempt reporting advisers', which covers advisers who manage *either* solely private funds subject to an assets under management ('AUM') ceiling *or* solely venture capital funds.[6] On 22 June 2011, the SEC published final rules to give shape to these exemptions.[7] As one might suspect from the name, 'exempt reporting advisers' – while exempt from full registration under the Advisers Act – will still be subject to record-keeping and reporting requirements with the SEC.

Given the expected increase in SEC-registered investment advisers resulting from the revocation of the existing 14-or-fewer clients' exemption, the Dodd-Frank Act also aims to alleviate the enhanced burden placed on the SEC by increasing the role that US States play in regulating US investment advisers. Subject to certain exceptions, US investment advisers with less than US$100 million of AUM will be prevented from registering with the SEC, thus leaving smaller asset managers to state jurisdiction and allowing the SEC to focus on larger investment advisers. It is expected that increasing this state-federal dividing line from the US$25 million threshold that applied prior to the Dodd-Frank Act will prevent thousands of investment advisers from selecting the SEC as their regulator and force them to become subject to the jurisdiction of one or more states.[8]

---

[6]   For purposes of the Dodd-Frank Act's references to 'private funds', a private fund is broadly understood to be any investment fund relying on one of two exemptions from regulation under the US Investment Company Act of 1940, as amended – those being sections 3(c)(1) and 3(c)(7) of that statute. Very generally, section 3(c)(1) exempts funds targeting 100 or fewer investors, and section 3(c)(7) exempts funds targeting investors that meet the definition of wealthy 'qualified purchasers.'

Also very generally, non-US domiciled investment funds typically apply these investor counts and eligibility requirements only to their US investors. A non-US fund with no US investors and that has not made a US offering typically would not be considered to be operating in reliance on sections 3(c)(1) or 3(c)(7) and would not be a 'private fund' under the provisions of the Dodd-Frank Act.

[7]   SEC final rule dated 22 June 2011 (Exemptions for Advisers to Venture Capital Funds, Private Fund Advisers With Less Than $150 Million in Assets Under Management, and Foreign Private Advisers), available at http://www.sec.gov/rules/final/2011/ia-3222.pdf. The authors of this chapter, together with colleagues at their law firm, also prepared a detailed summary of this and other SEC rulemaking published on the same day, posted to their firm's website, available at http://www.shearman.com/dodd-frank-act-rulemaking-sec-finalizes-exemptions-and-disclosure-requirements-for-investment-advisers-and-sets-compliance-for-early-2012-07-12-2011/.

[8]   For a discussion of the impact on US state law and state investment adviser registrations, see a letter to the SEC from the New York State Bar Association, *available at* http://www.sec.gov/comments/s7-37-10/s73710-128.pdf. See also

This US$100 million AUM threshold is not applicable to non-US investment advisers, assuming they have no physical presence in the US and, thus, cannot register with any state. As a result, unless such investment advisers fall within an available exemption, they will register with the SEC, regardless of their AUM.

2.1 The New Law of the Land in Brief

US regulation of investment advisers after the Dodd-Frank Act is thus to be divided broadly across the following types of firms: first, SEC-registered investment advisers, for which no exemption from registration and full-blown regulation is available; second, foreign private advisers that will be fully exempt; third, exempt reporting advisers – essentially comprising two classes of private fund managers – that will not be registered with the SEC and will not be subject to most SEC investment adviser rules, but will be subject to initial and ongoing SEC reporting; and fourth, family offices, certain commodity trading advisers and others able to rely on more specialized exemptions. US banks also continue to have a blanket exclusion from the Advisers Act.

2.2 Extension of Registration Deadline

The SEC's initial rulemaking efforts, published in October and November 2011, had come in for hundreds of detailed comments that required review and analysis by the SEC before final rulemaking could proceed.[9] As a result of this, and also severe budgetary constraints and political gridlock with which the SEC was contending at that time, there was widespread speculation that some form of extension of the new investment adviser registration requirements would be necessary. On 22 June 2011, it was finally confirmed by the SEC that the deadline for registration had been extended from 21 July 2011 to 30 March 2012.[10] That extension effectively continues

---

Section V of SEC final rule dated 22 June 2011 (Rules Implementing Amendments to the Investment Advisers Act of 1940), available at http://www.sec.gov/rules/final/2011/ia-3221.

[9] The authors of this chapter were among the many contributors of detailed comment letters on each of these rulemakings. Their letters to the SEC are *available at* http://www.sec.gov/comments/s7-37-10/s73710-79.pdf (investment adviser registration rules and exemptions) and http://www.sec.gov/comments/s7-25-10/s72510-85.pdf (exemption specific to family offices).

[10] For a public policy rationale for an extension, see a letter to the SEC drafted by the authors of this chapter, *available at* http://www.sec.gov/comments/s7-25-10/s72510-92.pdf.

the pre-Dodd Frank Act status quo for investment adviser registration rules until that later date.

2.3　The New 'Foreign Private Adviser' Exemption

The Dodd-Frank Act provides for a narrow exemption for what it calls 'foreign private advisers'. If a non-US fund manager qualifies, then it will be fully exempt from registration with the SEC (and unlike the 'exempt reporting advisers' it will have no record-keeping or reporting requirements under the Advisers Act).

In order to qualify for this exemption, an investment adviser must satisfy all of the following criteria:

- Have no place of business in the US;
- Have in total fewer than 15 US clients and US investors in private funds advised by the investment adviser;
- Have aggregate AUM attributable to these US clients and US investors in private funds advised by the adviser of less than US$25 million (or such higher amount as the SEC may deem appropriate, although the SEC presently does not propose any increase);
- Not hold itself out generally to the public in the US as an investment adviser; and
- Not act as an investment adviser to an investment company registered, or a company electing business development company status, under the US Investment Company Act of 1940 (as amended, the 'Investment Company Act').

The new foreign private adviser exemption is much more limited than the existing 14-or-fewer clients exemption. Notably, it requires that a fund manager look through its funds and count the US investors[11] in those funds when determining whether the threshold of '15 clients and investors' has been reached. Even very limited US connections – such as advising a non-US fund with *either* '15 or more US investors *or* US$25 million or more in US client investments – therefore will be enough to render the exemption unavailable. By contrast, under the existing exemption, 'look-throughs' are not required. The new exemption is less generous in more nuanced ways too. For example, investment managers must have *no place*

---

[11]　An 'investor' for this purpose generally includes any holder of equity or debt securities issued by a fund.

of business[12] *in the US* at all in order to take advantage of the exemption. Previously, having a *principal place of business outside the US* would have been sufficient.

Further, non-US advisers should watch for other guidance that may somewhat blunt the extra-territorial effect of the new law. For example, in its final rulemaking published on 22 June 2011, the SEC largely reconfirmed its position on the so-called 'Unibanco guidance'.[13] That guidance has allowed a limited form of 'piggy-backing' by a non-US firm on the registration status of an SEC registered investment adviser affiliate, so that a global business may be able to use a single SEC registration across multiple geographies and business lines.

A practical consideration thus far not addressed is the basis on which funds whose base currency is not US dollars should measure their assets under management for SEC registration purposes. Given the likelihood of currency fluctuations affecting the relative value of a given currency, it would be natural to contemplate a buffer so that non-US firms are not required to repeatedly register and de-register as the applicable thresholds are crossed.[14]

2.4 Exempt Reporting Advisers – Solely Managing Private Funds

One of the two new categories of 'exempt reporting adviser' covers any investment adviser that both (i) advises solely private funds; and (ii) in the aggregate, manages less than US$150 million in the US. Such advisers, labelled by the SEC as exempt 'private fund advisers', will be able to take advantage of this exemption regardless of the number of funds that they manage. The other side of this coin, though, is that if an adviser has

---

[12] A 'place of business' is any office where the investment adviser regularly provides advisory services, solicits, meets with, or otherwise communicates with clients, and any location held out to the public as a place where the adviser conducts any such activities.

[13] The 'Unibanco guidance' is set out and summarised in (i) SEC Staff Report, 'Protecting Investors: A Half-Century of Investment Company Regulation', Chapter 5, The Reach of the Investment Advisers Act of 1940 (May 1992); and (ii) an SEC Staff No-Action Letter issued to the Unibanco organisation on 28 July 1992.

[14] The buffer introduced by the SEC in its final rules unfortunately deals only with the $100 million State/Federal threshold. But the $25 million foreign private adviser and $150 million exempt reporting adviser thresholds for which no buffers were proposed will be most salient in the context of currency fluctuations. At least, however, the $150 million threshold (see immediately below) will only be tested once annually.

even a single client that is not a private fund, the exemption suddenly is not available.The US$150 million threshold is to be calculated annually (the original SEC proposal suggested quarterly calculations) and should take account of both contributions and redemptions of investor capital, as well as appreciation and depreciation in value of fund investments. Where an adviser's annual calculation indicates that it has reached the US$150 million threshold, having previously relied on the 'private fund adviser' exemption, that adviser generally will have a 90-day grace period within which it can continue to operate before it is required to apply for full SEC registration.

Under the SEC rules, there are significant differences with respect to how US and non-US entities are treated, to the benefit of non-US firms. When calculating whether the US$150 million threshold has been reached, a US adviser must include all assets of all private funds that it manages. By contrast, a non-US adviser may omit from the calculation any accounts and investment funds managed from outside of the US, irrespective of the amount of investments by US persons. As such, for non-US advisers, it is the location where investment decisions are made, and not where the fund is organized, that is central to the US$150 million threshold. The consequence is that many non-US fund managers with no place of business in the US that were steeling themselves for full SEC registration following publication of the Dodd-Frank Act, ultimately find that they are exempt from registration (albeit subject to some level of reporting and record-keeping requirements, as described below).

2.5   Exempt Reporting Advisers – Solely Managing Venture Capital Funds

The second category of exempt reporting advisers relates to managers solely of venture capital funds. A 'venture capital fund' is defined as a private fund that satisfies all of the following requirements:

- Holds no more than 20 per cent of its capital commitments in 'non-qualifying investments' (generally, investments will be 'non-qualifying' if they are anything other than equity securities of private operating companies acquired for the purpose of primarily providing operating or business expansion capital (not to buy out other investors));
- Does not borrow or otherwise generally incur leverage, other than limited short-term borrowing and certain guarantees, and its portfolio companies do not borrow in connection with or as a means to funding the fund's investment;

- Does not offer redemptions or other similar liquidity rights to investors except in extraordinary circumstances;
- Represents itself as pursuing a venture capital strategy to its investors and prospective investors; and
- Is not an investment company registered, or a company electing business development company status, under the Investment Company Act.

This definition is more generous to the venture capital community than the original definition proposed by the SEC. That original definition came under intense criticism because of its limiting nature (many common venture capital fund structures would have not met the requirements). But even with the more expansive terms, very few traditional private equity funds should be able to rely upon this exemption. The SEC has also refused to apply a beneficial interpretation of this exemption for non-US firms, unlike the US$150 million exemption just discussed, which is quite generous to the non-US community.

A venture capital fund manager relying on this exemption still will be subject to reporting and record-keeping requirements, as discussed below.

2.6 Exempt Reporting Advisers – Exempt Yes, but Still Reporting . . .

Assuming qualification under one of the exemptions just described, an exempt reporting adviser will not be required to register with the SEC, but will file a short-form version of the same registration form used by registered advisers (Form ADV) and in the same public format, with all filed information to be available online. Information to be filed with the SEC about the exempt reporting adviser and its advisory business will include the following: (i) basic identifying information about the adviser, (ii) the identity of its direct and indirect owners and its control persons (for this purpose, directors, certain officers, and similar personnel), (iii) financial industry affiliations, (iv) other business activities in which the adviser and its affiliates engage, and (v) disciplinary history of the adviser and its employees that may reflect on the firm's integrity.

An exempt reporting adviser also will be subject to the new fund-by-fund Form ADV disclosure described in the next section of this chapter.

2.7 Other Exemptions – 'Family Offices' and Certain CFTC-registered Commodity Trading Advisers

The Dodd-Frank Act treats so-called 'family offices' as special cases. Rather than being an investment adviser that is exempt from registration with the SEC, the definition of 'investment adviser' itself under the Act will not include family offices (which technically means that no exemption is necessary in their case). A 'family office' for this purpose is limited to an investment organisation that is controlled by and services the members of a single family.

Pre-July 2011, any investment adviser that is registered with the US Commodity Futures Trading Commission ('CFTC') as a commodity trader adviser and (i) whose business does not 'consist primarily' of acting as an investment adviser and (ii) who is not acting as an adviser to any registered investment company or business development company, is exempt from registration with the SEC under the Advisers Act. The Dodd-Frank Act tweaks this exemption to apply it to any investment adviser that is registered with the CFTC as a commodity trading adviser and who advises a private fund and whose business is not 'predominantly' the imparting of securities-related (as opposed to commodities-related) advice. If at any time that predominance test is no longer met, and there is as yet no guidance on how it will be measured, then a requirement to register with the SEC will be triggered.

3. EXPANDED FUND MANAGER REPORTING RULES

3.1 Expanded Fund-by-Fund Reporting on Form ADV

Under new rules generated by the SEC on its own initiative rather than at the behest of a specific Dodd-Frank Act directive, all advisers to private funds that use Form ADV, including exempt reporting advisers, will be subject to new fund-by-fund public reporting. The following non-exhaustive list provides a sense of the breadth of the disclosures that the SEC proposes to include on Form ADV regarding each private fund that an adviser manages:

- Name and place of formation of the fund;
- Name of the directors, general partner, or managing member of the fund;
- Details about master funds and feeder funds (whether or not the feeder is affiliated);
- Whether the fund invests more than 10 per cent of its assets in other funds;
- Whether the fund invests at all in funds registered under the Investment Company Act;

- Type of investment strategy employed (e.g., hedge fund, private equity fund, real estate fund);
- Gross asset value (a proposal to also require disclosure of net asset value has been dropped from the SEC's final rules, on the basis that the benefit of public disclosure was outweighed by the potential competitive harm of a fund's leverage strategy being publicly known); and
- Number of beneficial owners, and percentage of the fund owned by non-US persons.[15]

In the case of non-US funds for which the reporting adviser is a non-US firm, none of this reporting is required so long as a fund does not have US investors and is not marketed to US persons.

3.2 New Form PF

The Dodd-Frank Act directed the SEC to require that registered investment advisers to private funds maintain records, and file reports, containing information 'necessary and appropriate for the assessment of systemic risk' by the newly-organized Financial Stability Oversight Council (FSOC). The FSOC is a joint body of the primary US financial services regulators.

On 31 October 2011, the SEC and the CFTC completed a package of rules in response to that Congressional systemic risk mandate.[16] The two regulators now require SEC-registered advisers to file reports on a new Form PF that are:

- Broad-based in scope, providing for over 50 different high-level categories of reported information and literally hundreds of sub-categories of information – with the most detailed reporting proposed for fund managers with more than US$1.5 billion in AUM;
- Intrusive, in that the reports will collect information that firms view as highly sensitive and proprietary (regarding, for example, a fund's lenders and derivative counterparties); and

---

[15]   SEC final rule dated 22 June 2011 (Rules Implementing Amendments to the Investment Advisers Act of 1940), *available at* http://www.sec.gov/rules/final/2011/ia-3221.pdf.

[16]   SEC final rule dated 31 October 2011, Reporting by Investment Advisers to Private Funds and Certain Commodity Pool operators and Commodity Trading Advisers on Form PF, *available at* http://www.sec.gov/rules/final/2011/ia-3308.pdf.

- Administratively demanding, in that the reports will be both complex and prepared as often as quarterly (annually for smaller managers).

Importantly, the Form PF will *not* be filed by any firm falling within one of the new categories of 'exempt reporting advisers' discussed above. A non-US fund manager (i.e., a manager whose principal office and place of business is outside the US) also would enjoy special treatment and need not report on any private fund it manages that during the last fiscal year was itself not a US person and that was neither offered to, nor beneficially owned by, any US persons. This could well result in a non-US manager choosing to limit the availability of some of its funds to US investors.

When Form PF was proposed, it immediately generated sceptical commentary, including questions as to:

- How (and whether) the information from the form will be used once collected, e.g., what governmental monitoring will be conducted and what types of remedial steps might be taken by the FSOC/SEC/CFTC if a fund is determined to pose systemic risks;
- Whether these apparently 'disclosure-based' rules will morph into implicit or explicit regulation of the industry's investment practices, and;
- Whether the highly proprietary information involved will be appropriately secured – confidentiality of electronic information being of special concern in the wake of the Wikileaks State Department cables saga.

4.   SYSTEMIC RISK REGULATION

The Dodd-Frank Act's establishment of the FSOC puts in place a federal 'systemic risk regulator' to identify and monitor financial activities, practices and institutions that could pose a systemic risk to the US financial system. Under the Dodd-Frank Act, the FSOC has the ability to place a systemically significant company (including a fund group) under the supervision of the Federal Reserve Board (the 'Federal Reserve') if the prospect of material financial distress of that entity, or its nature, scope, size, scale, concentration, interconnectedness, or mix of activities, could pose a threat to the financial stability of the US. When making such 'systemic risk' determinations, the FSOC must take into account a number of factors such as (i) leverage, (ii) off-balance-sheet exposures, (iii) linkages to other institutions, (iv) importance to the American financial system (e.g., as a source of credit or liquidity), and (v) amount and nature of US financial assets. There is neither a statutory minimum on the amount of assets, or AUM, that would be necessary in order for a company to be found to be systemically important, nor an automatic systemic designation if the assets (or the AUM) of an entity exceed a specified amount. The Dodd-Frank Act allows the FSOC to place an institution that is headquartered outside of the US under Federal Reserve supervision if its US activities and connections are considered systemically important to the US economy.

In January 2011, the FSOC released a proposed rule relating to the designation of non-bank financial companies as systemically important with the proposal resubmitted, somewhat modified in October 2011.[17] It is expected that the FSOC will adopt a final rule at some point in 2012, with the first designations to occur shortly thereafter.

The FSOC's proposed rule incorporates each of the statutory factors and proposes a designation framework organized around six categories: (i) size, (ii) lack of substitutes for the company's financial services and products, (iii) interconnectedness with other financial firms, (iv) leverage, (v) liquidity risk and maturity mismatches, and (vi) existing regulatory scrutiny. The proposed rule, however, provides only limited guidance on how such factors would be applied in making designations. Some representatives of the fund industry have requested that the FSOC release guidance providing additional specificity on criteria for systemic risk designation prior to the adoption of a final rule.[18]

Given that the FSOC includes several banking regulators (as well as the Secretary of the Treasury), there has been some concern in the asset management industry that the rules governing systemically significant companies are geared toward banking entities, rather than investment funds.[19] And, at this point, it appears as though such rules could be incongruent with traditional fund operations. For example, if a hedge fund is tagged as a systemically significant company, it would appear to become subject to liquidity requirements, 'stress tests' measuring capital adequacy and counterparty exposure limits that could be unworkable for many fund managers.

Systemically significant companies will be subject to reporting requirements and the examination and enforcement authority of the Federal

---

[17] FSOC proposed rules issued 18 January 2011 *available at* http://www.treasury.gov/initiatives/Document/Nonbank%20NPR%20final%2001%2013%2011%20formatted%20for%20FR.pdf

[18] See, for example, Letter to the FSOC from the Investment Company Institute, dated 24 February 2011 and 19 December 2011.

[19] The FSOC is composed of ten voting members, four of which are the senior officials of US bank regulatory agencies.

Reserve, in much the same way as traditional bank holding companies (although in the case of a systemically significant company, with a greater emphasis on activities and operations of the company that could pose a threat to the financial stability of the US). Systemically significant companies will also be faced with the added requirement of developing and maintaining a 'resolution plan' to effectively carry out the rapid and orderly resolution of the company in bankruptcy during times of financial distress.[20] Under proposed regulations jointly issued by the Federal Deposit Insurance Corporation (FDIC) and the Federal Reserve in April 2011, resolution plans would need to be updated annually and an interim plan would have to be filed no later than 45 days after any event or change which results in, or could reasonably be foreseen to have, a material effect on the plan.[21]

Another safety mechanism put in place by the Act prevents systemically significant companies from becoming overly exposed to any single unaffiliated entity. The Dodd-Frank Act places a concentration limit of 25 per cent of the systemically significant company's capital stock and surplus on its aggregate credit exposure to any particular counterparty. The Federal Reserve is empowered to lower this 25 per cent limit still further, at its discretion. Exposures created through the use of derivative instruments and securities lending are included in this limit, which becomes effective 21 July 2013 (subject to a possible two-year extension).

In her Senate testimony, Sheila Bair, then Chairwoman of the FDIC and a member of the FSOC, reported that the staff of the FSOC was dividing non-banks into four categories for the purposes of the designation of systemically significant companies.[22] One such category is 'the hedge fund, private equity firm and asset management industries'.[23] This suggests that the FSOC staff both believes that funds and asset managers are among the

---

[20]   A 'resolution plan' will require, among other things, (i) a full description of the ownership structure, assets, liabilities, and contractual obligations of the company, and (ii) identification of the cross-guarantees tied to different securities, identification of major counterparties, and a process for determining to whom the collateral of the company is pledged.

[21]   FDIC and Federal Reserve proposed rule, issued on 12 April 2011, available at http://edocket.access.gpo.gov/2011/pdf/2011-9588.pdf.

[22]   See *Implementation of the Dodd-Frank Wall Street Reform and Consumer Protection Act: Hearing Before the Senate Committee on Banking, Housing and Urban Affairs*, 112th Congress, 2011 (Statement of Sheila Bair, Chairman of the FDIC on 17 February 2011).

[23]   The other three FSOC categories for purposes of designation of systemically significant companies are (i) the insurance industry, (ii) speciality lenders, and (iii) broker-dealers and futures commission merchants.

possible candidates for systemic designation and plans to closely review information about significant funds and advisers for the purposes of evaluating possible systemic designations.[24]

5. SWAPS AND DERIVATIVES REGULATION

While perhaps not directly applicable to all fund managers, the Dodd-Frank Act does create new rules relating to the trading of swaps and derivatives including, in particular, regulations addressing swaps clearing and exchange trading, registration of dealers and of major non-dealer swap participants, capital and margin requirements, position limits and regulatory reporting. Many of these new rules will be of real significance for private fund managers.

In addition to the new requirements for swap dealers, the Act introduces a new concept of a 'Major Swap Participant'. Any entity that is classified as a Major Swap Participant will be subject to regulation with the SEC and/or the CTFC, and will be subject to heightened prudential standards (including capital and margin requirements and increased business conduct, record-keeping and reporting requirements). It remains a possibility that some private funds could find themselves classified as Major Swap Participants and, as a consequence, subject to these heightened standards.

A Major Swap Participant is a person that is not a swap dealer and either (i) maintains a substantial position in swaps in any of the major swap categories, other than positions held for hedging or mitigating commercial risk and certain hedging positions maintained by employee benefit plans; or (ii) whose outstanding swaps create substantial counterparty exposure that could have serious adverse effects on the financial stability of the US banking system or financial markets; or (iii) is a financial entity[25] that is highly leveraged and maintains a substantial position in outstanding swaps in any of the major swap categories. The SEC and CFTC have proposed tests for Major Swap Participant status based on outstanding exposures and potential future exposure under swap positions.

---

[24] In order to assist the FSOC in making systemic risk designations, the Office of Financial Research (OFR), a new federal office created to support the FSOC, may request and collect information (including financial data and reports) from any fund or adviser. In addition, the FSOC may request that the Federal Reserve conduct an exam of a fund or adviser for purposes of making a systemic risk designation.

[25] 'Financial entity' for this purpose expressly includes private funds.

As with the Act's provisions relating to systemically significant companies, private funds may well not have been the primary target for the rules governing Major Swap Participants. But some private funds – particularly those hedge funds routinely engaging in swap trading – could find themselves subject to yet another layer of regulation as a result of these new rules.[26] Even if not directly regulated, private funds may be indirectly affected by the new requirements for their trading counterparties, including increased costs.

6. THE VOLCKER RULE

Blessed with perhaps more publicity than many (any?) other important changes brought about by the Dodd-Frank Act, the Volcker Rule generally prohibits covered 'banking entities' from engaging in proprietary trading and from investing in or sponsoring hedge funds or private equity funds. The Volcker Rule has been criticized as both over-reaching in curbing legitimate financial industry activities and not going far enough in its prescriptions.[27] Perhaps as a result of trying to be respectful of both sides of the equation, the Volcker Rule is, in its final form, somewhat disjointed and subject to complex exemptions and carve-outs.

Although a detailed analysis of the Volcker Rule is outside the scope of this chapter, it is worth noting its following basic ingredients:

- The Rule generally applies to banking groups (including any bank or non-bank subsidiary in the group) operating in the US. In practice, then, it captures virtually every major commercial and investment bank worldwide;
- The Rule's prohibitions affect every office and affiliate of US-based institutions, so there is no possibility for a US institution to shift business abroad to avoid the prohibitions;
- The prohibition on 'proprietary trading' should not cover customer-driven businesses;
- The prohibitions on sponsoring and investing in hedge funds and private equity funds are subject to a number of exceptions and

---

[26]   Section 764 of the Dodd-Frank Act.

[27]   The authors of this chapter, together with colleagues at their law firm, also prepared a detailed summary of the Volcker Rule posted to their firm's website, *available at* http://www.shearman.com/financial-regulatory-reform-update--the-volcker-rule-continues-to-garner-outsized-attention-in-the-wake-of-passage-of-fin ancial-reform-legislation-10-19-2010/.

technical fine points. For example, a banking entity is not prevented from 'advising' a fund that it does not 'sponsor'; and

- The Rule restricts many transactions and relationships between a banking entity and any hedge fund or private equity fund with respect to which the entity serves as fund manager, advisor, and/or sponsor.

The Volcker Rule was to become effective no later than 21 July 2012. Banking entities were to be given at least two additional years (i.e., no later than 21 July 2014) to conform or divest existing activities that are impermissible under the Volcker Rule.

On 18 January 2011, the FSOC issued a much-anticipated report on the Volcker Rule setting out recommendations to the five federal agencies that are required to adopt rules to implement the Rule.[28] While the FSOC study provides some guidance (especially relating to the prohibition on 'proprietary trading'), it fails to resolve many interpretative matters, largely leaving them to the individual agencies to resolve through their rulemaking. Rules interpreting and clarifying the scope of the Volcker Rules were issued in proposed form in October 2011.

The study makes ten recommendations, four of which deal with the relationship between entities subject to the Volcker Rule (banking entities) and hedge funds. Specifically, the study's recommendations include: (i) prohibiting banking entities from investing in or sponsoring any hedge funds or private equity funds, except to bona fide trust, fiduciary or investment advisory customers; (ii) prohibiting banking entities from engaging in transactions that would allow them to bail out a hedge fund or a private equity fund; (iii) identifying those funds that should be brought within the scope of the Volcker Rule prohibitions in order to prevent evasion of the intent of the Volcker Rule; and (iv) requiring banking entities to publicly disclose permitted exposure to hedge funds and private equity funds. The FSOC study also suggested that exempting venture capital funds from the prohibition on investment in hedge funds and private equity funds is a 'significant issue', implying that banking entity investment in venture capital funds could be permitted.

The study also includes thoughtful comments on dealing with the under-inclusiveness and over-inclusiveness of the definition of private equity and hedge funds that derives from sections 3(c)(1) and 3(c)(7) of

---

[28] The five agencies are the Office of the Comptroller of the Currency (OCC), the FDIC, the Board of Governors of the Federal Reserve System (the Board), the SEC and the CFTC. The report in question is available at http://www.treasury. gov/initiatives/Documents/Volcker%20sec%20%20619%20study%20final%201%2 018%2011%20rg.pdf

the Investment Company Act. For example, the study notes that entities such as commodity pools might need to be covered on the basis that they may share characteristics of traditional 'private equity funds' and 'hedge funds', including the use of leverage and how managers are compensated.

Finally, there is nothing in the study, and thus nothing published by federal regulators at the date of writing, that further clarifies an important – and likely to be much relied upon – exemption granted to non-US bank involvement in non-US hedge and private equity funds that are not offered for sale or sold to a US resident.

7.   OTHER DODD-FRANK ACT CHANGES OF SPECIAL INTEREST TO FUND MANAGERS

7.1   New Powers for the SEC to Define 'Client' and Other Terms

One significant and well-publicized change brought forth by the Dodd-Frank Act relates to something superficially minor: the meaning of the term 'client'.

As discussed above, the pre-July 2011 exemption from SEC registration on which many investment advisers – both US and non-US – seek to rely, is the so-called '14-or-fewer clients' exemption. When counting clients, an investment adviser is not required to look through the funds that it manages; a 'client' of a private fund manager is for the most part the private fund itself, and not an investor in that fund.

This has not always been free from doubt. In 2004, the SEC promulgated rules that reflected the SEC's belief that it could interpret the term 'client' differently for different parts of the Advisers Act. In practice, those new SEC rules gutted the 14-or-fewer clients exemption by requiring that investment advisers look through funds and count investors in those funds as clients. This led to a courtroom defeat for the SEC two years later in the so-called *Goldstein* case (named after activist hedge fund manager Philip Goldstein), which found the SEC's treatment of the word client in different contexts to be 'arbitrary and capricious' and to have exceeded the authority vested in the SEC by the Advisers Act.[29]

With the Dodd-Frank Act set to register hedge fund managers far more broadly than in the past, the underlying impetus for *Goldstein* – the case was fundamentally a battle over the SEC's 'back-door' repeal of the 14-or-fewer clients exemption – has been addressed. Yet the Act went

---

[29]   *Goldstein v SEC*, 451 F.3d 873 (D.C. Cir. 2006).

further than that in dealing with *Goldstein*. Indeed, the SEC is granted broad authority to define technical, trade and other terms used in the Advisers Act – and different definitions may be applied to a single term in different sections of the Advisers Act. As one exception, the SEC is expressly prohibited from defining the term 'client' to include an investor in a private fund for the purposes of sections 206(1) and (2) of the Advisers Act, both of which are broad, anti-fraud provisions.

While the SEC will be distracted by its Dodd-Frank Act implementation duties for some years to come, the SEC eventually will be disposed again to adopt rules under the Advisers Act on its own initiative. The new interpretive authority granted by the Dodd-Frank Act will then begin to show its scope.

7.2 Revisiting Investor Eligibility Standards

Private funds wishing to target US investors must do so in a manner that avoids the close regulation attaching to retail investment funds in the US under the Investment Company Act. To do so, private funds typically rely on section 3(c)(1) or section 3(c)(7) of the Investment Company Act. Very generally, section 3(c)(1) exempts funds targeting 100 or fewer investors, and section 3(c)(7) exempts funds targeting investors that meet the definition of wealthy 'qualified purchasers'. Also very generally, non-US domiciled investment funds typically apply these investor counts and eligibility requirements only to their US investors. The hedge fund world is thus divided for US law purposes between 100-person funds and qualified purchaser funds. While a qualified purchaser is generally an individual with US$5 million in investable assets or an institution with US$25 million in investable assets, the Investment Company Act itself imposes no eligibility requirement on investors in 100-person funds. Regulation of eligibility to invest in 100-person funds is left to other statutes, as described below.

In addition, private funds must avoid registration of their shares under the US Securities Act of 1933, as amended. Under the so-called 'Regulation D exemption', securities offered privately that target 'accredited investors' will be exempt from registration. The definition of an 'accredited investor' includes an individual who, either alone or with his or her spouse, has net worth of at least US$1 million. Prior to the Dodd-Frank Act, SEC rules allowed an individual's primary residence to be included when calculating net worth.[30] Congress concluded that this was no longer appropriate and,

---

[30] Rule 501 sets the standards for accredited investor status under certain exemptive provisions for private and other limited offerings under Regulation D.

accordingly, the Dodd-Frank Act provides that the net worth calculation for determining accredited investor status now must exclude the value of a person's primary residence. Since qualified purchaser funds already subject their investors to a high eligibility standard, this change largely affects only 100-person funds and effectively raises the floor for eligibility to invest in them.

The Dodd-Frank Act also directs the SEC to raise the eligibility standard for investors who may be charged a performance-based fee by a registered investment adviser. Again, this change should affect only 100-person funds.

7.3   Short Sale Reporting and Manipulative Short Sales

Under the Dodd-Frank Act, the SEC is required to adopt rules that will require periodic public disclosure on short sales by institutional investment managers, including the cumulative number of short sales of each security involved in such a transaction. The investment manager must make disclosures monthly, further increasing the reporting burden on hedge fund managers, in particular. It appears that these disclosure requirements are intended to arm the SEC with sufficient data to enable the SEC to determine where any manipulative short selling – which is to be made unlawful under the Act – has taken place. In the event of any manipulative short selling, the SEC will be able to adopt rules to ensure that appropriate remedies and enforcement are available.[31]

7.4   Fiduciary Standards

The Dodd-Frank Act requires the SEC to study the differences between investment adviser regulation and broker-dealer regulation, presumably with an eye to harmonizing the two regulatory regimes. Harmonization is hotly contested, primarily by the broker-dealer community, which is concerned that a new conduct standard based on an investment adviser's fiduciary duty of loyalty to a client will be extended to the relationship between brokers and their customers. That is, in fact, what an SEC study, concluded in January 2011, recommends.[32]

---

[31]   Section 929X of the Act amends Section 13(f) of the 1934 Act.
[32]   See SEC study, *available at* http://www.sec.gov/news/press/2011/2011-20. htm.

7.5 Self-Regulatory Organisation for Investment Advisers

The SEC is required under the Dodd-Frank Act to study the merits of a 'self-regulatory organisation' or SRO for investment advisers. What is presumably envisaged is a government-sanctioned private organisation like the Financial Industry Regulatory Authority (FINRA) that requires broker-dealer firms to be paying members of FINRA, to submit to FINRA's conduct rules and to submit to both examinations by FINRA examiners and to FINRA enforcement jurisdiction, in the event of alleged wrongdoing. The primary rationales for such an organisation are that it allows load-sharing between the government and a privately funded counterpart and provides for a structure for effective self-regulation by industry participants.

The investment adviser community is strongly opposed to such an organisation for their industry. That opposition is, in part, a 'better the devil you know' reaction, in that transitioning from sole regulatory jurisdiction by the SEC to a shared jurisdiction model with an SRO presents inherent uncertainties. There is also opposition based on the fact that FINRA has sought to position itself as the front-runner to serve as such an SRO. Investment advisers perceive FINRA as, at best, insensitive to their needs because of its brokerage industry focus to, at worst, actually beholden to the brokers and therefore having conflicts of interest in regulating investment advisers, which operate primarily as customers relative to brokers.

The relevant SEC study was concluded in January 2011. It has been read as either inconclusive or as generally favourable to the status quo in which investment advisers are regulated in the US solely by governmental actors.[33]

8. CONCLUSION

The Dodd-Frank Act is many hundreds of pages long yet, in some ways, it is little more than a skeletal outline of the many regulatory changes it contemplates. Much of the detail required for the implementation and the enforcement of the new legislation has been left for both existing and newly created regulatory agencies and committees to flesh out over the coming months and years. As is evident from the rulemaking promulgated by the SEC since the publication of the Act, even the rules intended to add flesh to the bones of the Act themselves frequently await interpretation, study and further regulation.

---

[33] See SEC study *available at* http://www.sec.gov/news/studies/2011/914studyfinal.pdf

What is clear is that many of the Dodd-Frank Act's provisions relevant to investment advisers can be treated as falling in two categories: those that *have* a significant impact on the ways in which investment advisers are regulated in the US, and those that *could have* a significant impact. In the first category one might find items such as removal of the 14-or-fewer clients exemption, with an inevitable increase in registrations as a result, and the burdensome and intrusive disclosures contemplated by Form PF. In the second category, one might place the possibility of a hedge fund being labelled as either 'systemically significant' or a 'major swap participant' and the possibility of investment adviser regulation incorporating a FINRA-style self-regulatory organisation.

Philosophically, the Act also provides a firm indication of Congressional willingness to extend its regulatory arm extra-territorially. But such a reaction to the global financial turmoil of the last few years is far from a US phenomenon. The EU's Alternative Investment Fund Managers Directive ('AIFMD'), which on its face is intended to create a pan-European regulatory regime for EU-domiciled fund managers, has enormous consequences for investment advisers and private funds located in the US and elsewhere outside Europe.[34] The monitoring of systemic risk, and the collation of information by regulators for that purpose, is a powerful driver behind many initiatives across the globe relating to fund manager regulation. Whether for good or for bad, much of the increasingly burdensome disclosure and reporting requirements imposed by those initiatives are justified as being necessary to prevent the build-up of systemic risk (or, at least, to assist regulators in identifying pockets of systemic risk and acting accordingly).

As a final note, and put gently, regulators are not resource-laden. The sheer volume of data landing on regulators' desks as a result of increased regulation and reporting may not serve to assist in the identification and mitigation of new risks to global financial markets and their participants. Instead, there is a real risk that the 'forest' of risks will become lost among the 'trees' of data.

---

[34]   For an account of the AIFMD, see Chapter 17 of this book.

15. German alternative investment fund regulation – wrong answers to the wrong questions?

*Norbert Lang**

1. THE LEGAL FRAMEWORK FOR ALTERNATIVE OPEN-ENDED FUND INVESTMENTS

1.1 The Investment Act of 2004

The purpose of the German Investment Act (Investmentgesetz – 'InvG'), which entered into force on 1 January 2004, was to modernize Germany's investment funds' regulation, start up a German hedge fund industry and implement the European UCITS II and III-Directives.[1] The InvG established a new legal framework for all types of open-ended funds. The Act replaced the former Capital Investment Company Act (Kapitalanlagegesellschaftgesetz – 'KAGG') and the Foreign Investment Act (Auslandsinvestmentgesetz – 'AuslInvG'). It was welcomed as an important step forward, which completely restructured the German fund provisions and harmonized the regulatory provisions for German and foreign open-ended investment funds, which were regulated in the two different aforementioned Acts before.[2] Hedge funds were for the first time regulated by German law. According to the draft of the InvG, the reason for the introduction of hedge fund-related provisions was to promote the

* Legal counsel SEB Asset Management.

[1] Directive 2001/107/EC of the European Parliament and of the Council of 21 January 2002 amending Council Directive 85/611/EEC on the coordination of laws, regulations and administrative provisions relating to undertakings for collective investment in transferable securities (UCITS) with a view to regulating management companies and simplified prospectuses OJ L 41, 13.2.2002, p. 20–34 and Directive 2001/108/EC of the European Parliament and of the Council of 21 January 2002 amending Council Directive 85/611/EEC on the coordination of laws, regulations and administrative provisions relating to undertakings for collective investment in transferable securities (UCITS), with regard to investments of UCITS OJ L 41, 13.2.2002, p. 35–42.

[2] Wallach 2004, p. 119 et seq.

existing German fund industry[3] and to build an up-to date legal regime for hedge funds.

1.1.1   Single-manager hedge funds

Because there is generally no widely accepted definition of the term 'hedge fund'[4] the InvG avoids using the term, using, instead, the expression 'Sondervermögen mit zusätzlichen Risiken' (investment scheme with additional risks). According to the definition in Section 112 InvG, a fund is considered an investment scheme with additional risks if it uses either leverage or short-selling strategies or both, and it is not restricted in the choice of its assets.

German hedge funds and hedge fund companies are subject to the supervision of the Bundesanstalt für Finanzdienstleistungsaufsicht (BaFin), while the take-up of the business of a hedge fund company requires authorization according to Section 7 InvG. The same applies, according to Section 43 (2) InvG, to the fund rules of a hedge fund, for which the prior approval of the BaFin is also necessary. This authorization requirement is the same for all German funds under the InvG, although the contractual conditions for hedge funds, according to Section 93 (1) InvG, also require prior approval if the hedge fund takes the legal form of a so called 'special fund' ('Spezialsondervermögen' Section 91–95 InvG). Special funds according to Section 2 (3) InvG are funds whose units are exclusively held by investors which are not natural persons on the basis of written agreements with the capital investment company. They have less formal and legal requirements than other funds and can't be publicly distributed. Except for hedge funds in the form of special funds, no prior approval of the BaFin is required for the fund rules of a special fund. A hedge fund can either be created in the form of such a special fund for institutional investors only, or as a fund in which non-institutional investors too are allowed to invest.

Section 120 InvG requires that persons responsible for the investment decisions of single-manager hedge funds have to have sufficient professional experience and practical knowledge about investments in hedge funds. Annual and semi-annual reports have to be issued, which have to include information about short sales during the reporting period and which have to be filed with the BaFin and, as far as the fund is not set up

---

[3]   Diskussionsentwurf eines Investmentmodernisierungsgesetzes (Discussion draft of an Investment Modernization Act) German Ministry of Finance, ZBB 2003, insert to issue 4, 3.

[4]   Kumpan (2006), 43 et seq.; Spindler/Bednarz (2006), 553 et sq.; Wilhelmi (2008), 862; Kovas (2003), 5.

in the form of a special fund, have to be published. Hedge funds have to observe the principal of risk diversification. According to Section 112(1) InvG, they are allowed to invest in all types of assets listed in Sections 2(4) No. 1 to 4, 7, 10 and 11 InvG, that is to say in securities, money market instruments, derivatives, bank deposits, shares of other investment funds, precious metals and interests in enterprises and silent participations within the meaning of Section 230 of the Commercial Code in an enterprise with its seat and management in Germany. Single manager hedge funds are according to Section 122(3) InvG allowed to tender assets [of the funds] as collateral for credit or derivative transactions, to prime brokers. Section 112 (1) InvG restricts the maximum investment of a hedge fund in non-listed equity to 30 per cent of the funds' assets under management. This investment limit was set to avoid the introduction of private equity funds in German law under the hedge fund label.[5] Single manager hedge funds are not allowed to invest in real estate to prevent closed-ended real estate investment funds – which, under German law, are considered to belong to the so-called 'grey area' of capital markets and are not regulated under the InvG – from enjoying the beneficial treatment reserved to a regulated investment fund.[6]

1.1.2 Fund of hedge funds
Section113 (1) InvG defines funds-of-hedge funds (FoHFs) as funds that are allowed to invest in German law single-manager hedge funds that are supervised by the BaFin, or foreign single-manager hedge funds, which, in terms of their investment policy, are subject to comparable legal requirements. What Section 113(1) InvG does not require is that the target funds be subject to comparable supervision, which means that off-shore hedge funds may be target funds too.[7] The home country of any target hedge fund should nevertheless be a state actively co-operating with Germany with regard to combating money laundering, in accordance with international agreements (Section 113(4) InvG), while its assets should be under the control of a custodian bank, a prime broker or another comparable institution (Section 113(3) InvG). Section 113(4) InvG restricts investments in a single manager hedge fund to a maximum of 20 per cent of the fund's value and allows a FoHF to only invest in no more than two funds of the same issuer or fund manager. FoHF can acquire all shares

---

[5] Köndgen/Schmies in Schimanski/Bunte/Lwowski (2007), § 113 margin no. 108.
[6] Wallach (2004), 122.
[7] Spindler/Bednarz (2006), 558.; Bednarz (2009), 125 et sq.

of a single manager hedge fund, but a FoHF is not allowed to invest in other FoHFs as the latter are not mentioned as eligible assets in Section 113(1) and (2) InvG. According to Section 113(2) InvG, besides investing in single-manager hedge funds, FoHFs are allowed to invest up to 49 per cent in bank deposits and money market instruments. Currency futures contracts can only be sold and put option rights relating to currencies or to currency futures contracts can only be acquired in order to hedge the currency rate of assets held in foreign currencies. Furthermore there are restrictions on leverage and short sales.[8]

Section 120 InvG requires that persons responsible for the investment decisions of FoHFs have to have sufficient professional experience and practical knowledge of hedge fund investments.

1.1.3   Redemption of units

The redemption possibilities for investors in hedge funds or FoHFs can, according to Section 116 InvG, be more restrictive than those for investors in UCITS funds. German law does not impose a daily redemption possibility in the case of hedge funds or FoHFs. Their contractual terms and conditions may, according to Section 116 first sentence InvG, provide that the determination of unit prices and the redemption of units will only take place on certain redemption dates, provided that this is possible at least once per calendar quarter. Section 116 sentence 3 InvG gives the fund company the possibility to oblige investors to announce their intention to redeem fund units up to 40 days in advance, if they are invested in a single-manager hedge fund, and up to 100 days in advance, if they are invested in a FoHF. The redemption price must be paid without undue delay after the redemption date, but no later than 50 calendar days thereafter.

1.1.4   Investor protection and distribution

Investor protection was one of the main topics of discussion during the law-making process.[9] In the early stages, the legislator's intention was to allow hedge funds to be distributed through so-called 'special funds' ('Spezialfonds'), which only institutional investors would be allowed to invest in. The argument against this originally intended restriction was that special funds are specific to Germany and so foreign investors would be forced to use an internationally unknown vehicle, which they most probably would not do. Another possibility under consideration was to

---

[8]   Spindler/Bednarz (2006), 558.
[9]   Köndgen/Schmies in Schimanski/Bunte/Lwowski 2007, § 113 margin no. 108.

impose a minimum investment threshold, so as to ensure investor protection.[10] But that solution was finally not adopted because, on the one hand, there was no reason why wealthy people should need less protection while, on the other hand, minimum investments might lead people to invest a bigger part of their cash fortune in a hedge fund than they would otherwise do, in order to reach the minimum investment threshold.[11] Finally a distribution-based solution was adopted to ensure investor protection. In Germany, single-manager hedge funds can only be distributed, according to Section 112(2) InvG via private and not via public placement,[12] which is only admissible for FoHFs.[13]

Public distribution is defined in Section 2(11) InvG, as distribution by public offering, public marketing or other similar ways. It can be understood as distribution to an undefined, unlimited group of people. Taking that definition as a starting point, the prevailing opinion understands private placement as an offering to a pre-defined group of persons, with either an existing business relationship to the offeror, or contacted on a selection basis.[14] However, according to Section 2(11) InvG, no public marketing is deemed to exist if, for example, the fund units are exclusively marketed to banks, private and public insurance companies, fund companies as well as to pension funds. The only reference to a fund by its name or the simple publishing of issue and redemption prices of a fund is not deemed to qualify as public marketing. Furthermore, no public marketing is deemed to exist if, for foreign investment units admitted to trading in a domestic regulated market or traded on a regulated or over-the-counter market, only the announcements prescribed by the relevant market's rules are made.

According to Section 117 InvG, a prospectus is required for the public distribution of FoHFs, with the simplified prospectus required for UCITS-funds not being admissible in their case. According to Section 117(2) InvG, the prospectus of a FoHF must include, in a prominent place, literally the following information 'Warning by the Federal Minister of Finance: Investors in these investment funds must be prepared and able to sustain losses of the capital invested up to a total loss.' Moreover, according to Section 121(3) InvG, investors must be specifically warned of the above risks prior to acquiring fund units. If a dispute were to arise over whether the warning was properly issued, the onus of proof would be on

10   Spindler/Bednarz 2006, 60.
11   Wentrup 2009, 313.
12   Spindler/Bednarz (2006), 558.
13   Bednarz (2009), 125 et sqq.
14   Bednarz (2009), 125 et sq.

the distributing entity. Additional information has to be included in the prospectus on the criteria according to which hedge funds are chosen by the FoHFs and on the extent to which those hedge funds use leverage or short-selling. Moreover, information about the fee-structure of the chosen hedge funds as well as information concerning the total of fees to be borne by the investor, have to be provided. Any restrictions of the redemption possibilities, compared to those applicable to UCITS funds, have to be mentioned in the prospectus in a prominent way.

1.2　The 2007 Amendment of the Investment Act

The German InvG was amended in 2007, partly because of the European Union's (EU) Eligible Assets Directive,[15] which had to be implemented in national law, partly because of national law developments and partly because a liberalization of German fund regulation was on the agenda.

This amendment signaled certain minor changes to the rules governing German hedge funds and FoHFs. In particular, amendments were made to solve some practical problems that had become evident since 2004. FoHFs got the possibility to defer the payment of the unit value to their investors for up to a maximum of 50 days after the redemption day until their underlying single-manager hedge funds had determined their unit value or had paid the unit value to the FoHFs. This had been tolerated by the German authorities before the 2007 amendment of the InvG.

Even with that amendment, contrary to many other countries, the use of so-called 'side-pockets' to separate illiquid assets from other more liquid investments is not allowed in Germany.[16] In many other countries, funds are able to establish a new class of fund units which participate only in the assets in the side pocket. Those fund units cannot be redeemed by the investor as long as the fund is not able to sell the side pocket assets.[17]

What the InvG excluded in 2004 was the possibility for FoHFs to make use of loans. As there was a great practical need for the use of short-term loans, the 2007 amendment of the InvG created the possibility for their

---

[15]　Commission Directive 2007/16/EC of 19 March 2007 implementing Council Directive 85/611/EEC on the coordination of laws, regulations and administrative provisions relating to undertakings for collective investment in transferable securities (UCITS) as regards the clarification of certain definitions OJ L 79, 20.3.2007, 11–19.

[16]　See for example http://www.finma.ch/d/aktuell/Seiten/aktuell-sidepockets-20090123.aspx where the Swiss financial authority describes that as in other countries under certain conditions side pockets are tolerable under Swiss regulation.

[17]　Kayser/Lindemann/Käks (2009), 206; Pütz/Schmies (2004), 59.

use at least to the same extent as in the case of UCITS-funds, that is in the form of short-term loans of up to 10 per cent of the fund volume. But even *after* this amendment, the possibility to take up short-term loans remains limited as, in contrast to the regulation for UCITS funds, for FoHFs the legislator has explicitly stated in the explanatory statement of the draft of the amending Act that this possibility is only introduced to ensure liquidity, and that the use of short-term loans to increase the level of investment is not deemed to be desirable.[18] Furthermore, the possibility to invest the fund's liquidity according to Section 113(2) InvG was extended by the possibility to invest not only directly in money market instruments or bank deposits but, also, indirectly via investment funds which may only invest in bank deposits and money market instruments.

The InvG did not mention, in 2004, prime brokers, as a result of which uncertainty prevailed as to the extent to which it was possible for hedge funds to use the services of a prime broker. In the years following the adoption of the InvG, the practice developed by the German authorities was to regard the use of prime brokerage services as possible, in principle. With the 2007 amendment of the InvG, what was only a practice has become the law. Under Section 112(3) InvG, as amended, custody of a hedge fund's funds can also be performed by a prime broker. Prime brokers have to have their seat in a Member State of the Union or in another Member State of the European Economic Area or in a state which holds full membership in the Organization for Economic Co-Operation and Development, which is subject to effective public supervision and which has an appropriate creditworthiness. According to the second indent of that section, the prime broker can be appointed either directly by the fund company or by the custodian bank. The appointment or the change of a prime broker has to be reported to the BaFin without delay. Fund assets can be transferred to the prime broker as collateral for securities lending.

According to Section 117(3), if the custody of the assets of a fund is transferred from the custodian bank to a prime broker, the warning concerning the risk of a total loss, under Section 117(2), must be supplemented as follows: 'The assets of this investment fund are not held in custody by a custodian bank in whole or in part.' If the prime broker has its seat outside Germany, the sales' prospectus must contain a typographically

---

[18]   Governmental draft of the act to change the Investment Act and other Regulation, BT-Drucks. 16/5576 v. 11.6.2007, 225, http://www.jura.uni-augsburg.de/fakultaet/lehrstuehle/moellers/materialien/materialdateien/040_deutsche_gesetzgebungsgeschichte/InvG_Aenderungsgesetz/invg_pdf/1605576.pdf

emphasized reference to that fact, together with a reference to the fact that the prime broker is not subject to state supervision by the BaFin. Here too, according to Section 121(3) InvG, the investor must be specifically warned of this risk prior to acquiring fund units.

Not all of the changes in the German hedge fund rules under the 2007 amendment of the InvG have led to further liberalization. The obligation to produce a prospectus for single-manager hedge funds distributed in Germany was even extended. Since that amendment, according to Section 121(3) InvG, German as well as foreign single-manager hedge funds only distributed via private placement, have the obligation to produce a prospectus which was not necessary before. The legislator invented the obligation to produce a prospectus for funds that are not publicly distributed for investor protection purposes, because of the possibility to distribute single-manager hedge funds via private placement to non-institutional investors. As a consequence, even if fund units are sold only via private placement, the prospectus liability in Section 127 InvG applies. The prospectus has to be translated into the German language, as Section 123 InvG stipulates. And in the case of an investor arguing that information contained in the prospectus which is of material significance for the evaluation of the units is incorrect or incomplete, the German translation of the prospectus leads. This gives investors the possibility to demand the takeover of the fund units in return for reimbursement of the amount paid from the fund company and from the person who sold such units in his own name on a commercial basis as joint and several debtors.

1.3   Investment Rules for Institutional Investors

It is only very reluctantly that the legislator has opened the possibility for regulated institutional investors to invest in hedge funds. Starting with the introduction of hedge-fund-related provisions in the German Investment Act in 2004, Section 3(2) no. 2 of the Capital Investment Ordinance (Anlageverordnung – AnlVO) gave insurance companies the possibility to invest up to 5 per cent of the assets they manage directly or indirectly, on behalf of their insurance holders, in hedge funds. But apart from this quantitative restriction for insurance companies, many more qualitative restrictions for insurance companies exist for investments in hedge fund, such as the necessity of a due diligence process before investing in a hedge fund, to the extent that the insurance company has to understand the investment strategy of the hedge fund and its performance characteristics, adjust its risk management mechanisms to integrate the risk profile of the hedge fund in the insurance company's risk management and monitor personal changes in the management of the hedge fund. Furthermore, organizational requirements exist, such as quarterly information from the board of directors and the supervisory board of the insurance company about all hedge fund investments. On top of that, the BaFin also has to be informed by the insurance company about each new hedge fund investment and the volume invested in hedge funds if hedge funds are among the restricted assets of the insurance company. All these requirements bring a huge administrative and documentation workload for insurance companies. This might be at least one reason why German insurance companies have been quite reluctant to invest in hedge funds.[19] Another important group of institutional investors, social insurance carriers, is much more restricted in the choice of assets than insurance companies, not being allowed to invest in hedge funds at all.

1.4 Hedge Fund Certificates

Even before the new hedge fund regime entered in force into 2004 many foreign and German fund companies and promoters looked for ways to access the German market. At that time no regulated German hedge funds existed, and it was almost impossible for foreign hedge funds to distribute their products in Germany, since public distribution of hedge funds was not allowed under the provisions of the AuslInvG. Moreover, even if units in foreign hedge funds were only distributed by private placement, the tax regime imposed by Section 18 (3) of the AuslInvG was applicable in public sales and private placements and, according to that regime, a fund that was neither admitted to public sale nor listed on a stock exchange was subject to a punitive taxation. As a result, alternative structures were developed for the sale of hedge-fund-like products in Germany, in particular 'index certificates' and 'performance-linked notes'.[20]

'Index certificates' are securities with or without maturity, the value of which is determined by an artificially composed reference asset. In practice, the issuer (which is usually a German bank) pays the amount stated in the respective reference asset to the investor, either at maturity or, in the case of so-called 'open-end certificates', at contractually fixed dates. The foreign investor works as a fund sponsor and invests the amount into different hedge funds. The return is paid back to the German bank. The German bank then divides the whole investment into certificates, which are distributed to individual investors. In the case of maturity of the certificate or in the case of cashing at the contractually fixed dates the amount

---

[19] Weitzel/Zeller (2006), 358 et sqq.
[20] Lang, *German Law Journal* (2004), 679 et seqq.

corresponding to the actual value of the index is paid back.[21] The other widely used model is that of 'performance-linked notes'. These operate in a manner similar to index certificates, subject to one important difference: the certificate is not linked, this time, to a defined index, but directly to a hedge fund or a FoHFs.[22]

In both cases the risks inherent to the investment are the same as or similar to those inherent to a hedge fund or a FoHFs. If anything, these products are even riskier compared to hedge funds since, besides the product risks, there is the emitter risk to worry about in their case. In both cases the certificates are regarded, from a legal point of view, as bonds that can be publicly distributed. And in both cases the possibility to publicly distribute those certificates exists without the prior need of an authorization of the product by the BaFin. This means whilst German hedge funds need, according to the InvG, a prior authorization by the BaFin and can only be distributed under the German private placement regime, performance linked notes that are linked to the performance of the very same hedge funds can be distributed via public placement. Furthermore, there are less transparency rules vis-à-vis investors for those certificates than for hedge funds, with cost transparency, in particular, being only rudimentary. According to section 3 of the Securities Prospectus Act (Wertpapier-Verkaufsprospektgesetz – 'WpPG') only a less detailed prospectus is needed for certificates. The only relevant distribution restriction is that only credit institutions and financial service institutions, to the exclusion of non-supervised agents, are allowed to distribute certificates.

When hedge funds were introduced into German law, a hedge fund certificate emitting industry had already existed for years in Germany. The legal framework applicable to the distribution of hedge fund certificates was more favorable then the rules for hedge fund distribution. There are fewer rules concerning tax transparency and the hedge fund certificates are less transparent for their investors compared with German hedge funds. The limited transparency of hedge funds and their tendency to avoid disclosing their investment strategies were also to the advantage of hedge fund certificates, leading to an increasing interest for the sale of shares in hedge funds wrapped as certificates rather than directly in regulated funds under the German InvG. However, from an investor protection perspective, certificates are riskier as there is, in this case, the emitter risk which

---

[21]   Luttermann/Backmann (2002), 1019 et seq.; Kayser/Steinmüller (2002), 1276 et seqq.; Lang *German Law Journal* (2004), 671.

[22]   Kayser/Steinmüller (2002), 1276 et seq.; Lang (*German Law Journal* 2004), 671.

is absent when investing in regulated hedge funds. Moreover, the fact that hedge fund certificates are quite vague both in terms of the description of the investment policy of their underlying funds and, also, in terms of their costs and fees does little to protect the best interest of investors.

1.5 Hedge Fund Strategies in UCITS Funds

The more liberal UCITS III rules (especially after the adoption of the Eligible Assets Directive, which clarified certain definitions, so as ensure a uniform application of the UCITS-Directive) were implemented in German law in 2007, leading to important developments as hedge fund managers were increasingly looking for a UCITS wrapping for their hedge fund and other alternative investment strategies, presented in the form of UCITS III investments. This is possible through several different techniques.

One possibility is through the so-called 130/30 strategy as a limited and pre-defined alternative to unlimited hedge funds strategies. A 130/30 fund is considered as a 'Long-Short Equity Fund', meaning that it goes both long and short at the same time. The '130' portion stands for 130 per cent exposure of the fund's volume to the fund's long portfolio and the '30' portion stands for 30 per cent exposure of the fund's volume to the fund's short portfolio. The gains resulting from the short positions are used to finance the additional 30 per cent invested in long positions.[23]

Another possibility is through indexes. The UCITS III rules and those of the Eligible Assets Directive make it possible for a UCITS fund to invest in derivatives that use financial indexes as underlyings. Such investments are possible under the condition that the financial indexes are diversified and constitute an adequate reference base for the market. The index may even be composed of assets that are *not* eligible under the UCITS regime. For instance, UCITS-funds are not allowed to invest in commodities but a derivative based on a commodities index that is diversified and constitutes an adequate reference base for the market can be part of the fund. As more and more hedge fund indexes were developed over the last years that are considered to be diversified and to constitute an adequate reference base for the market, the possibilities for UCITS funds to invest in derivatives using a hedge fund index as underlying have increased.[24]

The third way of using hedge fund strategies in a UCITS III fund is by wrapping single-manager hedge funds or FoHFs in a so-called Delta

---

[23] Kayser/Lindemann/Käks (2009), 211 et sqq.
[24] Kayser/Lindemann/Käks (2009), 247.

1-certificate. 'Delta 1' means that the value of the certificate changes one to one with the value of the underlying. Delta 1-certificates are eligible for UCITS III funds because they are regarded as securities, under Section 47 InvG, as long as they fulfill the requirements of Article 2(2) (c) of the Eligible Assets Directive, meaning that appropriate information and reliable valuation on them are available and the potential loss is limited to the amount paid for them. This applies even if their underlying differs from the assets eligible according to the UCITS-Directive.[25]

These techniques for the wrapping of hedge fund strategies – which, needless to say, are more interesting for institutional investors that are restricted to investments in regulated and transparent products only –[26] give hedge funds access to the more favorable UCITS fund regime, with their public distribution possibilities and their 'European passport', making their cross border distribution possible. This passport is expected to become even more interesting when UCITS IV[27] comes into force (this was to be implemented by the Member States into their national law by end of June 2011). As the UCITS IV-Directive aims, amongst others, at giving a European passport to single investment, its advent is expected to facilitate cross-border distribution.

1.6   Private Equity Investments

The setting up of regulated private equity funds is not possible in Germany. Private equity investments have been the subject of intense political discussion in Germany and no mainstream political party was willing, at the time of writing, to take the responsibility for allowing the establishment, in Germany, of open-ended private equity funds.

As seen above, hedge funds are restricted to a maximum investment of 30 per cent of the value of their assets under management (AUM) in non-listed equity. A restricted addition of non-listed equity is also possible in so-called 'Other Funds' ('Sonstige Sondervermögen') under Section 90g–90 k InvG, a fund type newly introduced into German law with the 2007 amendment of the InvG. Those 'Other funds' are non-UCITS funds and, besides investing in all assets that are eligible for UCITS investments under Section 90 h InvG, they are also allowed to invest in precious metal,

---

[25]   Kayser/Lindemann/Käks (2009), 211 et seqq.

[26]   Kayser/Lindemann/Käks (2009), 211.

[27]   Directive 2009/65/EC of the European Parliament and of the Council of 13 July 2009 on the coordination of laws, regulations and administrative provisions relating to undertakings for collective investment in transferable securities (UCITS) OJ L 302, 17.11.2009, 32–96.

un-certificated loan receivables, real estate fund shares and non-listed equity. However, according to Section 90h(4) InvG, a maximum investment limit of 20 per cent of the fund's value applies for investments in non-listed equity.

As described above, in the case of hedge funds, even if it is not possible to set up a regulated private equity fund in Germany, private equity investments can be sold in other ways than by distributing fund units. Private equity funds and private equity indexes can either be wrapped in certificates, while foreign-based private equity funds can be sold via private placement. It follows that funds can be set up outside Germany and then either wrapped as certificates and publicly distributed (with all the disadvantages for investors in terms of transparency and with the emitter risk as an additional risk factor) or sold as funds via private placement.

1.7 Real Estate Funds

Real estate funds, regulated under Sections 66 to 83 InvG, represent another class of German alternative investments. These are well established in Germany, so much so that they are not regarded as alternative investments but as a classical fund type, more comparable to a UCITS than to a hedge-fund or a private equity fund. German real estate funds are regulated by the InvG and by its predecessor act, the KAGG, since 1969.[28] Open-ended real estate funds are allowed to invest in real estate (Section 67 InvG) and in real estate companies via non-listed equity (Section 68 InvG). They have to hold a minimum liquidity of 5 per cent of the fund's volume and a maximum liquidity of 49 per cent (Section 80 InvG). Historically they have had a very low volatility. They are widely spread among retail investors, without any restrictions on their distribution, and they are regarded as liquid fund products. The price of a fund unit has to be calculated and published daily (Section 79(30) InvG) and investors can redeem their fund units daily without the need for a previous announcement and without the possibility for any deferral in paying back investor money.

Seen for a long time as liquid and non-speculative products for retail investors, several of the bigger real estate funds had to interrupt the redemption of fund units in end of 2005 and 2006. At that time outflows were caused by the interruption of the redemption of fund units linked to the announcement of a revaluation of the assets of a big real estate

---

[28] Baur 1997, § 44 margin no. 2.

fund. This led to heavy outflows for other real estate funds and so several of them had to interrupt the redemption of fund units too. The first reaction from the German legislator was to come with the 2007 amendment of the InvG, when the rules concerning the independent expert committee responsible for the valuation of real estate assets (Section 77 InvG) and the rules on the valuation of assets (Section 70 InvG) were revised.[29] During the financial crisis, several real estate funds had to once again interrupt the redemption of their units and, in October 2010, three open-ended real estate funds had to announce their dissolution as they were not able to restart the redemption of units after interrupting for a two-year-period, the maximum period admissible under to Section 81 InvG.

In the meantime, the lawmaker has already announced a new initiative in response to the interruption of the redemption of fund units of several real estate funds. The publication of the first draft law,[30] which provided for a global 10 per cent deduction from the value of the real estate assets in the fund, led to heavy outflows for real estate funds, forcing several amongst them to once again suspend the redemption of their shares. Meanwhile, a new draft-law was presented,[31] this time proposing to implement a holding period of two years for fund shares, a redemption fee of 10 per cent for fund shares redeemed in the third year and 5 per cent for fund shares redeemed in the fourth year. To suit the interests of private investors, the equivalent of € 5000 in fund shares can be redeemed per month without a holding period or redemption fee. The new draft law had not been adopted and was still under discussion at the time of writing. The fund industry was hoping for amendments to give funds the possibility to have different rules for big institutional investors with holding or announcement periods for that group so that only institutional investors are less flexible in their redemption possibilities. For retail investors, the industry wanted to maintain its ability

---

[29]   Roegele/Görke (2007), 396 et sqq.

[30]   Discussion draft of the 'Investor protection and capital markets function improvement act' http://www.bundesfinanzministerium.de/nn_1940/DE/BMF__ Startseite/Service/Downloads/Abt__VII/DiskE__Gesetz__Anlegerschutz__ Verbesserung_20Funktionalit_C3_A4t_20Finanzm_C3_A4rkte,templateId=raw, property=publicationFile.pdf.

[31]   Governmental draft of the 'Investor protection and capital markets function improvement act' http://www.bundesfinanzministerium.de/nn_1940/ DE/BMF__Startseite/Aktuelles/Aktuelle__Gesetze/Gesetzentwuerfe__ Arbeitsfassungen/20100921-Anlegerschutz__anl,templateId=raw,property=publ icationFile.pdf

to offer a flexible and liquid product without too many changes to the status quo.[32]

2. NUMBER OF GERMAN HEDGE FUNDS AND HEDGE FUND CERTIFICATES

A large proportion of the open-ended funds sold in Germany are funds domiciled in Luxembourg and almost every fund company that sells funds in Germany has an affiliated company in Luxembourg. Most hedge funds are based in off-shore jurisdictions,[33] with their managers acting out of London or New York.[34] In the light of the above, it seems quite astonishing that the German legislator, as a late-comer, expected to build up a German industry without setting any real incentives for the establishment of German based hedge funds and FoHFs. All hedge fund certificates publicly distributed on the German market before could continue being publicly distributed.

After a promising start in 2004 and 2005, where the total number of German hedge funds reached 42, with approximately two billion Euro in AUM, the number of funds and their AUM started declining and, in May 2008, there were not more than 38 hedge funds (18 single-manager hedge funds and 20 FoHFs) with approximately 1,5 billion Euro of AUM. At the same time, the number of hedge fund certificates and the total amount of assets invested in hedge fund certificates were constantly increasing.[35] In December 2009, 9 single-manager hedge funds and 19 FoHFs remained in operation.[36]

3. PROTECTING FINANCIAL MARKET STABILITY

The discussion around the impact of hedge funds on the stability of financial markets has intensified, also in Germany, since the start of the financial crisis.

---

[32] Press release of the German branch association BVI dated 22nd of September 2010 http://www.bvi.de/de/presse/pressemitteilungen/presse2010/2010_09_22/2010 _09_22_PI_Kabinettsbeschluss_OIFs-oa.pdf

[33] Graef (2008), 43.

[34] Steck (2004), 158 et seq.; Graef 2008, 43.

[35] Kayser/Lindemann/Käks (2009), 204 et seq.

[36] Finanzstandort Deutschland Report No. 6 – 2010 of the Initiative Finanzstandort Deutschland, 27.

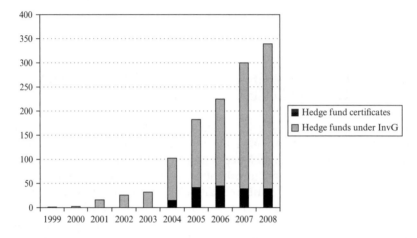

Note: As per May 2008.

Source: Busack & Sohl (2008), 29.

Figure 15.1   Number of German hedge funds and hedge fund certificates

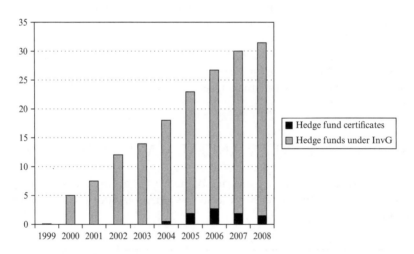

Note: As per May 2008.

Source: Busack & Sohl (2008), 29.

Figure 15.2   Assets under management of German hedge funds and hedge fund certificates

The German legal framework intended to ensure that capital market participants act in a fair and honest manner is based, for the most part, on European Directives. In brief, the relevant framework consists of rules of conduct, derived, in their actual version, from the MiFiD-Directive,[37] transparency rules, derived mostly from the Transparency[38] and the MiFiD-Directive and in rules prohibiting insider trading and market manipulation, based on the Market Abuse Directive.[39] Since the start of the financial crisis, the use of short-selling and leverage have also been seen representing a risk for financial markets.[40] As both leveraging and short-selling are typical hedge funds strategies, the whole debate has been linked to hedge funds, even if they are not the only ones to make use of those strategies.[41] With the subprime crisis turning into a public debt crisis and some of the EU Member States facing strong pressures, short selling hedge funds have come to be regarded as part of the problem, with calls to ban short selling becoming more intense. This led to the adoption of measures by the German legislator and to those topics being placed by the German government on the European agenda.

On 18 May 2010 the BaFin announced three new general decrees introducing temporary prohibitions of naked short selling of Eurozone government bonds[42] and of 10 leading German financial stocks,[43] together with a prohibition of entering into uncovered credit default swaps linked to Eurozone government debt,[44] taking effect from 19 May 2010 onwards. The BaFin justified its action by reference to the extraordinary volatility

---

[37] Directive 2004/39/EC of the European Parliament and of the Council of 21 April 2004 on markets in financial instruments amending Council Directives 85/611/EEC and 93/6/EEC and Directive 2000/12/EC of the European Parliament and of the Council and repealing Council Directive 93/22/EEC OJ L 145, 30.4.2004, 1–44.

[38] Directive 2004/109/EC of the European Parliament and of the Council of 15 December 2004 on the harmonisation of transparency requirements in relation to information about issuers whose securities are admitted to trading on a regulated market and amending Directive 2001/34/EC OJ L 390, 31.12.2004, 38–57.

[39] Directive 2003/6/EC of the European Parliament and of the Council of 28 January 2003 on insider dealing and market manipulation (market abuse) OJ L 96, 12.4.2003, 16–25.

[40] Graef 2008, 213 et sqq.

[41] Liebscher/Ott (2010), 842.

[42] www.bafin.de/cln_161/nn_720788/SharedDocs/Aufsichtsrecht/EN/Verfuegungen/vf__100518__leerverkauf__schuldtitel__en.html.

[43] www.bafin.de/cln_161/nn_720788/SharedDocs/Aufsichtsrecht/EN/Verfuegungen/vf__100518__leerverkauf__aktien__en.html.

[44] www.bafin.de/cln_161/nn_720788/SharedDocs/Aufsichtsrecht/EN/Verfuegungen/vf__100518__kreditderivate__en.html.

of debt securities of Eurozone countries and the significant increase in credit spreads of several Eurozone countries. According to the BaFin, large-scale short-sales of debt-securities and uncovered credit default swap (CDS) trading could lead to more volatility and jeopardize the stability of the financial system as a whole.[45] Those prohibitions were in place until 27 July 2010.

Meanwhile, despite heavy criticism from different quarters,[46] the German legislator has approved a new statute, which entered in force on 27 July 2010 and which aims at preventing supposedly abusive securities and derivatives transactions. The reference is to the Gesetz zur Vorbeugung gegen missbräuchliche Wertpapier- und Derivategeschäfte – 'WpMiVoG',[47] which introduces a prohibition of the naked short selling of shares as well as of debt instruments issued by Eurozone countries if these are admitted to trading on a regulated market in Germany (Section 30h WpHG); a prohibition of CDS, the reference obligations of which include an obligation of a Eurozone country, and which are not used for hedging purposes (Section 30j WpHG); and a transparency regime for covered short sales of shares admitted to trading on a regulated German market (Section 30i WpHG).[48]

The European Commission has over the last years been more reluctant than the German Government regarding restrictions on short sales. Nevertheless, the European Commission has in the meantime adopted a proposal for a regulation on short selling and certain aspects of CDS.[49] Interestingly, its draft still opts for a more liberal approach compared to the new German Act. While, in the proposed Regulation, the transparency requirements in Articles 5 to 8 are close to the new German Act, this doesn't include an unlimited prohibition of naked short sales, as the case is under German law. Instead, Article 12 of the proposal addresses

---

[45] BaFin press release, www.bafin.de/cln_161/nn_720788/SharedDocs/Mitteilungen/EN/2010/pm__100518__cds__leerverkauf__allgemeinverfuegungen__en.html.

[46] Möllers/Christ/Harrer (2010), 1169 et seq.

[47] Gesetz zur Vorbeugung gegen missbräuchliche Wertpapier- und Derivategeschäfte – 'WpMiVoG' dated 21.07.2010. BGBl 26.07.2010, part 1 No. 38 at p. 945 et sqq. http://www.bgbl.de/Xaver/start.xav?startbk=Bundesanzeiger_BGBl&bk=Bundesanzeiger_BGBl&start=//*%5B@attr_id=%27bgbl110s0945.pdf%27%5D

[48] Möllers/Christ/Harrer (2010), 1167 et seqq.

[49] EU-Commission, Proposal for a Regulation of the European Parliament and of the Council on Short Selling and certain aspects of Credit Default Swaps v. 15. 9. 2010. http://ec.europa.eu/internal_market/securities/docs/short_selling/20100915_proposal_de.pdf.

the potential risk of settlement failure and includes detailed requirements aimed at addressing that risk. To this end, natural or legal persons entering into short sales of such instruments must, at the time of the sale, have actually borrowed the instruments, entered into an agreement to borrow the shares or made other arrangements to ensure that the security can be borrowed so that settlement can be effected when it is due. Furthermore, trading venues, which according to Article 2(1)(r) of the proposal mean regulated markets or multilateral trading facilities in the EU, according to Article 13 shall be responsible to ensure that there are adequate arrangements in place for the buy-in of shares or sovereign debt where there is a failure to settle a transaction. Daily fines are to be imposed in case of non-settlement. Only in the case of adverse developments, which constitute a serious threat to financial stability or to market confidence, would the authorities be able to temporarily impose restrictions on short-selling and CDS transactions or limit natural and legal persons from entering into derivative transactions.[50]

4. PROTECTING GERMAN COMPANIES FROM PREDATORY INVESTORS?

4.1 The German 'Locusts' Debate

The debate on the need to protect German companies from private equity investors and hedge funds intensified when the term 'locust'[51] became a synonym for hedge funds in Germany. Leading politicians in Germany saw hedge funds and private equity funds as a plague and a menace for the German industry,[52] buying-off productive companies, only to break them up in parts and sell them off, while leaving valueless shells behind. The successful attack of two hedge funds on the management of the *Deutsche Börse AG* started up a debate that, irrespective of its motivation, developed into a political and legal one, on how best to protect German companies from

---

[50]   Möllers/Christ/Harrer (2010), 1167 et seqq.

[51]   The so called Heuschrecken (locust)-debate started in Germany when Franz Müntefering at that time Chairman of the Social Democratic Party (SPD) gave an Interview to the German newspaper 'Bild am Sonntag' which was published 17th of April 2005 saying that 'some financial investors are wasting no thought to the people whose jobs they destroy – they remain anonymous, have no face fall forth like locusts over companies, graze them and move on. Against this form of capitalism we fight.'

[52]   Seifert/Voth (2006); Schäfer (2007); Maier (2007).

activist shareholders that take advantage of the passivity of the majority of shareholders to use their voting rights in a way that gives them majorities in the decision making process, with only a minority of shares.[53]

On 12 December 2004, the management of *Deutsche Börse AG* made a take-over bid for *London Stock Exchange* (LSE). A group of hedge funds led by *The Children's Investment Fund* (TCI) bought in a short time enough of the shares of Deutsche Börse AG to block its planned take-over of the LSE. TCI's reasoning was that the price of £5,30 per share was, from the point of view of the shareholders of *Deutsche Börse AG*, too high. But the group of hedge funds was not only aiming on an increase in the market price of *Deutsche Börse AG* shares in case of a failure of the take-over bid. At the same time as they bought *Deutsche Börse AG* shares, they sold LSE shares short to depress their price. This meant that, even if the prices of *Deutsche Börse AG* shares didn't rise, *TCI* would still be able to profit from the sinking prices of the LSE shares, an inevitable effect of the failure of the take-over bid. This led to discussions on the need for stricter rules concerning the disclosure of holdings,[54] on what came to be regarded as acting in concert, and about the measures necessary to reduce the possibilities of minority activist shareholders to influence annual shareholder meetings. Additional transparency requirements were to be introduced, as a result, in German law in 2007 and 2008.

4.2   Transparency Requirements

When, in January 2007, the Transparency Directive Implementation Act (Transparenzrichtlinien-Umsetzungsgesetz, 'TUG') transposed the Transparency Directive into German law,[55] disclosure rules for shareholdings of 5, 10, 15, 20, 25, 30, 50 and 75 per cent were introduced. Beyond those EU-law based disclosure rules, an additional German disclosure rule for shareholdings of 3 per cent of a company was introduced in Section 21 Securities Trading Act (Wertpapierhandelsgesetz – 'WpHG').[56] Furthermore, the implementation of the EU Transparency Directive led to extended acting in concert rules in Section 22 WpHG, which attribute voting rights to anyone who bears economic risks in shares and has the possibility to influence the exercise of another's voting rights.[57] In addition, the entry into force, in August 2008, of the Risk Limitation Act

---

[53]   Wentrup 2009, p. 138 et seqq.
[54]   Wentrup 2009, p. 150 et seqq.
[55]   BGBl. I 2007, 10.
[56]   Wentrup (2009), 252 et seqq.
[57]   Wentrup (2009), 267 et seqq.

(Risikobegrenzungsgesetz)[58] brought about amendments to Section 25
WpHG. Since then, every investor that hits or crosses one of the thresholds in Section 21(1) WpHG that leads to a disclosure obligation, except
the 3 per cent threshold, has to, in addition, disclose its holdings in financial instruments bearing the right to acquire voting rights in this share.[59]
Financial instruments in this sense are, for instance, futures, forwards or
covered warrants.[60] Besides the transparency requirements in the WpHG,
there are transparency requirements in the Securities Acquisition and
Takeover Act (Wertpapierübernahmegesetz – 'WpÜG'), which, in Section
35 thereof, obliges anyone gaining direct or indirect control over a target
company to publicize this immediately and to make a take-over bid to
all other shareholders. According to Section 29 WpÜG 'control' means
control over at least 30 per cent of the voting rights.[61] A new draft law, the
Investor Protection and Capital Markets Function Improvement Act,[62]
which is expected to enter in force in the second quarter of 2011, is expected
to once again tighten the disclosure rules in the WpHG. Disclosure rules
concerning other financial instruments or non-financial instruments that
give their holders the possibility to acquire financial instruments giving
them voting rights are to be implemented. As a result, the rules for the disclosure of holdings in Germany will go beyond the requirements of the EU
Transparency Directive and the tendency today in Germany is to tighten
them even more.[63] This goes hand in hand with the increasing complexity
of the German transparency regime, which can create room for interpreta-
tional issues concerning the correct disclosure of holdings.[64]

5.   INVESTOR PROTECTION WITHOUT A CONCEPT

The preceding discussion provides a short overview of the current legal
framework for alternative investments in Germany, with an emphasis on
hedge funds and the discussions surrounding them.

---

[58]   BGBl. I 2007 at 3089.
[59]   Wentrup (2009), 254 et seq.; Bednarz (2009), 150 et seqq.
[60]   Schneider in Assmann/Schneider 2009 § 25 margin no. 14 et seqq.
[61]   Wentrup (2009), 264 et sq.; Bednarz (2009), 147 et seqq.
[62]   Governmental draft of the 'Investor protection and capital markets function   improvement   act'   http://www.bundesfinanzministerium.de/nn_1940/
DE/BMF__Startseite/Aktuelles/Aktuelle__Gesetze/Gesetzentwuerfe__
Arbeitsfassungen/20100921-Anlegerschutz__anl,templateId=raw,property=publ
icationFile.pdf.
[63]   Fleischer/Schmolke (2010), 846.
[64]   Wentrup (2009), 317 et seqq.

Summarizing that discussion, it would seem that there is no product-group-wide concept for investor protection in alternative investment products. This deficiency of the current legal framework leads to investor protection issues that have been detected and addressed for one product but ignored for others. This is true on an European level, where both the UCITS and the recently adopted AIFM-Directives,[65] do not address the issues arising from the distribution of certificates.

What is missing in German investor protection regulation is an overall model of the private investor.[66] Does he need protection from taking wrong or too risky decisions or does he only need fair, correct and appropriate information to take his decisions? When limiting the distribution of single-manager hedge funds, the goal seems to be to protect the investors by preventing them from buying those products. But, on the other hand, more and more information obligations are introduced in German law, which are not consistent with this preventive rationale. The latest example is that of a draft-law – the Investor Protection and Capital Markets Function Improvement Act – introducing an obligation for banks to hand out short, two-page-long product sheets for all of their products. This can only be helpful for a private investor who is able to understand the risks inherent in a product. What is more, the product warnings are not consistent. The governmental warning appearing on prospectuses applies only to single-manager hedge funds and FoHFs. No such warning exists in the case of certificates. This is all the more incomprehensible as, for certificates, the probability of a total loss seems more likely (on account of their emitter risk) than in the case of investments in open-ended funds.[67] Looking at other types of funds and taking, for instance, the volatility of an equity fund and the risk of losing substantial parts of an investment in equity funds, equity funds must be considered as risky for their investors; however, no governmental warning has to be printed on the prospectuses accompanying those products.[68] However, considering that hedge funds, in contrast to certificates or other fund products, require big minimum investments that prevent retail investors from investing in them, investors in them may be less dependent on product warnings than investors in other products.[69]

Looking at German hedge fund regulation over the last years, the

---

[65]   Proposal on a Directive on Alternative Fund Managers http://ec.europa.eu/internal_market/investment/alternative_investments_en.htm#proposal.

[66]   Lang, VuR (2004), 206.

[67]   Kayser/Lindemann/Käks (2009), 253.

[68]   Lang, *German Law Journal* 2004, p. 679 et sqq.; Lang, W.M. 2004, p. 59 et seq.

[69]   Graef 2008, p. 38.

impression that the German legislator gives is of being somewhat torn between wanting to build up a German hedge fund industry, preventing German investors from making risky investments in hedge funds and protecting German companies from aggressive activist shareholders, such as hedge funds and private equity funds. Moreover, the overall model of an investor that should lead the concept of what is necessary to protect him differs depending on whether the investor protection requirements derive from European or national, German investor protection standards.

6.   QUESTIONS TO BE ASKED

Some of the answers that the German legislator has given to the different problems with which modern capital markets are faced do not appear to be convincing. The reason for this might be that the German legislator is asking the wrong questions and that he often treats similar product groups differently.

Instead of asking, in a unitary manner, what kind of concept for the redemption of fund units would fit funds that invest in products that are largely illiquid, such as real estate funds and hedge funds, the question is asked for each product group separately. This leads to different answers to what is at least a similar problem.

Instead of asking how to protect investors from the risks arising from open-ended, regulated hedge funds, the question should be how to protect the investors from hedge fund-related risks independent from the product in the context of which such risks arise. This could lead to a product-group-wide answer, more investor transparency, as some requirements would lead to investor information that is more easily comparable, and even enhanced product-group-wide competition and a level playing field for legally different product types that entail the similar risks.

When it comes to private equity investments and the reluctance of the German legislator to legislate the creation of private equity funds in Germany, the questions seem to be the wrong ones too. If the question is how the legislator can protect German investors from investments in private equity funds, then investor protection from investments in publicly distributed private equity certificates and foreign private equity funds sold via private placement fall out of sight. And if German companies should be protected from asset stripping then restricting private equity investments of regulated German funds cannot help,[70] as foreign private equity

---

[70]   Spindler/Bednarz 2006, p. 605.

funds are investing on the German market by buying German companies without being subject to any legal barriers. If the question is how to protect German companies from asset stripping the answer has to be given either on German company law field or on an international level. What seems astonishing is that, on the one hand, the whole discussion about private equity funds is about their investment strategy and about their asset stripping of German target companies but, on the other hand, the political reaction is not to avoid asset stripping but just to avoid that regulated German private equity companies enter the German market while foreign private equity companies are allowed to use asset stripping techniques in Germany.

But even the question how to protect German companies from asset stripping by foreign private equity funds or hedge funds might be the wrong one. What can be stated is that the legislator is acting, especially in this field, on the basis of individual cases and case studies without any wider empirical basis. What is missing, is an analysis of private equity fund investments in German companies and the effects of those investments for the target companies. Instead, only singular cases have been analyzed and those singular cases have led to legal initiatives that are not based on a broad empirical basis and have been presented without a previous cost-benefit-analysis.[71] The question in this discussion should be whether or not German companies are really victims of private equity investors and hedge funds acting only with a view to their short-term profit and not in the long-term interest of the shareholders of their target companies. It should be asked whether activist shareholders really act to the long-term disadvantage of the companies they are investing in, problems which arise when hedge funds or private equity funds start investing in a company and how these problems should be addressed.[72]

Regarding the financial markets turmoil, the subprime crisis and the public debt crisis, even if the German regulator cannot be blamed for them, he nevertheless has the duty to prevent those crises from repeating themselves. Looking at hedge funds in this context, the question should be to what extent hedge funds have, through their short selling or other strategies, aggravated the crises. The question is not easy to answer as instruments such as CDSs are not sold on regulated markets. So it might be an approach to set-up a regulation that establishes transparency across markets, whether or not these are regulated.[73]

---

[71] Fleischer (2008), 191 et seqq.

[72] Lehmann (2007), 1895 et seqq.; Spindler/Bednarz (2006), 604 et sqq.; Kumpan (2006), 70; Engert (2006), 210 et seqq.

[73] Spindler/Bednarz (2006), 604.

Finally, when the German legislator is aiming to build up a German hedge fund industry, the first question should be what sort of industry that should be, where hedge funds are based and how they are acting. It should be asked what kind of regulation hedge funds really need and what kind of incentive is necessary to attract them to Germany. A framework allowing foreign hedge funds to publicly distribute their products wrapped as certificates but restricting German hedge funds on private placement might not be the answer to this. And even with the implementation of the AIFM-Directive in German law, those hedge fund certificates may remain outside the scope of regulation. What is necessary for the promotion of a German hedge fund industry is a consistent approach on the marketing of hedge fund products. What is also necessary is to build up a market for the selling of regulated hedge funds in Germany by setting a liberal framework for big institutional investors, such as, for example, insurance companies, to invest in hedge funds.[74] Furthermore, further liberalization of the German hedge fund regime is needed.[75] For example, it is questionable if for single-manager hedge funds, which are not publicly distributed, the requirement to redeem fund units at least quarterly is really necessary. Here the German InvG restricts the distribution on the one hand and on the other hand the rules for the redemption of units are stricter than for FoHFs, which can be publicly distributed and which at least benefit from the deferred payment option. The whole German concept of restricting distribution should be discussed.[76] It also seems questionable whether the credit rules for FoHFs really have to be stricter than for a UCITS III fund of fund. Furthermore, the prospectus requirement for single-manager hedge funds seems not to fit in the overall framework as long as the distribution regime remains unchanged, since the requirement for a prospectus is linked to public distribution. The admission of side-pocket solutions to separate illiquid assets from the liquid ones should also be discussed. These are only some of the issues. A well-considered legal framework for hedge funds is still a task to be accomplished.

Good answers require good questions and a consistent German capital markets regime with product transparency and a good level of investor protection needs a legislator asking the right questions. More than that, a law maker asking the right questions is necessary to build up an industry, not only for hedge funds but for all kinds of open-ended funds in Germany.

---

[74]   Weitzel/Zeller (2006), 367; Wentrup (2009), 312 et seq.
[75]   Wentrup (2009), 312 et seq.
[76]   Wentrup (2009), 312 et seqq.; Bednarz (2009), 159 et seqq.

BIBLIOGRAPHY

Assmann, Hans-Dieter and Uwe H. Schneider (eds) (2009), WpHG, 5th edition. Cologne, Germany: Verlag Dr. Otto Schmidt.

Baur, Jürgen (1997), Investmentgesetze 2. Teilband, 2nd edition, Berlin, Germany and New York, US: De Gruyter.

Bednarz, Sebastian (2009), 'Die Regulierung von Hedge-Fonds', Hamburg, Germany: Verlag Dr. Kovac.

Busack, Michael and Stefan Sohl (2008), 'Hedgefonds in Deutschland-Ein Marktüberblick'. Absolut-report, pp 28–35, Hamburg, Germany: Absolut Research GmbH.

Engert, Andreas (2006), 'Hedgefonds als aktivistische Aktionäre', ZIP – Zeitschrift für Wirtschaftsrecht, Cologne, Germany: RWS Verlag, pp. 2105–2113.

Fleischer, Holger (2008), 'Finanzinvestoren im ordnungspolitischen Gesamtgefüge von Aktien-, Bankaufsichts- und Kapitalmarktrecht', ZGR – Zeitschrift für Unternehmens- und Gesellschaftsrecht at p. 185–224, Berlin, Germany: De Gruyter.

Fleischer, Holger and Klaus Ulrich Schmolke (2010), Zum beabsichtigten Ausbau der kapitalmarktrechtlichen Beteiligungstransparenz bei modernen Finanzinstrumenten (§§ 25, 25a DiskE-WpHG), NZG – Neue Zeitschrift für Gesellschaftsrechtat pp. 846–54, Munich, Germany: C. H. Beck.

Graef, Andreas (2008), 'Aufsicht über Hedgefonds im deutschen und amerikanischen Recht', Berlin, Germany: Duncker & Humblot.

Kayser, Joachim and Steinmüller (2002), 'Hedge-Fonds im Überblick: Funktionsweise, aufsichts- und steuerrechtliche Behandlung aus Investorensicht', FR – Finanz-Rundschau, pp.1269–79, Cologne, Germany: Verlag Dr. Otto Schmidt.

Kayser, Joachim, Alexander Lindemann and Caroline Käks (2009), 'Aufsichtsrechtliche Entwicklungen auf dem deutschen Markt im Bereich Hedgefonds', Finanz Betrieb, pp. 204–213 and 247–254, Düsseldorf, Germany: Fachverlag der Verlagsgruppe Handelsblatt.

Kovas, Ashley (2003); 'Should Hedge Fund Products be Marketed to Retail Investors? A Balancing Act for the Regulator', Institute for Law and Finance Working Paper Series No. 10, http://www.ilf-frankfurt.de/ILF-Working-Papers.117.0.html.

Kumpan, Christoph (2006), 'Börsenmacht Hedge-Fonds : Die Regulierungen in den USA und mögliche Implikationen für Deutschland', ZHR – Zeitschrift für das gesamte Handelsrecht und Wirtschaftsrecht, pp. 39–71, Frankfurt, Germany: Verlag Recht und Wirtschaft.

Lang, Norbert (2004), 'Das Investmentgesetz – Kein großer Wurf, aber ein Schritt in die richtige Richtung', WM – Wertpapiermitteilungen at pp.53–9, Frankfurt, Germany: Herausgebergemeinschaft Wertpapier-Mitteilungen.

Lang, Norbert (2004), 'Das neue Investmentgesetz und das fehlende Anlegerleitbild des Gesetzgebers', VuR – Verbraucher und Recht, pp. 201–207, Baden-Baden, Germany: Nomos Verlagsgesellschaft.

Lang, Norbert (2004), 'German Hedge Fund Legislation: Modernised but Still Old-fashioned', *German Law Journal*, 669–77, www.germanlawjournal.com.

Lehmann, Matthias (2007), 'Die Regulierung und Überwachung von Hedgefonds als internationales Zuständigkeitsproblem', ZIP – Zeitschrift für Wirtschaftsrecht at p. 1889–98, Cologne, Germany: RWS Verlag.

Liebscher, Thomas and Nicolas Ott (2010), 'Die Regulierung der Finanzmärkte – Reformbedarf und Regelungsansätze des deutschen Gesetzgebers im Überblick', NZG – Neue Zeitschrift für Gesellschaftsrecht, pp. 841–6 Munich, Germany: C. H. Beck.

Luttermann, Claus and Julia Backmann (2002), 'Rechtsverhältnisse bei Hedge-Fonds ('Risikofonds') in Deutschland und in den USA', ZIP – Zeitschrift für Wirtschaftsrecht, pp. 1017–1124, Cologne, Germany: RWS Verlag.

Maier, Angela (2007), 'Der Heuschrecken-Faktor. Finanzinvestoren in Deutschland: Wer sind sie? Wie arbeiten sie? Wer profitiert wirklich?', Munich, Germany: Hanser.

Möllers, Thomas, Dominique Christ and Andreas Harrer (2010), 'Nationale Alleingänge und die europäische Reaktion auf ein Verbot ungedeckter Leerverkäufe', NZG – Neue Zeitschrift für Gesellschaftsrechtat, pp. 1167–70, Munich, Germany: C. H. Beck.

Pütz, Achim and Christian Schmies (2004), 'Die Umsetzung der neuen rechtlichen Rahmenbedingungen für Hedgefonds in der Praxis', BKR – Zeitschrift für Bank- und Kapitalmarktrecht, pp. 51–60 Munich, Germany: C. H. Beck.

Roegele, Elisabeth and Oliver Görke (2007), 'Novelle des Investmentgesetztes (InvG)', BKR – Zeitschrift für Bank- und Kapitalmarktrecht, pp. 393–400 Munich, Germany: C. H. Beck.

Schäfer, Daniel (2007), 'Die Wahrheit über die Heuschrecken. Wie Finanzinvestoren die Deutschland AG umbauen', 2. Aufl., Frankfurt, Germany: Frankfurter Allgemeine Buch.

Schimanski, Herbert, Hermann-Josef Bunte, Hans Jürgen Lwowski (eds) (2007), *Bankrechts-Handbuch Band II*, 3rd edition, Munich, Germany: C. H. Beck.

Seifert, Werner G. and Voth Hans-Joachim (2006), 'Invasion der Heuschrecken. Intrigen – Machtkämpfe – Marktmanipulation', Berlin, Germany: Econ.

Spindler, Gerald and Sebastian Bednarz (2006), 'Die Regulierung von Hedge-Fonds im Kapitalmarkt- und Gesellschaftsrecht', WM – Wertpapiermitteilungen, pp. 553–60 and 601–607 Frankfurt, Germany: Herausgebergemeinschaft Wertpapier-Mitteilungen.

Steck, Kai-Uwe (2004), 'Legal Aspects of German Hedge Fund Structures' in Theodor Baums and Andreas Cahn (eds), *Hedge Funds Risk and Regulation*, Berlin: De Gruyter, pp.135–160.

Wallach Edgar (2004), 'Hedge Funds Regulation in Germany', in Theodor Baums and Andreas Cahn (eds), *Hedge Funds Risk and Regulation*, Berlin, Germany: De Gruyter, pp. 119–131.

Weitzel, Michael and Sven Zeller (2006), 'Hedgefonds-Investitionen von Versicherungsunternehmen nach der neuen Anlageverordnung', WM – Wertpapiermitteilungen pp. 358–67, Frankfurt, Germany: Herausgebergemeinschaft Wertpapier-Mitteilungen.

Wentrup, Christian (2009), 'Die Kontrolle von Hedgefonds', Berlin, Germany: Duncker & Humblot.

Wilhelmi, Rüdiger (2008), 'Möglichkeiten und Grenzen der wirtschaftsrechtlichen Regelung von Hedgefonds', WM – Wertpapiermitteilungen, pp.861–8, Frankfurt, Germany: Herausgebergemeinschaft Wertpapier-Mitteilungen.

16. Hedge funds, private equity and alternative investment in Australia
*Alex Erskine**

INTRODUCTION

The Australian managed funds industry held AU$1.7 trillion (US$1.69 trillion) in assets and was ranked the fourth largest in the world and largest in the Asia Pacific region in December 2009.[1,2] The managed funds industry has grown by a compound annual growth rate of 11.9 per cent since 1992. The industry's funds under management (FUM) have nearly doubled since 2003.[3]

A number of factors have driven the growth of the Australian managed investment industry in general and the alternative investment sector in particular. Firstly, the Government introduced compulsory superannuation[4] (retirement) savings in the early 1990s. That resulted in a substantial growth in superannuation accounts (see Figure 16.1). Some superannuation monies were in turn invested in the alternative investments industries, facilitating growth and the achievement of economies of scale and scope.

* Alex Erskine is Chief Economist, Australian Securities & Investments Commission. Also contributing were Jeremy Bray, Li-Ling Chew, Ben Durnford, Dr. Pamela Hanrahan, Paulo Pinto, Trinh Quach, Dr. Shane Worner, Grantly Brown, Marie-Christine DeGreeff, and Geoff McCarthy. This chapter contains personal views which do not necessarily represent the view or policies of the Australian Securities & Investments Commission or its Commissioners. The contents of this chapter were finalized on 19 January 2011.

[1] Australian Trade Commission (2010), *Investment Management Industry in Australia*, Canberra, Australia.
[2] Exchange rate of AU$ = US$99.96 as at close of 18 January 2011. This exchange rate is used throughout the chapter unless otherwise stated.
[3] Australian Trade Commission (2010), *Investment Management Industry in Australia*, Canberra, Australia.
[4] Superannuation is the term used in Australia to describe the setting aside of income for retirement, generally known internationally as pension or retirement products. Australia's current 'superannuation guarantee' system was introduced in July 1992, requiring all employers to make tax-deductible superannuation contributions on behalf of their employees. The guarantee commenced with an employer contribution rate of 3% of salary. The current employer contribution rate is 9% of salary.

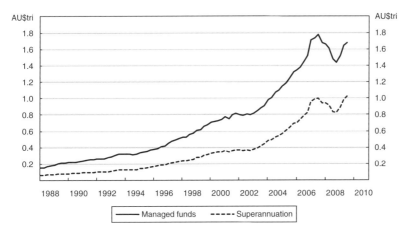

Note: Data to 30 June, 2010.

Source: RBA.

Figure 16.1   *Estimated assets of the managed funds and superannuation industry in Australia*

Secondly, the 1990s and the first half of the 2000s were characterised in Australia – as in many Western economies – by low inflation, low interest rates, and relatively stable and firm economic growth. In Australia, the consequent flow of funds into institutional investments was even more pronounced than in a number of other markets because the local economy was sheltered by a floating exchange rate and sound economic management from international turbulence (e.g. from the late-1990s Asian and Russian crises, the dot-com bubble and the ensuing early-2000s global recession) and benefited from the secular rise in commodity prices later in the 2000s.

A third factor has been taxation. Superannuation returns are taxed at lower rates than other investments and there have been special concessions for investors to transfer proceeds from asset sales into superannuation without triggering full capital gains tax. Tax arrangements have also favoured agricultural/forestry investment schemes.

The alternative investments industries in Australia are still small relative to mainstream investments (Figure 16.2). The combined assets of hedge funds, infrastructure funds, private equity, Australian real estate investment trusts (A-REITs) and agribusiness funds amounted to approximately AU$230 billion (US$229.9 billion) or around 13 per cent of the total managed funds industry as at mid 2010.

Australia's alternative investments industries were affected by the global

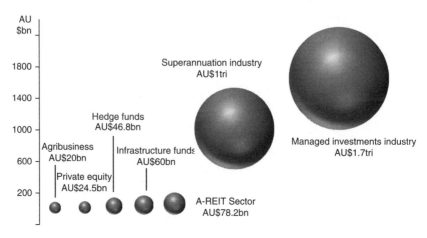

Note: Figures for Agribusiness, Hedge Funds, Infrastructure Funds and A-REIT Sector are as at 30 March 2010; figures for Private Equity, Superannuation industry and Managed investments industry are as at 30 June 2010.

Sources: Australian Bureau of Statistics, Austrade, AVCAL and RBA.

Figure 16.2   Estimated assets of the 'alternatives' components of the managed investments industry in Australia

financial crisis (GFC). As a whole, the alternatives segment saw falls in investment flows, funds under management and returns. There were a number of failures of hedge funds, property trusts and agricultural and infrastructure funds during 2007 to 2010, which revealed problems regarding the appropriateness of business models, adequacy of information disclosures, quality of advice provided by financial planners to retail investors and investors' understanding of the risk in alternative investments.

1.   REGULATORY OVERVIEW

Managed investment scheme (MIS) is the generic term used in Australia to describe a variety of structures for creating and operating collective investment schemes or projects. MIS's point of difference from other investments is that they involve an investor acquiring an asset other than a security (such as a share) or an investment with a prudentially regulated entity (such as a bank deposit). Approved deposit funds are regulated like superannuation funds and are excluded as MISs.

The MIS sector includes equity funds, bond funds, cash management trusts, property trusts, mortgage trusts (both those listed on public stock

Table 16.1 Summary of Managed Investment Schemes in Australia

Broad category	Investment arrangements	Assets
Portfolio-type investment funds, such as managed funds or mutual funds	These are the typical investment products offered by fund managers holding an Australian financial services license. They involve pooling financial assets. They may pursue passive or active investment strategies, be internally geared, and use derivatives. They may be focused on a particular sector (for example Australian equities) or be multi-sector or diversified.	Assets held in these funds range from highly liquid short-term debt securities through bonds and shares to less liquid longer duration listed and unlisted assets.
Property related schemes	These include listed property trusts, unlisted property trusts, property syndicates, funds for property lending, property securities funds, serviced strata projects, time share schemes, and investments in retirement village developments.	These schemes' assets lie along a risk spectrum, from income-producing high-quality tenanted assets to property-development projects and land banks. Property assets may be located in Australia or overseas.
Infrastructure investments	These are often held in listed trusts or 'stapled' structures (in which a unit issued by the MIS is stapled to a share issued by a company so they must be traded together).	These schemes' assets are long-lived and capital-intensive, producing relatively steady revenue flows. They include toll roads, airports, electrical power assets, pipelines and telecommunications assets. The assets may be located in Australia or overseas.
Agribusiness schemes	These are structured so that the investor is a 'grower' carrying on a primary production business (and therefore is entitled to special tax treatment with respect to the investment). The grower contracts with the RE to plant and maintain the land and harvest the produce.	These types of investments tend to be held for the medium to longer term. Their assets tend to be illiquid, and include plantation timber, horticulture, viticulture and aquaculture.
Other investments	MISs are sometimes used for particular and special investment projects.	The assets in these types of schemes can vary widely (from short term liquid assets to longer term illiquid assets) and tend to be exotic, for example films and syndicates for breeding and racing horses.

exchanges and unlisted trusts), property syndicates, trustee common funds with external members, hedge funds, limited partnerships, private equity investment schemes, investment platforms, serviced strata schemes, agricultural schemes (including forestry, horticulture, viticulture), and other alternate investments such as film schemes and horse racing syndicates. Time-sharing schemes are also MISs.

There are 5200 registered MISs in Australia, operated by 674 licensed operators, termed 'responsible entities' (REs).[5] However MISs are only required to be registered if their membership includes retail clients.[6]

2.   THE ROLE OF THE ASIC

There is no regulatory framework applying specifically to alternative investments in Australia. Instead, members of this sector are classified as MISs or companies and regulated accordingly. The role of the Australian Securities and Investments Commission (ASIC) in regulating registered MISs is set out below.

2.1   Licensing REs

An RE is a body that operates a registered MIS. ASIC may grant a licence to any public company which applies for a licence to be an RE. Licensees have ongoing compliance requirements relating to conduct and disclosure, provision of financial services and arrangements for managing conflicts of interests.[7] To enable it to form a view on these matters, ASIC collects information from applicants on a number of issues including, but not limited to, their responsible officers and risk management practices. ASIC may also impose conditions on licences (such as conditions relating to minimum financial resources) to address these matters.

2.2   Registering Schemes

As noted above a MIS may be required to be registered with ASIC. Note that ASIC neither vets nor approves the schemes. ASIC must register a

---

[5]   Data as at 30 June 2010.

[6]   Retail clients are generally clients that invest less than AU$500000, do not meet certain tests as to their minimum net assets (AU$A2.5 million) and gross income (AU$250000) and are not professional investors (see s761G of the Corporations Act).

[7]   See section 911A of *Corporations Act 2001* (the Act).

scheme unless it appears to ASIC that it does not have an appropriately licensed RE, or that its constitution or compliance plan does not comply with the law.

2.3 Monitoring Disclosure

Interests in a registered MIS generally must be offered to retail clients through a complying product disclosure statement (PDS). REs operating listed schemes must lodge their PDSs with ASIC. PDSs have a perpetual life, subject to an obligation to update for substantial changes. ASIC may (and does) examine PDSs individually or as part of a sample of a particular sector for pro-active risk-based surveillance.

2.4 Monitoring Conduct

ASIC supervises the conduct of REs, the holders of Australian Financial Services Licences (AFSL) and their officers and others acting on their behalf, to check compliance with legal obligations. This supervision is done on a risk-assessed basis and will often be triggered by either a breach notification from the RE, a report from a compliance plan auditor or compliance committee, a formal complaint, or ASIC's targeted supervision of entities or sectors identified as 'at risk'. ASIC can take or initiate a range of actions in relation to non-compliance, including administrative action such as licensing action or enforceable undertakings, civil action including civil penalty actions and criminal action through referral to the Commonwealth Director of Public Prosecutions.

The role of ASIC in regulating MISs that are not required to be a registered scheme involves:

2.5 Licensing

A number of the activities involved in the operation of a MIS may be financial services. This includes the dealing activities of the fund manager and the provision of custodial or depository services. Generally fund managers are required to have an AFSL covering their financial services. Licensees have ongoing compliance requirements relating to conduct and disclosure, provision of financial services and arrangements for the management of conflicts of interests.[8]

---

[8]   See section 911A of the Act

2.6   Monitoring conduct

Generally, there are no specific disclosure requirements for MISs that are not required to be registered schemes. A number of obligations still apply such as a requirement not to engage in misleading or deceptive conduct. However, as with REs, ASIC supervises the conduct of AFSL holders and persons who provide financial services on their behalf to check compliance with legal obligations in relation to their schemes. ASIC has the power to initiate a range of actions in relation to non-compliance.

3.   HEDGE FUNDS

3.1   Overview

While the global hedge funds industry saw a decline in both number of funds and assets under management in 2008–2009, there were signs in 2010 that the industry grew once again. FUM for single hedge funds and funds of hedge funds in Australia recovered to levels close to their peaks just prior to the onset of the GFC in September 2008.[9] While the collection of data on FUM for single hedge funds and funds of hedge funds is not systematic or mandatory in Australia, it is estimated that they represent only a very small slice of total assets in the managed funds industry (2.2 per cent and 1.0 per cent, respectively). Most hedge funds in Australia are small. Approximately 55 per cent of all hedge funds (that reported FUM data as at 30 June 2010; 296 in total) have AU$55million (US$54.9 million) or less in assets.

3.2   Hedge Fund Regulation in Australia

In Australia, the regulation of a hedge fund will depend on the fund's structure. Those funds that fall within the definition of a MIS in section 9[10] of the Corporations Act 2001 (the Act) and are retail MISs are

---

[9]   For the purposes of this section, hedge funds or funds of hedge funds considered to be 'Australian' are those that have been identified as domiciled or marketed in Australia. Estimates based on ASIC calculations as at 30 June 2010. Data sourced from www.fundmonitors.com.au, *Morningstar* and *Bloomberg*.
[10]   Section 9 of the Act defines MIS as (subject to certain exclusions):
(a)   a scheme with the following features

required to be registered under Chapter 5C of the Act.[11] The RE of a registered scheme is to operate the scheme and perform the functions conferred on it by the scheme's constitution and the Act. The RE is obliged to meet certain conduct and disclosure requirements under the Act, to provide a PDS if making an offer to a retail investor to acquire interests in the scheme and to prepare and lodge financial statements. Only retail MISs must have an RE, and that RE must be a public company.

Most hedge funds may fall under the definition of a MIS in section 9 of the Act but not be required to be registered under Chapter 5C.

Hedge funds that are structured as companies need to comply with relevant conduct and disclosure obligations under the Act that apply.[12]

Hedge funds also fall within the scope of the Australian Securities and Investments Commission Act 2001 (the ASIC Act) which contains some general consumer protections e.g. through the prohibition of unconscionable, misleading or deceptive conduct, false or misleading representations, bait advertising, harassment, coercion and pyramid selling of financial products. There are similar provisions in the Act in relation to misleading statements and also prohibitions on various forms of market misconduct, for example, insider trading, market manipulation, and so on. ASIC's usual investigation powers may be used in relation to hedge fund activity depending on the circumstances.

(i)   people contribute money or money's worth as consideration to acquire rights (interests) to benefits produced by the scheme (whether the rights are actual, prospective or contingent and whether they are enforceable or not);

(ii)   any of the contributions are to be pooled, or used in a common enterprise, to produce financial benefits, or benefits consisting of rights or interests in property, for the people (the members) who hold interests in the scheme (whether as contributors to the scheme or as people who have acquired interests from holders);

(iii)   the members do not have day-to-day control over the operation of the scheme (whether or not they have the right to be consulted or to give directions); or

(b) a time-sharing scheme.

[11]   See section 601ED of the Act.

[12]   For example, provisions in Chapters 6-6D which are in relation to conduct of control transactions, capital raisings and disclosure and continuous disclosure for listed investment companies (LIC) and the listing rules for LICs.

4.   HEDGE FUND ACTIVITY IN AUSTRALIA

4.1   Funds Under Management

The collection of FUM data for the Australian hedge funds industry has not been systematic.[13] (There is currently no mandated FUM reporting for all hedge funds operating in Australia.) This was particularly evident prior to 2008, when fewer than 200 firms were reporting their FUM data to a research house.[14] Since the middle of 2008, the number of funds reporting their level of FUM has been on a steady increase.[15] Single hedge funds and funds of hedge funds saw declines in their aggregate FUM in 2009, but reported FUM have subsequently recovered to figures close to the peak prior to the onset of the GFC (see Figure 16.3).

The Australian hedge fund industry is dominated by a small number of very large funds. The typical fund is very small. There were only 10 funds with more than AU$1 billion (US$0.9 billion) in funds under management and the median size of a hedge fund is approximately AU$32 million (US$31.9 million).[16] The FUM range of 'less than AU$5 million' accounted for 17 per cent of funds. Approximately 55 per cent of all 296 hedge funds that reported FUM data had less than AU$40 million (see Figure 16.4).

4.2   Comparison of Hedge Funds to Total Managed Funds

The total FUM of managed funds in Australia was AU$1.7 trillion (US$1.69 trillion).[17] The estimated total FUM of single hedge funds and funds of hedge funds represented approximately 2.2 per cent and 1.0 per cent respectively of the total FUM.

---

[13]   There is no generally accepted definition of what is a hedge fund; however, for the purposes of this chapter, we have relied entirely on the categorization of fund data providers.

[14]   This is based on the number of funds that voluntarily reported FUM data to research houses www.fundmonitors.com.au, *Morningstar* and *Bloomberg*.

[15]   The number of reporting funds is based on all the funds from www.fund-monitors.com.au, *Morningstar* and *Bloomberg*. As a result of the limited reporting by funds of their FUM, ASIC estimates that the actual FUM of hedge funds and fund of hedge funds would be significantly higher.

[16]   Estimates based on ASIC calculations as at 30 June 2010. Data sourced from www.fundmonitors.com.au, *Morningstar* and *Bloomberg*.

[17]   Data as at 30 June 2010. Reserve Bank of Australia (2010), 'Statistical Table B18 – Managed Funds, Australia', www.rba.gov.au, accessed 30 September 2010.

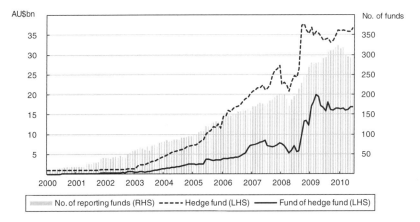

Note: A number of the top 10 funds only started to report their FUM in the middle of 2008 which explains the large increase in both the FUM of single hedge funds and funds of hedge funds during this period.

Sources: ASIC calculations, Data sourced from www.fundmonitors.com.au, *Bloomberg* and *Morningstar*.

Figure 16.3   Estimated growth of reported FUM (data up to 30 June 2010)

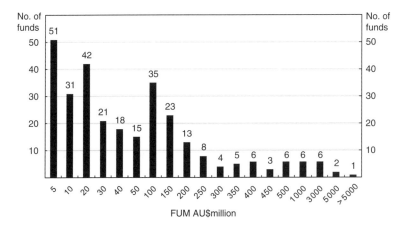

Note: The figures are based on only 296 funds that reported their FUM as at 30 June 2010.

Sources: ASIC calculations, Data sourced from www.fundmonitors.com.au, *Bloomberg* and *Morningstar*.

Figure 16.4   Number of funds by FUM range (as at 30 June 2010)

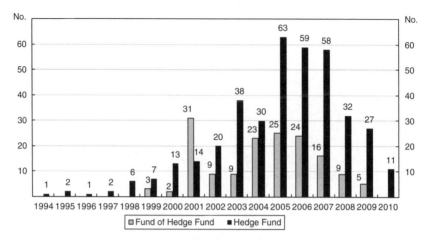

Sources: ASIC calculations, Data sourced from Australian Bureau of Statistics, www. fundmonitors.com.au, *Bloomberg* and *Morningstar*

Figure 16.5   Number of new funds established (data up to 30 June 2010)

4.3   Growth in the Number of Funds

The number of new single hedge funds being established each year has declined to 27 in 2009 from its peak in 2005 when 63 funds were created. There has also been a steady decline in the number of new funds of hedge funds being established since 2005. The GFC has no doubt had a significant impact on their decreasing numbers since 2008 (see Figure 16.5).

4.4   Investors

Australian hedge funds have benefited significantly from the growth of the superannuation industry in the last 20 years. The consolidated assets of superannuation funds have increased from AU$55 651 million (US$53 629 million) in June 1998 to AU$872 195 million (US$871 846 million) in June 2010.[18]

The government-owned *Future Fund* currently has the largest insti-

---

[18]   Australian Bureau of Statistics (2010), '*Catalogue No. 5655.0 – Managed Funds*, June 2010', www.abs.gov.au, accessed 30 September 2010. Exchange rates as at the indicated dates.

tutional pool of funds in Australia to invest, with AU\$67622 million
(US\$67594 million) in assets.[19] In the 2008–09 financial year, the Future
Fund allocated AU\$2694 million (i.e. 5 per cent of total assets) into alter-
native investments, of which approximately AU\$1300 million (US\$1299
million) was invested in hedge funds.[20] More recently, the Future Fund
has increased its portfolio allocation to alternative investments (including
hedge funds) from AU\$2776 million (4.6 per cent of total assets) in the
September 2009 quarter to just over AU\$7000 million (11.4 per cent of
total assets) in the December 2009 quarter.[21]

The growth of self-managed superannuation funds (SMSFs) has also
led to increased investment flow into hedge funds, as trustees look
to diversify their portfolios.[22] Since 2004, the number of SMSFs has
increased to 428198 funds, with combined total assets of AU\$390833
million (US\$390677 million).[23] The latest estimates are that the average
SMSF has assets totaling AU\$835580 (US\$835246).[24]

4.5　Impact and Lessons from the GFC

Among the earliest adverse effects of the GFC on the Australian hedge
funds industry were the suspension of redemptions from Basis Capital's
two Australian domiciled funds and Absolute Capital's two Yield

---

[19]　The Future Fund was established by the Future Fund Act 2006 to assist
future Australian governments meet the cost of public sector superannuation
liabilities by delivering investment returns on contributions to the Fund. Data as at
30 June 2010. Source: Australian Government (2010), 'Portfolio update at 30 June
2010', www.futurefund.gov.au, accessed 19 January 2011.

[20]　The financial year in Australia starts from 1 July to 30 June. The percentage
of assets invested into alternative assets to the total assets excludes funds received
from the sale of Telstra. Source: Australian Government (2009), 'Portfolio update
at 30 June 2009', www.futurefund.gov.au, accessed 19 January 2011.

[21]　Source: Australian Government (2010), 'Portfolio update at 31 December
2009', www.futurefund.gov.au, accessed 19 January 2011

[22]　SMSFs are restricted to a maximum for four members and are run by the
members of the fund who all must also be trustees, unless the fund has a corporate
trustee where all members of the fund are directors of the trustee. SMSFs are also
known as Do-It-Yourself (DIY) funds as trustees of the fund have control over
matters such as investment strategies. It is the control aspect which is a common
reason as to why an individual would establish their own fund.

[23]　Data as at 30 June 2010. Source: Australian Taxation Office (2010), 'Self-
managed super fund statistical report – June 2010', www.ato.gov.au, accessed 30
September 2010.

[24]　Data for the 2009 financial year. Source: Australian Taxation Office (2010),
'Self-managed super fund statistical report – June 2010', www.ato.gov.au, accessed
19 January 2011.

Strategies Funds in July 2007.[25,26] It was reported that Australian investors (individuals and superannuation funds) had invested AU$674 million (US$673.7 million) in the two Basis Capital managed funds.[27,28] Retail clients had access to these funds directly through their financial planners who promoted these funds as stable, low-risk and fixed-interest investments. The failure of these two funds brought to the forefront the direct exposure of retail investors and generated debate on issues such as whether hedge funds and other complex products should be available to all retail investors. The role of financial planners has also been questioned – especially in respect to whether they adequately understood and explained the level of risk to which their clients were exposed.[29]

In December 2008, hedge fund manager *HFA Asset Management* (now trading as *Certitude Global Investments*), announced that it was suspending withdrawals from three of its investment funds because of a lack of liquidity.[30] The liquidity problems experienced by the fund were driven by investors withdrawing funds to seek safe haven investments.[31]

The GFC had a significant impact on superannuation fund balances. The crisis led some investors and trustees to seek greater understanding of and control over the underlying exposures. The crisis highlighted the opaque nature of hedge fund strategies and investments, risk manage-

---

[25]   Basis Capital announced in July 2007 the suspension of redemptions from its two Australian domiciled funds, Basis Yield Alpha Fund and Basis Aust-Rim Diversified Fund. Basis Capital invested in the highest-yielding section of collateralised debt obligations, which were the first to take losses as US subprime defaults mounted in the middle of 2007.

[26]   Absolute Capital announced in July 2007 the suspension of withdrawals to its Yield Strategies Fund and Yield Strategies Fund NZD as it was exposed to the US subprime housing market.

[27]   For example, the WA Local Government Superannuation Fund had to write down its AU$8 million (US$7.9 million) investment in one of the funds to about AU$2 million (US$1.99 million).

[28]   Source: Barrett, Jonathan (2007), 'Problems worsen for Basis Capital', *Australian Financial Review*, 73.

[29]   In a media release dated 15 June 2010, law firm Slater & Gordon Ltd announced that it was continuing legal action against financial advisers who recommended the Basis Yield Fund to Investors. Source: Slater & Gordon (2010), 'Legal action continued on behalf of Basis Capital investors', www.slatergordon.com.au, accessed 30 September 2010.

[30]   In August 2010, HFA Asset Management changed its name to Certitude Global Investments Limited.

[31]   Units for HFA Diversified Investments Fund can now be redeemed on a quarterly basis subject to certain conditions. However, the latest investor updates dated 5 March 2010 for HFA Octane Fund and HFA Octane Fund Series 2 indicate that there are still redemption restrictions in place for both funds.

ment practices and valuation methodologies and the need for greater transparency for investors generally. There have been calls for more disclosure of hedge fund investments and risks to bridge the information disparity.

4.6 Looking Ahead

The International Organization of Securities Commissions[32] (IOSCO) published a report in June 2009 that agreed to six principles for the regulation of hedge funds to rebuild investor confidence through better investor protection, improved detection and avoidance of systemic risk and other regulatory risks posed by hedge funds.[33] These include requirements on registration of hedge fund managers (and, where appropriate, funds); operational and conduct requirements for fund managers; and requirements about disclosure to investors and regulators of activities by managers and their counterparties. IOSCO has also developed templates for collecting information from hedge fund managers to assist in identifying the systemic risks they may pose (individually and collectively). Pursuit of the principles should provide regulators with a greater understanding of the hedge fund industry and the operation of hedge funds. This recognises the fact that hedge funds can have multiple counterparties and service providers in different jurisdictions. Greater transparency and the facilitation of cross-border cooperation among regulators are also important objectives.

The Joint Forum[34] in 2010 also published a report titled 'Review of the Differentiated Nature and Scope of Financial Regulation – Key Issues and Recommendations' that noted four areas of concern regarding the regulation of hedge funds. The four areas discussed were the internal organisation, risk management and measurement of hedge funds; the reporting requirement and international supervisory cooperation; minimum initial and on-going capital requirements for systemically relevant fund

---

[32] IOSCO is an international association of securities regulators that was created in 1983. It provides a forum where securities regulators can exchange information, and co-ordinate supervisory and regulatory efforts.

[33] Technical Committee of IOSCO (2009), 'Hedge Funds Oversight' www.iosco.org, accessed 30 September 2010.

[34] The Joint Forum was established in 1996 under the aegis of the Basel Committee on Banking Supervision, the IOSCO and the International Association of Insurance Supervisors to deal with issues common to the banking, securities and insurance sectors, including the regulation of financial conglomerates. The Joint Forum is comprised of an equal number of senior bank, insurance and securities supervisors representing each supervisory constituency.

operators; and the pro-cyclicality and leverage related risks posed by the pool of assets.

ASIC is a member of IOSCO and the Joint Forum and will continue to monitor international developments advanced by these committees and their implications, recognizing that Australia's hedge fund industry is relatively small (compared to the UK and US) and, by itself, it is unlikely to have global systemic implications.[35]

5.   AUSTRALIAN PRIVATE EQUITY AND VENTURE CAPITAL INDUSTRY

5.1   Overview

Since its beginning with the first venture capital investments made in the late 1980s, the Australian private equity (PE) and venture capital (VC) industry has grown to become the fifth largest in the Asia-Pacific region. Today it is ranked 17th in the world in total investment value.[36]

According to the latest industry-wide figures released by the Australian Private Equity and Venture Capital Association (AVCAL), PE & VC firms raised a total of AU$1624 million (US$1624 million) in funds during the 2010 financial year (Figure 16.6).[37] This was 5 per cent below the amount raised in the previous financial year (and 73 per cent below the level raised during the market peak in the 2008 financial year) and illustrates the ongoing challenges faced by PE & VC firms in sourcing funding following the GFC.

Most of the new funding (90 per cent) was raised by PE firms, reflecting the dominance of PE over VC in the Australian market. Table 16.2 provides a breakdown of the various categories of investment for which these funds were raised.

The Australian superannuation sector is by far the largest provider of funds to PE & VC vehicles according to the most recent figures from the Australian Bureau of Statistics, with 56 per cent of total draw-downs in the 2009 financial year provided by local pension funds (up from 53 per cent in the previous year). The second largest source of funds was from

---

[35]   A speech by Tony D'Aloisio, Chairman, ASIC, 'Developments in the global regulator system'; Financial Services Council Annual Conference, Melbourne, 12 August 2010.

[36]   Thomson Reuters Financial – Calendar 2008 ranking.

[37]   Australian Private Equity & Venture Capital Association Limited (2010), *Australian Private Equity and Venture Capital Report – 2010 Yearbook*.

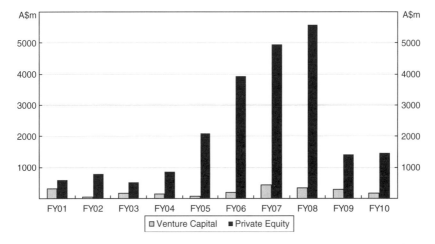

Source: AVCAL.

Figure 16.6   PE and VC funds raised in Australia by fiscal year

Table 16.2   Funds raised in the 2010 financial year by investment stage focus

Investment stage	Amount (AU$m)	No. of funds raising capital
Seed Stage	15.29	2
Early Stage VC	135.96	9
Later Stage and Balanced VC	17.03	3
Total Venture Capital	**168.28**	**14**
Generalist PE	397.75	4
Buyout/Later Stage PE	911.26	2
Turnaround PE	100	1
Growth/Expansion PE	47.06	3
Total PE	**1456.07**	**10**
Total PE & VC Funds Raised	**1624.35**	**24**

Note: The terms used in this table are standard AVCAL nomenclature. 'Seed stage' VC firms operate with start-up companies, helping to bring business plans into operation. 'Early stage' and 'later stage' refer to companies already in activity. A 'balanced' VC company can invest in multiple stages at any one time. The terms used in the PE section of the table are also standard. 'Buyout' PE firms seek to invest in established companies with a proven business model and track record. 'Turnaround' funds seek to improve the operations of target companies that have been recording poor results. 'Growth' funds target smaller firms seeking to expand their operations.

Source: AVCAL.

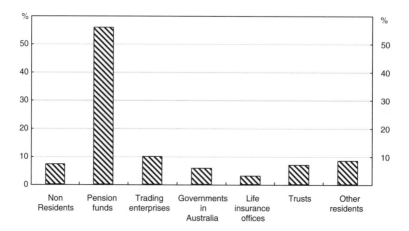

Source: Australian Bureau of Statistics.

Figure 16.7   Percentage of total investment in PE and VC vehicles – 2009 financial year

institutional investors ('trading enterprises,' with 10 per cent) followed by other residents (8 per cent).[38]

While the total amount of new funds raised in 2010 declined in comparison with the previous year, the total amount of funds invested by PE & VC firms increased during the 2010 financial year. A total of AU$2307 million (US$2306 million) was allocated by PE & VC firms across 304 investments in 178 companies (compared to AU$2121.86 million allocated across 302 investments in 202 companies during the 2009 financial year).[39] Among VC firms, the total amount of funds invested fell by 6.6 per cent in comparison to the previous year. There was a slight increase in the number of investments made by VC companies; however they chose to invest in fewer companies compared to the previous year (Figure 16.8).

In contrast to VC investment, the level of investment by PE companies rose by 13.6 per cent during the 2010 financial year, even while they cut back on the number of investments they made as well as the number of companies they invested in (Figure 16.9).

Of the funds invested by PE & VC firms in the 2010 financial year,

    [38]   Australian Bureau of Statistics (2010), '*Catalogue No. 5678.0 – Venture Capital and Later Stage Private Equity, Australia, 2008–09*, February 2010, www.abs.gov.au, accessed 1 September 2010.
    [39]   Australian Private Equity and Venture Capital Association (2010), Australian Private Equity and Venture Capital Report – *2010 Yearbook*.

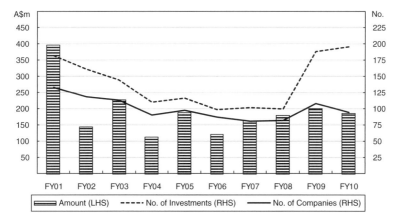

Source: AVCAL.

Figure 16.8   Investments by Australian VC funds by financial year

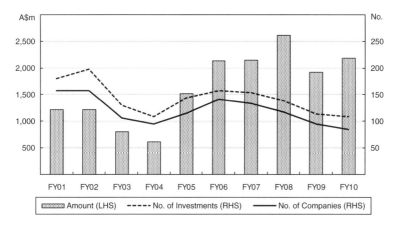

Source: AVCAL.

Figure 16.9   Investments by Australian PE funds by fiscal year

around 33 per cent were invested in refinancing the bank debt of firms that had hit the 'maturity wall' (the period in which many existing debt arrangements approach maturity).[40] This was followed by other[41] (21 per

[40]   Australian Private Equity and Venture Capital Association (2010), *Australian Private Equity and Venture Capital Report – 2010 Yearbook.*

[41]   Stages with fewer than three companies receiving investments have been aggregated into 'Other'.

Table 16.3 Distribution of investments in the 2010 financial year by stage of investee company

Stage of Investee Company	Amount (AU$m)	% of Total	Number of Investments	% of Total	Number of Companies	% of Total
Seed	1.86	0%	9	3%	7	4%
Start-up & early stage	116.14	5%	131	43%	69	39%
Later stage venture	85.66	4%	55	18%	28	16%
Growth/ Expansion	389.00	16%	59	19%	48	27%
Rescue/ Turnaround	46.15	2%	3	1%	3	2%
Secondary purchase/ Replacement capital	86.08	4%	12	4%	8	4%
Buyout	258.53	11%	21	7%	18	10%
Other leveraged buyout	98.17	4%	5	2%	3	2%
Refinancing bank debt	790.37	33%	5	2%	4	2%
Other	498.10	21%	4	1%	3	2%
Total Investment	**2370.07**	**100**	**304**	**100**	**178**	**100**

Source: AVCAL.

cent) and companies in the growth/expansion stage (16 per cent). Despite attracting a relatively small proportion of total funds invested, companies at the seed and start-up and early stage attracted the greatest number of investments made (46 per cent of the total).

The most popular investment sectors for PE & VC firms in Australia in the 2010 financial year were Consumer goods and retail (30 per cent of total funds invested), Energy and Environment (24 per cent) and Business and industrial services (15 per cent).[42]

---

[42] Australian Private Equity and Venture Capital Association (2010), *Australian Private Equity and Venture Capital Report – 2010 Yearbook.*

During the 2010 financial year, PE and VC firms moved 49 companies off their balance sheets, either through trade sales, write-offs, sales to management or other PE firms, or other means. The most prevalent method of exit was by trade sale (45 per cent) followed by sale of quoted equity (14 per cent), sale to management (10 per cent), write-off (10 per cent), other (8 per cent), IPO (6 per cent) and sale to another PE firm/sales to secondary private equity funds (6 per cent).[43]

5.2 Private Equity Regulation in Australia

Private equity funds, like hedge funds, do not always structure themselves as easily recognisable entities such as MISs (registered or unregistered). Some can be structured as MISs, and less commonly as listed investment trusts or as LICs.[44] The degree and nature of the regulatory oversight applying to them will vary according to their structure.

PE has been present in Australia for more than 20 years. The industry saw rapid growth around the mid 2000s, thanks to a low cost of funds, the search for yield and a general mis-pricing of risk. Following a PE fund-raising boom in 2007, legislative and regulatory bodies examined its implications.

In February 2007, the Takeovers Panel published 'Guidance Note 11: Conflicts of Interest' to apply to all takeover bids (regardless of the source of funding). The Panel recognised that private equity bids have a significant effect on markets and that the decisions as to the ownership of companies lie with properly informed target company shareholders.

In March 2007, the Reserve Bank of Australia (RBA) published a Financial Stability Review identifying several policy and regulatory issues, which were also raised in the March 2007 report issued by the Council of Financial Regulators (APRA, ASIC, ATO, RBA and Treasury).[45]

5.2.1   Corporate gearing
A significant increase in leverage of a PE-acquired company may encourage other companies to take on additional debt either as a defensive

---

[43]   Australian Private Equity and Venture Capital Association (2010), *Australian Private Equity and Venture Capital Report – 2010 Yearbook*.

[44]   We have observed that retail PE MISs are very rare.

[45]   Reserve Bank of Australia (2007), '*Private Equity in Australia*', Financial Stability Review. The Council of Financial Regulators consists of representatives of the APRA, ASIC, the Treasury and the RBA. The Australian Taxation Office (ATO) was also involved with preparation of the report.

strategy or in an effort to replicate returns. While this could be a problem in individual cases, the RBA noted that at that time corporate gearing in Australia was still relatively low and did not pose an immediate risk to the Australian economy.

5.2.2   Depth and quality of public capital markets

PE transactions involving the acquisition of listed companies result in reduced public reporting obligations of the newly private companies. Accordingly, investors would experience difficulties in comparing the performance of companies within and across sectors, and this may have implications for the efficiency of capital allocation.

5.2.3   Corporate conduct

Some PE transactions can lead to poor behaviour or misconduct that threatens the integrity of the markets where transactions occur. Conflicts of interest may arise where insiders can participate in the bidding consortium, though this was found not to be an area of major concern, as the issues are addressed by the Act (i.e. obligation to disclose price-sensitive information) and problems can be addressed by ensuring advisers and participants in PE transactions face robust and effective information barriers.

5.2.4   The exposure of the banking system

Risk may be underpriced and credit losses could turn out to be significantly higher than expected. The onset of the GFC proved that the RBA had good reasons to be concerned with underpricing of risk. However, the difficulties of the PE industry during and following the crisis did not lead to substantial losses by creditors.

5.2.5   The exposure of retail investors to PE

Investors are able to access these funds through the funds management industry, or through the purchase of shares in listed private equity funds. Retail investors are also indirectly exposed to private equity through their superannuation investments. The issue here is that the risks involved in PE are complicated and pricing is less transparent than for other alternative investments.

5.2.6   Taxation

In understanding the impact of taxes on PE deals at the earliest point possible, the ATO implemented a number of initiatives in its 2006/07 Compliance Program.

In August 2007, the Senate Standing Committee on Economics published the report 'Private equity investment in Australia', which looked at PE and its effects on capital markets and the Australian economy.[46] The committee concluded that further regulation of private equity activity in Australia was unnecessary since 'the overall exposure of the economy to this particular form of financing is quite low' and did not threaten financial or economic stability.[47]

5.3 Private Equity and Venture Capital Activity in Australia

The present operating environment remains challenging for PE & VC firms in Australia. An AVCAL survey, covering activity to June 2010, noted that both the value and volume of deal activity continued to decline in recent times as a result of the uncertain economic environment and the constrained supply of credit in the wake of the GFC.[48]

AVCAL reported that the Australian VC industry is facing a similar situation to the downturn in 2001, which resulted in VC funding all but disappearing, and, given the lack of new funding, this is likely to lead to a shakeout of the VC industry in Australia. Of the available funds that had been invested in the first half of 2009–2010 financial year, the majority went towards increasing investment in existing companies rather than investing in new companies.[49]

According to the AVCAL survey, the decline in private equity deal activity has been most pronounced at the top end of the market (deals with an enterprise value of greater than AU$250 million (US$249.9 million).[50]

The wave of secondary buyouts among PE firms is a relatively new and evolutionary development in the Australian market, with the sale of Study Group by *CHAMP Private Equity to Providence Equity Partners* recognised as the first major secondary buyout in Australia.[51]

---

[46]   Parliament of Australia, The Senate – Standing Committee on Economics, *Private Equity Investment in Australia*; August 2007

[47]   Mr Ric Battellino, Deputy Governor, Reserve Bank of Australia, *Proof Committee Hansard*, 25 July 2007, as quoted in The Senate, above n 5, 46.

[48]   Australian Private Equity & Venture Capital Association (2010), *Deal Metrics Survey*, July 2010.

[49]   Australian Private Equity & Venture Capital Association (2010), *Deal Metrics Survey*, July 2010.

[50]   Australian Private Equity & Venture Capital Association (2010), *Deal Metrics Survey*, July 2010.

[51]   Blinch, Jenny (2010), 'Picking up where they left off', *peiAsia*, (43), 15–18.

5.4   Looking Ahead

Significant refinancing is likely in the next two to three years. Several large PE deals, completed in the pre-GFC boom years of 2006–2007 and supported by bank debt with five to six year maturities, are due for refinancing. If the IPO market does not recover sufficiently before these maturities fall due then these firms will have to refinance their original deals. Similar challenges are faced by some foreign firms, such as CVC Asia Pacific and KKR, which financed their respective purchases of PBL Media and Seven Media Group with overseas bank funding.

Issues surrounding the taxation of PE transactions will likely continue as industry participants absorb recent determinations by the ATO regarding the circumstances under which profits on the share sales in company groups acquired in leveraged buyouts can be included in a vendor's assessable income.[52]

6.   AUSTRALIAN REAL ESTATE INVESTMENT TRUSTS

6.1   Overview

A-REITs are collective investment products that allow investors to gain exposure to capital appreciation and rental income from property, sometimes with tax deferred advantages. Real estate assets are packaged into managed funds that are professionally managed. In some circumstances the funds are listed on the Australian Stock Exchange (ASX), which allows investors to trade units in the marketplace.[53] A-REIT investments include office buildings, industrial estates, shopping centres, hotels, amusement parks and international real estate.

---

[52]   In 2009, TPG a US PE firm and the Australian Taxation Office were in disagreement over the tax treatment of the $1.5 billion profit TPG gained from the IPO of Myer Holdings Ltd.

Australian Taxation Office Taxation Determination (TD 2010/21): *Can the profit on the sale of shares in a company group acquired in a leveraged buyout be included in the assessable income of the vendor under subsection 6-5(3) of* the *Income Tax Assessment Act 1997?*

[53]   According to the ASX, there are 63 listed property trust entities.

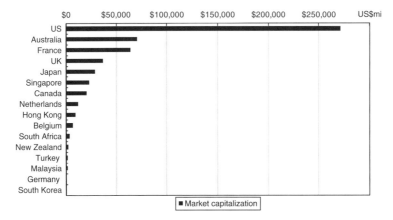

Source: Ernst & Young, 'Global REITs Report 2010: Against All Odds'.

Figure 16.10   Market capitalisation of selected REIT markets

6.2   A-REIT Activity in Australia

For over 40 years, Australia has had an active market for A-REITS, also referred to as 'listed property trusts'. The Australian market is now second only to the US and the biggest in the Asia-Pacific Region[54] According to *Ernst & Young*, in 2010 the global market capitalization of the REIT sector was US$568 billion, with Australia accounting for 12 per cent of the global market and the US for 47 per cent. See Figure 16.10.

The A-REITs sector is dominated by shopping mall-operator, the Westfield Group (40 per cent of the total). Six other groups collectively account for a similar percentage.

6.3   Impact and Lessons from the GFC

A-REITs were buffeted through the GFC. Over the last decade, the index of property stocks listed on the exchange has, overall, underperformed the broader market as represented by the All Ordinaries Index (Figure 16.11). The sector as a whole ended the 10 years to June 2010 27.3 per cent below

---

[54]   Australian Securities Exchange (2010), 'Fact Sheet – ASX-REITS: ASX-Listed Australia Real Estate Investment Trusts'.

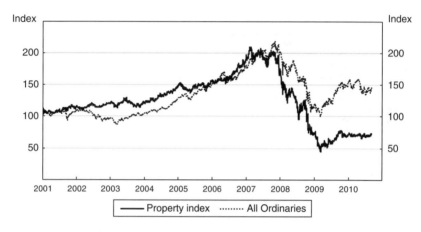

Source: Bloomberg.

Figure 16.11   Property index versus the All Ordinaries – March 2000 to June 2010

its March 2000 level, with the entire decline occurring during the GFC. At the same time, the broader market has returned 46 per cent.

Recently, A-REITs have recovered. From its lows in March 2009, the property index has outperformed the All Ordinaries Index, rising by 63 per cent compared to the broader index's 45 per cent to September 2010.

Since the GFC, many A-REITs have struggled since the GFC to roll over maturing debt, having made extensive use of unsecured borrowings to fund their liabilities. From 2006 to 2007, unsecured loans increased from 14 per cent to 25 per cent of liabilities. As well, property holdings valuations have fallen in line with exchange rate and interest rate fluctuations.[55] The value of property held by A-REITs dropped some 10 per cent during the GFC and has yet to recover.

6.4   Challenges Confronting the A-REITs Sector

In the early 2000s, A-REITs benefited from the 'great moderation', when the cost of capital was low and risk was under-priced. The market capitalization of listed A-REITs rose almost fivefold from AU$30 billion (US$29.9 billion) in 2001 to almost AU$140 billion (US$139.9 billion) by mid 2007.

---

[55]   Allens Arthur Robinson (2009),'Asia Pacific REIT Survey'.

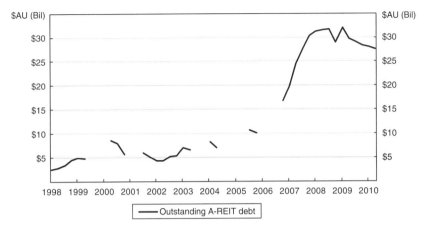

Note: Missing years, due to lack of data or incomplete source data.

Source: Australian Bureau of Statistics.

Figure 16.12   *Outstanding debt owed by A-REITs: December 1998 to June 2010*

6.5   Capital Structure

To comply with bank-imposed debt-leverage ratios, many property trusts have undertaken large capital raisings since the onset of the GFC. Problems afflicting Centro Properties Group in 2007 had focused concerns on A-REIT leverage.[56] Many of the larger A-REITs have not had significant problems raising equity capital, although their discounted security issues have diluted existing holdings and future earnings per share.

6.6   Access to Bank Lending Critical

The ability to refinance maturing debt provisions remains a key concern for the sector. As Figure 16.12 highlights, A-REITs significantly increased their debt exposures in the years before the GFC. PKF reported that 29

---

[56] Due to the sub-prime induced global credit crunch, in December 2007, Centro announced that it was unable to refinance AU$1.3 billion (US$1.29 billion) in short-term loans due to expire February 2008. As a result withdrawals and redemptions from Centro property trusts were suspended. In 2008, Centro's difficulties worsened as two security holders' class actions were initiated while the company was in the process of refinancing loans of AU$4.5 billion (US$4.49 billion).

per cent of outstanding debt held by A-REITs entities was to be refinanced in the 12 months to December 2009.[57]

6.7 Future Challenges

After the financial market turmoil of 2007–2008, Australia was the first OECD country to experience rising interest rates. The cost of debt and equity capital is likely to be a key challenge for A-REITs in future years. In addition, the strength of the Australian dollar may constrain some interest.

7. AGRICULTURAL MANAGED INVESTMENT SCHEMES

7.1 Overview

Agricultural managed investment schemes are collective investment vehicles, which pool capital for investment in agriculture or forestry. Within the agricultural MIS business model, investors receive an interest in an agricultural enterprise, on an allocated parcel of land. Agricultural MIS fall broadly into the following categories:

- forestry: their focus is on producing and harvesting timber products;
- non-forestry: their focus is, predominantly, on producing fruit; or
- land: their focus is on producing livestock

Agricultural MIS have two purposes:

- by investing in agricultural MIS, investors are entitled to a portion of the proceeds from what is grown or harvested on the parcel of land or from the selling of assets at the end of the project's life, subject to agreed management fees throughout the duration of the project's life; and/or
- by taking advantage of generous taxation treatments on agricultural production, an investor may deduct 100 per cent of the cost of the investment against other taxable income.

Investors do not own the land on which the scheme's assets are grown.

---

[57] PKF (2010), 'PKF REIT Monitor 2009/10: Survival turns to opportunity'.

7.2   Market Participants

As at July 2009, there were approximately 19 product managers with agricultural projects open for investment. Seven of these companies were listed on the ASX.[58]

7.3   Impact and Lessons from the GFC

Overall, agricultural investment schemes have not weathered the GFC well. Before the GFC, agribusiness MIS numbered 373; with 189 primarily dedicated to forestry products, 154 to other non-forestry products (for example, fruit and nut plantations) and the remaining 30 to agricultural land schemes.

However, the GFC had substantial implications for the agribusiness sector, especially forestry. In April 2009, Timbercorp, a forestry and agriculture company, called in administrators as it found itself facing AU$500 million (US$499.8 million) of debt. This was soon followed by Great Southern, announcing voluntary administration. Forest Enterprises Australia went under in April 2010, closely followed by the Rewards Group, a fruit and forests operation, in May 2010.

There were many reasons for the business failures. The Australian Bureau of Agricultural and Resource Economics reported that the GFC decreased demand for paper in Japan, depressing demand for tree plantations and wood chips. Others suggest that the preferential tax treatment of agricultural MISs and the drive for individual tax minimisation distorted the efficient allocation of capital, which drove overinvestment in the sector, leading to over-supply of product. As an example, 14 million m^3 of plantation timber is due to 'come online' in the next year, while Australia currently exports 4 million m^3 to Japan, plus another 5 million m^3 of native forest timber.[59]

The number of registered agricultural MIS has decreased, as shown in Figure 16.13. As at September 2010, the total number of agricultural MIS business was 281, a 25 per cent decline since before 2008. Over half of the failed schemes were forestry plantations, down 30 per cent to 133

---

[58]   Arafura Pearls; Forest Enterprises Australia Limited; Gunns Limited; Elders Limited; Macquarie Bank Limited; TFS Corporation Limited; and Willmott Forests Limited. Forest Enterprises Australia and Willmott Forests are now under external administration.

[59]   Australian Bureau of Agriculture and Resource Economics (2010), '*Future directions for the Australian forestry industry*'.

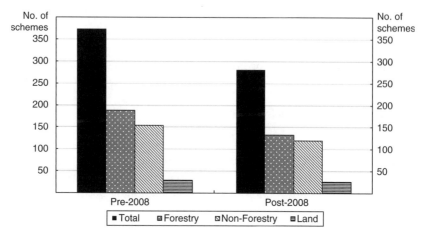

Source: ASIC.

Figure 16.13   Number of registered agricultural MIS businesses pre- and post-2008

registered entities. The numbers of non-forestry and agricultural land schemes declined to 121 and 27, respectively.

The number of new agribusiness offerings also declined following the GFC. Figure 16.14 shows that in 2009 the number of new offerings to the public declined by around 66 per cent to 24. The largest declines were in horticultural schemes. In addition, the number of existing projects has also declined from its peak in 2006 of 32 000 to just 7650.

The GFC has had other adverse impacts on agricultural MISs. Figure 16.15 shows the severity of the decline in both new capital raised and in revenue generated at the farm-gate. From its peak in 2006, capital raised has declined to AU$250 million across all new offerings; the weakest raisings since before 2003. Similarly, revenue raised from investments has fallen to pre-2003 levels. In 2009 revenue raised was AU$1.1 billion (US$ 1.09 billion), down from AU$6.5 billion (US$6.49 billion) a year earlier.

7.4   Issues Confronting the Agricultural MIS Sector

The tax treatment of agricultural MIS is known for its complexity and has been subject to uncertainty with the various taxation rulings and determinations on the topic issued by the ATO. Tax incentives for agricultural MIS have been blamed for a number of issues including contributing to an over-supply of certain commodities and distortion of the market for agricultural land.

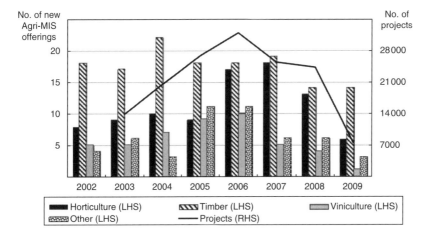

Source: Australian Agribusiness Group.

Figure 16.14 *Number of new agricultural MIS offerings and outstanding projects 2002–2009*

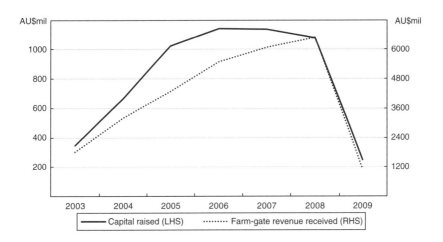

Source: Australian Agribusiness Group.

Figure 16.15 *Capital raised and revenue received from agriculture MIS 2003–2009*

8.   INFRASTRUCTURE FUNDS

8.1   Overview

Infrastructure funds are collective investment vehicles funding infrastructure projects by giving investors access to relatively stable assets with relatively high cash flows. There are also 'derivative' or 'aggregative' infrastructure investments which invest client money in a range of these funds and related companies. However, this section focuses only on funds which own infrastructure assets directly.

Companies create the funds by packaging infrastructure assets into a managed investment scheme with a trust structure, before selling or distributing interests in the funds to investors, often also with units in the trust stapled to shares of the operating company. The funds may also purchase long-term leases over assets, rather than purchasing them outright. This governance model marries aspects of listed REITs with aspects of traditional public companies. The resulting 'stapled' entities thus tend to have multiple boards.

The use of a trust structure, rather than a company structure, is in part to obtain pass-through taxation outcomes. The trust structure also overcame the provisions of the Corporations Act in place until 28 June 2010, which restricted companies to paying dividends only out of profits.

Assets favoured by Australian infrastructure trusts include toll roads, airports, power generation and distribution networks, water, gas pipelines, railways and rolling stock, and ports and stevedoring. Assets are mostly located in Australia, but some are located in North and South America, Europe and Asia.

Infrastructure assets are usually regulated monopolies or oligopolies in mature 'utility' industries, which generate stable and predictable revenues. Others, such as new toll roads, tend to produce steady revenue growth as they mature. Their physical assets generally carry a low risk of technological obsolescence, and are costly and long-lived, providing high barriers to entry. This makes infrastructure funds attractive to large institutional investors such as pension funds managing long-duration liabilities. The low volatility of cash flows also allows managers to raise the value of assets under management by lifting their gearing to relatively high levels.

One model for creating and operating infrastructure funds, since copied around the world, is that of Australia's *Macquarie Group Limited*. Under this arrangement, a financial institution seeks purchases and provides funding for infrastructure assets which it then places in an infrastructure fund that it has created for sale to investors. The sponsoring institution then manages the trust's assets externally, for a range of fees, and sometimes sells newly acquired assets to its funds.

Day-to-day control in registered schemes typically is vested in a RE external to the fund. Some of the funds issue special shares to their external managers, which give these managers the power to appoint the majority of board members, granting them a level of influence on the board well above their economic interests in the funds. Fund investment decisions tend also to be associated with or influenced by their sponsors. Termination fees attached to sponsors' management contracts tend to discourage funds' directors from taking this action in all but the most pressing circumstances, which tends to entrench the sponsors' external control of the funds.

In practice, the incentive and control structures of this model mean that infrastructure funds' operations have been characterised by:

- distributions being paid out of capital, rather than out of operational cash flows;
- high fees, only weakly related to cash flows, paid to external managers, and considerable difficulties in removing sponsoring firms as external managers;
- frequent and sizeable equity capital raisings; and
- high levels of debt and aggressive debt financing.

An alternative model, used by at least three funds operating toll roads, allows for an external manager to administer the projects in the development phase, with the option for the management company's securities to be 'stapled' to the fund once the project is completed. This model limits the influence and fees of the external manager, and ties the cost of buying out the external manager to the profitability of the project.

8.2   Infrastructure Funds Activity in Australia

There are 23 infrastructure funds listed on the ASX. In mid-2009 they managed assets with a combined value of around AU$90 billion (US$89.9 billion) across five continents. As of late 2009, there were 10 unlisted infrastructure investment funds operating in Australia. Seven were offered to wholesale investors only, the other three being offered at both wholesale and retail level. Most offer investors direct asset investments in infrastructure in a range of countries, with others offering access to equity investments in infrastructure companies, and others being 'fund of fund' managers. Unlisted funds tend to be considerably smaller than listed funds.

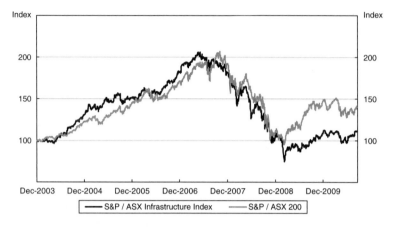

Source: *Bloomberg.*

Figure 16.16 *S&P-ASX Australian Infrastructure Index, December 2003*
to September 2010

8.3 Impact of the GFC

8.3.1 Effects on securities prices
The fall in economic activity, combined with limited access to, and higher
costs of, funding during the GFC weakened the balance sheets of many
funds, causing steep falls in the value of their traded securities.

Figure 16.16 shows the S&P/ASX Australian Infrastructure Index from
January 2004 to September 2010. The Index shows the average of the
prices of 15 infrastructure securities in the S&P/ASX 300 index, weighted
by market capitalisation.

While the index rose strongly through to mid-2007, the intensifying
global liquidity squeeze saw it peak and then fall as the value of the index's
underlying investments sank. After reaching a low in March 2009, the
index has recovered, and is now around 11 per cent above its January 2004
value.

8.3.2 Effects on individual infrastructure funds
The crisis tended to affect infrastructure funds according to their gearing
level at its advent. With their assets tending to generate strong income
flows, falls in income were moderate and could be offset by lower operating
costs. However, funds which were heavily geared, and/or had significant
near-term funding requirements, or which suffered from asset-price impair-
ment as a result of the crisis, tended to be the worst affected in the GFC.

The impact of the crisis on Australian infrastructure funds can be seen most clearly in the evolution of the funds created by investment banks *Macquarie Group* and *Babcock & Brown*.[60]

9. CONCLUSION

The broad alternative investment industry has benefited from the same conditions that promoted the growth of the managed investment industry in general in Australia. The 'search for yield' of the 1990s and early 2000s associated with mandated retirement savings, low unemployment, high corporate profitability and tax incentives have resulted in the development of a strong alternative investment sector in Australia.

Alternative investments in Australia are regulated in the same way as conventional investment schemes and are, as a general rule, accessible to retail investors. A number of factors – discussed below – may bring change to the way alternative investments have operated to date. Government-level reviews such as the Cooper Review[61] may impact the growth of the industry. One of the main areas of focus of the Cooper Review has been making superannuation funds more cost effective, with one of the recommendations of the review being a move to a new low-fee default superannuation account called *MySuper*. Under this proposal, superannuation fund managers would be restricted from investing funds in *MySuper* accounts into high fee alternative investment classes. If implemented by the Government, this proposal may have an adverse effect on the level of investment by domestic superannuation funds in alternative investments. However, another recommendation from the Cooper Review is to increase the compulsory contribution that Australians pay into their superannuation from 9 per cent to 12 per cent of their salary. The adoption and implementation of this recommendation by the Australian Government would likely have a positive effect on the overall level of funds that are allocated to alternative investments by domestic superannuation funds, since it would significantly increase the overall pool of superannuation funds.

---

[60] See also the 2010 publication by Trevor Sykes titled *Six Months of Panic* which recounts how the GFC developed and traces through its impact on Australia.

[61] On 29 May 2009, the Australian Government announced a comprehensive review of Australia's superannuation system: The Review into the Governance, Efficiency, Structure and Operation of Australia's Superannuation System). Website: www.supersystemreview.gov.au.

It is unlikely that the benign pre-GFC operating environment – characterised by low cost of capital and an under-pricing of risk – will return any time soon. Providers of alternative investments are likely to have to search for new sources of funding.

The alternative investment industry is also affected by demographic factors. The past three decades have seen the large 'baby boomer' demographic group save for retirement. This has contributed to generalised rises in asset prices and rapid growth in mainstream and alternative investments. However, from 2010 onwards this demographic group will start retiring in large numbers. This means that a substantial proportion of the Australian population will begin to spend – rather than accumulate – retirement savings. This may affect the growth prospects of the alternative investment schemes or change the sector's preferred product mix, with greater focus being placed on capital preservation and longevity-related products.

BIBLIOGRAPHY

Allens Arthur Robinson (2009), *Asia Pacific REIT Survey*, Sydney, Australia: The Trust Company.

Arnold, Martin and Peter Smith (2010), 'Bumpy road forces Macquarie to switch focus', *Financial Times*, 26 October.

Arnold, Martin and Peter Smith (2010), 'Macquarie in funds shake-up', *Financial Times*, 26 October.

Australian Bureau of Agricultural and Resource Economics (2010), '*Future directions for the Australian forestry industry*', Canberra, Australia: Australian Bureau of Agricultural and Resource Economics.

Austrade (2010), *Alternative Investments in Australia*, Sept, Canberra, Australia: Austrade.

Australian Bureau of Statistics (2010), '*Catalogue No. 5655.0 – Managed Funds,* June 2010', www.abs.gov.au, accessed 30 September 2010.

Australian Bureau of Statistics (2010), '*Catalogue No. 5678 – Venture Capital and Later Stage Private Equity',* Australia, 2008–9, February 2010, www.abs.gov.au, accessed 1 September 2010.

Australian Financial Review (2010), 'Private equity problem looms for PM', 15 September.

Australian Government (2010), 'Portfolio update at 31 December 2010', www.futurefund.gov.au, accessed 19 January 2011.

Australian Government (2010), 'Portfolio update at 30 June 2010', www.futurefund.gov.au, accessed 19 January 2011.

Australian Government (2009), 'Portfolio update at 30 June 2009', www.futurefund.gov.au, accessed 19 January 2011.

Australian Private Equity and Venture Capital Association (2010), *Australian Private Equity and Venture Capital Report – 2010 Yearbook*, Sydney, Australia: AVCAL.

Australian Private Equiry and Venture Capital Association (2010), *Deal Metrics Survey*, Sydney, Australia: AVCAL.

Australian Securities Exchange (2010), '*Fact sheet ASX-REITS: ASX-Listed Australia Real Estate Investment Trusts*', Sydney, Australia: Australian Securities Exchange.

Australian Taxation Office (2010), 'Self-managed super fund statistical report – June 2010', www.ato.gov.au, accessed 30 September 2010.

Australian Trade Commission (2010), *Investment Management Industry in Australia*, Canberra, Australia: Australian Trade Comission.

Bailey, Justin (2010), 'Flood of IPOs expected when market revives', *Australian Financial Review*, 22 September.

Barrett, Jonathan (2007), 'Problems worsen for Basis Capital', *Australian Financial Review*, 73.

Blinch, Jenny (2010), 'Picking up where they left off', *peiAsia*, **43**, 15–18.

Burgess, K. and Thompson, S. (2010), 'Private equity's back but investors aren't convinced', *Australian Financial Review*, 21 September, 49.

D'Aloisio, Tony, Chairman, ASIC (2010), *Developments in the global regulator system*, Financial Services Council Annual Conference, Melbourne, 12 August.

Ernst & Young (2010), 'Global REITs Report 2010: Against All Odds', London, England: Ernst & Young.

Parliament of Australia (2010), *Senate Select Committee on Agricultural and Related Industries*, Food production in Australia, Final Report, August, Canberra, Australia.

Parliament of Australia, The Senate – Standing Committee on Economics (2007), *Private Equity Investment in Australia*; August, Canberra, Australia.

Reserve Bank of Australia (2010), '*Statistical Table B18 – Managed Funds*', Australia, www.rba.gov.au, accessed 30 September 2010.

Reserve Bank of Australia (2007), 'Private Equity in Australia', *Financial Stability Review*, March.

RiskMetrics Group (2008), *Infrastructure Funds: Managing, Financing and Accounting, In Whose Interests?*, April, Melbourne, Australia, RiskMetrics Group.

Slater & Gordon (2010), 'Legal action continued on behalf of Basis Capital investors', www.slatergordon.com.au, accessed 30 September.

Super System Review, www.supersystemreview.gov.au

Sykes, Trevor (2010), *Six Months of Panic*, Sydney, Australia: Allen & Unwin, p. 201.

Technical Committee of the International Organisation of Securities Commission (2009), 'Hedge Funds Oversight', www.iosco.org, accessed 30 September.

17. The EU's AIFM Directive and its impact – an overview

Phoebus Athanassiou* and Thomas Bullman†

INTRODUCTION

On 29 April 2009 the European Commission published for consultation a proposal for a Directive on Alternative Investment Fund Managers (AIFM).[1] The stated objective of the proposal[2] was to establish 'common requirements governing the authorisation and supervision of AIFM in order to provide a coherent approach to the related risks and their impact on investors and markets in the Community'.[3] In substantive terms, the proposal sought to address the grave concerns expressed at the highest level in the wake of the global financial crisis,[4] but also prior thereto,[5] about the potency of the regulatory and supervisory frame-

*   Senior Legal Counsel, European Central Bank (ECB), Frankfurt am Main. The views expressed in this chapter are purely personal and need not reflect those of the ECB or the Eurosystem. Part of this chapter draws on some of the analysis in Phoebus Athanassiou, 'The AIFM Directive and the Future of European Alternative Investment Fund Regulation', OCHEL-Dice Report, 1/2010, 8–14.

†   Thomas Bullman holds a Bachelor of Business & Legal Studies and Master's Degree in Commercial Law from University College Dublin, and is a member of the Institute of Certified Public Accountants in Ireland. He is also a Senior Compliance Manager at Legal & General Investment Management Limited (LGIM). The views expressed in this chapter are personal and not those of LGIM.

1   European Commission, Proposal for a Directive on Alternative Investment Fund Managers (AIFM), Brussels, COM (2009) 207 final.

2   It is noted that the public consultation lasted less than six weeks, despite the guidelines stating that consultations should be open for 'at least eight weeks'.

3   European Commission, *supra* fn. 1, Recital 2.

4   The reference is, *inter alia*, to the European Parliament's Rasmussen and Lehne Reports; to the findings of the de Larosière Group; and, more recently, to the Commission Communication of 27 May 2009 on European Financial Supervision.

5   One of the most prominent examples is that of the furore caused in Germany, in 2005, by the thwarting, through a shareholder revolt spearheaded by UK-based hedge fund investor Chris Hohn, Head of The Children's Investment Fund, of Deutsche Börse's bid for the London Stock Exchange (LSE), leading to the res-

works of the European Union (EU) in the alternative investments field and, in particular, about the perceived lack of regulation and supervision of certain types of non-harmonised funds and their managers. The Commission proposal was to draw sharp criticism from many quarters, not least from the various components of Europe's alternative investment fund (AIF) sector: some considered it to be sweeping and unduly intrusive[6] or out of tune with recent regulatory recommendations;[7] others were of the opinion that it lacked in boldness or was too ambiguous.[8] In particular, while the Commission presented its proposal as a legitimate response to the risks posed by the AIF sector, exemplified by its perceived use of excessive leverage or speculative trading in the run-up to the financial crisis, many of those within the industry expressed the view that, as conceived and drafted, the proposal could severely damage the competitiveness of European investment funds, drive EU-domiciled fund managers off-shore and introduce strong elements of protectionism[9] to EU financial markets regulation, exposing European fund managers to the risk of retaliation from the US or other financial centres, should the latter follow the example of the EU. It is only after lengthy negotiations, leading to several hundred amendments to the original Commission proposal, some more significant than others, that, on 19 October 2010, the European Parliament and the ECOFIN Council were to reach an agreement on a revised set of rules, ending a long period of open-ended and intensive bargaining, mostly revolving around a handful of core issues thrown up by the original proposal.[10] Despite the immense political

---

ignation of Deutsche Börse's Chief Executive Officer and Chairman, and to the then Chairman of the ruling Social Democrats accusation of short-term investors, including hedge funds, of acting as 'locusts', greedily attacking German companies with no consideration for the jobs they destroyed.

6   Bundesverband Investment und Asset Management e.V., 2009; Swiss Funds Association, 2009; Finansinspektionen, 2009; AIMA, 2009; European Private Equity and Venture Capital Association, 2009.

7   In this regard, see Black (2009), 66.

8   Following the publication of the Commission Proposal, Poul Nyrup Rasmussen, President of the Party of European Socialists, stated that the draft directive 'has more holes than a Swiss cheese' and could have political consequences for Commission President Barroso's chances of securing a second term in office.

9   For an overview of the key issues arising from the Commission proposal see Thomas Bullman, 'The Draft Directive on AIFMs: European Protectionism or Attack on the Hedge Fund Industry?' – Parts 1 & 2, Bloomberg UK Financial Services Law Journal (2009) Vol. 1, No. 1 & 2.

10   Directive of the European Parliament and of the Council of 11 November 2010 on Alternative Investment Fund Managers and amending directives 2003/41/

capital invested by the Commission in its original proposal, the risk of its initiative being scrapped was ever present throughout the negotiations leading up to its adoption, testifying to the controversy that it sparked as well as to the complexity of the industries that it purported to regulate and the potency of the vested interests in the preservation of the *status quo ante*.

This chapter is divided in *three* parts. The *first* part provides an overview of the original Commission proposal, highlighting its strengths and weaknesses and explaining some of the reasons why changes to its text were necessary to help achieve its stated objectives without imposing an unwarranted regulatory straightjacket on Europe's AIF sector. [11] The *second* part provides an outline of the AIFM Directive, adopted on 11 November 2010, addressing the key issues of relevance to its scope, and examining its provisions on valuations, delegation, the appointment and responsibilities of depositaries, remuneration, and its 'third country regime'. A *third* part draws some tentative conclusions on the future of the European investment funds industry after the AIFM Directive has eventually been implemented by the Member States.

1.   THE COMMISSION PROPOSAL AND ITS DOWNSIDES: AN OVERVIEW

1.1   Outline of the Commission Proposal

The Commission proposal sought to introduce a comprehensive, harmonised regulatory framework for the managers of any collective investment undertaking other than those covered by the UCITS Directive,[12] where its manager was domiciled within the EU *or* the fund itself was domiciled or marketed in the EU.[13] While the Commission proposal captured all EU-domiciled AIFM, whether natural or legal persons, those managing small portfolios worth less than €100 million or less than €500 million (for non-

---

EC and 2009/65/EC and Regulations (EC) No. 1060/2009 and (EU) No. 1095/2010, OJ L174/1, 1.7.2011.

[11]   For an overview of the positive effects of hedge funds see Garbaravicius and Dierick (2005), 25–27.

[12]   Directive 85/611/EEC of the Council of 20 December 1985 on the coordination of laws, regulations and administrative provisions relating to undertakings for collective investment in transferable securities (UCITS), as subsequently amended.

[13]   European Commission, *supra* fn. 1, draft Art. 2(1).

leveraged funds with no redemption rights over a period of five years after their constitution) were to be exempted from its scope of application, on a *de minimis* basis.[14] Significantly, while the Commission proposal sought to regulate *managers* rather than *funds*, it affected both, with several of its provisions concerning the funds themselves.[15]

Under the original proposal, only authorised, EU-domiciled AIFM were to be allowed to offer their services and to market their funds to *professional*[16] investors within the EU.[17] Benefiting from the proposal's 'European passport', duly authorised fund managers could market their funds and offer their services throughout the EU, and not just in their home jurisdiction, subject mainly to a notification requirement to the competent national authorities of the host Member State(s).[18] The original proposal also imposed upon AIFM a wide range of transparency and information-reporting requirements vis-à-vis investors and regulators alike; some of those requirements were of general applicability, while others depended on the type of AIF.[19] The proposal also laid down detailed rules on the capital[20] and organisational[21] requirements of AIFM and on the regulation, by the Commission (through the exercise of delegated authority) of their use of leverage through the imposition of limits.[22]

---

[14]   *Ibid.*, draft Art. 2(2). However, since inception of these limits a major industry concern has been the practicality of applying these limits to smaller funds which straddle the threshold limits. It is unclear at what point an AIF should seek authorisation in such circumstances. This lack of clarity has remained in the AIFM Directive and forms a significant part of ESMA's Discussion Paper on policy orientations on possible implementing measures under Article 3 of the AIFM Directive, 15 April 2011.

[15]   Provisions of reference to AIF include requirements on liquidity management, depositaries, transparency, and the use of leverage.

[16]   European Commission, *supra* fn. 1, draft Art. 31. The professional-investors-only scope of the draft directive harks back to pre-financial crisis discussions on a possible harmonisation of the private placement regimes of the Member States. As retail investors already have access, in several Member States, to certain types of funds, draft Art. 32 provided that Member States may allow retail investor access to AIF, subject to the fulfilment of stricter, non-discriminatory regulatory requirements on the fund or the AIFM.

[17]   *Ibid.*, draft Art. 4.

[18]   *Ibid.*, draft Art. 6 read in conjunction with draft Art. 33.

[19]   *Ibid.*, draft Arts. 19–21.

[20]   *Ibid.*, draft Arts. 14.

[21]   *Ibid.*, draft Arts. 15–18.

[22]   *Ibid.*, draft Arts. 22–25. Leverage was only one of several areas where the Commission reserved itself a right to modify the requirements laid down in its proposal (others include short-selling, disclosure requirements, valuation standards and marketing rights).

The Commission proposal's 'third country rules' proved to be one of its most controversial features.[23] The original proposal prohibited EU-domiciled AIFM from marketing, within the EU, third country-domiciled AIF, earlier than three years after the eventual entry into force of the draft Directive,[24] and only where a number of conditions precedent to their marketing were fulfilled. Specifically, EU-domiciled AIFM wishing to market non-EU domiciled funds could only do so if the fund's country of origin had signed an agreement with its counterparts in the relevant EU Member State(s), *inter alia* agreeing to an effective exchange of information in connection with tax matters.[25] In the meantime Member States could allow EU-domiciled AIFM to market third country funds to professional investors in their territory subject to their own national private placement regimes. Non-EU AIFM wishing to market their third country authorised funds within the EU would need to approach the relevant Member State authorities and apply for authorisation, which could only be granted if tax and supervisory co-operation agreements were in place with the competent authorities of the host Member States, and if, in the view of the Commission (expressed through the exercise of delegated law-making authority), the AIFM's country of origin had introduced and effectively enforced prudential regulation and ongoing supervision requirements 'equivalent' to those of the Commission proposal, and granted EU-domiciled AIFM effective market access at least comparable to that granted under the Commission proposal to AIFM from the relevant third country.[26]

Finally, the Commission proposal required the Member States' competent authorities to cooperate for the exchange of the macro-prudential data necessary for the effective oversight of the AIF sector.[27]

The Commission's ambition to extend, through its proposal, 'appropriate regulation and oversight to all actors and activities that embed

---

[23]   Further evidence of this continued struggle can be found in the reference to the Call for Evidence issued by CESR after the AIFM Directive was adopted (see 'Implementing measures on the Alternative Investment Fund Managers Directive', Call for Evidence Ref CESR/10-1459, 3 December 2010). Four task groups were assembled but, noticeably, a 'third country regime' task force was left out, presumably due to the controversial nature of the Directive's third country regime.

[24]   European Commission, *supra* fn. 1, draft Art. 54 (1).

[25]   *Ibid.*, draft Art. 35.

[26]   European Commission, *supra*, fn. 1, draft Art. 39.

[27]   *Ibid.*, draft Articles 45–48. At the time of the proposal's publication, thinking had yet not crystallised within the EU on the post-financial crisis supervisory structure and, in particular, on the creation of the ESRB and the ESFS.

significant risks'[28] was no doubt both legitimate and sensible (and it was hailed as such by a number of institutional stakeholders).[29] That normative constraints making compulsory the authorisation and supervision of funds and/or their managers only applied, at the time of publication of its proposal, to *some* Member States, but not others, inevitably leading to regulatory fragmentation, supervisory difficulties and marketing inefficiencies, points to the conclusion that there was, indeed, room for regulatory intervention in this field.

Although many of the principles underlying the proposal are sound, where many have taken issue with the Commission's approach is on the detailed measures through which those principles were to be translated into concrete regulatory action. Leaving aside, for a moment, the costs that any regulatory drive would entail for the AIF sector and its investors, we briefly consider, in the following section, some of the Commission proposal's other, more 'conceptual', drawbacks.

1.2 Concerns Raised by the Commission Proposal

The Commission proposal raised concerns at various levels. For the purposes of this section we will only concentrate on the following four: (i) its 'one size fits all' rationale, (ii) its troubled relationship with the financial law *acquis* and the competition concerns to which some of its proposed measures gave rise (iii) its creeping protectionist and investor choice-limiting approach to the authorisation and marketing, within the EU, of non-EU domiciled funds and (iv) its lack of a clear regulatory focus. We briefly examine, below, each of these concerns.

One of the main concerns with the Commission proposal was linked to the, more or less, uniform regime that this purported to impose on a wide range of disparate and heterogeneous funds (not least in terms of their risk profile), including purely *national* ones, of no obvious relevance for systemic stability, many of which were *already* regulated domestically.[30] For instance, the inclusion in the scope of the Commission proposal of private equity and non-UCITS retail funds represented a notable shift from the hitherto approach of the Commission, which, since the launch of its public consultation in December 2008, had focused exclusively on hedge

---

[28]   European Commission, *supra*, fn. 1, Explanatory Memorandum, § 1.1. For an account of the Commission's rationales for regulating AIFs in general and hedge funds in particular, see McVea (2009), 35–41.

[29]   See, for instance, ECB, 2009, para. 3.

[30]   As drafted, the Commission proposal caught, besides hedge funds and private equity funds, real estate, commodity and infrastructure funds.

funds, considering them to represent risks for the financial system.[31] This is despite the fact that the introduction of an EU-wide regime to monitor the risks posed by hitherto non-harmonised funds could only be justified (and not just as a matter of law) in the case of certain funds, but not others.[32] A closely related (but distinct) point of concern with the Commission proposal is that several of its requirements (many of them inspired by the UCITS Directive, which caters for a different market and addresses a different set of public policy concerns) appeared unnecessary or singled out AIFM, despite the horizontality of the issues that they supposedly addressed.[33] The duty imposed on AIFM to appoint an 'independent' asset valuation agent for each AIF they manage,[34] the requirement for the assets of each and every AIF marketed within the EU to be deposited with a duly authorised, external depositary, with a registered office in the EU (a credit institution)[35] and the Commission's prerogative to dictate limits on the use of leverage by AIFM[36] are only some examples of prescriptions that appeared to discriminate against AIFM and AIF, without any clear public policy benefit, and which, what is more, would seem to *concentrate*, instead of *mitigating*, risks.

The Commission proposal's compatibility with the financial law *acquis*, at the time of its publication, was another major source of concern with its text. By including within the definition of 'AIF' both open-ended and listed, closed-ended investment funds – already subject to comprehensive regulation under the Markets in Financial Instruments Directive (MiFID),[37] the Prospectus,[38] the Transparency[39] and the

---

[31]   In a speech held in early 2009, European Commissioner for Internal Market and Services Charlie McCreevy stated that '[A]s far as private equity is concerned, the issues are very different – and have little to do with the financial crisis' (Charlie McCreevy, Opening Speech EC Conference on Private Equity & Hedge Funds Brussels, 26 February 2009).

[32]   It is telling that the G20 London Summit recommendations stressed the need to focus only on the 'systemically important financial institutions, instruments and markets' including on the 'systemically important hedge funds'.

[33]   ECB (2009), para. 8.

[34]   European Commission, *supra,* fn. 1, Art. 16.

[35]   *Ibid.*, Art. 17.

[36]   *Supra*, fn. 22.

[37]   Directive 2004/39/EC of the European Parliament and of the Council of 21 April 2004 on markets in financial instruments amending Council Directives 85/611/EEC and 93/6/EEC and Directive 2000/12/EC of the European Parliament and of the Council and repealing Council Directive 93/22/EEC.

[38]   Directive 2003/71/EC of the European Parliament and of the Council of 4 November 2003 on the prospectus to be published when securities are offered to the public or admitted to trading and amending Directive 2001/34/EC.

[39]   Directive 2004/109/EC of the European Parliament and of the Council of 15

Market Abuse[40] Directives – or by, effectively, imposing a double licensing requirement upon management companies that simultaneously managed UCITS *and* non-UCITS funds,[41] the Commission proposal appeared to place AIF at a disadvantage. By subjecting to more stringent rules AIF pursuing activities similar to those of harmonised funds, the proposal was also apt to generate competition concerns. The extra disclosure requirements for private equity managers – on top of those set out in the Transparency Directive – also threatened to distort competition, since wealthy individuals or the subsidiaries of multinational corporations (that private equity funds are, for instance, in competition with) would not be subject to the same regulatory requirements.

The Commission's ambition to regulate, through the proposal, the authorisation and marketing, within the EU, of third country funds was *ab initio* perceived as one of its most contentious features. The exacting requirements subject to which such authorisation was to be granted by the competent Member State authorities, in conjunction with the activation of the third country AIF EU marketing possibility not earlier than three years after the proposed rules' eventual implementation, made it unlikely that non-EU domiciled AIFM, not excluding those hailing from the US or other developed financial centres, could ever hope to secure an authorisation to market their funds in the EU. While the draft proposal's restrictive approach vis-à-vis third country funds could be defended for being consistent (at least prima facie), with the G20 Pittsburgh Summit's objective of enhancing transparency and quality of regulation in off-shore jurisdictions,[42] the restrictions on third country AIF and AIFM were arguably problematic, both because they restricted investor choice (effectively banning EU-based investors from placing money with off-shore funds

---

December 2004 on the harmonisation of transparency requirements in relation to information about issuers whose securities are admitted to trading on a regulated market

[40] Directive 2003/6/EC of the European Parliament and of the Council of 28 January 2003 on insider dealing and market manipulation (market abuse).

[41] However, it is worth noting that, pursuant to Art. 7(4) of the AIFM Directive, documentation provided as part of a UCITS management company authorisation procedure will not be required by the competent authority for the purposes of an authorisation application under the AIFM Directive, as long as such documentation is still up to date.

[42] A similar exhortation is to be found in the G20 Toronto Summit Declaration of 26–27 June 2010, which emphasised the need to 'strengthen financial market infrastructure by accelerating the implementation of strong measures to improve transparency and regulatory oversight of hedge funds . . . in an internationally consistent and non-discriminatory way'.

that did not satisfy European standards)[43] and because they were hard to reconcile with the G20 London Summit's call for regulators and supervisors to 'reduce the scope for regulatory arbitrage' as well as to 'promote global trade and investment and reject protectionism'. Moreover, given that the AIF sector operates mostly off-shore, a key issue thrown open by the Commission proposal was whether AIFM, with an emphasis on those operating out of the major European financial centres, would be willing to accommodate themselves to its proposed set-up, or whether they would seek to have as few dealings within the EU as possible, transferring their operations off-shore. The regulatory 'over-reach' of the Commission proposal (and its potential implications) aside, it is questionable whether the conditional opening of the European fund market to off-shore funds and their managers could ever be a legitimate internal market regulatory objective.[44]

Perhaps the greatest defect of the Commission proposal was its apparent lack of a clear regulatory focus on financial stability (as one would expect the case to be, given the timing and context of its publication)[45] or, instead, on investor protection (as very many of its provisions suggested). As a regulatory rationale, investor protection would appear to be inappropriate in the context of AIF, both conceptually,[46] and because the scope of the Commission proposal was explicitly limited to the marketing of AIF and to the offer of AIFM services to *professional* investors only. Financial stability would, on the other hand, provide an infinitely more compelling (even if not the only legitimate) regulatory rationale in this field. While these two regulatory rationales are by no means mutually exclusive, their parallel pursuit is bound to (and did, in the case of the Commission proposal) weaken the Commission's chances of attaining either. If the main focus of the proposal was on financial stability it would be sufficient that its scope of application extends over systemically relevant funds only, i.e.

---

[43]   The third countries' rules could have an impact not only on non-EU managers but, also, EU investors like pension funds (and therefore the pensions and savings of ordinary EU citizens). If AIFM could no longer accept subscriptions from within the EU unless they were authorised, restrictions of global capital flows would inevitably result.

[44]   Rather than restrict the cross-border distribution eligibility of foreign funds or facilitate, through an EU passport, legal and tax arbitrage phenomena, stronger incentives could be given for third country funds to transfer their domicile to the EU.

[45]   The Commission proposal was part of an overall regulatory package that included a new Credit Rating Agencies' regulation, a strengthening of the Capital Requirements Directive and a consolidation of the regulatory regime on insurance.

[46]   In this regard, see Athanassiou (2009), 52–59.

cross-border, highly leveraged ones with considerable assets under management (AUM). If, on the other hand, the main emphasis of the proposal was on investor protection, then its investor disclosure rules would appear inappropriate, as they were mainly geared towards the needs of retail, rather than professional investors (the only eligible investor group under the original Commission proposal).

1.3 Regulatory Principles

The criticisms that the Commission proposal attracted from various quarters suggested that its rules had to be (re)drafted, so as to enable it to achieve its objectives without undue 'collateral damage' and without going beyond what was necessary to achieve its legitimate objectives. Four broad principles could be followed to help achieve those objectives:

a) differentiate amongst different types of funds, exempting those with little or no systemic stability relevance from the scope of the proposed harmonised regulation;
b) drop protectionist elements or regulatory over-reach pretensions, mainly by overhauling the proposal's 'third country rules', so as to *inter alia* free up investor choice and avoid damaging the competitiveness of the EU's AIF sector;[47]
c) bring the proposal's organisational, investor disclosure, transparency and other reporting requirements in line with the realities of the business pursued by AIF (rather than blindly follow the model of the UCITS Directive) and with the risks that this genuinely entails; to avoid creating a false impression of oversight, the focus of reporting obligations would, in particular, need to be re-adjusted to capture information relevant to the monitoring of financial stability; and
d) improve legal certainty and rationalise restrictions on specific activities and/or investment policies, *inter alia* by removing (or reducing) the wide delegated law-making authority granted, under the proposal, to the Commission.

The next section will be devoted to an examination of the extent to which the revised Directive, as adopted, gives effect to the aforementioned

---

[47] Replacing the Commission proposal's third country rules with a reasonable requirement for 'prudential regulation and supervision' in the home jurisdiction of the third country AIF would not only be sufficient but it could also encourage off-shore jurisdictions to step up prudential controls over funds established in their jurisdiction.

principles and what that augurs for the future of the EU's AIF sector. It will further explore the similarities of the AIFM Directive, as adopted, with the Commission proposal, as well as the weaknesses detected in the Commission proposal that have been left unresolved in the final rules.

2.   AFTERMATH TO THE COMMISSION PROPOSAL: THE REVISED RULES AND THEIR ASSESSMENT

2.1   The AIFM Directive: Overview of the Final Text

The newly adopted Directive – which the Member States are to implement by June 2013[48] – is to apply to 'the managers of alternative investment funds (AIFM) which manage and/or market such funds in the Union'.[49] It captures all AIFM, including those domiciled outside the EU (provided that they *manage* an EU AIF or that they *market* any AIF within the EU, irrespective of its domicile).[50] The Directive covers all non-UCITS collective investment undertakings, 'which raise capital from a number of investors, with a view to investing it in accordance with a defined investment policy for the benefit of those investors'[51] and retains much the same *de minimis exemptions* as those in the Commission proposal.[52] By aspiring to regulate exhaustively the business of AIFM, the Directive goes to a level of detail that is unusual by pre-financial crisis European regulatory standards, and which has resulted in the length of its text being around three times that of the original Commission proposal.[53]

In summary, the Directive has much in common with the Commission proposal, from the EU-wide initial capital and own funds requirements that it imposes on AIF[54] to its detailed provisions covering a wide range of operating requirements and ongoing duties for AIFM and its retention of disclosure requirements for private equity funds with EU-based investors

---

[48]   *Supra*, fn. 10, Art. 63 (1).

[49]   *Ibid*, Art. 1.

[50]   *Ibid*, Art.2. The Directive captures all EU AIFM, managing one or more AIF, irrespective of the domicile of the AIF.

[51]   *Ibid.*, Art. 4 (1).

[52]   *Ibid.*, Art.3(2). Entities to which the Directive does not apply include holding companies, supranational institutions, national central banks, saving and pension schemes and securitisation SPVs (*ibid.*, Art. 2(2)).

[53]   As a commentator has aptly observed, the Directive is typical of the maximum harmonisation and 'non-optionality' wind, which has swept through many of the more recent Union legal acts (Moloney, (2010), 1355–1361).

[54]   *Supra*, fn. 10, Art. 9.

(imposing, for instance, an obligation upon them to disclose their business plan for any company they control). However, there are also certain noticeable differences between them, such as the welcome removal of all references to short selling and its use by AIFM,[55] and its transparency requirements in relation to the use of leverage by the AIFM[56] which entail the transferring of the power to impose limits on the use of leverage, in the interests of ensuring the stability and integrity of the financial system, from the Commission to the competent Member State authorities.[57]

On a closer inspection of the key features of the AIFM Directive, many of the concerns raised by the Commission proposal, such as scope and valuation, remain unresolved. When applying the Directive from a commercial perspective, a myriad of complex legal and regulatory issues emerge from how often a fund should be valued, and by whom, to whether or not a depositary is required or not. Due to the difficulty in applying a single set of regulatory rules to the fundamentally different areas of private equity funds and hedge funds it is highly likely that the final rules will retain a certain degree of controversy. The difficulty that the Commission has faced in creating this one-size-fits-all regime is exacerbated by the fact that the Directive itself exhibits something of an identity crisis. The Commission has not only tried to make of the Directive a 'catch-all' legal act for all non-UCITS fund managers: it has also shown signs of confusion in its attempt to indirectly regulate the fund itself through rules on leverage and disclosure. Many of the commercial complexities in applying the Directive's provisions, such as those on scope, emanate from the fact that AIFs are managed and distributed in different ways in jurisdictions such as Ireland or Luxembourg, on the one hand, and France or Germany, on the other. In Ireland and Luxembourg funds are predominantly managed and distributed through independent asset managers, whereas in Germany or France this tends to be done through subsidiaries of major banking organisations. Many aspects of the Directive which are seen as inappropriate, such as its scope and delegation provisions, can be linked to this

---

[55]   The issue of short selling is to be dealt with under a forthcoming European Parliament and Council Regulation on short selling and crdit default swaps.

[56]   Each AIFM will be required to set a limit on the leverage it uses and will be obliged to comply with these limits. In addition, AIFM will also be required to inform competent authorities about their use of leverage, so that the authorities can assess whether the use of leverage by the AIFM contributes to the build-up of systemic risk in the financial system. This information will be shared with the European Systemic Risk Board.

[57]   *Supra*, fn. 10, Art. 25.

commercial reality.[58] Arguably political motivations to regulate the hedge fund industry may not have fully taken into account such commercial differences across the European funds industry. Moreover, recourse to liability and transparency as mechanisms for controlling risk is widespread throughout the Directive, despite the fact that their suitability in seeking to achieve the Directive's objectives of investor protection and financial stability is under debate.

The remainder of this section is dedicated to reviewing the main provisions and the complex issues of the Directive that the European Securities and Markets Authority (ESMA) was charged with giving guidance[59] to the European Commission on by 16 November 2011.[60]

2.1.1 Scope-related issues

The Directive's scope has become the source of major international and cross-sector controversy,[61] given the somewhat confused and oversimplified approach that its text adopts with regard to the regulation of the complex structures and business models typical of the alternative investment industry, with its many distinct and heterogeneous constituent sub-sectors.[62] The Directive categorises investments as either UCITS or non-UCITS funds. However, in reality, there is no plausible way to view these categories as 'equal and opposite'. Furthermore, within the non-UCITS sphere hedge funds and private equity funds are fundamentally different in their legal structure, their strategies and investor base, as well as operationally and from a servicing perspective. The application of a one-size-fits-all approach to the industry's regulation

---

[58]   An example of this is the scope argument concerning who the AIFM is. In Ireland and Luxembourg management company structures are used that delegate all functions and do not have any employees. However, in France and Germany funds are governed by managers that are fully staffed. This difference is the root of the 'letter box entity' dilemma that the Directive poses for the Irish and Luxembourg funds industries.

[59]   ESMA's advice to the European Commission as part of the Level 2 process is built upon the feedback of four task groups which have been established. The AMF will chair the depositary group, the CBI will chair the scope group, BaFin will chair the group on authorisation/delegation/organisational requirements, and the FSA will chair the group on transparency/leverage/risk/liquidity.

[60]   The date for ESMA to furnish the European Commission with guidance was therefore postponed by 2 months from 16 September 2011 to 16 November 2011.

[61]   Hedge funds and private equity funds, for example, utilise different legal structures and therefore it is difficult to determine which entity within a complex cross-jurisdictional structure is the AIFM.

[62]   For a full discussion on the scope issues of the Directive see Bullman, Thomas 'Funds Law Update' (2011) 18(2) CLP 45.

lacks the clarity necessary for the issues arising in these heterogeneous spheres of investment from a valuation, delegation, and depositary perspective.

In applying the Directive it is essential to distinguish between two connected actors: the AIF and the AIFM. The Directive defines an AIF as '. . . any collective investment undertaking . . .' but does not further define what a collective investment undertaking is, or the circumstances subject to which this would be exempt from its scope of application (except where the fund is authorised as a UCITS fund, in accordance with the UCITS Directive).[63] The common understanding of this term is that it includes all open and closed-ended funds and all listed and non-listed funds. However, the Directive's provisions on valuation, for instance, may not be relevant to listed closed-ended funds, the value of which is determined by the equilibrium of buying and selling on an exchange. It follows that at no point can a closed-ended listed fund be subject to the same valuation procedure as a non-listed open-ended fund. Similar inconsistency can be seen in the depositary requirements placed on AIFs. Although the depositary obligations in relation to cashflow monitoring, safekeeping of assets, and record-keeping for a hedge fund may simply result in increased fees charged to investors, it is difficult to see how a depositary will be able to fulfill these obligations for private equity or property funds whose operations do not lend themselves so easily to being controlled in the same way.[64] The Directive scope issues extend past the AIF and AIFM, and have far reaching impacts for the existing valuation and depositary service provider models. The repercussions of these extra obligations on service providers

---

[63] Recital 6 exempts such vehicles as holding companies, pension funds, insurance contracts, family offices, joint ventures, and employee participation schemes or savings schemes. Recital 44 exempts reverse solicitations or passive marketing to investors. Recitals 12 and 13 support Article 3 in exempting AIFs that fall below certain threshold limits of €100million for hedge funds and €500million for private equity funds that are not leveraged and have a 5-year lock-up period. Article 59 also contains a grandfathering provision that exempts certain funds from being caught within the scope of the Directive. This clause covers any AIFs that have closed and take no further investment. However, even exempt AIFM have an obligation under the Directive to register with their Home State, provide information on their own behalf and for the AIFs they manage. However, a Home State registration process will exist for such exempt funds as per Art. 3.3.

[64] At a cost a depositary may be able to control a hedge fund's cashflow and stop unauthorised trades if necessary but only if the depositary has control over the assets in question. This is not always the case. In property funds it would be highly unlikely that a depositary could control every cash movement including payments to painters and decorators, and rent payments by tenants in the apartment block.

are yet unknown but they may decide not to offer these services to the AIF industry. Therefore, serious doubts apply as to the scope of application of the Directive, which is intended to capture all AIFs irrespective of their type or strategy.

Each AIF has to have a single AIFM to manage it.[65] However, identifying the AIFM from a pool of different actors within a complex hedge fund or private equity structure is not an easy task. A hedge fund business model may utilise a management company vehicle or a self-managed investment company vehicle, and it may have several investment managers. A private equity or property fund will have an operator, a General Partner and a Trustee that could all arguably be its 'AIFM'. As mentioned earlier, fund structures in Ireland and Luxembourg are managed and distributed in a different way from those in France and Germany, resulting in substantial difficulties in applying, in a harmonised manner, the Directive's rules throughout the EU.[66] What is also unclear is whether it is the investment discretion or the governance of the investment structure that is intended to be caught by the notion of an AIFM. This distinction is crucial as it may be the difference between the AIFM being considered a 'letter-box entity' and not. Jurisdictions such as France and Germany will favour the former, whereas Ireland and Luxembourg will favour the latter as it coincides with the models they utilise. As the Directive leaves it up to the AIFM (whomever that may be) to nominate itself for each AIF, and seek authorisation, this may lead to a situation where nominations of AIFM may evolve as a commercial decision based on national business models rather than as a result of a strict legal interpretation of the regulations.[67] Annex 1 of the Directive represents an attempt to shed some light on the issue by describing the minimum tasks to be completed by the AIFM as 'portfolio' and 'risk management'. Such AIFM can manage any number of AIF in any jurisdiction and can be either external to the AIF or be the AIF itself.[68] However, this is when the task of identifying which entity should be appointed as the AIFM takes on another level of uncertainty. The internal management option provokes the question

---

[65]   *Supra*, fn. 10, Art. 5(1)

[66]   'The AIFM Directive seen from a German Perspective', Freshfields briefing, November 2010.

[67]   Note also that an AIFM which seeks to benefit from an exemption under Art. 3(2) is also under an obligation to make their competent authority aware when they no longer comply with the criteria upon which the exemptions are based. After this notification the AIFM has 30 calendar days to apply for authorisation under Art. 7.

[68]   *Supra.* fn. 10, Recital 16 and Art. 5(1)(a)–(b).

of whether or not an AIFM's authorisation under the Directive must be supplemented by an authorisation under MiFID, a question that remains open.[69]

2.1.2   Valuation function

The Directive stipulates that the AIFM must establish and maintain appropriate and consistent procedures concerning the valuation of the AIF.[70] The AIFM must ensure a 'proper and independent' valuation of the assets held by the AIF, in accordance with the laws of the jurisdiction in which the AIF is domiciled.[71] The AIFM must further abide by transparency rules and make available to any investor the fund's net asset value (NAV) calculation. Such calculation must be undertaken at least annually for open-ended funds and as frequently as appropriate for closed-ended funds. The controversial aspects of the valuation provisions concern the related issues of (i) when a valuation is deemed to be necessary, and (ii) who can or should value the fund's assets. Firstly, the Directive requires a valuation to occur at least annually.[72] However, in relation to private equity funds, a yearly valuation is arguably unnecessary as the value of their investments is only certain once the AIF's assets have been sold and the investment realised. Secondly, the value of an investment made by a private equity fund is based on extensive due diligence by management. Therefore, the most appropriate valuer for such an investment is the AIFM itself.

In the field of hedge funds there are also valuation concerns surrounding whether or not the intention of the Directive is to impose obligations on the valuers to value the assets held in the AIF or to just calculate a NAV, albeit these are less controversial issues then those relating to private equity. However, in summary the valuation provisions of the Directive actually facilitate the hedge fund business models that operate within the industry by allowing internal and external valuation. It is not uncommon for hedge fund valuations to be undertaken within a group. The Directive therefore allows an AIFM itself to undertake the valuation process, provided that the valuation function is functionally independent from that of

---

[69]   Recital 7 and 16 tend to suggest that for investment firms offering services such as individual portfolio management, authorization under the AIFM Directive is not required. However, it is less clear if the reverse occurs and the AIFM itself is performing investment services for the AIF such as collective portfolio management.

[70]   *Supra*, fn. 10, Art. 19.

[71]   *Ibid.,* Art. 19(1)–(2)

[72]   *Ibid.*, Art. 19(3)

portfolio management and from the fund's remuneration policy.[73] Any conflicts of interest within the AIFM must also be managed and mitigated appropriately. The only cost to the AIFM in utilising the internal valuation option is that the AIFM's policies and procedures must be verified as appropriate by an external valuer or auditor.[74]

However, external valuation presents its own taxonomy of conflicts due to the model operated within the EU whereby administration and custody services are often provided by sister companies within a group. Therefore, an AIF's depositary may not act as valuer unless it has 'functionally and hierarchically separated the performance of its depositary functions from its tasks as an external valuer' and managed all conflicts of interest that may arise in such a situation.[75]

Further to this, it is specifically prohibited for a valuer to delegate its function to a third party after the valuer's appointment and notification to the AIFM's competent authority.[76] The concern here is that the Directive may act as an unnecessary impediment to the commercial operation of the valuation model. It is unclear if the prohibition on the delegation of valuation functions operates in its entirety or would it apply even if functions such as the valuation of side-pockets or sourcing prices for illiquid stocks were delegated to specialists. This brings us into the difficulties posed by the delegation provisions of the Directive.

2.1.3   Delegation arrangements

The Directive allows delegation as long as the competent authority of the AIFM's home Member State has been notified of the delegation before it takes effect, the delegation arrangements can be objectively justified, and the delegate has sufficient resources and expertise to perform its tasks.[77] The AIFM, as the entity charged with the responsibility for ensuring compliance with the Directive[78] must be able to monitor the delegate's activity and be in a position to replace the delegate in the interests of the AIF and investors should the need to do so arise.[79] A delegate may sub-delegate further based on the approval of the AIFM and to the same requirements being fulfilled as those outlined above.[80] However, no delegation over the

---

[73]   *Ibid.*, Art. 19 (4)(b).
[74]   *Ibid.*, Art. 19 (9).
[75]   *Ibid.*, Art. 19 (4).
[76]   *Ibid.*, Art. 19 (6).
[77]   *Ibid.*, Art. 20(1)(a)–(d).
[78]   *Ibid.*, Art. 5(1).
[79]   *Ibid.*, Art. 20(1)(e)–(f).
[80]   *Ibid.*, Art. 20(3)(a) – (c).

portfolio management or risk management functions shall be given to the depositary or to a delegate of the depositary because of the conflict of interest that this could give rise to.[81] No entity whose interest would cause a conflict with that of the AIF or its investors may act as a delegate of AIFM functions unless such entity has functionally and hierarchically separated the performance of its portfolio and risk management tasks from the other tasks that it performs which may represent the conflict of interest.[82]

Following on from this clarification is necessary in relation to the point at which an AIFM delegates so many functions that it becomes a 'letter-box entity' itself, void of any staff, policies, or procedures to ensure compliance with the Directive.[83] This is important because the Directive provides that an entity cannot circumvent the provisions of the Directive through delegating all of its functions. The difficulty for the industry is that hedge funds domiciled in jurisdictions such as Ireland use a management company or self-managed investment company structure which delegates all functions. Such governing structures are often staffed by non-executive directors who merely oversee the delegation of all functions to third parties. However, the question is whether or not such governance structures sufficiently oversee the delegation to the extent that they fulfill the Directive's requirement not to be a 'letter-box entity'.[84] If the management company or self-managed investment company is deemed to be a 'letter-box entity' then by default the UK-based investment manager is the only other entity that could be seen as the AIFM. This is an outcome that investment managers in the UK will seek to avoid at all costs and therefore clarification on this principle is necessary.[85]

2.1.4 Depositaries' responsibilities and obligations

The AIFM Directive provides for the appointment of a single depositary for each AIF in the Member State where the AIF is domiciled.[86] The depositary no longer needs to be an EU-based credit institution, as under

---

[81]   *Ibid.*, Art. 20(1)(i) – (ii).

[82]   To assure itself that no such issues exist the AIFM shall review its services provided by delegates on an ongoing basis according to Art. 20(3).

[83]   *Supra*, fn. 10, Recital 7 and Art. 20(2).

[84]   The Central Bank of Ireland is currently chairing the ESMA task force group on scope issues and will be responsible for giving industry feedback to ESMA on all legal and regulatory issues.

[85]   For an overview of delegation provisions of the Directive and how they aid in determining the AIFM in a complex structure see Bullman, Thomas 'Funds Law Update' (2011) 18(4) CLP.

[86]   *Supra*, fn. 10, Art. 21(1).

the Commission proposal.[87] The following entities may act as a depositary: (i) a credit institution with its registered office in the EU, (ii) a MiFID investment firm that has its registered office in the EU, and (iii) another category of institution which is subject to prudential regulation and supervision and the Member State in which such institution is domiciled has categorised it as being eligible to act as a depositary for a non-EU AIF only.[88] The depositary functions include such tasks as monitoring subscription and redemptions, ensuring the safe-keeping of the assets of the AIF, verification of the ownership of the AIF's assets, and ensuring that the valuation of the AIF's shares or units is carried out in accordance with the applicable national laws.

Of key importance to the alternative investment funds' industry will be the liability provisions associated with the depositary function. The depositary will always be liable to the AIF and investors *unless* the loss suffered by the depositary, or its delegates, was beyond its reasonable control and the consequences of such external events were unavoidable in the face of reasonable efforts made to avoid the loss. Furthermore, the depositary may be discharged of liability if it has delegated the custody function to a third party and the depositary's liability was contractually transferred to the delegate. However, this liability may not be easily transferred to third parties who are clearly going to be unwilling to accept it.[89] Concerning 'other losses', liability can only be established for a 'negligent or intentional' failure on the depositary's part to 'properly perform its obligations pursuant to the Directive'.[90] Despite representing an improvement over previous drafts, the Directive's depositary provisions point to a substantial increase in the level of liability taken on by depositaries, with a knock-on effect on their costs as well as on the prices for end-investors.

The scope of the Directive's depositary rules has also been controversial. An example of this is the list of financial instruments included in the scope of the depositary's custody duties which is in need of clarity and

---

[87]   *Ibid.*, Art.21(3). Eligible depositaries, under the Directive, include, apart from EU credit institutions, investment firms with their registered office in the EU, and other categories of institutions subject to prudential regulation and ongoing supervision in the Member States.

[88]   *Ibid.*, Art. 21(3)(a) – (c).

[89]   The AMF has been appointed as chair of the depositary task force group set up by ESMA. Top of its agenda is the definition of external events beyond the reasonable control of the depositary and the definition to be used for 'financial instruments'.

[90]   *Supra*, fn. 10, Art. 21(11) & (12).

reconsideration. The exhaustive list copied from MiFID[91] and applied in an ever-innovative investment sector seems inappropriate. Related to this is the lack of clarity in the Directive concerning the obligation of the depositary to monitor and control cashflows and oversee the instruction of transactions by the AIFM. In essence, under the current wording, the depositary is being turned into a quasi-fund manager, replicating some tasks that should be left to the fund manager or administrator.[92]

2.1.5 Third country provisions

Some of the Directive's most complex and controversial provisions have to do with its third country provisions and the wide taxonomy of rules governing the management and marketing of EU and non-EU AIFs by EU and non-EU AIFMs. To fully understand the impact of these rules these need to be broken into three groupings: (1) the EU passport, (2) the third country passport, and (3) the national private placement regimes.

The EU passport is automatic for EU AIFM's marketing or managing EU AIFs, upon authorisation under the Directive. This is the part of the distribution rules which are uncontroversial though. [93]

The third country passport has been the issue of greatest concern. As mentioned earlier in the chapter the major elements of controversy concerning the Commission proposal have been the provisions relating to the management and marketing of funds domiciled outside the EU.[94] To understand this passport more fully it is essential to review the Directive's detailed marketing rules. These differ, depending on the origin of the AIFM and/or the AIF (although there are overlaps across some of the different marketing scenarios). Concerning EU-based AIFM, the AIFM Directive's passport is to apply as of mid-2013. EU-based AIFM are to be allowed to *manage* non-EU AIF, subject to fulfilling the requirements of the Directive (except with regard to the appointment of a depositary

---

[91]   *Ibid.,* Art. 4(1)(o) which refers to the exhaustive list in Annex 1, Section C of MiFID.

[92]   *Ibid.,* Art. 21(6)–(8) outlines the obligations of the depositary which often entails control rather than oversight. Control over transactions is a fund management obligation and reconstructing the NAV calculation of a fund is an administration responsibility. The excessive duplication of obligations vis-à-vis the depositary will only result in the cost to the investor being increased or the depositary refusing to engage the business.

[93]   *Ibid.,* Art. 31–33.

[94]   *Ibid.,* Art. 36 and 40 provide for the marketing through national private placement regimes of non-EU AIFs by EU AIFMs and non-EU AIFMs respectively. Art. 35 and 39 provides for a third country passport for the marketing of non-EU AIFs by EU AIFMs and non-EU AIFMs respectively.

and the preparation of an annual report), and provided that appropriate cooperation arrangements are in place between the competent authorities in the AIFM's home Member State and the AIF's home jurisdiction.[95] Additional conditions are to apply to the *marketing*, by EU-based AIFM, of non-EU AIF, in the EU, under the Directive's passport regime,[96] with the marketing possibility for this constellation only becoming available upon the expiry of a two-year transitional period after the Directive's implementation by the Member States.[97]

Non EU-based AIFM wishing to manage EU-domiciled AIF are to do so subject to compliance with the Directive and after applying for a prior authorisation to be granted from the AIF's home Member State authorities,[98] while licensed AIFM wishing to market non-EU AIF are only to be allowed to do so once the conditions laid down in the Directive are fulfilled.[99]

The two year moratorium given to the holders of EU passports means that protection is offered to EU managers of EU-domiciled funds from non-EU competitors as the third country passport does not come into effect until mid-2015. It is this protectionist aspect of the third country provisions, which has provoked debate about retaliatory measures by the US.[100]

However, the Directive offers a more palatable solution by virtue of its retention of national private placement regimes for EU and non-EU AIFMs marketing non-EU AIFs within the EU. EU or non-EU-domiciled AIFM marketing non-EU AIFs will be able to use the national private placement regimes until at least 2018. Non EU-domiciled AIFM are to be allowed to market AIF to *professional investors* within individual Member State jurisdictions, under their respective private placement rules, provided that they meet, as a minimum, the Directive's specific requirements.[101] It will then be decided on a recommendation by the ESMA, after a review of the Directive in its entirety, whether the national private placement regimes will be terminated.[102]

---

[95]   *Ibid.*, Art.34.
[96]   *Ibid.*, Art.35.
[97]   *Ibid.*, Art. 63bis. It is foreseen that the current, national private placement regimes are to continue to exist side-by-side with the Directive's passport regime for another three years before being phased out.
[98]   *Ibid.*, Art. 37.
[99]   *Ibid.*, Art. 38.
[100]   *Ibid.*, Art. 63bis(1)
[101]   *Ibid.*, Art. 40.
[102]   It is noted that Art. 63(1)(ii) of the AIFM Directive provides that ESMA shall review and make recommendations to the European Commission on the

Finally, Member States may allow AIFM to market to retail investors in their territory AIF they manage in accordance with the Directive, irrespective of whether these are to be marketed on a domestic or cross-border basis or whether or not these are EU-domiciled AIF.[103]

2.1.6 Remuneration provisions

Contrary to the original Commission proposal, the Directive regulates remuneration-related issues.[104] Specifically, the Directive requires AIFMs to have remuneration policies and practices in place that are 'consistent with and promote sound and effective risk management' for all those categories of staff with 'a material impact on the risk profiles of AIF they manage', 'including senior management, risk takers, control functions and any employee receiving total remuneration that takes them into the same remuneration bracket as senior management and risk takers . . .'. The Directive entrusts ESMA with the task of establishing sound and proportional remuneration policies for the AIFM sector (in close collaboration with the European Banking Authority) and with ensuring their consistency with the principles laid down in an Annex to the Directive and in a relevant Commission Recommendation.[105] The ESMA's guidance on the sensitive issue of remuneration is anxiously awaited, and it remains to be seen how this will be implemented by the competent national authorities as well as what its interplay will turn out to be with the parallel Capital Requirements Directive regime.[106] For jurisdictions such as the UK who already operate a remuneration code, the Directive widens the scope of individuals caught under the remuneration provisions to include fund managers and not just senior management (or code staff under the Remuneration Code).[107]

---

termination of national regimes. The review will take place three years after the transposition of the Directive and under the terms outlined in Art 63(2)(a)–(d).

[103] *Supra*, fn. 10, Art. 41.

[104] *Ibid.*, Art.13.

[105] See Commission Recommendation 2009/384/EC of 30 April 2009 on remuneration in the financial services sector dated 30 April 2009, OJL 120, 15.5.2009, 22.

[106] See Commission Proposal of 13 July 2009 for a Directive of the European Parliament and of the Council amending Directives 2006/48/EC and 2006/49/EC as regards capital requirements for the trading book and for re-securitisations, and the supervisory review of remuneration policies SEC(2009) 974 & 975 final.

[107] See FSA Policy Statement 10/20 for details on the UK Remuneration Code.

2.2   The AIFM Directive: The US Comparison

Leaving aside the detailed nature of the Directive (and the complications that this entails, *inter alia* from the perspective of its future implementation by the Member States) other issues worth considering briefly are those of its consistency with (i) similar transatlantic regulatory harmonisation initiatives and (ii) the four principles identified earlier in the chapter by way of guidance for a qualitatively better outcome compared to the one achieved through the original Commission proposal.

Regarding the first of the abovementioned issues, the Directive no doubt shares a number of common features with the rules applying, at the time of writing, under the Dodd-Frank Act to hedge fund and private equity managers (as well as other private investment intermediaries).[108] For instance, both sets of rules envisage the mandatory registration of fund managers (although the AIFM Directive captures a broader range of managers) and both impose detailed reporting requirements upon them with regard to their use of leverage, their valuation procedures, and so on. However, the US rules for alternative investment managers remain more relaxed in comparison with those in the Directive. One key area where the US and the European rules appear to differ is in connection with the marketing of funds, in particular those domiciled in third countries. Although the new US rules will, no doubt, entail fresh obligations for EU investment funds and fund managers willing to operate in the US (as they will now have to register, bearing increased costs and disclosure requirements), these are nevertheless likely to be less demanding than those to be implemented in the EU.[109] Apart from suggesting that the transatlantic harmonisation in financial regulation advocated by the G20 in 2009 and 2010 is not likely to materialise any time soon, the differences between the EU and the US approach to the regulation of AIFM could give a competitive advantage to US-domiciled AIFMs and AIFs, over their EU counterparts.

---

[108]   Wall Street Reform and Consumer Protection Act (Pub. L. 111-203, H.R. 4173). The Dodd-Frank Act includes the Private Investment Advisers Registration Act of 2010, which substantially amends the registration and other requirements of the Investment Advisers Act of 1940 for private fund investment advisers by, *inter alia* eliminating the 'private adviser' exemption from registration with the SEC laid down in Section 203(b)(3) thereof.

[109]   The Registration Act provides, for instance, an exemption for 'foreign private advisers', with no place of business in the US, fewer than 15 US clients, less than US$25 million in aggregate AUM attributable to US clients and which do not hold themselves out to the public as investment advisers.

2.3 Assessment of the Directive Against Regulatory Principles

The picture emerging from an assessment of the final rules against the guiding principles identified earlier in this chapter is a mixed one. Throughout all preceding versions of the Directive, and in its current form, there has been a disconnect between the risks posed by specific funds and their subjection to comprehensive and uniform regulatory compliance obligations. An AIF's subjection to the Directive is essentially a function of its *size*, not of its risks, opening the door for the circumvention of its rules through the establishment of several, smaller funds, below the regulatory thresholds.[110] Moreover, what the wide definition of AIF, both under the original Commission proposal and under the rules finally adopted,[111] suggests is that, at least for certain structures (especially those that one would not ordinarily classify as AIFs, such as covered bonds, acquisition vehicles, managed accounts and index-linked or performance notes), it is difficult to decide whether or not they fall within the Directive's scope of application.[112] In the same vein, the fact that the capital requirements to apply under the Directive differ from those applicable to other, harmonised funds, raises doubts as to the level of capital necessary in the case of managers managing both AIF and harmonised funds. The phasing-out of many of the original Commission proposal's protectionist elements, evident in its controversial 'third country rules', is, on the other hand, a positive development: the Directive no longer prohibits market access for third country AIFM and their funds, it only makes it *more expensive* than it had been under the Member States' private placement rules. The Directive is, on the other hand, not appreciably different from its precursor in terms of the scope of the organisational, investor disclosure,

---

[110] This risk has been identified in Hanneke Wegman, 'EU Alternative Fund Regulation Proposal: Pros and Cons', European Company Law (2009) **6**(4), 150–151, 151. However, the AIF will still be required to register in its Home State under Art. 3(3) and provide periodic disclosures as well as monitor its proximity to the Directive's threshold limits which require full authorisation.

[111] The AIFM Directive only contains a generic definition of AIF, encompassing 'any collective investment undertaking, including investment compartments thereof, which raises capital from a number of investors, with a view to investing it in accordance with a defined investment policy for the benefit of those investors; and which does not require authorisation pursuant to Article 5 of the UCITS Directive, as amended.

[112] This is, perhaps, ironic, considering that the inherent risks of some of these structures (with an emphasis on equity index-linked or performance notes) are comparable to those of 'classic' AIF and that some of these structures are already freely accessible to the public.

transparency and other reporting duties to be imposed upon AIFM: the new rules are no more aligned with the realities of the business of AIFM than those originally proposed and it remains to be seen to what extent supervisors or investors will be able to benefit from the information that AIFM would, as a result, need to provide (what is more, at a significant additional cost). Finally, while the wide delegated law-making powers granted to the Commission under the original proposal are to be phased-out gradually,[113] that particular improvement over the original proposal has come at the price of the close involvement of the ESMA in no less than 11 different areas of relevance to the Directive's operation, running the gamut from the drawing-up of guidelines and recommendations through to the exercise of actual decision-making powers.[114] Given the likelihood that some, at least, of the delegated measures to be adopted by the Commission and of the technical standards to be proposed or adopted by the ESMA will be drawn from existing industry standards, it remains to be seen whether 'regulatory capture' phenomena will, eventually, be avoided.

It follows that the Directive is devoid of some, but not all, of the drawbacks of the Commission proposal, the spirit of which subsists in many of its final rules, and that several of the criticisms levelled against the original Commission proposal remain valid. However, considering the controversy surrounding the issue of the choice of the appropriate response to the AIF sector's growth, especially amidst the current turmoil (with the added public opinion pressure that this has put on regulators), the divided opinions over the sector's role in the financial crisis and the difficult compromises necessary between the conflicting positions of France and Germany, on the one hand, and certain other Member States, such as the UK, on the other, one is tempted to conclude that, even if not being an ideal piece of legislation, the Directive is less problematic than some may have originally feared.

---

[113]   Art. 54(1), according to which the powers to adopt delegated acts referred to in over two dozen of the Directive's Articles are to be conferred on the Commission for a period of 4 years following the entry into force of the Directive.

[114]   The ESMA's powers include the drafting of Level 3 technical standards, assessing the uniform application of the Directive across the Member States and monitoring the interaction of the competent Member State authorities with regard to the Directive's passport as well as the cooperation among the competent Member State and third-country authorities. It remains to be seen whether the ESMA will prove capable of delivering on its multifarious responsibilities under the Directive.

3.   THE FUTURE OF THE EUROPEAN AIF SECTOR

The adoption of the AIFM Directive after some 18 months of upheaval suggests that the era of fragmented and 'lighter-touch' regulation for Europe's AIF sector is rapidly coming to an end, with the implementation deadline of mid-2013 calling for immediate action by AIF, to ensure their readiness to apply the new rules. The process leading up to the adoption of the Directive has, no doubt, been edifying for the EU institutions involved in its preparation, confirming the need for Union lawmakers to seek, in a timely manner, the meaningful input of all relevant stakeholders before drafting their legal acts. The very tight schedule for the preparation of the original Commission proposal and the conflicting interests that it sought to serve have resulted in a text which, however much inspired by a handful of legitimate goals, was objectionable in several of its details. The final rules address some of the concerns raised by the original Commission proposal and comply, in some respects, with the four guiding principles highlighted earlier in this chapter. However, they also throw open several questions, most of which are of relevance to the future of the European alternative funds industry.

One obvious question is that of the impact of the Directive on the UCITS regime's rules: given that several of the Directive's provisions mirror and, in some respects, go beyond the UCITS standards (e.g. in relation to depositaries and their duties). A harmonisation 'upwards' of some of the provisions of the UCITS regime to match those of the Directive appears likely (not least in order to preserve a level playing field) between different types of vehicles that are, nevertheless, open, at least in part, to the same categories of investors, being in competition for the same resources.

Another question is whether the Directive's *sui generis* third country passport will not pave the way for other, similar third country passports covering activities in other financial market sectors. Rather unusually for a Union legal act, the Directive is to have consequences not only for the European but, also, for the global AIF industry, impacting EU and non EU-domiciled AIFM and AIF alike, as well as their service providers and investors. As we have argued earlier, it is questionable whether, as a matter of principle, the conditional opening of the European investment fund market to off-shore funds and/or their managers could ever be a legitimate internal market regulatory objective. However, it is not out of the question that the adoption of the Directive could establish a precedent with wide-ranging implications for the future of the European financial services landscape, if its third country passport were to be extended to foreign financial institutions active in the areas of banking, securities and insurance and to a parallel phasing-out of divergent national arrangements for the pursuit, by third country financial institutions, of financial business in the different EU Member States. The resulting centralisation of the currently decentralised authorisation process for third country firms wishing to operate within the EU could bring about seismic changes to Europe's financial services landscape, weakening the role of national supervisors and strengthening those of the ESMA and the Commission.

Perhaps the most crucial question is that of the impact of the Directive on the future growth prospects of the European AIF sector. The scenario that has, so far, been presented as the most plausible conceptually is that of an off-shore flight of AIFM to third country jurisdictions, where regulatory standards are lighter, with all the adverse implications of such a development for job-creation as well as for Europe's competitiveness and growth. Those speculating on the probability of an off-shore flight of fund managerial talent have pointed to the substantial compliance costs that the Directive's implementation will signal.[115] According to 2009 estimates, the one-off compliance costs of the original Commission proposal could reach €3.2billion, with the ongoing compliance costs reaching €311million.[116] The increased compliance costs for all players along the fund value chain – managers, custodians etc.– would inevitably be passed on to investors, in the form of higher fees. While discarding the off-shore flight scenario would be premature, an alternative scenario – which, in the authors' view, is no less plausible even if equally conjectural – is that of a massive conversion of AIFM (including overseas managers) to the UCITS discipline. Indeed, there is evidence to suggest that a substantial percentage of EU-domiciled hedge funds *already* meet the UCITS risk requirements and could, relatively easily, switch to the UCITS regime, trying to replicate, through it, at least to some extent, hedge fund strategies.[117] The liberalisa-

---

[115]   For instance, the Directive's depositary rules are inconsistent with current practice and stand to increase the risk that depositaries will have to take as well as their remuneration for it, resulting in increased costs that will inevitably be passed on to investors.

[116]   Charles River Associates, Impact of the proposed AIFM Directive across Europe, Report prepared for the Financial Services Authority, October 2009, 112. According to other estimates, the rules originally proposed by the Commission would cost EU private equity and hedge fund industries between €1.3 billion and €1.9 billion in the first year, with the annual recurring cost being estimated at between €689 million and €985 million (Persson, 2009).

[117]   The investment restrictions imposed by the UCITS framework limit the ability of UCITS to follow pure hedge fund strategies. UCITS cannot, for instance, engage directly in short-selling but they can invest in derivative instruments in order to limit their exposure to price declines; however, diversification rules apply

tion of the UCITS framework in 2002, through the UCITS 'Product'[118] and 'Management'[119] Directives, paved the way for this development, which the advent of the Directive may, however ironically, provide fresh impetus for. The uncertainties surrounding the interpretation of some of the provisions of the Directive (and how these are to be implemented in the different Member States) are apt to render that scenario likelier, strengthening the attraction, for hedge fund managers, of the tried and tested UCITS brand.[120] Post-financial crisis investor preferences, away from alternative investment funds and towards safer, lower-risk, regulated alternatives, could further reinforce the attraction of the tried and tested UCITS brand for AIFM. While a boost in the popularity of the UCITS brand could present a number of advantages (for instance, help keep managerial talent within the Old Continent or, even, attract new from abroad), and despite the fact that the ability to replicate hedge fund strategies within a regulated UCITS environment has substantial benefits (i.e. those of a recognisable brand, a wide investor base and a European passport), an unwanted consequence of the adoption of the Directive might be to bring about lasting changes to the character of the UCITS brand, leading to a watering down of its investor protection standards and to a deterioration in the brand's global reputation for safety, simplicity and quality of supervision. A massive flight of AIFM to the UCITS discipline, as a result of the entry into force of the Directive, and the more systematic pursuit, by the UCITS sector, of hedge-fund-like strategies, resulting in the offer of complex, structured products in a UCITS wrapper could, in the long run, render meaningless the distinction between alternative investment funds, marketed to qualified investors only, and UCITS-compliant funds, marketed to retail investors, blurring the borderline between traditional and alternative asset management vehicles,[121] intensify competition amongst

---

to the derivatives instruments held by UCITS. Similarly, the leverage that UCITS can employ is restricted to investment purposes. Other restrictions (e.g. on commodities investments) also restrict the ability of UCITS to replicate certain hedge fund strategies. Constraints such as the above may leave sophisticated investors with long-term investment policies preferring to invest with traditional hedge funds rather than with UCITS.

[118]   Directive (EC) 2001/108, [2002] OJ L41/35.

[119]   Directive (EC) 2001/107, [2002] OJ L41/20.

[120]   Investors have, over time, built confidence in the UCITS label and the safeguards of the UCITS framework are not just recognised in Europe but also beyond its borders.

[121]   This trend has been particularly evident in Europe after the regulatory changes in its harmonised funds towards more sophisticated financial products (including financial derivatives and indexes) and could, especially if aided by a

harmonised fund managers, compress UCITS sector returns and encourage greater risk-taking, with wider financial and, possibly, systemic risk implications. Those risks are unlikely to have been present in the mind of the Commission, and even less likely to have been accepted as permissible; however, if they were to materialise, they would make of the AIFM Directive a textbook example of regulatory failure.

Without prejudice to the above, from a commercial reality perspective, a widespread, voluntary migration of AIFM to the UCITS structure would appear unlikely, taking into account the fact that most hedge fund managers have no expertise in the operation and administrative requirements of a UCITS fund, no appetite for offering daily liquidity, and no desire to be bound by the investment restrictions and compliance monitoring procedures associated with retail products. AIFM migrations to the UCITS fund structure are more likely to be imposed by investors seeking to invest in more tightly and less risky regulated products.[122] However, it provides a compelling reason for AIFMs to assess the benefits and implications of using the UCITS label, especially when the national private placement regime option available to hedge funds is at risk of disappearing over the next few years.[123] In gauging the current trend of fund managers in redomiciling off-shore funds or setting up new structures within the EU, Ireland and Luxembourg, as natural choices for such redomiciling, have seen record levels of funds making the move to being serviced and domiciled in Europe.[124] Hedge fund managers are both setting up UCITS funds and also redomiciling AIFs within the EU. This is evidence of the continued

---

further relaxation of UCITS regulation, render AIF more mainstream and less easily distinguishable from UCITS funds, challenging the legitimacy of their different regulatory treatment, not least on grounds of competition. In this regard, see Athanassiou, *supra*, fn. 46, 41–42.

[122]   See ALFI study into Alternative UCITS conducted in association with Strategic Insight dated 25 November 2010 entitled 'Alternative and Hedge Fund Ucits in the Next Decade'. However, only a small percentage of alternative UCITS were being launched by hedge fund managers. These strategies were predominantly launched by traditional managers but were getting more interest from hedge fund managers.

[123]   Bullman, Thomas, 'Unintended regulatory consequences of the draft Alternative Investment Fund Managers Directive: UCITS III and the Irish dilemma – Part 1' (2010) 17(4) CLP 67 and 'Unintended regulatory consequences of the draft Alternative Investment Fund Managers Directive: UCITS III and the Irish dilemma – Part 2' (2010) 17(5) CLP 87 for further discussion.

[124]   See Irish Funds Industry Association press releases of 16 December 2010 entitled 'Ireland Comes out Top as European Hedge Fund domicile of Choice', and of 23 February 2011 entitled 'Irish Funds Industry Continues Expansion'.

struggle within the industry between avoiding uncertainty and preparing for change.

4. CONCLUSION

Whilst the final rules of the Directive are, no doubt, important, their actual implementation by the Member States and, no less crucially, their consistent application by the competent supervisory authorities in the various Member States will be equally important in determining the Directive's success and, ultimately, the future of the European AIF sector. At the time of writing, major question marks hang over both of these points. What was nevertheless clear was that for most of the rules laid down in the Directive to yield results and for the efficient monitoring of the cross-border dimension of the risks posed by the AIF sector to be possible, those rules would need to benefit from the revamped framework for supervisory co-operation and information-sharing amongst the competent national authorities and from Europe's nascent mechanism for the preservation of cross-border systemic stability and the management and resolution of crisis situations. Given the complexity of the Directive's rules, and the obvious need for cross-border cooperation for their application, at the level of national supervisors and macro-prudential stability watchdogs,[125] few other examples of harmonised regulation are likely to put the newly established EU-wide supervisory and systemic stability monitoring arrangements (with an emphasis on the ESMA and the ESRB) to a more demanding test than the Directive, making of it a measure of their failure or success. Although many have criticised the Directive as being disproportionate to the risks posed by AIFs, the jury is out on the genuine strengths and weaknesses of the new rules[126] and it will be some time before enough is known for a more comprehensive and conclusive assessment of the Directive and its impact on Europe's AIF sector and investment funds industry, at large.

---

[125] It is hardly surprising, therefore, that the Directive should give so much prominence to information-sharing and to coordination amongst the competent Member State-authorities as a pre-condition for the application of its rules.

[126] Eilis Ferran, 'The Regulation of Hedge Funds and Private Equity: A Case Study in the Development of the EU's Regulatory Response to the Financial Crisis' University of Cambridge Legal Studies Research Paper Series No. 10/2011, 28 which makes reference to the Directive being a proverbial 'sledgehammer to crack a nut'.

BIBLIOGRAPHY

ALFI (Association of the Luxembourg Fund Industry) (2010), Study into Alternative UCITS conducted in association with Strategic Insight entitled 'Alternative and Hedge Fund Ucits in the Next Decade', 25 November, available at http://www.alfi.ln/publications.statements/publications/alternative-and-hedge-fund-ucits-next-decade.

AIMA (Alternative Investment Management) (2009), Statement on European Commission Directive, 23 April, available at http://www.aima.org/en/announcements/aima-statement-on-european-commission-directive.cfm.

Athanassiou, Phoebus (2010), 'The AIFM Directive and the Future of European Alternative Investment Fund Regulation', OCHEL-Dice Report, 1/2010, 8–14.

Athanassiou, Phoebus (2009), *Hedge Fund Regulation in the European Union – Current Trends and Future Prospects*, the Netherlands: Kluwer Law International.

Black, Duncan (2009) 'The draft EU Directive on Alternative Investment Fund Managers: What's the Fuss About?', *Journal of Securities Law, Regulation & Compliance* **3**(1), 64–70.

Bullman, Thomas (2009) 'The Draft Directive on AIFMs: European Protectionism or Attack on the Hedge Fund Industry? – Part 1', *Bloomberg UK Financial Services Law Journal* **1**(1) and 'The Draft Directive on AIFMs: European Protectionism or Attack on the Hedge Fund Industry? – Part 2', *Bloomberg UK Financial Services Law Journal* **1**(2).

Bullman, Thomas (2010) 'Unintended regulatory consequences of the draft Alternative Investment Fund Managers Directive: UCITS III and the Irish dilemma – Part 1' *CLP*, **17**(4) 67 and 'Unintended regulatory consequences of the draft Alternative Investment Fund Managers Directive: UCITS III and the Irish dilemma – Part 2' *CLP*, **17**(5) 87.

Bundesverband Investment und Asset Management e.V. (2009), Stellungnahme des BVI zum Entwurf einer EU-Richtlinie für 'Alternative Investment Fund Managers' (AIFM), Frankfurt am Main.

Charles River Associates (2009), 'Impact of the proposed AIFM Directive across Europe', Report prepared for the Financial Services Authority, October, London, UK: Financial Services Authority.

Discussion paper on ESMA's policy orientations on possible implementing measures under Article 3 of the Alternative Investment Fund Managers Directive, 15 April 2011, available at http://www.esma.europa.eu/index.php?page=consultation-details&id=181

European Central Bank (2009), 'Opinion of 16 October 2009 on a Proposal for a Directive on Alternative Investment Fund Managers and amending Directives 2004/39/EC and 2009/. . ./EC'.

European Commission (2009), 'Proposal for a Directive on Alternative Investment Fund Managers (AIFM)', Brussels, COM(2009) 207 final.

European Council (2010), 'Proposal for a Directive on Alternative Investment Fund Managers and amending Directives 2004/39/EC and 2009/. . ./EC' – Issues note by the Presidency, Brussels, 5164/10.

European Council (2009), 'Proposal for a Directive of the European Parliament and of the Council on Alternative Investment Fund Managers and amending Directives 2004/39/EC and 2009/. . ./EC' – Presidency compromise proposal, Brussels, 15910/09.

European Parliament (2009), 'Draft Report on the Proposal for a Directive of the European Parliament and of the Council on Alternative Investment Fund Managers and Amending Directives 2004/39/EC and 2009/. . ./EC, Brussels', 2009/0064 (COD).

European Private Equity & Venture Capital Association (2009), Response to the Proposed Directive of the European Parliament and Council on Alternative Investment Fund Managers (AIFM)', Brussels, 26 June.

Ferran, Eilis (2011), 'The Regulation of Hedge Funds and Private Equity: A Case Study in the Development of the EU's Regulatory Response to the Financial Crisis' University of Cambridge Legal Studies Research Paper Series No. 10/2011.

Finansinspektionen (2009), 'Position on the proposed AIFM Directive', Stockholm.

FSA (2009), 'A regulatory response to the global banking crisis' ('Turner Review'), London, UK: Financial Services Authority.

FSA, Policy Statement 10/20 outlining the UK Remuneration Code, London, UK: Financial Services Authority.

Garbaravicius, Tomas and Dierick, Frank (2005), Hedge funds and their implications for financial stability, ECB Occasional Paper Series No. 34, August 2005.

Hanneke Wegman (2009), 'EU Alternative Fund Regulation Proposal: Pros and Cons', European Company Law, **6**(4), 150–151.

McVea, Harry (2009), 'Regulating Hedge Funds in the Shadow of the Recent Financial Crisis: The EU Response', in John Raymond Labrosse, Rodrigo Olivares Caminal and Dalvinder Singh (eds.) *Financial Crisis Management and Bank Resolution*, London: Informa, 31–52.

Moloney, Niahm (2010), 'EU Financial Market Regulation after the global financial crisis: more Europe or more risks?', *CMLR*, **47**, 1317–1383.

Persson, M. (2009), 'The EU's AIFM Directive: Likely Impact and Best Way Forward', London: Open Europe Report.

Swiss Funds Association (2009), 'Position Paper on the Draft AIFM Directive', Basel, Swiss Funds Association.

18. The domestic rooting of financial regulation in an era of global capital markets

Thomas Oatley* and W. Kindred Winecoff[†]

INTRODUCTION

The financial crisis that began in 2007 has forced academics and policy-makers to re-examine regulatory policy at the domestic and international levels. In an op-ed in the *Washington Post* during the height of the crisis, Prime Minister Gordon Brown (as he then was) called for 'cross-border supervision of financial institutions; shared global standards for accounting and regulation; a more responsible approach to executive remuneration that rewards hard work, effort and enterprise but not irresponsible risk-taking; and the renewal of our international institutions to make them effective early-warning systems for the world economy' (Brown 2008).

Similar responses were not only common following the current crisis, they continue a history of introspection following financial upheavals: in the United States (US), the Glass-Steagall Banking Act of 1933 – which established federal deposit insurance and separated commercial from investment banking – was a response to the waves of bank failures that exacerbated the Great Depression. In 2010, the United Kingdom (UK) reacted to the subprime financial crisis by moving to abolish its primary financial regulator, the Financial Services Authority, and giving its authority to several other agencies including the Bank of England and the Consumer Protection and Markets Authority, a new prudential supervision authority.

At the international level, the Basel Committee on Banking Supervision was formed to provide a platform for national governments to coordinate policy after policymakers mis-handled the liquidation of the German

* Thomas Oatley – Associate Professor, Department of Political Science, The University of North Carolina at Chapel Hill.

† W. Kindred Winecoff – PhD Candidate, Department of Political Science, The University of North Carolina at Chapel Hill, US.

Bank Herstatt in 1974, thereby sparking an international controversy. The Basel Capital Accord (Basel I), which established minimum capital adequacy requirements across the G-10 countries, was agreed following the exposure of banks in the G-10 countries to the Latin American debt crises in the 1980s. The Revised Common Framework (Basel II) followed the East Asian financial crises in the 1990s. The Basel Committee has developed a new agreement (Basel III) to address weaknesses in prudential standards that contributed to the subprime crisis, to be refined and implemented in the coming years.

The concern is for good reason. Not only have financial crises always been a recurring feature of the global economy (Reinhart and Rogoff 2009; Kindleberger 1978), they have increased in incidence and severity following the collapse of the Bretton Woods system (Bordo & Eichengreen 1999). Nevertheless, a healthy financial sector is a prerequisite for economic growth (King & Levine 1993), and there is some evidence that an open international financial system fosters economic growth.[1] Governments use regulations to resolve the tradeoff between the necessity of a robust financial sector, as a precondition for economic growth, and the potential for devastating collapses in the real economy if the financial sector breaks down as a result of excessive risk-taking. In short, governments use regulatory policy to balance private and public interests.

As governments consider revisions to domestic and international regulatory regimes, scholars and policymakers should also reconsider the causes and effects of regulation. Specifically, we should focus on why governments may wish to coordinate regulatory policy across national jurisdictions, why they may wish to maintain domestic control over regulatory policy, and what sort of policy coordination can be expected in the current climate given domestic and international constraints. Can we expect the current crisis to lead to the creation of a new, rigorous international regulatory agreement?

To answer this question, we look to theories of political economy and past instances of international regulatory cooperation and competition. In the next section, we discuss why financial regulation at both the domestic and international levels can be welfare-enhancing. We then provide a brief overview of international financial regulation up to this point in

---

[1]   There is some dispute on this point. Quinn & Inclan (1997) and Quinn & Toyoda (2008) find a strong association between capital account liberalization and growth, while Rodrik (1998) does not. Edwards (2001) argues that capital account openness affects developing and developed countries differently. The different results may be attributable to the fact that the different studies use different measures of capital account openness and study different time periods.

time before describing positive political theories of regulation. In the final section we provide an account of our expectations for the future of international regulatory policy in light of economic theory, regulatory history, and political theory. Our analysis suggests that we should not expect a strong international financial regulatory regime to emerge from the recent crisis. Instead, regulatory structures will remain fragmented and subject to domestic politics. Some cooperation at the international level is likely, but we expect it to be narrow and weak.

1.   SYSTEMIC RISK AND THE PRUDENTIAL REGULATION OF BANKS

The classic case for prudential regulation arises from the systemic risk that inheres to the banking sector. Commercial banking is an inherently risk activity. Commercial banks transform short-term and, thus, highly liquid liabilities (deposits and money market certificates) into long-term and relatively illiquid assets. Consequently, every commercial bank faces liquidity risk and solvency risk. Liquidity risk arises from the possibility that depositors will run on the bank; solvency risk arises from the possibility that the value of assets will drop below liabilities through default or other factors. Illiquidity and insolvency have the same impact: they prevent banks from repaying their creditors.

Systemic risk arises because liquidity or solvency problems at one bank can spread through the entire financial system. When one bank cannot repay an important creditor, the creditor is likely to begin encountering liquidity and solvency issues of its own. Illiquidity at the counterparty bank makes it difficult for this bank to repay all of its creditors who may then, in turn, confront liquidity problems. The interconnectedness of the banking system – the fact that one bank's assets are another bank's liabilities – can thus transform what might be otherwise a localized liquidity or solvency crisis into a systemic crisis.

Prudential regulation strives to reduce the likelihood of systemic crises. Such regulation seeks this objective through a number of channels. On the one hand, regulation can directly restrict bank activities. For example, regulations might govern the degree of allowable exposure to single correspondents in the interbank market. Alternatively, regulations might force diversification of bank assets across assets classes to limit exposure to negative shocks centered in a single asset class. Rules such as these strive to create a network of interbank assets and liabilities that can withstand the collapse of an individual bank, even a relatively large one.

Regulation can also strive to minimize the probability that individual banks will face insolvency by regulating bank capital. Bank capital includes shareholder equity and retained earnings (so-called 'Tier 1 capital' under Basel II) and undisclosed reserves, revaluation reserves, general provisions, hybrid instruments, and subordinated term debt (so-called 'Tier 2 capital' under Basel II). Such capital provides a cushion for unexpected losses. In the event of a negative shock, therefore, capital provides the funds needed to settle liabilities. Under the Basel II framework, the amount of capital that banks must hold is determined by the riskiness of the assets on their balance sheet. A balance sheet dominated by riskier assets requires banks to hold more capital.

The fundamental case for *international* regulation differs from this standard case only by virtue of the geographic scale of systemic risk. As national financial markets become more tightly integrated, network interdependencies inherent in financial systems increasingly extend across borders. Banks incorporated in one jurisdiction hold assets and liabilities of banks and non-bank entities incorporated in other jurisdictions. Consequently, the failure of a foreign institution can destabilize the local financial system. The most prominent illustration of such cross-border destabilization might be that arising from the collapse of the Credit-Anstalt in 1931, which some have characterized as the largest bank failure in history (see, e.g., Eichengreen 1995; Shubert 1991). International financial integration thus implies that domestic financial stability is dependent upon the financial health of foreign banks. Accordingly, governments gain an interest in the financial health of foreign banks and can potentially benefit from international measures that prevent foreign governments from under-regulating associated risks.

The potential benefits from international financial regulation are magnified by the extent to which governments use financial regulation to compete with each other as home states for financial institutions. Because compliance with regulation is costly, jurisdictions that impose relatively lax regulatory requirements gain a cost advantage over foreign competitors. In setting regulation within the context of globalized financial markets, therefore, governments must be aware of the impact of regulation on the competitiveness of local firms vis-à-vis foreign firms. At the minimum, governments wary of losing business to foreign jurisdictions will be reluctant to strengthen regulation even when they believe it necessary to do so. At the maximum, mercantilist governments will reduce the regulatory burden to attract firms into their jurisdiction. In globalized markets, therefore, unilateral national regulation can generate sub-optimal rules that fail to adequately manage the systemic risk inherent in banking. As a consequence, localized failures are more likely to spark international crises.

Changes in the financial sector over the past two decades also present opportunities for regulatory cooperation. The emergence of the 'shadow banking system' – in which traditional banking functions have increasingly been performed by investment banks, mortgage lenders, hedge funds, and other non-bank or quasi-bank institutions – has presented challenges for regulators. By the summer of 2008, lending by the shadow banking system in the US exceeded lending by the traditional banking sector (Geithner 2008). Unlike commercial banks, institutions in the shadow banking system do not take deposits, and so often escape many of the liquidity, leverage, and capital adequacy restraints imposed on commercial banks. These financial institutions are capable of spreading risk through the international financial system through the creation of asset-backed securities and derivative contracts, which are then sold to commercial banks and other institutional investors.

Over time, many large commercial banks began participating in these practices through structured investment vehicles, in-house hedge funds, and investment banking divisions. In the US, the 1999 repeal of Glass-Steagall wall separating investment from commercial banking encouraged this trend, although most European financial firms operated in a universal system already. The increased use of off-balance-sheet investment vehicles spread risk from the shadow banking system throughout the financial system. If the value of the assets underlying these securities and derivatives declines, then so does the value of the securities themselves. A decline in value of any asset can cause banks and other financial institutions to have difficulty paying their creditors, so a disruption in one corner of financial markets can ripple through the entire system. In this way, the systemic risk inherent in the traditional banking system is also present in the shadow banking system, but leading up to the subprime crisis regulatory safeguards did not keep pace with these financial innovations.

In short, the standard case for the prudential regulation of banking activities lies in the systemic risk associated with the interdependencies that inhere within financial systems. The case for international regulation resides in the recognition that in a global financial market the stability of local firms depends, in part, on the health of firms in foreign jurisdictions. This case for international regulation is strengthened by the recognition that the costliness of regulation makes governments reluctant to regulate unilaterally in a global market.

2.   A BRIEF OVERVIEW OF INTERNATIONAL FINANCIAL REGULATION

Although financial globalization creates a compelling case, on welfare grounds, for international financial regulation, in fact international regulation of financial institutions remains relatively under-developed. It is under-developed in terms of its organizational and institutional basis; it is under-developed in terms of its regulatory and geographic scope; it is under-developed in terms of its construction of specific regulatory practices; and it is under-developed in terms of the extent to which compliance is mandatory rather than voluntary.

One way to appreciate the current status of international financial regulation is to look at the current work of the Financial Stability Board (FSB). In April 2009, governments transformed the Financial Stability Forum into the FSB in an attempt to 'strengthen its effectiveness as a mechanism for national authorities, standard setting bodies and international financial institutions to address vulnerabilities and to develop and implement strong regulatory, supervisory and other policies in the interest of financial stability.'[2] Governments gave the FSB the mandate to identify vulnerabilities, to advise on solutions, and to give momentum to the ongoing multilateral effort to strengthen financial systems. In connection with this work, the FSB has identified twelve core standards necessary for sound financial systems.[3] Three of the twelve pertain to the macroeconomic framework; five pertain to specific aspects of the institutional and market infrastructure (accounting, auditing, corporate governance, insolvency, payments systems, and market integrity). The remaining three standards pertain to financial institutions: banking supervision, securities regulation, and insurance supervision.

A first observation to make, looking at the twelve areas above, is on the degree of organizational fragmentation. The International Monetary Fund (IMF) has responsibility for developing and monitoring compliance with standards for macroeconomic policy and data transparency. Responsibility for institutional and market infrastructure rests with the World Bank, the Organization for Economic Cooperation and Development, the International Accounting Standards Board, the Committee on Payment and Settlement Systems of the Bank for International Settlements (BIS), the Financial Action Task Force, and the International Organization of Securities Commissions. Banking, securities, and insurance regulation are likewise allocated to three different bodies: the Basel Committee on Banking Supervision, the International Organization of Securities Commissions (IOSCO), and the International Association of Insurance Supervisors (IAIS). Finally, the Financial Stability Board has some authority to coordinate the activities of these multiple groups.

---

[2]   http://www.financialstabilityboard.org/about/history.htm
[3]   http://www.financialstabilityboard.org/cos/key_standards.htm

Although international organizations dedicated to banking, securities, and insurance supervision do exist, only in the field of banking has cooperation within those organizations advanced beyond the formulation of non-binding principles and standards. The IAIS, for example, sets out principles that 'identify areas in which the insurance supervisor should have authority or control and that form the basis on which standards are developed'. Standards lay out best practices in particular areas. Neither the principles nor the standards in question are binding on IAIS members. IOSCO performs very similar functions. It has developed thirty standards for securities regulation based on three fundamental principles (IOSCO 2003). Yet, neither the principles nor the standards are binding obligations for IOSCO members. Moreover, in neither case do the commonly agreed best practices relate to specific regulatory requirements for specific types of institutions. IAIS provides no specific guidance, much less requirements, on how insurance firms must manage their assets and liabilities. Regarding capital adequacy, for example, IOSCO's primary framework says only that 'Capital adequacy standards . . . should be designed to allow a firm to absorb some losses, particularly in the event of large adverse market moves, and to achieve an environment in which a securities firm could wind down its business over a relatively short period without loss to its customers or the customers of other firms and without disrupting the orderly functioning of the financial markets. A firm should ensure that it maintains adequate financial resources to meet its business commitments and to withstand the risks to which its business is subject. Risk may result from the activities of unlicensed and off-balance-sheet affiliates and regulation should consider the need for information about the activities of these affiliates' (IOSCO 2003, pp. 34–5).

Only in the case of banking supervision have national regulators moved beyond the formulation of non-binding standards and principles to create specific regulatory targets. Working within the Basel Committee on Banking Supervision, national regulators have developed common capital adequacy regulations for commercial banks. The first version of these standards, enunciated in 1988 in 'The International Convergence of Capital Measurements,' provided minimum suggested capital requirements for commercial banks.[4] The agreement defined regulatory capital, developed a formula with which to weight the risk of

---

[4]   The 1988 Basel I version of 'The International Convergence of Capital Measurements' was incorporated into the 'Revised Framework' of Basel II along with other documents in a process that culminated in 2006. The original may be found at http://bis.org/publ/bcbsc111.pdf. The revised comprehensive version may be found at http://bis.org/publ/bcbs128.pdf.

different asset classes, and suggested specific risk-adjusted capital ratios that G-10 members believed appropriately encouraged sound banking practice. Governments began to revise this initial agreement in the late 1990s, refining how banks and regulators should measure and weigh the risk attached to specific assets.

Although international regulation has progressed furthest in banking, even here its scope is limited. The capital adequacy regulations formulated by the Basel Committee do not constitute binding obligations for the world's governments, or even for the governments that are members of the Basel Committee. As the Committee itself explains, 'The Committee does not possess any formal supranational supervisory authority. Its conclusions do not have, and were never intended to have, legal force. Rather, it formulates broad supervisory standards and guidelines and recommends statements of best practice in the expectation that individual authorities will take steps to implement them through detailed arrangements – statutory or otherwise – which are best suited to their own national systems' (Basel Committee on Banking Supervision 2009).

While the Basel Accord outlined broad standards, the interpretation and implementation of these standards was left up to national governments. Domestic regulators determined what accounting standard was used to measure the value of bank assets, and thus the required capital cushion. Some latitude was given to domestic regulators to determine what constituted regulatory capital, and what risk-weights were given to different asset types. The Accord included no provision for liquidity requirements. In fact, the original Basel Accord left so much to the discretion of national regulators, presented so many regulatory arbitrage opportunities for banks to exploit, and proved so inadequate to prevent pressures on the banking system during a series of financial crises during the 1990s, that a Revised Framework was commissioned less than a decade after the implementation of the original Basel Accord. The Basel II revision clarified many of the ambiguities in the original Accord, but was criticized in turn for promoting a 'one-size-fits-all' framework that was not appropriate for all countries, despite the fact that national regulators still retained some discretion over risk calculation and other aspects of regulatory policy. As a result, many countries delayed the implementation of the Revised Framework or only partially adopted it.

The inadequacies of the Basel Accord and Revised Framework were demonstrated by a series of international financial crises that culminated in the subprime mortgage crisis. Before and after these crises some governments maintained stricter domestic standards than those suggested by the Basel Committee, and some research indicates that market discipline places a greater constraint on bank behavior than Basel requirements

(Bernauer & Koubi 2009). There was no regulation of the shadow banking system at the international level, despite the fact that non-bank financial institutions are active across national borders, allowing risk to spread throughout the global financial system. The severity of the resulting sub-prime crisis provides strong evidence that the Basel standards were too weak to prevent banks from excessive risk-exposure.

Underscoring this point is the fact that, although accession to the Basel Accord is strictly voluntary, 140 of the 142 governments that responded to a 2006 World Bank survey claimed adherence to the Basel standards.[5] Such broad acceptance of the Accords indicates one of two things: either most governments do not consider the standards to be a major encroach-ment on their sovereignty nor a major burden to their banking sectors, or they claim adherence to the standard but do not actually achieve it. None of the following monitor compliance with the Basel Accord: the Basel Committee, the BIS, the IMF and the FSB. The lack of an enforce-ment mechanism means that there are many instances of partial- or non-compliance (Ho 2002, Walter 2008).[6] Either situation seems to indicate that neither the Basel Accord nor its Revised Framework presents a meaningful constraint on the behavior of banks or governments, which is its ostensible purpose. Considering that the Basel Accord represents the most prominent example of financial regulation at the international level, these facts demonstrate the weakness of both the *de jure* and de facto requirements of global financial standards up to this point.

In short, governments have not yet taken significant steps toward the realization of the potential gains to be had from the global regulation of financial services. In fact, the pattern of government activity and inactiv-ity revealed by the preceding discussion raises two puzzles. First, why do governments remain reluctant to develop strict, binding international financial regulations? This reluctance is especially puzzling when viewed in the context of other international regulatory frameworks. Second, why have governments been more willing to develop common specific regulations in banking than in securities and insurance? Answering both questions requires us to explore the political economy of financial regulation.

---

[5]   The data come from the Bank Regulation and Supervision database, described by Barth et al. (2008) and found at http://go.worldbank.org/SNUSW978P0

[6]   Many countries, including the United States, are still not yet fully in compli-ance with the Revised Framework of the Basel Accord.

3.   THE POLITICAL ECONOMY OF INTERNATIONAL FINANCIAL REGULATION

Early economic theories of regulation focused on the provision of public goods from which all actors in society benefit. According to this school of thought, regulation is to be used in the public interest to correct market failures or inefficiencies, such as negative externalities generated by some economic activities (Pigou 1932; Demsetz 1968). These occur when an economic action causes spillover effects that adversely affect others. The classic case involves a firm that creates pollution as a byproduct of production. Absent government intervention, the cost of cleaning up this pollution is borne by other actors or the society at large, not the firm that generates it. Regulation, through mandates or taxes, can be used to bring private and social costs in line to correct this market failure. In the case of finance, a function of regulation is to limit the capability of firms to generate risk that affects all of the actors in the system, not just the risky firm.

A second school of economic thought recognized that all regulations contain a distributional component: some actors will benefit from regulations, while others will suffer. Proponents of this view argue that regulations are a means for politically powerful interest groups to capture rents from the state, creating market inefficiency or failure where there was none before (Stigler 1971; Peltzman 1976, 1989). According to this view, regulations are of dubious social value, but strongly benefit those who are able to steer government policies in ways that protect their interests by limiting the competition they face. Classic cases of rent-providing regulations include barriers preventing new entry into markets, or granting of monopoly privileges by the state. In finance, regulations have been used to prevent foreign firms from entering domestic markets, or limiting the types of services they can provide.

Political economy analysis of regulation has incorporated both the public goods view and the rent-seeking view of regulatory policy into its models, and begins with the recognition that no matter how globalized financial markets have become, political accountability remains strictly local. And the governments that typically set the agenda for international negotiations, those who govern in the advanced industrialized countries, are held accountable by their population through regular national elections. As a result, the patterns of financial regulation we observe, in terms of its specific content as well as the degree to which it acquires an international component, reflect the imperatives of retaining office in electoral democracies.

First generation research drew on normative theories of regulation and political theories of international cooperation to explain international regulation as a process oriented toward public goods provision. Analysts working in this framework viewed national regulators as protectors of the public interest (Kapstein 1989, 1991, 1994). They set regulation in order to ensure systemic stability, although always subject to the need to reduce the impact of rules on the cost of doing business at home. International regulation, within this perspective, was a natural response to the expansion of capital markets beyond national borders. The central argument is that as financial markets become increasingly globalized, governments recognized that they were losing the capacity to regulate national markets effectively. Systemic stability came to depend upon common regulatory regimes that could only be established through international cooperation. And because banks were at the leading edge of financial globalization, national regulators initiated a process of international cooperation intended to reduce the risk of systemic instability in a global financial system. The initial result of this process was the adoption of minimum capital adequacy ratios by G-10 countries, which provided a buffer against systemic cross-national counterparty risks created by international financial transactions.

Second generation research draws on positive theories of regulation to emphasize the domestic and international distributional implications that drive financial regulation (Oatley and Nabors 1998; Simmons 2001). In this approach, politicians strive to balance two objectives when setting financial regulation. On the one hand, and in common with first generation models, the need to retain electoral support leads politicians to create regulation that provides systemic stability in order to reduce the probability that they confront a systemic crisis. On the other hand, politicians strive to enact regulation that maintains the competitiveness of the domestic financial sector in order to retain the financial and political support of the domestic industry. The politician's problem is that a trade-off exists between these two objectives: rules that promote systemic stability reduce the competitiveness of local industry, while regulation that enhances the competitiveness of domestic institutions relative to foreign competitors often increases the risk of systemic crisis.

This need to balance competing demands is evident in political debates about financial reform that emerged in the wake of the 2008 financial crisis. On the one side, the general public pressed for measures to limit excessive risk taking by financial institutions. Public opinion surveys conducted by the Pew Institute in 2009 and 2010 revealed an American public desirous of more stringent regulation of the financial services industry. In the February 2010 survey, for instance, 59 per cent of the respondents said that it was a 'good idea for the government to more strictly regulate the way major financial companies do business.' Only one-third of the respondents believed that tougher regulation was a bad idea (Pew Research Center for the People and the Press 2010). The regulatory reforms in the Dodd-Frank Wall Street Reform and Consumer Protection Act reflected this popular sentiment. One provision created a new regulatory authority charged with protecting consumer interests. Other provisions brought previously exempt activities, such as derivatives, into the regulatory orbit. Still other provisions limited bank activities and tightened regulator oversight of existing practices.[7]

While voters pressured politicians to 'punish' banks and restrict risky activities, financial institutions sought to thwart regulatory measures that would constrain the growth and reduce the competitiveness of the American financial sector. The Chamber of Commerce, for example, argued that although they recognized the need for reform, they feared that key elements of the proposal released in the spring of 2010 would place American financial institutions and the American capital markets more generally, 'at a distinct competitive disadvantage' (US Chamber of Commerce 2010). The American Bankers Association, although also generally welcoming the construction of a more modern regulatory framework, expressed concerns that the proposed regulatory reform was likely to impose unacceptably 'heavy new regulatory burdens' on the banking industry (American Bankers Association 2010).

Because finding a regulatory structure that satisfies these competing demands is difficult, and because these demands change over time, financial regulation tends to be unstable and marked by long periods of regulatory decay punctuated by sharp instances of re-regulation. Regulation tends to tighten significantly in the wake of a crisis. Market liberalization occurs slowly in response to the loss of memory of the most recent crisis. As mentioned above, the Glass-Steagall Banking Act of 1933 separated commercial from investment banking, a rule that persisted in the US until the Financial Services Modernization Act was passed in 1999. In the wake of the 2008 subprime crisis many American officials supported the re-establishment of the 'wall' between commercial and investment banking. The 'Volcker Rule' – proposed by former Federal Reserve Chairman Paul Volcker – serves much the same purpose by limiting the ability of commercial banks to engage in proprietary trading or sponsoring hedge funds. The sentiment also spread to Europe, despite the fact that European

---

[7]   Among the changes, Title X creates the Bureau of Consumer Financial Protection, to be located within the Federal Reserve; Title IV establishes regulations for hedge funds and other non-bank financial institutions; Title VII requires financial instruments such as credit default swaps and credit derivatives be traded through exchanges; Title VI included the so-called 'Volcker Rule', which banned some types of proprietary trading by depository institutions.

states have traditionally had universal banking systems. In the UK, a cabinet committee headed by chancellor George Osborne was established to examine whether to break up commercial and investment banks along similar lines (Evans 2010). Other national governments, and the European Parliament, debated taking similar measures.

Governments can enhance systemic stability following crises only if they can mitigate the consequent negative impact on industry competitiveness. In broad terms, governments have two options for reducing the negative consequences of stricter regulation: market closure or international harmonization. Governments opted for the first approach following the catastrophic failure of the financial system in 1929–1931. Most governments abandoned the gold standard, strictly limited the convertibility of their currencies, and effectively ended private cross-border financial transactions.

On occasion, governments opt for international harmonization. The Basel Accord represents one such instance of this response. Following the collapse of the Bretton Woods system of fixed exchange rates and capital controls, there was no institutional mechanism for cross-border cooperation to prevent or resolve financial disruptions. The crisis generated by American commercial bank exposure to sovereign defaults in Latin America in the 1970s–1980s necessitated government intervention in the financial sector. In response, the American public (and their representatives) demanded stricter regulation of the financial sector. The American banking industry argued that unilateral re-regulation would limit their competitiveness in global markets. An international agreement provided a way for American policymakers to appease both domestic audiences; stricter prudential standards improved system stability and thus made public intervention less necessary, while the international adoption of certain standards allowed domestic banks to compete against foreign banks on a 'level playing field'. The Basel Accord, which harmonized prudential standards across the G-10, checked both boxes.

Just as domestic regulations necessarily have distributional consequences, privileging some interest groups over others, so do international regulatory agreements. Observing this, one view expects the emergence of international standards to be largely a function of developments in the largest markets (Simmons 2001). Relative power determines whose rules will be proposed and accepted. Simmons argues that international regulations are a product of great power politics, whereby the dominant financial center initiates an international regulatory innovation that arises through a domestic political process similar to the one that led to the Basel Accord. This innovation represents a redistribution of wealth to the dominant state from weaker states and is thus Pareto-inferior relative to the status quo.

After major-power initiation, the other states in the system must choose whether to adhere to the new standard or oppose it and risk retribution from the stronger states. According to this framework, the Basel Accord was a redistributive agreement where the dominant centers (the US and UK) were able to coerce weaker states (including the rest of the G-10 and, especially, Japan) to conform to their preferred standard by threatening to limit access to their markets if the weaker states resisted (Oatley and Nabors 1998). By using their agenda-setting capabilities to change the status quo, the dominant states were able to provide a strong, credible threat so that weaker states were forced to accede to the new standard even though it may not have been in their interests.

Simmons does not closely examine what developments within a domestic polity might trigger a regulatory innovation in a strong state. Drezner (2007) argues that international regulatory harmonization occurs when gains from coordination exist for the dominant state, even if they do not for lesser states. He accepts Simmons' claim that states with large internal markets will be able to set standards for the globe by threatening to withhold access to those markets, but notes that the cost of adjusting to a new standard is also higher when the internal market is large, so powerful states will only push for a new standard when the gains from it exceed the costs of adjusting to it. Because these conditions do not often hold, this view expects relatively little international regulatory harmonization, but when it does occur it should reflect the interests of the most powerful firms and interest groups in the strongest states.

Another strand of research analyzes the incentives of regulators, who are in a principal–agent relationship with governments (Singer 2004, 2007). If regulators fail to maintain stability in domestic financial sectors, they run a high risk of being removed from office by their governments. Unlike governments, they have little incentive to promote the competitiveness of domestic industry, unless a lack of competitiveness affects the stability of the financial sector. Since regulators are held responsible for stability, *ceteris paribus* they prefer to keep regulatory authority for themselves rather than cede it to an international regulator, who may set standards that are suboptimal for firms under their jurisdiction. This equilibrium changes if a threat to stability emerges from foreign jurisdictions. In that case, national regulators may push for a broad international standard that addresses the cause of instability, while retaining as much autonomy as possible. The narrow focus on the Basel Accord seems to reflect this pattern, as does the composition of the Basel Committee itself, which comprises the primary bank regulators in the major industrialized countries.

These theories also help explain why the scope of international regulations has been narrowly focused on the traditional commercial banking sector and traditional banking activities rather than the shadow banking system and newer financial instruments, including structured investment vehicles, many over-the-counter derivatives, collateralized debt obligations, and credit default swaps. Many of these instruments allowed banks to move assets and liabilities off-balance-sheet, and thus evade capital adequacy requirements like those in the Basel Accord. In effect, banks and non-bank financial institutions were allowed to take on excessive levels of risk without being required to build up capital buffers as protection against default.

There are two reasons why newer innovations were largely unregulated before the subprime crisis. First, regulations are usually created as a reaction to a past crisis, not in anticipation of a potential future crisis. While there had been signs of the potential dangers of highly-leveraged derivatives trading following the near-collapse of the Long-Term Capital Management (LTCM) hedge fund in 1998, the subprime mortgage crisis was the first large-scale financial shock that heavily involved derivatives and other shadow banking vehicles. If regulatory policy generally reacts to crisis, and prior to 2007 there was no crisis involving these new financial instruments to respond to, then it should be no surprise that many activities undertaken in the shadow banking system were left unregulated.

Second, many of these vehicles were designed to mitigate the very risk they ended up creating. Many of these investments – including mortgage-backed securities and credit default swaps – were intended to reduce the exposure a bank had to default risk. In fact, many experts believed that derivative contracts made the financial system much more stable. In one prominent example from 2002, Senator Dianne Feinstein of California proposed legislation that would strictly regulate some types of derivatives. This followed the collapse of the Enron energy company, which had used derivatives and special investment vehicles to hide the holes in its balance sheet. But Federal Reserve Chairman Alan Greenspan was strongly opposed to the bill, claiming that derivatives helped diffuse risk in financial markets (Ip 2004). Before the subprime crisis, such beliefs were shared by many in public and private positions of prominence, as well as by the rating agencies, which routinely gave AAA or Aaa ratings to securities that eventually became known as 'toxic assets'. Given this intellectual climate, it is not surprising that most derivatives were left unregulated.

If we sum up the common expectations in these theories, we can converge on some general predictions regarding the likely necessary conditions under which financial regulation can occur at the international level. *First*, there must be a systemic financial crisis that threatens the stability of the strongest states' economies and alters their domestic political equilibria in favor of stricter regulation. *Second*, resolution of the fundamental causes of the crisis must require international coordination. *Third*, stricter regulations must adversely affect the competitiveness of financial firms in the dominant states relative to foreign firms, thus putting pressures on the government in the dominant states to shift regulatory policy in a way that advantages their domestic firms. *Fourth*, the new standard must privilege the interests of the firms in the dominant states by shifting the costs of moving to the new standard to foreign firms. *Fifth*, the new international standard must maintain policy flexibility for leaders to resolve domestic political tradeoffs. The history of international financial regulation supports this pattern. The extent to which the above conditions are satisfied in the context of the subprime crisis is examined in the following section.

4.   THE SUBPRIME MORTGAGE CRISIS AND EXPECTATIONS FOR FUTURE INTERNATIONAL REGULATIONS

Has the recent financial crisis altered the political equilibrium in powerful states toward stricter regulation? The answer appears to be 'Yes'. Many states have begun reforming their regulatory structures at the domestic level to improve prudence and emphasize financial stability. Additionally, the Basel Committee has updated its Accord with new capital adequacy, liquidity, and leverage requirements to be refined and implemented over the coming years. But should we expect a new, rigorous international regulatory standard in response to the subprime mortgage crisis? Positive theory and recent history suggest the answer is a qualified 'No': we should see some activity at the international level, but changes to the system are likelier than not to be narrow, focused, and limited. To see why, we must consider the causes of the crisis, its aftermath, and the incentives facing policymakers through the lens of the political theories discussed above.

The financial crisis and the recession that followed the collapse of the subprime mortgage sector in the US would seemingly provide an opportunity for meaningful policy changes at the international level. Financial crises are necessary conditions for enacting substantive regulatory reforms, and the international nature of this crisis would seemingly provide a window for the creation of a meaningful international prudential standard and enforcement mechanism. Necessary conditions are not always sufficient conditions, however, and the particular political dynamics present in this crisis leave little reason to think that this will lead to major international policy changes.

If we consider the subprime crisis in light of the likely necessary conditions for international regulation listed above we can see why this is the case. The first condition appears to hold: a systemic financial crisis has shifted domestic political equilibria in many leading states towards stricter regulation. While these debates are still ongoing, some reforms (such as the German ban on naked short selling, the reallocation of regulatory responsibilities and abandonment of 'light touch' in the UK, the Dodd-Frank legislation in the US, and the new Basel requirements) have already been initiated, and other reforms are likely to become law in the US, Europe, and elsewhere.

However the second condition – namely, that correcting the causes of the crisis should require international regulatory coordination – need not necessarily apply. To understand this, consider the proximate cause of the crisis: banks and other financial institutions in the US created large quantities of securities backed by mortgage assets located in the US, which they traded amongst themselves and sold to other investors, thus spreading mortgage risk throughout the financial system. In other words, from the American perspective the locus of the crisis was domestic, not foreign. The crisis did not occur because of a negative externality imposed by foreign firms or governments, so reforming the regulatory system does not require international agreement. Because lawmakers are ultimately held responsible by voters for the stability of the financial system, they will prefer to maintain regulatory authority rather than cede it to an international organization whenever possible. Thus, the location of the crisis provides incentives for policymakers in the US to focus on domestic, rather than international, reform. Because the American market is the world's largest, international reform is highly unlikely without their support, but even European governments can do much to reform their domestic regulatory structures to address their exposure to the crisis.[8]

It would be surprising to see no international response if opportunities exist for dominant states to put their firms at a competitive advantage through regulatory harmonization, the third condition for regulatory reform. The international nature of the crisis may provide such opportunities. Indeed, the G-20 has repeatedly called for greater international cooperation in monitoring national financial industries and coordination in responding to disruption, and has tasked the FSB with that purpose.[9] It has reiterated the role of the Basel Committee in crafting prudential stand-

---

[8] There are a variety of ways that this could happen, including changing the risk-weighting rules by which banks calculate their capital-to-assets ratios.

[9] See, e.g., the communiqué from the London meeting in April, 2009 that established the FSB, which may be accessed at http://www.londonsummit.gov.uk/en/summit-aims/summit-communique/. This has been emphasized in every com-

ards to be implemented by all its members, while acknowledging the need to 'help promote a level playing field, taking into consideration individual countries' circumstances' (Group of 20 2010).

Perhaps more importantly, American leaders have been hesitant to unilaterally initiate the sort of reforms that would put their firms at a competitive disadvantage, such as significantly increasing minimum capital-to-assets ratios that banks must maintain to hedge against default risk. In fact, US Treasury Secretary Timothy Geithner has been forthright in declaring the American administration's goal for revision of the Basel Accord: raise capital ratios in such a way as to not disadvantage American firms. 'By the end of this year [2010], we will negotiate an international consensus on the new ratios', he said in March 2010, while noting that '[American] major global banks have more capital today relative to risk than do many of their major international competitors' (quoted in Sorkin 2010). In other words, American banks would benefit if their competitors were also required to hold larger amounts of capital relative to assets, and would suffer if forced to do so while their foreign competitors were not, so the US government has insisted that stricter capital requirements be included in any new Basel revision.

This American demand has attracted complaints from European banks and governments. Because American banks already maintain higher ratios than many of their global competitors, such a revision would fulfill the fourth requirement for international regulatory reform. Even before the financial crisis, American banks were required to hold 50 per cent more Tier 1 capital than the Basel minimum to be considered 'well capitalized' by domestic regulators, and the definition of qualifying capital was stricter in the US than in many other advanced countries.[10] If the US were to unilaterally place even stricter regulatory requirements on their financial firms without other countries following suit, American banks would find it very difficult to remain competitive in globalized markets. But if foreign firms were also obligated to follow the new rules, American firms would be in a better competitive position.

For this reason, banks in Europe and Japan have resisted calls for a strong new regulatory standard. For example, the Association of German Banks issued a position paper in April, 2010 declaring that, while they were in support of regulatory reform 'in principle', they argued that the

---

muniqué, leaders' statement, and progress report since, the full list of which may be found at http://www.g20.org/pub_communiques.aspx .

[10]   Since the crisis American regulators have relied less on official numbers and more on 'stress tests' and other subjective assessments in determining the appropriate level of capital for banks to hold.

proposals under discussion by the Basel Committee 'are unsuited to achieving the declared aim of stabilising the financial sector' and would force German banks to raise at least €98 billion of new capital, and reduce loans by trillions of € (Association of German Banks 2010). The Japanese Bankers Association issued a statement disputing nearly every component of the Basel Committee's proposal, arguing that the proposed new rules would increase instability, decrease efficiency, and impair 'market soundness' (Japanese Bankers Association 2010). Japan's banking sector, battered after more than a decade of economic slump, would likely find it even harder than banks in Europe to attract enough new capital to meet stricter standards.

So the current political and economic situation is quite similar to that which led to the creation of Basel Accord in the mid-1980s: American domestic political incentives caused leaders to push for stricter regulation of the financial sector, while the financial sector responded by lobbying for the standard to also apply to their foreign competitors so they would not suffer a competitive disadvantage. The resulting agreement – Basel I – largely reflected American political and business interests, but was also relatively weak. It included no enforcement mechanism, no supranational authority, and left much to the discretion of national regulators. This type of agreement fulfills the fifth condition described above by maintaining policy flexibility for leaders to resolve domestic political tradeoffs, at least in dominant states.

A similar outcome is occurring today. The G-20 discussion of financial regulatory reform has focused almost entirely on updating the Basel Accord in light of the recent crisis rather than giving more authority to another institution. The resulting Basel agreement calls for increases in the quantity and quality of capital reserves that banks must hold against risk, new liquidity and leverage requirements, and a phase-in period of several years (beginning in 2013) for banks and national regulators to adjust to the new rules.[11] Perhaps as important is what is not in the agreement, such as rules regarding the organization or activities of the financial sector, official monitoring of compliance, an enforcement mechanism, or a transfer of regulatory authority from national governments to international bodies. The Basel Committee appears to have limited its jurisdiction to the most basic regulatory standards, leaving the more complex rules to national governments. National governments also appear to be unwilling to cede

---

[11]   The press release that summarizes the new rules may be accessed at http://bis.org/press/p100912.pdf. The full compilation of Basel III documents is located at http://bis.org/list/basel3/index.htm.

monitoring and enforcement functions to a supranational authority, and neither the Basel Committee nor any other international institution has asked for this role.

Basel III also appears to have similar distributional implications to Basel I. Analysis from Barclays Capital and German bankers indicates that the ten largest German firms will need to raise more capital to meet the new standards than the thirty-five largest American firms, while Nomura estimates that the sixteen largest European firms will need to raise twice as much capital (Jenkins 2010; Murphy et al. 2010). Because of this, Germany refused to accept the agreement unless full implementation was delayed until 2019. Japanese and British bankers also had concerns about capital standards and leverage requirements, respectively, that force them to raise more capital than their American counterparts. In short, Basel III appears to provide some competitive advantages to American banks relative to the pre-crisis status quo.

Does Basel III represent a significant shift in international regulatory policy? The previous discussion suggests the answer is 'No'. On the contrary, it may be considered a continuation of the status quo in structure and organization, and as with the Revised Framework, there is no guarantee that governments will strictly adhere to the new standards. Many of the most important regulations will be enacted at the domestic level, and are thus subject to domestic political constraints. Regulatory fragmentation across national jurisdictions will continue, as domestic political constraints force governments to tailor national regulatory policies to their local needs. In sum, if Basel I and II were not considered to be a strong, meaningful global standard, than Basel III is not likely to be either.

5.   CONCLUSION

Governments have strong incentives to maintain strong economic performance in their countries, and economic growth requires a strong, stable financial system to channel funds from investors to businesses. Breakdowns in the financial sector have severe and often long-lasting effects on economies, and incumbents are often punished for poor economic performance. As a result, governments have incentives to create policies that encourage a secure financial sector. However, too many restrictions on the financial sector will also dampen economic performance. Regulatory policy is often in flux because there is a tradeoff between financial stability and economic performance. Immediately following financial crises governments enact regulatory reforms to address the causes of the crisis. But over time, these regulations are weakened in order to promote economic growth, or become obsolete through new developments in the financial sector. If regulatory policy becomes too lax states are at risk of suffering another financial crisis. Therefore a cycle of crisis, re-regulation, deregulation, and repeated crisis tends to repeat itself over time, and has become more common in the post-Bretton Woods era.

The interconnectedness of financial markets across national borders presents an even greater challenge for policymakers. If regulators in one state enact stricter standards than those in another state, their firms will be put at a competitive disadvantage in globalized markets. This can destabilize financial markets and have adverse effects on economic growth. Moreover, a failure of firms in one jurisdiction can have negative effects on counterparty firms in other jurisdictions. In this way, even a localized event – such as Latin American sovereign debt defaults or a drop in home values in the US – can have negative effects across the globe. Because markets cross national jurisdictions, there is a strong case to be made that international financial regulations can be welfare-enhancing.

All regulations have distributional consequences. However, some international regulations will benefit some states more than others. The resolution of domestic tradeoffs is the motivation for governments to seek an international agreement, so they will try to influence the terms of any international agreement to satisfy the voters and firms in their jurisdiction. Since stronger states will be in a better place to steer the process than weaker states, any international agreement is likely to reflect the domestic political incentives facing incumbent governments in strong states.

For these reasons, a common pattern has emerged. Following international financial crises, states discuss ways to improve prudential standards. Many reforms are made domestically, but some desired reforms may adversely affect the competitiveness of domestic firms vis-à-vis their foreign competitors. In these circumstances, discussions are held at the international level and are led by the strongest states, which use their agenda-setting capabilities to propose international policies that help them resolve domestic political tradeoffs. Such proposals involve wealth redistributions, in the form of competitive advantages, from firms in weaker states to firms in stronger states. Governments of stronger states cannot resist these proposals without risking loss of access to the large markets in the stronger states. Governments of stronger states cannot extract too many concessions from weaker states without risking loss of cooperation. All governments are reluctant to cede too much authority to a supranational body, as this prevents them from using regulatory policy to resolve domestic tradeoffs. Thus, when an international accord is reached, it is often narrow, weak, and lacking in monitoring or enforcement mechanisms. Compliance varies from state to state, and regulatory policies beyond the scope of the agreement remain fragmented across jurisdictions.

Are there reasons to think that this pattern will be broken as a result of the recent financial crisis? The analysis presented here suggests the answer is 'No'. Regulatory authority will ultimately remain with national governments, which will reform their domestic regulatory structures in different ways according to local needs. Some international agreement reflecting the preferences of the strongest states is likely, but standards will be harmonized only along narrow dimensions, and are likely to be relatively weak.

BIBLIOGRAPHY

American Bankers Association (2010), Regulatory Restructuring: Letter to Senate Banking Committee (January 5), http://www.aba.com/NR/rdonlyres/76DCD307-2D7E-48A6-A10F-623175F0AEAD/64678/RegulatoryRestructuring_ABASenateLetter_010510.pdf

Association of German Banks (2010), 'Position of the Association of German Banks on the Basel Committee on Bank Supervision proposals on the capital and liquidity of banks.' Bundesverband Deutscher Banken, April 14.

Barth, James R., G. Caprio Jr. and R. Levine (2008), 'Bank Regulations are Changing: For Better or Worse?' *Comparative Economic Studies* **50**(4),537–563.

Basel Committee on Banking Supervision (2009), 'History of the Basel Committee and its Membership', Bank for International Settlements, Basel: Basel Committee on Banking Supervision. Available at http://www.bis.org/bcbs/history.pdf

Bernauer, Thomas, and V. Koubi (2009), 'Taking Firms and Markets Seriously: A Study on Bank Behavior, Market Discipline, and Regulatory Policy', Zurich: Center for Comparative and International Studies.

Bordo, Michael and B. Eichengreen (1999), 'Is Our Current International Economic Environment Unusually Crisis Prone?' in D.Gruen and L. Gower (eds), *Capital Flows and the International Financial System*, Sydney: The Reserve Bank of Australia.

Brown, Gordon (2008), 'Out of the Ashes', *Washington Post*, A1.

Demsetz, Harold (1968), 'Why Regulate Utilities?', *Journal of Law and Economics*, **11**(1): 55–65.

Drezner, Daniel W. (2007), *All Politics Is Global: Explaining International Regulatory Regimes*, Princeton: Princeton University Press.

Edwards, Sebastian (2001), 'Capital Mobility and Economic Performance: Are Emerging Countries Different?', *NBER Working Paper*, Cambridge: National Bureau of Economic Research.

Eichengreen, Barry J. (1995), *Golden Fetters: the Gold Standard and the Great Depression 1919–1939*, Oxford: Oxford University Press.

Evans, Simon (2010), 'British Banks Still Face Breakup Threat,' *Businessweek*, May 17. http://www.businessweek.com/globalbiz/content/may2010/gb20100517_189718.htm

Geithner, Timothy (2008), 'Reducing Systemic Risk in a Dynamic Financial System', remarks at the Economic Club of New York, June 9, 2008. http://www.newyorkfed.org/newsevents/speeches/2008/tfg080609.html

Group of 20 (2010), Communiqué, Meeting of Finance Ministers and Central Bank Governors, April 23, http://www.g20.org/Documents/201004_communique_WashingtonDC.pdf

Ho, Daniel E. (2002), 'Compliance and International Soft Law: Why Do Countries Implement the Basle Accord?' *Journal of International Economic Law*, **5**, 647–88.

IOSCO (2003), Objectives and Principles of Securities Regulation, http://www.iosco.org/library/pubdocs/pdf/IOSCOPD154.pdf

Ip, Greg (2004), 'The Deregulator: Greenspan's less visible role.' *The Wall Street Journal* November 19, A1.

Japanese Bankers Association (2010), 'Comment on the Basel Committee's Consultative Documents: "Strengthening the resilience of the banking sector", and "International framework for liquidity risk measurement, standards and monitoring"' April 15, 2010. Tokya, Japan: Japanese Bankers Association. Available at http://www.zenginkyo.or.jp/en/news/entryitems/news100435.pdf

Jenkins, Patrick (2010), 'German banks try to fend off Basel III.' *Financial Times* September 6, http://www.ft.com/cms/s/0/2d61f5ae-b9c3-11df-968f-00144feabdc0.html#axzz14omPQcIF

Kapstein, Ethan B. (1989), 'Resolving the Regulator's Dilemma: International Coordination of Banking Regulations', *International Organization*, **43**, 323–47.

Kapstein, Ethan B. (1991), 'Supervising International Banks: Origins and Implications of the Basel Accord.' In *Princeton University Department of Economics Essays in International Finance*, Princeton: Princeton University Press.

Kapstein, Ethan B. (1994), *Governing the Global Economy: International Finance and the State*, Cambridge: Harvard University Press.

Kindleberger, Charles P. (1978), *Manias, Panics, and Crashes: A History of Financial Crises*, New York: Wiley.

King, Robert G. and R. Levine (1993), 'Finance and Growth: Schumpeter Might Be Right', *The Quarterly Journal of Economics*, **108**(3), 717–37.

Murphy, Megan, N. Cohen, and B. Masters (2010),'US banks receive Basel III boost', *Financial Times*, August 18, http://www.ft.com/cms/s/0/0d54e652-ab01-11df-9e6b-00144feabdc0.html

Oatley, Thomas and R. Nabors (1998), 'Redistributive Cooperation: Market Failure, Wealth Transfers, and the Basel Accord', *International Organization*, **52**, 35–54.

Peltzman, Sam (1976), 'Toward a More General Theory of Regulation?' *Journal of Law and Economics*, **19**(2), 211–240.

Peltzman, Sam (1989), '*The Economic Theory of Regulation After a Decade of Deregulation*', Washington D.C.: Brookings Institution.

Pew Research Center for the People and the Press (2010), 'Midterm Election Challenges for Both Parties', http://people-press.org/report/589/midterm-electionchallenges-for-both-parties .

Pigou, Arthur C. (1932), *The Economics of Welfare*, London: Macmillan and Co.

Quinn, Dennis and C. Inclan (1997), 'The Origins of Financial Openness: A Study of Current and Capital Account Liberalization', *American Journal of Political Science*, **41**, 771–813.

Quinn, Dennis P. and A. M. Toyoda (2008), 'Does Capital Account Liberalization Lead to Growth?' *The Review of Financial Studies*, **21** (3), 1403–49.

Reinhart, Carmen M. and K.S. Rogoff (2009), *This Time Is Different: Eight Centuries of Financial Folly*, Princeton: Princeton University Press.

Rodrik, Dani (1998), 'Who Needs Capital-Account Convertibility?', in *Should the IMF Pursue Capital-Account Convertibility?*, Princeton: Princeton International Finance Section.

Shubert, Aurel (1991), *The Credit-Anstalt Crisis of 1931*, Cambridge: Cambridge University Press.

Simmons, Beth A. (2001), 'The International Politics of Harmonization: The Case of Capital Market Regulation', *International Organization* **55**(3), 589–620.

Singer, David A. (2004), 'Capital Rules: The Domestic Politics of International Regulatory Harmonization', *International Organization*, **58**, 531–65.

Singer, David A. (2007), *Regulating Capital: Setting Standards for the International Financial System*, Ithaca: Cornell University Press.

Sorkin, Andrew R. (2010), 'The Issue of Liquidity Bubbles Up', *New York Times*, March 30, B1.

Stigler, George J. (1971), 'The Theory of Economic Regulation', *The Bell Journal of Economics and Management Science* **2**, 3–21.

US Chamber of Commerce (2010), Letter Opposing the 'Restoring American Financial Stability Act of 2010' (RAFSA), in its Current Form,' http://www.uschamber.com/issues/letters/2010/100322rafsa.htm

Walter, Andrew (2008), *Governing finance: East Asia's adopt of international standards*, Ithaca, NY: Cornell University Press.

Index

A-REITs 407, 408, 428–432
Absolute Capital Management (fund) 83–84
Abu Dhabi 93, 327
  Investment Authority *see* ADIA
activist funds
  benefits and risks of 206–214
  characteristics of 199–204
  data on 198–199
  returns of 214–216
  targets of 204–206
ADIA 95, 100
administrators *see* service providers
AFSL 411, 412
AIF 443, 445
  and FSA, 142, 145–158, 160–167
  and future in the EU 467–471
  and liquidity concerns, 163–164
  and retail investors 141–142, 146, 148–150, 154–163, 166–168, 222, 391–392, 400, 408, 413, 418, 439, 463, 470
  and self-regulation *see* self-regulation
  in Australia 414–439
  in Germany 379–393
  in USA 15–26
  regulatory principles 451–452
  short selling 376, 395, 396, 397, 402 453, 490
  'side letters' 164–165
  valuation 163–164, 166, 251, 252, 419, 448, 453, 455, 457, 458, 464
AIFMD 144–145,148, 158, 167, 251–252, 442
  and comparison with new US regulation 464
  and interplay with UCITS 467, 468–471
  and investor protection 450, 451, 454, 469
  background to 444–447
  Commission proposal 444–451

  delegation provisions 458–459
  depositaries provisions 459–461
  final text of 452–453
  remuneration provisions 463
  scope 455–455
  third-country regime 461–463
  valuation provisions 457–458
Almunia, J. 272, 276
Alternative Investment Funds *see* AIF
Alternative Investment Fund
    Managers Directive *see* AIFMD
Amaranth Advisors (fund) 224, 293, 301
  collapse of 3, 7, 83, 306
  lessons from 303–304
  trading strategy 301–302
American Bankers Association 485
Asian countries *see* China (Peoples Republic of); Japan; Korea (South); Malaysia; Taiwan; Thailand
Asian Crisis 294, 303, 314, 335, 336, 407, 475
  and role of hedge funds 315–317
ASIC 410, 411, 412, 413, 414, 420, 425
Association of German Banks 491, 492
ASX 433, 437, 438
ATO 417, 425, 426, 428, 434, 440
Australia
  agricultural managed investment schemes 432–436
  and hedge fund activity 414–420
  and hedge fund regulation 412–413
  infrastructure funds 436–439
  private equity and venture capital industry 420–428
  real estate investment trusts 428–432
  see also AFSL; A-REITs; ASIC; ASX; ATO
Australian Financial Services Licence *see* AFSL
Australian Real Estate Investment Trusts *see* A-REITs